ORPHAN OF THE COLD WAR

Also by Margaret Joan Anstee

AFRICA AND THE WORLD (*co-edited with R. K. A. Gardiner and C. Patterson*)

GATE OF THE SUN: A Prospect of Bolivia

THE ADMINISTRATION OF INTERNATIONAL DEVELOPMENT AID

Orphan of the Cold War

The Inside Story of the Collapse of the Angolan Peace Process, 1992–93

Margaret Joan Anstee

St. Martin's Press
New York

ORPHAN OF THE COLD WAR
Copyright © 1996 by Margaret Joan Anstee
Map of Angola © 1994 by Michael S. Miller
All rights reserved. No part of this book may be used or reproduced
in any manner whatsoever without written permission except in the
case of brief quotations embodied in critical articles or reviews.
For information, address:

St. Martin's Press, Scholarly and Reference Division,
175 Fifth Avenue, New York, N.Y. 10010

First published in the United States of America in 1996

Printed in Great Britain

ISBN 0–312–16015–0

Library of Congress Cataloging-in-Publication Data
Anstee, Margaret Joan.
Orphan of the cold war : the inside story of the collapse of the
Angolan peace process, 1992–93 / Margaret Joan Anstee.
p. cm.
Includes bibliographical references and index.
ISBN 0–312–16015–0
1. Angola—History—Civil War, 1975– —Peace. 2. United Nations-
-Anogola. 3. Angola—Politics and government—1975–   I. Title.
DT1428.A57   1996
967.304—dc20   96–33803
                                                         CIP

For **Basil Davidson**, who first opened my eyes to the forgotten tragedy of Angola in October 1966, and against whose advice I went to see for myself a quarter of a century later

'Better is wisdom than weapons of war'

(Inscription on a banner embroidered by students of Newnham College, Cambridge, and carried in a procession of the National Union of Women's Suffragtte Societies on 13 June 1908.)

Contents

List of Plates	ix
Foreword	xi
Acknowledgements	xiii
Dramatis Personae	xv
List of Abbreviations	xxiv
Map of Angola	xxvi

PART I   THE CONTEXT: PERSONAL, NATIONAL AND INTERNATIONAL   1

1	A Late-Night Telephone Call	3
2	The Background	7
3	First Mission to Angola	15
4	A 'Small and Manageable' Operation, or Making Bricks without Straw	30

PART II   THE MILITARY AND SECURITY SITUATION – FEBRUARY TO SEPTEMBER 1992   45

5	The Military Conundrum	47
6	The Formation of the New Angolan Armed Forces	64
7	The Police Imbroglio	69
8	Alarms and Excursions	79

PART III   THE PREPARATION AND ORGANISATION OF THE ELECTIONS – MARCH TO SEPTEMBER 1992   85

9	The Prelude: March to May 1992	87
10	The Registration of Voters and the Electoral Campaign	99
11	Politics, Pride and Personalities	127

PART IV   DAY TO DAY LIVING   159

12	Life in Luanda	161
13	Vignettes from the Field	173

PART V   THE ELECTIONS AND THEIR AFTERMATH   185

14	The Moment of Truth	187
15	The Aftermath	199
16	The Débâcle	239

PART VI   OVER THE BRINK 263

17   The Bloodbath 265
18   The Slide into the Abyss 292
19   Cry Havoc… 328

PART VII   CONFLAGRATION AND MEDIATION 355

20   …And Let Slip the Dogs of War 357
21   Peace Talks in Ethiopia 380
22   From Addis Ababa to Abidjan 415
23   The Abidjan Marathon 447

PART VIII   MY FAREWELL TO ARMS 491

24   Going the Last Mile … and the End of the Road 493
25   Lessons of the Forgotten Tragedy of Angola 527
Epilogue 543

Notes 545
Index 548

List of Plates

1. A 'bairro popular' (shanty town) in Luanda
2. A view of the UNAVEM headquarters in Vila Espa, outside Luanda: 'container city'
3. The author inspecting FALA assembled troops with Major-General Unimna of Nigeria, February, 1992
4. Boy soldiers (UNITA)
5. The CCPM, photographed just before the elections in September 1992.
6. The author meeting with Jonas Savimbi, Head of UNITA (also in attendance are Gilberto Rizzo and Ebrima Jobarteh)
7. The crucial meeting between President dos Santos and Dr Savimbi on 26 September 1992, three days before the elections
8. A Soviet-made Ilyushin helicopter being unloaded from a giant Antonov cargo plane at Luanda Airport, to join the makeshift airforce hurriedly assembled for the elections.
9. Francisco Domingo, the sole survivor of a UNAVEM II helicopter accident, in which 15 people died, including four Russian aircrew, is carried off a rescue plane at Luanda Airport.
10. Onofre dos Santos, Director-General of the elections, and Dr Holden Roberto, Head of FNLA, during electoral registration
11. Angolan youth before the election, Luanda, September 1992
12. Women waiting in line to cast their votes in the Sumbe hinterland on 30 September 1992.
13. A cartoon of the author which appeared in the *Jornal de Angola* on 26 September 1992.
14. A UN medals' parade in UNAVEM Headquarters
15. Refugees fleeing from the fighting which erupted again after the elections
16. Inauguration of Abidjan negotiations, April 1993 (the author with Foreign Minister Essy of Côte d'Ivoire).

Foreword

This is the personal story of my experiences as Special Representative of the Secretary-General of the United Nations for Angola and Head of the United Nations Angola Verification Mission from February 1992 to June 1993. It is the distillation of a more detailed analysis of my mission, which interested researchers may consult in the Bodleian Library in Oxford. The aim of this book is to try to convey some flavour of what it was like to live through that turbulent time while at the same time recording the events as they happened.

No one who was there could regard it as other than a traumatic experience. In stark contrast to the ferocity of the conflict that has riven their country for 30 years, individual Angolans are amiable and relaxed, generous in their instincts and endowed with a charm and inveterate gaiety that combine traits both African and Lusitanian. While stoically enduring the most unimaginable sufferings, the Angolan people have long yearned for peace. At no time was that longing more tellingly expressed than on 29 and 30 September 1992. On those two historic days more than four million of them – over 90 per cent of the registered voter population, an unheard of turnout for any Western country of long democratic tradition – waited patiently in line (sometimes overnight) to make their preference known in the first democratic elections ever held in Angola, some of them having walked many long miles to the polling station. It was a logistical miracle that it had been possible to organise elections at all in that huge, war-ravaged country, practically devoid of infrastructure. It was a further miracle that the elections passed off peacefully, in an atmosphere of great serenity and civic responsibility. That in itself was testimony to the Angolans' wish for a democratic and peaceful outcome that would allow them to get on with their lives and develop the enormous riches of their beautiful land.

The ensuing débâcle was all the more shattering, above all for Angolans but also for foreigners committed to seeing the peace process through. And when our desperate efforts to retrieve the situation foundered, the tragedy developed into one of incalculable proportions.

Worse still, it was a tragedy that left the world unmoved and unaware. Former Yugoslavia, Somalia and Cambodia were constantly in the headlines and on the television screens. Angola scarcely rated a mention, although the toll of human death and suffering was on a larger scale than in Bosnia. In colonial times the Portuguese dubbed the south-eastern region of Angola, whose inhospitable terrain rebuffed their attempts at conquest over several centuries, as the 'Terras do Fim Mundo' – the 'Lands at the end of the world'. Now, in the late twentieth century, that epithet has come to take on a new significance for the country as a whole. That is why, whenever I had a chance to speak to a wider public from distant Luanda, I called it 'the forgotten tragedy', a phrase that caught on as did the later and equally true, expression 'the worst war in the world'. It is also why, even after I ceased to have any official connection with Angola, I could not disengage myself and have felt impelled to seize any opportunity to bring this shocking catastrophe to the attention of anyone willing to listen. It is why I have written this book. And it is why I dedicate it to the Angolan people and their survival.

There is another purpose. The Angolan operation began just before the great burgeoning of peacekeeping efforts in the wake of the Cold War. A new hope was vested in the United Nations and huge demands were made of it, accompanied by great expectations. But all too often, inadequate resources and ambiguous mandates have led to massive disappointment and accusations of ineffectiveness. Such oversimplistic reactions ignored the complexities of the situations the United Nations was called upon to deal with, more often than not with one hand tied behind its back. They also conveniently overlooked the fact that the United Nations is much more than the Secretariat and the UN forces and civilian staff on the ground, whatever their shortcomings. So the short burst of popularity for the UN after the Cold War has deteriorated into a crisis of confidence, still at its height as I write.

There are, inevitably, lessons to be learned from the UN's involvement in Angola – lessons for the Secretariat, for the member states, indeed for the international community as a whole. It is not my intention to attempt to 'whitewash' the United Nations – after 41 years in its service I am all too aware of its failings, many of them deriving from the very international character of its constitution and structure. One of its endemic problems has been a failure to analyse and learn from particular experiences – positive and negative – and to apply those lessons to future operations. What I do hope to do is to put the UN's role in Angola, its achievements (for there were some) and failures into some kind of perspective, and suggest the lessons that may be culled. Whether or not those lessons are acted upon will now depend on others.

Villa Margarita
San Pedro de Tíquina
Lake Titicaca
Bolivia   MARGARET JOAN ANSTEE

Acknowledgements

I owe an inmense debt of gratitude to my aunt Christina Mills. Not only did she bear uncomplainingly the loneliness and worry of my long absence in Angola, always having something cheerful and amusing to say when we did manage to speak and providing the brief haven of Knill whenever I could escape, but without her constant encouragement this book would never have been finished. She read every word of every draft and spurred me on at moments when daily reliving the tragedy of Angola seemed almost too painful to bear.

Many others have helped me, not least those who lived and worked with me in Angola. Particular thanks are due to colleagues in UNAVEM who made available their own notes, diaries or personal reminiscences, notably Colonel Roger Mortlock and members of the New Zealand contingent, which he commanded so superbly, Tom White, my ever-reliable Chief Administrative Officer, and Gaby Parry, who won the admiration of all for her work as electoral coordinator in the eastern region, based in Luena, Moxico Province.

John Flynn, now British Ambassador in Caracas, Venezuela, gave up valuable time to check my recollections of the ceasefire negotiations we conducted from the bowels of the British Embassy during the battle for Luanda, and of other aspects of that dreadful weekend, described in Chapter 17, and provided me with the other half of his historic telephone conversation with Jonas Sawimbi. Ambassador Antonio Monteiro, now Director General of the Portuguese Foreign Ministry in Lisbon, and Dr. Onofre dos Santos, formerly the Director General of the Elections, also filled in gaps in my memory of key events.

From further afield Professor Gerald Bender of the University of California and Shawn McCormick of the Centre for Strategic and International Studies in Washington were generous with advice and back-up information, as was Alex Vines of Africa Watch. In the final stages Professor Alan James of Keile University provided invaluable counsel on the reduction of the original text to its published length.

Logistical production of the text encompassed several continents and I owe thanks to Malena Pacheco Revilla in Bolivia, Jane Deem in New York, Paula Clay, Margaret Hofman and Katharine Paull in the United Kingdom and, most especially of all, Isabel Berclaz-Lewis in Geneva, without whose herculean efforts and technical expertise a final, edited and homonegeous typescript would not have seen the light of day.

Many friends and former colleagues were generous with photographs – more than could be accommodated in the space available. Appropriate acknowledgement is made on each of the plates included. Particular thanks are due to Marco Vercrusse for the photograph on the jacket and for others inside, as well as to Professor Bender for the *collages* and for his remarkable technical skill in making the newspaper cartoon suitable for reproduction. I am also grateful to the United Nations for the use of some of the photographs.

MARGARET JOAN ANSTEE

Dramatis Personae*

United Nations Headquarters

Kofi Annan	First Assistant Secretary-General (and Deputy to Marrack Goulding), then Under-Secretary General (from March 1993) in the Department of Peacekeeping Operations.
Horacio Boneo	In charge of electoral technical assistance.
Dr Boutros Boutros-Ghali	Secretary-General.
Virendra Dayal	Under-Secretary-General and Chef de Cabinet to the Secretary-General.
Jan Eliasson	Under-Secretary-General for Humanitarian Affairs.
Ambassador Gharekhan	Indian Permanent Representative to the UN, later Under-Secretary-General in the Secretary-General's Office.
Marrack Goulding	Under-Secretary-General (first in the Department of Peacekeeping Operations (DPKO) then (from March 1993) in the Department of Political Affairs (DPA)).
Major Hornsby	Field Operations Division.
James Jonah	Under-Secretary-General.
Alvaro de Soto	Assistant Secretary-General in the Secretary-General's Office.
Dmitry Titov	Angolan desk officer in DPKO.

UNAVEM II

Military

Brigadier Hussein Aly	Deputy Chief Military Observer (until August 1992).
Sergeant Adilson Barboza Costa	UNPO killed in Uige.
Lt Col. William Egar	UNMO, Capanda, then Chief Operations Officer.
Captain Essam	UNMO in Kuito/Bié (commended for gallantry).
Major Stephen Honest	Chief Operations Officer.
Colonel Jamwal	Chief of Staff, then Regional Commander, Lubango.

*In the functions which they occupied during the period covered by this book.

Colonel Hank Morris	Chief of Air Support Logistics Group (elections).
Colonel Roger Mortlock	Regional Commander, Huambo.
Brigadier Michael Nyambuya	Liaison Officer with FALA, then Deputy Chief Military Observer and ultimately Acting Chief Military Observer (December 1992– July 1993).
Major Ribeiro	Chief Police Observer.
Captain Waldicir Rosas	Medical Officer.
Colonel Cameron Ross	Chief of Staff.
Major Dennis Strilchuk	Head of Movement Control.
Major General Edward Ushie Unimna	Chief Military Observer (until December 1992).

Civilian

João Albuquerque	Author's spokesman.
Afonso Almeida	Interpreter/translator.
Senhor Andrade	Gardener at Vila Espa.
Hugo Anson	Senior Political Adviser
Antonio Moreira de Barros	Author's personal bodyguard.
Sammy Buo	Chief Electoral Officer (from May 1992).
Mr. Driggers	Flight engineer (electoral air support unit).
Deolinda Leitão Green	Secretary
Maria Grossi	Deputy Chief Electoral Officer.
Ebrima Jobarteh	Executive Director
Elizabeth Pantaleón	Personal assistant to the author.
Christian Prat-Vincent	Interpreter/translator
Peter Scott-Bowden	Special assistant to the author (from December 1992).
Sigurdsson (Sigi)	Author's personal bodyguard.
Manuel Aranda de Silva	Director, Humanitarian Coordination Unit (from April 1993).
A. Mpazi Sinjela	Legal Adviser.
Patricia Stott	Personal assistant to the author. (April/May 1992)
John Truman	Chief Electoral Officer (April/May 1992).
Thomas White	Chief Administrative Officer.

Other UN Personnel

Lucinda Matos de Almeyda	Deputy Head, UNDP electoral technical assistance team.
Maître Alioune Blondin Beye	Author's successor as Special Representative of the Secretary-General.

Dramatis Personae

Philippe Borel	Representative of World Food Programme.
Miguel da Graça	Resident Representative of UN Development Programme.
Sergio Vieira de Melo	UNHCR official, proposed successor to the author, rejected by Dr Savimbi.
Jose Julio dos Reis	Head, UNDP electoral technical assistance team.
Layashi Yaker	Executive Secretary, UN Economic Commission for Africa.

Joint Political and Military Commission (CCPM)

Colonel, later General, Higino Carneiro	Member of Government Delegation.
General Chilingutila	Member of UNITA Delegation.
Dr Abel Chivukuvuku	UNITA 'Foreign Minister' and Deputy Head of UNITA Delegation.
General Ciel Da Concepcão ('Gato')	Member of Government Delegation.
General Antonio dos Santos França (N'dalu)	Head of Government Delegation.
General Ita	Member of Government Delegation.
Ambassador Edmund de Jarnette	Head of US Observer Delegation. (From October 1992.)
Ambassador Yuri Kapralov	Head of Russian Federation Observer Delegation. (until November 1992.)
General 'Mackenzie'	Member of UNITA Delegation.
Ambassador Jeffrey Millington	Head of US Observer Delegation. (until October 1992)
Ambassador Antonio Monteiro	Head of Portuguese Observer Delegation.
General Armindo Lucas Paulo ('Gato')	Member of UNITA Delegation.
Engineer Elias Salupeto Pena	Head of UNITA Delegation (and nephew of Dr Savimbi).
Dr Vladimir Petukov	Head of Russian Federation Observer. Delegation (until November 1992).
General Rasoilo	Member of Government Delegation.
Interior Vice Minister Fernando de Piedade Dias dos Santos ('Nando')	Deputy Head of Government Delegation.
General Tadeo	Member of UNITA Delegation.
General Zacharias	Member of UNITA Delegation.

Dramatis Personae

'The Troika' (Senior Representatives of the three Observer Countries)

Minister Durão Barroso	Secretary for Foreign Affairs and Cooperation, later Foreign Minister of Portugal.
Ambassador Herman ('Hank') Cohen	Assistant Secretary of State for Africa, US State Department (up to January 1993).
Ambassador Karasin	Foreign Ministry, Russian Federation.

Ad hoc Commission of the Security Council (October 1992)

Ambassador José Luis Jesús	Permanent Representative of Cape Verde to the UN (Head of Mission).
Ambassador Valentin V. Lozinsky	Deputy Permanent Representative of the Russian Federation to the UN.
Ambassador Joseph E. Perkins	Permanent Representative of the United States to the UN.
Ambassador Ahmed Snoussi	Permanent Representative of Morocco to the UN.

Government of Angola/MPLA

Dr Manuel Baltazar	Governor of Huambo province.
Dr Lazaro Dias	Minister of Justice, later Deputy Head of Parliament and columnist.
H.E. Fernando J De França Dias van Dunem	Prime Minister, later President of Congress.
Dr Paulo Jurge	Governor of Benguela province.
Dr Antonio Paulo Kassoma	Minister of Territorial Administration (From May 1992).
Dr Victor Lima	Foreign Affairs adviser to the President.
H.E. Pedro de Castro van Dunem ('Loy')	Foreign Minister.
General João de Matos	Chief of General Staff, FAA (from December 1992).
Ambassador M'binda	Permanent Representative to the UN.
Dr João de Miranda	Vice-Minister of Foreign Affairs.
Dr Marcolino Moco	Secretary General of MPLA, later Prime Minister.
H.E. Venâncio de Moura	Vice Minister for Foreign Affairs, later Foreign Minister.
Dr Faustino Muteka	Head of Government Delegation at the Addis Ababa and Abidjan negotiations.

Dr Lopo de Nascimento	Minister of Territorial Administration until May 1992
General Pedro Neto	FAPLA, later head of the FAA Air Force.
Dr Pitra Neto	Minister of Trade.
Ambassador Jose Patricio	Angolan Ambassador to the OAS in Washington and liaison with US State Department.
General Santana Andre Pitra ('Petroff')	Vice-Minister of the Interior in charge of the police, later Minister of the Interior.
Admiral Gaspar Rufino	FAPLA, later head of the FAA Navy.
H.E. Jose Eduardo dos Santos	President of Angola.
Dr Norberto dos Santos	Minister of Social Affairs.

UNITA

General Andrade	General taken into Government custody in Luanda after the battle for the city.
Brigadier Apollo	UNITA Commander in Uige.
General 'Ben-Ben'	Chief of General Staff (and nephew of Dr Savimbi).
General Bock	Close military adviser of Dr. Savimbi.
Norberto de Castro	Spokesman on VORGAN, later member of Parliament.
Dr Jeremiah Chitunda	Vice-President of UNITA (until October 1992).
General Dembo	Vice-President of UNITA (after Dr. Chitunda's death).
'George'	Dr Savimbi's private secretary.
Dr Victor Hossi	UNITA delegate to NEC, later Dr Savimbi's nominee for Minister of Culture in central Government (never assumed post).
Dr Jaka Jamba	UNITA's 'Minister' of Culture.
John Marques Kakumba	UNITA representative in Abidjan.
Lt. Col. Katu	UNITA Commander in Quilenges, Huila province.
Alicerces Mango	Secretary-General of UNITA (until October 1992).
General Eugenio Manuvakola	Deputy Secretary-General, later Secretary-General of UNITA (after Mr Mango's death) and leader of UNITA Delegation at Addis Ababa negotiations.

Dramatis Personae

Dr Carlos Morgado	Dr Savimbi's nominee for Vice-Minister of Social Assistance in central Government (never assumed post).
Jardo Muekalia	UNITA representative in Washington.
General Numa	Commander at Caxito.
Mrs Fatima Roque	UNITA's 'Minister' of Finance.
Brigadier Paolo Sachiambo	Delegate to Addis Ababa and Abidjan negotiations.
Brigadier Samakuva	UNITA representative in London.
Marcos Samondo	UNITA representative to the UN.
H.E. Dr Jonas Malheiro Savimbi	President of UNITA.
General Jerónimo Ukeme	Delegate to Addis Ababa negotiations.
João Vahekeni	UNITA representative in Geneva.
Dr Jorge Valentim	UNITA's 'Minister' of Information, leader of UNITA Delegation at Abidjan negotiations.
General Wambo	General taken into Government custody in Luanda after the battle for the city.
Brigadier Wenda	UNITA liaison with UNAVEM Regional Command in Huambo

Other Angolan Personalities

Ambassador Almeida	Spokesman of National Electoral Council and Ambassador to Ethiopia.
Afonso Catumbo	FAPLA prisoner who escaped from UNITA
Dr Jorge Chicoty	FDA leader (later Deputy Foreign Minister).
Tito Chingunji	prominent UNITA member who was killed in late 1991.
Dr Daniel Chipenda	senior MPLA member, later presidential candidate for PNDA.
Francisco Domingo	electoral official, only survivor of the third helicopter crash.
Dr Tony da Costa Fernandes	UNITA's 'Foreign Minister' who defected in March 1992 with General Puna to form their own party.
Dr Paulo Pinto João	CNDA leader.
Dr Andre Kilandamoko	PSDA leader.
José Manuel Miguel	CSD leader.
Dr Sebastian Miguel	PAJOCA.
Monsenhor Alexandre do Nascimento	Cardinal Archbishop of Luanda.

Dramatis Personae

Dr Agostinho Neto	Founder of MPLA and first President of Angola (died 1979).
Dr Alberto Neto	PDA leader.
Dr Adriano Parrenã	PAI leader.
Dr Luis dos Passos	PRD leader.
General Miguel N'Zau Puna	UNITA's Interior 'Minister' who defected in March 1992 with Dr da Costa Fernandes to form their own party.
Dr Holden Roberto	President FNLA.
Dr Onofre dos Santos	Director-General of the Elections.
Wilson dos Santos	Prominent UNITA member who was killed in the late 1991.
Sra Analia María Caldeira de Vitoria P. Simeão	The only woman presidential candidate (for PLD).
Dr Antonio Caetano de Sousa	President, National Electoral Council.
N'Zita Tiago	Leader of FLEC/FAC.
Eng. Mfulupinga N'Landa Victor	PDP/ANA leader.

United States

Ambassador Madeleine Albright	US Permanent Representative to the UN.
Professor Gerald Bender	University of California.
Doug Bereuter	Member of Permanent Select Committee of Intelligence of the House of Representatives.
Robert Cabelly	Director, Department of Southern African Affairs, State Department.
Chester Crocker	Former Assistant Secretary of State for African Affairs and Co-Chair of the CSIS Study Group on Angola.
Ambassador Jeffrey Davidow	Deputy Assistant Secretary for Africa.
Major Fritz	Military adviser in Luanda.
Senator Nancy Kassebaum	Co-Chair of the CSIS Study Group of Angola.
Shawn McCormick	Assistant Director of Studies, CSIS.
Dave McCurdy	Member of Permanent Select Committee on Intelligence of the House of Representatives.
Mr Metelits	U.S. liaison officer, Luanda.
Ambassador George Moose	Assistant Secretary of State for Africa (from early 1993).
Tony Newton	US liaison officer, Luanda.
Richard Roth	Deputy Director, of Southern African Affairs, State Department.

Martin Olav Sabo	Member of Permanent Select Committee on Intelligence of the House of Representatives.
Bud Schuster	Member of Permanent Select Committee on Intelligence of the House of Representatives.
Nancy Soderberg	National Security Council.
Maurice Tempelsman	Co-Chair of the CSIS Study Group on Angola.
Ambassador Walker	US Deputy Permanent Representative to the UN.
Ambassador Jennifer Ward	National Security Council.
James Woods	U.S. Department of Defence (Pentagon).

Other Personalities

Pik Botha	Foreign Minister of South Africa.
Mr and Mrs Chambers	UK hostages taken by UNITA during the battle of Luanda.
Minister Amara Essy	Foreign Minister of Côte d'Ivoire.
Ambassador John Flynn	British Ambassador to Angola.
Dr Hage Geingob	Prime Minister of Namibia.
Colonel Bob Griffiths	Military Attaché, British Embassy.
Ambassador Gert J. Gröbler	Chief of the Directorate for Southern Africa, South African Department of External Affairs.
Sir David Hannay	UK Permanent Representative to the UN.
King Hassan II	King of Morocco.
Elizabeth (Sissy) Hejny	Author's housekeeper.
President Felix Houphoüet-Boigny	President of Côte d'Ivoire.
Mr Kruger	Acting Head of the South African Liaison Office in Luanda.
Karl Maier	*Independent* correspondent.
Ambassador Marker	Permanent Representative of Pakistan to the UN.
Ambassador Aziz Mekouan	Moroccan Ambassador to Angola.
Christina Mills	Author's aunt.
Dr Robert Mugabe	President of Zimbabwe.
M. Nicaud	ICRC representative in Luanda.
H.E. Sam Nujoma	President of Namibia.
Julian Ozanne	*Financial Times* correspondent.
Ambassador Rocha Paris	Portuguese Ambassador to Angola.

Colonel Fred Rindel	Senior Staff Officer of the South African Defence Force (SADF).
Ambassador Margaret Rothwell	British Ambassador to Côte d'Ivoire.
Ambassador Salim-Salim	Secretary General, OAU.
Ambassador Stewart	Permanent Ambassador of South Africa to the UN.
Ambassador Vorontsov	Permanent Representative to the UN of the Russian Federation.

List of Abbreviations

ACMO	Acting Chief Military Observer
CAO	Chief Administrative Officer
CASO	Chief of Staff for Air Operations
CCFA	Joint Commission for the Formation of the Angolan Armed Forces
CCPM	Comisão Conjunta Politica Militar (Joint Political Military Commission)
CEO	Chief Electoral Officer
CMO	Chief Military Observer
CMVF	Joint Ceasefire Verification and Monitoring Commission
CNDA	Convencão Nacional Democrática de Angola
COO	Chief Operations Officer
CSIS	Centre of International and Strategic Studies, Washington
DCMO	Deputy Chief Military Observer
DHA	Department of Humanitarian Affairs (UN)
DPA	Department of Political Affairs (UN)
DPKO	Department of Peacekeeping Operations (UN)
ECA	UN Economic Commission for Africa
EC	European Community
FAA	Forças Armadas Angolanas (Angolan Armed Forces)
FALA	UNITA forces
FAO	Food and Agriculture Organization
FAPLA	MPLA/Government forces
FDA	Foro Democrático Angolano
FLEC	Frente de Libertação del Enclave de Cabinda (Front for the Liberation of the Cabinda enclave)
FLEC/FAC	Radical arm of FLEC
FNLA	Frente Nacional de Libertação de Angola (National Front for the Liberation of Angola)
GPS	Global Positioning Systems
ICRC	International Committee of the Red Cross
MOVCON	Movement Control
MPLA	Movimento Popular de Libertação de Angola (Popular Movement for the Liberation of Angola)
NEC	National Electoral Council
NGO	Non-Governmental Organization
OAS	Organization of American States
OAU	Organization of African Unity
PAI	Partido Angolano Independiente

PAJOCA	Partido da Aliança da Juventude Operária e Camponesa de Angola
PC	Political Commission of CCPM
PDA	Partido Democrático Angolano
PDP-ANA	Partido Democrático para o Progreso da Alianza Nacional Angolana
PEC	Provincial Electoral Council
PLD	Partido Liberal Democrático
PRD	Partido Renovador Democrático
PSD	Partido Social Democrático
SAAF	South African Air Force
SADF	South African Defence Force
SC	Security Council
SRSG	Special Representative of the Secretary-General
UN	United Nations
UNAVEM	United Nations Angola Verification Mission
UNDP	United Nations Development Programme
UNDTCD	United Nations Department of Technical Cooperation for Development
UNFPA	United Nations Fund for Population Activities
UNHCR	United Nations High Commission for Refugees
UNICEF	United Nations Childrens Fund
UNITA	União Nacional para a Independencia Total de Angola (National Union for the Total Independence of Angola).
UNMO	United Nations Military Observer
UNOV	United Nations Office at Vienna
UNPO	United Nations Police Observer
US	United States
VORGAN	Voice of the Black Cockerel (UNITA radio)
WFP	World Food Programme
WHO	World Health Organization

Angola

Part I
The Context: Personal, National and International

Part I

1 A Late Night Telephone Call

People constantly ask: 'Why on earth did you take that mission on?' Like all good questions, it has a number of answers.

First of all, I was given very little time to reflect on my answer. Late at night on 5 February 1992 I was rung up in Vienna (where since 1987 I had been Under-Secretary-General and Director-General of the United Nations Office at Vienna) by the Chef de Cabinet of Dr Boutros Boutros-Ghali, who had assumed his functions as Secretary-General only a few weeks previously. I was in bed in a state of drowsy semiconsciousness, from which I was brusquely awakened by Virendra Dayal's opening words: 'The Secretary-General would like you to go to Angola as his Special Representative and to head the UN Angola Verification Mission there'. When I had collected myself sufficiently to ask a few questions, I was further electrified to learn that my answer was expected in 24 hours.

This is the kind of situation that concentrates the mind wonderfully, to paraphrase Dr Johnson. I knew enough of the Angolan problem to appreciate that, while the cause was very worthwhile, a considerable gamble was involved. Early next day I rang up an old friend who has been an acknowledged authority and writer on Angola for many decades. His advice was unhesitating: 'Don't touch it with a barge-pole', he said. 'It won't work. It's virtually an impossible mission and you'll only get hurt in the process.'

Why, then, did I perversely decide to go ahead? Perhaps stubbornness, rather than perversity, is the answer. From my early childhood my stalwart mother dinned into me a saying that still rings through my ears over 20 years after her death: 'Never say your mother had a jibber'. The origin of this strange phrase, which she claimed to be Irish, is obscure, but the reference is plainly to a horse that jibs at a fence. Hence I have spent a good part of my life hurling myself at obstacles of various kinds and differing degrees of difficulty, with predictably diverse results: sometimes crashing into the barricade itself; sometimes falling into the water on the other side; and, just occasionally, clearing the top with a clean pair of heels. Frequently, no doubt, it would have been easier just to edge round the side, but early upbringing will not be denied. In the case of Angola this option simply did not exist. It was all or nothing.

Not that I dashed at this particular fence without scrutinising the lie of the land. I consulted my colleague at headquarters, Marrack (Mig) Goulding, then the Under-Secretary-General in charge of peacekeeping, who had been British Ambassador in Luanda in the early 1980s. My question to him was brief and to the point: was there any chance of success? Mig's answer was more nuanced: it was certainly a difficult mission but he did not consider it a totally lost cause; with some luck it could be pulled off. More clinchingly he added that there had been some talk of the new Secretary-General asking him to take charge of the

Angola mission, and that he would have had no hesitation in taking up the assignment.

All of this I weighed up against some personal considerations. In six months it would be 40 years since I started work with the UN, in the Philippines, helping to set up one of the very first programmes of technical cooperation. For more than 20 years thereafter I had been constantly in the field, running operational programmes in Asia, Africa, Latin America and the Arab region. I had never wanted to work at headquarters but matters were taken out of my hands after the Pinochet coup in Chile, where I was serving as Resident Representative of the United Nations Development Programme (UNDP), when the DINA (the secret police) ransacked my house, regardless of diplomatic immunity. After due interval, UNDP had transferred me to New York in 1974. Thereafter I had remained in headquarters, and had been promoted to become Assistant Administrator of UNDP for programme policy and evaluation in 1977; Assistant Secretary-General of the United Nations, responsible for the Department of Technical Cooperation, at the end of 1978; and, in 1987, Under-Secretary-General and Director-General of the United Nations Office at Vienna with responsibility for all the programmes dealing with social policy and development and with the control of narcotic drug abuse and trafficking. In all these functions I had continued to be involved in the management of operational programmes worldwide. I had also been given special assignments in major disaster relief operations, including Bangladesh, the Mexican earthquake, the Chernobyl nuclear explosion and the burning oil wells in Kuwait as a result of the Gulf War. So I had had ample opportunity to keep my hand in, operationally speaking. But it was not the same as being 'in the front line'. I still chafed to get back to the field and regain direct contact with practical events, as opposed to the skewed presentations of reality served up in conferences and resolutions, where political gamesmanship, vapid compromises and costly arguments over punctuation seemed all too often to take the place of serious debate on major world problems. I had resigned myself to the probability that I was now too senior to be given a field post. And here, out of the blue, the opportunity had arisen. The temptation to end my career with a field mission was very great.

Moreover the nature of the assignment itself made it hard to refuse. The tragic suffering of the Angolan people went back a very long way in history. Most recently, war had ravaged their lives and consumed their country's potentially rich resources for the last 30 years. Now the end of the Cold War and the Peace Accords, signed at Bicesse in Portugal in May 1991, held out greater promise for a settlement than ever before. How could any responsible and caring person reject the opportunity of helping, however modestly, to consolidate this process? There was the added incentive for someone like myself who had worked for so long on development issues, that Angola was far from being a 'basket case'. It was blessed with vast resources, which, once peace was restored, offered the promise of rapid economic and social development, and greatly improved conditions of life for its relatively small population.

The 'woman thing' also came into the picture. By historical accident, or by virtue of belonging to a particular generation, I had been a pioneer in several areas not previously open to women. I had been one of the first women admitted to the British Foreign Service, the first woman field officer sent out by the United Nations; the first woman Resident Representative of what later became the UN Development Programme, involving the planning and management of development cooperation programmes in the field; the first woman to reach the levels of Assistant Secretary-General and Under-Secretary-General through the ranks, rather than as a political appointee. By coincidence I had just finished writing a chapter for a book being prepared by an American university in which women leaders recounted their experiences. Among other things, I had pointed out that 'peacekeeping' was the one area that women had not yet penetrated in the UN, recalling that, when the previous Secretary-General, Javier Pérez de Cuéllar, had considered appointing me as head of peacekeeping, an ambassador from a Western country had said that no woman could ever occupy such a position because it involved 'dealing with the military'. In my contribution, I had argued, more generally, that the only way to explode myths that women cannot perform this or that job, is for them to show that they *can*, and that it was therefore incumbent on women to seize any opportunity to do so, rather than shrinking back from it, as all too often happens. Peacekeeping being the one such myth not yet exploded in the United Nations, I found myself hoist on my own petard.

I realised that it was a case of 'damned if you do, and damned if you don't'. If I refused, it would be all too easy for those sceptical of women's capability in the peacekeeping area to say 'Well, it was offered to a women, but she refused'. By the same token, women could understandably feel that I had let them down by not rising to the challenge, and had been hypocritical in not adhering to my own precepts. Yet the risks involved in accepting were considerable. Success was by no means assured in the fraught and fragile situation prevailing in Angola. Failure would not only entail unspeakably tragic consequences but also the inevitable search for a scapegoat, a role for which the UN seems particularly well designed. And if the senior UN official were a woman, then the aforesaid sceptics would have a field day.

This is a more orderly presentation of the disparate thoughts that jangled through my head during those 24 hours. I cannot say that they had sorted themselves out by the time the deadline came. But by then I found myself impelled by a confused combination of forces towards that very high fence. I accepted.

Things then moved rapidly. On Friday 7 February the Secretary-General officially announced my appointment. I was to take up my assignment on 1 March. In true United Nations style, while a rather leisurely approach had been adopted as to whether to appoint a Special Representative at all, a proposal agreed in principle only in the autumn of 1991, once the appointment was made the individual was expected to get there the day before yesterday. In the meantime Mig Goulding was to lead a mission on 15 February to Luanda to pave the way and prepare the budget for the electoral components of the mandate.

In theory, this would give me a little time in which to wind up my office in Vienna, say my official farewells as Director-General and pack up my apartment. These were rather more daunting tasks than might appear, as I had the accretions of 40 years of international life to deal with, could take only the minimum of belongings to Luanda, and had the added problem, so familiar to senior women executives, of 'not having a wife' to deal with the domestic tasks. I was also to have an intensive briefing in New York before flying off to Luanda.

Even this plan went awry. Late on 14 February headquarters telephoned to say that Mig could not, after all, head the mission to Luanda, and could I therefore take his place?

So on Sunday 16 February, barely 48 hours later, I found myself on a plane to Brussels, where I caught the connecting flight to Luanda, armed only with information I had managed to glean from the various official UN documents that had been hurriedly despatched to me.

2 The Background

Angola, with a total area of 1 246 700 square kilometres, is larger than the combined territories of France, Germany and Italy. Strategically situated on the west coast of southern Africa, it is enviably blessed with natural resources, among them rich deposits of petroleum, diamonds and iron ore. The climate and topography range from the hot, humid, coastal fringe in the north and the high plateau in the centre, to the semi-arid bush lands of the south-east and the desert that stretches south along the coast from Benguela to merge across the frontier into the Namibian desert. The agricultural potential is equally promising. So too are the prospects for tourism in a country boasting an enormous variety of landscapes – from beautiful, empty beaches to high mountains, spectacular waterfalls and wild, uninhabited spaces where exotic wildlife will once more thrive if peace and order are restored.

Angola's history has not been as felicitous as its natural prospects. A colony of Portugal since the first discovery of its northern coastal areas in 1483 (the hinterland remained largely unexplored until the latter half of the nineteenth century), Angola was virtually – and tardily – catapulted into independence in the 1970s, more by the force of events occurring in Portugal itself than by any planned and gradual transfer of power to its dependent peoples.

Various indigenous movements of resistance, which were to play a prominent role in later events, had emerged: the Movimento Popular da Libertação de Angola (MPLA) in 1956, the Frente Nacional de Libertação de Angola (FNLA) in 1962, and the União Nacional para la Independencia Total de Angola (UNITA) in 1966. While they were the source of considerable harassment to the Portuguese colonial authorities, their effectiveness was diminished by dissension between the groups. Partly based on rivalries between their charismatic leaders (Agostinho Neto of the MPLA, Holden Roberto of the FNLA and Jonas Savimbi of UNITA), these rifts were exacerbated by ethnic loyalties and traditional affiliations with certain geographic areas of the country. The MPLA was strongly 'mestiço' and Kimbundo (the second largest ethnolinguistic category) in leadership and composition, with its territorial roots in the north-western part of the country. The FNLA had its base among the Kikongo further north still, along the frontier with Zaire. The main support for UNITA came from the Ovimbundu people, the largest ethnolinguistic category (nearly 40 per cent of the total population) whose core lived in the central highlands around the town of Huambo, the reminder spread out more widely.

The tiny northern enclave of Cabinda was formally incorporated into Angola as late as 1885, through the Treaties of Simulambuco. Its importance is quite disproportionate to its size, since it has proven reserves of oil in excess of three billion barrels – at present the yield is more than 500 000 barrels per day. Efforts to promote Cabindan independence began in 1956, and in 1963 the Front for the

Liberation of the Enclave of Cabinda (FLEC) was formed. The push for separation has continued unabated since Angola obtained its own independence, fuelled by a sentiment that the needs of its population have not been given sufficient attention by the central government: while Cabinda is the wealthiest province, upon which much of the development of the rest of the country depends, its standard of living is one of the lowest. During the intervening years the FLEC itself has splintered into two armed factions and several political groupings.

The divisions between the contending groups and the fierce resistance of the Portuguese make it improbable that independence would have been attained as early as 1975 (late as this was in comparison with other African countries), had not the authoritarian regime in Portugal been overthrown in April 1974 by an armed forces movement. The new metropolitan government proceeded to divest itself of the Portuguese colonies in Africa, and Angola was abruptly left to its own devices in 1975, which in effect meant abandoning it to the three major anticolonial movements to fight it out, with the added dimension of superpower conflict.

Some efforts were made to bring about a smooth transition. In January 1975 the Portuguese government signed the Alvor agreement with the leaders of the MPLA, the FNLA and UNITA, providing for a transitional, coalition government, comprising the three groups, and fixing 11 November 1975 as the date for total independence. Unfortunately the agreement broke down almost immediately, as conflict between the MPLA, the FNLA and UNITA intensified and was exacerbated by the increasing involvement of foreign powers. In late January the United States had authorised covert assistance to the FNLA, and over the following months more assistance was forthcoming from the United States, Zaire and South Africa for the FNLA and UNITA. On the other side the Soviet Union increased its arms deliveries to the MPLA, and Cuba also stepped up its help, not only training MPLA guerrillas but, later in the year, sending in combat troops. In October a South-African-led motorised force entered Angola from Namibia in support of the FNLA and UNITA, and advanced to within 100 kilometres of Luanda. This led to a massive increase in Soviet military supplies and Cuban troops, which reversed the military situation.

On 11 November 1975 the MPLA proclaimed the establishment of the People's Republic of Angola, with Agostinho Neto as its president. The FNLA and UNITA attempted to set up a separate regime in Huambo. Early in 1976, however, the South African troops withdrew to Namibia, and the MPLA achieved an apparent military victory, with the support of Cuban reinforcements, which eliminated the FNLA as a serious contender and drove the remnants of UNITA's army into the south-eastern bush. In February of that year the MPLA regime was accorded membership of the Organization of African Unity and was formally recognised by Portugal. Angola became a member of the United Nations in 1976.

There followed 16 years of internecine civil war, which further ravaged the Angolan countryside, halted development, destroyed the fragmentary infrastructure, cost an estimated 350 000 lives, permanently maimed and disabled another 60 000 people and sent hundreds of thousands of refugees fleeing across the borders into Zaire and Zambia. Internal conflict was almost certainly inevitable, given the fierce discord already rampant among the various nationalist groups during the anticolonial struggle, but was aggravated first by the abrupt nature of the Portuguese departure, and second by Angola's key strategic position – military, political and economic – which made it a valuable prize in the Cold War. There can be no doubt that the internal squabble among Angolans would have petered out much earlier, probably from sheer inanition, and would not have attained such horrific dimensions had this desirable piece of real estate not become a pawn in the struggle between the superpowers for dominance in southern Africa, where the strength and evolving role of South Africa were also of signal importance.

So the battle waged back and forth across this vast and rugged land, waxing and waning according to the seasons – wet or dry – and the varying fighting capabilities of the two sides, which largely depended on the support of their outside backers. The Soviet Union and Cuba assisted the MPLA regime, self-declared as Marxist–Leninist, while UNITA's military threat to the government quickly revived with considerable assistance from South Africa. The United States was initially prevented from giving any assistance to groups in Angola, unless specifically approved by Congress, by the so-called 'Clark Amendment' of 1976, but support was given to UNITA and its leader, Jonas Savimbi, in many other ways, including non-recognition of the MPLA regime as the government of Angola. The 'Clark Amendment' was repealed in 1985, after which direct United States assistance to UNITA began again.

No solution to the Angolan issue could be found in isolation from the interconnected problems in the region, and no progress could be made in the context of the Cold War. Thus, in his eight-year negotiations Chester Crocker, the Assistant US Secretary of State for African Affairs of the two Reagan Administrations from 1981 to 1988, linked Namibia's independence and the withdrawal of South Africa from Namibia with the withdrawal of Cuban forces from Angola, but the real breakthrough came only after Mikhail Gorbachev achieved power in the Soviet Union and the Cold War began to thaw.

In New York on 22 December 1988, a trilateral agreement was signed between Angola, Cuba and South Africa, as well as a bilateral agreement between Cuba and Angola, which provided, *inter alia*, for the withdrawal of Cuban troops by 1 July 1991 and the withdrawal of South African troops from Namibia. On this basis it was possible to complete Namibia's transition to independence, a process successfully concluded on 21 March 1990.

The first United Nations Angolan Verification Mission (UNAVEM) was established by the UN Security Council on 20 December 1988 (Security Council Resolution 626). UNAVEM's task was to verify the redeployment of Cuban troops northwards from the vicinity of the Namibian border and their staged and total withdrawal from Angola, to be completed by 1 July 1991. UNAVEM became operational on 3 January 1989 and by 25 May 1991 – more than one month before the deadline – all 50 000 Cuban troops had left. On 6 June the Secretary-General reported to the Security Council that UNAVEM had fully carried out the mandate entrusted to it.

While all this was going on, peace had not exactly broken out in Angola. The solution of the Namibian part of the equation meant that the internal Angolan issue could be addressed directly, but it continued to prove a hard nut to crack. In the wake of the New York accords, both President José Eduardo Dos Santos (who had succeeded President Agostinho Neto on the latter's death in 1979) and Jonas Savimbi gave signs of readiness to seek a political solution, but various attempts to mediate between them were unsuccessful. After a meeting of seven African heads of state in Luanda in May 1989, the two leaders met for the first time in June in Gbadolite, at a gathering hosted by the Zairian president, Mobutu Sese Seku, and attended by 18 African heads of state. A ceasefire was agreed. Unfortunately, confusion and misunderstandings over the conditions under which it would operate led to its almost immediate collapse.

Fighting resumed and developed into large-scale attacks by mid-August. Despite further mediation efforts by African states, little progress was made. At the end of 1989 the MPLA launched a major attack against Mavinga, a town in the south-east, which provided a strategic stepping-stone to the UNITA headquarters of Jamba. It was graphically code-named 'Final Assault'. At first they made impressive gains, but South African and US assistance to UNITA led to a stalemate by March 1990. Renewed attempts were made to get them to the negotiating table, with the United States and the Soviet Union initially in the forefront. Ultimately it was Portugal that opened up the way to the Bicesse Peace Accords. The mediator was the Portuguese Secretary of State for Foreign Affairs and Cooperation, José Durão Barroso (later Foreign Minister).

Agreement was only reached after six rounds of talks, interspersed with all manner of setbacks and changes of position by one side or the other and lasting just over a year. Fighting actually intensified during the last stages of negotiation, when UNITA laid siege to Luena, and continued even after the cease-fire came into effect on 15 May 1991, right up to the historic moment on 31 May in Bicesse, Portugal, when President dos Santos and Jonas Savimbi, the President of UNITA, shook hands and signed the documents officially ending 16 years of civil war.

The Bicesse Peace Accords covered all aspects of the convoluted conflict. First and foremost was the agreement on a ceasefire, stipulating the actions to be taken by both sides and a timetable for their completion. Of special importance was cantonment of the troops, together with their weapons, in 50 assembly areas scattered all over the country: 27 for Government troops and 23 for UNITA troops. This was to start on 1 July 1991 and be completed by 1 August 1991. Another important proviso obligated both sides to refrain from acquiring lethal material. By the same token, the United States and the Soviet Union agreed to cease to supply lethal material to any Angolan party and to encourage other countries to do likewise. (This became known as the 'triple zero option'). Border control posts were to be set up at 37 points along Angola's extensive frontiers, as well as controls at 32 airports and 22 ports.

The second attachment to the Peace Accords was entitled 'Fundamental principles for the establishment of peace in Angola'. These included, on the one hand, recognition by UNITA of the Angolan State, of President dos Santos and of the Angolan Government until elections were held, and on the other, the free participation of UNITA in political activities, in accordance with a revised constitution that the Angolan Government would draw up in consultation with all parties, based on the laws of a multiparty democracy. The peace process was to culminate in the first 'free and fair' democratic, multiparty elections conducted under international observation. Parallel with this process, a new national army was to be created.

Attachment III, 'Concepts for resolving the issues still pending between the Government of the People's Republic of Angola and UNITA', covered much of the same ground. One point requires special mention. Paragraph 4 stated unequivocally that *'overall political supervision of the cease-fire process will be the responsibility of the Angolan parties ...'* (my emphasis). Its verification would be the responsibility of the international monitoring group.' In addition, 'The United Nations will be invited to send monitors to *support the Angolan parties*, at the request of the Government of Angola'. (again, my emphasis)

The fourth and last attachment of the Bicesse Accords, the 'Protocol of Estoril', put flesh on all these manifold activities. It stated that the elections would take place between 1 September and 30 November 1992, preferably during the first part of this period – between 1 September and 1 October 1992; that is, 16–18 months after the ceasefire. This had been a major stumbling block upon which the negotiations had very nearly foundered. UNITA had wanted the elections to take place in very short order, a maximum of nine months, or less if possible. The Government had insisted that elections could not be properly organised in less than three years. The final compromise was the arithmetical one of splitting the difference rather than basing it on an analysis of the tasks involved. Moreover no provision was made for prolonging this period in the event of slippage in completing the measures needed to consolidate the peace process before the election.

Probably the most important of these was the formation of the Angolan Armed Forces. The basic, and crucial, principle was that the new Armed Forces were to be non-partisan and neutral, made up of officers and soldiers drawn from both sides. The total number of troops was to be drastically scaled down from the estimated total of 200 000 men then under arms, under the flags of the two rival groups, to 40 000, of whom 20 000 would come from FAPLA, the government army, and 20 000 from FALA, UNITA's army. An air force, totalling 6000 officers and men, and a navy of 4000 would initially be formed from

FAPLA personnal, since UNITA had only land forces, but UNITA elements would be trained as soon as possible. The new Armed Forces were to be in place, and fully operational, before the date of the elections. A tall order in itself, it also meant that all other troops would be demobilised and disarmed in the interim.

Stipulations about the role and composition of the police were much less specific. The neutrality of the police was to be verified and monitored by joint teams, comprising designated members from both parties and UN police observers. UNITA's participation in the police force, while envisaged, was ambiguously phrased. It was to be by 'invitation of the government'. UNITA was to be responsible for the personal safety of its highest-ranking leaders, and the government would give police status to those charged with this task.

Another element critical to the consolidation of the peace process and a united country was the extension of the central administration to all parts of Angola, since the government controlled only a small proportion of the territory. The principle was barely enunciated, however. The practicalities were to be studied later by joint teams within the framework of the Joint Political Military Commission, of which the better-known Portuguese acronym was CCPM.

The CCPM was to be at the apex of a complex network of joint monitoring mechanisms at every level, in every region, and on every subject germane to the Peace Accords. The CCPM's mission was defined as 'the overall political supervision of the ceasefire process. It will have the duty to see that the Peace Accords are applied, thereby guaranteeing strict compliance with all political and military understandings, and to make the final decision on possible violation of these Accords'.

In keeping with the concept that responsibility for implementing the Peace Accords lay with the Angolans, the only full members of the CCPM were to be representatives of the Government and UNITA, and meetings were to be presided over alternately by each side, with decisions taken by consensus. Representatives of the three observer countries – Portugal, the United States and the Soviet Union – were cited as part of the core composition of the CCPM with observer status. The United Nations was relegated to another category – 'The United Nations *may* be represented in *the capacity of invited guest*' (my emphasis).

The CCPM's subsidiary organisations were the Joint Cease-fire Verification and Monitoring Commission (CMVF), in the meetings of which the United Nations was also to be '*invited* to participate' (my emphasis); the Joint Commission for the Formation of the Angolan Armed Forces (CCFA), in which the United Nations would not participate, international assistance in this case being provided by France, Portugal and the United Kingdom; and the Political Commission, at whose meetings the United Nations was again to be represented upon invitation. The CCPM's mandate was to end on the date that the elected Government took office.

It will be observed that the United Nations was hardly accorded a central role. This flowed from the fact that the long negotiations had been mainly carried out by the three observer countries. There had also been some participation by the Organization of African Unity and African Heads of State, but virtually none by the United Nations. The United Nations had been represented only during the later stages, and then only at the military level, by the Deputy Military Adviser to the Secretary-General, who acted as 'a technical adviser on the cease-fire aspects';[1] there was no representation at the political level.

The nature of UN involvement in the implementation of the Bicesse Accords had been one of the fraught issues that bade fair to prevent agreement being reached at all. UNITA, no doubt on account of its deep mistrust of the Government, had wanted the UN to be entrusted with a major role of direct supervision of all aspects of the process, supported by adequate resources, including contingents of armed UN troops ('Blue Helmets'). The Government, conversely, had been reluctant to see the UN playing any part at all, and had insisted that its role should be minimal, on the ground that a major UN presence, with mandated supervisory powers, would trespass on Angolan sovereignty. The compromise reached was that the UN's role would be merely one of verification. Even this would be exercised at one remove, through the mechanisms of the CCPM, thus conferring responsibility for the successful implementation of the Bicesse Accords squarely on the Angolan parties.

Compromise is the essence of negotiation, without which agreement could never be reached, and the Bicesse Accords, in themselves a diplomatic triumph, due in large part to Minister Durão Barroso, could be no exception. But this particular compromise, and that over the timing of the elections, were to store up serious trouble for the peace process and for the United Nations.

The United Nations acted promptly to formalise its participation. On 20 May 1991 the Secretary-General informed the Security Council[2] that on 8 May he had received a formal request from the Angolan Minister for Foreign Affairs for United Nations participation and proposed that the mandate of the existing UN mission, UNAVEM, be expanded and prolonged to include verification of the ceasefire and of the neutrality of the Angolan police. He noted that the two sides had not yet decided which international organisation or organisations they would ask to provide assistance for the elections.

The Secretary-General's report envisaged 350 military observers, who would be stationed at UNAVEM's headquarters in Luanda, in six regional headquarters colocated with those of the CMVF, at each of the 50 troop assembly areas and at 12 'critical points' at certain ports, airfields and border crossings, as well as in mobile border patrols. Ninety police observers were to be deployed in teams of four in each province. There was to be an air unit and a medical unit. Civilian support personnel, numbering about 80, were to be drawn from the UN Secretariat and supplemented by locally recruited staff. The rank of the Chief Military Observer was to be raised to Major-General. This mandate of UNAVEM II would last from the date on which the ceasefire entered into force, namely 31 May 1991, until the day following the completion of the presidential and legislative elections. An addendum estimated the total cost for the full 18-month period at US$132.3 million.

On 30 May 1991 the Security Council adopted Resolution 696, establishing UNAVEM II for a period of 17 months. Immediate steps were taken to implement it. By the end of September 1991, military observers were in place in all the troop assembly areas in use by then, and police monitors were stationed in all provinces. This was a remarkable feat, considering the appalling logistical conditions, the remoteness of many of the locations and the two-and-a-half-month delay by UN member States in approving UNAVEM II's budget.

On 1 October 1991 Brigadier-General Péricles Ferreira Gómez of Brazil was succeeded as Chief Military Observer of UNAVEM II by Major General Edward Ushie Unimna of Nigeria. It was not until 5 December 1991 that the Angolan Government officially requested the Secretary-General to send UN observers to follow the Angolan electoral process and provide technical assistance. It was about this time also that the appointment of a political head for UNAVEM II, in the guise of a Special Representative of the Secretary-General, was mooted.

This was the context in which my appointment was made some two months later, and in which I made my first visit to Luanda.

3 First Mission to Angola

'The next morning I saw from the window of my descending plane a motionless white patch surrounded by the sun. It was Luanda.'[1]

The words are not mine, but those of Ryszard Kapuscinski, describing his arrival in Luanda 1975, in his book *Another Day of Life*. I did not read that moving book until the end of my mission – an inexplicable omission and yet that late reading proved more affecting, bringing out more starkly the awful affinities between 1975 and 1992–93.

Those affinities did not, however, extend to my first view of Luanda. The sun was indeed shining, but my impression was one of redness rather than white – a rufous desert bordering the blue waters of the southern Atlantic, as if the very earth was stained with blood. We did not fly over the city and that, seen from a distance, was no longer white, but a monochrome grey. As the plane swooped down, clusters of low hovels of an even more sombre grey came into view, intersected by mean and dingy streets.

It was blisteringly hot as the passengers straggled out, blinking in the glare of the sun, though it was barely 7 a.m.; the humid, foetid air seemed to have been breathed so many times, and by so many people, that it was almost drained of oxygen.

At the foot of the aircraft steps waited a car flying the UN flag, and a small huddle of people. I was greeted first by Major-General Unimna. He was a smallish, wiry man in his forties, with bright shrewd eyes and a pugnacious jaw. I had been warned that his personality was not of the easiest and it did not take exceptional insight to realise that it could not be pleasant to have a new chief put over your head when you had been running the operation for nearly five months. The fact that this was no reflection on his abilities, but rather of a tardy decision by the Security Council that the operation should have a political head, could not greatly assuage injured self-esteem; that that person was not only a civilian, but British *and* female to boot could only too easily be interpreted as adding insult to injury. Some senior staff told me early on that they thought General Unimna was only too happy to have someone on whose shoulders the responsibility for an increasingly complex mission, with growing political implications, could be squarely placed, but it would have been foolish to bank on that. I was conscious that our relations must be handled with consummate care. Fortunately they got off to an encouragingly cordial start at the airport and during the four days of intensive activity – briefings, official calls, discussions and field visits – that followed.

Others among the greeting party included the Deputy Chief Military Observer, Brigadier General Hussein Aly of Egypt, the Chief of Staff, Colonel Jamwal of India, the Senior Political Adviser, Hugo Anson of the United Kingdom and the Chief Administrative Officer, Thomas White of Canada.

After a brief sojourn in the VIP room to meet some Ambassadors who had come to greet me (prompted perhaps as much by curiosity as by protocol), we drove out to the UN encampment, Vila Espa, situated about 15 kilometres south of Luanda. I caught glimpses through the car window of the same blood-red landscape: raw earth with hardly a blade of grass or other vegetation, except for the occasional baobabs lifting their statuesque branches to the sun-burnished, unclouded sky like supplicants praying for rain – as well they might, for drought had stricken the area for several years past. Near the airport we had passed through the *musseque* (shanty town) of Rocha Pinto, a sprawling mass of one-storey buildings, the better ones made of cement blocks, the poorer of corrugated iron and ramshackle pieces of wood. The road that bisected the settlement was swarming with people amid a confused mass of antiquated vehicles, shuddering on the verge of final collapse. Roadside markets were in full swing, people were struggling to clamber on to buses and lorries, women (always the women) strode along with incredible burdens on their heads – crates of beer or soft drinks, bowls of laundry, buckets of water, even gas cylinders. There was an air of cheerfulness and gaiety, everyone smiling and laughing, despite the poverty and squalor. though, as I learnt later, Rocha Pinto had the reputation of being a dangerous place, renowned for brawls and violent crime, murder and even murkier goings-on.

After about twenty minutes we swept round a curve in the road and I saw a UN flag fluttering from a mast in the distance. Driving in through the gates to the camp was like coming upon an oasis. Suddenly there was green – a square of grass in the centre of the compound, studded with palm trees and acacias. Flowers proliferated. Fountains of brilliant blossoms spiralled from hedges of bougainvillaea, portulacae sprinkled the grass with purple, oleanders and frangipani bloomed in the tiny front gardens of the few small bungalows surrounding the square. Beyond, the dusty red earth took over again, and the houses gave way to white container units, used for offices and dwellings.

I was installed in one of the bungalows. The heat was almost unbearable after the winter chill of Vienna, and this, combined with the effects of the long overnight flight, made me wilt with fatigue. The programme organised for the visit allowed for no such human frailty. The original purpose was twofold: to review the present situation and to plan the electoral component. With the last-minute addition of myself to head the mission, a third function had been added, that of paying courtesy calls to the key players in the peace process. The team from New York comprised Dimitry Titov, the Angolan desk officer, Horacio Boneo, in charge of technical assistance for electoral processes, and Major Peter Hornsby of the Field Operations Division, covering administrative and logistical aspects.

First came a briefing of several hours by the Chief Military Observer and other senior staff. I was informed that, as of that morning (Monday 17 February 1992), UNAVEM's manpower strength was 335 UN Military Observers (UNMOs), 87 UN Police Observers (UNPOs) and 202 civilian staff, both international and local. The UNMOs were below full strength, largely because some had been loaned to the operation then beginning in Yugoslavia. UNAVEM personnel were already deployed in 84 locations: six regional headquarters, 48 troop assembly areas, 18 police locations (teams of three to four police observers, (UNPOs, in all 18 provincial capitals) and 12 critical points, as shown on the map below. In addition there were rapid reaction teams to respond to incidents where there was no UNAVEM presence, and mobile patrols to monitor such areas. Fourteen military medical personnel were also in place. The UNMOs were drawn from 24 member states: Algeria, Argentina, Brazil, Canada, Congo, Czechoslovakia, Egypt, Guinea-Bissau,

Note: The map reflects UNAVEM deployment of June 1992 as reported by the Secretary General to the Security Council on 24 June 1992 (S/24145).
Source: United Nations, map no. 3655, Rev 1, June 1992.

Hungary, India, Ireland, Jordan, Malaysia, Morocco, the Netherlands, New Zealand, Nigeria, Norway, Senegal, Singapore, Spain, Sweden, Yugoslavia and Zimbabwe. The UNPOs came from nine countries: Argentina, Brazil, Ireland, Malaysia, Morocco, the Netherlands, Nigeria, Sweden and Zimbabwe.

Most UNAVEM staff were living in very harsh conditions – conditions that the Secretary-General had described in his report to the Security Council in October 1991 for the period 31 May–28 October 1991 as 'in some cases ... amongst the most difficult that have ever been faced by UN peacekeeping personnel'. This had been brought home to me by some of the UNAVEM military observers whom I had seen in Vienna, en route to Yugoslavia. They had spoken of living in grass huts, in desolately lonely, malaria-ridden spots, and of having to shake snakes out of the roof before retiring to sleep. Their joy at being transferred to Yugoslavia was ill-concealed, though whether this euphoria was sustained in the light of subsequent events I cannot tell. Eventually some returned to UNAVEM.

Because of the remoteness of most of the sites and the devastated infrastructure – 70 per cent of the roads were unusable owing to landmines and destroyed bridges – UNAVEM's operations were highly air-intensive, absorbing nearly 50 per cent of the budget. There were three fixed-wing aircraft – a Beechcraft 200, an Antonov 26 and a C130 (the latter hired on request). Fourteen helicopters – Russian and Bulgarian – were distributed around the countryside at each of the regional headquarters. All were provided on contract. The helicopters and their crews came from Eastern Europe because this was the cheapest source in the international commercial market. They had no night-flying capability. I was warned that the air component would certainly have to be expanded once our mandate was extended to the elections. It was emphasised that the whole operation hinged largely on successful air operations.

Communications were also crucial and Tom White reported an urgent need for high frequency transceivers with fax and INMARSAT terminals. The delay in approving UNAVEM's budget had badly delayed acquisition of other vital equipment, such as Weatherhaven shelters for personnel up-country, vehicles, generators and communications equipment. The fact that UNAVEM, alone among all such UN missions, had no engineer unit had seriously hampered site review and repair, and the organisation of accommodation.

I was assured that the situation was generally calm, with no major violations of the ceasefire. There had been minor incidents, mainly due to lack of food in the assembly areas and non-payment of salaries to the troops. More worrying – and a major cause of these incidents – was the fact that virtually all aspects of the peace process were far behind schedule. The cantonment of all troops should have been completed by 1 August 1991, but nearly four months later, and despite a recent downward revision of the initial projection of total troop strength from 200 000 to 151 930 (114 600 FAPLA and 37 330 FALA), the goal had become even more distant. At Christmas there had been a sudden exodus of nearly 36 000 Government soldiers. In contrast UNITA troops had maintained a steady presence, except in the first half of January 1992. The last UNAVEM count, on 12 February 1992, showed that only 57 805 or 50.44 per cent of Government troops were in their designated areas, compared with UNITA's 34 996, or 93.75 per cent. The total for both was 92 801 out of a projected total of 151 930, or only 61.08 per cent. Although the situation had improved it was still far behind that of 31 October, as far as Government troops were concerned. Then 74 027 FAPLA effectives had been confined; now there were only 57 805. In contrast the number of FALA troops from UNITA had increased from 30 124 to 34 996.

Many problems lay behind this decline on the Government side: food shortages and non-payment of salaries; lack of medical facilities, lack of work and recreational facilities, and low morale. The troops in the UNITA assembly areas were more disciplined and, as guerrilla fighters, more inured to the rigours of life in the bush and better equipped to cope with them. The overriding factor causing desertions was the inordinate delay in starting demobilisation, which, according to the peace agreements, could not begin until cantonment was complete. General Unimna felt strongly that the peace process would collapse if there was insistence on completing one set of activities before starting another.

The CCPM met every Thursday afternoon. UNAVEM was always invited and General Unimna used these occasions to convey his worries over the delays. UNAVEM was also regularly invited to the two subsidiary bodies of the CCPM – the CMVF (the Joint Monitoring and Verification Mission, set up to verify observance of the ceasefire), and the Political Commission – but did not attend the CCFA (Joint Commission for the Formation of the National Army). General Unimna warned me that the meetings usually involved long, inconclusive discussions and arguments and put me on my guard about the attitudes of the two sides, both of whom liked to create and manipulate situations.

The CCPM was now considering a list of tasks not envisaged in its original mandate, which UNAVEM might be called upon to perform, such as verifying unconfined troops, transferring weapons from defunct assembly areas to centralised areas, various electoral duties, escort duties, communication and transport support, and assistance in public enlightenment. These could not be done without more military and police observers.

Despite all the caveats, the overall impression was not one of unrelieved gloom. General Unimna even expressed optimism: Angolans, generally, longed for peace and supported the process; life was fast picking up politically and economically; and he was confident of success, provided the number of UNAVEM observers was increased. There was a general feeling that the presence of the 'Blue Berets' had played an important confidence-building and stabilising role and that UNAVEM was a respected symbol of neutrality in which the Angolans reposed great trust and hope.

* * *

Similar expressions of guarded optimism, interspersed with concern over the delays, were conveyed to me by the three observers. Ambassador Antonio Monteiro of Portugal was the most knowledgeable. He had been born in Angola and spent his early years there. He was also the right-hand man of Minister Durão Barroso, and had been intimately involved with the negotiation of the Peace Accords, the implementation of which was his sole concern (a bilateral Portuguese Ambassador was accredited to the Government). Over a tête-à-tête dinner in his bijou house in Miramar, cheek by jowl with Dr Savimbi's recently acquired residence in Luanda (a proximity later to prove distinctly uncomfortable), he regaled me with insights into the process and the personalities engaged in it. Highly intelligent, dynamic and articulate, and blessed with a marvellous sense of humour, he was a charming as well as an informative host. His house was elegantly appointed with furnishings he had brought from Portugal, even for the relatively short period he expected to stay. Antonio believed in his creature comforts, and who shall say he was wrong? The contrast with the spartan surroundings of Vila Espa, the UN camp, was striking.

So, too, was that with the compound of the US mission, a huddle of prefabricated huts where I called on the US observer, Jeffrey Millington. The United States still had no official relations with the Angolan Government, and so no Embassy. Jeff had also been associated with the negotiations in Portugal. A career Foreign Service Officer, he was a bluff, genial man with a high colour and a rather boisterous, yet curiously self-deprecating manner. He was at times bluntly outspoken in a way rather surprising in a diplomat. Poor Jeff lived in the Hotel Presidente, the best hotel in Luanda, but one that was often bereft of water, electricity and a functioning lift. One soon discovered that he missed his wife and young family desperately and that the Angolan operation could not be over too soon for him.

The Russians, like the Portuguese, had a double presence in Luanda. The bilateral Ambassador was Yuri Kapralov, a relatively young man and a career diplomat, but one much in the mould of the new Russia. Observation of the peace process and the workings of the CCPM was the full-time responsibility of Vladimir Petukov, an older man who, perhaps unfairly, gave the impression of following a more traditionalist approach – he had spent many years in the Soviet Embassy in Luanda and had had close links with the MPLA and the Government during the heyday of Soviet dominance. Millington, for similarly obvious reasons, was reputed to be pro-UNITA. Such stereotypes are hard to throw off, and the reality is often infinitely more complex.

First Mission to Angola

I called on Ambassador Kapralov in the imposing mansion above the sea that for many years has housed the Soviet embassy. He gave me tea and a briefing, including the useful tip that, during the negotiations, the MPLA and the Angolan government had been most reluctant to accept a UN presence, a point not previously made clear to me.

Monteiro, Millington and Petukov were the men whom I was to see almost daily. Our roles were distinct, and to some extent complementary, but we shared the same goal. Monteiro and I were to be the only two to soldier on after the elections. They all made me very welcome. I had the feeling that they were glad, even relieved, to see me arrive. On further reflection, that was not an entirely reassuring thought.

* * *

On the evening of my arrival the UNAVEM Command Group organised a dinner party in a downtown restaurant with the senior members of the CCPM and the observers. The next morning I had separate meetings in the CCPM building with General Antonio França (N'dalu), leader of the Government delegation, and Engineer Elias Salupeto Pena, head of the UNITA delegation.

The CCPM was housed in a low, two-storied building near the centre of Luanda. Recently painted a pristine white, it stood out starkly against the dilapidated, peeling façades of the buildings around, all so typical of the rundown appearance of Luanda. It might have been a bright symbol of hope in the midst of the obvious consequences of war. Armed guards, a relic of that legacy, lounged lethargically round the door, as if they no longer had any clear mission to fulfil. General Unimna showed me our office – a dingy, windowless cell with one desk and a chair, an infernally noisy air conditioner, and an adjoining bathroom, where nothing appeared to work. A distinctly disagreeable odour hung about the place, which was already well-populated with voracious and aggressive mosquitoes, apparently unaware that a ceasefire had been declared.

General 'N'dalu' (to use his *nom de guerre*) spoke in Spanish, of which he had an excellent knowledge, as had so many MPLA members who had worked with the Cubans. General 'N'dalu' was a stocky *mestiço* of medium height, dapper and agile. In his early fifties, he had a very expressive and lively face, an impression reinforced by his twinkling eyes. He was one of a rare breed – a general who had fought at the front, led troops into battle and seen men fall, killed and wounded around him. Our conversation was inevitably rather general – part diplomatic courtesies, part overview of the situation as well as of the roles of UNAVEM II and the Special Representative. I came away with the feeling that behind the very *simpático* exterior lay an extremely shrewd person, likely also to be astute in negotiation.

Engineer Salupeto Pena was a very different kettle of fish. A member of the Ovimbundu tribe and an agricultural engineer, he was a nephew of the UNITA leader, Dr Savimbi. Like General N'dalu he was of medium height, but younger, probably in his late thirties. As he later told me, he had fought as a gunner and was consequently rather deaf. His complexion was almost pure black, and he had an imposing head with a broad brow and somewhat receding hair. His face wore a dreamy expression and his large eyes seemed to take a rather sorrowful view of the world at large. In contrast to General N'dalu's vivacious, sometimes almost staccato diction, his manner of speaking was slow and ponderous. He seemed to weigh every word, and employed almost to excess the Portuguese habit of repeating the last few words of a sentence for emphasis. Yet there was something studied about this apparently placid front, as if other, inner forces were being held in check by a great effort of will. We began with him speaking Portuguese and I Spanish, but then, in deference to General Unimna, we changed to English, which Salupeto Pena – like most members of UNITA, because of their long association with Americans – spoke reasonably well. He was courteous and welcoming, stressing the great store Dr Savimbi laid on the close involvement of the United Nations, and of the Secretary-General personally.

Encouragingly, both delegation heads stressed their side's total commitment to the Bicesse Accords; to the maintenance of the ceasefire and to the holding of democratic, multiparty elections to determine the future government of a united country. I comforted myself that, if these protestations were sincere, then that oft-quoted but elusive factor, 'political will', might yet overcome delays and stumblings along the road.

This was the kind of assurance I wanted to have directly from the two leaders themselves, President Jose Eduardo Dos Santos and Dr Jonas Savimbi. They had been consulted personally by Dr Boutro-Ghali (who knew them both) about my appointment and both, he had told me, had acquiesced with alacrity. At the airport I had already learned that Dr Savimbi would receive me on Tuesday 18 February at 6.00 p.m. No answer had yet been received from the 'Protocolo de Estado' about the meeting with President Dos Santos, and despite constant démarches by UNAVEM and interventions by several ambassadors during the next few days, none was forthcoming before my departure. This was disconcerting, if not downright alarming. What possible interpretation could there be except that, despite the assurances to the Secretary-General, one was not really welcome? Various Angolan 'old hands', while deploring the lack of reaction, consoled me that this was a common occurrence, perhaps meant to shore up the mystique of the Presidency. It was also all too possible, I was warned, that a messenger would rush in with a last-minute summons to the President just as I was on the way to the airport.

Accompanied by General Unimna and Hugo Anson I called on Dr Savimbi in his magnificent white mansion (he had a predilection for 'White Houses'), set in a commanding position on the heights of the elegant Miramar area, where most of the Embassies had their residences. This ample villa had been made available by the Government as part of the peace arrangements. The

First Mission to Angola

UNITA leader had returned to the capital the previous September, an occasion anticipated with trepidation, but which had passed off calmly, another seemingly good omen.

Mutual confidence was hardly rampant, however. The large, square forecourt was seething with UNITA guards, all armed to the teeth, whose dark, unsmiling expressions gave warning that they could very easily mean business if required, and quickly too. In contrast to these glowering countenances, a beaming Salupeto Pena emerged to greet us and ushered us through the imposing portico to the presence of Dr Savimbi. Savimbi rose to greet us from a large chair at one end of the main salon and motioned me to sit on his right-hand side, with my colleagues beside me. Mustered on the other side of the semicircle was an imposing array of his principal cohorts. Among them, in addition to Salupeto Pena, were Dr Jeremiah Chitunda, Vice-President of UNITA, Dr Tony da Costa Fernandes, Savimbi's 'Foreign Minister', various generals, Dr Abel Chivukuvuku, then deputy head of UNITA's delegation to the CCPM, and one woman, presented as the 'Minister of Finance', Fatima Roque, who stood out not only because of her gender but also because of her white skin.

The whole throng was effortlessly dominated by Dr Savimbi, a big man physically, built on the grand scale. He was wearing an elegant safari suit, well cut, but not sufficiently so to conceal evidence of a recently more sedentary life. Everything about him was larger than life – his hypnotic, piercing eyes, his hands, even his immaculately polished leather boots. The man simply exuded charisma. On that occasion he also exuded charm and sweet reasonableness. He spoke of his long-standing personal friendship and regard for the Secretary-General, his delight at my arrival and willingness to cooperate, his firm commitment to the peace process and to democracy. I made the appropriate responses and we then discussed the problems retarding the peace process. Dr Savimbi spoke in near-perfect English. I knew that he was a well-educated man, fluent in several languages, including French (he had studied at Lausanne in Switzerland) and his discourse gave ample proof of that. Soft drinks and beer were served, Savimbi partaking only of the former. Superficially it was a highly civilised and modern occasion. Yet my overwhelming sensation was of being a guest at a medieval court. And no amount of charm or European *savoir-faire* could mask the strength of Savimbi's personality, his will of iron and more than a hint of ruthlessness.

* * *

Earlier that afternoon I had met Dr Lopo de Nascimento, the Minister for Territorial Administration, responsible within the Angolan Government for organising the elections. A tall, thin man, he was reputed to be one of the more moderate and pragmatic members of the MPLA, as well as competent and intelligent. I had met him some years earlier when he was Minister of Planning and I was involved in providing development assistance from the UN. He spoke frankly of his hopes and fears for the process, and we agreed that the logistical and practical aspects of organising the elections presented immense difficulties on their own, leaving aside the political pitfalls. In addition to UNAVEM's observer function, the UN was providing technical assistance through the United Nations Development Programme, estimated to cost around US$12 million. No budget existed for this, and it was being financed by voluntary contributions from donor countries. Not all the money had been raised, and the Minister and I agreed that, in any case, the provisions in the project were frugal in relation to the immensity of the undertaking. The Minister's own conclusion, after a sober assessment of the practical and political minefields lying ahead, was that the elections were 'do-able' and had a good chance of being carried off successfully.

Another meeting – with the UNDP Resident Representative in Angola, Manuel da Graça, and the heads of the various UN organisations and Specialised Agencies – related to my responsibility, as Special Representative of the Secretary-General, to coordinate all UN system activities connected with the peace process. These included the repatriation of some 300 000 refugees from neighbouring countries, assistance for some 800 000 more people displaced within the country, and the provision of emergency food and medical assistance to large segments of the population, among them the troops in the assembly areas. Thus the representatives of the High Commissioner for Refugees, the World Food Programme and UNICEF, as well as FAO and WHO, had a key supportive role. We agreed to meet regularly and I asked for their collaboration with personnel and vehicles to observe the elections. Resources were so short that it would be a case of 'all hands to the pump'.

This became even clearer in a long meeting between the command group and the team from New York about our role in the elections. Organising elections was a relatively new departure for the United Nations, but already a significant volume of experience had been built up in Namibia, Nicaragua and Haiti. I felt ill at ease with the proceedings. I had no experience of such missions, decisions had to be taken in a hurry, given the scant six to seven months before the elections were due, and I was going to have to live with the outcome. My disquiet was hardly alleviated by the realisation that the Headquarters members of my 'team' (all of whom I had met for the first time only three days before) were operating from the premise of 'what the traffic would bear' rather than of what was needed to do the job effectively. I did not blame them. They, better than I, knew the prevailing atmosphere in New York and the extent to which member states' willingness to contribute imposed very real constraints on action. Moreover the odds were that a party line of frugality had been laid down for them before departure, a supposition borne out when I went to Headquarters shortly afterwards.

I suggested comparison with Namibia, where 1758 UN electoral and 1035 UN police observers supervised 358 polling stations,[2] but was told that that was a totally different and unique operation, and one that was no longer sustainable (*pace* Cambodia). More limited operations were to be the norm, on the lines of those in Nicaragua and Haiti, which Horacio Boneo, an affable and knowledgeable Uruguayan, had directed and which, I was assured, had worked out perfectly well on a sample basis, with teams of observers covering several polling stations each. Other international observers would be coming and all UN system staff in Angola would be pressed into service. The maximum allowable was 100 electoral observers, to be present from March until the voting date (still not fixed at that time) – five in each of the 18 provincial capitals and the rest in Luanda – to observe all the preparations for the election, including the registration and campaign phases. Their number would be increased to 400 for one month to cover the actual voting. I still expressed misgivings, given the enormous difference in size and quality of infrastructure between Nicaragua or Haiti and Angola, but Mr Boneo was confident that the proposals were adequate. Since I understood that he was likely to head the electoral side, I bowed to his superior judgement.

A staffing plan and budget were prepared for my own office, for an electoral division at our Luanda headquarters, and for the additional administrative and logistics support required by UNAVEM's expanded mandate. These estimates conformed to the same pattern of utmost parsimony.

* * *

A refreshing glimpse of what it all meant on the ground was afforded by a half-day field trip on Wednesday 19 February to two troop assembly areas in the northern province of Uige. In a proper spirit of evenhandedness, one of these was the realm of FAPLA (government), in the vicinity of Negage, and the other FALA (UNITA), at a place called Quipedro. Fortunately I had some field kit with me and someone produced a blue UN cap and neckscarf. We flew in the Beechcraft to Negage, which has an important airfield, but it bore a ramshackle appearance with derelict vehicles and bits of rusting machinery littered around. The UNAVEM team of five military observers and two policemen took us for a briefing and refreshments in the rundown building that served as their office and lodging. I was to see worse, but in the words of Major Hornsby, it was 'pretty grungy'.

We then flew to the FAPLA assembly area. I had been honoured with the VIP helicopter, reputedly once owned by the president of Bulgaria and which actually sported a loo (though hardly one that could be termed 'presidential style', as I discovered). As we circled to land I could see, scattered over a wide area of open ground, a motley collection of grass huts, tents and dugouts. A few men in

FAPLA uniform waved. There was a desultory air about the place, which was confirmed by the demeanour of the camp commander who met us and ostensibly briefed us – I say 'ostensibly' because he was unable to answer questions about the number of troops present or how many weapons were stored and where. His main concern was to take the opportunity to complain bitterly about the lack of food and tents, all of which he blamed on UNAVEM.

From Negage it was about an hour's helicopter flight to Quipedro, a marvellously scenic journey over wild, hilly country marked by rocky outcrops and huge stands of thick tropical forest, their almost impenetrable dark canopy splashed here and there with the bright crown – pink or scarlet or golden yellow – of a flowering tree. The assembly area was located on a series of hills, far from any habitation. Yet it had all the appearance of a settled community, with neat grass huts laid out in a regular pattern of streets. Vegetables and maize were being cultivated on patches of tilled soil. There were women and children, and chickens scampered between the huts.

We first visited our UNMO team in their newly installed Weatherhaven complex: a plastic-tented arrangement, providing office as well as sleeping and living accommodation. The toilet had not yet been installed, but it was a tremendous improvement on the grass huts in which they had been living till then, and a torrential shower made it easy to imagine how wretched their living conditions must have been. I was struck by the monotony and isolation of their life: five men, each of different nationality, keeping an eye on some 3000 UNITA troops, but having no other function but to fetch water from the river every day, count the troops on Wednesdays and the weapons on Fridays. The so-called road to Luanda ran nearby, but the capital was 258 kilometres away, and the road virtually impassable. Yet our men all appeared cheerful and committed. An Irish-Argentinean captain told me how he kept fit by jogging round the mountain trails. They were about to be rotated and a New Zealand officer had just arrived to take over as team leader.

Our reception at the assembly area confirmed the impression of orderliness from the air. A large contingent of troops was drawn up on one side of an open grassy space, as if on parade; on the other was a huge crowd of women and children. As we approached they broke into chanting and dancing. We visited various huts, all of them clean, tidy and reasonably comfortable, despite the rain and mud. Last of all came the huts where the weapons were stored. I had never before seen so many arms, row upon row of gleaming barrels neatly arranged on wooden racks, all freshly oiled. An all-pervading smell of weapon oil hung over the place. The contrast with the general sloppiness of the FAPLA camp was striking and the comportment of UNITA on cantonment to all appearances exemplary. I could not help murmuring to General Unimna, however: 'I know very little about weapons, CMO, but those guns look to me awfully ready for use!'

There was more dancing and singing and I mingled briefly with the women and children. Finally I was asked to address the troops, a daunting first experience but one to which I was to become accustomed. I often reflected how strange I must appear to them, as they had initially to me.

* * *

That Wednesday evening I was invited to dinner by the British Ambassador, John Flynn, and his wife Drina. John was a seasoned diplomat, and spoke excellent Portuguese and Spanish. He had served in the Luanda Embassy several years before, and was therefore well acquainted with the situation and the personalities. Drina, a vivacious and very pretty Uruguayan, gave me valuable advice of the feminine and domestic kind, which had been all too lacking in my other briefings. And I had the best meal since leaving Vienna, which cheered my spirits no end.

The question of my domestic arrangements had been the subject of some discussion in UNAVEM. It seemed to have been generally assumed that I would live in a suitably prestigious residence in town, the example being quoted of Maarti Ahtisaari in Namibia. Luanda was not Windhoek, however, and accommodation of a representational nature was almost impossible to come by. When it was, there was usually no water or electricity. Tom White, the Chief Administrative Officer, took me to see the house of the representative of the High Commissioner for Refugees, then empty during an interval between incumbents. It became clear, however, that the UNHCR was not exactly falling over itself to give the house to me – and this did not seem to me a good way of cementing harmonious inter agency relations. There was, moreover, the question of security. Robberies were on the increase, and there was broader concern for the security of the Special Representative. Antonio Monteiro voiced the contrary view, with some basis in reason, that my safety would be most in danger traversing the 15 kilometre stretch between the UNAVEM camp and town several times every day. The advice I got from all sides was conflicting and confusing. But the overwhelming consideration in my mind was that I should be near 'my troops' and I quailed before the domestic hassle of finding and organising a house.

That evening John and Drina advised that the camp was the best place. They also resolved a more difficult dilemma – whether to bring my Austrian housekeeper, Sissy, who had served me well for four years in Vienna. Luanda was a far cry from the city of music and waltz, and Sissy was of a rather nervous disposition and spoke only limited English. It might prove an expensive gamble (unlike national foreign services the United Nations does not contribute to the cost of domestic support). But Drina and John advised 'This is going to be a tough job. Be as comfortable as you can!' And so it was decided.

Living conditions were going to be important for morale, and next day I toured the whole camp. Outside the central square of bungalows – 21 in all – the camp was, as Major Hornsby again aptly said, 'pretty raw'. The cement paths and asphalt road changed abruptly into a wide expanse of the ubiquitous red earth that covered one's feet and legs with dust or mud, according to the season. Behind one of the bungalows, which was to serve as the main office for myself and General Unimna (I was also to have an office in a building downtown), there was a sizeable collection of prefabricated buildings and containers, arranged in neat squares and serving as offices. Alongside, more containers were going up to provide living accommodation, laid out in three round complexes, each with a separate ablutions block. Arrangements were well advanced for a dining and kitchen facility to serve the enlarged camp, under outside contract. A small store was already functioning where staff could buy basic foodstuffs, drinks and toiletries, but at exorbitant prices. It was clear that conditions were going to be crowded and pretty spartan.

* * *

On the last afternoon, Thursday 20 February, I was invited to attend my first weekly meeting of the CCPM. The meeting room was of medium size only, set in a well in the centre of the CCPM building, to which a few steps descended. Tables were arranged in a rectangle around an open space, with the heads and their senior aides seated along the longer sides – Government on the left and UNITA on the right – while the observers sat at the two ends: the Portuguese and the Russian at one extreme, at the other the American, alongside whom I was asked to sit with General Unimna. A small secretariat occupied a table at the back, while the overflow sat around the sides. There seemed to be an awful lot of men in battle fatigues. It was also stiflingly hot, the air conditioning being on the blink, and the mosquitoes much in evidence. That apart, the room seemed of a very suitable size and layout to permit businesslike negotiation of not too formal a kind.

A lot of time was taken up in wishing me welcome, and this was done very graciously by General N'dalu and Eng. Salupeto Pena, followed by each of the observers. Portuguese, being a wonderfully flowery language, with many a recondite and carefully crafted twist and turn of phrase, lends itself marvellously to such occasions, though it hardly contributes to brevity, or indeed clarity (luckily the latter did not matter much on this occasion). I hope that I replied as graciously, though in more sober Spanish (I could understand Portuguese, but learned to speak it only later). I took the opportunity to underline the need to speed up the various aspects of the peace process that must be completed before the fast-approaching elections, emphasising the need to start demobilisation, even though troop cantonment was still far from complete. Encouragingly, it was decided to start demobilisation immediately and complete it by the end of July.

* * *

When we got back to Vila Espa I had my own taste of the drawbacks of camp life: hot and tired after a long day, I got under the shower only to find there was no water. There was no electricity either. Sticky as I was, I had to struggle into my winter-weight clothes for the night plane to Paris. Even these could not be comfortably casual, in case a last-minute call to see the President materialised.

It didn't, of course. I was escorted to the airport and seen off by all the UNAVEM senior military and civilian staff and several ambassadors. During the long flight back to Europe I tried to disentangle the tangled skein of facts, thoughts and impressions that filled my mind, and composed a personal letter to the Secretary-General giving him my reactions to this crowded visit. Among them was my concern about the immensity of the task and expectations in relation to the resources and the mandate. The letter was faxed to New York the next day, on my arrival in Vienna.

Meanwhile, our plane arrived one hour early at Charles de Gaulle airport – before 5 a.m. There was no bus to the connecting terminal until 6 o'clock. The temperature was $-3°$ centigrade and it was bitterly cold. In my tired and light-headed state, Luanda no longer seemed quite real.

4 'A Small and Manageable Operation', or Making Bricks without Straw

As it happened I did not see Luanda again until 18 March. In the meantime my feet hardly touched the ground. When I arrived back in Vienna only 12 days remained before I had to hand over my office as Director-General on 1 March. Regular activities continued unabated, to which was added a round of official farewell calls and parties, including luncheons given by the President and the Foreign Minister of Austria. Nights and weekends were spent in a morass of packing cases and paper strewn all over the apartment and the office. Little yellow labels were stuck on furniture and other things proclaiming that their destination was Luanda (by far the smallest consignment), the United Kingdom, New York or Bolivia, where I ultimately hoped to retire, only to be modified as my housekeeper, Sissy, and I changed our minds, or they fell off of their own volition. Small wonder that, three years later, I am still trying to reunite different parts of the same piece of furniture, now scattered in different parts of the world. Such are the joys and hazards of international life!

En route for my official briefing at the United Nations headquarters in New York, I spent three days in England visiting my only close relative, my aunt Christina, whose house is set in an idyllic walled garden and a beautiful valley in the Welsh Marches. A secondary purpose was to stock up for Luanda, alarmist reports having warned me that most staple goods were hard to come by. Seven months of toiletry and pharmaceutical supplies devastated the stock of the chemist's shop in the local market town and the whole place came to a halt as they tried to add up the bill!

On 7 March I flew to New York for three days of briefing, and to sort out the budget and recruitment of personnel for my newly created office in Luanda and the new electoral component of UNAVEM II.

My meeting with the Secretary-General, Dr Boutros-Ghali, on 10 March was only our second encounter. Our first had taken place at the end of January 1992, and had not been a very propitious occasion. I had had a long agenda about the functions and future of the United Nations Office at Vienna, which the new Secretary-General would have to address with some urgency. As had been my custom with his predecessor, Javier Pérez de Cuéllar, I had listed the six or seven items at the outset so that he would have an idea of how much time needed to be devoted to each one.

Alas, we had never got beyond the first one: an account of my efforts, from Vienna, to help the Soviet Union and the Eastern European countries cope with the problems of transition to democracy and the market economy, and particularly my recent visit to Moscow with a high-level mission to advise on measures to counteract the social cost of the economic transformation. I had been convinced that the world community should, in its own interest, stretch out generous helping hands to the region and that the UN should play a key role in bringing this about. The new Secretary-General had not shared this view, however, and within minutes we had been locked in lively argument. I had found this radical change of style from that of his predecessor highly stimulating intellectually, and even exhilarating. Inevitably it had taken up much time, and I had been less than exhilarated when, as our exchange on this subject had come to a close, he had abruptly got to his feet and shaken my hand, so that I had had perforce to leave his office with several arrows still in my quiver!

The only other point discussed had been my own future. I had made it clear that I was not interested in prolonging my stay in Vienna, but would prefer an operational job. If that were not possible, I was quite happy to retire. Clearly this arrow, at least, had lodged in his mind because, barely a week later, came the offer of Angola.

This time our meeting went swimmingly. In the three years since then Boutros Boutros-Ghali has often received a bad press, not least for his management style and his relations with his senior colleagues. I must say that in all our personal dealings over the next 17 months he was always courteous and sometimes even charming. At times he was tough and impatient – he is a hard man who does not suffer fools gladly – but then he has grave and urgent responsibilities. I also found him to be opinionated and argumentative, but the latter characteristic did allow one to put one's view forward and I did not find that he would brook no contrary view, as some have said. But perhaps I was fortunate in having some independence, since I originally accepted a mission of seven months only, and thereafter the organisation had more interest in my staying on than I had in doing so. I shall never forget a gesture that I greatly appreciated in July 1992, when UNAVEM II was subjected to virulent accusations by the Government that it had a pro-UNITA stance. The Secretary-General, arriving late at night in Paris after a gruelling visit to Moscow, took the trouble to telephone me personally in the UNAVEM camp to express his complete confidence in myself and UNAVEM, a splendidly encouraging message to pass on to the troops.

The Secretary-General's report proposing the extension of UNAVEM's mandate to cover the elections, and the all too modest additions of staff discussed during my initial visit to Luanda, had been presented on 3 March,[1] but had not yet been considered by the Security Council. That body eventually gave its approval in Resolution 747 (1992) on 24 March, by which time I was already back in Luanda.

The report summarised the present state of play, recalling that the Angolan government had requested assistance with the electoral process, confirming my own appointment and describing my first visit to Angola. In reviewing the peace process, the report commended the avoidance of any major violation of the ceasefire, but expressed serious concern that implementation of key aspects was well behind schedule, singling out as the most worrying, the unsatisfactory situation on the confinement of troops as well as the delay in implementing the CCPM's decision of 20 February to start demobilisation. Other areas of concern related to joint police monitoring teams, the extension of the central administration to all parts of the country and the mutual release of prisoners. It is worth recalling these strong warnings, which give the lie to those armchair critics who later claimed that the United Nations had not drawn timely attention to the shortcomings of the process.

The report laid out in some detail the 'Operational Plan for United Nations Observation of the Elections and the Enlargement of UNAVEM II'. This specified that the United Nations electoral mission 'will be an operation limited in scale, similar in approach to the United Nations Observer Mission for the Verification of the Elections in Nicaragua (ONUVEM) and the United Nations Observer Group for the Verification of the Elections in Haiti (ONUVEH)'.[2] Terms of reference were set out, as well as the disposition of the additional staff. UNAVEM II's headquarters in Luanda would be enlarged by the establishment of my office, with a staff of 18 (including an executive director and staff, a legal adviser, a political adviser and a small information unit), and an electoral division headed by a chief electoral officer with five international staff. Electoral division offices would be established in all 18 provincial capitals and be supervised by six regional electoral offices colocated with the regional teams of the military components of UNAVEM II. Three phases were foreseen: registration of voters, the electoral campaign, and the poll itself. For the last of these the number of observers would be increased to 400, but only 200 would come from outside. The 100 United Nations observers already in the country would be supplemented by 100 from UNDP and other United Nations agency personnel stationed in Angola, plus volunteers from selected non-governmental organisations (NGOs). One hundred of the additional observers would be drawn from the United Nations Secretariat; the rest from member states.

The report acknowledged[3] that 'this proposed operational plan and the preliminary estimates ... are very modest for observing and verifying the first-ever elections in Angola, especially when compared with the costs currently projected for other recently initiated United Nations operations. Given the vast size of Angola, its difficult terrain and its degraded administrative infrastructure, the allocation of an average of only five observers to each province (i.e. approximately one United Nations observer per 100 000 inhabitants) would obviously allow for only sample observation.'

The contradictions of logic in such a statement are self-evident. But they reflect the Secretariat's perception that the Security Council wanted 'a small and manageable operation', a phrase repeatedly used in my discussions at senior levels of the organisation. In vain I commented drily that, from my brief experience of Angola, it was certainly not small nor, as far as I could see, did it appear to be particularly manageable.

The Security Council could not act immediately on the Secretary-General's report because an all-important addendum containing the cost estimates had not yet been prepared, a signal indication of the pressures on Secretariat officials dealing with financial and administrative aspects of peacekeeping operations. This became painfully evident to me in other respects as I made my rounds, trying to select personnel for the additional posts and ensure their rapid appointment to Angola. With barely six months to go before the elections, there was no time to be lost. It was a dispiriting and frustrating experience. Although outside recruitment was not excluded, most posts had to be filled by existing staff because of tight buogetary constraints. The competition for the several peacekeeping missions being mounted at that time, some in more desirable-sounding locations, was considerable and Angola usually ranked last on the list of preferences of the volunteers, except the most hardy and adventurous. Some, having served in Namibia and thoroughly enjoyed the experience, anticipated similar delights in Angola. They were to be sorely disillusioned and tedious problems later arose in the case of those who did not adapt.

My biggest disappointment was the news that Horacio Boneo would not be coming as Chief Electoral Officer, as I had earlier been assured, but was to head a special unit at Headquarters to oversee all UN electoral missions. His talents and experience had been my guarantee that the Angolan mission would somehow manage to achieve its objectives, despite its severely limited resources. The fact that the person who had deemed the resources adequate would also be responsible for proving this to be the case, had somewhat assuaged my own very real doubts. Now that straw had been snatched from me. Moreover, as a Uruguayan Boneo could understand Portuguese and make himself understood. An anguished search ensued for a replacement. The only available candidate with anything like the right experience was an American member of the Secretariat, John Truman, who had served in Namibia and had some knowledge of Spanish, though he admitted it was rather rusty. The difficulty was medical clearance: he had a severe back problem and had undergone serious operations, which put in question his capacity to withstand the rigours of a rugged operation as Angola bade fair to be. To my relief the doctor gave the green light a few days later.

The selection of other senior staff gave rise to more headaches. I felt it important that my immediate collaborators should, as far as possible, be people with whom I had worked before, so that no valuable time would be lost in adjustment, and there would be mutual confidence and understanding. I also wished to have people with at least some knowledge of Spanish, since Portuguese speakers were hard to come by. Unfortunately it did not work out that way. I had several people in mind, but either they were not available or could not be released. The overriding consideration, which was made very clear to me, was that the Secretary-General wished me to give preference to staff from developing countries, Africa in particular. Normally this would cause me no problem: over a professional life spent working in and for developing countries, including countries in Africa, I have developed a high regard for the capacities of their nationals. But it is quite another thing to impose conditions – any conditions – on the selection of staff, at very short notice, for a difficult operational mission, particularly if outside recruitment is virtually excluded, as it was in this case for budgetary reasons (the idea was to slim down the number of headquarters staff by sending them out on field missions). Inevitably this led to compromises, some of which were later to make an already difficult mission even harder. Language was also a major constraint. Portuguese not being an official language of the United Nations, it was difficult to find people in the Secretariat with knowledge of it (and Portuguese nationality was not exactly appropriate for senior posts in UNAVEM II). Most of the people eventually selected did not even have Spanish. Thus nearly all the senior officials of UNAVEM II, with the exception of myself and one or two others, could only operate through an interpreter. No matter how proficient, this can never satisfactorily substitute for direct, face-to-face exchanges, especially in delicate political negotiations.

It was with more than a lingering sense of foreboding that I flew back to Europe to tie up the last loose ends of my previous existence. A spring weekend in the Welsh Marches and a walk on our windswept hills – themselves once the site of bitter conflict but now contested only by skylarks in exuberant spring song – did much to calm the spirit and to store up memories upon which to draw during the long months ahead in a very different environment. On Sunday 15 March I was back in Vienna. The movers arrived early on 16 March. They took two days to empty the apartment, and just thirty minutes after they had left with the last packing case I finally departed for the airport.

* * *

I arrived in Luanda at 7.15 a.m. on Wednesday 18 March, feeling exhausted. Perhaps fortunately, there was little time to brood. I barely had time to settle into my little bungalow and greet the Angolan maid, Maria, before I had to accompany General Unimna to a CCPM meeting.

It is symptomatic that the very first cable I sent to the Secretary-General, on 20 March 1992, reiterated my concern about the number of major tasks that must be accomplished within a very tight timetable, a concern reinforced by the fact that the financial implications of the enlargement of UNAVEM's mandate had still not been submitted to the Security Council. This was no mere formality: without the Council's approval the arrival of urgently needed staff would be delayed. I appealed for exceptional steps to break the logjam. Later that day the Secretariat presented the financial implications to the Council.[4] The total cost, including all the additional civilian personnel and their travel, premises, vehicles, aircraft operations and the public information programme, was US$18.75 million.

The Council was then able to adopt Resolution 747 (1992), on 24 March, approving the expansion and the proposed course of action. It also exhorted the two parties – the Angolan Government and UNITA – to cooperate fully with the Special Representative and UNAVEM II, and to comply with the Peace Accords and the agreed deadlines, 'and to this end to proceed without delay with the demobilization of their troops, formation of a unified national armed force, effective operation of joint police monitoring units, extension of the central administration and other major tasks' – in short, all the issues singled out as problem areas in the Secretary-General's report. Other paragraphs referred to the 'free and fair multi-party elections, to be held in September', calling upon the Angolan authorities and parties to finalise preparations and 'to make available as soon as possible all available resources for the electoral process'; encouraging 'all States to contribute voluntarily'; requesting 'the United Nations programmes and Specialized Agencies to provide the assistance and support necessary', and urging 'the parties to establish as soon as possible a precise time-table for the electoral process in Angola'.

My days were full of meetings and organisational problems. Ambassadors were beating a path to my door, avid for information. I had a meeting with the Acting Minister for Foreign Affairs, Venâncio de Moura, though President dos Santos continued to elude me. On the UNITA side I again saw Engineer Salupeto Pena, this time accompanied by Abel Chivukuvuku, now UNITA's 'Minister of Foreign Affairs', since just before my return there had been the dramatic defection from UNITA's ranks, amid a flurry of accusations and counteraccusations, of two of Dr Savimbi's oldest and closest associates – 'Interior Minister' General Miguel N'Zau Puna and 'Foreign Minister' Tony da Costa Fernándes. There were visits, by air, to all the provincial capitals to make contacts and arrange accommodation (a major challenge) for the electoral teams. The CCPM was meeting at least twice a week, and on 31 March, less than two weeks after my arrival, the demobilisation process was finally launched in two assembly areas, one Government, one UNITA, near Luena, the capital of Moxico province in the eastern part of the country.

It was a joyous occasion, which the CCPM attended *en masse* – General N'dalu, Engineer Salupeto Pena, the three observers, and myself and General Unimna – as well as a horde of journalists. UNAVEM provided helicopters in Luena to ferry everyone to and from the two camps, there were upbeat speeches by General N'dalu in the FAPLA assembly area, Camitongo, and by Salupeto Pena in the FALA area, Chicala, each delivered with the former arch-enemy standing by the orator's side, each strikingly similar in their emphasis on peace, elections and the hopeful prospects for a united, democratic and prosperous future. The troops were delirious with joy at the prospect of civilian life. As usual the UNITA troops were the more disciplined of the two, drawn up in serried ranks in a vast parade. The FAPLA troops broke ranks and danced in a frenzy of enthusiasm. The FALA men also chanted and danced, but with the of controlled spontaneity typical of their regime, and sang songs of praise to Dr Savimbi. In each camp the ceremony began with the symbolic presentation of demobilisation papers, a set of civilian clothes and a very small amount of cash (110 000 kwanzas, then equal to about £58) to the first set of six men, in which the two delegation leaders, the observers and General Unimna and I took part. It had all been arranged in such a hurry (characteristically the CCPM, having dragged its feet for over a month after its decision on 20 February to start demobilisation, despite considerable pressure from ourselves, had launched the Luena ceremony with virtually no notice), that it occurred to me to wonder, no doubt with typical feminine practicality, whether the trousers I was handing to my allotted Government and UNITA soldiers would fit the recipient!

In the Government camp lines of tanks, heavy military vehicles and guns, in disuse for nearly a year and under constant observation by the five-man UNAVEM team resident there, were grim reminders of what was being left behind. UNITA's weapons were smaller and confined in weapons stores, again under observation by a resident UNAVEM team. We walked in shimmering heat through the bush – the low, tawny scrub that covers vast expanses of eastern Angola – to thatched huts where refreshments were served. I had to be reminded by General Unimna to keep to the narrow paths winding through the long grass, not (as was my first reaction) because of snakes, but to avoid the risk of treading on one of the millions of mines that have wrought such havoc among civilians as well as soldiers, giving the country the dubious record of having the largest number of amputees in Africa, and probably second only to Afghanistan in the world.

We had started very early but, in typical Angolan style, the timetable was vastly behind schedule by the time we sat down to lunch in the governor's palace in Luena. (Despite all the supply problems, the Angolans were remarkable for being able to produce large banquets at the drop of a hat.) This was a truly auspicious occasion. Everyone was in high spirits and there was much camaraderie, exchange of jokes and general bonhomie between the two formerly warring sides. The choice of Luena held its own significance – it had been the scene of the last great battle before the ceasefire, when UNITA laid siege to Luena in an effort to capture a provincial capital for the first time. Where we were now giving civilian handouts to the newly demobilised, hundreds of soldiers and civilians from both sides had been killed barely 12 months earlier. It had been the last place for the guns finally to fall silent, though they had continued firing for a few hours beyond the deadline of 15 May 1991.

The occasion was thus infused with a sense of drama, as well as a feeling that, at long last and despite all the procrastination and frustrations, the process was moving forward and a decisive new chapter was being opened. I think we all felt a deep sense of relief and of hope that somehow we would attain the objectives, even if the way of doing so was far from perfect. Antonio Monteiro was particularly euphoric, this being the first time he had returned to the town where he had lived as a boy.

No doubt this optimism seemed naive to those with the benefit of hindsight, when the process later collapsed and Luena was again besieged by UNITA for many long months, suffering destruction and privations far exceeding any experienced there during the earlier 16 years of civil war. I can only say that it is exceedingly hard to judge unless – as we all were – one is at the core of such a life-and-death undertaking, with so much at stake. Perhaps it was a straw at which we clutched. But what else could we do but try to move forward with hope, and make the best use of our scant resources? It was becoming increasingly clear that the outside world was unlikely to bring anything more to bear on the situation other than words.

* * *

My own euphoria was short-lived enough. I got back to the camp – after dark and a 14-hour day – to find an urgent message to telephone Mig Goulding. When, with difficulty, I got through to New York it was to receive a douche of cold water. The Secretary-General was displeased because Dr Durão Barroso, the Portuguese Secretary for Foreign Affairs and Cooperation, had visited him the previous day and expressed concern about the adequacy of UNAVEM'S resources, assuming that this was at my instigation. The Swedes had spoken on similar lines to the desk officer. I was reminded, somewhat acerbically, that 'in-house' problems of staffing and administration should not be taken up with the Secretary-General by member states and I should not encourage them to do so.

The conversation was brief and I was given no time to refute the mistaken assumption upon which this baffling rebuke was based: Headquarters had other problems to attend to. I sent off a cable late that same night, pointing out that the people on the ground – both Angolans and diplomats – needed no encouragement from me to feel deep concern about UNAVEM'S resources. Security Council Resolution 747 had caused dismay in the CCPM. Engineer Salupeto Pena had launched a broadside, citing the far more generous budgets assigned to Namibia, Cambodia and Yugoslavia, and had been strongly supported by General N'dalu and the Portuguese and US observers. Both UNITA and the government had clearly inferred that Angola was being short-changed because Africa was an 'also-ran' in the race for the attention and resources of the United Nations. One European Ambassador had referred to Angola as 'a footnote in the international agenda'. The Portuguese had a special interest and stake in the process and I had been told by Antonio Monteiro that the Minister would convey his concern to the Secretary-General, but I had been foiled in my attempts to warn the latter in advance because, as frequently happened in those early days, the satellite had been out of action we had no communication with New York for 24 hours. As for the in-house delays in providing the staff and equipment for which resources *had* been made available, I rejected the suggestion that I had discussed these with Member States. It must have been obvious to any interested observer that I was running a virtual one-woman show on the civilian side and that, six weeks after my first visit to Luanda, only *one* of the additional staff envisaged had arrived and I was still without a qualified secretary with good English and dictation skills. I asked that my cable be shown to the Secretary-General.

Despite all these explanations the controversy rumbled on, lowering morale among the senior staff of UNAVEM by leading them to feel that Angola did not rank high in the peacekeeping stakes in New York. My cables did not increase my popularity at Headquarters, especially in personnel and administrative quarters. I was beginning to realise that I was fighting an almost impossible battle on several fronts at once. Matters were not improved by the prominence given in some international media of a sombre joke I had made about Security Council Resolution 747 – that I had been given a 747 Jumbo to fly but provided with fuel sufficient only for a DC-3!

Mig continued the dialogue by letter, but use of the UN pouch led to long delays. It was only on 23 April that I received from him a brief record of the meeting with Durão Barroso. The offending reference was not much more than a passing remark, in the midst of some flattering comments about the impression I had made in Luanda, but it had sparked the Secretary-General's testy riposte that the problems were the same everywhere, whether it was Yugoslavia or Cambodia, and his Special Representatives should not think they were 'les seuls au monde'. This comment overlooked the fact that the budget for Angola was only US$118 million for the year, compared with an initial US$2 billion for Cambodia. Durão Barroso had made the comparison with Namibia, and Mig insisted to me that it was not apt, since in Angola the UN was simply to *observe* the elections, as in Nicaragua and Haiti, and not *supervise and control* them, as in Namibia. I argued that the one to four difference in funding was still considerable, if one considered the larger size of Angola, its population of 10 million and its estimated six million voters, in contrast to Namibia's population of 1.8 million and between 600 000 and 700 000 voters. Moreover Namibia had a functioning infrastructure and administration, whereas Angola was totally ravaged by war and the central administration covered only a small proportion of its vast territory.

My arguments, however convincing they seemed to us on the ground, proved academic. It was patently clear that UNAVEM was not going to get any more resources. Mig did admit that, even for the more limited type of electoral mission envisaged for Angola, the plan prepared by Boneo required less resources than he had expected, but since Boneo had assured him they would be sufficient, he had accepted his judgement. The Secretary-General would not welcome going back to the Security Council with a revised operational plan, and even if he did the resources might well not be forthcoming, as current difficulties with mounting the new operations in Cambodia and Yugoslavia showed.

A visit to Luanda by Mr Boneo in the meantime threw light on his thinking when preparing the plan. He had initially been adamant that the transport element contained in the UNDP technical assistance project – four-wheel-drive vehicles, second-hand vehicles and 600 motorcycles – was sufficient. At a lively session with him on 17 April our Regional Commanders gave their unanimous view that, from their experience on the ground, this was a totally impractical suggestion. (The New Zealand Commander in the south-eastern region of Mavinga brought the house down by saying that he had ridden a motorcycle since his teens, but would certainly not venture to do so, or let any of his officers do so, on the deep sandy tracks around his base: neither they nor the motorcycles were likely to survive!) The same opinion was expressed by the UNDP regional coordinators in charge of the Special Relief Programme, and by the logistics expert working on the UNDP electoral project. All were convinced that air support was absolutely essential.

At the end of these discussions Boneo remarked, I thought revealingly, to the Regional Commanders: 'You speak as military men, starting from the premise of the resources that you need to do a particular job. I am an economist and I therefore start from the premise of the resources that are available and then tailor the job to fit them'. I then intervened, as chairperson, saying that, while I too had trained as an economist and believed in cost-effectiveness, we had to find a solution between the two extremes whereby we specified the minimum amount that was essential to do a reasonable job and then, if we did not get it all, it would be clearly understood that some corners would have to be cut.

In recounting this incident to Mig, I recalled that, during my briefing visit, the emphasis at headquarters had been very much on what the traffic (that is, the main contributors to the United Nations) would bear, rather than what the real needs were. The number of electoral observers had been predetermined by a psychological barrier – the figure of 100 – and although I had voiced concern over this, I had not been sufficiently *au fait* with the operation and the country to be able to argue very effectively. Even the US Assistant Secretary of State for Africa, Herman (Hank) Cohen, who had visited Luanda the previous week, had gone away convinced of the need for air support (despite Mr Boneo's having contradicted me in his presence about the need for it, before he had his baptism of fire at the hands of the Regional Commanders).

During Easter I brooded over UNAVEM's predicament. Not only was the Security Council a non-starter as a source of additional resources, but procedures for obtaining money through formal UN channels were too cumbersome and it was already late in the day. I concluded that the only way out was to seek timely contributions *in kind* from donors, in the form of transport (including the loan or hire of aircraft), services (for example printing) and supplies (for example paper), as well as perhaps personnel. I suggested to Mig that such an approach might even have wider relevance, given the international community's desire to have bigger and better UN peacekeeping operations at cut-price rates, on the one hand, and the UN's limited operational capacity on the other. Might we not use Angola as a pilot exercise in bringing about a new form of international in-kind support for peacekeeping, which governments might find easier to provide than having to ask increasingly recalcitrant parliaments, sometimes in their own election years, for more money as such? Moreover different sources had to be tapped in the donor countries: the traditional agencies providing development cooperation are usually unwilling, and indeed unable for legislative reasons, to provide money for helicopters, for example, whereas departments of defence, in a period of détente and disarmament, might well be willing to provide such support.

My resolve that the only solution for Angola was to seek innovative, non-traditional ways of overcoming the problem would require some pretty smart and decisive action on our part. I declared my readiness to visit some key capitals and expressed the hope that headquarters would likewise make *démarches* at the highest level.

I had also hoped that the conceptual argument could rest there and we could get on with the action along the lines I had proposed. Action did indeed follow, with valuable support from New York for my initiative, but Headquarters was determined to have the last word on the underlying issue. On 1 May 1992 the Secretary-General himself wrote me a letter that did not reach me until a week later, owing to what the covering cable described as a 'muck-up' at Headquarters. Despite initial expressions of admiration for the 'vigour and energy' I had brought to my tasks, the letter could only be described as a thinly veiled rebuke. All the old arguments about resources were reiterated: comparisons with Namibia were inappropriate; the mandate from the Security Council would permit only a 'comparatively modest operation'; and member states would not approve any substantial increase in resources for Angola. This was not only guidance for me: I was instructed to convey the Secretary-General's thinking to all my interlocutors in Luanda. He further instructed me to discourage the government about the degree of logistic support it could expect from the donor community (thus curtailing my 'fall-back' strategy also). Unrealistic expectations, especially about the provision of helicopters, might, if unfulfilled, provide a pretext for the Government to try to postpone the elections. The letter ended with an assurance of his full support in my 'arduous task'.

The words were encouraging, but the underlying message was unmistakable. It was also mystifying. Why was a letter necessary when Mig and I had already thrashed out the matter and my alternative strategy had been agreed? And who had written it? Mig had told me that he had not shown my initial cables on this to the Secretary-General, partly because the latter was busy but also because he did not want to exaggerate a 'passing exchange'; instead he would find a suitable opportunity to reassure the Secretary-General that I was not orchestrating a deliberate campaign about the adequacy of resources and administrative support for UNAVEM. Clearly the Secretary-General had not felt reassured. Worse still, he appeared to have blocked my only course of action.

I spent a long sleepless night trying to work out what to do. I decided that my only course – if I did not throw in the sponge there and then (and, dispirited as I

A 'Small and Manageable' Operation 41

felt, I dismissed that option – one could not 'jib' at that stage) – was to apply my 'vigour' and 'energy' to achieving *ad hoc* solutions, whatever Headquarters said.

That story comes later. In the meantime I had an immediate decision to take: whether to send a bland reply of acquiescence or continue to defend my corner at the risk of exacerbating already irritated feelings still further. I decided to run that risk, since it was not clear to what extent the Secretary-General had been informed of the earlier exchanges, or was aware of the reasoning behind my stance. I was determined to try to make the Angolan operation a success, against all the odds, not least because of the Angolan people themselves, and to derive from it whatever lessons might help to make other future peacekeeping operations less fraught with difficulties and more likely to succeed.

So I wrote back, assuring him that I well appreciated the limits of UNAVEM's mandate and resources and the need to avoid giving an erroneous impression of what we could do, but pointing out the singular characteristics and dangers of the Angolan operation, which made Haiti and Nicaragua inappropriate as models. The Security Council might want a 'small and manageable' operation, but neither epithet appeared very apposite for Angola.

I had constantly impressed on (often reluctant) authorities that the elections were a *sovereign,* national undertaking; the problem was that Angola needed the help of the international community and the United Nations to enable it to exercise that sovereignty, and I feared that the operation might collapse as much from sheer administrative incapacity, and especially a lack of adequate logistical support on the part of the Government, as from political difficulties. If that happened the United Nations would be blamed, however unfairly, by both the Angolans and the international community. It was because adequate logistics were essential for a successful outcome that I had proposed a strategy of pursuing innovative ways of improving the Angolan government's capacity to carry out its key role, through in-kind support from donor countries.

My own testing of the waters had shown that donor countries shared my concerns and were willing to help, not simply on account of the importance of the Angolan process, both *per se* and for all of southern Africa, but also because they felt the need to offset the perception in many national quarters (Government and other), as well as among African Ambassadors in Luanda, that Africa was a lower priority. Ambassador Cohen had followed up his recent visit with discussions in Pretoria and at UN headquarters. Cables that I had received from Headquarters instructing me to take certain steps, as well as *démarches* in New York to obtain help from Norway, Germany and Switzerland, had given me the impression that my strategy had been accepted. Now I had the impression that misunderstandings still persisted and I was receiving cross-signals.

Far from providing a pretext for a postponement of the elections, I believed that the international support, supplementing national resources, might act as a spur to a process that could otherwise die of inanition. That very day the EC countries had delayed declaring their contribution until the Government appointed a Director-General of the elections, thus providing a useful lever in support of our own, unavailing efforts to get the Government to make this key appointment.

Finally, I conveyed my apprehension that distance and communication only through the written word were distorting factors and that a *viva voce* discussion would be helpful. Although it had been foreseen that I would visit New York when necessary, I had not envisaged going there so soon, but as the Secretary-General had to report to the Security Council again in June, I suggested that it might be appropriate to plan a visit for some time in the next few weeks.

That suggestion was taken up and I spent three days at headquarters, from 25 to 27 May. My talks with the Secretary-General went well and, as was so often to prove the case in my direct dealings with him, I gained the impression of a much greater meeting of minds than through the medium of written and cabled communications between New York and Luanda. I pointed out that the problem we faced was inherited from the past, before he had been elected Secretary-General and I appointed to Angola: it stemmed from the assignment of an inappropriate role to the United Nations as a result of compromises hammered out by a group of member states, in negotiations over peace accords in which the organisation itself had had only a tardy and peripheral role. I voiced my conviction that, ideally, the United Nations should never agree to monitor peace agreements that it had not itself helped to forge; it should certainly never agree to do so without being sure that both its mandate and the resources provided by member states were adequate for the task. If satisfactory assurances on both counts could not be obtained, then the Secretary-General should reserve the right to refuse to take on the mission. The Secretary-General said he fully agreed with these views, and was indeed ready to say 'No' if necessary, as he has shown on a number of subsequent occasions.

In the case of Angola, however, the die was cast, whether we liked it or. We had to grapple with an almost impossible situation and make it work. During my brief sojourn at headquarters I met with members of the Security Council and senior colleagues in the Secretariat, and we launched the 'lease-lend', 'make-do and mend' strategy I had proposed from Luanda. At the time this was a wild gamble, but it worked. We eventually mounted, in support of the elections, the largest UN air operation of this kind – including the 'unrealistic' number of helicopters – that the organisation had ever had anywhere, and all without any budget. We did so by begging and borrowing, and though we never went as far as stealing we certainly used every innovative and imaginative process we could think of to achieve our objective – elections in Angola that would reach every corner of the country and permit all eligible voters to exercise their civic right.

* * *

In the meantime it was not proving easy to disburse even those resources that were available. During our protracted correspondence Mig Goulding had expressed his doubt about the UN's capacity to manage operations on this scale, not only because of the resource problem and lack of any working capital or reserve stock of equipment, but also because procedures had become extraordinarily sclerotic. He wrote enviously of Sir Brian Urquhart's comments about the speed with which the Congo operation had been mounted in 1960, adding wryly that cutting corners in the good old way practised then, and in 1973 in Sinai, was no longer possible. The last time it had been tried, when setting up UNIMOG between Iran and Iraq in August 1988, the result had been an auditors' report three inches thick! In my reply I said that I felt it imperative for those of us directly responsible for peacekeeping operations to get to the Secretary-General the message that the United Nations would simply not be able to cope with the increase in such activities unless there was a much more streamlined field-oriented administration for that purpose, with a single line of command, under one person with proven experience of complex international field operations. (I strongly believed that the Field Operations Division, which handled all the administrative underpinning of peacekeeping missions, should be transferred from the Department of Administration and Management to Mig's own Department of Peacekeeping Operations.) This eventually did happen, but not until a year later, in the second half of 1993.)

We were dogged by bad luck as well as bureaucracy. John Truman, the Chief Electoral Officer, had been a most welcome early arrival at the beginning of April. He and I had immediately begun to organise the Electoral Division, and had visited all provincial capitals to meet the local authorities and make practical arrangements for the installation of electoral teams. Alas, in less than a month the strain had begun to tell; he became visibly haggard and was clearly in almost constant pain with his back. I suspect, also, that his physical condition was not helped by the realisation of just how daunting the task ahead was. There was no help for it but to arrange for medical evacuation. So, just over four months before the elections we were again without a key official.

My joy at finally getting a qualified English-speaking secretary at the end of April was not destined to last long either. For about three weeks Patricia Stott, an old friend from Geneva, transformed my life. Then she suddenly fell ill – malaria was diagnosed and the routine treatment prescribed. But this was no routine attack. Had I not moved Patricia from her container to my house, she would almost certainly have died. Luckily I was working late one night and discovered in time that she had wandered off towards the camp gates and the surrounding bushland (where every night there was sporadic shooting) in her nightdress and a high state of delirium. Twice afterwards in my bungalow she lapsed into a terrifying coma, foaming at the mouth, from which she was resuscitated with great difficulty by Captain Waldecir, a marvellous military doctor attached to the Brazilian medical unit. It was a very close shave with death. It turned out that she was suffering jointly from cerebral malaria (an often fatal disease) and typhus. She, too, had to be medically evacuated. Happily she eventually made a good recovery, but I was back at square one as regards the secretary I so desperately needed.

An executive director, *de facto* my deputy on the civilian side, arrived in the second week of April. He was Ebrahim Jobarteh, a national of the Gambia, and a long-serving staff member of the Secretariat who had occupied a number of posts in administration and finance in New York and had served in Namibia. I had never worked with him before, but he had reputation of knowing the ins-and-outs of the bureaucratic maze of New York and of being adept at finding ways through it. It was already apparent that skills of this kind would be very necessary.

By this time additional administrative staff and members of the initial electoral team of 100 observers were also beginning to trickle in. And while struggling with these administrative and financial problems, we were simultaneously pressing the government and UNITA to fulfil their military obligations under the Peace Accords and to prepare for the elections.

Part II
The Military and Security Situation – February to September 1992

5 The Military Conundrum

Any lasting solution of a long-standing civil war depends on a satisfactory resolution of the military element. There can be no hope of forging a unified, stable and democratic state so long as opposing armed factions roam the land. Angola was no exception. It is equally self-evident that the dissolution and disarming of the existing armies, and the creation of a unified national force, demand a high degree of commitment and sincerity on the part of all sides to the conflict, qualities not easy to come by in the atmosphere of mutual suspicion, distrust and often deep-rooted hatred that is invariably spawned by long years of strife. Again Angola bore tragic witness to these verities.

The subtleties of such a process usually find little echo in the clinical language of peace accords, thought they must necessarily be in the minds of the negotiators. The Bicesse Accords set forth a straightforward proposition. Within 60 days the armies of the Government and UNITA were to be confined to 50 specified assembly areas, dotted in remote areas all over Angola, together with their weapons and matériel; demobilisation would then start, simultaneously with the selection of soldiers and weaponry from both sides to form the new, combined Angolan armed forces.

From the outset, major difficulties of concept and application began to appear. There was, for starters, the vexed question of just how many troops we were talking about. At Bicesse, a round total of 200 000 on the government side and 50 000 on UNITA's had been estimated. After only a few months these numbers were revised downwards, with the realisation that both sides had almost certainly swelled their numbers rhetorically during the negotiations in order to strengthen their respective bargaining positions. Such uncertainties affected UNAVEM's monitoring capacity, and the relevance of the meticulous records of men and weapons we counted weekly and regularly presented to the CCPM, particularly as regards the comparison between figures and percentages reported at different stages of what became a prodigiously long and difficult operation. The only figure that remained constant was the 50 000 troops that would constitute the new Angolan armed forces.

Contrary to what has since been alleged, from early on the United Nations had given public notice of the problems. Secretary-General Pérez de Cuéllar, in his report to the Security Council on 31 October 1991,[1] drew attention to the delays and consequent dangers to the peace process that were already beginning to appear: 'Both parties were slow in establishing joint monitoring groups, deploying their troops to the Assembly Areas, and granting UNAVEM authorizations to conduct reconnaissance in those areas, many of which were subsequently changed to other locations'.[2] UNITA was particularly singled out for its reluctance to allow UNAVEM personnel into its areas. It was not until 9 August 1991 (nine days *after* the cantonment of all troops should have been completed) that

UNAVEM was at last granted permission to reconnoitre reconnaissance the assembly areas designated for FALA (UNITA) troops.

The two and a half months' delay by the UN member states in approving the mission budget after the Security Council's decision to establish UNAVEM II had hardly helped, causing serious logistical difficulties. Notwithstanding, by 30 September 1991 UNAVEM had effected deployment to all of the 46 areas in which the forces of the two sides were assembling. Of the remaining four, two assembly areas were under discussion by the Joint Cease-fire Verification and Monitoring Commission (CMVF) while the two areas in the Cabinda enclave – Dinge and Chimbuanda – could not yet be established because of security problems.

The deadline for the completion of cantonment was postponed from 1 August 1991 to 15 September 1991, but even a month after that, on 22 October, only 60 per cent of the projected totals were in assembly areas – 68 968 FAPLA personnel (against a total of 115 640) and 26 968 FALA personnel (against a total of 49 800), making a combined total of 95 634 confined troops. The two sides mainly blamed this unsatisfactory situation on logistical problems arising from the remoteness of the assembly areas. FALA was moving its troops, often with their families, over very long distances on foot. FAPLA's forces had traditionally been deployed in towns and they lacked transport to move them and their heavy equipment to the assembly areas.

Even when the CMVF had succeeded in establishing its joint monitoring groups, there was difficulty in getting them to function. UNAVEM filled the vacuum by itself monitoring some aspects of the Peace Accords, and both sides welcomed this. So it was that, in early September 1991, UNAVEM started the regular counting of troops in every location – the beginning of a system that continued right up to the elections.

Meanwhile five incidents had flared up, but had been resolved by the CMVF and UNAVEM. One of these had been particularly serious. In Malange, UNAVEM and FALA teams had stumbled upon the body of Colonel Pedro Macanga, a UNITA political officer who, it was presumed, had been ambushed the previous night. The situation had become dangerously tense. FALA said the circumstances pointed to FAPLA being responsible, while FAPLA retorted that the killing had taken place in a recognised FALA area. Both sides had been prevailed upon to exercise restraint and not allow the killing to jeopardise the peace process. But the Malange incident would come back to haunt us months later.

At the end of his report of October 1991, the Secretary-General praised the fact that the ceasefire had held for over five months, while deploring the delays in the cantonment process, 'a state of affairs which undermines confidence and, at worst, could imperil implementation of various other aspects of the Peace Accords'. He nonetheless recognised the genuine logistical difficulties involved, and had tried to help by launching an emergency programme to relieve food shortages in the assembly areas. The report also raised the need for proper custody of weapons, 'which, in many cases, are not properly controlled and guarded in the Assembly Areas'. Mig Goulding recommended various measures on this to the CCPM in October 1991. They were still relevant when I arrived nearly four months later because the CCPM had done nothing about them.

Indeed custody of armaments was never properly resolved. While the theory was clear, there were very real obstacles in practice. During my visits to New York in March and May 1992 I was besieged with queries by Security Council members as to why the 'double key' system, which had worked so well elsewhere, had not been applied in Angola. Under this system arms are stored in a safe building, one key remaining in local hands, the other with the United Nations. I had to explain that it could not operate in a situation where weapons were mainly – and perforce – housed in grass huts rather than in solid buildings that could be padlocked; that there were no funds with which to construct such buildings; and that Angola presented particular difficulties that made it impossible to apply procedures used successfully in El Salvador or Nicaragua.

What the October 1991 report makes clear is that the seeds of the ultimate débâcle were being sown from the beginning – long before my arrival – and the Secretary-General was not letting them pass unnoticed in his reporting to the Security Council.

Nor were other warning signs absent in the period before my arrival. In January 1992 a particularly nasty incident occurred when a party of seven British tourists, travelling through Angola to Namibia, were ambushed and four of them killed in the vicinity of the southern town of Quilenges, where UNITA was strongly represented. The incident became a *casus belli*. UNITA produced a supposed FAPLA commander, who testified that organised troops of FAPLA soldiers had been ordered to terrorise UNITA supporters and civilians roaming through UNITA-held territory. The Government denied the story and the 'FAPLA commander' was found to be a phoney. To make matters worse, UNITA troops prevented the CCPM and the UN from completing the investigation on the ground. Then questions arose as to whether the attack had been carried out by random UNITA troops as a simple act of theft and without orders from Savimbi. The problem was never solved and became a smouldering issue on the CCPM's agenda, rekindling old animosities every time it came up.

I described in the previous chapter how the new Secretary-General, in his report of 3 March to the Security Council, and the Council itself, in its Resolution 747 of 24 March, again expressed concern about the delays in cantonment and starting demobilisation, and how the CCPM, whether in response to all these promptings or as a result of some mysterious maturation process of its own, finally launched the inaugural demobilisation ceremonies on 31 March.

We had already agreed that the Secretary-General should try to reinforce the process with parallel personal letters to President dos Santos and Dr Savimbi, which I would deliver personally. A secondary, but significant, intention was to prod President dos Santos into receiving me. Everyone was getting very jittery that, two months after my appointment and two weeks after my return to Luanda, I had still not seen the leader of one of the two conflicting parties.

The Secretary-General signed the letters on 2 April. That same day, with the suddenness that I was to come to find typical of events in Angola, I was summoned to an audience with President dos Santos. His residence at Futungo de Belas was not far from the UNAVEM camp, on a promontory overlooking the sea, surrounded by well-kept, sweeping gardens, marred in my view by outsize sculptures in the larger-than-life Marxist mould. The palace itself, a handsome, modern building encircling a huge swimming pool, had been a gift from Cuba.

I found myself being greeted by a handsome man of medium height, youthful-looking in spite of slightly greying hair, and dressed in a well-cut suit – attire which I later discovered he alternated with equally finely tailored safari outfits. His demeanour was grave and reserved, to the point that I sensed a trace of shyness or timidity, absurd as this seemed. The contrast with Dr Savimbi's flamboyant personality could not have been more vivid. He was accompanied by Minister Lopo de Nascimento and Victor Lima, his foreign affairs adviser, a tall, good-looking but invariably lugubrious character who was said to wield a great deal of influence and was much sought after by Ambassadors when they could not get direct access to the President.

The President was extremely gracious and courteous, and was evidently anxious to dispel any misgivings about his delay in receiving me. They had tried to contact me on the last day of my initial visit in February, he assured me, only to find that my aircraft had already left. Since Sabena left every night at the same time, around 7.00 p.m., this did not cast a very favourable light on the efficiency of the President's collaborators, but the last-minute character of the exercise did ring true, coinciding as it did with all the warnings I had received from older hands about the manner of organising presidential audiences. There was still the puzzling question of why no one at UNAVEM had ever received the call, even after my departure, but this was clearly not the occasion to quibble about technicalities. The President was, in any case, winningly profuse in his apologies.

Our first conversation lasted over an hour, during which the atmosphere became palpably more relaxed. After the ritual exchange of courtesies, our talk ranged frankly and widely over all facets of the peace process. As regards the military aspects, I emphasised our grave concern about the delays in cantonment, especially on the FAPLA side, where the situation was, if anything, deteriorating. This underlined the urgent need for rapid demobilisation, and the President and I exchanged mutual congratulations that it had already started two days earlier in Luena and agreed on the need to keep up the momentum.

Next day the Secretary-General's letters came. They were similar in content, in that they expressed some satisfaction with progress so far, especially the start of demobilisation and the announcement, that very day, of the dates for the elections, but urged much greater speed and determination in tackling the many things to be accomplished before then. Each letter was then tailored to fit the areas of foot-dragging on either side. The letter to the President dwelt on the need to accelerate the formation of the new Angolan armed forces, as well as to establish proper monitoring of the police and constitute a joint police force; while that to Dr Savimbi urged cooperation in facilitating the extension of the central administration and the establishment of public security throughout Angola so as to ensure the free circulation of persons and goods and the normal conduct of political, economic and social activities.

Although I had so recently seen President dos Santos, I had no option but to ask to visit him again to hand over the Secretary-General's letter. After an abortive attempt by his entourage to contact me on a field trip in Namibe, at the customary one hour's notice I eventually saw him on 14 April. Dr Savimbi once again granted me an appointment with great alacrity, on 7 April, and again I had the impression of being received by a feudal lord, in a carefully orchestrated scenario: he sat in the middle, as if on a throne, with all his barons on one side facing the visitors arranged at his right hand. The atmosphere was just as cordial, open and reasonable as on the previous occasion, especially as regards the actions to be taken in the military context.

Although clouds loomed on the horizon, there was still room for cautious optimism. A political report we sent to New York in early April noted a number of positive developments, among them the start of demobilisation, though at the same time we expressed our worry at the increase in violent incidents between individuals and groups in the main towns, as well as in the countryside, and conveyed our particular concern about Cabinda. The three observers shared our general assessment in a joint declaration on 9 April at a CCPM meeting. They congratulated the parties on starting demobilisation, as well as on the announcement of the date of the elections, but urged more rapid progress on all fronts. Thus we were all drawing attention to shortcomings but at the same time trying to jolly the two sides along the right path. These efforts were, however, far from effective. At the end of my message to New York on the observers' declaration there was a sobering phrase: 'I regret to add that, although this was the first CCPM meeting in two weeks, little or no progress was made on any front'. And this, alas, was to prove 'par for the course'. The CCPM was a very strange animal.

Proof of that was given at its meeting a week later, on 16 April, when a CMVF report, giving the demobilisation figures up to 8 April, was presented. Inexplicably, this would have been noted without comment, had I not taken the floor to indicate UNAVEM's deep concern about the figures. I pointed out that, as of 15 April, FAPLA had demobilised 9994 men, or 48.66 per cent of the 20 537 that should be demobilised in the experimental first phase, due to end on 30 April, while FALA had demobilised only 180 men, a mere 6.45 per cent of the 2790 that should be released during the same period (180 was the number for the experimental period only, and had already been met at the ceremony on 31 March in Luena – i.e. *no* progress had been made in the intervening 16 days). Our Regional Commanders had told me that the FALA commanders in their respective regions attributed this to lack of instructions from the CCPM. There thus seemed to be some confusion.

Engineer Salupeto Pena was quick to reassure the meeting that it was indeed UNITA's intention to demobilise more men, but it was unable to do so because of serious problems over the timely submission of correct documents, demobilisation money and civilian clothing. Speaking for the Government, General N'dalu admitted that considerable logistical problems had been encountered. The views then exchanged around the table threw up the perennial problems of transport and access to remote parts of the territory

I intervened a second time to point out that this foreshadowed the practical difficulties that would have to be faced on a much larger scale for the election, and that even those FAPLA soldiers who had been demobilised had had to remain in their assembly areas for lack of transport. Thus a large number of ex-soldiers in civilian clothes were still in those camps, with all the attendant dangers, including the risk they would spend their pathetically small gratuity before rejoining their families. At this point General N'dalu mentioned that he had asked US Assistant Secretary Cohen to provide C130 aircraft to carry the demobilised soldiers home.

No decision was arrived at, but at least the problem had been highlighted to the parties concerned, as well as to the observers, who had seemed to be unaware of it. What was inexplicable was that no one would have so much as commented on the clear disparity of the figures had I not charged in. Particularly incomprehensible was the apparent lack of concern on the part of the Government. Surely the clear indication that its forces were being demobilised rapidly while UNITA stood still should have flashed all sorts of warning lights? In fact these were the first signs of a new phenomenon: UNITA continued to maintain an exemplary 90 per cent or more as regards the cantonment of its troops, but in demobilisation it lagged far behind the Government, which scored the highest percentage in that area. A rather ominous picture was beginning to emerge.

The Government's apparent passivity was all the stranger because at about that time, it began to voice its concern about UNITA's alleged 'hidden army', for which fairly astronomical figures were cited: in the region of 20 000 men. The Government delegation complained to the CCPM about the alleged concealment of FALA troops in the Jamba–Licua–Mucusso area in the far southeast, near the Namibian border (Jamba was Savimbi's guerilla headquarters). Foreign Minister 'Loy' expressed the same fear at UN Headquarters during a visit to New York. The CCPM, at its 37th meeting on 17 April, proposed that the CMVF should investigate this allegation 'in the presence and with the support of UNAVEM'. The item then figured on the agenda of the 38th meeting, under the customary 'Relatorio' (report) of the CMVF, but could not be discussed because the latter body had not yet taken action (a sadly familiar sequence of events in the CCPM machinery). To facilitate an investigation we had asked FAPLA to provide more precise information, if necessary on a confidential basis, on locations, troop numbers, supply routes and depots, but had been told that it could only be provided by the local population, who were too scared to do so. The Government planned to move 30 of its troops from Menongue in the southern region to Mucusso in the south-eastern region to investigate whether troops were being concealed there, this unilateral action apparently raising no UNITA objection.

Ambassador Gröbler of the South African Department of External Affairs visited me on 5 May and General Unimna and I explored this issue with him. We expressed our concern that persistent rumours about hidden armies was hardly conducive to diminishing distrust, nor to creating an atmosphere of stability. The Ambassador said that South Africa shared this worry, especially as the Angolan government had alleged to him that some white men had been seen among these supposed troops. He had assured them that his government had nothing to do with this, and that President de Klerk would deal summarily with anyone found to be involved in such an undertaking. Colonel Rindel, a senior staff officer of the South African Defence force, who was also at our meeting, expressed the view that it was simply not feasible to sustain a 20 000-strong force in that area and promised to give UNAVEM any information coming to South Africa's attention through its continuing contact with Jamba.

Facts were, however, a very scarce commodity. The CMVF and the CCPM finally got their act together and three CMVF teams (comprising Government and UNITA representatives) were sent to the area, accompanied by UNAVEM and the military advisers of the three observers. Even this would not have been possible had not UNAVEM, once more exceeding its mandate, provided transport. From 26 May to 2 June the teams flew over the area in UNAVEM helicopters and visited locations in Cuando Cubango province. They could not find the alleged concealed army, but at five localities observations pointed to the existence of several hundred undeclared UNITA troops. One of our ablest officers, the commanding officer of the Zimbabwean contingent, Colonel Michael Nyambuya, then the UNAVEM liaison with FAPLA, accompanied the teams. I can well remember his indignation when the hunt was called off by the Government two or three days before its scheduled termination. Once more, the reason why the Government should take a decision that was apparently at odds with its own interests is obscure. Did it mean that the whole thing was a smoke screen with no foundation in fact? Or did the government participants simply bridle at living and travelling conditions that, by all accounts, were far from salubrious?

The CMVF reported to the CCPM that its team could find no evidence of a large, concealed army, but only of some UNITA 'logistical' bases with about 300 FALA troops, who should be included in the count of unassembled troops and the suspect areas monitored on a regular basis. On 6 June General Unimna and I obtained Dr Savimbi's agreement to this and action was taken accordingly. The Secretary-General reported these developments to the Security Council on 24 June.[3]

With the CCPM's decision, the bizarre episode of the 'hidden army' was closed to all formal intents and purposes. But rumours continued to rumble on, and do so to this day: I still get questions about the mysterious 20 000 men whose existence the combined efforts of the CCM, the observers and UNAVEM never managed to prove. This does not mean to say that it was a case of smoke without fire, and perhaps a fire considerably more significant than the 300 'logistical' units turned up by the investigation. Let us not forget that this wild and remote region of south-eastern Angola was known in Portuguese times as *Terras do Fim Mundo,* 'The Lands at the End of the World'. Moreover a man who is an armed guerrilla at one moment may be a peasant in civilian clothes peacefully going about his farm work the next, and who is to know the difference? The incident is symptomatic of the enormous difficulties inherent in any peace process of this kind, and in this particular case of the puzzling twists and turns of the Government, which did not seem ready or able to follow through consistently on matters vital to its interest. But perhaps it had other fish to fry, and this was simply a sideshow.

Meanwhile we continued to pound away at the central issue of demobilisation. On 28 April we reiterated to headquarters our worries about FALA's numbers, though noting they had edged up very slightly to 380, or 12.67 per cent of the first phase. That same day I took the matter up vigorously with Dr Savimbi at a luncheon he gave in my honour. My host expressed dismay and professed not to know that FALA's demobilisation was falling behind. In our presence, he instructed his collaborators to rectify the situation and overcome the logistical obstacles they cited in justification. 'We have a better record on troop cantonment than the government', said Savimbi, 'and we should do the same on demobilisation'. Was this sincere, or merely a consummate piece of showmanship? Certainly UNITA's showing improved, but never at the rate we would have liked. I took up the question of logistical support with General N'dalu when he came to a private dinner with me in the camp on Thursday 30 April, and he agreed that urgent measures must be taken to improve matters.

In addition to the clinical question of figures there was also the human one of what was going to happen to these people; how were they going to be helped to adjust to a civilian life that few of them had known even briefly, some never? How were they going to be absorbed into an economy destroyed by the war, and be trained and helped to find jobs in an already overburdened employment market? There were a number of schemes and programmes aimed at tackling these questions, especially in vocational training, and some governments had supporting funds. At a donors' meeting on 30 April, Engineer Salupeto Pena, speaking on behalf of the CCPM, presented a number of projects for the social reintegration of demobilised soldiers. These would require external funding of some US$447 million, in addition to local costs. He said that a request had already been made to the European Community for US$171.7 million. There were more immediate needs of a logistical nature – supplies and transport – standing in the way of achieving even the first-phase target of demobilising 23 000 troops by that very date, 30 April.

The Military Conundrum

None of the donors reacted. By then their minds and their funding priorities were fixed on matters directly related to the elections. Nor, to my knowledge, were any of the projects in the CCPM's paper ever implemented. Sporadic vocational training programmes were undertaken, with foreign support, but their scale was totally inadequate to the needs. Might the outcome have been different had more satisfactory arrangements been made? Fear of the unknown must have played a large part in the personal calculations of men who had known no other life than war, and particularly in the case of a guerrilla force such as UNITA. As Dr Savimbi never tired of reminding me, these men had their whole *raison d'être* in FALA. Unlike their opposite numbers in FAPLA, most of them had no homes to return to, much less jobs, having spent their life on the move, taking their families and goods and chattels with them and setting up self-sufficient villages wherever they went. This was why their assembly areas were so much better organised than those of the Government. It was also why, when demobilised, they stayed where they were, irrespective of the availability of transport, having nowhere else to go. Another of Savimbi's pet themes was that his men had had an identity and self-respect while they were active in UNITA's forces, a sense of being 'someone'; so how would they fare when ejected into an unknown world of anonymity?

The observers and ourselves were not the only ones to be alarmed by the slow pace of demobilisation. During the first week of May I met the leaders of the other political parties that had by then acquired legal status. They all sang a common refrain: why the delay in the confinement of troops? Slow demobilisation and the formation of the new armed forces led to the spectre of there being not one, but *three* armies in place at the time of the elections in September. This, combined with the proliferation of weapons among the civilian population, the decline in law and order, and the slow progress in extending the central administration, added up to a very grim prospect and they exhorted the UN to act more decisively to improve action on all these fronts. I was hard put to make them understand the limitations of the UN's role and capabilities, and that their very valid concerns should be addressed to the CCPM and the National Electoral Council.

In response to all these urgings, the CCPM worked out, with the help of UNAVEM, a new and accelerated demobilisation plan, to come into effect on 26 June. Instead of demobilising bit by bit across the board, there would be concentration on individual assembly areas, which would be visited by a complete, integrated demobilisation team. The troops and arms designated for the new Angolan armed forces would be taken at once to their designated centres. The remaining troops would be demobilised in one fell swoop and sent home, and then the assembly area would be closed down. Eight assembly areas were to follow this process initially, four from each side. They should have been closed down by 14 July, but this deadline was not met either.

The CCPM also adopted directives for the custody and/or disposal of arms, the drafts of which had been languishing in the CMVF's hands for many weeks, despite our protests. As assembly areas closed, weapons and other armaments selected for the FAA would be stored in regional and central warehouses under proper custody, with heavy armaments in designated field areas; the rest were to be destroyed on the spot. The FAA would be the ultimate custodian of all weapons outside police hands. Like so much else, the procedures did not work well in practice. In addition to customary administrative inefficiency, there was a genuine lack of secure storage facilities and transport was again a major obstacle. I authorised the use of UNAVEM planes and helicopters – again going far beyond our mandate – to carry the arms from the assembly areas to the regional storehouses, with UN military observers accompanying the consignments. But the process was far from complete by the time of the elections. Furthermore these arrangements could not address the problem of the thousands of weapons in private hands.

In his report to the Security Council of 24 June,[4] the Secretary-General expressed concern that, by 17 June 1992, only about 74 400 (49 per cent) of the total of 151 930 troops had been confined: for the Government, 42 600 or 37 per cent of 114 600; for UNITA, 31 700 or 85 per cent of 37 330. While the emphasis was now on demobilisation, it too was well behind schedule because of the lack of civilian clothes, funds, vehicles and aircraft. As of 20 June only around 20 000 troops had been demobilised, barely 13 per cent of the total of 150 000. In the case of the Government, the percentage was 16 per cent; in that of UNITA, only 4 per cent. The report also pointed out that additional international assistance would be needed, both for immediate logistical problems and for the longer-term problem of social integration and development. In a statement made by its President on 7 July,[5] the Security Council, appealing to member states to provide assistance expeditiously and pragmatically to resolve the logistical constraints, firmly reminded the two parties of their central responsibility for the success of cantonment and demobilisation.

Notwithstanding these exhortations, I was still only able to report to New York nearly one month later, on 6 August, that a mere 34 per cent of the total FAPLA and FALA troops had been demobilised, although some progress was being made on the loan of C130s by the United States. During my visit to Washington, from 21–22 July, I had pushed this matter very hard with both the Congress and the Administration, receiving positive responses. On 24 July the Secretary-General had written a personal letter to President Bush about Angola, *inter alia* thanking him for making available three of these large transport aircraft to support demobilisation and the elections. The planes eventually came in August and gave a much-needed boost to demobilisation, but by then it was already late in the day and they stayed only a few weeks.

It was also far from plain sailing. The C130s operated out of Luanda airport, from a hangar next door to that occupied by UNAVEM. The US Air Force team was constantly complaining of administrative hold-ups and poor planning by the Angolan authorities, leading to a less than optimum use of this costly service. Jeff Millington kept bringing these complaints to the CCPM, where renewed promises would be made to rectify the situation, but I still saw innumerable instances of the problems on the ground in my frequent visits to Assembly Areas. Administrative incapacity, as much as lack of transport, was responsible for the slow pace of progress.

I seized every opportunity to voice at the highest level my concern about the delays and inefficiencies. By now I was meeting regularly with the two leaders and had established a good *rapport* with both. The President often received me accompanied only by Mr Lima; encounters with Dr Savimbi were always of a group nature. Early in August 'Nando', Vice Minister of the Interior, and deputy head of the government delegation to the CCPM, and Engineer Salupeto Pena, head of the UNITA delegation, issued a joint statement that, while the new Angolan armed forces (FAA) would not be completely formed by the date of the elections, both FAPLA and FALA would be disbanded by then. President dos Santos then ordered that demobilisation *must* be completed by 31 August, the deadline fixed by the CCPM, and that all possible resources be mobilised to that end. In a meeting with myself and the three observers, hurriedly called by Dr. Savimbi on the evening of 19 August (I had been on a trip to Lubango and Namibe and arrived travel-stained and weary, still in my field kit), the UNITA leader stressed the need for the immediate dissolution of FAPLA and FALA, and the finalisation of the structure of the FAA before the elections.

In what was almost an echo of this conversation, President dos Santos reiterated to me on 21 August that demobilisation and total disbandment of the two forces were critical to the conservation of peace and must at all costs be completed before the elections. He thought that the main problem derived from the fact that the principal military leaders from both sides had not yet been integrated into the new structures, and he said he was taking action to get early decisions on this.

Notwithstanding all these public and private assurances, many Angolan and foreign observers were still assuming that both the Government and UNITA were somehow keeping some separate élite troops at hand, but no one could prove anything.

Even normal, open demobilisation did not pick up as it should have done. The deadline of 31 August came and went. When I met Foreign Minister 'Loy' on 3 September, he expressed his own conviction that demobilisation and disbandment were now virtually impossible before 27 September, the election date, and launched into a diatribe against UNITA, painting a grim picture of its warlike intentions, which he attributed to UNITA's growing fear that it would lose the elections. The population was scared, and there was a general expectation that UNITA would take up arms if it lost. This was why it was delaying demobilisation, moving arms and troops about the country and leaving demobilised troops in its assembly areas. He greatly feared that there could be a bloodbath. He had raised these fears with Assistant Secretary Cohen, and had not been convinced by the latter's assurance that the international community would never countenance such a development and would react vigorously.

'What could the international community do?', he demanded, with considerable heat. 'Sanctions? They won't have any effect on UNITA and will only hurt most of the poor people who have suffered so long from this war. The United Nations should draw up a contingency plan, including the immediate dispatch of a large contingent of Blue Helmets.'

Beguiling as this proposition was, it blithely overlooked the fact that it was the Angolan Government itself that had insisted there should be *no* Blue Helmets, and that the UN mandate should be strictly limited and marginal in order to conserve the country's sovereignty. Once again I had the thankless task of pointing out how little leverage UNAVEM had, and why. This did not mean we were not doing our utmost, often exceeding our mandate, I assured him, to try to ensure the consolidation of the peace process. We had, however, to work through the CCPM machinery, and it would he helpful if the Government would present a formal complaint with chapter and verse of the alleged troop movements by UNITA, so that a thorough investigation could be carried out according to the established norms. No such hard information was forthcoming. The Minister softened his doom and gloom prognostications and said – surprisingly in view of what had gone before – that he remained reasonably confident that the elections and the installation of the new government would take place.

This conversation was part of a concerted diplomatic strategy by the Government. Victor Lima had been sent on a lightning diplomatic mission to various quarters, and the next day in New York he transmitted to Assistant Secretary-General Alvaro de Soto a letter from President dos Santos to Mr Boutros Boutros-Ghali. Lima said that the Government was concerned about UNITA's military activities and feared a new war might be in the making. The President had expected increased tension as the elections drew near, but not that it would take a military turn. A memorandum attached to the letter enumerated troop movements by UNITA, which seemed to be aiming to occupy strategic positions. Most serious, said Lima, was that this was taking place under the very noses of those who were supposed to 'control' it and who seemed to notice nothing (a clear and disparaging reference to UNAVEM, but one that greatly exaggerated its function). Passivity would only encourage UNITA to indulge in violence.

Once again UNAVEM became the convenient scapegoat, and the Government performed an agile *volte face*, bemoaning the very limitations of the UN role, on which it had previously insisted, and by-passing the joint mechanisms set up under the Peace Accords. The record of the New York conversation gave no indication as to whether Mr Lima had been reminded of the facts. Back in Luanda we went through all the allegations in the memo, and contacted all our Regional Commanders and field teams. The list was a hodge-podge of minor items mingled indiscriminately with potentially serious ones, and hard facts were scarce. Once more it was difficult to prove anything in the general mix of speculation, allegations and counterallegations. Simultaneously UNITA was conducting its own similar campaign against the Government, about the antiriot police.

The Military Conundrum

On 7 September, only three days later, President dos Santos and Dr Savimbi held a long-heralded meeting together. Did President dos Santos, I wonder, express the same concern about UNITA's troop movements to Dr Savimbi as he had to the Secretary-General? I cannot even surmise on this point, because all that was divulged was the apparently heartening news that they had agreed to disband both FAPLA and FALA, and replace them by a single, unified FAA, at least formally, by 27 September. Dr Savimbi did raise UNITA'S concern about the antiriot police and some progress towards an accommodation appeared to have been made.

Coinciding with this important encounter, the so-called Troika of senior officials from the three observer countries – Assistant Secretary Cohen, Minister Durão Barroso and Ambassador Karasin – paid a strategically timed visit to Luanda on 7–8 September. They issued a joint declaration that underlined the importance of the commitment by both sides to the integration of the military leaders of FAPLA and FALA into the FAA, as well as to the abolition of the armed forces of both parties before the elections.

On 9 September I reported to Headquarters that provocations and acts of intimidation were increasing, but that both sides seemed at pains to avoid overreaching or pushing each other too far. There were continuous reports of UNITA troop movements, but despite its best efforts UNAVEM had been unable to substantiate any of significant dimensions. All the Angolan parties, including the two principal ones, the MPLA and UNITA, continued to express their concern about the 'reserve forces'. Three weeks before the elections only 41 per cent of Government and UNITA troops had been demobilised: 24 per cent of these were still in the assembly areas with their weapons stored near at hand; and 32.5 per cent of total Government and UNITA troops had not been verified. The smaller political parties were publicly voicing their anxiety about where all these 'missing' 65 000 (a figure based on the original total of 200 000, which was later reduced) troops were, and what they could do.

In the face of this ambiguous and dangerous situation I asked the Secretary-General to exert his influence on the two leaders. On 9 September he again wrote to both of them saying that I had conveyed to him my concern about the delay in demobilisation and in establishing proper arrangements for the storage or disposal of weapons and ammunition, and urging prompt action to disband the two armies and form the FAA. Both letters dealt with President dos Santos' concern about UNITA's intentions and actions, as conveyed in his letter to the Secretary-General, but in different terms. To the President, the Secretary-General said he had asked me to ensure that UNAVEM investigate every alleged incident, and reminded him that in August I had arranged such investigations through the joint mechanisms of the CCPM and the CMVF, but that the results had not substantiated the allegations that there were unauthorised, large-scale FALA contrigents outside the assembly areas. The Secretary-General pointed out that such concerns was likely to be widespread until demobilisation and the formation of the new army were complete, another reason why it was essential to speed up the process.

The letter to Dr Savimbi referred to President dos Santos' complaint and the Secretary-General's commitment that UNAVEM would thoroughly investigate all such allegations, expressing the hope that UNITA would cooperate. He also addressed UNITA's parallel concern about the formation of the antiriot police by the Government, as did I when I met Dr Savimbi on 9 September.

* * *

That was also the date on which the Secretary-General's last report to the Security Council before the elections was finalised, although due to pressure of work at Headquarters it was not released until 17 September. In the light of later events the delay probably did not make much difference, but at the time I was dismayed that its important messages, which might just possibly prod the two parties into some more energetic action to resolve the military situation, could not be imparted while there was still time.

The Secretary-General could still say that there had been no major violation of the ceasefire, despite noticeably rising tension and incidents of political intimidation. But he also had to point again to alarming deficiencies in the fulfilment of the peace process, notably in cantonment and demobilisation. More than one year after the original deadline the number of confined troops remained dangerously low, especially with regard to FAPLA, and had declined in relation to the latter part of 1991. The reasons given were the same: the troops had chafed at being confined so long, and, despite significant international relief aid, shortages of food and medicines had occasionally led to riots, especially in the FAPLA areas. The Government had confined no troopsat all in its two assembly areas in Cabinda, arguing that it needed the FAPLA troops there for combat duty against armed FLEC factions that were claiming independence for the enclave. UNITA had only 100 soldiers in its own assembly area in Cabinda.

Demobilisation provided some incentive for absentee soldiers to return to the assembly areas to receive their papers, money and civilian clothes, but it was a slow process, hampered by problems of organisation, transport, logistics and resources. As of 2 September, the Secretary-General informed the Council, only 61 994 troops or 41 per cent of the combined total had been demobilised: 54 737 or 45 per cent for the government, and only 7257 or 24 per cent for UNITA. The deadline of 31 August had proved unrealistic, and the best that could be hoped for was that 'with strong political will and sustained efforts demobilization can be completed before the elections'.

The new procedures instituted by the CCPM and increased international assistance had helped to speed the process somewhat, and demobilisation was now being undertaken in 26 assembly areas (14 Government, 12 UNITA). UNAVEM was providing logistical support, but the key ingredient was political will. UN military observers were to remain in the assembly areas until these were formally closed by the CCPM, on verified completion of the selection and transport of troops either to the FAA or to their home destinations, and the transfer of weapons and other military matériel to the designated storage areas, each area to be guarded by a 50-man team (25 from each side) and verified by the joint monitoring teams and UNAVEM. Several assembly areas were near closure, but none had yet filled all the conditions.

The Secretary-General's report welcomed the directive, but pointed out that most weapons were still stored in the assembly areas and countless numbers were in private hands, and this not covered by these arrangements. Time was running out, warned the Secretary-General, and 'Unless drastic efforts are made, there is a dangerous prospect that several armies will continue to exist in Angola'.

The Security Council considered this report on 18 September 1992, and the President issued a statement yet again calling on the Angolan parties to take 'urgent and determined steps' to complete certain essential measures stipulated by the Bicesse Accords, among them the 'demobilization of the remaining Government and UNITA troops, the collection and centralized storage of weapons'.

* * *

These were precisely the concerns engaging much of my attention in Luanda. Unfortunately, while the Bicesse Accords obliged us to operate through the joint consultative machinery, those bodies were still not demonstrating much dynamism, even though the election dates were creeping inexorably nearer. In the week commencing 7 September the CCPM had no meeting at all until late on Friday 11 September: the weekly heads-of-delegation meeting on Tuesday was cancelled because of the Troika's visit, while the Thursday plenary had to be postponed because the two sides' Chiefs of General Staff, whose presence was needed for the discussion on demobilisation, were in Malange. They were still not back on Friday, and it was initially proposed that the subject of demobilisation be dropped from the agenda, but General Unimna and I insisted that it be retained, in order to voice UNAVEM's concern about the serious and escalating disturbances that had recently arisen.

A particularly grave incident had ocurred in M'banza Congo the previous day. In their mad anxiety to get away, demobilised FAPLA troops had tried to storm the US C130 planes that had come to transport them to their destinations. The planes had taken off again, empty, in accordance with security instructions. Several hours of mayhem had ensued, and the local authorities, including the Vice Governor and the police, had prudently disappeared into the surrounding bush. Our tiny UNAVEM team of military police and electoral observers had been the only objects upon which the rampaging and disappointed soldiers could vent their pent-up wrath. The camp had been attacked and our personnel, all unarmed, had been in danger of losing their lives. We had spent another sleepless night in Vila Espa in sporadic radio contact with them. We had not been able to take them out by air, because night landing was not possible in M'banza Congo, which was accessible only by helicopter. Instead we had planned a daring night escape by road. The team in M'banza Congo had decided to stay and stick it out, however, and a new plan had been developed. At first light on Friday 11 September a UNAVEM helicopter, carrying the Deputy Chief Military Observer, Brigadier Nyambuya, other UNAVEM personnel and representatives of the CMVF, had flown into M'banza Congo, immediately followed by the US C130 planes. In the meantime our local UNAVEM team (civilians, including women, as well as the military and police) had managed to calm the soldiers with news of imminent rescue and marshalled them in groups on the airfield, according to their various destinations, so that they could be boarded in an orderly way. The demobilisation had then continued without further incident, but there is no doubt that an even uglier situation could have developed had it not been for UNAVEM's initiatives, and above all the bravery and dedication of our team on the spot.

I recounted this incident to the CCPM and described it as symptomatic of an increasing and disturbing phenomenon: the collapse of organisation and authority, of which I cited other recent examples in Funda and Lobito. Although everyone understood that demobilisation could not now be completed by 27 September, expectations had been raised by the declarations of President dos Santos and Dr Savimbi after their meeting of 7 September, but there would be a growing and dangerous focus of instability in the assembly areas if the process was not at least speeded up. The risks were accentuated by the loss of control over armaments and ammunition, and I called for renewed and more vigorous efforts to get them stored in the regional deposits, under FAA control. For both these purposes it was urgent to improve the coordination of demobilisation among all the national authorities (that is, both Government and UNITA). Without that the support being provided by UNAVEM, over and above its mandate, could not be effective.

General Unimna emphasised the urgent need for all concerned to be informed of the lists of the 50 000 troops that would make up the new Angolan armed forces, since uncertainty was a further destabilising factor, including among the officers. The US observer also expressed concern that the C130s were not being used properly and that their pilots and crews were being put at risk by the lack of organisation. The CCPM decided that the General Staff should urgently deal with this matter, but while some of us urged that they should meet over the weekend, since only fourteen days remained to the D-day of 27 September, they set the meeting for the morning of Tuesday 15 September. The findings were to be presented to the heads of delegation in the afternoon.

The following week, in contrast, saw a flurry of meetings of the CCPM, which at last – and all too late – had galvanised itself into action. On Monday 14 September the Chiefs of General Staff discussed arrangements for expediting the demobilisation, which was also on the agenda of the Heads of Delegation meeting the next day. Three priorities were agreed: control and storage of weapons in the regional depots; formation of personnel for the FAA; and demobilisation of the remaining troops. Various commissions were set up to carry out the revised plans, and assurances given that clothes, money and transport were available for the fourth and fifth phases of demobilisation. A major bottleneck was the lack of polaroid cameras – yet another illustration of how insignificant logistical problems can have huge consequences. As I wrote after the meeting, the theory seemed fine, but past experience did not make me sanguine about its translation into practice, particularly with only ten days to go before the deadline for disbanding the two armies and twelve before the elections.

My prognostications were all too correct. When I saw President dos Santos on 23 September, he recognised that FAPLA and FALA could not be demobilised by the time the new Angolan armed forces (FAA) were due to take over on 27 September. He felt, however, that if the key appointments of the new FAA Chief of General Staff could be made before the elections, then the remaining FAPLA and FALA troops could be put under the command of the FAA until demobilisation was completed. This arrangement was agreed between the President and Dr Savimbi at their meeting two days before the elections. They jointly declared that.

> Today, 27 September 1992, the People's Armed Forces for the Liberation of Angola (FAPLA) and the Armed Forces for the Liberation of Angola (FALA) are formally abolished, and from now on there will only be the Angolan Armed Forces (FAA) which will report directly to CCPM until the inauguration of the new Government resulting from the elections.

The declaration went on:

> Since there remain some administrative activities to be carried out for the complete encorporation into FAA and integration into civilian life of some military personnel of the two former Armed Forces, these activities will be carried out from now on by the Chiefs of Staff of the Angolan Armed Forces and verified by UNAVEM II in order to achieve the abovementioned requirements as soon as possible.

But the new Angolan armed forces, upon which the burden of completing unfinished business was now laid, was facing its own difficulties and debilitating compromises.

6 The Formation of the New Angolan Armed Forces

The formation of the new Angolan armed forces (the FAA) was inextricably linked with the of cantonment, demobilisation and disbandment of the two armies. In retrospect it seems absurd that the UN was left out of the whole issue under the Bicesse Accords, and mandated only to observe and verify cantonment and demobilisation. While it was perfectly sensible to give the British, French and Portuguese the task of training the new force, the enterprise constituted such a critical element in the process that UNAVEM should at least have been given a role of verification and a seat in the CCFA (the Joint Commission for the Formation of the Angolan Armed Forces, under the CCPM). In practice UNAVEM was drawn willy-nilly further and further into the issue.

I was already reporting to Headquarters on 28 April that, according to Portuguese, French and British sources, it was now unlikely that more than 20 000 soldiers out of the total 40 000 envisaged could be selected before the elections. Since training courses were nearly six months behind schedule, only some of these 20 000 could be trained by that time. Courses for 500 sergeants and corporals (250 from each side) had started in Benguela the previous week.

Concern over the delays led to shortcuts being sought. On 1 May, Mig Goulding informed me that, at a meeting in New York, US Assistant-Secretary Cohen had commented that most probably the new national army would not be in place before September but did not consider that this should prevent the elections from taking their course. He saw some merit in an idea, mentioned to him by General N'dalu, that a way out of the difficulties would be simply to transfer the required number of personnel from the existing Government and UNITA forces into the new army, without retraining, and demobilise the rest.

Senior UNAVEM military personnel maintained close contact with their military counterparts in the CCFA, where proposals for compromise solutions were also brewing. On 11 May I conveyed to New York the news that Government and UNITA members of The CCFA, together with the Portuguese, French and British military advisers, had agreed to present a new plan to the CCPM. On leaving the assembly areas, FAPLA and FALA troops would either go 'home' if demobilised, or, if selected, to the FAA. The latter group would go to barracks, if these had been completed, or to temporary camps (tents), if bilateral assistance could be provided to equip them. If enough camps could not be set up, then the troops would stay in the assembly areas, which would then become assembly areas of the FAA. Three phases were envisaged: the first would be the selection of the General Staff and other essential units, including logistics, numbering some 13 000 men; the second, other priority units, including engineers, amounting to an additional 10 000 men; the third, the remainder. The plan was to train, or start training, between 13 000 and 23 000 men by the time of the elections, but to complete by then the selection of all 40 000 soliders who were to come from assembly areas. All the selected troops, whether in temporary camps or assembly areas, would be under FAA command. It was considered that this was the best that could be attained, but that it might be jeopardised by delays in providing logistical support, which was the government's responsibility.

Once again the problem of logistics raised its ugly head. There was a genuine lack of premises to house the new troops, in addition to the problem of transporting them from the assembly areas. The British provided aid to build a barracks at Uige, which was inaugurated before the elections; other barracks were under construction or being rehabilitated, but were behind schedule and too few in number. Makeshift arrangements were the only way out, but they too presented difficulties. The very idea of tents was repugnant to some of the Angolan military, who considered that barracks were a *sine qua non*. Colonel Nyambuya, with his experience of the formation of the unified Zimbabwean army, was invaluable in dealing with such plaints. Zimbabwe had been in a much more favourable position than Angola as regards its economy and infrastructure, but even there there had been insufficient barracks to house the new army and many of its troops had willingly stayed for some time in tented camps. But an even greater snag than the overblown expectations of the Angolan military was the lack of money or local facilities to provide even tents, much less that strong symbol of unity, uniforms.

The UN became involved in trying to resolve these deficiencies, an unexpectedly difficult task. On 12 June President dos Santos, in the course of a meeting with the Secretary-General in Rio de Janeiro during the Earth Summit, indicated that the Government wanted to launch an international appeal for funds for barracks and tents. In his report to the Security Council of 24 June, the Secretary-General drew attention to this need for external assistance and the President of the Council included an appeal to that effect in his statement of 7 July.

For my part, I was exploring various avenues for the provision of tents. The United States seemed far and away the most likely to be able to send a sufficient number quickly, and I took the matter up during my visit to Washington on 21–22 July. There I encountered an unexpected obstacle: while there was the utmost good will, I was told that it was legislatively impossible because Congress had prohibited the Administration from giving military assistance to Angola! In vain I pleaded with members of Congress and the Administration that this was hardly typical military aid, but rather assistance that would be crucial to the consolidation of a vital *peace* process. I had to make these *démarches* unofficially because, with characteristic leisureliness, the Angolan Government did not submit a formal request to the Secretary-General for tents until the first week in August, nearly two months after the President's meeting with Dr Boutros-Ghali. Foreign Minister Loy's note requested 50 tents for 30 persons each, and 200 tents for 120 persons each. I cabled Headquarters on 6 August, recounting my unsuccessful *démarches* in Washington, and suggesting that they might have better luck in pursuing this directly with the US government. Back came the reply on 13 August: the United States had no legislative authority to provide assistance to the Angolan military and advised an approach to the United Kingdom, France and Portugal. Soundings had already been taken in those quarters in any event, and on 12 August I was able to report that the United Kingdom hoped to provide 100–200 tents. The issue disappeared from view in the confusion of subsequent events, but I doubt whether the total required was ever attained. Sadly, they were never needed.

On the equally vexed issue of uniforms, the former colonial power, Portugal, came to the rescue. Thousands of uniforms were manufactured, post-haste, and airlifted to Angola. It would be interesting – and probably sobering – to know how many of them were actually used.

Such details may seem like minutiae to the impatient reader. I include them because they are illustrative of the many small but potentially disastrous pitfalls attendant upon a process of this nature. Individually inconsequential, they can collectively add up to a formidable obstacle. This experience shows how extremely difficult it was to obtain even a relatively modest number of non-lethal items to sustain the peace process in Angola, while planes and tanks and guns poured in to peacekeeping operations in other parts of the world.

There was one positive development. On 6 August I reported to New York that the FAA's commanding officers had been appointed. General 'Wiyo' of UNITA was to lead the Army, Admiral Gaspar Rufino of FAPLA the Navy and Major General Pedro Neto, also of FAPLA, the Air Force. They were all well-regarded officers (I knew 'Wiyo' and Neto personally through the CCPM) and the announcement lightened everyone's spirits. I also had to report that tension was rising, and that the previous week General Unimna had warned the Troika that the main dangers lay in the military and police areas. Pointing to UNAVEM's latest verification figures, he noted that only about 10 per cent of the FAA had been trained and only 24 per cent of FAPLA and FALA demobilised. On a more optimistic note, Ambassador Monteiro had added that at least the command structure of the FAA had been agreed and the 50 000 personnel selected.

Although President dos Santos and Dr Savimbi agreed on 7 September that FAPLA and FALA would be disbanded and replaced by the FAA, there was an ominous difference of opinion between them on the timing of the appointment of the Chief of General Staff of the FAA and of senior posts in the Ministry of Defence. On 9 September Savimbi informed me that he had told the President that UNITA was not agreeable to these appointments being made *before* the elections. According to him, it had been agreed that they would be decided by the new government. When I met President dos Santos on 23 September, he expressed considerable concern over what he termed UNITA's 'reticence' about the appointment of the Chief of General Staff before the elections. The Government felt this to be essential, and he gave no indication that he had agreed to the postponement of the decision.

In his last progress report to the Security Council before the elections, tardily released on 17 September,[1] the Secretary-General warned that the formation of the FAA was 'running woefully behind schedule'. High-ranking officers from both sides had been sworn in to head its command structure but only 19 per cent of its effectives had so far been formed, while 59 per cent of the Government and UNITA armies had still not been demobilised. The Secretary-General noted the intention to speed up the demobilisation of all troops not wanted for the FAA, so that the new force would come into existence before the elections. 'Much depends', he added 'on a solution being found to the acute problem of finding tents to accommodate the troops selected for the new Armed Forces' – another example of the negative power of logistics. The Security Council once again urged the rapid completion of the FAA in a statement made by its President on 18 September.

In Angola the atmosphere became progressively more fraught as the month of September advanced. The disbandment of FAPLA and FALA and the designation of the FAA Commander-in-Chief could only be agreed and authorised by the two supreme commanders of the existing armies – President dos Santos and Dr Savimbi. Their last meeting before the elections was tantalisingly postponed time and again, and sometimes seemed dangerously close to not taking place at all. Rumours, mostly of the doom and gloom variety, abounded in Luanda. There was evidently much cliff-hanging and jockeying for position on both sides.

And then, just when we had all given up hope, the two leaders met on Sunday 27 September, just two days before the elections, and took the critical joint decision to disband their respective armies and declare the FAA as the only unified armed force of Angola. They also resolved their differences about the timing of the appointment of the Chief of General Staff, hitting upon a compromise – one that could not fail to cause some 'frissons' among those of us most closely connected with the process. The appointment would be made immediately, but there was to be not one, but two, Chiefs of General Staff; in short a joint top command, comprising General N'dalu and General Ben-Ben (a nephew of Dr Savimbi and Chief of Staff of FALA).

The next afternoon, on the eve of the first day of voting, their swearing-in ceremony was held at the main barracks. We all went. General Unimna and I represented UNAVEM. All the observers and their military advisers were there, as were many Ambassadors and an array of national and international media. It was a very moving occasion. The troops marched up and down the dusty road in the stifling heat. The officers and men who were being incorporated, drawn up in solid phalanxes, were sworn in, FAPLA and FALA mixed. The two joint Chiefs of Staff were also sworn in. The sight of all these arms being raised together in joint salute, having for so long been raised against one another, and the sound of their voices proclaiming in unison their a common allegiance to Angola could not fail to impress the occasion with a high degree of solemnity that in turn seemed to endow it with credibility. The identical uniforms – that strong symbol

– reinforced this impression. FAPLA and FALA were indistinguishable. One had to look twice, and hard too, to identify well-known faces and slot them mentally into their former allegiances. Nonetheless I had to confess that I found the new uniform rather drab – dark brown with a dark brown beret. I said to someone that I supposed the brown beret was the result of mixing the green of the FAPLA berets with the red of FALA. At the time I considered this to be a whimsical remark – perhaps even a superficial feminine comment – only to find out later that this was exactly what had happened. It was another symbolic compromise.

The reception that followed the formalities was an occasion of great euphoria, with much back-slapping and mutual congratulation, and there was a very pervasive atmosphere of brotherliness and unity in a common purpose. None of us who were there could forget for one moment the intense precariousness of the situation. But one would not have been human had one not gone away at the end of the ceremony thinking, wishfully perhaps, that things might somehow work out, despite all one's misgivings, because, in the final analysis, everyone wanted done with war.

7 The Police Imbroglio

The issue of the police was arguably as crucial as that of the military, but it had been given much less emphasis in the Peace Accords. Uncharacteristic as it was of its consummate bargaining skills, UNITA seemed somehow to have missed a trick by not insisting on more precise provisions. The issue was important for two reasons. First, it was essential to maintain a reasonable degree of law and order for the holding of free and fair elections but bound to be problematic in the wake of prolonged civil strife, with a central administration covering only part of the country. Second, a unified and neutral police force had to be established. All of this was inextricable from the whole question of security, itself a tangle of common criminality on the one hand, arising from the parlous living conditions and long-running civil strife, and on the other of military-type incidents, which might either be the result of misunderstandings or deliberately provoked.

The Peace Accords envisaged joint police monitoring teams, verified by UNAVEM, and the creation of a representative joint police force, into which persons from many quarters and affiliations would be incorporated. Again difficulties emerged from the very start. There were delays in setting up the joint teams, which prevented the UNAVEM police observers from discharging their functions. They were further hampered by having insufficient Portuguese speakers. It was not until 20 June 1992 that, after considerable pressure from me, the Security Council increased the number of police observers to 126. Argentina and Brazil then increased their existing contingents and Colombia sent a group, which greatly eased the language problem.

Misconceptions about the role of the UNAVEM and of the joint verification groups persisted, despite repeated attempts to make it clear that neither had any executive responsibility for the maintenance of law and order, which remained with the existing police force. Their job was simply to verify that the latter carried out their duties in a politically neutral manner and respected the human and political rights of individuals.

UNAVEM teams of three or four police observers were in place in all 18 provincial capitals by October 1991, but the two Angolan sides did not complete the designation of their joint monitoring teams (through which UNAVEM had to work) until early 1992 and they were not fully deployed until June of that year, despite constant pressure by UNAVEM. But even then both sides had difficulty in providing transport, communications and office space. Once again it fell to UNAVEM to try to fill the logistical gap. The Secretary-General's next report, of 24 June 1992, recognised that the joint monitoring system was almost entirely dependent on UNAVEM's transport and communications facilities, which were neither intended nor sufficient for this purpose. Other severe constraints related to the lack of radios, offices, funds and identity cards. The Secretary-General urged that greater international cooperation be provided, but little was to be forthcoming in this area.

The police monitoring activities were misunderstood by many Angolans as an attempt to institute an alternate or parallel police force, alongside the existing police. A further problem was UNITA's tendency to flout the Government's authority and the responsibility of the Angolan police to maintain law and order when their followers were alleged to have committed criminal acts or disturbed the peace. As late as 9 September 1992, less than three weeks before the election, the Secretary-General was still warning the Security Council[1] about the weakness arising in the Government/UNITA police monitoring mechanism because of mutual mistrust, political interference by the two parties and inadequate logistical support. Security Council resolutions and statements were peppered with references to the importance of making the police monitoring operation work properly, but its exhortations seemed to fall on deaf ears.

There was also difficulty in distinguishing between common-or-garden criminal acts, which came under the general heading of civil law and order and were therefore the responsibility of the police, and those of a military nature that constituted a breach of the Peace Accords and required the CCPM's attention. The difficulty was compounded by of the proliferation of weapons among the population, as well as the fact that many civilians wore military uniforms or fatigues, simply because they had no other clothes.

In our first meeting on 2 April President dos Santos had expressed concern about the proliferation of arms, and the tendency to deal with common criminal acts in a political way through the CCPM. I had told the President that I shared his concern, and seized the opportunity to stress that effective police monitoring and the creation of a joint, neutral police force were a *sine qua non*. The creation of a joint police force, like the formation of the FAA, involved the incorporation and training of UNITA elements. This process had hit a stumbling block: UNITA claimed that the government had offered too few posts (the first batch of trainees was to number only 183) and at too low a level. I had expressed the hope that concessions might be made on both points. The President had replied that individual recruits would be welcome 'as Angolans, but not as UNITA cadres'.

The police training issue came to occupy a lot of time and cause considerable frustration. UNITA wanted between 7000 and 8500 places in the police, including senior positions, but the Government was willing to offer only 1200. The Government argued that, since the Peace Accords specified that UNITA's participation was to be at 'the invitation of the Government', it was not under the same binding obligation as in the case of other clauses. UNITA reacted by refusing to send any trainees at all. I made numerous attempts to try to persuade the Government to be more generous, and privately urged Engineer Salupeto Pena to break the *impasse* by accepting the posts that *had* been offered as a first step towards broader participation, rather than refusing to do so pending a better offer.

The Police Imbroglio

Even when UNITA did agree to send 183 UNITA men to a first police training course in Luanda, the way was far from smooth. Transport once again posed a seemingly insuperable obstacle. After lengthy discussions in the CCPM, the Government agreed to send a plane for them and I rashly thought the problem resolved. Not a bit of it. An almost farcical element intervened. Salupeto Pena informed the next CCPM meeting that a regrettable mistake had been made by those on the ground: the plane had returned, not with the police trainees, but with UNITA troops selected for training and incorporation into the FAA! I was frankly incredulous. Were they engaged in a crude game of playing for time? Was the Government sincere when it pleaded logistical difficulties and lack of aircraft? Were both sides, playing out an elaborate charade of foot-dragging, aimed at who knew what Machiavellian ends? At moments like these I felt as if I was caught up in an Angolan 'Alice in Wonderland' situation, in which the potentially sinister elements far outweighed the merely comic or bizarre.

The 183 UNITA police recruits eventually attended the course but 144 of them failed, so only 39 were integrated into the police force! UNITA accused the government of nefariously organising this outcome. The Government retorted that UNITA had made a poor selection and that a high proportion of the would-be recruits were not even literate. It was hard to believe that either side was genuinely committed to building a joint police force.

Meanwhile an even more dangerous issue had arisen, to muddy the waters further. The first signs, although serious, gave no inkling of the dimensions that would ultimately be reached. Exchanges of views between the two sides in the CCPM, even on the thorniest of subjects, were usually remarkably civilised at that stage. The two would seem to dance around one another in some kind of elaborate saraband, punctuated by long, sonorous speeches richly embellished with flowery phrases and compliments. Cordiality and bonhomie were the name of the game. Sometimes the atmosphere became almost ebullient, spiced with humour and private jokes. In less charitable moments one ceased to be beguiled by these charm-laden demonstrations of apparently good-humoured, mutual tolerance and wished they would just get on with the business in hand and, more particularly, talk less and act more. At one meeting, in April, this tradition was rudely broken by a visibly angry Salupeto Pena. The cause of his wrath was an assignment of equipment for the police, including some lethal items, which the Government had purchased from Spain, and which had now arrived at the port of Lobito. The Government had waited until the last moment before officially informing the CCPM of this shipment, as it was legally obliged to do, and correct verification procedures had not been observed. UNITA claimed that all this was distinctly fishy, and contrary to the Peace Accords, especially the so-called 'triple zero' clause. The Government said that this was normal equipment to enable the police to maintain law and order, especially in emergency situations. The debate raged back and forth over several meetings and gave rise to public accusations, as well as to one of the most extraordinarily vituperative exchanges of diplomatic notes (if that is the term) between UNITA's 'Foreign Minister' and the Spanish Ambassador that I have ever seen.

The lethal Spanish equipment proved to be the tip of a large iceberg – the Government's decision to set up an 'antiriot' or 'emergency' police force. This became a real *casus belli*. More angry exchanges took place in successive CCPM meetings, eventually boiling down to the issue of whether or not the Government had the right to set up a special antiriot police unit and what its purpose was. The Government's allegations about UNITA's 'hidden army' and UNITA's accusations about the Government's intentions in setting up the antiriot police, though never formally linked, came to form an ominous point and counterpoint of the relations between the two sides, reflecting mutual suspicion of each other's intentsions, or perhaps just negotiating positions. Figures flew back and forth across the table, amid a barrage of accusations and counter-accusations, but hard facts were elusive. Dr Savimbi first raised the issue with me during our meeting of 31 July, but rather as an afterthought in a discussion about electoral preparations and my talks in Washington. He and his colleagues alleged there was a wide distribution of antiriot police in various parts of the country, and an increase in their number. We agreed that all such matters must be pursued through the CCPM. (As a further complication the new police units sported light-blue berets almost identical to those of UNAVEM, which gave rise to dangerous confusion.)

On 6 August UNITA alleged that Dr Savimbi's residence in Huambo had been attacked by antiriot police. An emergency CCPM meeting was held, at the behest of an exceedingly belligerent Salupeto Pena, and a joint investigative mission was despatched to Huambo. General Unimna represented UNAVEM. According to the official mission report presented to the CCPM, Dr Savimbi had been conducting a meeting with his aides in 'The White House' when four vehicles of the antiriot police had driver at speed through the Presidential Guards' security barricade in front of the residence, sounding their sirens. UNITA considered this to have been an act of provocation and intimidation, claiming that the antiriot police paralleled FAPLA and had been set up to harass UNITA and FALA. The Government admitted that the police had driven through the barricade, but pointed out that it had been erected on a public road that UNITA had no right to block. There had been no ill-intent, only a mistake. The Government was surprised that the CCPM paid so much attention to this matter while lending only deaf ears to similar complaints by the Government.

After a vituperative discussion, a consensus was finally reached that the police had indeed acted incorrectly, and a special commission was set up to investigate the circumstances further. A full CCPM group would visit Huambo again on 11 August and a CCPM meeting would be devoted to discussing the antiriot police.

General Unimna had told me that, while the observers and UNAVEM had been having their first meeting with the parties in the office of the Governor of Huambo, UNITA sympathisers had staged a demonstration around the building. A Government police guard had been beaten up and another had had his service pistol seized. The UNITA demonstrators had arrived in vehicles, suggesting that the event had been organised rather than spontaneous. It was hard to tell whether the Government police had acted foolishly or deliberately, or whether UNITA had purposely overreacted. What was clear was that, from then on, the issue hotted up in an atmosphere of tension and deteriorating relations that worsened as the election date drew nearer.

On 13 August, Salupeto Pena requested that a special 'Heads of Delegation' meeting on the subject of the antiriot police be held on Saturday 15 August. Almost simultaneously Mig Goulding sent me a memorandum presented by Marcus Samondo, the UNITA representative in New York, alleging that massive contingents of Government troops dressed in antiriot police uniforms had converged on the cities, and that large numbers of FAPLA personnel in the assembly areas had been 'converted' into antiriot police. He claimed that 970 antiriot squad units had been detected in Huambo alone (as I pointed out to Mig, since each unit consisted of 10 men, this meant no less than 9700 antiriot police, which seemed rather unlikely), and troop movements had been observed around Huambo, Lubango, Uige and Negage, and Benguela. FAPLA commandos famous for the part they had played in the civil war were, according to Mr Samondo, now commanding these paramilitary forces in the cities. UNITA, he assured us, was exercising all restraint, but dialogue was urgent and the international community must help to defuse this dangerous situation.

I assured Headquarters that dialogue was indeed underway, and expressed surprise that Mr Samondo had not seen fit to mention the actions already taken by the CCPM. I also voiced my concern about the tenor of UNITA's reports on this incident, as widely published abroad, and the fact that Mr Samondo had made no such allegations at a meeting I had had in Luanda with him and other UNITA representatives only a few days earlier, on 8 August. We should not forget, I suggested, that UNITA had a formidable propaganda machine; it should be encouraged to resolve its grievances through the CCPM before bruiting them abroad.

The special Heads of Delegation session on Saturday 15 August began inauspiciously with a demand by UNITA for immediate action by the CCPM on incidents in Malange, Benguela province, Bié and Huambo. It then concentrated on a long letter of the previous day from Engineer Salupeto Pena to General N'dalu, alleging that 30 000 FAPLA troops had been transferred into the antiriot police and reiterating UNITA's concern about the Spanish equipment. The letter also claimed that no less than eight schools were training antiriot police. These actions, it continued, formed part of a Government strategy to make the elections impossible, or at the very least to provoke UNITA, impede voter access to polling stations in UNITA areas and, in the event of an MPLA defeat, take power by force. UNITA demanded the disbandment of the antiriot police, their concentration in FAPLA assembly areas and subsequent demobilisation. It also wanted an official declaration by the Government that the later would not resort to force, whatever the election results might be (an ironic request in the light of what happened subsequently).

After an inordinately long and tortuous exchange it was decided that the following day a CMVF delegation would investigate the situation in Malange. There would be joint verification of the allegation that 30 000 FAPLA personnel had been transferred into the police. The Government was to provide, by Monday 17 August, full information on police numbers. General N'dalu advanced the information that the antiriot police (which the government preferred to call 'emergency police') numbered only 2500. The entire police force was only 39 830, considerably less than the ideal ratio of one policeman to every 100 000 inhabitants, which in Angola would require a total of 100 000. He said that there were only two police schools, in Luanda and Lobito, and these were for 'normal' police. The antiriot police were being trained in a single, special school in Luanda. Moreover UNITA elements – 70 officers, 50 drivers, 100 sergeants and 1000 agents – were being admitted into a course now beginning. A further agreement reached was that the government would suspend all deployment of police over the weekend. For its part UNITA undertook not to attack the police and would strictly observe the rules governing security personnel for high UNITA officials (another bone of contention because UNITA guards were numerous and very heavily armed). The attributions and behaviour of the antiriot, or emergency, police were to be jointly reviewed and the joint police monitoring groups strengthened. The incorporation of UNITA elements into the police was to be accelerated. The last decision bore eloquent testimony to the dangerous flashpoint that had been reached – a duty officer was to remain in the CCPM building permanently over the weekend in case an emergency arose.

Jeff Millington circulated a statement made by Assistant Secretary Cohen in Washington the previous day. This identified the antiriot police as the principal cause of rising tension but recognised that UNITA had acted overzealously in bringing heavily armed security personnel into urban areas, and in limiting the activities and movements of some of the civilian population. The United States had raised these issues with UNITA and called on both parties to resolve these tensions and avoid provocation.

Under instructions from Washington, Jeff afterwards handed me an aide-memoire. This document reiterated that the antiriot police were a major source of tension and stressed that the United Nations must now strengthen the police monitoring efforts as quickly as possible so that a climate of confidence could be restored, and maintained, throughout the electoral period. I asked Jeff to assure Washington that we were doing everthing possible to strengthen joint police monitoring, but reminded him of the very real difficulties, ranging from the attitude of the two parties and logistical constraints, to UNAVEM's own limited mandate and resources.

Tuesday 18 August saw another marathon Heads of Delegation meeting, in which the observers and UNAVEM tried to guide the parties towards an understanding. General N'dalu said that the total strength of the police, including the 'emergency' police, was 39 830. The 'emergency' police numbered only 1030, and their projected total was 1516, to be attained by December 1992. It had been the practice to incorporate personnel from the armed forces into the police even before the Peace Accords came into effect, and the Government had so far recruited only 4080 demobilised FAPLA troops into the police.

I pointed out that it was customary for governments, including those with a long-standing democratic tradition, to have at their disposal a special police force, trained to deal with emergency situations and breakdowns in public order that exceeded the capacity of the normal police (I cited some recent television coverage of street demonstrations in Europe that had got out of hand and had been dealt with in this way). The essential point was that there should be complete transparency, that such forces were used *only* in emergencies, did not patrol the streets on a regular basis, and their composition was such as to give assurance of neutrality. Hence I urged that agreement should be reached that the formation of an emergency police force was acceptable, *provided* it was kept small and confined to barracks at all times, except when there was a genuine emergency, and that it was a truly neutral force, in which UNITA elements would be adequately represented, as well as recruits from other non-MPLA sources, since Angola was now to be a multiparty democracy.

At the meeting of 10 August, to which Dr Savimbi had urgently called the observers and myself, he had laid particular emphasis on UNITA's anxieties over the antiriot police. He had told us that he had just agreed with General N'dalu and Deputy Interior Minister 'Nando' that it would be part of the agenda for the forthcoming meeting between him and President dos Santos, then scheduled for 24 August.

On 21 August I had an audience with President dos Santos. The President's attitude was very statesman-like. He emphasis was on building the basis for the future and he made fewer accusations against UNITA than on previous occasions. I wondered privately whether that meant he was now confident of victory. When we got to the subject of the antiriot police, the President dismissed UNITA's complaints as political propaganda. The severe deterioration in the security situation had shown the need for a strong police force. The Government intended to use the police to ensure there was no political intimidation. I took the same position as I had in the CCPM, and as I had also done with Dr Savimbi. I particularly stressed the need for transparency, especially to verify quickly UNITA's allegation that 30 000 FAPLA troops had been incorporated into the emergency police, as well as to clarify their deployment and the rules of conduct established for them. I also urged the incorporation of non-MPLA elements, particularly members of UNITA, into the force. The President agreed but pointed out that UNITA's first batch of candidates had not qualified, and that over 1000 places had been reserved for them.

When the postponed meeting between the two leaders took place 7 September, the Troika were in town and the eagerly awaited news of the outcome was brought hot-foot by a jubilant General N'dalu and Engineer Salupeto Pena to a working dinner by the waterfront. On the antiriot police, they informed us, there had been an almost hour-long discussion. Although no firm conclusions had been reached, both delegation leaders had seemed satisfied that progress had been made towards an accommodation. The Government had affirmed its willingness to incorporate 8000 UNITA elements (thus meeting UNITA's original demand) into the police, including the antiriot police. It was apparently also agreed that an unspecified 'international body' should verify the composition of the police (presumably the UN, although this was not specified). Nothing ever came of the latter, quite sensible, proposal.

Nonetheless the police issue smouldered on and became a hot campaign issue on the hustings. Thus, when the chief of the national police said the government would no longer tolerate the intimidation and disturbances caused by UNITA supporters, UNITA promptly branded this as a 'declaration of war' on UNITA. The Government, for its part, reacted angrily to criticisms of the antiriot or emergency police by the US State Department.

In his report to the Security Council on 17 September, the Secretary-General conveyed his anxiety on this score, as on so many others. He noted that joint Government/UNITA police monitoring continued to be fragmentary and that only a few dozen UNITA elements had been incorporated into the police. A heightened political temperature was to be expected as the election date approached, but the climate was not helped by the proliferation of weapons or by rumours and allegations about the intentions of both sides. The Government alleged that UNITA was maintaining and deploying hidden reserves of its best troops and systematically installing armed units in the main population centres. UNITA was deeply apprehensive about the antiriot or emergency police, which UNITA contended was a 'parallel army'. The statement issued by the President of the Security Council on 18 September confined itself to saying that it was 'essential that the police should operate as a neutral, national force.'

The Secretary-General also took up the issue in letters of 9 September to President dos Santos and Dr Savimbi. That to Dr Savimbi endorsed the line I had been taking, which was also reflected in his report to the Security Council. Many governments, he pointed out, including those with an established democratic tradition, found it necessary to set up exceptional police forces. The principles that must be observed were transparency about its composition, the incorporation of elements from outside the government, and deployment only in real emergencies. He hoped that agreement could be reached on these lines. For all the oratory and debate it unfortunately never was.

And yet my meeting with Dr Savimbi on 9 September seemed to confirm the impression that some progress had been made during the summit meeting two days earlier. Dr Savimbi expressed the view that President dos Santos was not fully informed about the antiriot police: the fact, for instance, that some FAPLA officers had merely changed their uniform for that of the antiriot police. Dr Savimbi said that, after he had given several examples of this kind, the President had told General 'Nando' that there must be complete transparency. At this point I reminded Dr Savimbi of the UN's view, as stated in the CCPM by myself, and by the Secretary-General in his letter. Interestingly, Dr Savimbi said

The Police Imbroglio

he had no objection to the antiriot police as such, agreeing that they should not be deployed in the same manner as regular police, nor incorporated into the latter.

But when the CCPM heads of delegation met on 15 September, we seemed to be back where we started. Verification of the antiriot police by the joint investigative group set up by the CCPM was progressing painfully slowly. The Government gave figures for the continuous incorporation of UNITA nominees in general police training courses, but said UNITA had refused to take part in the latest course for antiriot police. Dr Savimbi subsequently said, in a campaign speech, that, if UNITA won the election, it would immediately do away with this special police force.

There could have been no clearer sign that, on this issue too, the two sides were poles apart.

8 Alarms and Excursions

The CCPM also had to deal with specific incidents that placed the peace process in jeopardy. Many were the product of deficiencies in the Peace Accords, or in their application. Some were genuine misunderstandings, others calculated brinkmanship. Not infrequently it was a combination of the two. Some were blown up out of all proportion to their significance, others were genuinely serious. All of them undermined the fragile confidence that had built up since 31 May 1991, and increased mistrust and suspicion. The ceasefire held – even if sometimes by a hairline – simply because, when push came to shove, neither side wanted to imperil the elections, which each expected to win (at least in the latter stages). The elections were the critical watershed.

The case of one FAPLA private soldier, Afonso Catumbo, took up several CCPM meetings. It erupted at about the time of my arrival and UNAVEM made a considerable contribution to its eventual solution. Catumbo had been captured by UNITA in 1987, at the battle of Lomba river, and had last been seen by the International Committee of the Red Cross (ICRC) in Jamba (Dr Savimbi's bush headquarters in the far south-east of Angola) in September 1989, as a prisoner of war. He was on the list of *reclamados* given to UNITA by the ICRC, in the context of the exchange of prisoners foreseen in the Peace Accords, a matter frequently on the CCPM's agenda. Catumbo escaped, and on 24 March 1992 sought refuge with the Mavinga CMVF monitoring group, which was accompanied by UNAVEM observers. Mavinga was the site of our south-east Regional Command, which had just been taken over by Colonel Roger Mortlock, the commanding officer of the New Zealand contingent. As he told me later, he had been in charge 'minutes rather than hours' when faced with this incident and a posse of irate FALA 'police', some thirty in total, 'all with their weapons facing inwards'.

After heated debate the government and UNITA agreed, in UNAVEM's presence that the prisoner should be handed back to UNITA, on the latter's commitment to assure his safety and hand him over to the ICRC. The handover was to take place at Licua, the FALA 'critical point' in Cuando Cubango, on 7 or 8 April, and to be witnessed by the UNAVEM team there, but Catumbo was not presented and disappeared from view for three weeks. Meanwhile there was no troop count at the FALA assembly area in Mavinga on 1 April because the FAPLA monitoring group protested against the handling of the Catumbo case.

Mystifying delays intervened. The matter made local headlines and caused some stir internationally, particularly in the United States. It even threatened to block progress in the CCPM. I took the matter up with Dr Savimbi on 7 April and repeatedly intervened in the CCPM. On 17 April, at one of these sessions, the US observer demanded an explanation from UNITA as to why Catumbo had still not been released. Engineer Salupeto Pena, with an air of great puzzlement, said he could not imagine what had gone wrong. UNITA *had* delivered Catumbo to Licua as agreed. As if in unequivocal proof that this must be so, he added 'The Special Representative of the Secretary-General took this up with Dr Savimbi, who immediately gave instructions after the meeting that the prisoner should be handed over'. The US representative insisted that UNITA should clarify what had happened. I also followed up through UNAVEM channels. Catumbo turned out to be back in Jamba and, according to UNITA, did not want to leave. (UNITA was fond of proclaiming that ex-FAPLA prisoners loved the life in Jamba so much that their one overwhelming desire was to make their home there permanently.) In the meantime a UN military observer who had seen Catumbo during the Mavinga incident flew to Jamba on 23 April and spoke to him. The man was clearly terrified, showed scars on his body, and was so desperate to leave that, when he heard he had to wait for the formal ICRC procedure for his release to take place a few days later, he made a break for the UNAVEM helicopter as it was about to take off. The helicopter was surrounded by FALA personnel, who struck Catumbo several times. When protests were made later, UNITA tried to claim that UNAVEM had incited the man to escape.

The story had a happy ending. On 28 April the ICRC collected Catumbo and transported him to Luanda. It was a typical example of an apparently straightforward matter turning into a monstrously convoluted web of intrigue and crossed wires, in which it becomes impossible to unravel the underlying motives or the true facts.

Quilengues, in Huila province, was always a centre of unrest, not least because of the particularly rumbustious local UNITA commander, Lieutenant Colonel Katu. This was the area where the British tourists had been killed in January 1992. On 6 April a serious incident occurred in the small town of Chongoroi (Benguela province), 60 kilometres to the north of Quilengues, after a FALA soldier had been killed there by a Government policeman. About 40 heavily armed FALA soldiers, under the command of Lieutenant Colonel Katu, attacked Government buildings. They took weapons from the police armoury and stole fuel from the town's generators to burn down some houses. After intervention by some Catholic priests the FALA soldiers returned to Quilengues, taking five Government policemen with them as hostages. The policeman who had killed the FALA solider was later arrested. The CMVF monitoring group, was rapidly despatched to the area in a UNAVEM helicopter on 7 and 8 April, together with UN military observers. They concluded that Katu had violated the ceasefire by moving his troops from the FALA assembly area at Quilengues and that the Government policeman should be detained and sent for trial. The stolen weapons were returned through UNAVEM, and the five hostages were released. These decisions, endorsed by the CCPM, defused a potentially very dangerous situation, interestingly enough by sharing blame between the two sides.

At the end of April there were two tragic incidents affecting civilians, in both cases Portuguese. In Luanda a Portuguese priest, who had long served the community in Angola, was killed. In the other incident two Portuguese families, including young children, were murdered on a beach on which they had camped *en route* from Luanda to Cabo Ledo. To my knowledge the responsibility for those killings was never satisfactorily established. This was at a time when the Government and UNITA, despite their soft words in the CCPM, were becoming ever more voluble in accusing each other of alleged violations of the Peace Accords, lack of commitment to the peace process and preparing for renewed hostilities. Incidents of this kind were grist to the propaganda mills of both sides. There was a supposition that the two Portuguese families had been the victims of common robbers, now a growing danger as a result of the economic situation and the wide proliferation of arms. But the Government accused UNITA of perpetrating the killings, and UNITA returned the compliment, alleging that the government had staged them in order to cast the blame on UNITA. Then, on 2 May, Dr Savimbi made a speech with distinctly xenophobic overtones, in which he reminded foreigners that they had their own countries in which to live. The Government did not fail to take advantage of this message of 'Angola for the Angolans' to accuse UNITA once more of the beach murders, as well as the murder of other foreigners in Luanda. UNITA's riposte was to lodge responsibility with the Government, because of its incapacity to maintain law and order (though, as we have seen, when the Government took steps to improve law and order by strengthening the police, UNITA was not exactly supportive).

Tit-for-tat exchanges of this kind intensified wearisomely during the following months. It did not matter that some were relatively petty: the cumulative effect was to raise tension and test the inherent fragility of the Peace Accords even further.

Some of them were extremely serious. Malange was a case in point. Situated some 200 miles to the east of Luanda, and capital of the province of the same name, Malange was an MPLA stronghold. The balance of power in the surrounding countryside was held by the other side and UNITA, taking advantage of the new access to urban centres afforded by the Peace Accords, aimed to gain a foothold in the city. The situation was aggravated by the presence of a large FAPLA assembly area, which was much nearer to the city than was normally the case, and by the murky activities of a mysterious and louche character known as 'Fubu' and his followers. It was not very clear whether 'Fubu' (sometimes spelt 'Fubo') denoted an individual or an organisation, though a member of UNAVEM claimed to have seen him in the flesh. UNITA said the nefarious activities of this gang were supported and even fomented by the Government, an allegation the latter vehemently denied, claiming that 'Fubu' was a common criminal.[1]

UNITA supporters were not behind in launching provocative actions. The clashes between the two sides centred on one particular *bairro* (quarter) of Malange, and by early July the mounting spiral of violence seemed imminently liable to spin out of control. An emergency meeting of CCPM Heads of Delegation was called early on 13 July and for once they reached a speedy agreement: matters were so grave that the Delegation heads must themselves go immediately to Malange. We all went home to change into field clothes.

For once it was not UNAVEM that was providing the transport: the Government had rustled up one of its ancient Russian Antonovs. Owing to a communication problem General Unimna and I were the last to arrive, and as soon as we had hurried up the narrow iron ladder the back hatch was closed and the engines roared into ear-shattering life. In the gloom we could discern the whole of CCPM – heads of delegation, the observers and all their advisers – crouched facing one another on metal benches arranged along the sides of the huge aircraft. I was the only woman. It was about mid-day, and in the middle of the plane there was a large carton filled with individually packed snacks, which we all fell upon with considerable appetite. The flight to Malange took about an hour in the slow, lumbering aircraft. The windows were too small and too high for us to see out and there was a sense of claustrophobia, which heightened the feeling of foreboding. The demonic din of the engines and the shuddering and shaking of the ungainly craft made conversation difficult, if not impossible, even at shouting pitch. Each was left to his own thoughts, which, to judge by the solemnity of the countenances, were uniformly gloomy. Mine were no exception. It occurred to me to wonder what would happen to the peace process if the Antonov (Angolan maintenance being notoriously haphazard) went down, taking the cream of the CCPM and the observers and UNAVEM with it. More immediately, the hard metal bench and the curve of the fuselage were distinctly uncomfortable and my back was emitting familiarly ominous signals when, to the relief of all of us, we landed at Malange.

The Governor and the local MPLA and UNITA representatives were on the airfield to meet us, and we were whisked off in a convoy of cars and jeeps to a large hall in the Governor's office. The local leaders of the two sides were extremely belligerent in their presentations, especially the Brigadier who spoke for UNITA. Among other things, the UNITA office in the affected *bairro* had been destroyed and its compound threatened. It was decided that we must visit the *bairro* and inspect the damage, so the motorcade set off again. When we got there, after passing through an ominously deserted market place (Angolan markets are always pullulating with people, noise, bustle and colour) there were suddenly hundreds and probably thousands of people in the narrow streets, running alongside, peering inside the vehicles, climbing on bonnets and roofs, banging on the windows and shouting incomprehensibly. Most seemed to be MPLA, but General Unimna and I, travelling in a UNAVEM jeep with some of our local team, thought we identified UNITA supporters in the background.

Under the pressure of this mass of people our convoy ground to a halt, and someone further up the line decided we should walk the rest of the way. This turned out to be quite a distance – I would say a mile – and our progress was impeded by the pounding mob in our midst. It was hard not to become separated from the rest of the group. Although several paces behind, I managed to keep General N'dalu and Engineer Salupeto Pena in sight at the head of our valiant little column, though neither of them were very tall. Salupeto Pena's ebony face was grey – he must have wondered if he was being led into a trap. I am sure my own face was several degrees paler than usual. My fear at that point was more of being knocked down and trampled underfoot than anything else, and I was glad to have a burly Dutch police observer at my side (it had not yet been considered necessary for the Special Representative to have a bodyguard).

After what seemed an eternity we arrived near UNITA's local headquarters. At that point large stones began to rain down on the roof of the damaged building and the atmosphere became distinctly nasty. The situation was saved by General 'Gato' of the Government. Both sides had a General 'Gato', so-called because they had so often escaped death as to be credited with the cat's proverbial nine lives. The Government's General 'Gato' had the reputation of being a talented, astute and courageous general. His appearance belied this, being more that of a dilettante. He was good looking, with fine, aquiline features, always impeccably dressed, and invariably had several gold chains hung about his person. By a happy chance, he also came from Malange and was a local hero. Now this elegant creature gave testimony of his famed courage by leaping onto some higher vantage point and haranguing the exalted crowd. Miraculously the tension was broken.

But all was not yet over. We still had to find our way back to our vehicles, through the cramped streets and the still excited and heaving crowd. As we did so, the first shots rang out. Their source was difficult to determine, but it was uncomfortably close. Not all in the crowd were friendly and in some cases their animosity clearly extended to UNAVEM. Nonetheless we struggled back to our vehicle safely, and wasted no time in driving out of the *bairro* as fast as we could. We had lost all the other members of the cavalcade, but one by one they filtered back to the original meeting place. In the Governor's office there the conclave resumed. It was not very clear what had been achieved by our visit to the scene of the crime, apart from heightened blood pressure all round. Subsequently there were voices suggesting that the mob scene had been carefully stage-managed by the local Government representatives, but once more no clear picture of what had really occurred ever emerged.

I do not recall the details of the arguments that rolled back and forth, sometimes in smaller cabals in a side-room, in which General Unimna and I took part. After many hours some kind of truce was cobbled together, and we agreed to regather in the morning. Peace was restored for the night, or so we hoped, since we now had no alternative but to stay the night, partly on account of unfinished business, partly because our aircraft could not take off in the dark.

We repaired to the dining room of the Governor's palace where the usual imposing meal had been set out for this large and unexpected invasion of dignitaries, by now grubby, tired and extremely hungry. Not for the first time I found myself wishing that this extraordinary display of logistical mastery by the Angolans was not restricted to the culinary and gastronomic areas, but might sometimes extend to fields more immediately germane to the fulfilment of the Peace Accords.

There was also the question of where everyone was to sleep. The most senior people, including General Unimna and myself, were to be housed in the Governor's ample mansion. But our UNAVEM team had invited us to spend the night in their Weatherhaven camp. The General stayed in the palace but I opted for the camp, so as to talk more informally with the team and savour their living conditions at first hand. We drank some whisky together (much needed after the rigours of the day) and talked a great deal, mostly by candlelight as the generator failed. I was allotted a tent and the two women electoral observers liberally showered on me their precious store of toilet water, shampoo and hair conditioner as well as a hair dryer and a toothbrush, most of which (except the toothbrush) I had no time to use, much less the inclination, knowing how hard they were to come by and how carefully hoarded. I slept in my underwear, largely undisturbed by a few things that went bump in the night in the town around us. At 6.30 in the morning there was a discreet tap, and outside stood Peter Scott-Bowden, the head of the electoral team, with a steaming cup of early morning tea. I felt there was still hope for the world and Angola, and for myself. There was even water for a shower. (I later learned from General Unimna that he had had a palatial room and private bathroom, but *no* water!)

After a quick breakfast the team drove me to the outskirts of Malange to visit a Norwegian missionary who was living there with his small son and running a hospital. It was a beautiful morning, glades of eucalyptus shining grey-green in the sun, and a wide panorama of low hills and fields spread before us in a deceptively peaceful scene. From outside its high walls we inspected a huge agricultural college, whose ornate Italian architecture struck a strange contrast with the rural scene around. Not a soul stirred, not even a caretaker. It looked like a white elephant. I don't suppose any students ever did occupy it. When the war broke out again, Malange was under siege by UNITA for many months and the people there were close to starvation point. Many lost their lives or limbs to mines or gunfire when, desperate for food, they ventured into that rich and idyllic countryside, which greeted us with such a smiling countenance on that memorable morning.

We were back in town in time for the renewed meetings between the parties, which I had to leave at midday for an urgent commitment in Luanda. One of UNAVEM's Russian helicopters ferried me back, as its solitary passenger, but it did not have sufficient fuel and we had to land at Capanda, where a vast dam was being built as a joint enterprise between the Angolan Government, Russia and Brazil. We had a two-man observer team there, headed by an Irishman, Lieutenant Colonel Bill Egar. They met me and, while the helicopter was being refuelled, hurried me off for a quick lunch in the huge canteen used by the men working on the dam. They numbered thousands and there must have been at least several hundred at one sitting on that day. I also glimpsed some of the huge engineering works, an unreal and anachronistic spectacle in the midst of a singularly barren landscape. Yet the bustling, business-like activities of the place, in the middle of nowhere, also pulsed with optimism, a tantalising hint of the great potential about to be realised, opening up a grand future for Angola and its people.

Not long afterwards Capanda lay in ruins, its modern machinery destroyed or looted, its thousands of workers, Angolan and foreign, dispersed in flight, many of them dead.

The immediate problem of Malange was solved, but only temporarily. It continued to simmer dangerously and once or twice the CCPM had to take drastic measures when it threatened once more to erupt.

These kind of occurrences were very much the stuff of our everyday lives, though Malange was particularly grave. There were many other incidents both before I came and during the rocky run-up to the elections. All over Angola, tiny UNAVEM teams were working every day with the Government/UNITA joint monitoring groups to defuse potentially dangerous incidents, that could blow up unexpectedly and expand into major threats to peace and the ceasefire. I have cited only a few, just to give the flavour of the negotiations and convey how flimsy was the veil between peace and aggression, which, if rent, could all too easily lead again to outright war. There was a terrifying degree of brinkmanship and cliff-hanging on both sides. What saved us each time was that, when the cliff-edge came vertiginously near, neither side wanted to take the fatal plunge while the elections were in the offing. They scrambled back in the nick of time. Perhaps they did so for genuine reasons, perhaps because they thought the time was not yet ripe.

Part III
The Preparation and Organisation of the Elections – March to September 1992

9 The Prelude: March to May 1992

When I took up my duties in March virtually nothing had been done to organise the first democratic, multiparty elections which, according to the Bicesse Accords, would have to take place towards the end of September. Only about 180 days remained.

About 10 political parties were beginning to emerge, in addition to the two giants, the MPLA and UNITA. The Government had organised a multiparty conference in January 1992 to discuss issues such as the draft electoral law, the law on the formation of political parties, the date of the elections, the simultaneity of the presidential and legislative elections and changes to the constitution. UNITA had refused to attend, on the grounds that, as one of the two signatories of the Peace Accords, its status was equal to that of the Government and it would not accept being lumped together with the new parties. The Government accordingly held separate consultations with UNITA, but little action followed these meetings.

As was the case with troop cantonment and demobilisation, I now had to goad the CCPM into speedier action on the elections. UNITA, from the fortunate position of having no responsibility for organising them, waxed loquacious on the subject. At an unusually heated Heads of Delegation meeting on 30 March, the Government's insistence that the election date could not be fixed until the National Electoral Commission was set up provoked the veiled threat that UNITA might not go through with demobilisation. Antonio Monteiro and Jeff Millington argued vigorously (the latter in particularly strong terms) that it was essential to announce the date for voting. I echoed them, citing Security Council Resolution 747, particularly the operative paragraphs 6 and 8, which urged the Angolan authorities to finalise the organisational arrangements for the elections, make resources available as soon as possible and establish a precise timetable for the electoral process.

We were all dispirited by the tone of the exchanges in the CCPM, and afterwards Antonio told me that he was asking the Portuguese Permanent Representative to the UN to convey grave concern to the Secretary-General. Jeff Millington was requesting Washington to exert pressure on the Angolan Ambassador (who was accredited to the Organization of American States since the United States had no formal diplomatic relations with Angola).

I could see that General N'dalu was also worried, but our interventions in the CCPM had had some effect: he confided to me that, as a result of them, there was a good chance that the date of the election would be announced by President dos Santos at the People's Assembly the following Thursday, 2 April. The issue was high on my own agenda for the President, but I was still without word as to when I would see him.

UNITA was also keeping up constant pressure. On Wednesday 1 April I met Engineer Salupeto Pena and 'Foreign Minister' Abel Chivukuvuku at UNITA's main offices, a drab building in the centre of the city, swarming with the usual large complements of guards armed to the eyeballs. Chivukuvuku made the running for UNITA; his vehement, almost aggressive manner and flashing eyes, contrasted with the normally placid demeanour of Salupeto Pena. Reiterating UNITA's concern that the Government had still taken no decisions on vital election preparations, he added a decidedly less veiled threat than the one Salupeto Pena had made at the CCPM. 'UNITA', he said, 'has made clear to the government that our agreement with them under the Bicesse Peace Accords ends on 30 November and that, after that date, if the elections have not been held, then anything could happen.' He repeated this last phrase for greater effect, injecting the most sinister meaning into the word 'anything'.

While recognising the legitimacy of concern over the delays, and that the election ball was in the Government's court, I pointed out that the major responsibility lay with UNITA for other necessary preconditions for free and fair elections, such as allowing the extension of the central administration to the whole country and the free circulation of people and goods, since large areas of territory remained under UNITA's sole control. Chivukuvuku replied that UNITA had told the Government it would welcome the extension of the central administration to all their areas, including Jamba.

The next morning, 2 April, I had my first audience with President dos Santos. In the anteroom I had been told by Minister Lopo de Nascimento that the election date was about to be announced, and it was a great relief when the President confirmed this, indicating that the last days of September had been chosen and that the relevant laws would be approved that afternoon. He stressed his preoccupation with the adequacy of international financial support for the elections, citing an estimated cost of US$30 million, in contrast to a plethora of promises so far not substantiated with hard cash, and voiced the hope that the announcement of a firm date would break the present vicious circle – the widespread scepticism on the part of both donors and the international media as to whether the elections would indeed take place – enabling us to lobby for more help with greater conviction and a greater likelihood of success.

The President strongly criticised UNITA's attitude to the extension of the central administration and the free circulation of people and goods. 'Administration' meant more than two officials and an office. As for Jamba and other UNITA-held areas, the situation there was totally undemocratic and could hinder the process of registration and voting, and even prevent it from taking place at all. I told the President that I had repeatedly taken up both matters with UNITA, most recently the previous day, and would continue to do so. The President also expressed the hope that UNAVEM could investigate the human rights situation in UNITA-controlled areas. I was obliged to point out that, since human rights had not been included in our mandate, I had neither the resources nor qualified people to undertake such a task. I forbore to add that if I had they would have to investigate both sides.

Later that day the President announced that the elections would take place on 29 and 30 September. On 3 April the People's Assembly approved the Electoral Law. And then, on 5 April Dr Savimbi returned to Luanda after a six-week sojourn in Jamba. This lengthy absence, coinciding with the widely publicised defection of two of his closest and most powerful aides, had given rise to the wildest surmises in the rumour-ridden diplomatic cocktail circuit, all equally and predictably dire in their general purport.

Savimbi's public utterances were a judicious mix of temperateness and more than a glint of underlying steel. His speeches in Luena on 4 April and in Luanda the next day carried the same threefold message: there was no crisis in UNITA, despite the defections of Tony Fernandez and General Puna; he personally accepted the moral responsibility for any errors committed by UNITA; and he reiterated the warning that UNITA's agreement with the Government under the Peace Accords was finite in nature. This time the deadline was brought forward to 30 September. If the elections had not been held by then, there would be trouble. Threats were not lacking on the Government side either. The main one was that there could be no elections in areas controlled by UNITA unless the central administration was effectively extended there. My own comment to New York, based on the judgement that both sides wanted the elections to take place, was that both threats would help to push the electoral process along.

But we were still not out of the woods. The essential next step was to appoint the National Electoral Council and the Director-General of the elections. Precious days and weeks passed and nothing happened. Everyone was jittery, sensing conspiracy behind even some of the most straightforward situations.

Under the Electoral Law the Council was to be chaired by a judge of the Supreme People's Court elected by the Court. It would consist of one magistrate, designated by the President of the Court; five citizens of recognised merit and moral and professional aptitude, designated by the Head of State; the Minister of Territorial Administration; the Director-General of the Elections, designated by the Head of State after consultation with the political parties; one representative of the National Council of the Media; and one representative of each political party, or coalition of parties, competing in the elections. Each candidate for the office of President of the Republic could designate a representative to the Council but no member could be a candidate in the legislative or presidential elections. The Council was to have two organs: the Directorate-General of the Elections, and the Provincial Electoral Councils. The Provincial Councils, in turn, would have two organs: the Provincial Directorate of the Elections, and Municipal Electoral Offices.

The Electoral Law was published in the *Diario da Republica* on 16 April 1992, but it did not galvanise anyone into immediate action. The rumour mills continued to churn away, producing every possible kind of conjecture and a general theme of gloom and doom. One of the most popular theories going the diplomatic rounds was that the Government and the MPLA, convinced there was no hope of winning the election, were in general disarray and were using the delay as a breathing space in which to consolidate their financial assets abroad, and so guarantee themselves a rapid and comfortable getaway to Europe, most probably Portugal. The more extreme exponents went so far as to claim that the elections would never take place at all and power would pass to UNITA by default.

My colleagues and I strove to keep ourselves outside, and above, the maelstrom of speculation. Our job was to observe and verify the elections, and hence do everything possible, within our limited power, to ensure that those elections took place. But as the weeks drifted by without appreciable progress, or any acceleration of the snail-like advance on troop cantonment and demobilisation, it was hard not to be contaminated by the general atmosphere of mounting dismay. I did my best to counteract this by exerting steady, but I hoped diplomatic, pressure wherever and whenever I could.

The UN operation, although also behind schedule, was taking shape considerably faster than the process it was supposed to observe. The UN's role was twofold: UNAVEM would obsere and verify all stages of the electoral process, according to Security Council Resolution 747; and technical assistance would be provided by experts recruited by the UN Development Programme (UNDP) and the UN Department of Technical Cooperation for Development (UNDTCD) and funded by voluntary contributions from member states. Observers were beginning to trickle in and were being fanned out to the various provinces. The technical assistance team was also taking shape, under the leadership of a courteous and diplomatic Brazilian, Jose Julio dos Reis, who had good electoral experience but was perhaps of too gentle and unassuming a character for the rough and tumble of Angolan politics. In addition his English was rather limited. His second-in-command was a dynamic and mettlesome Portuguese lady, Lucinda Matos de Almeyda, loquacious in both her native language and her own colourful brand of English, who was also well-qualified and had connections in high places in Portugal. Both made a sterling contribution in their different and often complementary ways.

On 3 April, the day after the announcement of the election date, my staff and I met the UNDP Resident Representative, Miguel de Graça, and Mr dos Reis to identify the essential steps along the critical path to the elections. I asked that two sets of information be urgently provided. The first related to the budget: the amount available from the Government; the amount already provided, or formally committed, by donor countries; and the gap that still need to be filled. The second requirement was a revised, realistic timetable for the elections, highlighting the steps that must be taken during the critical month of April, and then the 'break points' over the next six months by which certain key actions must completed, together with alternative solutions if these targets were not met, as well as contingency planning for resources that might be required at short notice from donor countries to 'save' the process.

The list of 'Essential steps to be taken before the end of April', which I then presented to the national authorities, was daunting. In addition to the establishment of the National Electoral Council, the appointment of the Director-General and the promulgation of the various laws, the Director-General's office had to be staffed and at the province level, the Provincial Electoral Councils had to be installed, provincial electoral plans prepared and detailed inventories of requirements drawn up.

Logistics were clearly going to be a formidable obstacle. On the organisational and legal aspects, we could only urge the Angolan authorities to speed up. But we could, and did, get on with planning how the phenomenal practical difficulties might be overcome, in the hope that the other matters would fall into place sometime, somehow.

The underlying assumptions were that about four million people would be eligible to vote; that 40 per cent of the registration and polling sites would be accessible only by air; and that 60 per cent of the planned 1400 registration teams would be mobile and the remaining 40 per cent static. The plan distinguished between the needs for the registration period and the intensified requirements over the two days of voting. It embraced four-wheel-drive vehicles, trucks, helicopters and light aircraft able to land almost anywhere, polaroid cameras, diesel and aviation oil, communications of all kinds, tents and camping equipment, combat rations (for the Angolan registration and electoral teams), jerry cans for water and fuel, and so on. Ten helicopters, or light aircraft, would be required for the registration phase, which could be staggered; and no fewer than 84 would be needed for the intense two-day period of voting, when all areas would have to be reached simultaneously.

Logistical support continued to be a bone of contention with Boneo, despite our discussions in Luanda. On 29 April he faxed me, contending that an air operation, while desirable, could not be financed. We also had a protracted philosophical exchange on accessibility as a guarantee of 'fairness'. He submitted that, in a context of scarcity it would be difficult to equate 'fairness' with a distribution of registration sites that allowed every citizen to reach one of them, and that, fairness should be pursued by ensuring that scarce resources were used in a way that did not discriminate against any of the contending parties. The flaw in this appealing argument, as I pointed out, was that by far the largest number of remote and inaccessible places lay in areas presumed to favour UNITA. My own strongly held view was that we must do our utmost to overcome the constraints and see that all eligible voters were reached. If these efforts ultimately proved unsuccessful, then at least this would be shown to have been for reasons of *force majeure* rather than any lack of planning or foresight on our part. It was imperative that we indicate from the outset the minimum resources needed for a reasonable outcome and to ensure free and fair elections. If the required resources were not forthcoming, only then should we see what modifications needed to be made. I appreciated the difficulty of obtaining assistance, especially in transport, through traditional development cooperation channels, another point stressed by Boneo, and that was why I proposed trying to obtain loans in kind, especially of military aircraft to be used for peaceful purposes.

Boneo also stressed that UNAVEM's limited mandate and resources precluded 'first level verification', which would have to be undertaken by the Angolan parties, and only allowed 'second level verification', which could be used as an instrument of last resort by the Angolan parties if their complaints were not properly handled by the national electoral authorities. I had perforce to agree. There was no way in which I could get the number of observers increased, whereas I did believe I had a sporting chance of augmenting the logistical and material resources by hook or by crook. But I pointed to the fundamental flaw that parties other than the MPLA and UNITA were so thin on the ground that they could not be present during registration and voting except in a limited number of probably urban locations. Moreover the limited nature of our role was not understood by most of those following the Angolan electoral process, both within and outside the country, despite my efforts to disseminate the Secretary-General's view that the elections were a sovereign Angolan affair, with modest assistance from the United Nations.

Following that argument to its logical conclusion, one could argue that taking a dominant role in trying to fill the logistical *lacunae*, instead of just sticking to our last and letting the Angolans muddle through, could compound the misperceptions of the UN's role still further. Certainly we were already far overstepping our mandate. But I was temperamentally incapable of standing idly by and watching the ship go down for a 'ha'porth o' tar' that the international community could provide with little pain. Besides, it was clearer to me by the day that logistics were becoming a political factor – an essential element in determining whether the elections would be 'free and fair': if minimum logistical requirements were not met, then a large part of the population would be deprived, *de facto*, of their right to take part in one of the most crucial junctures of their history, though virtually all had suffered from the prolonged horrors of the civil war.

Even the 'ha'porth o' tar' was hard to come by, however. I took my 'shopping list' to the Minister of Territorial Administration, and to the CCPM. The latter body, with an exasperating display of its customary dilatoriness, had been constantly rescheduling a long-promised meeting on the elections, largely, I suspect, because the Government delegation had no progress to report. Then, on 20 April, a Heads of Delegation session was called at short notice to discuss the convening of a donors' meeting to address the severe humanitarian situation resulting from prolonged drought in some areas and excessive rainfall in others. This was thought to have reached a degree of gravity that could endanger the peace process. I urged that the meeting be used also to appeal for assistance in support of the elections and present a detailed inventory of what was needed.

Both General N'dalu and Engineer Salupeto Pena immediately accepted this suggestion, stressing the critical need for air support.

There followed a great burst of activity by the CCPM, which met in almost daily session from 23 to 29 April, sometimes even twice a day. Papers were prepared on electoral needs (this document entirely reflected our proposals, but it still proved impossible to get a clear indication of what the Government could provide), on demining, on demobilisation and on the humanitarian emergency. The meeting with donors was to take place on 30 April. One CCPM meeting was taken up by an extraordinarily convoluted and lengthy discussion about who should be invited, and in what form and style the invitation should be couched (the Angolans are a fair match for the Portuguese in their obsession with the niceties of protocol). Clearly, one might think, they meant to do things properly. I was therefore mystified to discover, as I prepared the ground with key Ambassadors, that none of them had any inkling that a meeting was to take place. When I expressed concern at a CCPM meeting (less than 48 hours before the great appeal to donors was due to take place) a crestfallen silence ensued: it transpired that no one had actually got round to sending the invitations out! This was an all too typical example of the CCPM's predilection for talk and formality rather than action. The omission was hastily rectified, but it meant that donors had indisputable grounds on which to claim they had had no time to consult their capitals. The meeting, jointly chaired by General N'dalu and Engineer Salupeto Pena, could thus serve no larger purpose than the presentation of the four papers. The only decision taken was to hold a second meeting a week later, on 7 May.

As General N'dalu introduced the paper on the elections, the conference room was plunged into stygian darkness (power cuts occurred with boring regularity in Luanda), which some of those present took to be a disquieting omen. Fortunately light was soon restored. N'dalu laid particular emphasis on the need for transport, especially air support and helicopters. Salupeto Pena introduced the other three papers, but in the ensuing discussion the representatives of the donor countries spoke only of electoral matters.

John Flynn, the British Ambassador, asked three very pointed questions. What was the calendar for the elections, and were any delays expected? Would UNITA and the other parties be included in registration teams to ensure the exercise was free and fair? And since extending the central administration was causing such difficulty, might not an 'impartial organisation' (he meant the UN) assist the CCPM by investigating the nature of the problems? John told me later that his remarks had been prompted by hearing the new Minister for Territorial Administration declare, on the radio, that the elections would probably have to be delayed because of problems with extending the central administration, problems that 'were not the Government's fault'.

The representative of the Portuguese bilateral Embassy raised another highly pertinent question. Could the Government indicate the extent of its own commitment? For example how many vehicles and helicopters were available to meet the needs listed in the paper? General N'dalu had to reply that the Government had 'unfortunately' not yet had time to prepare such an inventory, for which I had long been pressing.

In this way the donors used the meeting to push the Government to take action on the elections – a kind of implicit conditionality – and this was its most important outcome.

At end of the meeting General N'dalu, perhaps prompted by Salupeto Pena, unexpectedly asked me to speak about emergency humanitarian aid. I extended my remarks to the electoral process and stressed the interrelationship between the two: democracy was of no use if one was hungry and stability could not be achieved either before or after the elections in such conditions. Having learned that some EC Ambassadors had received the impression from Mr Boneo that no further resources were needed to support the elections, I underlined the critical importance of logistics, transport and communications, explaining that in earlier assessments the external resources needed had been based on an inadequate knowledge of the country outside Luanda, as well as on the assumption that only very limited international resources would be available. The requirements had therefore been tailored to fit this premise rather than what was actually needed. Furthermore those earlier assessments had also assumed that registration and voting could not be carried to tens of thousands of people in remote areas, because of practical and resource limitations. This was unacceptable, in my view, as an *a priori* assumption and contrary to the very concept of free and fair elections. If, in the end, it turned out to be impossible to reach certain areas, then that would be a different matter but it was imperative to make an all-out effort to do so.

I was spreading this message to anyone who cared to listen, and getting support in unexpected ways and from unexpected quarters. We spent some time, ultimately unsuccessfully, in negotiations with the Norwegian Government about the use of the helicopter wing they keep permanently earmarked for UN purposes. The Polish Chargé d'Affaires informed me that his country could provide helicopters, as well as small light aircraft that could land virtually anywhere. The problem was that Poland, being in dire economic straits, hoped that payment could be made, while I, having no budget, was trying to scrounge whatever I could on an in-kind loan basis. The Chargé came back saying that aircraft could be provided free of charge, provided their transport to Angola could be arranged. This was to prove a recurrent saga, more voracious of time than productive of results, but we had to explore every opportunity on offer.

Meanwhile Assistant Secretary Cohen paid a brief but highly useful visit to Luanda. Antonio Monteiro gave a working lunch for him on 13 April, after which I had a tête-à-tête meeting with him. It was the first of many encounters with Hank Cohen and I found him sympathetic to my problems of mandate and resources, and unexpectedly forthcoming in suggesting solutions, some of them highly unorthodox. He spoke of the possibility of the annual US National Guard exercise taking place in Angola, in which case helicopters would be available and could be used for electoral purposes.

Shortly afterwards Cohen came up with an even more surprising proposition in a meeting with Mig Goulding in New York on 30 April. After consulting President dos Santos, who had given his full consent, he had approached the South African government about air support, Pretoria having been his next port of call after Luanda. 'Pik' Botha, the South African Foreign Minister, no doubt eager to find a new and positive role in the Angolan situation, had, he reported, reacted enthusiastically. Cohen had also urged the Japanese to contribute and had asked the European Community, of which Portugal then held the Presidency, to use part of the 171 million ECUs allocated for development purposes in Angola to support the elections. He also confirmed that the State Department was pursuing the idea of a US National Guard exercise.

Events on the South African front moved rather swiftly. On 4 May a South African team – headed by Ambassador Gert J. Gröbler, chief of the Directorate for Southern Africa in the South African Department of Foreign Affairs – arrived in Luanda for talks with the Angolan Government. The next day he called on me, accompanied by Colonel Fred Rindel, senior staff officer of the South African Defence Force (SADF) and two officials from the newly opened South African Liaison Office in Luanda.

Ambassador Gröbler stressed the great importance South Africa attached to the peace process in Angola, both with regard to the changes taking place in his own country and to the stability of the whole southern African region. He conveyed a similar message to one I had received in New York from the South African Permanent Representative to the United Nations, Ambassador Stewart, namely that the South African Government was committed to a totally impartial stance on Angola, and was anxious to provide cooperation to ensure a successful outcome. He referred to the improving relations between South Africa and Angola, and to the assistance already provided by South Africa through the World Food Programme for feeding troops in the assembly areas, in demining and in vocational training for demobilised soldiers. Ambassador Gröbler told me that following Hank Cohen's discussions in Pretoria, Pik Botha had confirmed to him South Africa's keen interest in providing aircraft (helicopters and light planes), fuel, communications and maintenance facilities for the elections. I stressed that any South African assistance must be negotiated with the Angolan Government. He well understood this, saying that he had met officials of the Ministry of Foreign Affairs on his arrival the previous evening, and would be seeing them again to pursue all these ideas. He was also seeing Engineer Salupeto Pena, and I suggested he should try to speak to General N'dalu and the Minister for Territorial Administration.

Afterwards I spoke privately to Ambassador Gröbler, warning that, although the situation had improved, many sensitivities remained for historical and other reasons, and expressing the hope that the African National Council (ANC) could be associated with any initiatives. Gröbler told me that the possibility had already been raised during one of his department's regular foreign policy meetings with the ANC, and had been welcomed: the ANC too was very anxious to help ensure that the Angola process went well. He promised to see that the matter was taken up in another such meeting soon. He also mentioned that this kind of initiative would have to be handled very carefully within South Africa, because of the many complexities on the home front.

Ambassador Gröbler seemed to epitomise the new approach then gaining momentum in South Africa. And the prospect of South African aircraft – which in the past had created such devastation through their bombing raids – being used to help bring peace and stability, seemed a harbinger of a new spirit of reconciliation burgeoning throughout the region. One could not but be alive to the tremendous dangers attendant upon such a dramatic turnaround, but the assurance given to me afterwards by Venâncio de Moura, Vice-Minister of Foreign Affairs, that the Government welcomed these developments, infused me with hope that we might indeed be witnessing the dawn of a new era.

Things were gradually beginning to move on other fronts too. Hank Cohen had voiced a concern we all shared: that the training of Angolan field staff for registration and polling duties could prove as big a problem as logistics. The possibility of using some US personnel for training was mooted, but never came to anything. But some progress was being made. In the third week of April a first voter registration training seminar for provincial officials was organised by the Government, with the help of the UN technical assistance project and UNAVEM, and revealed an encouraging degree of interest and enthusiasm among the participants. Curiously enough, planning and organisation at the provincial level seemed considerably more advanced than at the centre, where we still awaited key decisions on the National Electoral Council and the Director-General. The British firm De la Rue had been contracted by the Government to provide registration kits. The firm's representatives had arrived in Luanda and were training national officials to use them.

The appointment of the Director-General was a key decision, as the success and fairness of the elections would largely depend on the organisational capabilities and integrity of this person. Names continued to be bandied about. In the second week of April an ostensibly most reliable source, Lopo de Nascimento, informed Julio dos Reis that Dr João Batista Kassuwma would be appointed. This did not happen, however. Lopo himself was a hot favourite and considered eminently suitable by many on account of his experience in senior governmental posts, his personality and moderation, and the generally high regard in which he was held. This particular speculation received a boost when, on 10 May, with the disconcerting suddenness with which things were wont to happen in Angola, he was replaced as Minister by Antonio Paulo Kassoma, until then Minister of Transport and Communications.

Yet still no action followed. We all continued to hammer away at the Government. At the CCPM on 9 April, the Portuguese, Russian and US observers issued a strongly worded joint declaration, exhorting the two sides to collaborate jointly with me and to hasten preparations for the elections, especially the appointment of the National Electoral Council. On 20 April I was received by the new Minister. He was very different from his ascetic and faintly quixotic predecessor, being well-fleshed to the extent of distinct portliness, his embonpoint accentuated by a somewhat rolling gait and ample cheeks like polished blue-black ebony. His manner was suave, his expression invariably smiling. According to some Ambassadors he had the reputation of being a consummate 'wheeler-dealer' and was an astute negotiator. He greeted me warmly and assured me that a Director-General, either provisional or definitive, would be appointed shortly. He agreed to raise with the President our concern about the dangers of a two-day election, because of the difficulty of guarding the ballot boxes overnight, a concern I had already voiced in the CCPM. Our suggested compromise, in the event that it was no longer possible to confine voting to 24 hours, was to dedicate the first day to voting in the remoter areas, reachable only by air, and the second to mass voting in urban and other areas of easier access, thus reducing the risk of fraud, or claims of fraud, through overnight retention of the ballot boxes.

It was not until three weeks later, when we had almost abandoned speculation along with hope, that on Saturday 10 May the Government performed one of its characteristic *tours de force*, scattering messengers hot-foot all over town to deliver invitations to the swearing-in of the National Electoral Council and of the Director-General that very afternoon. The hastily arranged ceremony, at 5 p.m. at Futungo de Belas, bore none of the hallmarks of precipitate preparation. It went off like clockwork, as if planned for weeks ahead as a militarily precise operation. At the sumptuous reception that followed, with champagne and mutual congratulations flowing in equal profusion, President dos Santos beckoned me aside and said: 'Please convey my warm greetings to the Secretary-General and tell him I have kept my promise. It has just taken rather longer than I had hoped because of the difficulties of getting agreement on a candidate for the post of Director-General'.

The President of the Council was to be Dr Antonio Caetano de Sousa, a judge at the Supreme Court, as required by the Electoral Law. The Director-General might be described as a completely dark horse, were this not a misnomer, since he was a white Angolan-Portuguese, Dr Onofre dos Santos. That name had never surfaced during the wildest speculations of the preceding weeks. During the previous weekend, news had got around about someone living in Portugal but precision had been conspicuously absent. Now more information was rapidly forthcoming: he was a lawyer, born and brought up in Angola, who had joined the FNLA in its palmier days and had been very close to its charismatic leader, Holden Roberto. When things deteriorated in Angola he had settled in Portugal, where reportedly he had flourishing business interests. Politically it was an inspired choice: the new Director-General was not affiliated with either of the two main contenders. His connections were with a party now considered as coming third after the MPLA and UNITA (albeit a long way behind), but which had a long tradition and had played a prominent role both in the struggle to banish Portuguese colonial power and immediately after independence.

Moreover his success in the private sector in Europe gave hope of managerial efficiency.

I was to work very closely with Caetano de Sousa and Onofre dos Santos. They were as different as chalk from cheese. Caetano de Sousa was a quiet man, surprisingly diffident in manner for an Angolan, his compatriots usually being characterised by their ebullience. He had a strong, deep voice and spoke very slowly, measuring his words and using them sparingly. Caution was his watchword. Onofre was a charismatic figure with a shock of untamed grey hair and the air of a man in a permanent hurry, as well he might be, seeing that he had been appointed just 20 weeks before the elections. Portuguese, as spoken in Portugal, is a quick-fire language in almost any circumstances (Caetano's case being a noteworthy exception to prove the rule). Onofre fired it off in salvoes with the rhythm, and often the impact, of machine-gunfire. He also spoke excellent English, an advantage not shared by Caetano. He was not only a first-rate organiser with a gift for communication and public relations, but also brimmed over with imaginative ideas. He was a born risk taker, as evidenced by his having left a comfortable and lucrative position in Portugal to engage in this extremely hazardous adventure into the unknown.

At first the two worked pretty well in tandem, and often received me together. But as the strains and pressures mounted the discrepancies between their personalities and, above all, their respective styles and perceptions began to take their toll of what, in any circumstances, could only have been a very sensitive relationship. I maintained a good rapport with both of them, but more and more on a bilateral basis. Caetano and Onofre soon began to disagree on some basic points of policy (for example the use of De la Rue to handle the voting process as well as registration, instead of a cheaper alternative), and this drove the rift deeper, although outward appearances were kept up. Caetano came to appear the more passive and acquiescent of the two, and was increasingly perceived in some quarters as a 'Government Man'. Much of the criticism failed to take account of the fact that Caetano had to walk a more difficult tightrope than Onofre. He had been appointed by the establishment and would have to continue to live with it when all the hue and cry over the elections had died down. Onofre had all the virtues and advantages of being truly independent, and could return to his former life in Portugal. At the end of it all, while I could at times have wished Caetano to be more decisive, I concluded that he had performed his balancing act rather well.

Onofre I came to admire greatly. Arriving like a *deus ex machina* on a scene of considerable disarray, he threw himself into his task with a will and reignited the flames of hope and optimism that had begun to flicker dangerously low.

But on my side I had suffered another dispiriting setback with the sudden medical evacuation of John Truman. We now had a Director-General for the elections, but I was again without a Director to head UNAVEM's electoral division.

10 The Registration of Voters and the Electoral Campaign

The National Electoral Council (NEC) was sworn in on Saturday evening. On Monday 11 May 1992 Mr Kassoma, the new Minister for Territorial Administration, summoned me to his office to tell me that the NEC had already met and taken a number of key decisions. The most important one was that electoral registration would begin nine days later, on 20 May, and end by 31 July. This was contrary to the Electoral Law, which stipulated that the dates of the registration period should be announced 30 days in advance. The delays in setting up the NEC, and the consequently very short time now remaining before the election date, made it impossible to meet this condition. In any event, everyone throughout the country was chafing for registration to begin. The drawback was that there would be precious little time in which to organise the administrative and logistical requirements.

Provincial Electoral Councils would be set up in Luanda on 13 May, in Huambo and Bié on 14 May and in Benguela and Huila on 15 May. These were the five most heavily populated provinces, and it was here that registration would begin on 20 May, and extend progressively thereafter to less densely inhabited areas. The NEC gave high priority to civic education and recommended to the CCPM that the extension of the central administration to the whole country must be completed by 20 June.

Six parties had been legalised by now and I had already met with the leaders of five of them the previous week: Luis dos Passos of the PRD, José Manuel Miguel of the PSD, Jorge Chicotiy of the FDA, Paolino Pinto João of the CNDA, and Sebastian Miguel of PAJOCA. The FNLA was also hoping to gain legal status in the next few days, and in the continuing absence of its leader, Holden Roberto, I had met with his representatives, Mr Kabango and Mr Kambandu. Another encounter had been with Daniel Chipenda, an influential Ovimbundu figure in the MPLA. My aim was to broaden the outreach of UNAVEM and strengthen the multiparty approach as the only available antidote to the increasing polarisation and confrontational attitude of the two main contenders.

***

After several postponements, the second follow-up meeting with donors to obtain logistical and administrative support was held on Friday 15 May. At my insistence, a paper had at last been prepared showing which of the electoral requirements submitted to the first meeting could be met by the Government.

The main problem was helicopters, the Government having first taken the position that the only ones available, being military, could not be used for elections. It was eventually agreed that they could be used, provided they were painted another colour and with electoral insignia. More would be needed from foreign donors but the bilateral Portuguese Ambassador, Rocha Paris, then President of the EC group, assured me that a favourable attitude now prevailed, provided that a reasonable share of the burden was borne by the Government. As one Western Ambassador put it: 'The Angolan Government has got money' (he meant from sales of oil and diamonds), 'and if it doesn't, then it ought to have it'.

The second meeting, chaired by Engineer Salupeto Pena of UNITA, went much more smoothly. The list of invitations issued by the Government had been expanded to include some European and African Ambassadors not present at the first one, as well as South Africa, whose representative did not, however, speak. A big innovation was that representatives of the private sector (mostly oil companies) were invited. This was at my request, as I was determined to tap all possible sources of support, including the most unorthodox, and the private sector had as much interest as anybody in helping to make the elections a success.

The most encouraging reactions came from the EC, the United States and Sweden, although there was still considerable vagueness about exactly what could be expected and it was hard to distinguish between genuinely new commitments and those already known. The EC representative was favourably disposed to giving additional funds, including funds for helicopters, but the details were still being worked out. Jeffrey Millington's intervention was also encouraging, but even vaguer. In addition to providing US$4.5 million to the UNDP technical assistance project, which was already earmarked for specific purposes, the US Government was 'considering additional ways of helping'. He explained to me in private that this related to the various modalities for air support. Sweden said that, as well as the 10 million Swedish kroners already pledged to the UNDP project, they were considering additional funds for observers, and perhaps for transport. Portugal pledged 40 additional vehicles, and the United Kingdom announced the imminent arrival of 20 Land Rovers, plus a metal bridge for the Huambo–Lubango road (the EC was also to provide six metal bridges). Denmark promised a contribution, to be announced later, and the Netherlands said that its contribution of US$225 000 to the UNDP project might be increased.

The Spanish Ambassador suggested that the US$4 million credit already provided by Spain for irrigation pumps, but not yet spent, could be diverted to the electoral process. A jovial character, he got a laugh by inserting a pregnant pause after the Spanish word *bombas* (which can be translated as either 'bombs' or 'pumps'), before going on to reassure everyone that he was referring to pumps for agricultural use. This obvious reference to the controversial supply of Spanish equipment for the antiriot police was a bit chancy, to say the least, but even Salupeto Pena joined in the laughter. The Ambassador also suggested the use of the soft credit of US$20 million granted to Angola during the earlier visit of Prime Minister Felipe Gonzalez. Afterwards he told me he was confident that Spain would be ready to provide light aircraft, as it had done in Namibia. Even Egypt pledged a contribution of US$10 000 in addition to the camping material it had already supplied.

Finally, the private sector spoke up: the representative of Cabinda Gulf said his company was ready to provide helicopters at low cost, as well as maintenance teams. The Conaco representative followed suit, indicating that his company, too, was prepared to help with air transport.

When everyone had had their say, the Minister of Territorial Administration announced that, because of the increased number of registration and electoral brigades, the cost of the De la Rue contract would rise from US$15 million to US$18 million. This was being paid by the Government. He added a special appeal for food and camping equipment, which, with characteristic Angolan optimism, he requested to be available on 20 May, only five days later!

To keep up the momentum a third donors' meeting was held on 12 June. It got off to a good start with Minister Kassoma's announcement that the Government would increase its budgetary support to the elections by an additional 3.5 billion new kwanzas in local currency and US$15 million in dollars. It would also provide, immediately, 50 more jeeps and hoped to add 50 Land Rovers by the end of June. Other advances in land transport were reported: Portugal said that 23 of the 40 vehicles it had promised, would arrive at the end of July, while 10 of the 20 Land Rovers provided by the United Kingdom were already in the country and the remaining 10 would arrive in July.

The position on air support had also improved, though the overall picture remained nebulous. The most concrete response came from the EC, which pledged two million ECUs in cash for air activities, in addition to the 2.5 million ECUs already committed for other aspects, as well as the possibility of food for the electoral brigades; and from Italy, which promised a bilateral contribution of one million ECUs for air support, especially helicopters and light planes. The United States confirmed its cash commitment: US$1 million for seminars, US$1.5 million for the UNDP technical assistance project and US$2.8 million for air support. This represented an addition of only US$800 000 over the previous contribution of US$4.5 million, with a reordering of its use to enable US$2.8 million to be earmarked for air support. Sweden reconfirmed its unearmarked contribution of 10 million Sweden kroners for the UNDP project, but said it would not be able to provide helicopters. Denmark announced a contribution of US$500 000, but it was earmarked for civic education.

This meeting ended with a strong appeal by the NEC President, who stressed the urgent need for transport (land and air), food and money. I echoed these sentiments, giving our view that, while registration had started reasonably well, it was already confronting the predicted logistical and practical difficulties, and these must be resolved quickly. It was essential for the air operation to begin in early July at the latest. In the meantime the most urgent need was for land transport to deal with the large concentration of eligible voters in urban and suburban areas. I suggested that the private sector, which had promised air support, might also lend vehicles. Some speakers had required assurance that the contributions would be adequately coordinated, and I was able to assuage their concern by pointing to my own broad terms of reference as Special Representative of the Secretary-General, and to the expected arrival of an air logistics group.

By the middle of June I was able to inform the Secretary-General that our strategy had already resulted in offers for the provision of an impressive part (though still by no means all) of the required air and land transport, communications equipment and food. Since only a limited amount had arrived by then, however, I stressed the vital need to translate pledges into deliveries. These concerns were reflected in the Secretary-General's next report to the Security Council.[1]

The orchestration of air support, which was being provided by different sources and under varying conditions, would pose a complex logistical problem that would exceed the capacity of the national authorities. Virtually all those who had indicated a willingness to provide air support made clear to me, privately, that they would prefer to make them available to UNAVEM II, under my direct control, so as to ensure they were used to maximum effect and within a well-organised logistical planning framework. Direct supervision by UNAVEM would have been ideal from an operational viewpoint but was precluded by the nature of the UN mandate, not to mention our exiguous budget. The elections were being organised by the national authorities as a sovereign affair, in keeping with the philosophy of the Bicesse Accords to put the Angolan parties squarely in the driver's seat. At the same time operational efficiency was hardly their most outstanding characteristic, and without some assurances on this score it was going to prove even harder to get the indispensable air support. After considering various alternatives, we decided that the most practical way of meeting the legitimate concerns of donors would be for aircraft to be made available through the UNDP technical assistance project. UNAVEM's role was to be one of advisor and catalyst, but we would monitor the process carefully and be ready to step in if things went wrong. We would assist directly by expanding our existing aviation fuel support system, which covered the whole territory. This approach was agreed with the Government and with Headquarters but there still remained the matter of ensuring adequate logistical and operational coordination, which required special professional skills.

My brief visit to Headquarters on 25–27 May had given me the chance to discuss the problem with Mig Goulding, who had come up with the excellent suggestion that the Salvadorean operation, ONUSAL, might be persuaded to loan the services of a retired Canadian Colonel and pilot, Hank Morris, who had conducted a similar operation in Central America. Together we had presented the proposal to the Secretary-General, on 27 May, and he had readily agreed.

Mig thought extremely highly of Colonel Morris, and, knowing his exacting standards, his judgement was more than good enough for me. Nor was I disappointed. Hank was to prove one of the best things that ever happened to

UNAVEM II. A refreshingly breezy character, bursting with energy and innovative ideas, he was the quintessential 'can do' person, never fazed by the most intractable and unexpected of problems, and we were to have more than our fair share of those. He also had the advantage of speaking Spanish. Later a highly competent American, called Driggers, who had worked with Colonel Morris in Central America was contracted as flight engineer, while the Canadian Government generously provided two additional air logistics officers. This small group worked closely with the Director-General for the elections and myself, as well as with Major Dennis Strilchuk and his doughty band of desperadoes, who performed daily and nightly miracles on Movement Control at the airport.

Although the decision had been taken at the end of May, the idea did not become reality until perilously late in the day, in late July. Problems of money arose once more. I had understood that the services loaned from El Salvador would be a 'goodwill gesture' by the UN, even though the group would work primarily within the framework of the technical assistance provided by UNDP. It was in this guise that, in all good faith, I presented the matter to General N'dalu and Minister Kassoma on my return to Luanda and obtained their official agreement. UNITA also welcomed the idea. In early July I was dismayed to find that funding was to be sought from the modest EC contribution envisaged for providing much-needed aircraft. I warned Headquarters that the unit could well be interpreted as a 'Greek present' by the Angolans, and that there was thus a political as well as a financial angle. I appealed for some way to be found of 'absorbing' any additional costs within the UNAVEM budget. After a predictably reluctant initial response, I was told that other options were being considered, including absorbing the expense against shortfalls on other items of UNAVEM's budget.

The South African air unit did not start to arrive in Luanda until Thursday 9 July, when an advance party came to set up arrangements; the remainder of the unit became operational on 15 July. The initial phase of the registration had therefore to be carried out without significant air support, although UNAVEM had pitched in whenever it could, ferrying registration brigades and kits to various parts of the country. Given transport limitations and the scant time for planning and preparation, it was small wonder that registration got off to a disturbingly slow beginning: fewer than 100 000 voters were registered during the first two weeks. By 16 June – four weeks after the process had begun – the pace had quickened only slightly, with 370 000 voters registered. After six weeks the number had risen to 750 000 but between three and four million people still needed to be registered in the remaining period of little more than a month. It began to look increasingly doubtful whether the process could be completed by 31 July. In addition to the transport difficulties, communication problems had impeded the transmission of registration data and lack of food for registration teams was also adversely affecting progress.

Gradually the problems began to be ironed out through Onofre dos Santos' flair and leadership and the grim determination of Angolans to make the process succeed, ranging from the registration brigades, who sat for hours under the blazing sun or struggled through the bush on foot with exiguous rations to reach the thousands of isolated settlements scattered over the countryside, to the many people even further afield who walked hundreds of kilometres, sometimes spending several days on the trek, to ensure their eligibility to vote. Spreading information about the election was a major headache in a country where much of the population was illiterate and had no access to mass media such as television. Radios were more widespread, and their programmes were used to good effect. Even megaphones were ordered to get the message across in remote communities. Provincial officials, most of them extraordinarily dedicated, played a highly significant role. And, small though our little band of UN observers was, it was now functioning in all the provinces and its very presence and high visibility – with its white vehicles and the blue UN caps and arm badges of the electoral teams – in areas that had seen few or no foreigners during the long war years were already having a positive impact. Their daily meetings with local officials and party representatives, as well as their constant availability to answer questions or resolve disputes, promoted transparency and built confidence among the people that the electoral process would be free and fair.

* * *

The UN observers formed a heterogeneous and interesting group. A few had been recruited from outside – academics with an interest in Angola or southern Africa – but the majority were volunteers from the secretariats of the UN and the Specialised Agencies, and the fact that they had chosen Angola rather than one of the more fashionable and appealing peacekeeping missions on offer generally denoted a high level of commitment and readiness to face hardship. Many had quite extraordinary stories to tell of their experiences. Interestingly there was a high proportion of women, mostly from the higher ranks of General Service UN staff (the UN distinguishes, often arbitrarily, between the 'Professional' and 'General Service' categories). Many of these women had professional qualifications and most of them positively blossomed under the redoubtable challenges of the Angolan assignment, which contrasted strikingly with the humdrum (though usually highly responsible) administrative posts they had occupied in those far-distant European and North American cities. The women often had an advantage over the men in being able to get close to the local population and win their confidence.

Whenever I could extricate myself from the endless meetings and negotiations in Luanda, I hopped on to the Beechcraft, with a helicopter link at the other end, to visit the UNAVEM teams. During the weeks running up to the election I visited every provincial capital at least once, as well as going further afield to the troop assembly areas and field registration stations. In conformity with my policy of making optimum use of all available resources, instructions had gone out that there must be maximum teamwork between all components of the mission: military, police and civilian. UN police and electoral observers made particularly appropriate joint teams. The military's role in the elections was less obvious but it provided logistical and security support, and in many cases very much more. My concern that we would be very thin on the ground, even with the reinforcement of 300 electoral observers for the actual voting, had led me to insist to Headquarters that we would need to augment them by using UN military and police observers as well. There had been an animated exchange with New York as to whether the military should wear uniforms or civilian dress. I had argued for the former, on the grounds that their blue berets, neck-scarves and UN armbands would confer a special status, and differentiate them from normal military personnel, and that this would underscore their role as guarantors of the process. It was a great relief when the UN Legal Office said that they could perform these functions in uniform.

The team approach worked better in some places than others. The determining factors were personality and leadership qualities, and particularly the attitude of the senior military man in those places where the sites coincided with UNAVEM's Regional Commanders; in some, cooperation between the military and civilians was made more difficult by cultural hang-ups, including implicit sexual discrimination. The experience of living together in the same camp, facing the same dangers and hardships, either strengthened the communal approach where a mutual predisposition to work together already existed, or acted as a further divisive factor where no such inclination was present. The policy of rotating military observers between different posts, so that hardships would be shared more equitably, helped to keep any tension within check. (Electoral observers, stationed exclusively in provincial capitals, were not rotated for reasons of continuity, though living conditions varied greatly from one capital to another.)

At UNAVEM Headquarters we eventually filled the gap left by John Truman's departure. The time factor, the unavailability of anyone suitable in Headquarters and the all-too-familiar problems and delays of outside recruitment led us to the inescapable conclusion that we must find someone from our own midst to be Chief Electoral Officer. My initial choice was John Truman's deputy, Maria Grossi, a Brazilian professor who had excellent theoretical grounding in electoral matters, and had served in Haiti and Nicaragua. Tall, dark and very slim, Maria not only conveyed an impression of restrained elegance, but had a quiet, warm personality, which helped to breed confidence and gave added weight to her invariably sensible and well-balanced counsel. Moreover Portuguese was her native tongue. It was Maria herself who raised objections. She did not want the administrative and managerial responsibilities, nor, she added with characteristically unassuming modesty, did she feel she had the capacity for them. In her reluctance I noted more than a trace of the tendency among highly competent women to underrate their own capabilities.

My blandishments were of no avail; Maria was adamant. The choice therefore fell on Sammy Buo, a Cameroonian Secretariat member working in the Electoral Division, who had spent much of his UN career in political research and analysis, although with little experience of operational management. Maria remained as deputy, and in the long run this was probably the best arrangement since, relieved of day-to-day administrative work, she came to play an indispensable role liaising with the NEC and the Director-General, Onofre dos Santos. While I would have liked to have seen another woman in a key position in UNAVEM's male-dominated hierarchy, Buo's appointment, along with that of Dr Sinjela of Zambia as legal advisor, meant that we had a strong core of Africans in senior posts, in addition to those already occupied by General Unimna and Jobarteh. (Ironically, in one particularly virulent attack, after I had left the mission, I was accused of surrounding myself with Americans instead of Africans who were more familiar with the psychological subtleties of the situation. Since there had only been one such American – John Truman – and he had departed, this demonstrates how difficult it is to convince biased opinion with mere facts.)

* * *

The NEC held meetings on 20 June and 11 July to review the voter registration process with provincial electoral authorities, in the presence of representatives of the political parties as well as Ambassadors and UNAVEM staff. The second meeting was conducted with a good deal of 'panache', the announcement of the numbers registered being heralded by a vibrant display of traditional drummers in full regalia – feathered head-dresses and loin cloths – who surged into the hall on a great tidal wave of sonorous rhythm that immediately seized everyone's attention. The drummers were the living incarnation of the images that adorned the posters being put up everywhere, with the poignant legend 'Volta a sorrir Angola' – 'Angola smiles again' – above the words 'Elecoes libres e justas' – 'Free and Fair Elections'.

This time there really was something to smile about. The numbers registered had reached an estimated 2.6 million, a more than 250 per cent increase over the 750 000 reported on 20 June. Another cause for jubilation was that the target of 2.5 million set on the latter occasion had been surpassed. The meeting did, however, confirm the urgent need for better land and air transport and communications facilities, and also identified the late payment of salaries to registration teams, as well as the inadequacy of food and shelter for them, as serious obstacles still to be overcome. It also aired the continuing controversy over the estimated total number of eligible voters. Onofre dos Santos suggested that the number might be closer to 4.5 million, rather than the five million figure hitherto generally accepted. With the end of the registration phase approaching, we were concerned that the lower estimate was being advanced in anticipation of the total figure falling short of the higher expectations raised earlier.

Speculation was already widespread about the possible extension of registration beyond 31 July. In our view such a prolongation was by now inevitable, to cover, for instance, returning refugees. Furthermore, although a great spurt had been made, registration of the remaining two million or so voters would encounter even greater difficulties since they were located in the most inaccessible areas, where air transport was indispensable.

In these circumstances the arrival of the South Africans could not have been more timely. As one would expect of the SAAF, they were an exceedingly tough and professional group of flyers. They came equipped with four helicopters and two fixed-wing aircraft, and with everything required for their operation and maintenance. One of the aircraft arrived with the advance party and was temporarily housed in the UNAVEM hangar at the airport. That night or the next, during the shooting spree that invariably enlivened the hours of darkness at the airport, a stray bullet hit the plane. Fortunately the damage was easily repaired and the South Africans took the incident (which was clearly fortuitous – the UNAVEM hangar frequently received the fallout from the activities of the trigger-happy owners of Kalashnikovs) in their stride.

The agreement between South Africa and the Angolan Government envisaged that the South African air support would continue through the remainder of the registration period and right up to the end of the voting. The Government was to provide accommodation. Within a day or two a hangar was made available, but no accommodation was forthcoming for the crews. Meanwhile they camped in the hangar in the most basic and insalubrious of conditions. Soon the main centre of their operation was transferred to Malange, nearer to the difficult areas they were to fly to, mainly in the eastern half of the country, as well as in the rugged northern areas of Uige province, but a base was retained at Luanda airport. Still the Government did not honour its commitment to provide living accommodation, which was unobtainable in the capital city without some Government intervention for example by putting one of its compounds or some other installation at their disposal. This apparently minor hiccough was to become a major problem.

Meanwhile the South Africans set to work with alacrity and consummate efficiency. No air support from other sources had yet materialised and, as far as registration was concerned, it was already pretty late in the day when the South Africans themselves came, but they did so in the nick of time. Without their help it would have been impossible to reach the remoter parts of Angola and an appreciable number of voters would have been disenfranchised. If that had happened the 'free and fair' nature of the elections would have been undermined long before the actual voting and I would have had to make a statement to that effect.

As it was the registration figures took an encouraging jump in the second half of July. On 31 July the Director-General announced the glad tidings that

4 303 266 voters had been registered. It was still the case, however, that not everyone had been reached, and the NEC president announced an extension of registration until 10 August.

By the same date 13 presidential candidates had completed all the necessary formalities. No less than 24 Angolan political parties had been legalised, or were about to be legalised. Many were very small and fragmented, and confined to specific areas of the country.

The news of the extension of the registration date was welcome. I issued a statement, locally, which was also used by the Secretary-General's spokesman at the noon press briefing of Monday 3 August in New York, in which I praised the achievements so far of the registration exercise. The Troika, who had visited Luanda the previous week, shared this view. At the same time we all underlined the many problems still to be resolved if the September elections were to be peaceful and national reconciliation and a stable political climate were to flourish, singling out the demobilisation of the two rival armies and the creation of a single unified armed force before the election date as paramount among these. My communiqué also emphasised the urgent need for increased logistical support from the international community during the next critical weeks, particularly in communications and through the loan of air and land transport.

The last point was key. The extension of the registration period gave a necessary breathing space, but it was a very short one. The NEC estimated that about one million eligible voters remained to be registered during those 10 days. These were tucked away in the most inaccessible corners of all, particularly in the provinces of Cuando Cubango, Moxico and Uige, which meant even heavier reliance on helicopters. Unfortunately there were some dark clouds looming on the horizon.

* * *

Predictably there had been fierce opposition by MPLA hardliners to the assistance being provided by the South Africans. Much of this was based on their understandable reaction to the role of South Africa during the 16 years of civil war and the trail of death and destruction left by its bombing raids. But there was another more immediate element behind these protestations: the people who were being helped to vote through the helicopter support were mainly in traditionally UNITA-occupied territory. Two points seemed to escape those antagonists who thought somewhat simplistically along these lines. First, living in UNITA-occupied territory did not necessarily make a person a UNITA supporter (quite the reverse in some cases, and there were to be surprises in the eventual voting results); and second, if access to these areas was inhibited, then I would not be able to declare the elections 'free and fair'.

The outcry broke into outright clamour as a result of an insensitive action by the South Africans. Fed up with the abysmal conditions in which their men were living, they brought a military supply-cum-hospital ship into the port of Luanda to serve as a floating camp. I received differing versions from the two sides as to the extent to which this move had been cleared with the Angolan national authorities beforehand. This was by now irrelevant anyway, as the arrival of the ship provided a highly emotional pretext for those who wanted the South Africans out.

Rumours were already rife when I spoke to President dos Santos on 30 July. By this time we had an easy personal relationship, and at the end of our talk I conveyed my concern about a possible breakdown in the arrangements between South Africa and the Angolan Government. I was very conscious that this was a bilateral issue, and of the political sensitivities involved, and merely wished to express the hope that some mutually acceptable *modus operandi* could be rapidly agreed, since the South African contribution had been critical in making possible the excellent registration results attained so far, and would be even more vital in the coming weeks, as well as during actual voting. Furthermore a breakdown would convey the wrong signal to other donors, whom I was trying to persuade to provide similar support. The President, in his customary moderate way, said that he well understood the crucial nature of the South Africans' help. He considered that they should continue, but confided that he faced significant internal resistance within the MPLA. The problem had been exacerbated by the arrival of the ship. I suggested that the solution was for the Government to live up to its commitment to provide accommodation for the South Africans. The President assured me that this would be done rapidly and South Africa accordingly removed the ship.

By then, however, irretrievable damage had been done. On 6 August a representative of South Africa informed us that Ambassador Gröbler had received a telefax from the Angolan Ministry of Foreign Affairs on the previous day, saying that the Angolan Government regretfully had to ask South Africa to withdraw its air support units when registration closed. Onofre dos Santos was out of the country, but that evening General N'dalu raised the matter with me. Moderate as always, he expressed his concern and surprise and said that he was urgently seeking a solution. Meanwhile the Portuguese had expressed their serious concern to the Vice-Minister of the Interior, 'Nando'. Jeffrey Millington too was extremely worried, particularly since the South African presence had arisen from Hank Cohen's initiative, and had informed Washington.

Our efforts failed. The next day the South African liaison office told us that the Government had formally requested South Africa to withdraw its electoral air support unit *forthwith;* it should not even remain until the close of registration. The acting head of the office, Mr Kruger, had been summoned to meet Foreign Minister Van Durem 'Loy' and Vice-Minister Venâncio de Moura at short notice the previous day, 6 August. They had, in his words, 'politely but firmly' requested South Africa 'to withdraw all the relevant aircraft and men with immediate effect, that is on 7 August'. The Minister reportedly tried to soften the blow, saying that the Government had thought the departure of the ship would have eased the situation, 'but various elements in the MPLA and the Government are unhappy with the South African presence'.

Mr Kruger expected that SAAF C130 aircraft would evacuate all the aircraft and men by 12 or 13 August. He had told 'Loy' that South Africa was withdrawing its men with great regret, as it had genuinely hoped to help, and that it intended to play down the nature of the withdrawal. Comments to the press would merely say that South Africa had been invited by the Angolan government to assist with the registration of voters, and now that that process had been completed South Africa's participation had come to an end. De Moura had replied 'we will back you on that'. To us Mr Kruger confirmed that South Africa was going to 'bow out gracefully', and with the realisation that past conflicts in the whole region of southern Africa would take 'longer than we thought and will need much patience to heal'.

While it was right and proper for South Africa to gloss over its precipitate departure, the reality was that registration had not been completed. Although the departure of their air unit was staggered over several days, operations stopped literally from one moment to the next on 6 August. This not only left a large number of people unregistered, but totally disrupted a carefully orchestrated logistical plan. The planes had been shuttling to and from various locations, dropping registration brigades and kits in one place, and leaving them there while they retrieved teams from other areas and transported them to their next destination, before returning to pick up the first team. This neat little jigsaw was thrown into complete disarray. Registration brigades were stranded in the back of beyond, without sufficient food, and sometimes in environments that were hostile politically as well as physically. Not only was the registration process deprived of their services for its few remaining days, but many of them suffered considerable privation. Some of them were 'lost' – in the sense of our having no news of them – for a week or more while they struggled back out of the bush on foot.

* * *

This unfortunate turn of events also had looming political implications. On 31 July, 24 hours after my audience with President dos Santos, I had had a meeting with Dr Savimbi. He had expressed satisfaction with the figures just announced by the NEC, and with the decision to extend the registration period. But he had emphasised that the gap was still very wide and hinted strongly that a longer extension period might be required. It was obvious that any shortfall in the number of registrations that could be imputed to the premature withdrawal of the South African air unit could be a major source of controversy.

The conversation had also demonstrated that there was still disagreement over the total number of voters. Dr Savimbi – no doubt for tactical reasons – was espousing the very high estimate of 6.1 million, while the NEC was now working on the basis of 5.3 million. I had to stress that, in the absence of a proper census, UNAVEM had no objective yardstick by which to judge these figures, and that the only practical solution was for the NEC, of which UNITA was a member, to reach agreement by consensus.

The untimely departure of the South Africans made it all the more important to speed up decisions on air and other transport and communication support from elsewhere. It was clearly impossible to bring in, at the drop of a hat, replacements that could fill the yawning gap left by the South Africans for the mere three or four days left for registration, but we had also counted on their being there right through the voting itself. Although some aircraft were beginning to trickle in, we were still worryingly far from having firm commitments for all the outside help needed.

The EC had promised to fund the leasing of aircraft, but we had not yet seen the colour of their money. Jeff Millington confirmed that the United States was prepared to provide US$2.8 million to finance air transport and wanted a breakdown of how it might best be used – a request that was not easy to fulfil without knowing what was forthcoming from other sources. Less encouragingly, he told me that Assistant Secretary Cohen's proposal for a National Guard exercise with the accompanying C130 aircraft now looked distinctly bleak, owing to reluctance on the part of the US Department of Defence and a 'general lack of interest in Africa in Washington'. On a brighter note, he thought it might be possible to obtain a C5 aircraft to ferry to Angola the helicopters and light aircraft offered by Poland.

The Earth Summit in Rio de Janeiro, which began a few days after Millington's conversation, provided an opportunity for high-level intervention, since the dignitaries attending included President George Bush, President dos Santos and the UN Secretary-General. At my suggestion the Secretary-General raised the urgent need for logistical support, especially helicopters, in a private conversation with President Bush, who promised to pursue the matter. I also advised President dos Santos to discuss these needs with both the Secretary-General and President Bush.

But despite our combined efforts, cables criss-crossed between Mig and myself without recording any developments that could give real encouragement.

* * *

Then suddenly, in July, a breakthrough occurred from a totally unexpected quarter. Shawn McCormick, Assistant Director of African studies at the Centre for International and Strategic Studies in Washington (CSIS), telephoned me out of the blue one day and invited me to Washington to address the CSIS Study Group on Angola on the topic 'The Role of the United Nations in Angola: Prospects for a Peaceful Transition to Democracy'. He also offered to put me in contact with influential people in Washington who could help me to get the logistical support so desperately needed. I responded with gratitude, but did not anticipate that one person (and a very young person, as I was soon to discover) was likely to sway the course of events.

I was totally wrong.

The CSIS Study Group on Angola boasted a prestigious membership – virtually anyone who was anyone in Washington in relation to Africa and Angola, ranging from members of both houses of Congress and high officials in key departments of the Administration to chief executives of firms in the private sector with an actual or potential interest in Angola. Its three co-chairs were Senator Nancy Kassebaum, Chester Crocker and Maurice Tempelsman. The latter was scheduled to chair the session at which I would speak on Wednesday 22 July.

I arrived in Washington on Monday, 20 July. Whirlwinds are supposed to be short in duration, but the one that snatched me up into its vortex at Dulles Airport did not loosen its grip for a moment during a hectic but productive 48 hours. Its animator was Shawn, who drove me pitilessly through an amazing array of speeches, meetings, working lunches and dinners and media interviews. But he did so with a charm and efficiency that brooked no complaint, however great the physical and mental fatigue (my visit coincided with weather that exceeded even Washington's norm for heat and humidity). In a matter of hours this remarkable young man opened practically all of the most important doors in Washington.

On Tuesday 21 July I had a succession of high-level meetings in the Pentagon and the State Department, and in the White House with the National Security Council, as well as discussions with the UNITA representative in Washington, Jardo Muekalia, and the Angolan Ambassador, José Patricio. In the evening there were drinks with Chester Crocker, the former Assistant Secretary of State for African Affairs, followed by a dinner with representatives of the private sector, hosted by Chevron.

During the whole day I had been pushing hard for American financial and logistical support from whatever source to ensure that demobilisation, the formation of the new army and, above all, the elections were successfully carried out. Within my philosophy of mobilising every possible kind of support, I also aimed at securing help from the private sector. Chevron in Angola had already indicated its willingness to make its planes available to ferry electoral personnel and material. That was the origin of the dinner and the burden of the song I sang for my supper. Asked how I would sum up the situation in one sentence, my tired brain managed to come up with the not inapposite refrain 'Pay now, or repent later!'

The next day, Wednesday, was equally hectic. The whole morning was taken up with the session of the CSIS Study Group, followed by lunch on Capitol Hill with selected members of Congress: Dave McCurdy, Bud Schuster, Doug Bereuter and four staff members. This was one of the most important contacts of all, and I was encouraged by their clear recognition across the bipartisan divide that the Angolan operation had been underfunded, and that something must be done, and quickly, if it was not to founder.

In the afternoon the CSIS had arranged for me to speak to a larger audience. Well over a hundred people attended, comprising officials of both the executive and legislative branches of government, and representatives of the private sector, international organisations, the media and the academic world. Ambassador José Patricio, and Jardo Muekalia were both there but, as I recall, did not speak. After that I met a group of journalists and gave one or two radio interviews. By the time I arrived in New York late that night I was totally exhausted, but at the same time buoyed up by the feeling that my message had got across in most of the places where it mattered in Washington.

I spent the next day, 23 July, in NewYork to talk to the Secretary-General, Mig and some members of the Security Council. I arrived back in Luanda on 27 July. I had been away only a little over a week, but felt we had made a great leap forward.

* * *

To follow up my Washington visit and his own conversation in Rio de Janeiro, the Secretary-General addressed a personal letter to President Bush on 24 July. Referring to my meetings in Washington, he said that he had been glad to learn that a decision about the loan of three C130 aircraft, to assist both with demobilisation and the elections, was likely that week. He had also been given to understand by me that further, much-needed assistance – helicopters, road transport, food, tents, mobile kitchens and the like – and perhaps even a National Guards exercise might be possible, if a policy decision was taken at the highest level that this was a critical area deserving exceptional measures. Here he gave his own opinion that a great deal was at stake in Angola and that assistance now, of a relatively modest nature, could prove a crucial investment in the future stability not only of Angola, but of the whole of southern Africa. With the elections now 10 weeks away, time was very short, but a brief, one-shot effort could still make a vital difference. The Secretary-General also spoke on the phone to Brent Scowcroft, the President's National Security Adviser.

President Bush was to receive another urgent message about Angola on 28 July. This one was from the Permanent Select Committee on Intelligence of the US House of Representatives, and was signed by some of my luncheon companions, drawn from both the Democratic and the Republican parties: its Chairman, Dave McCurdy, Bud Schuster, Martin Olav Sabo and Doug Bereuter. The letter referred to an earlier one, of 4 June, expressing concern that the elections might not take place at all and urging immediate action to ensure a successful conclusion to the US policy of encouraging democracy in Angola. With 10 weeks to go, the Committee still feared the process to be in serious jeopardy, and cited their recent meeting with me as underscoring the need for immediate assistance. The Committee believed that certain components of the US military, operating under UN auspices, could provide such assistance (a veiled reference to a National Guard exercise, which they had told me they supported). It also emphasised the significance of democratic elections in Angola as a model for other sub-Saharan African countries, adding that Angola deserved the same consideration and support from the United States as that enjoyed by Eastern Europe and the former Soviet Union. It would be tragic, they said, if, for want of a modest amount of help, the goal of self-determination was not realised in Angola.

President Bush replied encouragingly to the Secretary-General on 5 August, assuring him that the United States was committed to seeing this foreign policy priority through to a successful conclusion. The letter brought the long-awaited confirmation that the Department of Defence would provide three C130s for approximately six weeks to assist with demobilisation and support the electoral operation. (A White House spokesperson, Judy Smith, had already announced this decision on 29 July, while accompanying President Bush on a trip to California.) The President went on to refer to the Secretary-General's telephone conversation with Brent Scowcroft, in which he had reiterated the request for helicopters. He said that it did not seem feasible to use US aircraft to transport the Polish helicopters to Luanda, and suggested that perhaps helicopters could be rented in the region. The President had requested that every effort be made to identify other resources to meet some of the needs mentioned in the Secretary-General's letter.

The Angolans themselves had been active in pressing for support. Immediately after my visit Ambassador José Patricio sent an eloquent letter to Congressmen and Senators. Members of the powerful American lobby supporting UNITA were also pushing for a positive response to my appeal. It was encouraging that both sides saw advantage in ensuring an effective electoral operation, but one of the lobbyists for UNITA, Christopher Lehman, warned me that the bureaucratic obstacles in Washington remained substantial.

The needs still to be met were also alarmingly substantial. Our list was updated in early August. The newly arrived flight coordinator, Mr Driggers, reduced the requirement for helicopters to 40, which would, with the 14 UNAVEM helicopters, make a total of 54, but increased the number of fixed-wing aircraft from eight to nine, including six Beechcraft. The shortfall in land transport was also causing concern. Of the 1386 four-wheel drive vehicles needed, less than half had been provided, mainly from government sources; 743 still had to be found by mobilising all available vehicles, including those of Government ministers, as well as private sector and individual sources.

Moreover the US response, though high-level and encouraging, was not exactly speedy in execution. I had been cheered by a fax from the UN

Information Centre in Washington, on 13 August, informing me about a Pentagon proposal for Angola, code-named 'Operation Provide Transition'. This was a direct result of my visit and aimed to use military capability to provide logistical support. But when I mentioned this to Jeff Millington at a CCPM meeting a couple of days later I was dashed to learn that he had poured cold water on the idea, arguing that such a 'massive US presence' (certainly an overstatement) could cause misunderstandings, because of past US support of UNITA. I appreciated his wish to avoid any repetition of the South African experience, but my own informal soundings in Luanda indicated that the Government would gladly accept such an offer.

I conveyed to Mig, in New York, my apprehension that the negative comments Jeff had already sent to the State Department could well nip a promising initiative in the bud and cancel out my endeavours in Washington. Moreover it was becoming clearer every day in Luanda, after the experience with registration, that support on this 'massive' scale was essential. As only one example, five days after registration had ceased, dozens of brigades were still stranded in remote areas without food, because of the unavailability of helicopters to rescue them. Although some air support was promised from other sources, the shortfall was still very large (Norway had said it could not provide its peacekeeping wing of helicopters; and Headquarters had drawn a blank with the Germans and the Swiss, to whom they had suggested that, while neither could contribute directly to a peacekeeping operation, they might perhaps loan aircraft to support a non-military action such as an election).

Mig quickly contacted Jeff Davidow, who said that the Administration had provided US$2 million through the World Food Programme to rent aircraft for the elections, which was about to be supplemented by a further US$2.1 million. (The curious choice of WFP as a conduit was to cause many administrative headaches.) The three C130s of the US Air Force were already in Angola. In addition, all sorts of papers were moving around Washington in order to get more logistical resources to Angola, 'ranging from fuel bladders to helicopters'. Jeff Davidow asked for me to be assured that any concerns conveyed through his namesake in Luanda had not deterred his own efforts to press for a larger American response.

The next development occurred in the last week of August, barely a month before the elections. Jeffrey Millington was away and his deputy, Tony Newton, on instructions from Washington, requested more details on the requirements, as well as an update of contributions already received and of the shortfall still to be met. I undertook yet another review of a situation that was changing daily and conveyed the results on 27 August. Reciting many needs in the area of food, tents, camping equipment, mobile kitchens and four-wheel-drive vehicles, I emphasised that the acute need that would spell the difference between success and failure was still air support and communications. It would be extremely serious if logistical and transport shortcomings could be used either as an excuse for not reaching all voters or as a pretext for not accepting the results of the election. In giving the new figure of 40 helicopters and nine fixed-wing aircraft, I stressed that the estimates made no allowance for malfunctions or unforeseen developments. It would thus be desirable to have a few more as a safety valve. Confirmed contributions, totalling US$5.5 million, including US$2 million from the United States, would pay for the lease of the nine fixed-wing aircraft, basic HF communications, logistical support, food, the transportation of fuel to up-country sites and the operating and positioning of 16 helicopters. Contracting for these items was underway. There was still a gap of 24 helicopters, which could be bridged either by cash or in kind. The total cost for the 40 helicopters and nine fixed-wing aircraft, plus the requisite logistic support, was calculated at US$9.7 million. Hence there was a shortfall of US$4.2 million (US$9.7 million less the US$5.5 million of this already contributed). Total donor pledges amounted to US$8.5 million, but since only US$5.5 million had been received, there was still a shortfall of US$3 million, including a further US$2 million from the United States. We understood a problem had arisen with the latter because of the need for Congressional approval. If the pledged, but uncommitted, US$3 million became available very soon, it could be used to contract an additional 17 helicopters. But even if we got all of the promised US$8.5 million in time, there would still be a deficit of US$1.2 million, this sum representing the funds required to contract the remaining seven helicopters. Alternatively they could be provided in kind.

I suggested that the United States could also help by providing six communications satellites for Luanda and the five main operational centres up-country to ensure essential voice communications; and by supplying six to eight light utility helicopters for the liaison flights transporting smaller loads of personnel and cargo, and for medical evacuation if necessary.

Of course the ideal way of handling all of this would be through Hank Cohen's original suggestion of holding a US National Guard exercise in Angola. Earlier legal and bureaucratic problems within the United States had been ironed out during my Washington visit. The members of Congress whom I had lunched with had been enthusiastic about the proposal, which was also the thrust of 'Operation Provide Transition'. Ironically it was the Angolan Government that, when officially consulted, dealt the final blow. On 27 August the Vice-Minister for Foreign Affairs, Venâncio De Moura, speaking on the President's instructions, told Jeff Millington that the Government could not accept US helicopters for reasons of sovereignty, even for the peaceful purpose of providing transport and communications for the elections. I was never able to find out who was behind this decision, which was so much at variance with what I had been told. MPLA hard-liners again? Perhaps unfairly, I felt the outcome could have been different had Jeff himself not had doubts. The Angolan Government had, after all, requested the helicopters in the first place. The only possibility now left was for the United States to provide cash for helicopter rental and assistance in communications.

The loan of two planes by the Chevron Company also ran into difficulties over insurance and the ambiguities of its status and official attachment, and fell through. The road to finding adequate support for the elections was proving a rough one.

* * *

Unpleasant difficulties were simultaneously rearing their heads on another front, exacerbated by the untimely departure of the South Africans, which made it impossible to register the expected number of people by the extended deadline of 10 August. I wrote two letters to President Caetano urging the NEC to consider a further, brief, extension. Appeals were coming in from provinces with the most rugged terrain, and the Director-General too felt that more time was needed. The NEC met to consider this matter on Tuesday 11 August, and I visited President Caetano beforehand to reiterate my concerns. Notwithstanding the NEC decided not to extend registration beyond 10 August. A secret vote was taken, with only three members voting for further extension, despite an impassioned appeal by Director-General Onofre dos Santos.

It was a very difficult situation, since the NEC's decision, adopted by a large majority, was a *fait accompli*, and there was scant chance of getting it changed. After discussing various options with my UNAVEM colleagues, I decided to request a meeting with the NEC President, the Director-General and the Minister for Territorial Administration, at which I would make the UN's position clear. I would also speak in similar terms to President dos Santos at my next meeting with him.

We were not the only ones to be concerned. At the CCPM meeting on Thursday 13 August, Engineer Salupeto Pena complained bitterly about the NEC's decision, saying that UNITA would probably send a letter of protest to President dos Santos, requesting reconsideration. Nor was the donor community well pleased. No doubt anticipating such an eventuality, several speakers at the NEC meeting had, I understood, argued that this was a sovereign decision upon which international opinion had no bearing. Notwithstanding, Jeff Millington and John Flynn told me that they expected to be instructed by their capitals to express concern to the Government, and the three observers at the CCPM were considering similar joint action.

My meeting with the Angolan electoral authorities took place on Friday 14 August, and was a far from enjoyable experience. Minister Kassoma was in the chair – opposite us sat President Caetano and Ambassador Almeida, now the NEC spokes person and an ardent MPLA stalwart. I sat to the Minister's right, with Ebrima Jobarteh and Maria Grossi beside me. The Director-General, Onofre dos Santos, arrived late and sat down on the UNAVEM side of the table,

I suspect unwisely for him, and certainly embarrassingly for us. The seating looked confrontational before we had even begun to talk.

I worked up to my theme as diplomatically as possible, starting off with our congratulations for the impressive manner in which registration had been undertaken and stressing that the conduct of the elections was a sovereign national responsibility. At the same time the UN had been mandated by the Security Council to verify that every phase was free and fair and that involved a judgement of whether eligible voters had been denied the right to register. Problems had arisen in certain provinces, where the effects were reflected in the registration figures. I cited the logistical causes, among them the premature withdrawal of the main external air support and the problem of registering refugees. These aspects could not go unremarked in my public assessment of the registration exercise or in the report the Secretary-General had to make to the Security Council before the end of August. I therefore enquired whether the NEC could authorise an extension of some days – on an exceptional basis, and as provided in the Electoral Law – for the areas most affected and for the refugees. This enquiry, I stressed, far from being an attempt to interfere with a sovereign decision, was prompted by a desire to pre-empt criticism focusing on one aspect of what had, in all other respects, been a job well done. The extension could not ensure the registration of *all* eligible voters, but it would unequivocally demonstrate that maximum effort had been made to do so, and this was in the interests of all concerned, including the Angolan Government.

Mr Kassoma's face was smiling as usual, but his eyes were not. He said it would be impossible for the NEC to authorise even a limited extension. Efforts must now concentrate on the all-important next stages, and besides the 10-day extension beyond 31 July had shown that prolongation did not produce a significant additional number of registrations (here he blandly sidestepped the impact of the withdrawal of South African air support). As for the refugees, their organised return had only just started and would not be completed even by the date of the election. NEC President Caetano spoke next and reiterated virtually all the same considerations. It was left to Ambassador Almeida to put the boot in, with the blunt comment that the NEC could not reverse a decision because of pressure from the UN or the international community. He spoke, his gaze fixed on me more than a little pointedly, about deep sensitivities in the country over undue external influence; no one would understand why the NEC changed its decision.

Onofre dos Santos spoke last, and forcefully contradicted most of what the three previous speakers had said. He expressed his displeasure that the decision had been taken without consultation with him and repeated all the arguments he had made to justify an extension during the NEC's debate. Contrary to the Minister's opinion, the number of additional registrations between 31 July and 10 August *had* been significant – no less than 400 000 – and would have been even more so had air support remained constant throughout. In Uige province alone, he estimated, 100 000 voters had yet to register (a figure that tallied with those of our observers). Then he suddenly executed a complete *volte face*, conceding that it was probably not feasible to reverse the NEC decision or reopen the process of registration. He estimated the total number of registered voters to be around 4.8 million, and appealed to me to minimise the lack of coverage and emphasise what had been achieved. The abrupt change of tack was surprising, but I understood his dilemma. He had to work with these people, whose views he did not share, and he was determined that the elections should go forward in the best manner possible.

Minister Kassoma seized on the last part of the Director-General's intervention and appealed for my *comprensão* (understanding). I replied that Angola, and all those responsible for making the peace and electoral processes work, had had my understanding from the outset, for I well understood the difficulties they faced. But by the same token they must be equally understanding that the UN had mandated responsibilities it must fulfil. And there it had to be left.

* * *

Headquarters were not at all keen about my taking up with President dos Santos the non-extension of the registration period, but an audience had already been requested on the general status of the peace and electoral processes, and I thought it important that he be made aware of the implications and underlying issues. As so often happened, I saw Dr Savimbi first, on 19 August, and was received by the President on 21 August.

In the interim the NEC announced that 4.86 million eligible voters had fulfilled the registration formalities; that is, 92 per cent of their estimate of a total voting population of 5.3 million.

I have already referred to some aspects of the meeting called by Dr Savimbi on 19 August, especially that of the antiriot police. But the main message of his clearly orchestrated diplomatic campaign with various national and foreign groups was the safeguarding of the electoral process. He expressed concern over registration, using a higher estimate of the total number of eligible voters than the NEC, and deploring the failure to reach some of the population in remote (usually UNITA-strong) areas. He claimed that UNITA had lost 5–600 000 potential votes in Moxico province alone, plus a significant number in Uige. We were all struck by the air of moderation with which he advanced his complaints. He emphasised that he was not crying over spilt milk but wanted to avoid any recurrence of such difficulties in the final, and vital, phase of voting. Presumably this attitude was based on the calculation that UNITA was still going to win, despite the shortfall in registration, and it would therefore be foolish to do anything that might impede the process or offer any pretext to the Government to postpone the elections, a constant fear in the minds of UNITA. Dr Savimbi accordingly stressed the need to ensure proper organisation, logistical support and international observation so that all those who had registered were given a fair chance to vote. He proposed that voting should be extended to a third day.

I described my efforts to persuade the NEC to agree to an extension, but counselled strongly against adding an extra day for voting: we were already exercised about the difficulties of maintaining ballot security over two days, and a second intervening night would complicate the problem further. I argued instead for the need to ensure proper logistical organisation, and described my own campaign to obtain additional support in air transport and communications.

In my meeting with President dos Santos, it was not until the last part of a wide-ranging review of all the pending problems that we reached the subject of the elections. I told him about my meetings with Minister Kassoma and Dr Savimbi and stressed that, since it had not been possible to register all eligible citizens given the decision not to extend registration (which I regretted), it was all the more essential to ensure that the same problems did not recur during voting and that all those who had been able to register would be given full opportunity to exercise their vote. The President said he agreed fully and assured me that the Angolan authorities would do everything possible to ensure maximum efficiency and coverage during the election proper. I remarked that, apart from the very necessary political commitment to this end, proper organisation and logistical support were essential, and outlined the present status of our efforts to obtain more help from abroad.

The general atmosphere permeating these two meetings gave grounds for a certain optimism, but this was almost immediately dashed when the meeting between the two leaders, scheduled for 24 August, did not come about. According to television reports, later confirmed to me by General N'dalu, Dr Savimbi simply did not turn up. He gave no prior notice of his non-attendance, nor did he send an explanation or apology. According to hearsay he was 'detained in Huambo on other business'. We were all left wondering about the meaning of this development which could be interpreted simply as a cavalier act of monumental bad manners, or, more likely, one with serious political implications. Savimbi's absence was all the more mystifying because he had told us of the things he intended to raise with President dos Santos, and had expressed the hope that a joint commitment might emerge that a 'government of national unity' would follow the elections, no matter who won. The aborted meeting was not held until 7 September, an ominous delay of two weeks at a particularly crucial time.

* * *

The failure to extend registration had repercussions in the field, especially in the provinces of Cuando Cubango, Moxico and Uige. Some of these took on a distinctly ugly character, as the following extracts from the notes of one of our electoral observers stationed in Luena, the provincial capital of Moxico, indicate:

13 August
Mr Maseka, President of the Provincial Electoral Council, appears at the UNAVEM camp looking troubled. Leo Pavillard, the UNDP Regional Coordinator, and one of the people from the electoral office fetching back the registration brigades, are being held 'hostage' at Lumbala N'Guimbo by an angry crowd who had walked many kilometres to register, but arrived too late. The pilot had managed to take off – with people hanging on to the tail while the plane was already moving – and return to Luena. The President of the Provincial Electoral Council and Sr. Christiano, the UNITA member on the Council, return to Lumbala and manage to calm things down, chiefly Sr Christiano who, Leo tells us later, gave the local UNITA people a good dressing down for not keeping order (this is completely UNITA 'territory'). The brigadistas are brought out on the next flight, clearly very shaken and vowing never to go back to Lumbala. Finally, after dark and guided in by car lights, the plane brings Leo and the electoral people.

A well-orchestrated and well-behaved group of UNITA supporters demonstrates at the gate of the UNAVEM compound, protesting that not all potential voters who wished to register have been given the opportunity to do so. They have not in Moxico. The decision not to extend the period of registration is a source of disappointment and resentment for UNITA. The area around the provincial capital, which mainly supports MPLA, is fully registered.

The Lumbala N'Guimbo hostage affair, and other similar incidents, kept us constantly on our toes in Luanda, and in order to defuse them we were frequently obliged to intercede with the NEC or with one or other of the two main contenders. Fortunately we were usually sucessful and none of these incidents blew up into major proportions, as they might have done if not swiftly and sensitively dealt with.

* * *

Another matter occupying much time was the drafting of an 'Electoral Code of Conduct'. Maria Grossi was particularly helpful in adapting the precedents in Namibia and Nicaragua to the special needs and circumstances of Angola. I constantly emphasised to all the parties the importance of adopting the code before the electoral campaign began. The draft was extensively debated in the NEC and all the parties, including the MPLA and UNITA, appeared to want the code. An insuperable problem arose, however, because some parties insisted that the

Government, and not just the MPLA, should also sign it. The Government contended that the code defined the conduct of the political parties and should therefore be signed only by them. It was never possible to resolve this difference of opinion, and so the electoral campaign had to start without an agreed code.

Voter education was another area of prime importance. Onofre dos Santos brought great enthusiasm and imagination to this task, as well as a talent for infusing it with a particularly Angolan flavour. A great hit in Luanda was the representation of a traditional meeting place, set up in the main thoroughfare, where participatory activities drew great crowds of people and dispensed civic education in a most pleasurable form. Civic education courses, often using the medium of short plays in local languages, and trial voting exercises were provided to provincial officials, who then trained more people there, and these in turn fanned out to the surrounding countryside. Our UNAVEM electoral teams were closely involved in these activities, providing advice and land and air transport.

Human rights had been cursorily dealt with in the Bicesse Peace Accords and did not figure at all in UNAVEM's mandate, but it was a subject that could not be ignored. Mustering our scarce human resources, and with the cooperation of the UN Centre for Human Rights in Geneva, Amnesty International and other NGOs, we organised Angola's first ever seminar on human rights. It began on 31 August, to coincide with the launching of the electoral campaign. The main inaugural speech was given by the then Minister of Justice Lázaro Dias, who impressed me as a pleasant, mild-mannered man. He was certainly extremely affable to me. Just how deceptive this impression was, I discovered to my pain some months afterwards when he attacked me virulently in the *Jornal de Angola*. But that is a tale for later.

The seminar could not achieve much of itself, but it brought the issue of human rights to public attention and encouraged Angolans to strengthen their own activities and pressure groups.

* * *

The electoral campaign opened officially on 29 August, as scheduled. Only two of the parties – the MPLA and UNITA – were equipped to carry out a full-blown campaign countrywide. Both were stepping up their rhetoric and increasing pressure on each other in the key central and northern areas. Both were also preparing contingency arguments to question the freedom and fairness of the elections if they lost. Not unnaturally they were also giving overt signs of their conviction that they would win, the MPLA now more genuinely, and with increasing confidence. UNITA had never been in doubt about its destiny, but most impartial observers were finding it increasingly difficult to predict who would win.

Both President dos Santos and Dr Savimbi embarked upon a punishing schedule of speaking at large rallies. They were shown nightly on television, and made interesting viewing. President dos Santos had always been considered a poor public speaker, diffident and dull, and this was thought to put him at a disadvantage *vis-à-vis* the flamboyance and charisma of Dr Savimbi. The campaign proved quite a revelation. José Eduardo dos Santos grew into the unaccustomed role of presidential candidate with extraordinary speed. The message was the same – a moderate one – but the content of his speeches and the manner of their delivery changed dramatically, and he began to look as if he was actually enjoying himself on the hustings. Yet, while exciting a rapturous response from the crowds, he contrived never to deviate from the calm demeanour of a statesman who knew what he was about and who preached peace, unity and prosperity. Of course much of the audience's response was orchestrated. Everyone had MPLA caps, T-shirts and flags. The MPLA had engaged a Brazilian public relations firm, which put on a highly organised campaign, modern style. Another factor helping dos Santos was the presence of his wife, who was intelligent as well as decorative and often campaigned on her own, especially among women's groups. The MPLA spread the load, despatching prominent party members to campaign in the regions of their own ethnic origin.

The followers of Dr Savimbi had always been well-drilled. The following description by a UNAVEM observer is fairly typical:

21 July
Savimbi visits Luena. We hang about all morning awaiting his arrival, having received an invitation from the UNITA office to meet him. We get short shrift in the line-up, not even eye contact as he shakes hands, in a pea-soup green suit, looking powerful. The 'rent-a-crowd', trucked in by UNITA from its strongholds away from Luena (which is MPLA territory) have been singing and dancing for hours in the sun coached by a conductor. Behind us in the line-up is a row of old men rather weakly fluttering little paper flags. It's not exactly a spontaneous demonstration. He then goes outside the airport to say a few words to the locals – a half-hour address in Chokwe, punctuated at intervals by chants of what sounds like 'yo-yo-yo, yay-yay-yay', which the crowd echoes.

Savimbi's first speeches were typically fiery, colourful and aggressive. He played the crowd, often speaking in the appropriate local language, introducing little jingles and catchy slogans, and even breaking into an undulating jig, which was greatly at odds with his large, rather ungainly frame but produced roars of delight from the assembled masses. As he often favoured a gaudy UNITA T-shirt, which accentuated his girth, and an equally gaudy campaign cap with an excessively large peak, the effect to a Western eye bordered on caricature, an impression accentuated, no doubt deliberately, by the state television, which took cruel delight in filming him from the most unflattering angles. But the crowds loved it and he swayed their emotions by sheer force of personality.

Savimbi never delegated the speech-making. His was unmistakably a one-man show. He was invariably accompanied by his closest advisors, all with high military rank, and often wore a gun holster, so the image of a guerilla leader remained strong, accentuated by the pugnacious nature of his utterances. As the campaign wore on he modified his style towards more nuanced and statesman-like declarations of intent, but later the more aggressive tone crept back. Many people thought, with the benefit of hindsight, that his contentious manner had alienated some voters who would otherwise have opted for UNITA. Although one suspects that Savimbi was probably less receptive of advice that dos Santos, both leaders, to varying degrees, tried to adapt their performance to offset the negative perceptions of their parties among the general public – disdain in the case of the MPLA and fear in that of UNITA.

The smaller political parties were active in varying degrees, but were handicapped by lack of resources. Difficulties of access to the provinces were a particular gripe, not only because of limited transport capabilities but also on account of alleged intimidation by both Government and UNITA supporters. Another preoccupation related to the Government-controlled national radio and television, whose impartiality they questioned. According to the procedures laid down by the Council of Social Communication, all parties had the right to equal time. Unfortunately much of the allotted television time was not fully used by many of the smaller parties, and audiences were treated to didactic films about handicrafts in unidentified corners of the globe to fill the unused spaces. Some who did use their time gave lack-lustre monologues, sadly lacking in charisma or even vestigial interest. For the rest of the time the Government TV and radio stations were producing their own programmes, including the news, which could be quite subtly slanted. In a country where very few people had TV sets, or could read newspapers, the radio was of particular importance. I considered it a major drawback – a tragedy even – that UNAVEM had no resources or mandate to operate its own radio station, as was so successfully done in Cambodia. UNITA had its well-established Vorgan radio and television service, but that too was biassed. What was desperately needed, in a situation in which hostile propaganda continued unabated, was a totally impartial radio channel, and this, sadly, was not possible.

The electoral campaign turned out to be more peaceful than any of us had dared to hope, but there were a number of heart-stopping incidents. Two occurred in the very first week of the campaign, in Huambo and Kuito/Bié. In the former case, in Longonjo, UNITA supporters attacked a convoy of cars returning from an MPLA rally with the leader of the MPLA campaign, Kundi-Payama. He was not harmed, but one person was killed. The incident was immediately investigated on the spot by the CCPM, in the presence of UNAVEM observers. The CCPM also managed to defuse an almost equally serious situation in Kuito/Bié, where an incident sparked off by UNITA firing at a FAPLA colonel approaching their headquarters resulted in tanks appearing on the streets and shots being fired at the governor's palace. The investigations showed that the origins of both events were complex and by no means one-sided. Both were symptomatic of a dangerous atmosphere where fear and mutual suspicion could lead to trigger-happy reactions.

The following notes by the UNAVEM observer in Luena illustrate how a small spark could erupt into a large fire:

> One day an argument arose in the open-air market on the outskirts of Luena over the price of some rice. Some UNITA supporters from the tail end of a rally became involved, insults were exchanged and in the resulting fight three people were killed. The police, heavily armed, intervened; in their turn FALA elements were brought in and soon an all-out battle was going on in Luena, its epicentre the police headquarters opposite the UNAVEM camp. The whole camp took refuge at the far corner of our office building, moving to one side or the other depending on the direction the shooting was coming from. At one point an agitated FAPLA general came into the camp to speak to the Colonel, who soon mustered up a few 'volunteers' to go out and try to make peace – to no avail. Driving out from a side street between UNITA and the police, their car was peppered with bullets and discretion dictated retreat. Two of the UNAVEM police had their car confiscated at gunpoint by the Angolan police (it was three days before they could persuade them to return it) and had to walk back to camp, dodging the fighting. The battle eventually petered out towards evening.

Tension rose higher as the election date drew nearer, heightened by the postponement of the meeting between President dos Santos and Dr Savimbi at the end of August, and further still when their vital last meeting before election day (to dissolve their respective armies and set up a joint command) remained in doubt until the very last moment.

In his last report to the SecurityCouncil before the election, released on 17 September,[2] the Secretary-General warned that the political situation had deteriorated significantly, particularly in Malange (where problems had again erupted in August), Huambo, Saurimo and the provinces of Benguela and Bié. There were reports of intimidation and provocation by both Government and UNITA supporters. The Secretary-General urged both leaders to foster restraint among their followers and in the media. It was also essential for all parties to pledge themselves to accept the results of the elections, as verified by UNAVEM II. The report drew attention to my unavailing efforts to have the registration period extended beyond 10 August, and stressed the consequent need to ensure that all those registered were able to vote. The President of the Security Council, in a statement on 20 September, expressed similar concerns and made similar appeals. The Council again underlined the importance of adequate logistical planning and support and urged the donor community to move speedily to provide the requirements identified in the Secretary-General's report.

Meanwhile, behind the organising framework of the elections, a tangled political web was evolving and we had to try to discern what was happening at what was, after all, the heart of the whole exercise.

11 Politics, Pride and Personalities

There is an alarming tendency in Western international policies – post Cold War, and in the midst of continuing economic recession in most parts of the world – to preach universal remedies in the starkest terms of black and white. On the economic side, the road to liberty and prosperity lies infallibly in reliance on market forces, structural adjustment, and economic stabilisation programmes aimed at reducing the role of government by dismantling the public sector and privatising everything in sight. On the political side it lies in embracing democracy and carrying out, as quickly as possible, 'free and fair', multiparty elections. The problem with this engagingly simple – and very possibly simplistic – approach is that when you try to follow the precepts, reality has the uncomfortable habit of getting in the way. There is also the bland and highly tempting assumption that democracy can be equated with the holding of elections. This is a very dangerous assumption. Democracy cannot be created overnight, least of all in places with a long history of authoritarian rule or civil war.

In Angola the process of transformation had to contend with both. On the Government side was the MPLA, moulded in the monolithic Marxist tradition and under the constant scrutiny and surveillance of the Soviet Union and Cuba ever since independence. On the other side was UNITA, headed by a larger-than-life leader, trumpeted by the United States – one of his two main foreign supporters – as the champion of democracy in southern Africa, a role in which Savimbi increasingly came to see himself. What this really meant was that he was considered to be the only bastion against the menace of creeping Communism in southern Africa. Certainly South Africa, the other main supporter of UNITA, saw its interests in cruder terms: at that stage in its history it could hardly set itself up as a defender of the democratic ideal. But labels and symbols, presented with a sufficiently smooth veneer of public relations and rationalisation, tend to stick, and the perceived image overrides reality. In this case the reality of sustaining a guerilla campaign against an entrenched government for 16 years, in unbelievably harsh terrain and living conditions, meant iron discipline and autocratic leadership. UNITA had these in full measure. It just would not have been possible for it to survive as a movement without them. Democracy did not figure large in UNITA's internal practices either.

As for the Government, it seemed to me that the admixture of Angolan and Lusitanian culture and temperament, deriving perhaps from the greater degree of *mestiçaje* and closer contact with the Portuguese of the coastal peoples, was hardly conducive to the strict maintenance of a rigid Communist regime, even at the height of the Cold War. Once those shackles were removed there was a pendulum-like reaction in the opposite direction, the kind of excess of individualism and pent-up democratic yearnings that from Vienna I had observed in Eastern Europe and the Soviet Union, which made it very difficult to organise anything. Of course hardliners remained, and could at times still exert considerable influence. But from my observation there was a great deal more liberalization, politically, on the government's side than on UNITA's, and it went far beyond *de rigueur* formalities such as changing the country's name from 'Republica Popular de Angola' to simply 'Republica de Angola' (this happened in 1992), or drafting a new constitution. But it still could not be called democracy.

With the exception of the FNLA, which was one of the original 'Big Three', most of the other parties were new, for no opposition had been brooked during the heyday of Communist rule. No less than 15 of them sported the word 'Democratico' or 'Democracia' somewhere in their official title, but in most cases there was only a rather vague notion of how to go about making it a reality in Angola. With 25 parties eventually legalised, of whom 18 presented candidates for the 220 seats in the future Legislative Assembly, fragmentation was rife and geographic coverage usually limited. The problem was often compounded by the presidential ambitions of party leaders, reflected in the phenomenal number of official presidential candidates. Some of the parties seemed to have been created as a springboard from which to launch such dreams, rather than as a political platform presenting principles and policy proposals on which the electorate could make a dispassionate judgement, as shown by the abysmal quality, and sometimes non-existence, of party political broadcasts.

All these factors demonstrated the enormous amount of ground to be covered before there could be any proper understanding of what democracy entailed. By the same token it pointed up how unrealistic were the arrangements made at Bicesse: a timetable of barely 16 months to lead up to elections designed to foster reconciliation and overcome the physical and psychological problems engendered during 16 years of war, with the onus for this near-miracle being placed on the two sides to this painful and deep-seated conflict.

Given the totally polarised and confrontational situation between the two main contenders for power, the most desirable course would have been the emergence of some kind of buffer between the two. Indeed the number of different political groupings that sprang up did seem to evidence a significant number of people whose motto could well be 'a plague on both your houses', but it was no doubt too much to expect them to perceive the wisdom of forging some kind of common cause between them. The very number of parties, and the highly personalised nature of most of them, together with their lack of political experience and maturity, conspired to put such solutions beyond reach.

We did our best to help and encourage these smaller parties, meeting with them frequently both individually and collectively. On 7 August 1992 I convened a meeting of all the registered parties. This was in the very last days of registration and coincided with the crisis over the withdrawal of the South African air support unit. The 'rec hall' was packed, the torrid atmosphere of the discussion mirrored in the stifling heat of the overcrowded room where the ancient air conditioning units, a legacy from the original oil camp, were, as usual, on the blink (there was always a difficult choice between leaving these units on, in which case their incredible noise drowned all debate, or switching them off and running the risk of tempers flaring). Twenty-four parties were invited and virtually all turned up, with the signal exception of the MPLA and UNITA. Clearly they considered this gathering of 'small fry' beneath their attention. This gave the smaller parties the chance to speak more openly than they might have done had the two 'biggies' been present, but it also meant that the opportunity to have a really tough and frank debate was lost. It was also depressingly obvious that fragmentation and self-interest were the order of the day.

The general concerns expressed by the smaller parties were remarkably similar:

- The elections had scant chance of being free and fair, mainly because of intimidation and difficulty of access for their members to major parts of the country.
- Delays in the confinement of troops, demobilisation and the formation of the new army raised the spectre of *three* armies being in existence in September.
- The slow extension of central administrative control to cover the whole country.
- The proliferation of weapons and the general decline in law and order.

The call, predictably, was for the UN to act more decisively and intervene directly. My constant explanations of the limitations of our mandate – not to mention resources – were of little avail. It seemed impossible to make people understand how constrained we were by decisions of the Security Council and the agreements reached at Bicesse. The clamour for a greater UN role became even more vociferous at this meeting, including a demand for the despatch of 'Blue Helmets' (that is, armed UN troops). Rather wearily I had to explain yet again that it was not in my gift to bring this about. This was met with general incredulity – no one seemed able, or willing, to grasp the fact that my role as Special Representative of the Secretary-General was far from omnipotent. I felt the irony of my position the more keenly having been convinced from the outset that UNAVEM needed wider powers and the wherewithal to carry them out. Both the Government/MPLA and UNITA came in for harsh criticism and fear was expressed about UNITA's intentions and the ruthlessness of its forces.

* * *

Considering the emphasis on individuals rather than policies, it was curious to note that few of the leaders showed charismatic qualities of leadership.

Holden Roberto was the party chief whom one expected to stand head and shoulders above the rest. The FNLA had been one of the three major Angolan liberation movements, along with the MPLA and UNITA, tracing its roots back to 1957, and had established the Revolutionary Government in Exile of Angola in 1962. UNITA had in fact been the last of the three to be formed, having been set up in 1966. Savimbi's first party affiliation had been with the FNLA: he had been for a time 'Foreign Minister' before breaking away in 1964.

Roberto had been a forceful leader and had received considerable support from abroad, from Zaire in particular but also some from the United States and China. During the period immediately preceding independence the FNLA had appeared to be the strongest movement militarily, if not politically. In November 1975, when Luanda had been a powder keg, FNLA forces advancing from the north had looked likely to take the city by storm. But they had been routed by Cuban/MPLA forces using Soviet guns, in what came to be known as the 'Battle of Death Road'. For a while the FNLA had made common cause with UNITA, but had then split away again. It had never recovered its former military strength and it was UNITA that had come to occupy the forefront as the main opponent of the MPLA Government. Holden Roberto had been exiled in France, reportedly a sick man.

For whatever reason, Holden Roberto did not appear in Luanda until the latter part of June 1992, when we had a long meeting. I found myself facing a slightly built, grey-haired man: 'spry' was the adjective that came to mind, borne out by the animated tone of his discourse, which, at his request, was conducted in French. Still, his was not a very imposing presence and it was hard to visualise this neatly suited, rather insignificant looking person, in the role described by Ryszard Kapuscinski, writing of the events of 1975 in *Another Day of Life*:

> Since morning, the whole city has been staggering and trembling, and the window panes are rattling, because the artillery has opened fire all out: Holden Roberto has announced that he will enter Luanda today. He's asked the populace to remain calm. Yesterday his planes dropped leaflets, pictures of Holden with the caption, 'God rules in Heaven, Holden rules on earth'[1].

While that vision had proved ephemeral, Roberto clearly felt he had a major role to play. He told me that the multiparty meeting in January 1992 had been his idea, and that he had written to the Secretary-General giving his strong view that the United Nations should have been given the mandate to *supervise* the peace process and the elections, supported by 'Blue Helmets'. He spoke a lot of good sense, but little about remedies for the problems he so eloquently described. For the future, he was pessimistic. His remarks were almost virulently anti-UNITA and anti-Savimbi. UNITA had many soldiers waiting abroad, he claimed, prophesying all too presciently: 'Il y aura une autre guerre' – 'There will be another war'. Savimbi, according to him, would never give up Jamba 'and the United States knows it very well'. He had some words of criticism, albeit less harsh, for the government: the MPLA was at one and the same time 'both football players and referee'. About the CCPM he was contemptuous: 'it simply doesn't work'. Holden Roberto's speeches before the elections frequently invoked reconciliation and the name of God (not in any personal comparisons this time), demonstrating a wish to be seen as a statesmanlike older figure, standing above the conflict.

Many of my other interlocutors among the smaller political parties talked good sense too. I think particularly of Luis dos Passos of the Partido Renovador Democratico (PRD), José Manuel Miguel of the Partido Social Democratico (PSD), Jorge Chicoty of the Foro Democratico Angolano (FDA) and Alberto Neto of the Partido Democratico Angolano (PDA). Some seemed to share Holden Roberto's rather apocalyptic vision of what the future might hold. It was therefore all the more incomprehensible that their common concerns did not add up to make a common cause.

Another interesting character with an historic, almost legendary past in the liberation struggle was Daniel Chipenda. Born into a leading Ovimbundu family, he had worked closely with Agostinho Neto but in February 1975 he and his troops, mainly Chokwe, had joined the FNLA. Later the Chipenda forces were incorporated into the South African forces as the Thirty-Second Battalion, or the 'Buffalo Battalion', and were used against SWAPO in support of UNITA. In 1987, in another of those bewildering *voltes face* so typical of Angola, Chipenda returned to the welcoming arms of the MPLA and was appointed Ambassador to Egypt.

I met him on the eve of the MPLA's Party Congress, at which a plan was reported to be afoot to make him Vice-President in order to attract the Ovimbundu vote, but he pooh-poohed this notion. It was true that the MPLA had no leader from the south but making him Vice-President would not, in his view, solve the problem. He personally did not think that national reconciliation could be obtained: rather the goal should be national *harmonisation* and he advocated a coalition government after the elections. Perhaps his most ominous remark was: 'The MPLA underestimate Savimbi. They are thinking like Europeans, not Africans, and they have been in power too long'. Unless this European bias was corrected, he considered that plans to use him to attract the Ovimbundu were unlikely to succeed. At the Congress the idea of making Chipenda Vice-President was shelved. Instead he was entrusted with the organisation of the MPLA's electoral campaign, with Lopo de Nascimento as his deputy. This should have put him in a very key position to influence the direction of thinking and policy in the party. But Chipenda's new functions did not last long. Before July was out Chipenda had resigned from the MPLA and joined the swarm of presidential hopefuls, proposed at the last minute by the Partido Nacional Democratico Angolano (PNDA).

Probably the only other candidate known to the public was Luis dos Passos, who had agreed to run on the resignation of its former leader, Joaquin Pinto de

Andrade. Luis dos Passos' most eye-catching public appearance during his candidature was almost certainly at his sumptuous social wedding to a beautiful and equally telegenic bride, attended by everyone who was anyone. Alas, not by me! My invitation arrived too late – a common hazard in Luanda.

There was only one woman candidate among the 13, despite the key role played by Angolan women in national life. She was Mrs Analia Maria Caldeira de Vitoria P. Simeão, an attractive and personable lady, invariably accompanied by her highly eccentric husband, whose presence could be guaranteed to enliven any gathering in unexpected ways. He spent the general meeting with the parties drawing caricatures and slogans, which he presented to me afterwards. They were engagingly pro-feminist, a refreshing note in an overwhelmingly 'macho' society, but it was not certain that all of his antics advanced his wife's candidature.

The number of presidential candidates became reduced from 13 to 11 due to the withdrawal of Dr Andre Kilandamoko of the Partido Social Democratico Angolano (PSDA) and Engineer Mfulupinga N'Landa Victor of the Partido Democratico para lo Progresso da Alianza Nacional Angolana (PDP-ANA), who announced that their parties would support Dr Savimbi, as did the Convenção Nacional Democratica de Angola (CNDA), led by Mr Paulino Pinto João. The candidate of the Partido Social Democratico (PSD), Do José Manuel Miguel, had his candidature rejected by the Supreme Popular Tribunal because of a past conviction for raping his niece. The Partido Angolano Independiente (PAI), led by Mr Adriano Parreira, said it would support the MPLA.

The real issue remained the struggle between the giants. The MPLA, as we have seen, had its own share of internal upheavals and dissentions. UNITA suffered a much greater jolt with the defection in February of two of Dr Savimbi's closest henchmen and confidants, General Miguel N'Zau Puna and General Antonio Fwaminy da Costa Fernandes. Both were Cabindans, both had been with Savimbi virtually since the birth of UNITA and both had held consistently senior positions in the movement. The two defectors announced that they had left because Savimbi had ordered the killing of two young men prominent in the movement and their families: Tito Chingunji and his brother-in-law, Wilson dos Santos, both well-known outside Angola. N'Zau Puna publicly blamed Savimbi's guards for the killings. After a trial in Jamba – allegedly presided over by Salupeto Pena – Chingunji's two children, one a baby, were said to have been done to death by their heads being bashed against a tree. It transpired that, over a number of years, nearly all Chingunji's family – his parents and all but one of his nine siblings – had met their deaths in what was claimed to be a vendetta by Savimbi. The two defectors had other fearsome tales of cruelty and blood lust to recount, among them allegations of women being burned alive for witchcraft.

There could hardly have been a more damaging blow than this to Savimbi, the man supported by influential members of the US Congress as an exemplary anti-communist 'freedom fighter' and defender of democracy and human rights in

Angola. The US Secretary of State, James Baker, wrote to Savimbi demanding a full account of what had happened to the two men.

UNITA closed ranks immediately and embarked on a blanket operation of damage limitation. Abel Chivukuvuku was quickly appointed to succeed da Costa Fernandes as 'Foreign Minister'. Reemerging from Jamba after an unexplained six-week absence, which in retrospect must have been linked to the events just related, but was then described as 'a period of reflection', Dr Savimbi insisted that there was no crisis in UNITA. At a press conference in Luanda he claimed that he had had nothing to do with the violent deaths of Chingunji and dos Santos, and had been unaware of them until late February. He accused one of his own accusers, N'Zau Puna, of having carried out the killings in November, when he himself had been in Luanda, not returning to Jamba until 20 February. N'Zau Puna and da Costa Fernandes contended that the killings had taken place in August, when Savimbi had still been in Jamba, and that he had ordered them. Tragically there was no way in which any outsider could penetrate Jamba to undertake an independent investigation. Savimbi rode the storm, as he had ridden so many in the past and would continue to do in the future. But it may well be that these renewed allegations of ruthlessness and cruelty cost him votes among those outside Jamba who felt secure enough about the secrecy of the ballot, and who might previously have been UNITA sympathisers.

There were to be more mundane complications. I was repeatedly asked by the President and the Deputy Minister of the Interior, 'Petroff', to provide protection for the two defectors, but there was no way in which the UN could assume this responsibility. Despite repeated allegations by both the Government and UNITA that the other side was plotting to kill them, they both survived to tell the tale. Tony da Costa Fernandes is now the Angolan Ambassador in London. The two generals had formed a group called 'UNITA – Tendencia de Relexao Democratica', whose declared aim was to militate for the democratisation of UNITA, but it did not seem to make much public impact, although the UNITA leadership made clear in the CCPM its extreme irritation that the Government/MPLA had assisted the two dissenters to set up offices in Luanda, flying the UNITA flag.

UNITA eventually held its first Convention from 29 August to 1 September in Lobito and adopted an electoral manifesto. The final communiqué recommended that UNAVEM II be extended, a government of national unity formed, human rights protected, the antiriot police abolished immediately, freedom of the church and of public information guaranteed, foreign relations established with all countries except Cuba, and a solution to the Cabinda question negotiated with the FLEC.

Both parties boasted well-organised propaganda machines. The Government had the newspaper *Jornal de Angola*, the radio programme 'Angola Combatiente' and state television, while UNITA had its 'Vorgan' television and radio station, – The 'Voice of the Black Cockerel', transmitting out of Jamba, and began to publish a weekly newspaper in Luanda: *Terra Angolana*.

* * *

The release of all civilian and military prisoners in accordance with the Bicesse Accords was a particularly sensitive issue that occupied long hours of often fruitless debate in the CCPM. Overseeing the actual release was the business of the International Committee of the Red Cross (ICRC), but we often had to provide transport, or information on the spot. By April 1992 the Government had released 940 prisoners and UNITA 3099. Both sides claimed that the other still held prisoners, however, and the ICRC had its own list of missing persons.

Problems over the release by UNITA of 20 Government military and civilian prisoners in Jamba, including one woman, blew up into a major but typical crisis in July. After many postponements it was agreed that a CCPM delegation and an ICRC representative would fly to Jamba on 11 July to witness the release. As recounted to me later by Major Ribeiro, our chief police observer, it was a dramatic experience. The group came back with only 12 of the 20 prisoners, resulting in traumatic televised scenes at Luanda airport among the families who had been waiting for hours for husbands, sons and brothers whom they had not seen for many years. It proved impossible to clarify whether this calamitous outcome was the result of UNITA machinations (it inexplicably took two hours to refuel the plane at Jamba during which several prisoners 'changed their mind'), genuine human reasons (some of the men had formed 'second families' in Jamba) or logistical bungling by the Government (the Government plane was two hours late); it may well have been a combination of all three.

Small wonder that the release of prisoners was yet another issue undermining mutual trust that was still not resolved before the elections.

* * *

The extension of the central administration to the rest of the country was another of those amorphous topics that occupied hours and hours of the CCPM's time, causing long, impassioned speeches and reams of virtually illegible documents. (Document reproduction techniques in the CCPM were decidedly dodgy, which, coupled with invariably last-minute circulation, was perhaps why every agenda item had to be prefaced by someone reading out loud the verbatim text of the relevant report. Or was this some hallowed Portuguese tradition, inherited from colonial times? Anyway, it was the most monumental time-waster.)

A big effort was made to meet the original deadline of 20 June. A special CCPM meeting was held on 2 June with the Minister for Territorial Administration, Paulo Kassoma. At that date, nine of Angola's 165 municipalities and scores of its 542 communes were said not to be covered by government administration, but the numbers fluctuated every week. The Government exerted pressure by the simple but effective means of stipulating that there could be no registration of voters in places where its administration was not effectively installed.

The two sides agreed to form a special group, which, accompanied by representatives of the three observer countries and of UNAVEM, would visit 'problem' municipalities and communes to investigate the situation *in loco* and find practical solutions. UNAVEM had perforce to offer the use of its small fleet of planes and helicopters to transport the group, a job quite outside its purview, there being no others available.

The situation varied enormously from place to place, depending on local circumstances and the personalities and attitudes of the local UNITA bosses. Even when Government administrative personnel found a reasonable reception, however reluctant, they faced other problems. Often they were dumped in some outlandish location without offices, pay or food supplies, and were conveniently forgotten by the central or provincial authorities. It is hard to believe that the Government did not have the means to supply these needs. A more likely explanation was customary inefficiency and a generally lackadaisical approach to such matters. Our Commanding Officer in Luena told me of how he had, at the Government's request, transported a lone administrator in his UNAVEM helicopter to a remote place in Eastern Moxico, deep in UNITA country. Days later the man staggered back to Luena, on foot, ragged and hungry, having received no money or food from the Government and having been intimidated by a hostile population.

The overall situation had changed little by the time the Secretary-General presented his report of 17 September to the Security Council.[2] All 163 municipalities had been covered but 54 of the 542 communes – that is, one in ten – remained without Government administration. This was yet another example of logistical deficiencies acquiring political significance. In an emergency CCPM meeting on 16 September, the Minister for Territorial Administration took the line that the situation had deteriorated since registration with the withdrawal of some administrators, due to hostile local reception, while UNITA maintained its familiar stand that, where people had registered, they should also be given facilities to vote. After a lot of wrangling another group was set up, this time to reinstate the Government's representatives in communes abandoned since registration. UNAVEM observers accompanied and monitored this process. Nonetheless, as late as 23 September, six days before the elections, UNITA was complaining that several more administrators had left their posts, for reasons not of UNITA's making. General N'dalu maintained that they had been forced out, but added, a little wearily I thought, that the Government was no longer going to insist on 'effective administration' being in place: just one administrator would do to justify the holding of the vote. In this not very satisfactory way the matter was patched together, virtually on the eve of the elections.

* * *

The arguments over extending central administration opened up an even more explosive issue: Jamba. Jamba had been, to all intents and purposes, almost a separate kingdom, or enclave, and most certainly a law unto itself. In the old days you had to pass through immigration and passport control at the airport, a practice that continued for a while even after the signing of the Bicesse Accords. Dr Savimbi had expressed special concern about the extension of the central administration to Jamba. He was, not unnaturally, keen to ensure that the inhabitants of Jamba should not lose the opportunity to exercise their vote in what was expected to be 100 per cent support for him and for UNITA. The issue went wider, however, than merely planting a token administrator there. The Bicesse Accords stipulated that there should be free circulation of people and goods and Jamba was notoriously a 'closed shop', difficult to get into and even more difficult to leave (unless you happened to be a specially invited guest). This question was not within our mandate, but again we could hardly dismiss it as irrelevant. In his personal letter to Dr Savimbi of 9 September, the Secretary-General said he was aware of President dos Santos' concern over Jamba and of Dr Savimbi's frequent declarations that Jamba was open to anyone; tensions would be greatly eased if this could be demonstrated in a practical way. It could be no coincidence that Dr Savimbi not only raised the matter with me on 10 September, but also told the NEC President that Jamba would be open for all political parties to campaign there.

In the CCPM General N'dalu welcomed Dr. Savimbi's statement and urged some rapid follow-up. Engineer Salupeto Pena took the comfortable position that Jamba was completely open, that the parties had only to go there. But he also reminded everyone, rather less encouragingly, that Jamba was a long way away and that even if one managed to fly to the airport, the town itself was still far distant and there was no transport between the two. This distinctly blinding glimpse of the obvious was followed by an elaborately polite, but disingenuous explanation that UNITA, to its profound regret, was unable to provide any assistance. Superficially the matter appeared to boil down to one of practicality rather than principles, but that was clearly a far too simplistic interpretation. The three observers insisted that this problem must be resolved if the elections were to be free and fair. Jeff Millington threw this hot potato into my lap without any prior consultation, proposing that UNAVEM should act as 'intermediaries and interlocutors', and suggesting that we could provide transport. Caught on the hop I offered a UNAVEM aircraft to ferry representatives of the CCPM and interested political parties to Jamba. I recognised that a visit undertaken with the elections only 12 days or less away smacked of tokenism, but even a token appearance of representatives of other political affiliations would be important, as General N'dalu was quick to agree, and could not fail to make a dramatic impression on the cloistered inhabitants of Jamba. The idea was welcomed in the CCPM, including by UNITA. I also talked to other political parties, most of whom were warmly supportive. Some were already trying to organise an initiative of their own, including a 'peace march' to Jamba.

Despite much feverish activity on all sides, however, none of it happened. Once again I had, as in the case of the 'hidden army', the disconcerting experience of the Government pushing very hard on an issue, and then, when one provided the practical means of solution, inexplicably lapsing into masterly inactivity. As for the political parties, who had also protested loud and long about the inaccessibility of Jamba, I suspect that when the opportunity was opened up an element of caution, and perhaps even of fear, crept in. And then time ran out on us.

* * *

It was not only UNAVEM and the observers on the spot who were trying to steer the process in the right direction. Any number of would-be intermediaries flocked in, in well-meaning attempts at mediation.

Our most diligent and regular visitors were the Troika: Assistant Secretary Herman Cohen of the United States, Minister Durão Barroso of Portugal and Ambassador Karasin of the Russian Federation. Their visits were strategically timed to coincide with key milestones in the timetable of the peace process. They always met with the two leaders and each time issued a declaration giving credit where due, but pinpointing the failings and enjoining the two sides to do better in whatever areas they were found to be particularly deficient.

The three seemed to work in great harmony, though they were as different as chalk from cheese. Ambassador Cohen was the archetypal elder statesman who had seen it all; he had had a long experience of Africa and had been associated from 1987 with the latter part of the complicated negotiations on Namibia and Angola, conducted by Chester Crocker, whom he had succeeded as Assistant Secretary of State for Africa in 1989. A wise and gentle man, he showed a genuine affection for Africa and Angola, and when one penetrated his reserve, one discovered a marvellous sense of humour. It would be hard to imagine a greater contrast to this self-effacing career diplomat than Durão Barroso, a brilliant, self-confident young man who had conquered some of the highest offices of state at a very early age. His was a modern, forward-looking vision, blessed with imagination as well as a natural aptitude for negotiation which he had applied to excellent effect in spearheading the year-long negotiations, at Bicesse.

Karasin fell somewhere in between the two. Russia's role in the Angolan situation, because of the latest turn of events in its own territory, was more historical than actual. He was a seasoned diplomat, had a pleasant, low-key manner and, when he did intervene, spoke much good sense.

I found it agreeable and helpful to work with them, and had special cause to be grateful to Cohen and Durão Barroso, who both went out of their way to support me outside Angola and bolster my scarce resources.

* * *

The various religious groups, who were experiencing a kind of renaissance after the years of Marxist rule, also did their best to foment peace and reconciliation. Christianity had been imposed on Angola by the colonists, but native religions and beliefs remained strong, intertwined with the imported faith. It is estimated that some 40–45 per cent of Angolans are Catholic; they are mostly in Western Angola. Protestants are estimated at between 10 per cent and 17 per cent. The latter's missionaries tended to do their proselytising in the interior, being driven to those remoter places by the Catholic domination of the areas near the coast. Thus there was a strong Protestant following in the Ovimbundu tribe and many members of UNITA received their early education in Protestant schools. Savimbi's father had been converted to Protestantism and founded churches and schools along the Benguela railroad, for which he worked. Savimbi himself made his first sortie abroad, to study in Lisbon, on a scholarship from the United Church of Christ.

In the years following independence the Catholic hierarchy in Angola had been constantly at odds with the MPLA Government, but the situation began to ease with the signing of the Bicesse Accords and the decision to hold democratic elections. UNITA had declared its tolerance for all religions in 1983.

The Catholic Cardinal and Archbishop of Luanda, Monsenhor Alexandre do Nascimento, was a very influential figure, whom I visited at fairly regular intervals in his rose-coloured palace tucked away in a quiet cobbled square of old Luanda. I also met delegations from other denominations, who asked to see me from time to time and were often composed of a mix of foreigners and Angolan citizens. All the different religious affiliations did their best to support – and later tried to save – the process.

The Cardinal was a large, powerfully built man with a broad, calm countenance, so black against the snowy white of his soutane that he might have been carved in ebony. A native of Malange, he spoke slowly, in measured tones, as if weighing the meaning of every word. When we first met he was busy organising the visit of the Pope, who arrived on 4 June and stayed six days. All public activity came to a virtual halt. His itinerary took him to Huambo, Lubango, M'banza Congo (the site of the first church in Angola) and Cabinda. His consistent message was a general appeal for peace, tolerance, forgiveness and reconciliation. The Pope was received by President dos Santos, and there was more than a hint of surrealism about the whole event, not least in the Angolan red and black flag on the side of the aircraft provided by the Government, which still prominently sported the hammer and sickle. The visit was a huge popular success. Hundreds of thousands of people turned out, and for a few days much of the country lived in a paroxysm of religious fervour. This was perhaps not surprising. What was unexpected was that the visit was organised with a degree of efficiency to which even a short stay in Angola made one become swiftly unaccustomed.

The culminating point was a huge celebration of Mass in Luanda, in the vast square dominated by the unfinished monument to President Agostinho Neto, like some abandoned lunar rocket. A red-carpeted and canopied dais was constructed for the occasion. Nearby, massed choirs – perilously perched on rickety stands but swaying energetically and rhythmically to the music, regardless of their imminent collapse – bellowed out joyous melodies more reminiscent of African revivalist chants than Catholic sacraments, under the enthusiastic batons of priests and nuns, soberly clad in religious robes, but also carried away in an ecstasy of rhythm. People had been pouring in since dawn: whole families, decked out in their colourful best; large groups from schools and churches, uniformed in the papal colours of yellow and white; and hundreds of priests and nuns. The huge square was a cacophony of colours, a swaying mass of exalted humanity. It was estimated that at least half a million people attended. President dos Santos was present, but Dr Savimbi was not.

For a few days the whole of this turbulent country experienced an extraordinary lull. To many it was an augury that presaged new hope, symbolised most tellingly in the extensive television coverage of the Pope standing between the President and Dr Savimbi and surrounded by other Angolan political leaders. Others predicted that the Pope's visit would be followed by orchestrated campaigns of destabilisation on both sides, and it was they who were nearer the truth.

* * *

As if on cue, immediately after the Pope's departure the atmosphere between the Government and UNITA deteriorated dramatically. The CCPM meeting on 11 June was the most acrimonious I had yet attended. UNITA presented a memorandum claiming that the Government had launched an all-out campaign to harass UNITA supporters all over the country between 3 and 9 June, the inference being that the security clampdown surrounding the Pope's visit had been used to make life uncomfortable for its people. Salupeto Pena recited a long litany of UNITA's complaints, stressing repeatedly that, for the first time, the Peace Accords were in real danger and that there would be a return to armed struggle.

As if all this were not bad enough, UNITA's General 'Gato', a good-looking, rather fiery young man who had replaced Chivukuvuku as deputy head of UNITA's delegation to the CCPM, entered the fray, excitedly waving a photocopy of an article in that very day's *Independent* newspaper of London, with a banner headline proclaiming: 'West warned of plot to kill Jonas Savimbi'.

This did not come as a complete surprise to me. Ten days earlier, when I had stopped in London on my way back from Washington to lobby the Britiish Government for more logistical support for the elections, the Foreign Office officials I met had dropped some dark but not very explicit hints about information they had, pointing to orchestrated troubles later that month, designed to make postponement of the election inevitable, including a possible attempt by MPLA elements to assassinate Savimbi. They had been considering a démarche to the Angolan Government, either alone or with other governments. While we too had heard disquieting rumours of possible trouble afoot (though certainly nothing as serious as an assassination attempt), solid facts were hard to come by since we had no 'intelligence' capacity in the military sense of the term. On my return to Luanda I had learned from the British Ambassador, John Flynn, that he had been instructed to see President dos Santos. Now these suspicions had erupted in the international press and the CCPM.

In the CCPM General N'dalu gave UNITA an equally vigorous and hard-hitting reply, along with assurances that there was no campaign against UNITA. The need for tight security during the Pope's visit had led to a number of arrests, and not only of UNITA supporters. General N'dalu was particularly vehement in rejecting any suggestion of a plot to eliminate the UNITA leader; he was the one man on the Government side whom the UNITA leaders held in some esteem, and his words always carried weight with them. But they were not easily mollified on this occasion, and it was only after further heated exchanges that agreement was reached that UNITA would provide further evidence of the allegations, which the two sides would discuss outside the orbit of the CCPM. Whenever some truly grave issue came up, they always sorted it out amongst themselves in private, by-passing the CCPM, which was very much a talking-shop, although perhaps useful in allowing steam to be let off before the real issues were tackled.

I was never able to ascertain satisfactorily whether there was any fire behind the considerable smoke billowing around the alleged assassination plot. At any rate, nothing happened, though the incident inevitably accentuated UNITA's already deep-seated paranoia – alleged lethal intentions against the UNITA leader were to be a recurrent theme during the rest of the CCPM's existence.

* * *

The UN Secretary-General, Dr Boutros-Ghali, was also following the situation from afar and could be relied on to intervene, through telephone calls and personal letters to the two leaders, when I advised him that the situation required it. A more direct way of influencing affairs would have been for him to pay a personal visit to Angola. When he had spoken to me at the time of my appointment he had said jovially, 'I can at least promise you one thing – I shall come and see you there'. He had, it seemed, pleasant and nostalgic memories of Luanda, which he had visited as an official guest of the Government when Egyptian Deputy Minister of Foreign Affairs. Indeed he had waxed quite lyrical: 'A beautiful city', he had mused, time having perhaps blurred his recollection, or possibly the rigours of protocol and an official programme had protected him from close contact with the daily squalor of that otherwise idyllic setting, 'You will love it'.

During the first months of my time in Luanda this visit was still very much on the cards. The President raised it with me at every audience, reiterating his great desire that it should happen soon. Dr Savimbi was equally keen. The problem was choosing the right time. We never seemed to be able to fix a date that would be appropriate in the calendar of the peace process and could be accommodated in the Secretary-General's own heavily crowded schedule. Once the electoral process was in full swing it became increasingly hard to choose a timing that would not be liable to some political interpretation. Timing in relation to other visits also had to be considered – the Pope's for instance, and there was also a possibility of the Portuguese President, Mario Soares, coming to give a boost to the process. Although President dos Santos in particular was not happy about it, it was eventually decided that the visit should take place after the elections. As a result it never happened. That was unfortunate, especially as the Secretary-General visited most of the other main peacekeeping missions in operation at that time, but the circumstances made it unavoidable.

* * *

As electoral fever became more fraught, so did the situation of UNAVEM as it tried to maintain its impartial stance. Out of the blue strong criticisms of our supposed inclinations towards UNITA began to circulate on the Government side.

The row blew up without warning when President dos Santos visited Luena on Saturday 22 August. Local *sobas* (tribal leaders) and a group of women complained to him that UNAVEM was siding with UNITA in Moxico province. The same allegations were made to me, publicly and very disagreeably, when I visited Luena on Friday 28 August as part of my hectic round of visits to all provincial capitals and UNAVEM regional commands to ensure that everything on our side was ready for the big test of the election. The culminating point was a meeting with local officials and party representatives, where the Vice Governor violently accused UNAVEM of favouring UNITA, mainly it seemed by giving lifts to

FALA soldiers but refusing to do the same for FAPLA! He also cited the actions of someone who did not even work for UNAVEM. In refreshing, if bewildering, contrast the local electoral authorities were loud in their praise of UNAVEM'S work, the only voice in support of the Vice Governor coming in a blurred gabble from an individual whose incoherence could only be attributed to the local brandy, to which he was reputedly very partial. When later, in front of TV cameras at the airport, I challenged the Vice Governor to produce more substantial arguments for his attack he could only come up with one example: UNAVEM had not retrieved the registration brigades stranded in the bush. This gave me an excellent opportunity to point out that UNAVEM was once more being blamed for something that was the responsibility of the national authorities, but I forbore to mention that the problem would never have arisen had these same authorities not cancelled, at no notice, the South African air support.

On my return to Luanda I learned that on the previous day, 27 August, President dos Santos had joined in this attack during a political rally in Malange, criticising UNAVEM as 'impotent and ineffectual' and saying it must be 'perfected'. His remarks had provoked a very ugly response by the crowds: Immediately after the rally people had driven past our camp in Malange, shouting threats and abuse. Later, strong indications emerged that this episode had been orchestrated by Government security forces through the mysterious and sinister 'Fubu'.

A rising crescendo of sarcastic articles against UNAVEM in the official Government press and vicious attacks on the radio followed, but not one of them cited specific instances. It was crystal clear that all these 'coincidences' added up to a deliberate, if ill-advised, strategy on the part of the Government and the MPLA that related to the elections. Several diplomats expressed their fear that the intention was to muzzle UNAVEM in its role of verifying that the voting was free and fair, and they linked the attacks to the Government's reluctance to accept some of the air support proffered (adequate air coverage would ensure that voting took place in remote areas, which were primarily UNITA's stronghold).

We concluded that it was best to ride out the storm as coolly and calmly as possible, and that the necessary defence of UNAVEM must avoid putting it on a collision course with the President and the Government. I despatched a personal letter to President dos Santos, which was, with some difficulty, delivered to the presidential palace (it was Saturday and even in moments of acute crisis the offices there seemed strictly to observe a five-day week!) I told him that I had learnt with deep concern of his dissatisfaction with UNAVEM, and was therefore seeking an urgent audience to clarify the grounds for it and agree on remedial action. I could only conclude that there must have been some recent development of which I was unaware since, when I had last seen him on 21 August (only six days before the speech), the President had made no criticisms but rather had requested an extension of UNAVEM after the election. I stressed the dangers of the media campaign against UNAVEM, which was based on flimsy evidence or a misunderstanding of our role, as well as the grave implications for the security and morale of my staff.

A flurry of diplomatic activity followed. The three observers and several key Ambassadors made their views known to the Government in no uncertain terms. Theirs was much more than a quixotic defence of the United Nations. The interpretation among many was that the Government wanted to manipulate UNAVEM as part of a Government/MPLA strategy to control the election process, and prepare for possible defeat. If it lost it could say that UNAVEM was partly to blame and its verification faulty; if it won, then the argument could be that UNAVEM had improved its performance after intervention by the President. These tactics were, however, seen as dangerous because, if the MPLA won, its expressed doubts about UNAVEM, which would have to validate the results, could boomerang and present UNITA with a useful counterargument.

The Secretary-General was attending a meeting of the non-aligned countries in Indonesia, and Mig Goulding and I arranged for him to take the matter up with Prime Minister Van Dunem, who was leading the Angolan delegation there. At their meeting on 31 August the Prime Minister assured the Secretary-General that his Government had full confidence in me and in my objectivity. It did, however, object to the behaviour of certain UN observers, but again he did not substantiate his allegations.

The attacks were discussed at a CCPM Heads of Delegation meeting the next day. The three observers expressed their keen dismay and General N'dalu was visibly discomfited, while UNITA was in the comfortable position (for UNITA, that is, but certainly not for us) of springing to the defence of UNAVEM. Dr Savimbi, to our acute embarrassment, was doing likewise in his frequent campaign speeches.

There was no prospect of my seeing the President, who had gone to Seville to inaugurate the Angolan stand at the International Fair, and so I asked for an appointment with Foreign Minister 'Loy', which was granted with extraordinary alacrity on 3 September. We went over the ground once again and the Minister assured me that it was certainly not the Government's intention to weaken UNAVEM and that the President would make a statement to that effect in a day or two.

Meanwhile Victor Lima, without any official word to us, was well on his way to New York, where he presented to Assistant Secertary General Alvaro de Soto a letter from the President to the Secretary-General. Contrary to what the Prime Minister had suggested in Djakarta, this did not expatiate upon UNAVEM's reputed failings, but complaints about UNITA's conduct. Lima did raise the UNAVEM issue orally, but again without anything specific being said. The Government proposed that an enquiry should be made into the accusations against UNAVEM. The problem was that chapter and verse about the 'accusations' were never forthcoming, neither then nor later.

One great consolation was that we had the prompt and wholehearted support of the Secretary-General himself. He cabled a message from Moscow and, on his arrival later that night in Paris, telephoned to tell me personally that I enjoyed his complete confidence, and to wish me *bon courage*. He must have been even more exhausted than I and his words of encouragement, and his resigned comment that this kind of attack was the normal fare of peacekeepers, did much to restore my deflated spirits. The Secretary-General also referred to the incident in his report to the Security Council of 17 September, pointing out that the role of an impartial observer is always difficult, being open to different interpretations by the two sides, and reiterating his fullest confidence in me and the UNAVEM staff. He also issued a strongly supportive press statement in New York, which was widely publicised in Angola.

Support also came from other quarters outside Angola. The Troika, who visited Angola at that time, made no bones about their dismay over the attacks during their discussions with government authorities, and in their communiqué they reaffirmed their trust in UNAVEM. Likewise the President of the Security Council issued a strongly worded statement on 20 September expressing support for UNAVEM and enjoining both sides to ensure our security, a very necessary injunction since hostile attacks on our staff in the provinces were mounting, something that had never happened before, while government media continued to churn out derogatory comments about UNAVEM.

On 15 September I received a reply from President dos Santos to my letter to him of 29 August. It was dated 8 September and was delivered through an unlikely channel, being handed to my spokesman a week later by the special assistant of the President's Secretary for External Relations. The tone of the letter was courteous in the extreme, the argument as circuitous as the route by which it had reached me. Blaming UNITA for acts of violence and unauthorised movements of troops, the President said that 'many negative reactions and complaints' had been received of the 'passive attitude' of UNAVEM, which the population did not consider to be impartial or neutral. The main message was that there was no hostile attitude to UNAVEM, only a desire on the part of the Government to 'restore' UNAVEM's authority and prestige.

My requested audience with President dos Santos took place on 23 September. The President was more concerned to discuss the overall situation and the subject of the criticism of UNAVEM came up only at the end. I said that the unsubstantiated allegations were prejudicing UNAVEM's negotiating influence, and seriously affecting the morale, security and safety of its personnel. It would be helpful if the President could make a strong supportive statement. The President replied, without hesitation, that he intended to do this. Throughout the meeting he was extremely positive about UNAVEM. It was as if the incident, with whose consequences we were still wrestling, had never happened!

But no Presidential statement ever came out in support of UNAVEM. Violent abuse, threats and ocsasional acts of violence continued to rain down on UNAVEM personnel. We somehow learned to live with them and tried to 'muddle through' in the age-old and well-perfected tradition of Angola, a phrase that was beginning to acquire an ominous familiarity. It was also rapidly becoming the *leitmotiv* of the UN's peacekeeping mission there, for the simple but cogent reason that we had been left with no alternative.

* * *

Another fainter, but constant theme was 'What to do about Cabinda?' This oil-rich enclave covers 14 000 square kilometres and has only 120 000 inhabitants, but a secondary war was being waged there, diverting resources from the main task in hand and providing ample fuel for new acrimony. Furthermore, no matter who won the elections, the survival of Cabinda, with its vast oil revenues, as an integral part of the Angolan economy was vital to the country's reconstruction, development and potential prosperity. The matter was not within UNAVEM's mandate but failure to hold simultaneous elections in Cabinda because of the ongoing conflict could have serious consequences for the future stability of the country, and so compromise the peace settlement.

The subject of Cabinda came up regularly in the CCPM, and in every one of the periodic meetings I had with the two leaders. The UNITA was leadership clearly caught between the temptation, on the one hand, to exploit the potential for making trouble for the Government, whether by accusations of non-compliance with the Peace Accords, because FAPLA troops were not confined to assembly areas, or by outright meddling in the conflict; and, on the other, the realisation that, if they made too much mischief, they would be storing up trouble for themselves if, as they hoped and believed, they came to power after the elections. The Government, for its part, sought a political as well as a military solution.

Representatives of the CCPM visited Cabinda on 27 May and decided that the Government's troops should be partly assembled and that priority should be given to Cabinda in deploying units from the new army, thus meeting the security requirements to fight the FLEC in a way compatible with the Peace Accords and acceptable to both the Government and UNITA. (This sensible decision was subsequently foiled by the interminable delays in getting the FAA established.) A Provincial Electoral Council was established and began the process of registration, despite threats from the FLEC.

On the political front various initiatives were taken. On 14 April the President told me that he was trying to negotiate a settlement directly, but in June 'Petroff', then the Vice-Minister of the Interior and himself a Cabindan, told me that it had come to naught, although he seemed sanguine about a viable solution being found through a conference in Gabon, due to start on 18 June. I was given to understand that only Cabindans were involved, including the various factions of the FLEC, but on 19 June the *Jornal de Angola* announced that President dos Santos had spent some hours in Gabon the previous day in connection with the meeting.

Early in July, President dos Santos and other Government leaders held talks in Luanda with moderate FLEC leaders, the FLEC President and founder, Rank Frank, and Francisco Sebastião of the Organização De União Nacional De Cabinda, but the radical leader of the FLEC/FAC, N'zita Tiago, was not involved. A more formal meeting between the various factions of the FLEC and Government representatives was planned to be held in Geneva on 29 July, but was postponed until early August while efforts were made primarily through the French Government to persuade N'zita Tiago, who lived in Paris, to attend. The Secretary-General offered, through me, his good offices but the Government did not take it up.

By 4 August the situation in Cabinda was becoming more fraught by the day. UNAVEM's position, and that of our team in the field, was extremely difficult and this led us to establish some underlying principles to guide our actions, based on the premise that the Cabinda issue *per se* was an internal problem of a sovereign state and outside UNAVEM's mandate, but that, despite all the difficulties, UNAVEM should carry out its appointed task transparently, impartially, and in the best way possible. Since the electoral process was likely to be seriously flawed in Cabinda, public observations to this effect would have to be made at the proper time.

By the end of the registration period only about 15 per cent of the estimated 84 000 voters in Cabinda had registered, while the political stalemate remained unbroken because the armed factions of the FLEC, led by N'zita Tiago and José Tiburcio, had still not been persuaded to join the proposed talks in Geneva.

The Government and UNITA at least agreed on one thing: no independence for Cabinda. They differed on how to deal with the problem. Dr Savimbi's statement in an interview that he favoured only a negotiated solution and that UNITA would not participate if the new armed forces were sent there, provoked a controversy in the CCPM, but that body never came to grips with the Cabinda issue. Instead it was relegated upwards, and placed on the agenda of the 'summit' meeting between President dos Santos and Dr Savimbi on 7 September, On the negotiation front, Lopo de Nascimento told me on 9 September that the postponed Geneva meeting would now take place in Gabon, expressing confidence that N'zita Tiago would attend. No progress was made, however, and Cabinda was still in dangerous limbo when election day arrived.

* * *

Of vital interest to the peace process was the relationship between the two leaders. Their very different personalities and styles of leadership may have been due in part to their different trajectories: Dr Savimbi had broken away early from the FNLA to form UNITA, of which he had always been the sole and unopposed leader. In contrast President dos Santos had slipped almost by historical accident into the leadership of the MPLA as a result of Dr Agostinho Neto's death soon after independence. The choice of this rather self-effacing man had been a surprise to many, and he had had to grow into the job.

The two leaders were said to be divided not only by ideology and the mistrust engendered by a long civil war, but also by deep personal animosity. Even after the signing of the Peace Accords in Bicesse, and the strained handshake that followed for the benefit of the media, this was no de Klerk–Mandela relationship. Theirs was not a close association where personal and political rivalry was suppressed for the overriding national interest. These two men were prepared to fight out their political destinies to the end. In South Africa the winner of the free and fair election was never in doubt; in Angola, although many observers considered Savimbi the favourite, his victory was by no means certain.

Pride was involved too. Savimbi's pride in himself was very evident, to the point of resembling arrogance. Some thought it even approached megalomania. He was a man with a mission and a Messianic view of his role in history: he saw himself as the man born to govern Angola and to lead the people out of the wilderness. Dos Santos' pride was of more modest proportions, less extrovert, but there nonetheless. He was, after all, Head of State, and so invested with the impalpable but unmistakable aura that goes with that position, in addition to the visible authority it carries. He was also, I sensed, a man who took pride in maintaining a steadfast purpose – in this case leading his party and Government to victory in the elections – even to the point of obstinacy. The gulf of personal mistrust between the two was so vast as to be probably unbridgeable. I hardly ever attended a meeting with either that did not contain some comment of suspicion or disdain – even contempt – for his rival.

President dos Santos had all the panoply of power and authority to bolster his position: the palace at Futungo de Belas, with its imposing salons and reception rooms; the official receptions he gave, with food-laden tables arranged around the huge swimming pool and brightly clad Angolan dancers to entertain the guests. Dr Savimbi was not to be outdone, however. He had lived for years as a self-styled Head of State in the very *sui generis* capital he had created for himself in Jamba. His title as head of UNITA was 'President'; that was what he was invariably called by his followers, and it was clearly the form of address that everyone else was expected to use. Now he had his 'White House', which, if not a palace, had certain palatial qualities. He too gave grand receptions from time to time. The first one I attended was held in the Hotel Presidente on 6 April to mark his return to Luanda after his unexplained six-week sojourn in Jamba, at which he made a long and rambling speech, though we all took comfort from its moderation of tone.

A month or so later Dr Savimbi sent out invitations to a dinner-ball, a rare social occasion in Luanda. It was held in the Hotel Panorama on the Ilha on Saturday 16 May, but Savimbi himself did not attend. Vice President Jeremiah Chitunda did the honours, with Engineer Salupeto Pena at his side. The CCPM was there in force, as who was anyone on all sides of the political spectrum, plus the usual stalwarts from the diplomatic corps. I found Chitunda a very taciturn dinner partner and my efforts to contribute to what ought to have been a convivial social atmosphere were not helped by the fact that Salupeto Pena was engrossed with his son, a bouncing baby boy, not much over a year old. His paternal pride was understandable, but this was, to say the least, a singular occasion on which to give it public expression and his son was an unusual guest.

Even when the music struck up Chitunda remained stolidly seated and silent. Antonio Monteiro rescued me and we joined the happy, jigging throng that was rubbing shoulders on the nightclub-sized ballroom floor. Angolan rhythms are infectious, and even Salupeto Pena gyrated, albeit sedately, with his wife. Everyone seemed to be enjoying themselves, whatever their party affiliations. The music conjured up a fiesta atmosphere, and the happy mingling between the two sides stirred hope for some more harmonious future for Angola. It seems almost incredible that, only five months later, both Chitunda and Salupeto Pena were dead and the country was teetering on the brink of a return to all-out war.

* * *

The infrequency of the personal encounters between José Eduardo dos Santos and Jonas Savimbi, and the touch-and-go manner in which they were held, raised both fears and expectations, fuelled speculation and heightened the impact on the highly volatile and nervous 'market' of investments in Angola's future democratic stability.

Three such 'summits' meeting took place between my arrival on the scene and the elections. The first was on 29 May, very near the anniversary of their historic handshake and the signing of the Peace Accords. Both seemed to regard the outcome as positive, although both remained concerned about the serious delays in implementing key provisions of the Peace Accords. Afterwards Savimbi made some remarkably upbeat comments on Radio Angola, which he confirmed in a meeting with me on 4 June. He told me that he had had a 'very good', frank and wideranging meeting with the president, and reiterated:

> I give you my word of honour that I will not begin a war, even if we lose the elections [a rare admission, indeed, that this could ever be on the cards]. 'That is a guarantee ... I can tell you that even if some officers on either side might want to start another war, the troops on both sides do not want that.

The next meeting – only the third in the 15 months since they had signed of the Peace Accords – was originally scheduled to take place on 24 August. The imminent start of the electoral campaign, the tension arising from a number of serious incidents, and the many untied ends needing joint action before the election made this an absolutely critical meeting. Hence the various postponements, and especially the reason for the first one – Savimbi's failure to turn up – were greeted with alarm and foreboding. Fear that the process was dangerously stalled brought the three members of the Troika hurrying back to Luanda.

A deadly game of poker was being played out. Yet again, in curious contrast, when it did take place on 7 September the meeting was acclaimed by both sides as very positive. I have described the jubilant arrival of General N'dalu and Salupeto Pena (who had accompanied their leaders at the meeting) at the dinner with the Troika in the Barracuda Restaurant on the Ilha, where we all sat anxiously watching television and awaiting news. The news brought to us by the two participants was encouraging. The meeting had lasted two and a half hours, and both concurred that it had been conducted in a most cordial and positive atmosphere and had dealt with virtually all the issues now crucial to success. Both leaders reaffirmed their commitment to hold the elections on 29–30 September and respect the results, and agreed that whoever won would form a government of national unity and reconciliation. Other important points referred to the replacement of FAPLA and FALA by the FAA by 27 September, and to the antiriot police, as has been described in earlier chapters. Both leaders agreed to request a brief extension of UNAVEM after the election, and the CCPM was also to be prolonged for a judicious period to facilitate dialogue during the transition. They both considered Cabinda to be an integral part of Angolan territory: UNITA agreed that it would no longer object to the deployment of FAPLA troops there, on the understanding that their numbers would be reduced, they would be integrated within the new FAA and would adopt a defensive, and not an offensive, position against the FLEC/FAC. Lastly the two leaders agreed to meet again before the elections, most probably between 24 and 27 September.

The Troika highlighted the importance of the agreement on a government of natural reconciliation, in which the losers might also have some stake, in their subsequent joint declaration. Some confusion arose in the international press, however. Prestigious journals such as the *New York Times* and the *Financial Times* reported that President dos Santos and Dr Savimbi had agreed that whoever won the elections would form a *coalition* government. Both the MPLA and UNITA at once publicly rejected this notion, making clear that the victor would form a government of *national unity and reconciliation*. In other words, representatives of various political affiliations, including those of the main rivals, would be invited to participate in the new administration, a concept rather different from that of a coalition.

At our meeting on 9 September I once again had the impression that Dr Savimbi was pleased with the summit meeting and with the atmosphere in which it had been conducted, although he had a slightly different interpretation of some of the points from that given to us by General N'dalu and Salupeto Pena. President dos Santos was also reasonably upbeat about the general picture when I saw him on 23 September, even though his mistrust of and complaints about UNITA's intentions had multiplied.

Predictably, however, tension and incidents mounted to a crescendo during the three weeks between that summit encounter and the elections.

* * *

The political campaign was hotting up, and the MPLA and UNITA were lavishly dispensing gifts and organising food, drink, music and dancing to attract support. Each repeatedly warned their followers not to react to provocation by the other, though not always with conspicuous success. Still, it was nothing short of a miracle that there was no major clash when, by unfortunate coincidence or lack of planning, the two leaders visited Namibe on the same day, 15 September, to speak to large rallies of their supporters. While there was still much jockeying for position and brinkmanship it looked as if both sides regarded the election route as their best bet, but both sides had fall-back positions.

In the week of 14 September armoured Kaspir vehicles of mysterious provenance (and South African manufacture), never before declared or verified, suddenly appeared on the streets of Huambo in order, according to UNITA, to protect their leader during his campaign visit there. This occurrence led Dr Savimbi to appear unannounced at the UNAVEM camp in Huambo, at midnight and in his pyjamas (he had evidently risen from sleep), to explain at some length to an astonished Colonel Mortlock that the Kaspirs had been brought in without his knowledge. He then amazed the Colonel further by inviting him to pray with him, there and then, for peace in Angola. He also prayed that he would govern well, if victorious in the election, and accept failure with dignity if he lose. The problem was that the vehicles were undisputedly still there. The CCPM was galvanised into action and despatched the CMVF for on-the-spot an investigation. On the other side, while the FAPLA command structure was rapidly disintegrating, there was reason to believe that the antiriot police force was providing a haven for its best troops, but no way of proving it.

Up until the third week of September major clashes had been avoided, but then a very nasty incident occurred in Kuito/Bié, in which Presidential guards were beaten up by UNITA personnel. UNAVEM played a key role in bringing about a solution. For our pains, UNITA then criticised us as being on the side of the Government, which at least allowed me to point out to the President that the perception of impartiality varies greatly according to the eye of the beholder.

The various churches were also trying to exert a calming influence. Cardinal Alexandre do Nascimento was being studiously neutral in his public utterances, although many Angolans saw the Catholic church as continuing its historical trend of favouring the established secular power, at that time the MPLA Government. I cannot say that I detected any such bias in my personal conversations with him. If there was any nuance to be discerned it may have been some fear of UNITA, perhaps unsurprising in a native of Malange. For its part, the Episcopal Conference of Angola and São Tomé issued a statement on the peace process on 3 September, which was welcomed as 'courageous and realistic' by Marcolino Moco, the Secretary-General of the MPLA

The Security Council President's statement of 18 September expressed concern at the recent deterioration in the political and security situation, and endorsed the Secretary-General's appeal to President dos Santos and Dr Savimbi to exercise leadership 'at this critical juncture' and ensure that their followers acted with restraint and tolerance. It also underlined the importance of forming a government of national reconciliation after the elections.

The main way in which leadership could be demonstrated by the two contenders for power, and public confidence shored up, was by holding their further promised meeting and getting on smartly with the formal dissolution of their separate armies and the appointment of the Chief of General Staff for the new one. Everything had looked to be back on course, if tardily, after their meeting on 7 September. But nothing is ever plain sailing in Angola. Along with the rash of new incidents and fresh squabbles within the CCPM, it began to look dreadfully possible that the vital meeting might not happen before polling day. Dr Savimbi's electioneering caravan was roaming all over the country and his speeches were seen as increasingly aggressive. One phrase of his, frequently quoted by alarmists and opponents alike, was 'If UNITA does not win, then it means fraud!'

On 22 September Foreign Minister 'Loy' summoned me urgently to his office to convey his grave concern about UNITA's latest actions, which he described as tantamount to a war strategy: UNITA, he claimed, had increased its forces and had only pretended to demobilise by moving troops from one assembly area to another. He said he was not so much concerned by the individual incidents as by his perception that they were adding up to a consistent pattern. Dr Savimbi had adopted 'an extremely aggressive attitude' following his visit to South Africa, where he was known to have met President de Klerk, Foreign Minister 'Pik' Botha and a number of South African generals. South African supplies and technical support were still being received in Jamba, and the Government had been 'reliably informed' that no help had been given to UNITA without President de Klerk's personal knowledge (the source of this information was not divulged).

The Minister requested that the United Nations put as much pressure as possible on Dr Savimbi, so that 'he behaves as he ought to behave'. The Government's interpretation was that UNITA was now afraid it would lose the elections and was setting in train a spoiling operation, either to prevent the elections from being held at all, or, if they were, from being considered 'free and fair'. A cynical interpretation, on the other side, of the reason behind the Minister's démarche could have been that it was the Government that had the jitters and was trying to preempt the impact of a possible defeat. By now the general confusion was so great and rumour so prevalent that even the most impartial observer might have been forgiven for finding it difficult to distinguish fact from fabrication, or even mere wishful thinking, and would have found it impossible to judge sincerity, or otherwise, of intent.

In contrast the President was relaxed and confident when I saw him the following day: 'We are satisfied with the process', he said, 'Our overall assessment is positive'. (I could never decide whether the variations in the views expressed by senior members of the Government were the result of a deliberate tactic, or simply of poor coordination.) There was no mention of South Africa, but the President did stress that UNITA was still a military organisation rather than a political party, and (now a familiar theme) that it was deploying large numbers of troops under the pretext of protecting UNITA leaders and facilities. He was disturbed by what he considered to be the inflammatory tone of his opponent's recent speeches and said the Government was convinced that UNITA had a plan to eliminate MPLA leaders. (If so – and strangely – the Government delegation never brought this up at the CCPM, which was constantly wrestling with parallel accusations by the representative of UNITA about attempts to assassinate *their* leader.) The Government, he assertted ,had shown restraint in reacting to the incident at Kuito/Bié, but there was a real danger over the next few days that a repetition of such incidents could derail the process. Some sectors of the population had 'had enough' of UNITA's provocations and might take the law into their own hands. He too called on UNAVEM to exert a moderating influence on UNITA.

I told the President that we remained 'cautiously optimistic', but that we were very concerned about recent incidents and doing all in our power to calm the situation. I also expressed the fervent hope that the two leaders would hold their promised meeting before the elections. The President assured me that, as far as he was concerned, it would take place before 27 September, only four days later) with the clear implication that the onus to make sure that happened rested with his opponent.

* * *

I was by now deeply worried as to whether the vital meeting between the leaders would take place, as well as conscious that I was expected to do something to make it happen. My despondency was not assuaged by a further long and very acrimonious meeting of the CCPM that went on until late that night.

Immediately after the meeting I sought out Engineer Salupeto Pena and told him I was anxious to talk urgently to Dr Savimbi, and was ready to go anywhere in Angola to do so (the UNITA leader was still campaigning in the northern provinces and there was no date for his return, which was further increasing uncertainty and apprehension). Salupeto Pena said he would get a message to his leader that very night, late as it was, and let me have the answer the following day.

Arranging the time and place of my meeting with Dr Savimbi became my overriding preoccupation for the next 36 hours or so, interspersed with two more long meetings of the CCPM. Frequent messages kept reaching me from UNITA, each saying something different about where and when Dr Savimbi would see me. The Beechcraft was on permanent standby at the airport, and I was ready to travel at a moment's notice. At one point we were told to go to M'banza Congo on Thursday night or early Friday morning, but at the last moment the venue was changed to Uige, where Dr Savimbi was expected to arrive at 3 p.m. on Friday 25 September. That enabled me to attend the morning meeting of the CCPM, where I found my three observer friends sunk in uniformly low spirits. Antonio Monteiro seemed quite the most dejected of the three, perhaps because his mood present contrasted so greatly with his normally cheerful demeanour. They all thought it essential that I see Dr Savimbi, but were not sanguine about the results.

I spent many of the intervening hours thinking about how I should approach the issues I had to take up with Dr Savimbi, but I still felt distinctly nervous. Well before three o'clock we landed in Uige and were taken to the UNAVEM Weatherhaven camp.

There followed what seemed to be interminably long hours of waiting, punctuated at intervals by UNITA emissaries driving up in a flurry of dust to report on the latest state of play. Dr Savimbi's programme was well behind schedule and he would be arriving late; Dr Savimbi was arriving in half an hour and would see me immediately afterwards; Dr Savimbi had arrived but had found that a huge rally had been waiting for him under a broiling sun in the stadium and did I mind if he made his speech and met with them first? There was only one answer to that question. My main object was to see him, and I could hardly complain about the courtesy they were showing by giving me a blow-by-blow account of developments. The tedium and suspense were killing, however, and did nothing to bolster my confidence. I wanted to get this difficult meeting over.

At last the summons came. It was already dark when one of the UNAVEM police observers drove us down to the UNITA headquarters and we penetrated the usual serried ranks of armed guards. Dr Savimbi was accompanied by Dr Chitunda, Dr Valentim, his 'Minister of Information', and a third high-ranking official. He had already endured four political rallies that day in different places, and looked and sounded extremely tired. His eyes were bloodshot and had a curiously glazed look. As usual, I greeted him in Portuguese, out of courtesy. Normally he would then switch to English out of reciprocal courtesy to those of my UNAVEM colleagues who did not understand Portuguese. On this occasion, however, we continued in Portuguese, a sure sign, I felt, of his extreme fatigue.

The meeting lasted well over an hour and, as I had anticipated, was exceedingly difficult. This was a Savimbi I had heard about, but never before seen. The urbanity and sometimes joviality of manner that he customarily demonstrated at our meetings all but disappeared. He was aggressive, argumentative and domineering, at times appearing to be struggling with pent-up rage, at others rambling in his discourse, which was, however, dismayingly consistent in its negative tone. He spoke favourably of UNAVEM but was vituperative and uncompromising in his accusations against the Government and the MPLA. While I tried to counter some of his arguments, I did not feel that I had been successful in budging any of his opinions. He did not seem to be listening. The whole tone was completely at variance with that of our last, rather positive, meeting only just over a fortnight previously. Jobarteh afterwards expressed the view that drink or drugs, or possibly both, were responsible for the sea-change.

Dr Savimbi enquired why I had travelled all the way to Uige to see him. I replied that I had done so because this was an exceedingly critical moment, with only 72 hours left before the elections; that I had seen President dos Santos two days earlier and wished to see him also in order to urge both leaders to meet and to appeal to their supporters for calm and rejection of violence: the important thing now was for everyone to vote. I was concerned by the recent escalation of violent incidents, which gave a disquieting impression that both sides might be losing control over their rank and file. The process was becoming caught up in a vicious circle of rumours and speculations that could all too easily develop into a vicious spiral. The fact that several recent CCPM meetings had been delayed for hours because of the non-appearance of Engineer Salupeto Pena and UNITA, that there still had been no Chiefs of General Staff meeting owing to the disappearance of UNITA's General 'Ben-Ben', coupled with rumours of UNITA troop movements, had contributed to the rise in fear and tension. Urgent action was needed to draw back from the brink. The meeting between the two leaders was crucial and I hoped it would result in a joint declaration reiterating their commitment to peace and to the elections, their readiness to accept the election results and that whoever won would install a government of reconciliation. I hoped that it would also contain a joint message of confidence in UNAVEM, whose capacity for exercising effective moral persuasion depended on its image and its acceptability to both parties. As for the elections, I was satisfied that, so far as the mechanisms, logistics and observation arrangements were concerned, significant fraud would be very difficult. The biggest danger in my view was violence, and if this reached large proportions the elections could not be verified. Even if it did not reach this extreme, the winner's victory would be hollow if the process was flawed by violence and the new government would not command respect internally or externally.

Dr Savimbi agreed that there had been an escalation of violence and launched into a tirade against the Government in which the recurrent theme was the antiriot police, which, he claimed, was 'a parallel army'. He did not see why UNITA should demobilise its army if the Government was putting its best troops into this new force. If the Government brought out the antiriot police during the elections, that, he said, 'would mean war' (a remark in disturbing contrast to his many previous assertions to me that there would not, and could not, be any more war in Angola). I reminded him of the three conditions I had repeatedly put forward at the CCPM and which were reflected in the Secretary-General's letter of 9 September, namely that such a police force must be transparent, representative, and not used on patrol but kept in reserve for emergencies. When Dr Chitunda said that none of these conditions had been fulfilled, I reminded him that all these issues had been thoroughly discussed at the CCPM and a group set up to investigate the allegations. There was also agreement that on voting day, only electoral police would be at the polling stations, the normal police being stationed at least 500 metres away and the antiriot police in their barracks, unless serious disturbances broke out. But Dr Savimbi and Dr Chitunda brushed aside these arguments and continued as if the matter had never been discussed at all in the CCPM or any agreements reached.

Dr Savimbi felt the main danger was the situation in Malange, which he considered unresolvable. When I said there had been agreement to demobilise both sides rapidly in that area, he retorted that the FAPLA Fifth Brigade, confined near Malange, had simply been dressed in civilian clothes. Another serious problem was that the Government had brought out tanks on some occasions. 'If tanks continue to be used, we are not going to put up with it and will use anti-tank weapons.' He had urged his followers not to retaliate to MPLA provocations, but there had been many deaths and it was becoming more difficult to restrain his rank and file. At one point he seemed to admit my contention that both sides might be losing control of their supporters, saying 'We, the leaders of the parties, are not responsible for any of the violence. Our militant supporters frequently take it upon themselves to act, and we are informed later'.

I pointed out that the Government was expressing similar concerns to us about UNITA, citing recent movements of FALA troops and the security arrangements for high UNITA officials. FALA was demobilising at a much slower rate than FAPLA and, in the latest UNAVEM verification of 23 September, not one additional man had been demobilised on the FALA side since 16 September. Was this, I enquired, a reflection of his earlier remark that UNITA would not demobilise so long as the antiriot police continued in existence? And would the two armies be disbanded on 27 September as agreed? I had serious concerns about this as, when I had left the CCPM meeting to fly to Uige, it looked as if UNITA was suggesting that the crucial meeting between the Chiefs of General Staff might not take place until after the meeting of the two leaders. Dr Savimbi (who did not adopt a consistent position throughout the meeting) said that the Chiefs of General Staff meeting certainly had to take place beforehand and the two armed forces should be disbanded on Sunday 27 September. He inferred that General Ben-Ben's non-appearance was because General Alberto Neto had allegedly kept him waiting for a full day in Huambo two weeks previously for a similar meeting. It hardly seemed the moment, I thought privately, for such childish displays of injured vanity.

I stressed that my greatest fear was the level of mistrust each of the parties showed about the other's actions and intentions, leading them to adopt defensive positions of an escalating nature that could all too easily tip over into offensive action. This was why the meeting between the two Presidents was absolutely key, as well as a calming joint message to the populace at large. Both Dr Savimbi and Dr Chitunda chillingly said they did not set much store by such meetings, which they described as a one-way conversation in which President dos Santos made commitments he did not fulfil (which was exactly what President dos Santos was saying of Dr Savimbi). Dr Savimbi said that the Government had made a statement to Portugal that the MPLA would win the elections, which he considered, in view of the overwhelming support for UNITA, could only mean that the MPLA intended to indulge in fraud and dirty tricks. I was unaware of any such statement but Dr Savimbi was on record as saying that if UNITA did not win, then it would mean that there had been fraud, and I promptly said that it was very dangerous to predict in advance that a certain outcome would be fraudulent.

At the end I reiterated my concerns about violence, pleading that it would be tragic if we were to fail after all that had been achieved and at this crucial moment of decision. I had transmitted the same message to President dos Santos, who had assured me that he would abide by the results of the vote. I myself, and UNAVEM, would be on call day and night to resolve any emergency situation that might arise. Dr Savimbi said that, provided the Malange situation and the antiriot police issue could be resolved, he saw no danger to the process. But he did not think it was worth talking to the President, whom he considered unreliable and lacking in commitment. He trusted General N'dalu, but asserted that he did not have the ear of the President. His final words were that UNITA would try everything to avoid violence.

Despite this slightly more conciliatory tone I did not feel very reassured. Nor were the circumstances of our departure from Uige such as to inspire confidence. There were no lights at the airport, and aircraft were not supposed to operate after nightfall. By now it was 9 p.m. and pitch-black. The local UNAVEM team marshalled their few vehicles at intervals along the airstrip with headlights blazing. By this somewhat erratic illumination the little Beechcraft bumped and roared along the rough runway. No one said anything but we all breathed a sigh of relief when, after what seemed an eternity, we were safely airborne. We were tired, hungry and dispirited as we dined on some equally tired sandwiches and discussed what to do next. It was not just that the omens for the meeting between the two leaders did not look good; we had been left in very considerable doubt as to whether Dr Savimbi would agree to meet at all.

Back at last at Vila Espa, I called Mig Goulding, and urged that the only hope now was for the Secretary-General to telephone Dr Savimbi that very night. Our next problem was to establish how he could get through to the UNITA leader. That meant getting in touch with Salupeto Pena, but as usual the local telephone system had gone on the blink. Antonio Monteiro, anxious for news of our visit to Uige and unable to get through, had come in person. My tiny living room was now swarming with people. A UN Military observer from Guinea-Bissau, Major Mbalu, was despatched to locate Salupeto Pena and had to scour the town before running him to earth. The radios would not work inside my house, and so in the early hours of the morning there was a procession of people walking up and down in front of it, myself included, radios pressed to ears. I managed at last to speak to Salupeto Pena, who radioed Savimbi to wake him and alert him that the Secretary-General would call, and gave me the number. By then it was about three o'clock in the morning and we were all exhausted.

* * *

The next evening, Saturday 26 September, the meeting we had feared to be in jeopardy took place. I cannot claim it would not have happened without the Secretary-General's intervention, but most observers in Luanda believed it to have been very important at that exceedingly critical moment when the peace process was balanced on a knife edge.

The meeting lasted two hours, and was reported by some of those there as having gone reasonably well. In declarations immediately afterwards, Dr Savimbi was quoted as saying 'the meeting was held in a very good atmosphere and, while many people think of war, we think of peace'. He made another statement of a conciliatory nature at a UNITA social gathering that evening, in stark contrast to his tone in Uige only 24 hours before.

Late on Sunday 27 September a joint communiqué and a declaration on the disbandment of FAPLA and FALA were issued. They stated that the functions of the Chief of General Staff would be carried out jointly by General Antonio dos Santos França ('N'dalu') and General Arlindo Isaac Chenda Pena ('Ben-Ben'). It would be a transitory arrangement and the new government would make the final selection. This, then, was the not fully convincing compromise through which Dr Savimbi's reticence on this point had been overcome – another compromise in a long series of such.

But the peace process had survived – just – yet another cliff-hanging experience. The sense of relief that this engendered heightened the euphoria that permeated the swearing-in of the two Joint Chiefs of General Staff of the FAA the next afternoon, Monday 28 September, barely 14 hours before the polls were due to open.

Part IV
Day to Day Living

12 Life in Luanda

Luanda, according to those who knew her in palmier days, was the most beautiful city in Africa. Even the most censorious observer of the squalor I found in 1992 could not fail to discern traces of faded elegance. Conceived by its original architects to enhance the graceful sweep of a wide, curving bay and natural harbour, the city immediately reminded me of Rio de Janeiro, except there were no steep hills or *Corcovado* dominating it.

Luanda had been a white city, built by whites for the comfort and self-aggrandizement of whites. When the Portuguese empire crumbled in 1975, the original *raison d'être* for Luanda, capital of the flagship of Portuguese imperialism, crumbled too. Ryszard Kapuscinski captured that moment poignantly in *Another Day of Life*: 'Luanda was not dying the way our Polish cities died in the last war.... The city was dying the way an oasis dies when the well runs dry: it became empty, fell into inanition, passed into oblivion'. He described how everything that could possibly be packed was stowed into crates and shipped abroad, and made a graphic distinction between the 'wooden city' that sailed away and the 'stone city' that remained.

> I managed to see how the city sailed away. At dawn it was still rocking off the coast, piled up confusedly, uninhabited, lifeless, as if magically transformed into a museum exhibit of an ancient Eastern city and the last tour group had left.... I stood on the shore with some Angolan soldiers and a little crowd of ragtag freezing black children. 'They're taking everything from us', one of the soldiers said, without malice.... The soldier ... smiled and added 'But anyway we've got a home now. They left us what's ours'.

That wasn't very much. Kapuscinski goes on to say: 'On the streets now there were only thousands of cars, rusting and covered with dust. The walls also remained, the roofs, the asphalt on the roads, and the iron benches along the boulevards'. Water was running out and

> Rumours circulated that the black quarters would descend upon the stone city. Everyone knew that the blacks lived in the most awful conditions, in the worst slums to be seen anywhere in Africa, in clay hovels like heaps of smashed cheap pottery covering the dust around Luanda. And here stood the luxurious stone city of glass and concrete – empty, no one's.

Kapuscinski describes how quickly the decline set in:

> The city was dirty and neglected, so people assumed that the garbage men had flown to Europe a long time ago. Then it turned out that they had left only the

day before. Suddenly ... the garbage began piling up.... It appeared on the sidewalks, in the roads, in the squares, in the entrance ways of town houses, and in the extinct market places. You could walk through some streets only with great effort and disgust. In this climate the excess of sun and moisture accelerate and intensify decay, rot and fermentation. The whole city began to stink.

Subsequently the city filled up again and the Angolans tried to pick up the pieces of their flawed heritage. But it was an almost impossible task, as war continued to rage across the country. Luanda was never occupied by the forces opposing the MPLA, but its water and power services were frequently sabotaged by the guerrillas and it became hopelessly overcrowded with refugees from the fighting.

Sissy filmed the waterfront from the front seat of my car. From that judicious distance, and a moving base, Luanda was restored to its old colonial glory. Some buildings had been meticulously restored and stood out against their squalid surroundings. The white-balconied National Bank of Angola is one such, and the Museum of Anthropology another, their walls washed in the traditional deep pink of Portuguese architecture. The white mansions and embassies of Miramar gleamed high on the bluff above the port, and nearby the old cemetery was another oasis of whiteness – white walls, white tombstones and a forest of white frangipani. The rest however, when viewed from close to, was sadly down-at-heel and seedy. The buildings were dirty and dilapidated, their windows broken, shutters hanging from a single hinge, the dingy balconies of overcrowded apartment blocks permanently festooned with ragged laundry. The beautiful harbour was silting up and had become a floating sewer. Some of the poorer people, in a pathetic quest for cleanliness and oblivious of passing traffic, could be seen vigorously lathering themselves in pools of filthy, stagnant water in the middle of the street, water whose origins one could only too well imagine. Refuse was piled high wherever one looked, provoking an almost intolerable stench, and derelict lorries and decaying, rusty cars lay about everywhere.

One could almost imagine that no garbage men had ever been found to replace those who left in 1975 and that some of these vehicles were the same ones Kapuscinski had seen abandoned 17 years before, for his description of the city after the exodus of the Portuguese remained all too true to life. There was one very important difference. This was not now a dead city, an abandoned city. This was a city pulsating with life and energy. Dilapidated vintage vehicles that looked as if they, too, should be put out to grass, roared around the pot-holed streets, in terrifying displays of erratic driving, a triumph of virtuosity over reason. Every day saw small new shops opening and the markets were bustling hives of activity. It was good to see the returning air of normality, the carefully piled little mounds of fruit and vegetables, the ample market women, eager to bargain, the live ducks and chickens, even if some products were still in painfully short supply. Things had greatly improved since the signing of the

Peace Accords. There was a new sense of hope, of a tangible future. Everyone was sick of war and eager to seize the fruits of peace.

It was still a violent society, however. Every night there was shooting and looting in the port. Every night tracer bullets raced across the night sky over the airport, and Vila Espa. Our hangar at the airport, with its planes, trucks, machinery and stores, was a permanent temptation to armed robbers. The movement control team (MOVCON) slept at the airport, in primitive conditions under the command of a maverick Canadian, Major Dennis Strilchuk. There were many midnight chases and narrow squeaks. The road between the UNAVEM camp and the city was distinctly unsafe after dark. Some of the shooting seemed quite random, and not of criminal intent: people had guns, and nothing much to do, so it became a form of entertainment to pass the time. One such man would wander around the perimeter of Vila Espa, letting fly almost every night. There were more serious incidents too, including attempts at robbery even by the locals we had hired to guard the camp. On one occasion we discovered that buildings cheek by jowl with the main entrance to the camp were crammed with weapons, and occupied by disgruntled FAPLA elements, impatient for demobilisation and threatening to use their guns if we did not give them food and water. Predictably, we did, but then I intervened with the Vice Interior Minister, 'Petroff', who had them removed to a more suitable site. Eventually Headquarters allowed us to hire the services of an international security group to guard the camp; retired SAS men were prominent among them, as well as very smart Ghurkas, whose efficiency and discipline inspired confidence.

The element of violence and criminality was much at odds with the demeanour of the ordinary Angolans with whom one came in contact. They were invariably warm, friendly and very polite, and seemed, as individuals, very peaceable. They were also almost perpetually smiling, though goodness knows most of them had little to smile about. The women in particular were magnificent. They are the real workers of Angola, as in so much of Africa. They are the hewers of wood and the carriers of water – the carriers of virtually everything, mostly on their heads. It is they who have borne the brunt of all these long years of war, trying to feed and care for their families in unbelievably straitened circumstances while their men were away at the front, losing husbands, sons, brothers in the senseless battles, or receiving them back often maimed for life. Angola has one of the highest levels of amputees of any country in the world. I had never before seen so many young men hopping around on one leg, or missing an arm, or totally incapacitated.

The indomitable and caring spirit of the women was demonstrated in an incident in which Sissy was the protagonist. She insisted on shopping in a market that was notorious for violence but where, she said, the prices were lower and the produce fresher. One day, when she was buying a melon from a stallholder with whom she often dealt, there was a sudden burst of shooting only a few yards away. Sissy is highly strung at the best of times and had never heard a shot fired in anger in her life. She panicked, but the market women pushed her under the stall and crouched beside her until calm was restored. Even then they insisted on escorting her back to the car. This, to me, demonstrates an extraordinary sense of solidarity between women, white and black, Angolan and foreign, particularly since neither could speak the other's language. After all their suffering one could not have blamed the two Angolan women had they just shrugged their shoulders and left this strange white woman to look out for herself.

* * *

On my arrival in Luanda I had domestic help in the buxom shape of a statuesque Angolan lady, with the appropriately dignified name of María do Fátima, who sailed gently around the house like a galleon before a barely perceptible breeze, and in a generally becalmed state of mind. I did not want to eat the rather heavy Angolan food, but chicken breasts boiled with cauliflower for four hours between breakfast and lunch was going too far in the way of blandness!

Sissy's arrival changed all that. As usual, the early morning flight from Europe landed ahead of time, and when my car sped up to the foot of the aircraft steps nearly all the passengers had left. Sissy stood alone, looking decidedly anxious, clasping a lugubrious-looking teddy bear almost as big as herself, and predictably strung around with about twice as much hand-baggage as any sensible person would try to carry or prudent airline allow.

She soon explored the markets, and started concocting recipes from local fruits and vegetables, some of which we had never seen before. Meat usually came from Windhoek, the source of most supplies for the mission; a plane went there once a week, also transporting some UNAVEM personnel for brief rest and recuperation. Vegetables were the most difficult to obtain, though I later supplemented them from my own little garden. With Sissy's arrival I could begin to entertain representatives of the two sides, the observers and Ambassadors at discreet working dinners and lunches. This was a great boon professionally as well as personally. There were very few restaurants in Luanda, and I soon became a well-known figure, through the attention of the media. Rumour and gossip being rife, I could not have avoided speculation as to whom I was seeing and why. As it was, I could receive them in my little bungalow in total privacy. There was another attraction that induced my guests to drive out from the city – Sissy was a superb and inventive cook. I was told that my house was beginning to be known as one of the best restaurants in town, and when I left I have no doubt that those who came to see us off were sadder to see Sissy go than myself!

The house itself was simple. The front door opened into a very small living area, with a dining table on one side and a very cramped seating area on the other. The main bedroom was almost entirely occupied by a large bed, around which one had to manoeuvre to get to the wall mirror and shelf that served as a dressing table, a cupboard and the shower room. There was a smaller bedroom for visitors, a second shower room, a smaller room still that losed as a study, and a kitchen and scullery. Only the General, the Executive Director and myself had sole use of a bungalow. The others were shared between at least three people. The furniture was sparse, impersonal, and the same everywhere. I had identical sofas in my home, my camp office and my downtown office, and so often wondered where I was! But there was air-conditioning (periodically), and the kitchen – the site of nightly orgies by very large cockroaches – was reasonably well-equipped. Domestic dramas were not infrequent, as for example the time when the dishwasher kept flooding the kitchen, a heinous crime in a place so short of water. The UNAVEM repairman was received by María do Fátima, who was her customary distrait self. When Sissy went into the kitchen she found not the dishwasher but the *washing machine* in small pieces all over the floor and the repairman scratching his head and saying 'I can't find anything wrong with it!' Result: we were without both machines for several days.

Those members of staff living in containers, as many as 300 at the peak of the operation, had to contend with much more cramped conditions, but had air conditioners and the same basic furniture. The worst part was having to use the communal shower and toilet blocks. Initially the hygiene in these left a good deal to be desired, but it improved after I made a personal inspection and called in our Brazilian military medical team. It improved still further with the construction of narrow concrete walkways, so that people no longer trod red dust or mud everywhere. There were also complaints about the food in the cafeteria. Some improvements were introduced but inevitably dissatisfaction erupted from time to time. There were many domestic details, critical to staff morale, in which one had to take an interest.

Vila Espa was like a small city, self-contained, providing all its own services. Behind the bungalows and the prefabricated cabins and containers housing the offices and living quarters there were fuel stores, vehicle maintenance and repair shops, water storage, the cafeteria, the bar and the tiny shop. Every drop of water and fuel for the considerable fleet of vehicles had to be brought in daily. Each morning the big tankers roared into camp just after dawn. Ostensibly the camp was on the public electricity supply but that was frequently cut off, and then an ancient generator sputtered resentfully into life. Water was often scarce and rationed to certain hours.

When there was still only a military and police mission working hours had been from 7 a.m. to 2 p.m. With the expansion of the mission's mandate to electoral matters they were changed to 8 a.m. to 5 p.m., but all the key people had perforce to work very much longer hours, seven days a week. We were permanently on call and there was always some crisis. My day began at 5.30 a.m. and I was usually on the go non-stop until it was time for bed. The first hour or so was my jealously guarded private time when I did my back exercises and swam my daily kilometre in the pool (a mile at weekends). In this precious interlude I could quietly review the hurdles to be surmounted during the rest of the day as well as keep myself fit.

The very early morning was the best time in Luanda, cool and fresh even in the hottest season. It was very quiet, hardly anyone was about except a few eager beavers jogging or exercising, and even the trigger-happy gunmen had gone home to bed. The bird life, in contrast, was much in evidence. Silvery skeins of white egrets flew over towards their feeding grounds, followed by graceful flights of ibis in perfect formation. Sometimes the egrets descended *en masse* on the grass square in the middle of the camp, and two often perched on the fence round the pool. I christened them Ernest and Ernestina. A big grey heron used to cruise over in lonely state. Swallows nested under the roof of my porch in a long tubular mud nest, with a bulge in the middle for the eggs or fledglings. The nest was cunningly constructed to fit the contours of the corrugated plastic. and had a front and a back door – and it was a delight to see the parents whizz in through one side and out the other, barely braking their incredible speed. Flocks of delightful little 'cordon bleu' finches abounded, so-called because they (very appropriately) sport UN-blue heads, breasts and rumps (our observers, though, wore blue only in their berets and neck scarves!)

The bird life survived in spite of an army of semi-feral cats. They mostly lived under the containers where they regularly produced hordes of kittens and kept down the rat population. One feisty and battle-scarred old tom cat, whom I christened Thomas, appeared to be responsible for a good deal of the paternity and was lord of the clan. At our first encounter, when I ventured to stroke him, he bit my hand severely and a tetanus jab had to be swiftly administered by Dr Waldecir, but we soon became friends. I was given a pretty calico kitten, whom we christened 'Missy', and whose antics were refreshing at the end of a stressful day. When young, she insisted on sleeping by my feet inside the bed, and paraded around the camp curled about Sissy's shoulders. But she was a wild little thing, always ready for a scrap, letting fly with tooth and claw at the slightest provocation. We speculated that her bad temper was due to mistaken identity and that she thought she was a dog, for she was always growling. She became known as the 'guerrilla cat'. A grown tabby cat, at first very wild and timid, adopted us, looking in the first instance for food. I christened her Grizel, because she was always miaowing pathetically. She became so tame that she had her kittens under the dresser in the living room, and doggedly kept bringing them in even when set up with a box and some old sweaters on the verandah. As if there were not enough crises, one night I found myself – scantily clad, barefoot and ankle-deep in dirty water – rescuing the kittens from my flooded verandah when a torrential tropical storm suddenly struck the camp at 2 a.m.! Alas, though saved on that occasion, none of the kittens survived for long. Just before we left Missy had her first kittens; both were stillborn. All life seemed precarious in Angola.

A few minutes of tranquillity were sometimes to be snatched at sunset. The sun goes down in Luanda in a great panoply of riotous colours, like the backcloth of some vividly painted battle scene. Blood-red was often the dominant colour, and the whorls and torn veils of tinted cloud gave an impression of torment and chaos. In the foreground, by the fence near my house, stood a

Life in Luanda

baobab tree, silhouetted black and stalwart against the lurid sky, its branches upraised as if to still the tumult, while overhead the skeins of egrets and ibis glided back to their roosting places in the marshes along the shore. The baobab and the homeward flight of the birds seemed to diffuse a calming influence, an assurance of continuity and a certain stability in the order of things. Wishful thinking, no doubt, but such things were important in a life otherwise steeped in tension and with no time for distraction.

Not that many distractions were available. It was in any case dangerous to stay out late at night and after a few incidents we had to warn people to be careful. Luanda is surrounded by wonderful beaches, but most became out of reach as the security situation worsened. A favourite haunt was the Ilha, a former island in front of Luanda's waterfront, to which it is now joined by a narrow causeway. The Ilha has beaches on both sides; the one facing the harbour was totally polluted, but the oceanward shore was usually more salubrious, depending on the vagaries of the tide.

Further afield lay the beautiful white strands of Moussoulu. Moussoulu is a long tongue of land, a peninsula that begins further down the Atlantic coast and curves back to taper off near the city. It is mostly sand, with sparse vegetation and only a few dwellings of fisherfolk. The land approach was very rough and took several hours, but by boat it was only 20 to 30 minutes from a little port not far from the UNAVEM camp. Of course, one had to take a boat, and UNAVEM had every kind of transport except the maritime variety! There were public passenger boats, usually ludicrously overcrowded, and some Embassies and companies had their own vessels and were generous with invitations. A few of them even had small houses on the peninsula, though the mosquitos at night were said to be legion and merciless. Most weekends one could find a good cross-section of the Diplomatic Corps picnicking and swimming on Moussoulu, but I only managed to get there three times in seventeen months.

Within the camp there was a basketball court, where matches were organised between the various contingents, and a tennis court with a dubiously pitted surface. I gingerly took up tennis again after 30 years of not playing, conquering my fear of making a public spectacle of myself, under the patient coaching of one of the Swedish policemen. Although I was able to play only rarely, it was marvellous therapy, obliging me to forget everything else and simply concentrate on hitting that elusive ball.

The swimming pool was not very large, and often very crowded, except at the early hour at which I swam. Its upkeep caused problems, as materials became hard to get and the filter decayed. I continued doggedly to swim even during the *cazimbo* (the two or three depressing months of heavy, clouded weather in the middle of the year that is the Angolan equivalent of winter), when the water became very chilly. It also became green and thick but I still swam on, though I complained mildly to Tom White that I had spied a kingfisher watching expectantly from the fence, which seemed a significant omen. (It was a woodland kingfisher, which rather spoilt my argument.) The final straw, however, was the arrival of frogs, mating frogs to boot, which I found in possession of the pool at dawn. I had to engage the help of the Ghurka guards, who patrolled the grounds at first light to switch off the security lights, to help me scoop out the offending animals. An observer would have found the scene indescribably comic: as I stood there incongruously clad in my bathing suit the Ghurkas, invariably disciplined, saluted me smartly before extricating the frogs and again when the operation was completed. I lodged another complaint with Tom about the unauthorised occupants of the pool and a series of somewhat ribald memos about copulating frogs began to circulate in the camp.

The pool was the scene of a more tragic event. One night when I got home late after a CCPM meeting, Tom came to tell me that a Russian airman had been found drowned. With other crew-members he had been drinking and generally larking about in the water. No one had noticed that he had not surfaced, but when they at last saw the body, his inebriated companions ran to tell the barman, rather than rushing to pull him out. The autopsy showed that the dead man had almost certainly suffered a heart attack before drowning. This was the first of the Russian coffins which we had to send off to Moscow from Luanda airport. More would follow, but for other reasons.

Our large group of Russians, who flew and maintained the Russian helicopters and the Antonov, lived up to their national reputation of putting away sizeable amounts of alcohol (as, to a lesser extent, did the Bulgarians, who also flew some aircraft) but they were always dead sober on the job, and performed feats little short of miracles with their elderly, battered machines in that far from friendly terrain. One could not grudge their whooping it up a bit in their free time. The snag was that the recreation hall was only a few yards from my house, to which I had been moved from the one I had occupied during my first visit on the ground that it was too near the noisy old generator. It was a case of out of the frying pan into the fire. It was also a less advantageous location from the security point of view, being isolated at the end of the compound and near the perimeter. The Russians were not the only offenders. I felt guilty when a curfew had to be put on festivities after eleven o'clock, but I had to sleep. The time of the curfew was extended to the small hours for special functions, usually a celebration of the national day of one of the contingents, which, if large, spilled over to the swimming pool and even the basketball court. They were sometimes solemn affairs, with speeches about the particular country's history or affiliation with the United Nations; sometimes very jolly with music and dancing, though the men greatly outnumbered the women. They were homespun occasions, but provided a welcome distraction from a monotonous routine for people long absent from their homes and families, as well as an opportunity for forging a spirit of community.

The recreation hall was a pleasant gathering place at the end of the day. Little tables with gay umbrellas were placed along the pool, and coloured lights hung overhead. A considerable effort was made to give people an alternative to confinement in their quarters. The New Zealanders set up a much appreciated Cotton Reel Club in another part of the camp. All of this came to an end after the elections; the recreation hall closed and evening social life was concentrated in the starker surroundings of the Blue Beret Bar, near the cafeteria. These may seem trivialities, but it is hard for anyone who has not experienced it to comprehend how difficult it is for people with different backgrounds and nationalities, often without a common language, to live in large numbers cheek by jowl in an extremely constricted space over a long period of time. The media and the general public often seem to think that personnel on UN peacekeeping missions should have no enjoyment at all and that any recreation is a sin. They forget that these are human beings like themselves.

Soon after I left UNAVEM the *Daily Mail* published a column attacking the UN's peacekeeping efforts, and including a brief, sneering paragraph on Angola, saying that the UN had organised – from the rooftop bar of the best hotel in town – elections that had promptly dissolved into resumed civil war (thereby implying cause and effect!). I wrote to the editor pointing out that the UN had not been mandated to organise the elections, only to observe and verify them; that I had been in charge of this operation and had never set foot in the aforementioned bar; no doubt some of my UNAVEM colleagues had but I did not blame them, considering the conditions in which they normally lived, especially in the field. I presumed that journalists also patronised that bar, but without having their morals and their efficiency being put into question. The *Daily Mail* did not have the grace to publish the letter. Instead I received a form letter saying they received many letters and could not publish them all. The truth is not always convenient.

* * *

There was a good deal of official social life before the elections. Most of the Ambassadors of the major countries gave lunches or dinners in my honour and there were the customary receptions on national days or to greet important visitors. These occasions provided an opportunity to meet personalities involved in all aspects of the peace process, including the key figures in the new political parties. They were the hub of all the latest and often conflicting rumours. On occasion they also provided some useful, hard information.

My evenings were never short of visitors. There was no dearth of problems requiring consultation within UNAVEM and the camp. Since telephone communication with the city was abysmal (we could call New York by satellite more easily than reach the Government, UNITA or the observers), people would arrive unannounced to discuss some particularly pressing problem. As my front door opened straight into the living room there was no escape, and no privacy. One always had to be suitably attired, mentally and physically, to face whatever might arise. It was an 'open door' policy with a vengeance.

Whenever a military contingent returned home from UNAVEM, a medals parade was held by the flagpole outside the bungalow that General Unimna and I shared as office space. The practice of giving UN peacekeeping medals was extended to the police observers as well, but never to the civilian staff. Such occasions, which were conducted with military formality, made a welcome interlude in the normal routine. I handed out the medals, and General Unimna did the difficult job of pinning the bars on to the officers' uniforms. Then I said a few words of commendation and farewell. Where possible I included a few words in the language of the departing contingent, some of whom had sparse command of English. This became a major bone of contention with the General, who insisted that only English should be used, despite the fact that, with the exception of Portuguese, all the other languages were official languages of the United Nations.

Every Monday at 8 o'clock I held a meeting of senior staff from the military, the police and civilian components to review the current situation. I felt it important that everyone should be aware of the evolving, overall context in which they were making their contribution, as well as of what their colleagues were doing. It was a standard technique that I had long found to be helpful in forging a team approach and spirit. More restricted and more frequent meetings were held between the General, the Executive Director, the senior political adviser and myself to discuss urgent policy matters.

Every two weeks a more general meeting took place with the resident representative of the United Nations Development Programme, and the representatives of all the UN agencies stationed in Luanda: UNICEF, the High Commissioner for Refugees (UNHCR), the World Food Programme (WFP), the United Nations Fund for Population Activities (UNFPA), the World Health Organization (WHO) and the Food and Agriculture Organization (FAO). These were held in our downtown office, which had been set up in a government building in the centre of Luanda to house the electoral division and provide offices for myself and my senior staff, which would make us more accessible to our main interlocutors in the peace process. Our administrative staff had done a splendid job of sprucing up very tatty and dirty premises and setting up communications. The snag was that the offices were on the fifth floor, and the lift did not work. It was a gruelling climb in the clammy heat, and soon most Ambassadors, at least, preferred to drive out to the base office in Vila Espa.

The main purpose of the meetings with the UN agencies was to brief them on the latest developments and discuss items of common concern, such as security – a permanent anxiety, especially up-country – and the humanitarian situation, since under the terms of my appointment I was to coordinate all humanitarian activities of the UN system that related to the peace process.

* * *

Among my main distractions were knitting, reading and listening to the BBC World Service. The latter pastime was not wholly relaxing (particularly later on when that service was constantly interviewing me by satellite telephone), but it served a therapeutic purpose in reminding me that there was another world where other lives, other crises were being played out.

At first I concentrated on books about Angola, and tried to devote one hour every evening to learning Portuguese, having armed myself with various tomes of the 'teach yourself' variety before leaving Vienna. The choice of more general literature was necessarily eclectic, depending on what I had been able to snatch up during my rapid passage through airports or short sojourns in England. Conrad figured large. I reread *Nostromo,* and for the first time *Heart of Darkness.* I also read John Updike's *The Coup.* The quest for power and influence as the principal motor of so many human endeavours was prominent in all of these. *Heart of Darkness* had an especially sobering message to impart. A more soothing antidote was Trollope's *The Small House at Allington,* which transported one into a totally different world but still one in which, beneath the genteel exterior and apparent tranquillity of country life, passion runs high and the levers of power are ever at work. In contrast *Three Letters from the Andes,* exquisitely written by Patrick Leigh Fermor, provided total escape to a part of the world that has a special place in my life and heart, and a timely reminder of the adobe house on the shores of Lake Titicaca to which I hoped to repair once all this was over.

There was also my tiny garden, which surrounded three sides of my house and was badly overgrown when I arrived. I find gardening a most absorbing occupation, providing an outlet for frustrations and anger in its cutting and slashing aspects and the tearing up of weeds (I give them the names of my latest *bêtes-noires*), as well as tangible satisfaction when something actually grows and bursts into flower. Enlisting the support of João, a young Angolan boy who was studying and earning money by gardening, I sallied forth one Saturday and bought bourgainvillea of various hues, ferns and foliage plants to brighten up my verandah, on which I ate lunch most days and breakfast at weekends. Most I purchased from an elderly Portuguese who had hung on in Angola through all the vicissitudes, cultivating his small nursery and who was now more exercised by the persistence of the drought, which threatened his life's work, than encouraged by the peace process. 'It hasn't rained enough this year', he mourned 'It hasn't rained properly for years. But what can you expect? They've cut all the trees down. Just look about you – all the land around Luanda is bare, going back to desert.'

João had an accident that injured his back and he was forbidden to garden. Only then did I discover Senhor Andrade, a thin wisp of a man who headed the team of gardeners employed in the camp by its owners, the Angolan national oil company, Sonangol. Senhor Andrade (like so many others in Angola, including my driver, Brito) was from Cape Verde. He had lived over 20 years in Angola, married an Angolan, and had a large clutch of children, some of whom – small boys mainly – used to turn up on Saturdays. Senhor Andrade (I never learnt his first name or called him anything else) had been trained as an agronomist and horticulturist. He cared about plants and knew how to make them flourish. He replaced the spindly grass in front of the house with a brilliant carpet of portulacae, and planted frangipani and some exotic species of hibiscus. We used to meet after breakfast on Saturdays. Together we made a tiny vegetable garden at the back of the house, and a compost heap. I brought seeds from England – lettuce, spinach, tomatoes, carrots, onions, leeks, parsley, broccoli and my favourite runner beans, which I had introduced successfully into Ethiopia nearly three decades earlier. (The local paper on the Welsh border later trumpeted, in almost banner headlines 'Kington beans provide salve in Angola', a statement that lent itself to considerable misconstruction.) The beans did well, and we had a good crop in the *cazimbo* until the hot season came round again and Senhor Andrade mournfully informed me that we had 'pollenisation problems'. There was a glut of lettuce, so I was able to supply my neighbours in the camp with salad. Most of the other things did well too, and supplemented the poor supply of local vegetables, thus varying our diet. The broccoli didn't 'broc', but we pressed its leaves into service nonetheless as vitamin-rich greenstuff.

Like many gardeners, Senhor Andrade was a philosopher. He also followed the Angolan situation closely, having irrevocably thrown in his lot with its people. I learnt a lot from him during our Saturday morning encounters. I came to think of him as a kind of touchstone to intelligent popular thinking, bereft as I was of close daily contact with the man and woman in the street. All along I somehow felt that through him I had a finger on the pulse of what was going on in ordinary people's minds. Senhor Andrade adopted a very sober, cautious approach to the peace process. His voice always restrained any wishful impressions that perhaps, after all, everything was going to work out. After the elections, when all had fallen into disarray, his demeanour became almost funereal. His wife's family lived in Wako Kungo, which was overrun by UNITA. They had, he thought, managed to flee, but his wife was without news. There was still none when I left Angola, months later. Senhor Andrade continued to work with his beloved plants but grew sadder and even frailer in appearance, though he was still relatively young. One could see he felt that all the hopes he had invested in Angola, all his efforts (and he was a hard-working man) now lay in ruins.

Senhor Andrade's team of gardeners, plodding about the camp in their orange dungarees were also interesting characters. There was a very old Cape Verdian, nearer 80 than 70, who was perpetually pushing heavy wheelbarrow-loads around the camp, with an equally constant smile and a cheery greeting. Others were Angolans, all of whom lost someone of their family in the terrible fighting in Luanda at the end of October. One young Angolan man endeared himself to everyone by his unfailing courtesy and friendliness. Shortly before I left he was stupidly killed in a bizarre road accident, leaving a young wife just about to give birth to their first child. The whole camp mourned.

And when I departed from Angola, the farewell I took of Senhor Andrade was one of the most emotional – for me that is. I felt I was leaving behind a true and trusted friend to face a very uncertain fate.

13 Vignettes from the Field

If our lives were circumscribed, this was as nothing compared with the conditions in which our field teams – military, police and civilians – found themselves. I visited as many of their far-flung outposts as possible, though I could not hope to cover them all, since my presence was often required in Luanda. Sometimes I was away as many as three days a week on inspection trips, which started at 7 o'clock in the morning or earlier and lasted until well after dark.

My visits encompassed all aspects of UNAVEM's work – military, police, elections, humanitarian issues and administration. General Unimna also periodically inspected military and police operations, and we sometimes combined our trips. I was, in any case, always accompanied by a Staff Officer, and quite often by a senior military observer and the head of the police component, as well as appropriate members of the civilian staff. We used to invite Ambassadors of the countries that had provided troop contingents to UNAVEM to accompany us. They did not have many opportunities to get out of Luanda, and it enabled them to visit their compatriots and get the feel of the operation on the ground; from our point of view it was a useful diplomatic and public relations exercise. We also gave seats, when available, to television crews and journalists who were anxious to get up country to see for themselves. Surface travel was either exceedingly slow or totally non-existent because of the destruction of roads and bridges, and the proliferation of mines. The CMO and I usually travelled to the main points of destination (normally Regional Commands and provincial capitals) in the Beechcraft, which only held some eleven passengers, so it was not possible to accommodate many outsiders. They were, moreover, obliged to sign a statement absolving the United Nations of all responsibility in the event of accident, which must have given them pause for thought.

The drill on arrival varied little. We were met at the airport by the local UNAVEM team – military, police and civilian (electoral and administrative), the former drawn up in military formation and saluting smartly as the plane arrived. The provincial Governor or his representative, the local UNITA representative, the joint CCPM monitoring units, made up from both Government and UNITA personnel, were usually there also, and in the later stages, the provincial electoral authorities and representatives of other political parties would likewise greet us. Our first call was always at the UNAVEM camp, where we were briefed on the local situation and reviewed administrative and logistical problems, of which there were many. In most places almost everything had to be supplied from Luanda, even basic foodstuffs being hard to come by locally. Supply flights visited all main areas once a week, and carried eagerly awaited mail back and forth; outlying posts were served by helicopters fanning out from the regional centres. Inevitably there were slip-ups and complaints, but considering the appalling difficulties the system worked well.

The system of rotation, while not always conducive to continuity, helped to even out the hardship and reduce complaints – the switches between headquarters and the field, especially, generated more understanding of mutual difficulties. The duty stations were graded according to the harshness or isolation of the living conditions, and considerable effort was made to see that no officer stayed only in hardship areas (though some of them actually preferred them). This rotation centred mainly on the military observers, who often had to serve right out in the wilds. Police and electoral observers were based in provincial capitals, but conditions varied from place to place, and adjustments were made as necessary.

After the briefing I would call on the Governor or other provincial officials. The UNITA representative was often present at such meetings, otherwise I would call on him separately. We would already have seen the joint CMVF monitoring teams at the UNAVEM base camps and heard their presentations and problems. Later, when electoral preparations were more advanced, there was also a general meeting with the electoral officials and party representatives.

Then there were visits to assembly areas, usually in one of the Russian helicopters outposted in the Regional Commands. These were dilapidated boneshakers with uncompromisingly hard metal benches along the sides, which always seemed about to rattle into a thousand pieces, but which, with their experienced pilots, managed to stay in the air, fly low over hills and treetops and whir down to land in the most unlikely places, in a great swirl of dust and flying stones that scattered the waiting reception line in disarray.

During those months of 1992 I was able to travel the width and breadth of Angola, penetrating into its most remote corners. I felt myself privileged but at the same time frustrated because, apart from visits to the towns and brief sorties into wilder areas in the vicinity of our helicopter landing sites, my vision of Angola was primarily from the air. These bird's eye views only whetted my desire to come to know the country more intimately. The beauty of the landscape and its immense variety are arresting; it ranges from the high plateau, indented with jagged precipices and cliffs, to tropical jungle with canopies of flowering trees, with all the intermediate stages of open forest, scrub, savannah, and even, in the far south towards the Namibian border, long stretches of arid desert. When we flew back to Luanda at night, vast expanses of darkness lay below, interrupted occasionally by circles of flickering fires where unseen people were settling for the night and keeping wild animals at bay. We would descend into Luanda airport in darkness, with all the plane's lights extinguished, to avoid the attentions of another and more lethal kind of predator – men with guns.

You could not look upon the natural wonders of Angola without realising what a splendid country this could be, and what almost unlimited potential it offered, with its small population, its rich natural resources – minerals, diamonds, petroleum and a good supply of fertile agricultural land – and the enormous possibilities for tourism. As always there was an 'if', and a very big 'if' –

if only peace and a stable democratic government could be consolidated. But the mere sight of all those untapped opportunities spurred one on to renewed efforts to see things through, despite all the apparently insurmountable obstacles.

The obstacles were all too evident in the course of these excursions upcountry. Sometimes we flew low over hill-top villages that were totally deserted, their roofless houses gaping open to the sky, the people having fled from what had once been pleasant, self-contained rural communities. Even larger centres of habitation did not present any more promising an aspect. Many of the airfields at which we landed – even the bigger ones – were virtually deserted and the the buildings damaged. Crashed and downed aircraft lay around where they had fallen, with no attempt being made to remove the wreckage or even salvage the scrap metal. It was moving to see, in the midst of a vast emptiness, two or three white, four-wheel-drive trucks with the UN emblem painted on the side and flags flying, and a row of 'blue berets', all of different nationalities, neatly lined up and ready to salute as the engines died, the door of the plane opened, and its rickety steps lowered. I have to admit that I was not always quite up to the solemnity of these occasions. Once I emerged before the engines had sufficiently reduced power and the force of the jet blew me into an ignominious crouching position, clinging for dear life to the ladder. I was always cracking my head on the low doorway, which led one Regional Commander to exclaim solicitously 'Do be careful, Ma'am – we only have one Beechcraft'. So much for sympathy!

Not everything was destruction and desolation. The towns near the coast had escaped the ravages of war. Benguela bore all the aspects of a pretty seaside resort dozing beside the Atlantic Ocean. Brilliantly flowering flame trees bordered the road from the airport, like welcoming banners, a legacy from Portuguese times. Inside the town, more trees of yellow blossoms lined streets that were swept and clean, in contrast to the garbage in Luanda. A tranquil, almost somnolent atmosphere pervaded the place. This was in large part due to the Governor, Paulo Jorge, though he was far from a calm or tranquil person. A *mestiço*, not very tall, and always looking ready for action in the short-sleeved safari suit that was his characteristic mode of dress, he radiated energy from every pore. He had been an effective Foreign Minister a few years earlier, and made no bones about his continuing allegiance to the basic tenets of the MPLA, of which he was a founding member. He came over as an indisputably tough character, but a likeable one, a live wire with whom you could engage in a forthright sparring match. That is exactly what we did on our first encounter in his official residence, a beautiful Portuguese palace. Our exchanges included some very pithy comments on his part about UNAVEM, as well as some troubling observations about the prospects for peace. I came to regard him as quite the most striking of all the provincial Governors.

Lobito, the Atlantic port adjoining Benguela, was, like most ports, a more unruly community. It had, moreover, a growing UNITA presence alongside the traditionally large number of MPLA supporters, and so was always ripe for conflagration. There had already been one major incident, which our local

UNAVEM team of military observers had helped to quell, and there were more to come, some very serious.

On my first visit to Benguela the UNAVEM team was lodged in a private house with many deficiencies. For the electoral observers about to arrive we found a splendid new apartment building owned by a Portuguese, and eventually everyone moved into these relatively plush surroundings. Our team in Lubango was well housed too, occupying a hotel consisting of separate low buildings scattered throughout a pleasant garden. Lubango was a coveted field station, another well-kept and tree-lined town bright with blossom, and set in a bowl of cloud-dappled hills which one of our Irish contingent aptly commented brought him nostalgic memories of home.

Our police group in another coastal town further north – Sumbe – was not so fortunate. They were living in a decaying house in the most squalid conditions, which only major and expensive repairs could correct. The leader of the group was a fresh-faced young Irishman with a splendid sense of humour. He and his colleagues (all from different countries) certainly needed humour to stomach their surroundings. The Irishman admitted to me that his worst day had been the first, when he had nearly turned round and gone back. By the time I met him, however, several months later, he was in his element, settling disputes between the Government and UNITA in the local joint police monitoring group at night sessions round his scruffy table, and even writing begging letters in English for a group of Mexican nuns who, with perhaps more optimistic religious fervour than sense, were trying to build a seminary costing US$1 million in a country where most people didn't have enough to eat. We decided to establish a Weatherhaven camp forthwith, and on my next trip I found our team, now reinforced by electoral observers, encamped in a much more salubrious place near a white, palm-fringed beach.

At the southern end of Angola's Atlantic seaboard, Namibe, a seaside oasis in the midst of a vast desert stretching further southwards still to the Namibian border and beyond, also had its share of silvery strand. This was another place where the UNAVEM team lived in a hotel, a modest affair, but a paradise compared with the police group's quarters in Sumbe. Paradoxically the team in Namibe seemed less happy and united; discomfort may have its benefits!

As you moved further inland, to areas that had been more directly stricken by the conflict, conditions worsened. In one of the long, breathless letters I sent to my aunt during those early months (they became even more breathless, but shorter as the pace hotted up, and eventually were replaced by staccato telephone calls), I enthused over the climate of Huambo and the scenery of the high plateau, adding that 'as so often, the town was filthy and down-at-heel, ravaged by war and poverty'. Some of the smaller towns, such as Menongue and Kuito/Bié, were perking up with peace and making an effort to clean themselves up. This was also true of some larger ones, such as Malange, Luena and Saurimo, and indeed Huambo itself. Some, however, had a very long way to go. I shall not easily forget my first visit to Ondjiva, the capital of Cunene, another southern province bordering on Namibia. The desolate, abandoned little airport prepared us for what was to come. The only sign of life was a single white UN vehicle, with a blue-bereted officer standing stiffly to attention beside it. He was a member of the Spanish contingent, one of our two-man mobile border patrol stationed at Santa Clara, a frontier crossing into Namibia, some miles to the south. For the moment he was alone at the post. He told me that, far away in Spain, his wife was about to give birth to their fifth child.

As we drove into the town there were plenty of people to be seen in the dried-up river bed, mostly brightly dressed women and children, the women washing clothes and hanging them on rocks and bushes, the children desporting themselves in the tiny trickly of muddy water. But the town beyond was virtually no more, gone, obliterated by one of the savage South African air bombardments and never rebuilt. Eyeless and gaping, the shattered walls and empty rooms of what had once been attractive little houses with tiled roofs lay open to the sky. People somehow managed to live among the ruins. There was only one intact building that I remember, the Governor's pristine residence, which had just been rebuilt and was now watched over by a single, not very friendly guard, lolling in the front garden. The Governor, we were told flatly, was away. It looked as though plans might now be afoot to restore Ondjiva as the provincial capital and transfer the administration there from Xangongo. Since a Weatherhaven camp was obviously the only answer we selected a suitable site, but as it turned out the administration did not go back to Ondjiva and we had to accommodate everyone in Xangongo.

Our departure from Ondjiva that late afternoon was as memorable as the arrival. As we took off the sun was riding low in the sky, softening with gentle amber light the harsh contours of the encroaching scrubland and the skeletons of a few derelict buildings. In the middle of those macabre surroundings, a solitary figure in a waste of desolation, the Spanish officer in the blue beret stood once again stiffly to attention by his white vehicle with its UN flag and markings. As the Beechcraft gained height I observed from the window that he had remained in that position, and probably did so until our plane was no more than a silver speck in the distance. He may well have felt that we were his only fragile link with the world he had left behind to come to this God-forsaken place. To me his rapidly diminishing figure seemed a very fragile bastion against the inhumanity of war, of which we had seen so many manifestations that day. But it still looked a very important symbol.

Months later I visited Ondjiva again and this time drove to Santa Clara. It was quite a busy frontier post but still a rather benighted spot. The same Spanish officer was there, now accompanied by a Moroccan. After our briefing he took us out into the bush to visit a nomadic encampment nearby. Sheltering behind a thick thorn palisade, the encampment was home to people who wandered to and fro at will, as their forefathers had done for centuries, making nonsense of the frontier, an invisible line in the sand, and of any effort to maintain border control. Before we left the small Weatherhaven camp at Santa Clara we were given refreshments. They included a magnificent Spanish omelette made by our host.

Cooking in the wilderness seemed to be a favourite way of passing time. Another remote observer post was located at Sambo on a barren hilltop, not far from Huambo by helicopter but many hours' drive over bad roads. The five military observers there had the task, along with the resident joint CMVF group, of monitoring an assembly area containing several thousand FALA troops. It really was the middle of nowhere. In the centre of the tiny cluster of UNAVEM tents the team had erected a signpost with five arms pointing in the directions of their respective homelands, with the distances – to Spain, to Algeria, to New Zealand (I do not recall the nationalities of the other two). It seemed a dubious therapy to be constantly reminded just how far away one was from distant loved ones. More sensible was their practice of having cooking competitions in which each produced a meal representative of his country's cuisine. Goodness knows what they were like, as some of them confessed to me that they had never cooked before, but it probably proved a better means of communication than language, of which there was not a common one between them. And who knows, perhaps they returned home as better husbands!

These men confessed to me that they felt vulnerable. For the moment they had good relations with the FALA Commanding Officer of the assembly area, whom I met: an imposing personality in his late thirties who had been fighting for Savimbi since his teens, but who looked forward, he told me, to taking up a professional career in Benguela after the elections. But they were an easy target if ever things should go wrong. Their fears were prophetic. When hostilities broke out again in January 1993 the Sambo team (a different one by then) was violently harassed by UNITA supporters in an orchestrated act of intimidation. Two of our men, a Swede and an Argentinean, were beaten up. When we got them back to the UNAVEM clinic, the Argentinean was much more severely affected psychologically than one of his compatriots from Huambo, who had had an even narrower escape, with a bullet lodged near his heart. As the beaten man kept telling me, the problem was not his injuries, painful as they were, but the fact that the people who had administered them were those with whom he and his colleagues had lived closely for months, whom they greeted every day, and with whom they had thought to have a civilised relationship, approaching friendship.

The living conditions of the troops in the assembly areas were often parlous, despite consignments of WFP food and UNICEF medicines. The FAPLA areas were worse off, being usually more disorganised than UNITA and not as self-sufficient. But UNITA had its difficulties too. In May 1992 I went with General Unimna and some Ambassadors to Kuemba, Cuanza, Quirimo and Mussulo in the central region. This was a sensitive area because UNITA had marched its troops, with their families, from its designated assembly area to another, 100 kilometres away, on the ground that food had been insufficient. At one place the UNITA commander told us that there was a serious outbreak of influenza and diarrhoea, causing children to die daily. The sick were housed at some distance in derelict buildings – another deserted settlement – on the old Benguela railroad, which had long slipped into disuse because it was constantly blown up by UNITA. It was the middle of the day and blisteringly hot. We had to walk a long way through the bush to reach the place, where a pathetic sight awaited us. A few bedraggled women in bundles of rags huddled in the corners of filthy, abandoned buildings with blackened, suppurating walls, clutching emaciated babies whom they were vainly trying to comfort. One of the men, who said he was a doctor, took me round and showed me his 'clinic': on a rickety table in a similarly disgusting building I saw a few instruments and, as the sole supply of drugs, *one* sachet of UNICEF rehydration salts, much vaunted because they save babies from dying from diarrhoea and cost less than one US dollar per packet. When I got back to Luanda I asked the UNICEF director to send a supply immediately, but I was only too conscious that the same tragedy was multiplying all over the country, without respect for ideological or political affiliations.

UNITA's main base in the far south-east, the mysterious non-town of Jamba, had never appeared on any map, though it had for years been Dr Savimbi's headquarters and boasted an international class airstrip that had seen the coming and going of many internationally known people, US Senators and Congressmen, journalists and a constant flow of South African dignitaries and supplies. Yet the town itself could not easily be discerned from the air, being composed of grass-roofed huts, scattered over a wide area under the concealing canopy of the bush and indistinguishable from their natural surroundings. UNAVEM had two military observers in Jamba, under the umbrella of our South-Eastern Regional Command, located further north in Mavinga.

On Saturday 25 April 1992 I visited Mavinga and Jamba. In Mavinga I was met by the Regional Commander, then Colonel Mortlock of New Zealand, and after a bumpy ride to the camp on a track that must have become totally impassable in the wet season, followed by the usual briefing, I was flown by helicopter to the nearby FALA assembly area, strapped to a jump seat by the open door so that I could have a better view. Colonel Mortlock joined us for the onward flight to Jamba in the Beechcraft. The reception on our arrival was mind-boggling. A large concourse of young girls and youths were frantically dancing and chanting to the beat provided by equally frenetic drummers. As the aircraft ladder went down, a shy little girl presented me with a posy of paper flowers (the real kind don't grow in this parched region) and General 'Ben-Ben' came to greet me, followed by other dignitaries. He was the top UNITA general, doing the honours on behalf of his uncle, Dr Savimbi, who was in Luanda. He was also a brother of Engineer Salupeto Pena, although, apart from the same large, dark mesmeric eyes, they were not really alike. General 'Ben-Ben' was taller, with a more athletic and muscular build, as befits a military man. Perhaps as befits a guerrilla leader, there was also a slightly swash-buckling, even piratical, air about him. Like his uncle, he certainly had charisma, while his brother made more of a bureaucratic impression.

After some speeches and refreshments in the small airport building, we set off for the centre of Jamba, about 15 kilometres distant, along a dusty dirt track running through thin forest of low acacias, through which one glimpsed scattered dwellings. I rode with General 'Ben-Ben' in the first vehicle which, to my astonishment, turned out to be a British Range Rover. American pop music blared at full blast from the car radio. Sections of the trail were lined with smiling, chanting people waving UNITA flags, and behind us a long convoy of trucks churned up an impenetrable cloud of white dust.

After we had visited the quarters of our two observers – grass huts – there was a large and long-drawn-out luncheon followed by more speeches and the presentation to me of an elaborate carved wooden apparatus. In the centre of this was a large cylindrical pot, with a lid, and lined with yellow plastic foam. The central pot was surrounded by several similar, smaller pots, connected to it and to one another with spokes like an open wheel. I felt it impolite to ask what on earth it was for, and no one has been able to tell me since.

After lunch we made a rapid tour of the installations tucked away in this remote corner of the bush: a 'hotel', where I was shown the clean and comfortable-looking grass hut where I would have slept had I been staying the night; a well-equipped hospital, in which I saw a baby girl, only three hours old, already looking very much a little person, and fervently hoped that her future might be a better and more peaceful one; the Vorgan radio station – 'The Voice of the Black Cockerel', UNITA's emblem, which, from these unlikely surroundings, broadcasts as far as Europe; a printing shop already churning out UNITA propaganda for the elections; and a clothes factory. When I expressed surprise that the latter seemed exclusively to produce dark green military uniforms, as worn by the FALA troops, I was blandly told that they had a tremendous stock of this green cloth that must be used up and would be worn by civilians! It added a practical reason for the ever-present difficulty in distinguishing civilians from guerrillas, and hence in verifying what was actually going on at any point in time.

My arrival at each port of call was greeted by a doggedly enthusiastic crowd of young people, excitedly dancing and chanting and waving UNITA flags. When I came out they had mysteriously evaporated. Before long, I realised that I was seeing the same persons at each place, glowing black faces still beaming, arms and legs still wildly gyrating. It was a marvellously organised 'rent-a-crowd' operation – they were being trucked from point to point. The whole exercise nearly came unstuck, however, when our Range Rover indiscreetly passed the lorry that was rushing the 'spontaneous popular demonstration' back to the airfield to see me off.

There was a curious sequel. We were always meticulous about ensuring we visited Government and UNITA assembly areas, and other key points equally. I never went to Jamba again. But nearly four months later, on 12 August 1992, I visited Mavinga once more, this time accompanied by some journalists and a state television crew. This occasion was much more concerned with the election, but I also visited the assembly area to see how demobilisation was progressing. As usual, in the FALA assembly areas I was expected to address serried ranks of troops drawn up in a square, and the usual animated groups were present, cavorting and belting out songs in praise of Savimbi. It was a routine visit. Some weeks later people began to comment to me about a curious scene shown on television where, it was said, I was consorting with a large group of UNITA troops in *Jamba*. I had not seen it, but then a virulent attack on me appeared in the *Jornal de Angola*, following a series of articles questioning the impartiality of UNAVEM. The tone was very unpleasant, enquiring what on earth I was doing in Jamba, and, even more pointedly, what were all these UNITA troops doing there, when they should be confined in assembly areas? Even President dos Santos raised it with me personally. I explained that the scenes portrayed on the television were of the Mavinga assembly area, where I had been going about my legitimate business, and not of Jamba, where I had been only on one occasion, months earlier, in April. 'You must issue a *démenti* at once' advised the president. So I did, and it was published, but not given the same prominence as the original attack. A charitable interpretation would be that the national television had made a genuine error in substituting Jamba for Mavinga. But the mistake was so gross, and coincided so conveniently with the orchestrated campaign against UNAVEM, that it is hard to be charitable, especially since the national television crew had been with me in Mavinga and it was their footage that was used.

There could be no greater contrast to the esoteric surroundings of Jamba than the traditionally MPLA provincial capitals of Luena (Moxico), Saurimo (Lunda Sur) and Dundo (Lund Norte) in the north-east. The first two were the epitome of Portuguese colonial towns. Dundo was a surprising revelation. The nearby diamond mines were its *raison d'être*, and it was a neat town of square bungalows, set in well-kept gardens, which had been built by the British. It looked like a small British suburban town transplanted into the centre of Angola. During the pre-electoral period this was a relatively calm area, though there was a serious incident in Saurimo on 12 July, coinciding with the crisis in Malange, when several FALA/UNITA personnel were arrested by government police, and another on 3 August, when a FALA soldier was killed and UNITA claimed he had been shot by Government police.

The diamond industry in Lund Norte province was also a source of tension between the Government and UNITA. The Government had, somewhat ill-advisedly, passed a law lifting the monopoly on diamond mining and making it no longer illegal for individuals to hold diamonds. This had led to a flurry of small-scale mining activities by individuals, and by UNITA, which attacked the richer veins first, instead of following a rational process of extraction. De Beers complained that the carefully controlled world market was being disrupted by the flood of illegal diamonds from Angola. Diamonds were a tempting source of ready money for individuals suffering economic hardship or demobilised soldiers returning to civilian life to find they had no jobs or source of income, as well as for an organisation such as UNITA, which needed to finance its electoral and other operations.

Some of the most volatile areas were to the north of Luanda itself – M'banza Congo, capital of the province of Zaire, bordering on the country of that name (which was always a source of support for UNITA), Uige, capital of the province of the same name, N'dalatando, and Caxito, this last very close to Luanda. UNITA had a strong following in many of these areas, as did Holden Roberto's party, the FNLA.

My last routine trip in that area was to Uige on 2 September, when I met all the local authorities and visited a nearby assembly area occupied by FALA troops. There was a big parade and the customary chants and dances. This took place in front of an open grass shelter, in which I sat with my UNAVEM colleagues, the joint CMVF monitoring group and the FALA officer in charge of the assembly area. The assembled troops were arranged in a three-sided square, of which our grass hut formed the fourth, and at a considerable distance. Although I had managed to develop a parade-ground volume of delivery for such occasions, I did not think my lungs and larynx could bridge this gap, so when I stood up to speak I asked the commanding officer if the men could be brought a little nearer. The effect was electric. He barked an order and in seconds the men had advanced in perfect formation to within a few feet of me. I was totally surrounded. There was something very frightening about this instantaneous, machine-like discipline. I remember feeling glad that this was a friendly occasion; I would not like to have met them in less auspicious circumstances. As I had observed about their weapons on an earlier occasion, UNITA still looked very ready for business. I delivered my message of peace and democracy as clearly and forcefully as I could, and hoped it would sink in. Just before the helicopter left I was, to my embarrassment, presented with a handsome pair of live Bombay ducks. I could not imagine coping with them at Vila Espa, but there was no way I could refuse without causing offence and so the crate, with its loudly protesting occupants, was loaded on to the helicopter. In Uige I passed this gift on to our local team, suggesting they could provide a supply of eggs, for food was short. When I returned a week or two later for my meeting with Dr Savimbi, I was told that one of them had *drowned*. It did not seem an entirely likely story.

Not all of the omens were dire. When I visited N'dalatando on 14 August, my helicopter landed in the middle of the town. Before the blades had stopped whirling it was flanked by two large groups of opposing supporters – MPLA on one side and UNITA on the other – shouting slogans and waving banners as they closed in on both the helicopter and each other. It seemed a sure recipe for instant, disastrous conflict, with myself in the middle. As I climbed out of the helicopter, however, the two groups parted to let me through, exchanged some lively but basically good-humoured badinage, and pranced on their separate ways to the appointed meeting place. On such occasions as these you felt that, perhaps after all, the seeds of democracy, tolerance and cohabitation were beginning, however insecurely, to take root.

Similar feelings predominated when, on 27 August, *en route* between Xangongo and Santa Clara in the south, I visited the FAPLA assembly area of Cahama. Mass demobilisation was in process. The American C130s were coming in relays to the nearby airfield to transport those who had completed the formalities. The formalities were agonisingly slow, the one Polaroid camera was defective – a good example of how one detail can paralyse a whole process – and the queues long, but spirits were high and good humour prevailed. Many had already changed into civilian clothes. Some of them told me they had not seen their families for seven years or more. They were overjoyed at the prospect of reunion and it was difficult not to be infected by the general jubilation, and the feeling that a new phase of life in Angola was indeed about to begin.

Part V
The Elections and their Aftermath

14 The Moment of Truth

While Herculean efforts were going on to maintain political commitment to the process, no less a labour of Sisyphus was in progress on the physical organisation of the elections. The D-Days of 29 and 30 September loomed very near now.

For us it was 'all hands to the pump'. All leave and 'compensatory time off' were cancelled from 15 September. The staff of other UN organisations stationed in Luanda had responded magnificently to our request to serve as observers, and all UN vehicles that were even marginally roadworthy were pressed into service. Some non-governmental organisations (NGOs) also cooperated. Every international plane that arrived at the airport disgorged hordes of official and unofficial observers, journalists, and TV cameramen – all bent on taking part in that new spectator sport, election watching. There were to be some 800 international observers in all: 400 through the United Nations, and 400 to come directly from governments and specialist organisations.

The first group was our responsibility; the second was looked after by the NEC, with Ambassador Almeida in charge. Briefing sessions were held in Luanda before the observers went to their posts around the country, and Vila Espa was bursting at the seams – there were even traffic jams! People were living and sleeping in the most basic conditions. In the field they were even more difficult, especially as regards food, though the supply planes had been ferrying necessities of life to the far corners of Angola. Many people savoured for the first time the delectable joys of 'MREs' (meals ready to eat) – American forces' basic rations, of which one million had been provided by the United States. Rumour had it that they were leftovers from the Gulf War, so presumably with a long shelf life. But no one who was busy, hungry and out in the bush was looking at labels!

Fearing sporadic and perhaps even more general outbreaks of violence, we had made our security plans as elaborate as possible, but it was not feasible to anticipate every contingency. I addressed every briefing session, and security was one of the issues with which I had to deal. Fortunately the presence of 'old hands' who had done it all before, in Namibia, or Nicaragua, or Haiti, provided a steadying influence. There was, however, one pair of newcomers who required an inordinate amount of hand-holding. For the first time ever, Japan was sending two electoral observers. There had been much correspondence, the Japanese Government insisting on a guarantee that they would not be sent to any dangerous location and, even more specifically, that they would not leave Luanda. It was impossible to agree to such discriminatory treatment. I said that we would do everything possible to ensure their safety, as for all the other 398 observers, but the Japanese do not easily accept less than total compliance with their wishes. There were representations in New York, I was bombarded with telephone calls and visitors from the Japanese Embassy covering Angola (there was no Ambassador locally) and a high official from the Foreign Ministry in Tokyo was sent to Luanda to talk to me. When the two young men arrived they had strict instructions that they must see me and no one else, and be briefed by me personally! A compromise was reached: one stayed in Luanda, the other (as I recall) went to Lubango. One could understand the Japanese anxiety that no untoward happening should mar this first excursion in international peacekeeping (in Cambodia, a little later, there were Japanese fatalities) but the excessive demands made on our overburdened mission made one wonder whether it was worthwhile.

By the skin of our teeth, and after anguished and sometimes argumentative cables to Headquarters, we obtained INMARSAT sets and distributed them, thus greatly enhancing communications. The conference room in the downtown office was turned into a control room, bristling with wires and machines, and linked also to our communications office in the camp. Fleets of four-wheeled-drive vehicles had been shipped in and flown to their respective destinations up-country, where they would transport observers to those polling stations that could be reached by land.

Miraculously we had managed to assemble a miniature air force. The efforts described earlier resulted in additional contributions of some US$10 million for the airlift. After exploring possibilities of providing facilities in kind, the donors had ultimately decided that the most cost-effective way was to provide cash to hire the required aircraft, but little time was left in which to organise it all. Bids were sought and the best proposal was submitted by SkyLink, the company that provided UNAVEM's own air support and knew well the difficult flying conditions. They mainly used Russian surplus military aircraft with heavy cargo capacity, the cheapest obtainable on the international market. Russian crews came with them. The assembled fleet comprised 40 Russian helicopters (MI-17) carrying 3.5 tons of cargo each; and 10 fixed-wing planes (one Antonov-26, three Hercules C130s, and six Beechcraft and King Air planes). Together with UNAVEM's fleet of 14 helicopters and two fixed-wing planes – an Antonov-26 and a Beechcraft – this constituted the largest air operation ever assembled for a mission of this nature, most of it without any budget. Mammoth Russian Antonov-124s roared in over Luanda, each ferrying four of the helicopters. The last batch arrived on Friday 18 September, just in the nick of time to carry out familiarisation flights before the work began in earnest.

* * *

The air operation still had to face major setbacks, and in some cases tragedy. On three Saturdays running UNAVEM helicopters carrying electoral personnel and staff, crashed, all in remote sites in the northern province of Uige. The first was on 12 September and could not be located until 4 a.m. on Sunday morning because of loss of radio contact and the difficulties of night flying. At dawn a rescue operation involving seven helicopters, two Beechcraft and two C130s was mounted. At lunchtime I went to the airport to meet the C130 that brought back the injured – miraculously none of the 24 people on board were killed, but some of them immediately had to be flown to Windhoek in the Beechcraft for adequate medical attention. The tail rotor had hit a tree on take-off and an inquiry was immediately set up, but before its findings were complete a second accident happened on Saturday 19 September. Again there were no fatalities, and this time there was immediate radio contact and rescue was speedier. A tail rotor had hit a tree on landing.

But our relief that the gods, if not exactly favourable, had spared us the tragedy of death was immediately tempered by concern over the almost unbelievable coincidence that there should have been two accidents, two Saturdays running, to two identical helicopters operating in the same province, out of the same provincial airport. Uige was a particularly sensitive province. It was one of the most difficult to penetrate, being studded with curiously shaped angular mountains and high, jagged outcrops of rocks that abruptly reared up above an impenetrable mass of tropical forest. This craggy landscape was more often than not shrouded in swirling clouds and mists. Moreover the province was a strong source of support for UNITA, and the redoubtable terrain had made it impossible to register an estimated 100 000 of the people who were eligible to vote. Should we suspect sabotage or simply attribute the double catastrophe to a hostile natural environment?

Immediately after the furst crash we had grounded all flights out of Uige, and sent technicians to examine the aircraft there for defects or signs of tampering, as well as guards we could ill spare from Vila Espa to search the surroundings thoroughly and keep vigil day and night. Nothing suspicious was found, and flights had to be resumed if voting materials and facilities were to reach all those who had been registered in Uige province.

On the next Saturday (26 September) I was exhausted, having had very little sleep after the odyssey of my flight to Uige the day before to talk to Dr Savimbi and the subsequent all-night efforts to put the Secretary-General in direct touch with him. My spirits improved in the early afternoon with the news that the meeting between the two leaders would almost certainly take place that evening. And then at three o'clock, as if at the predestined hour, came the familiar radio emergency-call – another UN helicopter had disappeared in Uige province. A grim joke began to circulate in UNAVEM headquarters: if it is Saturday and 1500 hours, prepare for news of a helicopter crash and another search and rescue operation. This time we were not so lucky. The helicopter was again a Russian M-17, in this instance carrying election materials and ballot boxes, 12 members of the Angolan electoral staff and four Russian crew. It crashed while circling the village of Cassangongo, north-east of Uige, seeking a suitable landing site. Again a tail rotor hit a tree. The exact whereabouts of the crash were unknown at first and there was another anguished search through the night, hampered by low cloud and dangerous flying conditions, and this time by gunfire from the ground.

It was not until 11 o'clock on Sunday morning that the crash site was located. The rescue team found that everyone had perished, except one young Angolan, Francisco Domingo, who had suffered multiple fractures and spent the night surrounded by his dead comrades. He had shared the last minutes of one of the pilots who, before he expired, had just managed to send out the emergency signal that had given the first alert. The bodies of the Angolan officials were taken to their place of origin, Damba. Those of the slain Russian crew members came back to Luanda in the C130, together with the injured Angolan. It was a very sad group that witnessed the lowering of the huge back hatch of the Hercules, this time with no relief to temper the horror. There was only one stretcher to be carried off; the rest were shrouds. A few days later, when the sad formalities had been completed, we were all at the airport to see the coffins leave for Moscow, after a simple but moving ceremony.

The young Angolan's legs had been badly smashed and recovery would take long. He had nowhere to go, and so we took him into the UNAVEM clinic and he soon became a familiar sight in the camp. He was a native of Uige, and in his early teens he had been kidnapped, or press-ganged, by UNITA to join the FALA troops. He had not enjoyed the harsh conditions, and when signs of peace had begun to appear he had managed to escape to Uige, only to find that his parents had disappeared. He had become an electoral official with great optimism, and then suffered this terrible accident and the horror of a night in the bush, surrounded by the corpses of his companions. He was scared to go back to Uige lest he fell into the hands of UNITA again. He was not yet twenty. In a typical but incomprehensible Angolan way, he was not at all bitter – his face was invariably beaming even when, propped on his crutches, he leaned against the wire fence watching the UNAVEM men playing basketball or kicking a football around. He was mad about soccer. I asked Captain Waldecir apprehensively one day whether Domingo would ever play football again. He said he thought he would, but it would take a long time. When I left Luanda for good, nine months later, Domingo was still in the camp, but gradually becoming more mobile. His story was almost poignantly symbolic of the Angolan experience with peace and democratic elections.

The enquiries into the causes of the accidents could find no trace of evil-doing or anything approaching sabotage, shooting, or mechanical or technical defects, only pilot error, and hostile weather and terrain. In the case of the third and worst accident, it appeared that the crash had been precipitated by all the passengers rushing to one side to get a view of the village and the landing site.

* * *

The air operation was in full swing. Twenty five thousand people had to be flown to and from the 5800 voting stations during the elections. They were carried in 320 flights, which originated in each of the six distribution centres (hubs) and spread out like wheel spokes to all the polling stations, however remote. Six hundred and twenty metric tons of materials – ballot boxes, stationery, kerosene lamps, communications, equipment, tents, fuel and food – also had to be carried by plane to the polling stations. The Russian M-17 helicopters, the only ones that could reach the most inaccessible areas, carried 3.5 tons of cargo each. Six million litres (1.5 million gallons) of aviation fuel were required for this gigantic operation. The Angolan Government provided the fuel, but since there were few stores at airports outside Luanda, it had to be prepositioned across the country.

The planning of this intricate network of flight patterns and the supporting logistics had been done in only a few weeks by Colonel Hank Morris and his team. The six main hubs were in Luanda, Malange, Luena, Kuito, Menongue and Mavinga, which could receive fixed-wing aircraft. But they had very little else – airports were dilapidated, air traffic control skeletal – and were now to see more activity than at any other time in their existence, even at the height of the civil war. This was true even for Luanda. During the election days, all international flights were suspended and the borders closed but the airfield looked like a mini-Heathrow, with phalanxes of planes and helicopters, all hastily painted white instead of military grey, and bearing either the UN emblem or the attractive logo of the Angolan elections, a dove of peace. It was a living example of 'swords beaten into ploughshares'.

The existing, rudimentary air control facilities could not handle this volume of traffic. Hank Morris had told me a few weeks before that it was imperative to bring in a team of experienced air traffic controllers for each of the hubs. But how to get them? Again the lack of any budget seemed an insuperable stumbling block. The best way was to seek military air traffic controllers and I hit on the idea of asking Mig Goulding whether a few countries might provide such personnel in kind, in the manner that they were providing contingents of troops. Some money would be needed for travel and *per diem* but the sums would be relatively small. Mig thought this a viable idea, and obtained favourable reactions from several member states. However there remained the problem of language. English is the universal language of air traffic control, but these men, scattered around the provinces, would have to deal with local people unlikely to have any English. In the end, Argentina and Portugal supplied the specialised air force officers required. Angola thus provided another 'first' in the annals of inventive approaches to cost-effective peacekeeping.

There were other technical problems. The difficulties of the terrain were even greater than anticipated. Forty sets of global positioning systems (GPS) tracking equipment had to be bought and connected to three or four satellites in stationary orbit, so that each helicopter could follow its exact route and land within 12-feet of its targeted destination. Thus high technology also played a vital role in ensuring that the elections were free and fair. Extra satellite communications facilities and fuel bladders were provided by the United States.

On 22 September the fixed-wing planes flew to the six operational centres, loaded with supplies. From each centre helicopters then fanned out to the least accessible polling stations, carrying the required materials and international observers, mostly on 28 September. On the 29th and 30th, the two polling days, the same helicopters moved the international observers from station to station, so that they could have maximum coverage. The 400 UN observers were transported around their appointed areas by our own UNAVEM helicopters or vehicles. In the final tally the 200 two-person UN observation teams visited a total of 4480 polling stations.

When the voting closed on 30 September, the ballot papers were to be counted in each polling station and then flown to the provincial electoral centres. As each centre completed the exercise, the results were faxed to the NEC in Luanda. Fax and radio communications had had to be specially installed.

UNAVEM brought in a special consultant to carry out a 'Quick Count' analysis of the presidential election. This device rapidly analysed the results in a carefully selected mathematical sample of polling stations, and served as a secondary check of the freedom and fairness of the elections. The UN had used it with enormous success in Namibia, Nicaragua and Haiti, coming in every case within a few decimal points of the correct percentage; in Nicaragua it had been politically decisive. Nobody had any illusions that the 'Quick Count' could play such a pivotal role in Angola. It was a much larger undertaking, and prey to many more imponderables, but it would still be a useful double-check.

* * *

Although we had done all in our power to make sure that everything would be 'all right on the day', everyone in UNAVEM awaited the two D-days with apprehension bordering on dread. I know I did. I had long feared that violence was almost inevitable and my relief that the two leaders had met, and the joint Chiefs of General Staff sworn in at the eleventh hour, in no way blinded me to the extreme volatility of the situation. Every one of my political reports to headquarters since March had warned that the whole thing could go up in smoke at any time.

Contrary to the general conviction among many 'Angola watchers' that UNITA was bound to win, I had also emphasised that there could be no way of gauging which side would be the victor, and it might well be a close-run thing. As the elections drew nearer, many who had put their money on UNITA began to have second thoughts. The MPLA had run a clever campaign and its presidential candidate had performed much better than anyone could have expected. Its political propaganda had often been brilliant: the decision to use its final party political broadcast time, not to present its own candidate or programme, but simply to show clips of Savimbi ranting at campaign rallies had been a daring

The Moment of Truth

masterstroke. It had been assumed that the MPLA government's record of inefficiency, bureaucracy and, above all, alleged widespread corruption would weigh heavily against its parliamentary hopefuls and President dos Santos in the minds of the voters. Now, after the violent incidents that had marred the preceding months and weeks, it looked as though fear of UNITA might act as a counterbalance to the perceived venality and ineptitude of the Government. To anyone with an open mind, there could be no certainty as to how the voting would turn out. The contrast with what happened in South Africa a year and a half later is illuminating. There too the fear of violence was very great. But there was never any doubt as to who would win if the elections were free and fair. The only question could be, by how much? That certainty about the victor injected an element of stability into an otherwise highly precarious situation in South Africa that was notably absent in Angola.

On Monday 28 September I issued a statement, in which I congratulated the Angolan people on the maintenance of the peace process, the impressive success in registering the great majority of the adult population for the election and the generally peaceful electoral campaign. I referred to the slow progress in demobilisation and in establishing the FAA, but expressed the hope that the joint declaration by the two leaders on the disbandment of FAPLA and FALA would alleviate such concerns. I called for a further demonstration of leadership, restraint and tolerance by the major parties, and for all parties to pledge themselves to respect the results of the elections and look forward to building a new future, rather than look back in rancour to the tragic past, so that the remarkable achievements of the past sixteen months would not be jeopardised. This was, I reminded everyone, a truly historic moment, and the world would be watching.

* * *

Tuesday 29 September 1992 dawned. I followed my usual routine, hoping it would have a calming effect on my nerves. I was up with the light, did my back exercises at 5.30 and swam my kilometre in the pool at 6 a.m. As I showered and dressed I listened to the BBC World Service. The Angolan elections were the first item of international news that day, and the local correspondent, Anita Coulson, was already reporting from downtown Luanda on the long queues of so far orderly and calm voters who had also been up since dawn.

During the morning I found myself in an unnerving state of limbo. Used to working at full tilt almost round the clock I suddenly had nothing to do, except sit in my tiny hot office in the camp and listen to the radio. My staff were all frantically busy, patrolling the polling stations in Luanda and its surroundings, or monitoring the situation all over the country through the messages sent in by the outposted teams. We had agreed that I should stay at Headquarters, close to our central communications, so that, should anything go wrong, I would be on hand to take whatever decisions the situation might demand.

It was one of the longest mornings I ever remember spending in UNAVEM. It was too early for any proper news to come in, and the radio was mostly occupied by queries from our mobile teams on how to handle specific situations. When lunchtime at last came, the information reaching us from every quarter showed that, after an initially slow start in some places, voting was gathering pace in an atmosphere of general calm. That reassurance enabled me to escape for an hour or two in the afternoon. I went alone with my driver into town, stopping, unannounced, to visit polling stations on the way. All other business had stopped for the elections. Only the polling stations were hives of activity – rather slow activity in some cases, because everyone was taking pains to ensure that the voting procedure was followed to the letter, and some of the voters, performing this function for the first time in their lives, did not discharge it very speedily. The lines were long, and the heat and humidity laid a sultry pall over the shimmering city, encircled by the burning blue rim of the ocean. But tempers were astonishingly good (except for one man at a school, who demanded roughly of me, what on earth I thought I was doing: he clearly thought that I was trying to jump the queue!), the novelty and excitement of the event, as well as the extreme seriousness with which it was being taken by the people, offsetting the tedium and discomfort of the long wait.

I went on to the suburb of Viana just outside Luanda, a *bairro* in which UNITA seemed to have obtained a considerable foothold in the otherwise traditionally MPLA capital, and where earlier events had suggested there could be trouble. I made radio contact with some of our mobile teams, and joined up with them. They were mostly in schools, health centres or other communal buildings, usually in the most precarious and even ramshackle conditions, but they functioned thanks to the enthusiasm and dedication of everyone involved, from the electoral officials and the representatives of the parties to the voters themselves. Here in the vicinity of the capital many other parties, besides the MPLA and UNITA, were represented, watching every development with an eagle eye. In one station there was a lively discussion on some point of procedure, but the exchange was amicable as well as animated and was brought to a satisfactory outcome by a suggestion from our team.

I returned to Vila Espa, incredulous but content. Later that evening Sammy Buo brought me the assessments of the first day from our 19 provincial centres around the country. Even from areas that had been notorious trouble spots the reports were almost unanimously worded – 'generally calm', 'high turn out', 'no violence'. No major incidents had occurred anywhere. Where minor disorders had arisen, they had stemmed more from an excess of zeal on the part of the voters than from deliberate mischief. Although in many areas the crowds had been huge, they had been calm and disciplined, and any restive behaviour was attributed largely to fatigue, hunger or thirst from waiting for long hours under the hot sun. There were also reassuring reports that civic education programmes had paid off in familiarising voters with the procedures, although, predictably, the better-educated voters had completed the process more rapidly than others. In some places voting materials had not arrived in time for the starting hour of 7 a.m. By then, large numbers of citizens eager to vote had assembled and the delays had provoked some agitation, though not major violence, and in most cases the problems had been speedily solved.

Over the two days of voting UNAVEM was often the key mover in bringing about solutions, by transporting late voting materials and electoral officials to their destinations. Our vehicles also carried food for polling officers because the NEC did not have sufficient transport. Curiously, such needs proved greatest in the Luanda area. As the brief tropical twilight began to fall on the first night there were anguished calls for food, water, kerosene lamps and bedding material for those who would spend the night in the polling stations, guarding the ballot boxes. This vigil was going on all over the country. Everyone stayed: the polling officers, the representatives of the parties assigned to the particular station (including, invariably, both the MPLA and UNITA) and in some cases international observers. Clearly the philosophy of the Angolans was that if everyone watched everyone else, no mischief could be perpetrated. From Vila Espa we could only respond, after dark, to unforeseen emergency calls for basic creature comforts in areas reachable by road from Luanda. We stripped the camp of kerosene lamps, candles and matches, because even in this relatively built-up area there were long breaks in the electricity supply, and my repeated warnings of the need to purchase and distribute large supplies of lamps had gone largely unheard.

In many parts of Angola little groups spent the night of 29 September without food, huddled together in the polling stations in whatever wraps they could find (nights can be surprisingly cold there, especially in highland areas), their dark faces in some places barely visible in the flickering candlelight, in others merging indistinguishably into the surrounding blackness. No one dared to sleep. Outside, in the rural areas, the long patient lines of those who had trudged through the bush, sometimes for several days, also waited, hungry and sleepless, for the dawn and for their turn to come. What in other countries has become a routine, run-of-the-mill event, in Angola took on the air of a vigil, sanctified by fasting and privation, almost of a holy crusade in pursuit of the elusive grail of democracy and peace.

I, in contrast, slept better than I had for a long while, even if it was only for a few hours. I was up betimes to have news of what had transpired during the night. Nothing had happened. The hours of darkness had passed peacefully everywhere and at 7 a.m. the polling stations opened their doors again, everyone stretched their stiffened limbs in the early warmth of a still beneficent sun, and the voters began, like somnambulists, to file through the booths once more. In some places, especially where there had been delays the day before, the stations opened at first light. The parties had agreed beforehand that the hours of voting could be extended to permit everyone who had been registered to cast their vote, but lighting problems in many places limited that possibility to the hours of daylight.

We had agreed that, if the first day passed peacefully, I might visit a rural voting area in a place from which I could return very quickly if something went wrong. Sumbe, the capital of Cuanza Sul, was an obvious choice, barely an hour's flight down the coast and with a large rural hinterland. Once I was satisfied that the second day was proceeding as uneventfully as the first, I flew down there at noon and drove with some of the provincial electoral officials and our own observers to voting stations on the outskirts of the town. Sumbe was a small, sleepy town at the best of times, lulled by enervating sea breezes. On that Wednesday, 30 September, it was even more somnolent than usual. The election had been organised super-efficiently, virtually everyone had voted on the first day, and now only a few stragglers were lounging round the polling stations. There was disappointingly little to see.

Out in the countryside it was a different story. After a bone-shaking ride of about 45 minutes we came to a small school perched high on the peak of an arid hill and dominating the undulating landscape all around like a lighthouse. There was no village to speak of, only one or two shabby huts, a bleak, forlorn place where the soil was more like sand and there was scarcely a blade of grass. The population lived scattered over open, treeless country that stretched emptily to the far horizon, eking an impoverished living from a land sucked barren by long years of drought.

The sun was not long past its meridian, beating fiercely down, and there was no shade. Beneath its full glare were two long lines of voters, the women decorously separated from the men – a pattern common to most rural voting stations – some of them sitting or half-lying in the dust, their babies on their backs or suckling at their breasts, small children running around them. There were older people too, aged crones who walked with difficulty, bent old men leaning wearily on sticks. Whole families had made the long pilgrimage here, as if to a community outing. But there was no holiday air abroad, rather one of serious purpose. A few of them were talking softly to one another, but most were silent, contemplating this great event in their lives when for the first time they might have a say in their own future. They were quiet and disciplined and the atmosphere inside the polling station was the same.

The procedure was painfully slow, but absolutely correct. I talked to some of the waiting voters who could speak Portuguese. They were reticent, and yet they exuded a quiet confidence. They knew very well what it was all about. I was struck by the fact that they were all very thin. This might seem a surprising comment were it not that in Luanda, and in the provincial capitals, even poor Angolans, doomed to marginal lives in the *musseques*, tended towards a certain plumpness. However deficient their diet in many vital aspects, the staples of Angolan cuisine fostered an unmistakeable *embonpoint*. These people were in a different category altogether, the deprived and frugal denizens of a deprived and frugal land. Emaciation and indigence were the common characteristics that sprang to mind as one surveyed them and their surroundings – a small gaggle of people in a hostile landscape. It was this physical impression that heightened the contrast with the robustness of their attitude and their aims. They wanted to vote, they wanted peace, they wanted a better life, and they had, uncomplainingly, made great sacrifices to make their desires clear. Some of them had walked for two days. All those whom I saw had, at the end of the long trek, spent the night outside the polling station, squatting on the dry, dusty earth, impervious to the pangs of hunger and thirst, all stilled by their overwhelming passion to vote. It was impossible not to be moved by this sight, nor to be shamed by the casual, even indifferent approach of Western voters, who take their democratic privileges for granted, often to the extent of not exercising them at all.

I could tell that two young American observers, who had seen other elections before, shared my wonderment. As if in unison they said, 'This is textbook, absolutely textbook. We have never seen anything that so scrupulously followed all the rules'.

They had visited a number of similar stations, as I was to do on the way back to Sumbe. In one of them we ran into a small group of Dutch observers who, like the Americans, were not attached to the UN team. Their views completely reflected those I had heard earlier. Knowing the limitations and the background of Angola, they could not believe that things could be going so smoothly, nor that election procedures could be so efficient.

Reflecting on the experience during the flight back to Luanda, it seemed to me that the scene at the school epitomised all that the elections meant to the ordinary men and women of Angola – the hopes and fears, the sacrifices, and above all the sheer doggedness of that long vigil in the heat and dust, and the pride and satisfaction, almost disbelief, with which they afterwards held aloft their indelibly stained hands to show that they had voted.

The news when I got back to the camp was of similar scenes all over the country, all unfolding in the same unruffled calm, with no reports of major incidents of violence, intimidation or interruption. After the brisk start on the first day, the pace had been slower because the majority had already cast their votes. There were some problems, mostly resolved to everyone's satisfaction with the intervention of UNAVEM. Some polling stations experienced a shortage of voting materials (electors were not required to vote at the place where they had registered and it was therefore impossible to predict accurately the number likely to turn up), and once again UNAVEM jumped into the breach to transport additional supplies, as well as blankets and food. Problems of lighting again arose, in some places causing operations to be suspended before the appointed time of 7.00 p.m., while in many others it was impossible to start counting the votes immediately after the close of the poll as the instructions required. UNAVEM again managed to find and distribute hundreds of lamps. At our urging Dr Caetano, the President of the NEC, announced on national television and radio that, in polling stations without lighting, counting could instead begin the following morning, 1 October. That meant a second night's vigil over sealed ballot boxes for the electoral officials and the party watchdogs. He also urged that all polling stations remain open until 7.00 p.m. and that all eligible voters who arrived before that time should be allowed to vote, no matter how long it took. This, of course, was only possible where there was lighting.

The turnout everywhere was reported to be massive, and tranquil. There was an isolated incident in Luanda, where armed UNITA elements surrounded a school building in which a polling station was located, but it ended peacefully through the intervention of a CCPM joint police monitoring unit, with the support of UNAVEM police observers.

An air of subdued euphoria pervaded the UNAVEM camp in Luanda that night. Everyone was too exhausted to celebrate, and in any event most were working into the small hours again, attending to problems and observing the counting of votes. But as they went about their tasks, everyone was smiling in quiet jubilation, mingled with an overwhelming sense of almost disbelieving relief that all should have gone so well.

Angola had not only had its first democratic election. It had also had the two most peaceful days in 30 years of continuous warfare.

* * *

One would like to be able to add that these had been the only two days in that long history of bloodshed when no shot had been fired in Angola. There had, however, been one ominous incident, early on 30 September, about which I learned on my return from Sumbe. It was apparently unconnected with the elections but its potentially disastrous consequences could not be ignored.

The incident had occurred in Miramar near the residence of Dr Savimbi, which was virtually a fortified garrison with a huge complement of the security guards allowed for the protection of UNITA leaders under the Bicesse Accords, for which no limit had been specified. His house was located in a quarter containing, besides many Embassy residences, Government villas occupied by Ministers and other senior officials, as well as the charming little house that was the pride and joy of Antonio Monteiro. One house was occupied by a Deputy Minister of the Interior, Armindo Espiritu Santo, and, like the other Government villas, was guarded by police. On the pretext that it was being used to plot an attack on the life of Dr Savimbi, armed UNITA men had stormed the premises, shot the guards and taken over some of the surrounding houses. One unfortunate policeman had tried to save his skin by running away. He had been shot down in cold blood in the tiny garden of Antonio Monteiro's house. Antonio had heard the shots and was confronted by the bleeding corpse lying before his front door.

Once again, the CCPM had to meet to discuss a tragic incident of which we had seen all too many during the preceding months. It was a gruesome reminder of the great tensions and dangers that still had to be overcome if Angola was to have lasting peace.

15 The Aftermath

With morning, harsh reality began to impose itself in other ways on our short-lived elation. There was some good news. Preliminary estimates showed that over 80 per cent of Angola's 4.86 million registered electors had voted. Later, the final figures raised this to 92 per cent or a total of 4.4 million voters, an outstanding performance by any standards, certainly by those of Western democracies where it is considered a triumph if even 50 per cent of the electorate turn up at polling stations on their doorsteps. The security situation and the general atmosphere throughout the country were both calm. Following the Miramar incident, the number of security forces in Luanda increased significantly early on Thursday 1 October, but by mid-day they were less conspicuous. Nonetheless the air was full of anxiety as to whether the next great challenge, acceptance of the results, would be equally peacefully met. Everyone was on tenterhooks to hear the results, but by next morning it was disturbingly clear that the vote counting would take far longer than anticipated.

This was not only because of delays due to lack of lighting or transport. Ironically, the major problem was an *excès de zèle*. Everyone took their responsibilities with deadly seriousness: our observers told of electoral officials and party representatives sitting together for hours and hours, through more long nights, counting and recounting the votes, checking and rechecking possible anomalies and investigating queries. By all accounts the proceedings were invariably amicable – to the extent even of the MPLA men saying to the UNITA representatives 'Here, I think this one is really yours', and *vice versa*. Many UN observers told me how struck they were by the general spirit of camaraderie, and the sense of 'we are all in this together, and so much is at stake that we'd better get it right'.

But this painstaking approach did not make for quick results, and lengthy suspense was dangerous. Some results came in quickly, but mainly from Luanda and nearabouts and these were inevitably skewed. The processing of results was also complicated by difficulties with the NEC's computers and by frequent power cuts. Against our strong advice the NEC had moved from the dilapidated but functional building we shared downtown to a refurbished colonial edifice – very elegant, but the new generator had promptly burned out.

I was faced with a dilemma. My public statement on the freedom and fairness of the elections could not be made until the NEC officially announced the final results, but now it was clear that this might take up to eight days. I was under great pressure to say something and total silence could be misinterpreted in the generally tense atmosphere. Late on Thursday 1 October I made a brief progress report on television and radio, as well as through a press communiqué, which was also issued at the noon briefing at UN Headquarters in New York the next day. I have been criticised in some quarters for issuing a statement at that point, but the text was studiously non-committal and meant to have a calming effect. It merely congratulated the Angolans on an excellent turnout and their demonstration of civil responsibility, warned that the counting would take several more days and counselled patience and serenity in the interim.

At 10.30 a.m. the next day, Friday 2 October, Engineer Salupeto Pena and 'Foreign Minister' Chivukuvuku asked to see me. To our relief both UNITA men were smiling and relaxed. Chivukuvuku said they wanted to give us, at Dr Savimbi's express request, UNITA's view of the situation. Their news was encouraging. UNITA considered that UNAVEM had done 'a very good job' and that the election process had generally gone well. There had been some problems, particularly in Luanda and Malange. UNITA was putting together a complete picture and would present its position in due course. The main reason for their visit was UNITA's concern about the way in which the Government was presenting unofficial election results through the media, virtually claiming it had already won, when the NEC had received only a small proportion of the results, mainly from urban areas (traditionally MPLA sympathisers). This was creating nervousness and could lead to real danger. Chivukuvuku alleged that in some areas MPLA groups were crowing over UNITA groups, claiming victory, and were beginning to settle old scores. UNITA feared that vote counting might even be disrupted and an assertion made that, up to that point, the MPLA had been winning. They appealed to UNAVEM to help put some discipline into the process. The election results should be announced only by the NEC, especially since UNITA considered that 'everyone still has very good prospects' of winning the elections. I proposed that the NEC should appoint a single spokesman to announce the results and Dr Chivukuvuku agreed that UNITA would take up this matter officially with the NEC.

I immediately went to see Dr Caetano de Souza and Dr Onofre dos Santos, who readily agreed to appoint an official spokesman. Dr Caetano subsequently selected Ambassador Almeida, who was arguably not the best choice, being the Government's appointee on the NEC and someone who made no secret of his strong MPLA affiliations.

In the early afternoon John Flynn, the British Ambassador, visited me and we agreed that the situation did not look too bad, provided the counting process could be speeded up and the results presented more objectively. At six o'clock I saw the Vice Interior Minister, 'Petroff', who confirmed that the security situation seemed under control, despite the Miramar incident, though he angrily denounced UNITA for refusing to return the body of the slain policeman. I told him I had made an appeal to Dr Savimbi through Engineer Salupeto Pena for its return.

When my senior colleagues and I assessed the situation that evening, our mood was one of guarded optimism. The UNITA representatives had had no major criticisms of the handling of the elections – indeed they thought they had gone well – and their concerns were legitimate. So far, so good, was our summing-up that Friday night.

* * *

Barely 12 hours later that view suffered a severe reverse. At lunchtime on Saturday 3 October, Antonio Monteiro called me. He was greatly exercised about a 'Message to the Angolan Nation', that had just been broadcast by Jonas Savimbi, which he described as 'distinctly warlike'. We at once sent our liaison officer to UNITA to obtain the text.

It was hard to tell how far the speech was a prepared one. There was a consistent theme, which suggested a structured approach and a degree of premeditation, but there was also a lot of repetition, which was characteristic of the UNITA leader's 'off-the-cuff' style. The speech began unobjectionably enough, recalling UNITA's long struggle and many sacrifices to achieve peace and democracy, and appealing to 'all UNITA militants to remain calm and serene'. The next sentence, however, could be variously interpreted, depending on your view of UNITA's intentions: 'Each one at his post should accomplish the orientation that he or she had received'. Anyone inclined to detect an ominous ring would have found it echoed in the next passage:

> It is a pity for me to tell you that the MPLA wants to cling to power illegally, tooth and nail, by stealing ballot boxes, beating up and deviating polling list delegates and distorting facts and numbers through its radio and television network. I appeal to all the Angolan people to remain serene. I appeal to all UNITA militants to remain vigilant as in the past. At the right time, we will give an adequate response to the MPLA manoeuvre.

A virulent attack on the MPLA followed, accusing it of wanting to retain power 'as it did in 1975'. It was, Dr Savimbi went on, 'the duty of us freedom fighters, those who through their blood and sweat brought about democracy to this country, to tell you that the MPLA is not winning and cannot win'. The reality, in contrast to the 'inflated numbers' propagated by the MPLA was that 'in all provinces, UNITA is ahead both in the presidential and parliamentary results, in a noble and just recognition of those who fought for the country's liberation'. He attacked the NEC (of which UNITA was a part), challenging it not 'to repeat only what the Futungo de Belas Presidential Palace is saying', coupled with a barely disguised threat: 'All its [the NEC's] manoeuvres through the falsification of numbers and tampering with the computers, will lead UNITA to take a position which will deeply disturb the situation in this country'.

The speech continued, 'just as we said in 1975, to the late President, Dr Agostinho Neto: "It is easy to start a war, but to prolong and win it is difficult." If the MPLA wants to opt for war, it knows that such a war will never be won'. After this bellicose statement he claimed that 'We want Angola to live in peace', adding, with significant emphasis, 'and that the electoral process be transparent and honest in such a way as to convince Angolans and not foreigners'. He added for good measure, 'as far as we are concerned' (it was not clear whether this was a royal 'we' or referred collectively to UNITA as a whole), 'it will not depend on any international organization to say that the elections were free and fair. It will only depend on the observations of all Angolans as to whether all registered Angola voters actually voted, and whether all the ballot boxes were not tampered with or stolen and that everybody has a tranquil conscience that they participated freely in the act of citizens determining the path to be followed by Angola'.

More coded messages hinted at a possible violent reaction by UNITA to the MPLA's alleged corruption and fraud, usually incongruously rubbing shoulders with impassioned pleas to the Angolan people to remain calm. A fine spate of rhetoric towards the end was typical: 'Angolans resident in Luanda should be calm. Angolans in the north should be serene. Angolans in the central highlands, the western part of the country and the south should be confident. When necessary, we will assume our responsibilities'. Yet the next sentence, seeking to reassure, generated only ambiguity and unease: 'We would like that none of us, be it the MPLA, UNITA or some other political party should have the courage to plunge this country into war once more. History will never forgive those ambitious men who only derive profits and money and never render service to the people'.

In his final words, Savimbi claimed his speech aimed to 'calm down all Angolans' (it had quite the opposite effect); to alert the NEC 'not to be instrumental in the Futungo de Belas Presidential Palace fraud'; and to thank UNAVEM, the UNDP and other international organisations. This last remark was more than a little blunted by the next: 'We would also like to say that Angolan interests come first as far as we are concerned than any accommodation with international opinion, which is foreign opinion'. The final sentence was another rhetorical call: 'Angola should be calm. Angola should be serene. Angola should be confident. With Angola the future is secure'.

It was difficult to make head or tail of the real intention behind these sibylline and often contradictory utterances. If it was meant as a warning shot across the bows, and no more, the timing seemed extraordinary, especially after the general satisfaction registered by Savimbi's two senior CCPM representatives the day before. Nothing had come to light in the interim to justify the escalation from concern over the manner of announcing the results to these virulent accusations of major fraud. Was it a panic reaction to the initial results, which, coming from areas of readier access known to favour the MPLA, appeared to show a slide towards the Government in both legislative and presidential elections? If so, it revealed a degree of naivety incompatible with Savimbi's personality and sophistication. But whether this was the impulsive reaction of an unquiet mind, or a calculated first step in a series of premeditated actions, the episode bore all the signs of destabilising an already very fragile situation. I was deeply worried and called Mig Goulding that Saturday evening to tell him so.

Later on Saturday afternoon the CCPM met. Bewilderingly, in view of his leader's speech, Engineer Salupeto Pena (the only UNITA representative present, a rare occurrence in itself) still maintained the same generally positive view as on the previous day, albeit with some new qualifications. UNITA considered the voting had gone very well, despite some incidents, among which figured, for the first time, the allegation that scores of votes had gone missing – with the intervention of the antiriot police – and that 20 ballot boxes had disappeared. The process was far from finished, he said, and UNITA questioned the delays in the transmission of results from certain provinces. He repeated his concern about the announcement of unofficial results by the media, saying that this had led to 'aggressive euphoria' by MPLA militants, especially in Luanda, forcing people to flee from their homes. He asserted that people had entered Angola from Namibia to vote. If the alleged frauds were not properly examined, there was a risk that UNITA would not accept the results (the first time that such a possibility had been mentioned, and in direct contradiction to the joint declaration made by Dr Savimbi and President dos Santos the previous Saturday). These concerns had led Dr Savimbi to make his radio speech, of which UNITA was distributing texts 'so as to avoid misinterpretations'. Since the text was riddled with ambiguities, this remark could only be described as disingenuous.

The Government, in contrast to UNITA, was present in force, in the persons of General N'dalu, Vice Interior Minister 'Nando' and the Vice Minister of Foreign Affairs, Venâncio de Moura. They noted that some of UNITA's complaints (for example the alleged deviation of voting kits) had already been dealt with. General N'dalu said there had been few possibilities of fraud, since party agents had been able to follow every detail of voting and counting, while the international observers had confirmed that so far everything had gone well. The Government could not stop the media from publishing unofficial results, or party members from prematurely boasting of victory. However all parties, including UNITA, had to control their militants. The police had been 'nervous' in recent days, but UNITA also had to control the behaviour of its supporters and its security troops, particularly around Dr Savimbi's house in Luanda. UNITA had been impeding proper investigation into recent incidents, such as an attack on the national radio station and the killing of the policeman near Miramar. The Government had information that troops in FALA uniforms were moving in Nharea (Bié province); Alto Zambeze, Cazombo and Luchazes (Moxico province); and Uige and Malange provinces. These troop movements were disrupting the collection of ballot boxes. The Government considered that the CCPM, the CMVF and the NEC should investigate all complaints, and warned that it was 'very dangerous' of Dr Savimbi to say that the NEC was committing fraud and was controlled by Futungo de Belas. It would also be very serious if Dr Savimbi was warning that UNITA would not accept electoral results announced by the NEC and verified by UNAVEM.

Not a whit abashed, Engineer Salupeto Pena repeated UNITA's position that, unless all its allegations were properly investigated, there was a risk that UNITA would not accept the election results. He was surprised at the reports of FALA troop movements, and would like to see proof. He also claimed surprise that the CCPM group investigating the Miramar incident had not yet been able to function properly. UNITA had given orders that people should not be prevented from moving freely around Dr Savimbi's residence.

In what I hoped would be a calming intervention, I emphasised that UNAVEM remained determined to ensure the transparency of the electoral process in every way possible, even though this meant going beyond mere observation and verification. We would investigate every complaint backed up by hard evidence, and take proven irregularities into account in making our final evaluation, but I reminded Engineer Salupeto Pena that the Electoral Councils were the main channels for dealing with alleged fraud, and that the machinery for this had been accepted beforehand by all parties.

Salupeto Pena then launched himself into an impassioned outburst. Reliance could not be placed on the NEC. Angola was in crisis, he declaimed. It was all very well for the international observers, he went on bitterly, they would leave the country and go home, and the unfortunate Angolans would have to live with the results. UNAVEM should intervene more directly. His remarks seemed hardly credible only a few hours after his leader had decried the usefulness, and even relevance, of international verification. One was left with the unavoidable impression that it would be accepted only if its pronouncements said what UNITA wanted said. Months of experience in the CCPM had perfected my capacity to turn the other cheek, and I forbore to point out the anomalies in Salupeto Pena's statement, simply saying that we were well aware of how critical the present juncture was for all Angolans. All the UNAVEM staff, and I in particular as the Special Representative of the Secretary-General, were deeply conscious of our responsibilities, which we intended to carry out to the maximum of our ability. On that note the meeting closed.

I immediately walked round the table to Engineer Salupeto Pena and said that, in view of UNITA's allegations, I felt it to be of the greatest importance for me to have an urgent meeting with Dr Savimbi. He promised to convey my message. Normally Savimbi responded with great alacrity to such requests. This time a blanket of silence fell. I waited all Sunday in the camp, but no message came. This was not directed against me only: I learned from various sources that Savimbi had received no visitors and spoken on the telephone to no one at all for the past several days.

* * *

All who had observed the elections were unanimous in their accolades. On 1 October the European Community congratulated the Angolan people 'for the success of its first exercise in democracy' and urged all sides 'to work together for the reconstruction of Angola'. Observers from the European Parliament and Canada later expressed broad approval of the ballot counting, describing it as 'free and secret' and saying they had observed no fraud or bias, thus confirming the experience of the UNAVEM observers. The Zimbabwean Deputy Parliamentary Speaker said that Angola's elections set an example for other African countries, a sentiment echoed on 5 October by Ambassador Ba, a high-ranking electoral observer from Senegal. It was hard to avoid concluding that UNITA's allegations were a petulant response to the initial indications that the MPLA and President dos Santos had gained more votes, an impression fortified by its failure to substantiate its accusations.

The Americans were embarrassed by Dr Savimbi's speech and Assistant Secretary Cohen sent a personal appeal to him not to disrupt the process. Jeffrey Millington, earlier considered to favour UNITA, stated publicly on 3 October, after talking to President dos Santos, that the elections had been impressive, that he was unaware of any fraud and that the ballot counting, though slow, was going smoothly. He challenged UNITA to give proof of Savimbi's charges that the all-party NEC had tampered with the results. In Washington, Jeff Davidow tried to play down Savimbi's speech, saying that the United States had confidence in UNAVEM's verification (US observers, sent bilaterally and independently of UNAVEM, all concurred in the verdict of fair play), that he interpreted Savimbi's remarks as aimed at 'calming down the situation', and that procedures existed to investigate allegations of fraud.

During the weekend we tabulated our 'Quick Count' of the presidential elections, based on 166 polling stations. The results were dramatic. They showed President dos Santos as getting 49.2 per cent, Savimbi 38.2 per cent, and the rest (including spoiled or blank ballots) 12.6 per cent. If the sample was true, it meant that there would have to be a second round between the two protagonists, since neither of them would have achieved the required 50 per cent. But we had no option but to keep them in reserve as a yardstick against which to judge the accuracy of the official results, when finally announced. We dared not publish them earlier, partly because – this being the first time the technique had been attempted in a country of such size and complexity – we could not be sure of the margin of error, but more importantly because the estimated number of votes for President dos Santos fell short of 50 per cent by just 0.8 per cent. Only a small margin of error could mean that the second round would not be required. The second round was the nub of the question. If Dr Savimbi could be made to understand that all was not lost for him, that he would have a second chance to win the presidency, then he might be dissuaded from taking some precipitate and irretrievable step that would plunge the country back into chaos. This was the main reason why I was desperately anxious to see him: while it would be too risky to give him the exact percentage of our Quick Count, I could at least assure him that we had strong indications there would have to be a second round, to clinch all the other arguments against reacting too soon, and too rashly, to the initial results.

But Dr Savimbi remained invisible, and indeed *incomunicado*. I passed the message through Salupeto Pena, but it was not the same thing by a long chalk.

* * *

The mystery about Dr Savimbi's whereabouts and intentions deepened. On Monday 5 October the crisis deepened also.

The NEC President convened a meeting, at 3 p.m., of NEC members, party representatives, CCPM delegation heads and UNAVEM, to reduce tension and mistrust by clarifying the procedures being used. It lasted four hours and was an unmitigated disaster. The representatives of some parties, including UNITA, took over the agenda with a well-orchestrated chorus of 'widespread fraud'. Dr Caetano's attempt to explain how the NEC was going about its business was derailed by one of the small parties angrily declaring that the party representatives were not students to be lectured at, but were there to present their grievances, a cry that was taken up by others.

Those in attacking mode began to give voice, with a bevy of small parties rehearsing a litany of criticisms that ranged from lack of transparency (overlooking the fact they had thwarted the NEC president's attempt at transparency) to very general accusations of alleged fraud. It was obviously a carefully calculated build-up to the crescendo provided by UNITA. Later it was alleged that the parties who had expostulated the loudest had received generous offers of pecuniary support from UNITA.

The Secretary-General of UNITA, Aliceres Mango, insisted that the NEC should not publicise definitive results (a fresh element), and that if it dared to do so it would have to take responsibility for 'the consequences for the country'. An even more violent broadside followed from Dr Chivukuvuku, who sang a very different tune from that of only three days before. He went further than the now almost monotonous refrain of 'widespread fraud' to proclaim that 'UNITA categorically rejects the process', adding that UNITA would reconsider its position only if the NEC together with the political parties, reexamined all the data received, verified excess voting material supplied by De La Rue, had the NEC computer system examined by experts from the political parties, and investigated alleged irregularities, such as the behaviour of the police and the disappearance of voting kits and ballot boxes.

The defence of the electoral process was led by the MPLA Secretary-General, Marcolino Moco. In a clear reference to Dr Savimbi's speech, he said that the MPLA did not understand why 'some parties' were launching declarations of war. The MPLA would not cast the first stone, and whoever wanted to start a new war should ask themselves against whom they intended to wage it. He reminded everyone that there was a proper mechanism to investigate complaints, that is, the NEC. Other parties and some presidential candidates expressed their general satisfaction, emphasising that all parties were represented in the NEC; and that instead of criticising the NEC, they should make better use of it. Every specific complaint (as opposed to general, unsubstantiated allegations) should be investigated but not used as a pretext for questioning the whole peace and electoral process. The Angolan people would not accept another war.

After this verbal duel, Dr Caetano promised that the NEC would compare its data on election results with those presented by the presidential candidates, or by UNAVEM. He made clear that any allegations of fraud must be specific and presented in writing; some complaints by UNITA were already being investigated and replies would be presented shortly.

It was a lame finish to a thoroughly unsatisfactory meeting. My assessment was made all the gloomier by the increasingly aggressive tone of Vorgan broadcasts, by a surge of Government allegations (also unsubstantiated) about movements of FALA troops, and by outbreaks of violence in some provinces. In an attempt to resolve this dangerous impasse I invited General N'dalu, Engineer Salupeto Pena, and the directors of the MPLA and UNITA election campaigns, Mr Kundi Payhama and Dr Chivukuvuku, to a private and unpublicised meeting with me the next day, Tuesday 6 October, at 11 a.m.

* * *

A worse blow still was to fall that night. Reaching the camp at about 8 p.m. I received the news that General 'Ben-Ben', the new joint Chief of General Staff, and all the senior UNITA generals had abandoned the FAA, to which they had sworn undying allegiance only one week before. They had issued a 'Declaration of the FALA in the FAA', a title indicating they had never considered themselves as integrated into the new joint army. It was signed by General 'Ben-Ben' and 10 other generals, including Chilingutila, Wambu, Zacarias, and 'Mackenzie' from the CCPM. The declaration claimed that massive electoral fraud had undermined the democratic process and that all the generals, officers, sergeants and soldiers from FALA were abandoning the FAA in 'profound protest'. They did not wish to return to war, but in order to 'avoid the worst' they posed three conditions:

- The electoral process, which had been 'marred by frauds and violations on a scale never before seen in the history of emerging democracies', should be reviewed or cancelled outright.
- The NEC should not publish any results, either provisional or definitive, without a decision on the complaints made by political parties.
- Account should be taken of the fact that many voters had been intimidated by the antiriot police.

They said they were ready to return as soon as serious negotiations took place between the MPLA Government, the UNITA leadership, and all representatives of the 'genuine' opposition to resolve the crisis. 'We are soldiers, and our sole desire is to serve our country and true democracy.'

This bombshell caused a predictable furore. Late on Monday night General N'dalu called an emergency meeting of the CCPM Heads of Delegation for 11 a.m. on Tuesday morning and asked me to postpone the private meeting I had arranged with the two sides; I still planned to hold it, although its slim chances of producing a breakthrough looked bleaker than ever. The US, Portuguese, British and French Ambassadors met through a large part of Monday night; they had wanted me to join them but the telephones were not working and the heavy security arrangements deterred them from coming to the camp. All four countries had been involved in the formation of the FAA, and all but Portugal were members of the Security Council. After consultation with their capitals, they agreed that the rapidly deteriorating Angolan situation should be discussed in informal consultations among Security Council members in New York, the following day (Tuesday). I cabled some briefing notes to the Secretary-General but it was difficult to see what the Council could do, except issue admonitory statements.

I, too, had a sleepless night, wondering what on earth I could do to stem this headlong slide back into disaster. I concluded that only a very personal approach to Dr Savimbi, appealing to his place in history, could have any chance of success. As if by telepathy, a cable arrived from Mig Goulding, enclosing a personal letter that the Secretary-General had decided to write to Dr Savimbi on the Sunday after his radio broadcast, and which I was to deliver by the fastest available means. The letter, written in French, recalled their long association and Dr Savimbi's decisive role in Angolan history, and made an emotional appeal to him to face the new challenges 'avec cette magnanimité et cette humilité qui sont inséparables de la grandeur'. He reminded Dr Savimbi of what his hero, General de Gaulle, had said at a low point in his fortunes in 1950 – 'On peut être grand, même sans beaucoup de moyens; il suffit d'être à la hauteur de l'histoire' – and recalled another famous phrase of de Gaulle's: 'Quand une décision est lourde, difficile, incertaine, il faut regarder vers les hauteurs: là, il n'y a pas d'encombrements'. The letter went on to say that Angola would have greater need of him than ever in the new stage following the elections, which the United Nations was convinced had been carried out correctly. This was why, the Secretary-General said, he was appealing personally to him to bring together all the Angolan people, through moderation and scrupulous respect for the verdict of the urns, and for peace. Savimbi's stature, enhanced still further by a spirit of magnanimity, could serve the whole of 'notre cher continent africain'.

It was a magnificent letter, a *tour de force*, and an answer to my prayers.

Mig's cable said that although UNITA's abrupt departure from the FAA a day later had raised great doubts about Savimbi's intentions, the Secretary-General still wanted the letter to be sent. Evidently the Secretary-General later had second thoughts, for another cable came from Alvaro de Soto, saying that the Secretary-General would leave it to my judgement as to whether or not to deliver the letter. I replied that I was convinced that only a very personal approach of this kind could have any chance of success, and that no one could do this with more eloquence and authority than the Secretary-General. I wrote a personal note to Dr Savimbi, enclosing the facsimile text and reminding him that I had asked to see him.

Armed with this I set off for the CCPM, since the best way of ensuring the safe delivery of the letter was through Salupeto Pena, Dr Savimbi's residence and office in Miramar being now a bastion that no mere messenger, even one with a blue beret, could penetrate. Several hours of waiting ensued in the insalubrious and deadening heat of my office in the CCPM building. The emergency meeting of the CCPM Heads of Delegation could not start, owing to the non-appearance of the UNITA delegation, a favourite tactic of theirs that had been used with infuriating frequency during the tense days before the elections. News gleaned from the other delegations as we hung around, providing lunch to the mosquitoes but getting none ourselves, gave little ground for comfort; there was still no news of Savimbi's whereabouts and it was widely assumed that he had fled the city. Even more worryingly, General 'Ben-Ben' too had disappeared, and was said to have travelled to the interior. General N'dalu, visibly and uncharacteristically anxious and irritated, tried to contact Salupeto Pena. In the end it was 1.15 p.m. when the UNITA delegation wandered in, nonchalant and unapologetic, saying they had been trying to contact their leader.

General N'dalu explained that he had called the meeting to discuss what he termed 'a serious violation of the Peace Accords' as a result of the exodus of the ex-FALA FAA generals and the electoral stand-off. Engineer Salupeto Pena at once embarked on his familiar catalogue of accusations of massive fraud, demanding the immediate setting-up of a large, multiparty investigative commission, as well as immediate suspension of the further publication of results, whether provisional or definitive. Otherwise UNITA 'would not be responsible for the consequences', nor would it accept any results without an exhaustive examination of what he described as 'a major scandal'. But he also stressed that UNITA was looking for solutions that did not mean war; its sole intention was to safeguard the transparency of the process and the democratic future of Angola.

At a further meeting that evening at the NEC, four commissions were set up, composed of UNITA representatives, technical personnel of the NEC and the Directorate General of the Elections, the UNDP technical assistance team and UNAVEM. They would cover the following areas: comparison of polling records; investigation of allegations in the provinces; the whereabouts of surplus materials of De La Rue; and communications and computers. There was also agreement that, while this investigation was going on, the vote-counting process must not be held up. We took this to mean that, in spite of earlier UNITA objections, provisional results would continue to be announced. The statutory deadline for the announcement of the results, 9 October (a maximum of eight days from the closing date of the polls), was clearly unattainable, but it was agreed that the work must be completed as expeditiously as possible and we snatched some comfort from Salupeto Pena's reiteration that UNITA did not want war and his implied affirmation that UNITA would accept the results, provided this exercise demonstrated transparency and resolved the issues raised.

At the CCPM meeting I had handed over the Secretary-General's letter to Salupeto Pena and Chivukuvuku, with the reminder that I had been waiting four days for a meeting with Dr Savimbi. Salupeto Pena reacted with an unexpectedly stormy outburst: nobody understood the tremendous strain under which the UNITA leaders were working. They were not sleeping and Dr Savimbi was not only unable to see anyone, but could not even speak to anyone by telephone, not even General N'dalu, who had been seeking contact since the previous week. Their leader's whole time was taken up by his efforts to restrain his commanders from going out with their troops to fight, on account of the 'scandalous' handling of the election results. When the tirade died down, Salupeto Pena said, more calmly, that Dr Savimbi would be reminded and the letter would be got to him.

The clear implication was that Dr Savimbi was no longer in Luanda. I watched carefully as the meeting proceeded to see what was done with the letter and was astonished when Chivukuvuku tore it open and read it, despite the word 'Personal' on the envelope. This seemed quite at variance with Savimbi's autocratic style, and added strength to the supposition that he was not in Luanda, but somewhere beyond the reach of a fax.

* * *

Angola was discussed informally by the Security Council that day. Then, in a formal meeting, the President read out a statement that – after praising the way in which the presidential and parliamentary elections had been held – expressed concern about reports the Council had received 'according to which one of the parties to the Peace Agreements is contesting the validity of the elections', and about the announcement by 'certain generals of the same party' of 'their intention' to withdraw from the FAA. After this masterpiece of circumambulatory drafting, the Council called upon 'all the parties' to respect their obligations under the Peace Accords, especially the election results. 'Any challenge must be settled through the mechanisms established for that purpose.' The final paragraph announced the Council's decision to send to Angola an '*ad hoc* Commission, composed of members of the Council to support the implementation of the Peace Agreements, in close cooperation with the Special Representative of the Secretary-General'.

I think the idea of this commission originated from the Secretariat. Mig had mentioned the possibility and I had advised against it, preferring the Council to restrict itself to a strong statement (certainly stronger than the language actually used). I felt that a commission was unnecessary, in the light of that day's developments, and could even be counterproductive by injecting a new element at a very delicate stage. In my view, such a possibility should be kept in reserve, in case the fraud investigation did not provide satisfaction and the potential military threat increased.

But the die was cast. The next day the Security Council announced the members of the mission: Ambassador José Luis Jesus of Cape Verde, who would lead it; Ambassador Ahmed Snoussi of Morocco; Ambassador Valentin V. Lozinskiy of the Russian Federation; and Ambassador Joseph E. Perkins of the United States. They would arrive on Sunday 11 October.

* * *

The Secretary-General's letter did not defuse the situation. In the NEC on Tuesday evening (6 October), Dr Chivukuvuku accosted me in a decidedly belligerent manner. It seemed unlikely that Dr Savimbi had yet seen this strictly personal letter, and subsequent information made clear that he could not have done, though the text might have been communicated to him orally. Chivukuvuku demanded my response on two points. First, did the letter mean that the UN had already decided that the elections were free and fair? This was an obvious reference to the sentence 'L'Organisation des Nations Unies, convaincue que les élections se sont déroulées de façon correcte, envisage l'avenir avec confiance'. I told him it simply meant that the Secretary-General felt the organisation of the elections and the actual voting had gone extremely well, as had been recognised by everyone, including UNITA (he agreed with me on this). I reminded him that I had made crystal clear that the UN would not make any announcement on whether the elections were free and fair until the final results were announced and all allegations and complaints clarified.

His second point was that the tone of the letter indicated that the Secretary-General considered Dr Savimbi had already lost. I said this was certainly not the case as the Secretary-General was perfectly aware that even the preliminary counting was far from complete and stressed that the letter should be regarded as a strictly personal message from an old friend and fellow African. Dr Savimbi's declaration of Saturday 3 October, the day before the letter was written, had had considerable international repercussions and caused alarm in many quarters; and it was in this context that it should be viewed.

Chivukuvuku belaboured the same points over and over again, and exuded the acute paranoia that seemed to be guiding Dr Savimbi's and UNITA's actions. I had the impression that he positively *wanted* to believe these perverse interpretations and resented any logical arguments that were likely to provide a more innocuous sense. Was UNITA perhaps determined not to be deflected from its strategy by any inconvenient facts? I thought I had satisfied Chivukuvuku's doubts, but he still went around declaiming to anyone who would listen, his original interpretation of the letter and the perfidy of the Secretary-General, as if we had never had our conversation, and I had to spend much time correcting his deliberate misinterpretations.

Early next morning (Wednesday 7 October) our suspicion that Dr Savimbi had been smuggled out of Luanda several days previously were confirmed. According to General N'dalu, the UNITA leader had been hidden in a coffin and taken in this macabre manner from Miramar to Luanda airport, whence a UNITA plane had flown him to Huambo. He said that the Government had known every detail of the plan, but had done nothing to prevent his departure. I was seeing General N'dalu to give him the statement of the President of the Security Council. The General said that the Government welcomed the statement and would like to see the *ad hoc* Commission arrive as soon as possible.

Salupeto Pena's reaction was very different. Chivukuvuku was with him. I was amazed to find that they were unaware of the statement as their information system was usually impeccable and speedy. Salupeto Pena said that the statement, and the despatch of the Commission, would push UNITA's backs further against the wall, while encouraging the Government and the MPLA. Both he and Chivukuvuku claimed that, had it not been for the statements of Assistant Secretary Cohen, Jeffrey Millington and Prime Minister Anibal Cavaco Silva of Portugal, the FALA generals would still be in the armed forces, which seemed to bear out my feeling that paranoia, rather than logic, determined their actions. I pointed out that it was this action that had escalated alarm about UNITA's intentions and prompted the Security Council's reaction; if the Council's actions provoked a further reaction on UNITA's part, rather than dialogue and negotiation of an acceptable solution, then we were in for a vicious spiral that could only end badly. Moreover it was one thing to allege that the elections were fraudulent and insist on proper investigations, but quite another to link this to the armed forces, a pivotal part of the Peace Accords. Both then said that UNITA did not want war but neither would it accept fraudulent results.

It became dispiritingly clear that UNITA was operating on the premise that the investigations must prove the allegations of fraud, and would not accept any other outcome. When (not if) the fraud was proven, asserted Chivukuvuku, UNITA would work out a solution with the Government, which could take the form either of another full election, or of elections in areas where fraud was proven, these to be organised entirely by the United Nations. Much disturbed by UNITA's intransigence, I cautioned them in the strongest terms that they should not prejudge the investigation, but UNITA's tactics were by now blatantly obvious.

When I asked again about the prospects of my seeing Dr Savimbi, Dr Chivukuvuku told me 'confidentially' that they had smuggled Dr Savimbi out of Luanda because the Government had ordered all UNITA leaders to be prevented from leaving the capital, only to discover from General N'dalu that morning, that this was a misunderstanding. I did not let on that I already knew of their leader's departure, merely commenting that this once more illustrated how the high level of mutual mistrust could lead to overreaction. I added that I was prepared to go anywhere in Angola to meet their leader.

Significantly, neither of the two mentioned something else I had learned from General N'dalu – that Savimbi wanted to see him in Huambo and that, subject to the President's agreement, he might be going there that day, or the next. Savimbi's message had said that a 'political solution' must be sought. It was not clear what this phrase embraced, but an obvious key question was: what position could be found for Savimbi, in the event of a victory by President dos Santos, that would be commensurate with his stature and acceptable to him? The President had sent him a letter a few days previously, promising that any Government of his would work closely with UNITA, which presumably meant offering some key positions. But that still left open the situation of the leader. In any case the two prongs of UNITA's strategy were clear: to fight hard to win the elections, including trying to prove fraud; and to secure a dignified solution for their leader.

The Government was taking steps to protect its own position. Foreign Minister 'Loy' was on his way to New York with a personal letter from the President to the Secretary-General. The letter, dated 6 October, categorised the actions of Savimbi and UNITA as threats to the peace and democratisation process. It appealed to the Secretary-General to exert his influence to make him and his organisation accept the people's will, and asked him to submit the issue to the Security Council, which he hoped would take a strong position to impede the return to war. The President was obviously unaware that the Security Council had already taken a position that day, or that the Secretary-General had written to Dr Savimbi.

When handing over a copy of the letter to Hugo Anson, Victor Lima said that the Government was determined to avoid war, if possible, and still believed it would be avoided, but he added 'we have the means to hit them very hard if that is what they choose. War would be a disaster. We shall neither start one, nor sit back if war is forced upon us'. He also said that the President was planning to make a positive statement, emphasising reconciliation and offering guarantees for the security of Dr Savimbi and UNITA, but only after the definitive electoral results were officially announced.

It was imperative that the election results, of which the compilation was nearing completion, should not be announced until the investigating commissions presented their findings, but the NEC seemed bent on publishing the results on 9 October, come hell or high water, and I was having great difficulty in restraining them. On 8 October I requested an urgent audience with President dos Santos for that afternoon, to make sure he understood the perils of such a course.

As I was trying to arrange this appointment, my personal assistant, Elizabeth Pantaleón dashed in to say that Dr Savimbi wanted to speak to me. The man who had been playing so hard to get for nearly a week was waiting patiently on my secretary's phone. Dr Savimbi was extremely affable, and measured in his statements. He expressed warm thanks for the Secretary-General's letter. He did not comment on its contents, but the manner in which he spoke was in reassuring contrast to the cavalier reaction of Chivukuvuku. Dr Savimbi then said that he had just had a meeting with N'dalu and Salupeto Pena and wanted to tell me that the election results were not important; what was important was the transparency of the process. It was essential to establish this and ensure the support of all Angolans for the results. I replied that these were precisely my concerns and that, when he called, I had been requesting an urgent audience with President dos Santos to make these very points.

Dr Savimbi said that the investigative commissions had found discrepancies between the number of polling records and those shown in the computers. There was obviously no time in which to recount the votes but he would like these aspects elucidated. I assured him of our full cooperation and told him that many UNAVEM observers were participating in the commissions so as to guarantee total transparency. When I reminded him of my request for a meeting he said he was always happy to see me and we agreed to meet in Huambo the following day at 11 a.m.

I was certainly not about to be sanguine, but it did appear that we might make some progress, if we could keep cool heads and see the fraud investigation through before the results were announced. As I told the Secretary-General, when I informed him about this first conversation with Dr Savimbi since the election, my Celtic hunch was that his letter might have done the trick.

Later that day the Secretary-General received Foreign Minister 'Loy' and asked him to transmit urgently to President dos Santos his strong advice that the results should not be published until the four commissions had done their work. On the basis of Dr Savimbi's telephone conversation with me, the Secretary-General believed there was a need to help him save face, and get his supporters to accept that the election results should be respected. If they were announced before the commissions completed their enquiries, Savimbi would forever be able to say that this showed that something 'fishy' had occurred. 'Loy' undertook to transmit that message that very evening to President dos Santos, whom I was now to see early the next day, before flying to Huambo. 'Loy' did, however, express his fear that Savimbi would use the interval to prepare military action as the Government had information of many UNITA troop movements.

Another surprise was in store for me before the day ended. I received an unexpected midnight visitation in my house from Salupeto Pena and Chivukuvuku. I hastily called in Jobarteh and Maria Grossi, while Sissy provided refreshments, for they seemed both tired and hungry. They had come to see me at Dr Savimbi's request to follow up his telephone conversation. They seemed subdued, almost chastened, and were much calmer and more reasonable than in our recent encounters. UNITA was no longer insisting on an open-ended investigation into 'widespread fraud', they said, but had whittled down their demands to two areas: discrepancies in polling records and investigation of the left-over material of De La Rue, an issue related to the supplementary polling stations. There was considerable discussion, during which Chivukuvuku nodded off several times, plainly exhausted, and at about 2 a.m. they took their leave.

The next morning I was received by President dos Santos at 8.30 a.m. Immediately afterwards he had a meeting with the three observers. Our position, presented separately, was the common one of urging postponement of the announcement of the results to give the commissions time to finish their work. I told the President about my telephone conversation of the day before with Dr Savimbi – he knew I would be seeing the latter later that morning – as well as about my midnight visitors and the reduced, more manageable demands they had presented. Then I gave all the reasons why we thought it essential to allow more time for the investigations. We knew this could not be long: our technical advisers working on the commissions had suggested a week.

The President had addressed the nation the previous evening, pleading for calm, reconciliation and unity 'now that the election results are about to be announced within a few hours', but he indicated his readiness to consider a postponement provided it was no longer than 48 hours. I warned that this might not be enough. The President said he could not hold the situation for long; he was being pressurised by his supporters and feared violent repercussions, especially in Luanda, if the delay was longer. Moreover he was worried by UNITA's warlike stance and that they would use the interval to prepare themselves militarily. It was a difficult political dilemma, to be handled with maximum sensitivity, but he authorised me to tell Dr Savimbi that he was ready to arrange a 48 hour postponement.

I went straight from Futungo de Belas to the UNAVEM hangar at the airport, where I found General N'dalu waiting to brief me about his meeting with Savimbi the day before. He also transmitted a further message from the President, authorising me to tell Savimbi that he would like to have an early meeting with him.

Chivukuvuku, looking perkier than the night before, was also there, as he was to accompany me to Huambo. He insisted that I must first see a Côte d'Ivoire delegation, headed by a Minister of the Côte d'Ivoire Presidency, also at the airport and about to leave for Abidjan. The reason soon became apparent: the Minister had seen Dr Savimbi in Huambo and purported to be convinced that fraud had been 'widespread'. President Houphoüet-Boigny had long supported Savimbi, and the delegation was singing the UNITA song. I explained the investigation process and said we would keep an open mind until we had the outcome. This was not enough for the Minister, who tried to convince me that I should, without more ado, declare the elections totally flawed.

It was noon when we landed in Huambo, where the UNITA black cockerel flag was flying over the airport. Colonel Mortlock and most of the UNAVEM team were waiting, as were local UNITA representatives, and we drove directly to Savimbi's 'White House'. I was glad that Chivukuvuku was with us. The road outside was barricaded, and full of guns, guards and vehicles. Even thus escorted I had the barrel of a rifle shoved menacingly into my face by an over-eager thug. Inside Savimbi was waiting for us, surrounded by the usual large retinue, including Vice-President Chitunda, Jorge Valentim and at least two generals. We were only four. It was a marathon meeting, lasting over two hours, but I felt I was on a better wicket than in Uige, two weeks before. Despite the strains of the past few days Savimbi appeared more consistent, more relaxed and less tired, in contrast to his collaborators, some of whom followed Chivukuvuku's example of the previous evening and fell fast asleep.

I told Dr Savimbi about my meeting with President dos Santos and conveyed his messages. He thanked me, stressing the importance of the UN role and then, following a favourite ploy, invited his colleagues to speak first. A torrent of invective was unleashed about fraud and the NEC, first by Chitunda, whom I had never seen so loquacious or agitated, and then by the rest. The only favourable words were addressed to UNAVEM. It was a superb piece of theatre that allowed Savimbi to intervene with the voice of sweet reasonableness. He repeated his line that it was not important who won: transparency and the proper elucidation of grievances were the key to stability, both immediately and in the longer term. A longer time was necessary, and the 48 hours proposed by the President was not enough. If the MPLA was so sure it had won fairly, then it should allow more time. Fortunately he agreed that it should not be an open-ended or lengthy extension. I told him about the President's concern that he could not hold the situation indefinitely.

Dr Savimbi said that his own problems were much worse. As I had just been able to see for myself, his followers were indignant, and exceedingly difficult to control. I told him that the President had said he feared a delay would simply permit UNITA to prepare militarily. This was greeted with general laughter and Savimbi gave me a long explanation of why war was out of the question – 'suicidal' was his term. What he feared most was civil strife, looting, general violence and even secession. He repeated several times that UNITA would never contemplate war. What they wanted, as he had told General N'dalu, was a 'political solution'.

I pointed out that the withdrawal of the generals from the FAA had given a different impression, led to the Security Council statement and the despatch of the *ad hoc* Commission, and generally caused alarm, nationally and internationally, about UNITA's intentions. A fundamental tenet of democracy was that the military do not become involved in elections. This action had given a whole other dimension to the problem and violated the Bicesse Peace Accords. I was interested to note several heads nodding in apparent agreement. Dr Savimbi said that the Generals' withdrawal had been 'controllable pressure'. I contended that control of its effects could prove very difficult and that the issue was in any case a different one: this kind of pressure was not consonant with democracy. I reiterated the views I had expressed in Uige – that the greatest danger came from the high degree of mistrust on both sides – and stressed the importance of reconciliation.

Dr Savimbi asked me to convey three messages to President dos Santos: there should be transparency in dealing with the fraud allegations and sufficient time should be allowed to make that possible; UNITA guaranteed that it would not go to war; and he was ready to meet the President in the very near future. He added that he would also be glad to receive the Security Council Commission.

It was always hard to get any kind of personal message across to Dr Savimbi, surrounded as he was by his well-rehearsed Greek chorus. On this occasion I took a gamble and asked to see him alone for a few minutes. He took me into an anteroom out of earshot of the main salon. I mentioned the Secretary-General's letter to clarify the misconceptions it had created in Dr Chivukuvuku's mind, but Savimbi said he did not share these. I then recalled the Secretary-General's remarks about his role in history. His great hero, Churchill, I pointed out, had suffered unexpected defeat in the elections after the war, a war that he had brought to a victorious conclusion. Yet he had continued to play an important role as the leader of 'His Majesty's Loyal Opposition' – a role that, perhaps overoptimistically, I tried to explain – and five years later had been voted back into power. Whoever won the Presidency in Angola, I suggested (and I made it clear that there was every possibility, in our view, of a second round), would have an unenviable task: a totally war-devastated country to be reconstructed, an economy to be transformed into the market mould, and an electorate filled with the unrealistic expectation that peace and democracy would bring a prosperous life overnight. Instead things might well become more difficult before the tide turned. The international financial institutions would require economic stabilisation and restructuring programmes as a condition for their support, and initially this would bring more hardship. There would be a pendulum effect and whoever led the opposition would have an excellent chance of being elected to power the next time round. It was important to remember that, while this was the first election in Angola, it was not the last and that change and alternation were central to democracy. Finally I suggested that the present tension could be dissipated, and UNITA would acquire a better image and a more sympathetic hearing, if the FALA generals returned to the FAA immediately. Savimbi listened attentively and appeared to be receptive to my words. But it was impossible to gauge what he was thinking.

* * *

On my return to Luanda I drove straight from the airport to see the Minister for Territorial Administration. To my dismay I found that the investigatory commissions had made no progress because of dissension over their mandate.

It was decided to call a meeting of the CCPM and the electoral authorities later that night to expedite the work.

Exasperatingly, after a lot of hanging about the meeting was postponed until the next morning (Saturday 10 October), thus wasting more of the extension I had with such difficulty obtained. The meeting should have been quite short, as both the Government and the NEC had made concessions to UNITA about the length of time that would elapse before the announcement of the final results, as well as on the mandates of the commissions. Nonetheless it dragged on for four hours, because UNITA kept going back over earlier perceived wrongs, and even introduced totally new aspects, a ploy that reinforced the view that their intention was to filibuster and to keep changing the rules of the game. I was twice forced to intervene energetically, first to point out that we now had a brief of opportunity to satisfy UNITA's concerns and this chance should not be squandered, which meant we should concentrate on what could be done over the next few days, rather than dwelling on the past or getting lost in minutiae. Then, when the UNITA delegation started insisting once again on an open-ended time-frame for this exercise, I had to remind Engineer Salupeto Pena sharply that this was totally at odds with what I had agreed with Dr Savimbi the previous day.

At last it was agreed that investigations should be carried out in all the provincial capitals on the polling records, the left-over electoral material, the supplementary polling booths and, where necessary, on specific allegations. The work was to be done by commissions comprising the provincial electoral authorities, the UNAVEM electoral observers posted in each place and representatives of UNITA and other parties. Each enquiry was to start at 6.00 p.m. that evening and be completed within 48 hours. Like the NEC and UNAVEM, UNITA had people *in situ* but insisted it must send out special representatives from Luanda to the 11 provinces it considered most critical. When that was conceded UNITA said it had no way of transporting them! I offered UNAVEM planes to carry them (my makeshift 'air force' was more or less still intact) and requested that I be urgently informed of the number, names and destinations of the passengers. Predictably these were not provided until late that night, which meant that the planes I had already had standing by had to postpone their departure until first light on Sunday. Even then some of the UNITA people arrived late, or not at all, and had to be sought out by UNAVEM. For a party notoriously eager to investigate and pluck out fraud, and to whom every possible facility to do so had been offered, it was an extraordinary performance.

A further meeting of the CCPM and the NEC was convened for Saturday evening in the NEC building. General N'dalu, Maria Grossi and I arrived first and were in the anteroom to President Caetano's office. Suddenly there were sharp bursts of automatic fire below the window. The secretaries dived panic-stricken under their desks. Maria (who told me she had never before had such an experience) looked distinctly nervous. I said 'Get away from the window', and we managed to retain some of our dignity by standing pressed against the wall.

General N'dalu, in what seemed a foolhardy display of bravado, or perhaps a demonstration of his famed courage on the battlefield, was leaning out of the window and bellowing into the street below. My mind was working on two levels. One inner voice was saying 'How foolish of him'. The other, more ominously, was saying 'This is it. The balloon has gone up. And here we are, caught in the NEC building, which is now probably under siege by people wanting to destroy all the election results'. Such were the apprehensions pervading those days that this melodramatic vision appeared only too probable.

The firing below continued, but moved a little further down the street. After a while, and some more shouting, General N'dalu withdrew his head from the window, roaring with laughter. 'Excess of zeal' was the comment he made when he had recovered his breath sufficiently to speak. It transpired that a ragged street urchin had been surprised committing a minor theft and when he had fled the police, on guard for other purposes, had lost their heads and fired into the air, which had then provoked a panic reaction from others, unaware of the mundane cause of the first outburst. Calm was soon restored, but we had all had a good fright, and General N'dalu agreed with my comment that we were handling a tinderbox, which any stray match could ignite.

* * *

As there was no direct flight, late on Saturday 10 October the members of the *ad hoc* Commission of the Security Council arrived at Brazzaville, where I had sent my Beechcraft, with a staff officer to escort them to Luanda.

Their arrival could not have been more dramatically timed. A few hours later a large bomb exploded at dawn under a car parked outside the Hotel Turismo, which housed many UNITA personnel and their families. It caused only structural damage, blowing out windows as high as the sixth floor, but it led to a violent armed confrontation and outbreaks of shooting in Rocha Pinto and the Gamek suburb near our camp. UNITA, claiming it was under attack by the Government when shots fired from an unmarked passing car injured two of their guards, began spraying the square in front of the hotel with machine-gun fire and launched grenades at the police station opposite. They also took hostage 12 antiriot police who were investigating the earlier bomb blast. Later the Government made the counterclaim that UNITA had itself planted the bomb in order to provoke just such an incident. Heavy and indiscriminate firing went on for hours and some civilians were killed in crossfire. It was a Sunday morning and people were on their way to the beach. One man appeared to have been arbitrarily shot because he was wearing an MPLA T-shirt. The CCPM was hastily called to the spot and we sent UNAVEM military and police observers, led by Brigadier Nyambuya, to help negotiate the release of the hostages and restore peace and order.

The planned briefing of the Security Council mission could not start until noon, as the shooting made it difficult to transport them from the Hotel Presidente to the camp. Ambassador Jesus told me they wished to see the two leaders that day. I warned that experience made me less than sanguine about the prospect of seeing President dos Santos on a Sunday, even without a bomb incident, although I had requested an appointment. Dr Savimbi was ready to see them, but the latest turn of events might make it impossible for the Beechcraft to fly to Huambo.

The briefing in our cramped and oven-hot conference hut was punctuated by menacing noises outside and continually interrupted by officers bringing me the latest update. I read out each message, in a deadpan voice. 'Heavy firing continues around the Hotel Turismo.' 'Shooting has broken out in Gamek and Rocha Pinto, between here and the airport.' 'Mortar fire at the crossroads [200 yards from the camp] has forced the Beechcraft pilots [on their way to the airport to fly the group to Huambo] to return to camp.' 'The airport has been closed.' The latter piece of news seemed to be gainsaid by a deafening roar of engines overhead. Until then the visitors had borne up pretty well, but now one of them burst out 'Then what on earth is that?' Tom White disappeared outside, returning to report laconically, 'Those are our helicopters, ma'am, landing on the road as they can't get into the airport'.

We would not have been human if we had not derived some vicarious pleasure from the discomfiture of Security Council pundits finding themselves in the middle of the kind of incident upon which they normally pontificated in the well-padded confines of the Council Chamber.

Spirits were restored by an *al fresco* and suitably lubricated – although very late – lunch in my carport (the house being too small), and by the news that the road to the airport was now safe and the airport open, although firing still continued around the Hotel Turismo. But the afternoon was well advanced, and meetings with Dr Savimbi being notoriously long and Huambo airfield without lights, the group might have to stay there, a prospect they clearly did not relish. We had agreed over lunch that I would not go to their major meetings, so that their interlocutors would not be inhibited by my presence, but that members of my staff would be there to take notes. In any event the outbreak of fighting in Luanda required me to stay in the capital.

After seeing them off I drove to the Hotel Turismo. A terrible scene of destruction greeted me, and some of the wounded were still being loaded into ambulances. In the devastated hotel I witnessed the release of the government police hostages, and spoke to Engineer Salupeto Pena and General N'dalu. The incident had been resolved, but with difficulty and loss of life. Recriminations continued as to who was responsible for what. Everyone was glum and downcast. The omens did not look good.

The Security Council Ambassadors did get back to Luanda that night, their take-off from Huambo made possible by a colonnade of vehicle headlights organised by Colonel Mortlock. As I stood on the tarmac waiting for them, their return to Luanda was lit by a different kind of illumination, an even greater number of tracer bullets than usual, racing above our heads to weave an eerie, coruscating pattern on the dark backcloth of the African night sky. If there was any message to be gleaned from those hieroglyphic streaks and swirls it was hardly one of hope. I did not tell our visitors that their arrival path had been criss-crossed with fire. I thought they had had quite enough for one day.

Over sandwiches at the camp they described their meeting with Dr Savimbi. They had been given the works and came back visibly impressed by UNITA's claim of fraud. A main element was a computer printout showing an identical number of votes for different parties in three provinces, Bié, Lunda Norte and Cuanza Norte. I explained that this was an initial computer error, immediately rejected by the NEC, a minor but important detail that UNITA had conveniently forgotten to mention. I also advised them not to prejudge the thorough investigation now underway with UNITA's full participation, or their meetings next day with the NEC, Onofre dos Santos and President dos Santos.

The next morning, they told me later, Onofre dos Santos put on a bravura performance and dealt summarily with UNITA's examples of fraud, particularly their favourite exhibit, the computer printout that had been presented in Huambo. The Director General confirmed that this was one of the first products of the computer system, which was immediately discarded as an error and the programme perfected. He added that he had explained this to UNITA many times, and that its representatives, who haunted the NEC building, were aware of the arrangements to get the computers working correctly. As with Dr Chivukuvuku's criticisms of the Secretary-General's letter, it was as if nothing had been said, and the same table and the same arguments were trotted out to every visitor. The members of the Security Council Commission were no exception, and they too had fallen for it, until they heard the explanation. Apart from his obvious technical and managerial competence, the frankness, dedication and integrity that Dr Onofre dos Santos had exuded impressed them greatly.

In the afternoon the Commission members had an audience with President Jose Eduardo dos Santos, of which they also spoke well. They were becoming more keenly aware of the intractable complexities of the personalities and positions that riddled the political and constitutional problems we were trying to solve in order to avoid a slide-back into war.

They were not the only high-powered dignitaries on the scene. Pik Botha, the South African Foreign Minister, had also arrived, a visit initially welcomed by the Government, who told me they thought it crucial to get South Africa, as well as the United States and the United Nations, to make Dr Savimbi see sense. He was installed on a Greek ship that had suddenly appeared in the port of Luanda and was now serving as a 'luxury' floating hotel, moored off the Ilha. No doubt its enterprising owners had calculated that there was a need for presentable accommodation for the procession of international bigwigs sweeping into Luanda, and that their investment was secure since, at the first sign of trouble, they could weigh anchor and set out to sea (which was what they did, not much later). I was asked to see the Minister there, but on the way I received a message on my car radio that I was expected immediately at Futungo de Belas, so had to turn around.

I had originally asked to see the President to tell him personally about my meeting with Dr Savimbi and the latter's messages, which I had already transmitted through intermediaries. In the intervening two and a half days the situation had evolved greatly. The President told me that it had become increasingly difficult to postpone the announcement of the results. Although neither of us directly mentioned the possibility of a second presidential round, the President clearly realised that it was virtually inevitable and was prepared for it. The deadline for completing the fraud investigations in all the provinces was only a few hours away, and I begged him to hang on a little longer, so that it would be unequivocally clear that proper steps had been taken and ample opportunity had been given to investigate UNITA's allegations. The President agreed but reiterated his scepticism about UNITA's intentions: its procrastination and prevarication during the last few days had done nothing to reassure him or his followers.

After that there was a CCPM meeting at 6.30 p.m. to discuss Sunday's incidents and the fraud investigation. I went on to a dinner hosted by the Moroccan Ambassador in the Hotel Presidente for Ambassador Snussi and members of the Commission. It was midnight or later when we broke up. Ambassador Jesus was kind enough to worry about my returning to the camp without security cover. I assured him that I often did just that, but as my driver Brito and I sped through the dark, deserted streets, the atmosphere seemed even more sinister than usual. No one was out in the open. Figures moved in the shadows, and I devoutly hoped that these were police. I was very relieved when the lights of the camp at last glowed above the dark surrounding plain.

At 6.30 a.m. the next morning there was an urgent call from Engineer Salupeto Pena with a personal message from Dr Savimbi: would I use my good offices to obtain a stay on the issue of the final results, on the understanding that, within the ensuing 72 hours, a meeting would take place between Dr Savimbi and President dos Santos, which he (Salupeto Pena) and General N'dalu would prepare? This meeting should take place outside Angola in a neighbouring country, for example Namibia or Zambia. I rang General N'dalu, who was seeing the President about this new development at 9 a.m., and he promised to meet me at 10 a.m. In the event he was held up in constant consultations until late afternoon, when he told me that the President would under no circumstances accept a meeting outside Angola. He said the Government anticipated that the final results would apportion less than 50 per cent to President dos Santos. In that event, and even if the end result was marginally over 50 per cent, the Government was ready to accept a second round, on certain conditions: a longer interval than the one month foreseen in the Electoral Law so as to enable the integrity of the FAA to be restored and the Bicesse Peace

Accords once more honoured; demilitarisation (a very tall order); and a larger role for the United Nations.

At 5.30 p.m. I met Salupeto Pena and Chivukuvuku to tell them that President dos Santos would not accept a meeting outside Angola. The possibility of a second round was discussed, but the UNITA representatives categorically said that this was not acceptable because of the alleged fraud.

My next appointment was with the Security Council Commission at the Hotel Presidente. They had rather abruptly decided to leave ahead of schedule, and would travel the next morning to Windhoek to write their report there. I had hoped they would stay to witness the outcome of the fraud investigation, but Ambassador Jesus told me that none of them liked the turn that events were taking; they sensed serious trouble looming and did not want to be caught in Angola. I found them putting the finishing touches to the joint statement they were to present to a press conference. Predictably, it did not contain any earth-shaking revelations.

After listing the various meetings they had had, the Commission emphasised that the Peace Accords must be fully implemented and the integrity of the electoral process upheld, with all claims of irregularities investigated and the results made public. They noted with 'grave concern' the recent increase in violence and appealed for peace to be safeguarded, demobilisation completed and the FAA consolidated. Any resumption of armed confrontation would 'meet with the strongest condemnation of the international community'. They expressed satisfaction with the assurances they had received from both leaders to curb violence and resolve their differences through dialogue and peaceful means, and welcomed the prospect of a government of national unity. The final words were of support for my staff and myself.

I recounted the events of my day, and we discussed the prospects. They saw them as unequivocally gloomy. Ambassador Perkins, whom I had come to respect during those few days as a thoroughly decent and sensible man, exploded angrily: 'This was a UN mission done on the cheap – a totally false economy on the part of the international community'.

It is always pleasing to have one's views corroborated, especially from the highly placed, but my satisfaction was tempered by sadness that the realisation had come so late – perhaps too late to save Angola. At least the Commission had been convinced that it was essential, in the event of a second round, to strengthen UNAVEM and make its role more central. They spoke of a blanket UN coverage of at least one observer for every polling booth. I said that this would be very desirable but, on the basis of my bad experience in trying to obtain more resources, felt obliged to point out that it would be costly, involving even larger air and logistical support, which member states might not be ready to contemplate. I was encouraged when Ambassador Perkins affirmed categorically: 'The necessary resources *must* and *can* be found'. If that was the US position, then surely the rest would follow.

One positive outcome of the Commission's visit, whatever its impact on the Angolan political situation, was their realisation, however tardy, of just how desperately underresourced UNAVEM had been, as well as having its hands tied by an excessively limited mandate.

They were also greatly exercised about their four-to five hour-trip to Windhoek in the Beechcraft, although we had arranged for a stopover in northern Namibia. Apart from the Russian, they were all big men and had found even the short hop from Brazzaville intolerably cramped. Ambassador Perkins was especially plaintive on the subject, and the fact that there were no toilet facilities aboard. Emboldened by his earlier remarks, I mentioned that we too suffered when flying the width and breadth of Angola, and was rash enough to suggest that a small executive jet would meet everyone's requirements, including theirs, much more satisfactorily. Alas, Ambassador Perkins was the first to banish the very notion as far too extravagant!

The Commission's last appointment was with the South African Foreign Minister, and Hugo Anson and I accompanied them. The encounter between this group of distinguished Ambassadors and Pik Botha was one of the more bizarre of the many strange experiences I had in Angola, and the esoteric surroundings of the 'floating hotel' heightened the sense of unreality. The evening was wearing on by the time we clambered up the companionway and were ushered into a large saloon, with a bar at one end, and armchairs and small tables scattered over the rest. Scores of aides were hanging about, or drinking at the bar, as well as journalists anxious for a quote. Minister Botha was ensconced in one corner, holding court – no other description would suffice – and still talking to Onofre dos Santos. There was a large glass of whisky in front of him, and it seemed unlikely to have been his first. He waved us to sit down and proceeded to conduct the meeting simultaneously with ourselves and the Director General of the Elections. I could see that Ambassador Jesus, a very distinguished and experienced diplomat, was not pleased. I shared his reaction but there was little we could do. The Minister offered us drinks and after my long and exhausting day I, too, was glad to have a whisky. Ambassador Jesus would only accept water.

I had heard a good deal about Pik Botha, but the reality exceeded all the imaginings. Big, burly and ebullient, he dominated the proceedings. Nobody else could get a word in edgeways. He'd got it all sewn up. There had been massive fraud but he, the *deus ex machina*, had got the solution. Without allowing Ambassador Jesus even to fulfil the diplomatic niceties of telling him what the Commission was about, or what findings it had reached, he launched into an emotional tirade describing his meetings with President dos Santos the day before and, for four and a half hours that same day, with Dr Savimbi. Dr Savimbi had given him 'proofs' of widespread fraud, which he found scandalous and intolerable. 'As an African' (Ambassador Jesus winced visibly) he could not accept a different standard of democracy from that of 'Western colonialist countries', 'we are not a pile of rotten cabbages to be buggered about like this'.

He had taken with him journalists from the *Financial Times* and the *Independent*, who had stayed throughout the meeting, and told him their newspapers would reveal the scandal to the world. (I ran into both correspondents, Julian Ozanne and Karl Maier, the next day and was assured that no such headlines had appeared. They seemed as surprised at having been included in top-level secret talks as we were to hear about it. Goodness knows what Dr Savimbi thought, but perhaps he enjoyed the exposure.)

The familiar recital of allegations followed, and no one was allowed to utter a dissenting word or explanation. Some did not stand up to even preliminary scrutiny, for example the allegation that election materials were being 'hidden' in banks in Luanda that very night (when Dr Onofre was able to speak, he pointed out that all parties, including UNITA, had agreed that sensitive materials should be kept in banks for maximum security); and that a ten-minute electricity cut had been engineered in Luanda to enable ballot boxes to be stolen under the cover of darkness (much later, I enlightened him that electricity cuts occurred every day and around the clock in Luanda in a totally unpredictable fashion). And then came the *coup de grâce*. Like a magician producing some exotic bird or animal from his sleeve, he flourished a familiar-looking piece of paper: the computer printout showing identical results. This, he roared at full blast, would not be acceptable 'in any civilised country'. Again much later, Dr Onofre commented mildly, and with only the faintest glimmer of irony, that it had not been accepted in Angola either.

Mr Botha was at pains to exonerate UNAVEM and myself from any blame. Turning towards me, seated on his left, he patted me encouragingly on the knee and intoned 'This lovely little lady here has been doing her very best' (it was my turn to wince, not least since I happen to be tall and far from petite, which made the comment even more patronising) but the resources of the United Nations and the provision of 'only 800 [sic] observers' had been pitifully inadequate, especially in comparison with what had been done for Namibia. He described this as 'a disgraceful abandonment by the UN [clarifying he meant member states] of its responsibilities', and he intended to say so to the Secretary-General that very evening. He stressed that his main aim had been to persuade President dos Santos and Dr Savimbi that they should meet. During their talk Savimbi had been called out, and returned to say that he had just received a message from President dos Santos indicating his readiness to meet him any time, anywhere, including outside Angola, for example in Pretoria or Cameroon. This was puzzling, since this message must have been relayed only shortly prior to General N'dalu's informing me that President dos Santos would *not* accept a meeting outside Angola. I checked later with General N'dalu, who said it was simply not credible that such a message could have been passed.

As for the FAA, Dr Savimbi had explained that the ex-FALA generals and officers had left because the Government had refused to pay them and their emoluments had had to be borne by UNITA. I commented that, if this were the case (and it did not jibe with the declarations made by the departing generals) then it could easily be resolved since I knew the Government had the resources and the intention to cover these expenses.

Minister Botha's main message was that the fraud allegations must be properly investigated (again, when I had the chance, I pointed out that this was already being done) and that the election results must not be published because this would mean WAR! (The word was bellowed out, making the people at the other end of the saloon jump and their glasses rattle.) He also stressed the need for a face-saving device for Dr Savimbi, and described his efforts to convince him of his place in history and in the future. He would be meeting President dos Santos early next day to express his concern about the irregularities and to try to 'persuade' him to meet Dr Savimbi and work out a solution.

Ambassador Jesus was sitting opposite me, and during this unstoppable torrent of words his gaze several times met mine in a look akin to despair. He confessed to me later that he had very nearly walked out. When at long last he was allowed to speak, he described the Commission's activities and the main points of their press statement. He added, rather dryly, that the Minister would be well advised to follow their example and have a meeting with the NEC, an experience the Commission had found extremely illuminating in relation to Dr Savimbi's allegations.

I told the Minister that a second round for the presidential election seemed very much on the cards and that General N'dalu had indicated to me the government's readiness to go ahead with it. The same did not seem to be true of UNITA and I suggested that, since he had so much influence with the latter, it would be of great assistance if he could persuade them to agree also.

The meeting finished very late. As it closed the Minister presented me with a box of chocolates, an unusual diplomatic gift, but very welcome in the frugal conditions in which we lived. Although I sped back to the camp, I was too late to warn the Secretary-General of Mr Botha's impending call. Mig was already on the phone to tell me that it had already taken place. Among other things, the Minister had told the Secretary-General that neither of the two sides would accept a second round and he was therefore trying to broker a deal based on a government of national unity, involving the full participation of UNITA. I explained that this was based on a false premise, since I had clearly conveyed to him the Government's willingness, even *desire*, to have a second round. The minister had also said that salary was the main problem in relation to the armed forces. The next day (14 October) both General N'dalu and Engineer Salupeto Pena confirmed to me that this was nonsense, Salupeto Pena adding that he had had to advise Mr Botha that he had completely misunderstood Dr Savimbi, who had simply been giving an additional example of the generals' discontent; the basic issues remained the same.

I was by now worried that Minister Botha's intervention might further muddy waters that were already pretty murky. One of the biggest dangers was that the confusion reigning everywhere might be compounded by the plethora of well-meaning mediators. Perhaps the Government felt the same. At any rate,

The Aftermath

President dos Santos did not receive Mr Botha on the morning after our meeting and sent General N'dalu and Vice Foreign Minister de Moura to see him instead.

South Africa was engaged in an all-out diplomatic offensive to resolve the Angolan problem. Its Permanent Representative to the United Nations had conveyed details of his Foreign Minister's proposals to the Secretary-General in New York, and its Ambassador to Portugal had made a similar *démarche* to Secretary of State Durão Barroso in Lisbon. These proposals involved a large role for Dr Savimbi and UNITA, amounting to a coalition and the virtual scrapping of the elections. Antonio Monteiro told me and General N'dalu that Durão Barroso was very concerned, and had spoken to Hank Cohen. Antonio's instructions were that the Bicesse Accords must be adhered to, otherwise Portugal and the United States would withdraw from the process.

Earlier that Wednesday morning I had seen the members of the Security Council commission off to Windhoek, where they wrote their report in more tranquil surroundings before returning to New York. Their visit had not defused the fraught situation nor, in my view, could it have been expected to, but it did have the effect, not to be underestimated, of underlining the Security Council's deep concern and continuing close interest in Angola. I also found their strong support of UNAVEM and myself extremely valuable.

* * *

Continuing my own efforts to arrange an early meeting between the two leaders as the only hope of real progress, I was encouraged to learn from Engineer Salupeto Pena, on the morning of Wednesday 14 October, that Dr Savimbi was now ready for the meeting to take place inside Angola, in any place except Luanda, and that General N'dalu had been informed. I stressed that, since it was an Angolan process, the two Angolan sides should sort out between themselves the matters to be discussed, and the solutions to be proposed. We were there to facilitate and to act as intermediaries, if desired, but matters must be settled squarely between them.

There was also better news about the fraud investigations. All the provincial commissions had completed their work with the exception of two (Huambo and Kuanza Sul), which expected to do so by 6 p.m. The main problem now was to transport their bulky reports to Luanda. An oral report indicated that, although some irregularities had come up, major fraud did not seem to have been proved.

The situation was evolving by the hour. During the afternoon I learned that the President would, after all, receive Minister Botha, but only to tell him politely that his intervention was not needed. At 7 p.m. the counting of the votes was at last completed, but it was agreed that they would not be announced until after a meeting next morning between the NEC, the CCPM and myself. By this time it also looked probable that the meeting between President dos Santos and

Dr Savimbi would take place the following day, although the location was still under discussion. My last note for that day read: 'There is great tension throughout the city in the general expectation that the results will be announced tonight, and streets were deserted by 7 p.m., except for armed guards. We must hope that an accommodation will be reached between the two leaders before the results are made public'.

* * *

One of the things that helped me to survive in Angola was that, when I could get to bed, I usually slept soundly. That night was no exception. But not for long. I was deep in a dream, back in my childhood in the midst of the German blitz during the Second World War, when I suddenly realised that the noises were real, very near and very frightening. The whole world seemed to have exploded around the camp, reverberating in a cacophony of sound, the thud of bombs or heavy artillery, the crepitation of rifle fire, the thump of mortars. Through my window the sky seemed to have burst into flames.

'This is it' I said to myself as I lunged simultaneously for the telephone and for my radio to call General Unimna and Tom White. 'They have started fighting one another for real. But why tonight?'

But no one knew what was happening, only that the source of the explosions was very near the camp, and that UNAVEM itself might be under attack. On the radio the voice of one of our military observers was shouting 'I have never seen anything like this. This is no picnic. This is war! Don't panic, don't panic, DON'T PANIC'. The disembodied voice over the crackling of the radio rose to a crescendo more likely to have the opposite effect until sharply shut up by Tom White.

Everyone in the camp must have been awake by now and listening to their radios, and a calming message replaced the panic-button call, ordering everyone to stay under cover, except those investigating the explosions. General Unimna was trying to reach his Angolan military contacts to find out what it was all about. There was a loud banging on the front door, and I opened it to find Sigi, my newly arrived bodyguard. Headquarters had at last heeded our pleas and sent half a dozen UN security guards, who were allowed to carry side arms. This was the first call on Sigi – a gentle giant from Iceland, where he had been a policeman – though what the poor man could do was far from clear.

I dressed quickly and put on my borrowed flak jacket (only the military had these, but the Swedish contingent had insisted on lending me one and when they left the New Zealanders did likewise. It was many months before the UN sent such protection for me and other civilians). Sissy was up, and in contrast to the hysterical outbursts with which she greeted every water or electricity cut was reacting with commendable *sang froid* and making tea, having acquired the traditional English response to a crisis.

At this hectic time I kept daily notes to remind myself of the sequence of fast-moving events. That particular entry read:

UNAVEM camp is rocked by heavy explosions which continue for several hours. For what feels like an unconscionably long period of suspense, it seems armed conflict has broken out or even that UNAVEM is under attack. It transpires that an ammunition dump only a thousand yards away has blown up. (The explanations next morning, vary from 'accidental' to allegations of UNITA sabotage.) UNAVEM staff react calmly, which makes me very proud of them, especially as many have never before been in such a life-threatening situation. The main fear, once the origin was discovered, is that this could provoke panic and armed conflict among the population, as happened after the bomb explosion on Sunday. CMO takes prompt action with General 'Gato' to get the Government to broadcast a message enjoining calm and explaining the cause of the explosions, which reverberated throughout Luanda, while the spectacular fire could be seen for miles. In the morning we discover that a mortar bomb has exploded inside the camp, damaging a number of cars and perilously near two houses and one block of residential containers. Another had fortunately not exploded. Two houses in the neighbouring Gamek compound, where a few of our staff are accommodated, were burnt down. The roadside nearby is littered with heavy debris. UNAVEM had a very lucky escape.

Much later there were allegations not only that the sabotage had been the work of UNITA but that UNAVEM had been the intended target.

The next morning, after I had inspected the damage, I left, rather bleary-eyed, for the floating hotel, where I had been bidden to breakfast with Pik Botha. He too had been up most of the night. His aides told me that he had been pacing the deck, watching the huge conflagration lighting up the city and surrounding countryside and, when he learned that our camp was in danger, had with difficulty been restrained from coming to the rescue in person! I liked him much better on this occasion, not just because he had been worried on our behalf, but because he was calmer, and this time ready to listen. My notes again:

8.30 to 10 a.m. (Thursday 15 October) At breakfast Pik Botha was much more reasonable than the other evening and it was possible to put him straight on some of his misconceptions about fraud and earlier one-sided perceptions. He had sent one of his senior aides on a private aircraft to Huambo early today to arrange for Dr Savimbi to be brought to Luanda to meet President dos Santos. Botha considered it essential that the two leaders meet *before* any final election results are announced. His aim was to get the two leaders to state publicly their resolve to: (1) ensure that the FAA operates as an integrated defence force; and (2) settle all differences through dialogue rather than violence. He was ready to stay longer in Luanda to achieve this.

10.00 a.m.   To the CCPM for daily meeting now being scheduled; no meeting took place. Instead, General N'dalu briefed me about the meeting he and Antonio Monteiro were about to have with the President. Antonio Monteiro is extremely pessimistic about prospects for a peaceful outcome, given UNITA's rapid regrouping of the former FALA and its strong armed concentrations in Bié, Huambo, Benguela and some parts of the north. The President felt at a disadvantage since, as Head of State, he must keep within the law and observe the Bicesse Accords. Moreover all his troops were now concentrated in the FAA, and hence under the control of the CCPM, which UNITA could paralyse. Antonio thought an emergency meeting of the Security Council might be needed. General N'dalu was unusually sombre but not quite so gloomy. He said it was clear there would be a second round, but did not see how it could take place without complete demilitarisation and proper fulfilment of the Peace Accords. This could take at least six months, during which an interim government would be necessary; this could be a main subject of the meeting between President dos Santos and Dr Savimbi. It would also, he added, require much greater UN involvement, perhaps including 'Blue Helmets' during the transition period, including full responsibility for the organisation of the elections, as in Cambodia.

11.15 a.m.   To the NEC, where I met with President Caetano and received the printout of the definitive results of the presidential elections: President dos Santos has 49.57 per cent, Dr Savimbi 40.07 per cent. (This is remarkably close to our own Quick Count: 49.2 per cent for President dos Santos and 38.2 per cent for Dr Savimbi.) Legislative elections: MPLA – 53.74 per cent, UNITA – 34.10 per cent. I ask the NEC President to analyse the investigative reports as a matter of extreme urgency. He says he thinks it can be done by that evening and assures me that no action will be taken on them or on publishing the results without a prior meeting with myself. I point out that the CCPM should also be involved.

12.30 p.m.   Back to the UNAVEM camp. General N'dalu and Antonio stop by after seeing the President. He wishes to delay publication of the results until the reports of the investigation are known, and probably needs to see me urgently later in the day. General N'dalu speeds off to meet with Engineer Salupeto Pena to discuss subjects for the 'summit' meeting.

3.00 p.m.   I send an urgent personal cable to the Secretary-General, asking him to telephone Dr Savimbi immediately, to make the following points:

1. The indispensable need for an urgent meeting with President dos Santos. I explained that the two leaders were supposed to meet in Luanda that day, the President promising that the election results would not be released until afterwards, on condition that Dr Savimbi made a declaration about the return of the generals to the FAA. This had fallen through and the emissary sent by Pik Botha to persuade Dr Savimbi to come to Luanda had had no success. Dr Savimbi was reluctant to come to Luanda for security reasons but the Government had guaranteed his safety and I had promised an 'international cordon' of blue berets and flags at the meeting place.
2. The ex-FALA generals should be reintegrated into the FAA as soon as possible.
3. A personal appeal to him to conform to the Peace Accords and the electoral process.

3.30 p.m. Engineer Salupeto Pena comes to see me with General 'Gato' of UNITA. It is clear that their position has, to some extent, softened, though Salupeto says there is a difference of views between Luanda and Huambo (the former are more hardline), which Dr Chivukuvuku has flown to Huambo to try to clear up. For the first time, he tells us, Dr Savimbi is in a minority, by implication taking a more moderate position than many of his immediate collaborators, though Salupeto makes clear that whatever the leader decides would be followed by the rest. He outlines three scenarios: (1) total annulment of the elections; (2) acceptance of the results by UNITA and a second round, but under certain conditions; (3) war. At first he seemed to favour option (1) but later swung towards option (2), provided that the legislative elections were repeated in some provinces. I interjected that this could only happen if shown to be necessary by the fraud investigation, and he concurred. His other conditions were remarkably similar to the Government's, albeit with some nuances: *viz.* responsibility for organising the elections to lie fully with the UN; and demilitarisation, but UNITA would only disband FALA if the antiriot police were also disbanded. He insisted that all this could be done within one month before holding the second round, a view with which I had strongly to dissent. He claimed that FALA could be disbanded in three days but went on to say ominously that, meanwhile, 'I am rearming all my people in Luanda'. He and General N'dalu were preparing the meeting of the two leaders for the next day, 16 October, in Luanda, and we discussed the possibility of an 'international security cordon', and even of the UNAVEM camp as a venue. UNITA would welcome such arrangements, he said. I reply that they are possible but must be acceptable to both sides.

5.00 p.m. I receive an urgent call to see the President. He is calm and statesmanlike as he has been throughout. He wants to know the status of the fraud investigations. I suggest that prompting from the Presidency to the NEC might help to speed things up (this was later done); my people were preparing to work throughout the night on our own analysis, which should be ready by 10.00 a.m. on Friday. The President did not feel that Minister Botha's efforts had much bearing on events or see any need for him to prolong his visit. He expected to meet Dr Savimbi the next day (Friday) in Luanda. I told him of my conversation with Salupeto Pena about ways of dispelling Dr Savimbi's security fears.

6.30 p.m.   On leaving Futungo, I receive a radio message that Minister Botha wishes to see me urgently. He tells me he has good news: Dr Savimbi will be arriving the next day between 3.00 p.m. and 4.00 p.m., and will meet with President dos Santos in Futungo. Mr Botha himself intends to act as intermediary and requests UN cooperation, which I say I have already promised to both sides, but only on their joint invitation. At our breakfast meeting, Minister Botha had favoured a second round (a change from his position of Tuesday night), but he now veered back to a modified version of his earlier idea whereby Savimbi would accept the results without a second round and there would be a transitional government of "national unity" of perhaps a year, with power sharing. His argument is that, between them, they constitute 90 per cent of popular support. The idea envisages a very minimal role, if any, for the newly elected parliament. The UN presence, he says, must be maintained and the UN should organise the elections. I point out that this plan is unlikely to be acceptable to the President and the MPLA, who seem fixed on due legal process. Minister Botha replies that he has just met with Foreign Minister 'Loy', who had expressed great concern that a second round would only increase the dangerous polarisation of this country and was even now on his way to Futungo to discuss his (Botha's) ideas with the President.

8.30 p.m.   Back at the camp, I learn from Mig Goulding that the Secretary-General has telephoned Dr Savimbi and received the rather puzzling comment that, 'provided the results are announced today, I will be at Futungo at 14.00 hours tomorrow to meet with President dos Santos'. This is in remarkable contradiction with his earlier insistence that the results should not be published until the investigation is completed. Light begins to be shed on this *volte-face* a little later.

9.30 p.m.   Antonio Monteiro and Jeff Millington come to my house, at their request, for a working dinner. They (particularly Antonio) express doubts about the viability of Pik Botha's proposals. In any case, General N'dalu and Engineer Salupeto Pena are quietly working away on their own agenda for the meeting. Durão Barroso has just telephoned Antonio to tell him that Dr Savimbi has announced the presidential results on Portuguese television, claiming them as a victory for himself and proof that there was fraud. At about midnight, Mig calls to say that the Secretary-General has had a second conversation with Dr Savimbi that put a slightly different gloss on this latest unexpected turn of events and attitudes. I am also informed that the Troika will probably arrive this weekend.

The Aftermath

7.30 a.m. (Friday 16 October). The UNAVEM staff's analysis of the reports of the investigative commissions is brought to me. The overwhelming conclusion is that, while irregularities have been found in some places, there is no evidence of fraud on any major scale and the irregularities were not one-sided. UNITA representatives have taken part in all the investigations and subscribed to the findings.

Around 10.00 a.m. I receive a message from Minister Botha that Dr Savimbi is not prepared to travel to Luanda today unless the results are declared *beforehand* and asking me to use my influence with the NEC. I say I will, but that there are other factors and personalities involved.

11.00 a.m. A meeting is held of the NEC, the CCPM and UNAVEM. Confusion has been caused by the fact that, last night, the NEC spokesman, casting around to find some new way of explaining how yet another day has gone by without publication, stated that the results were being held up because 'some modifications might occur'. This caused alarm in UNITA, probably reflected in Dr Savimbi's insistence on publication before his meeting the President. The matter is settled to the satisfaction of both sides by President Caetano's immediate statement on the radio that there will be no further modification in the voting results. These are to be announced at 10.00 a.m. on Saturday morning.

The Council produced a document summarising the reports of the provincial investigating groups, containing conclusions agreed *unanimously* by its members late last night, including a UNITA delegate representing Dr Savimbi (Mr Benguela). UNAVEM representatives had witnessed all this. The conclusions point to some irregularities but no evidence of improper actions amounting to fraud. There is a pregnant pause. It seems that the matter must now be settled, given the unanimous agreement on the findings by all concerned, including the UNITA representative. All eyes are on Mr Hossi, UNITA's main delegate to the NEC. Mr Hossi closes his file. It seems for a moment that we are faced with a *fait accompli*. But before we can relax in a sigh of relief, Mr Hossi, with a fine sense of diplomatic timing, takes the floor to say that UNITA did not agree, but did not want to intervene in the Council's conclusions; they were reserving their fire 'for a later stage'. There is stunned silence, broken by Antonio Monteiro who rather forcefully asks whether they had stated their reservations in the NEC last night. Mr Hossi replies smoothly that it was not considered worthwhile, since UNITA had known from the outset what the outcome of the investigation would be. UNITA remained convinced that there was widespread fraud and would present its views separately. The fact that the UNITA representatives had signed the provincial commissions' reports is brought up, but is clearly not considered either relevant or binding. Mr Hossi[1] remains impervious to all arguments and entreaty and finds nothing illogical in UNITA having insisted on the investigation and taken part in it when it had prejudged the outcome from the start and would accept no other. He is plainly acting on precise instructions, presumably part of a wider strategy.

The meeting broke up in disarray. We are all dismayed and depressed.

12.30 p.m. I receive a message from Mr Botha that he is extremely pleased with Caetano's statement on the radio, has informed Dr Savimbi and still hopes the meeting between the leaders will take place that afternoon.

1.15 p.m. I call in at the CCPM building to ascertain the arrangements for Dr Savimbi's arrival and the meeting with President dos Santos and learn that it will now take place next Monday.

2.00 p.m. Another message from Minister Botha! Dr Savimbi is not happy with the NEC President's radio message (agreed beforehand by Salupeto Pena, who expressed complete satisfaction with its contents) and that he (Botha) is still striving to arrange the meeting for this afternoon. I tell him that it is now to be on Monday. It looks like a typically Angolan solution, side-stepping the 'Pik Botha solution', probably by mutual consent.

5.00 p.m. To a meeting of the CCPM to review the present situation and recent troop movements only to find it is postponed. An OAU delegation, headed by the presidents of Cape Verde and Zimbabwe will arrive on Sunday 18 October. The Troika will also gather in Luanda on Monday, so, as I comment dryly to Headquarters, there will be no lack of mediators.

That evening I received an urgent message to go and see Pik Botha. When I got to the boat he was telephoning President de Klerk, but I found Engineer Salupeto Pena and another UNITA representative waiting for him and we chatted together. When the Minister arrived he greeted me cordially and asked me to wait a few minutes with Ambassador Gröbler, courteously escorting me to a table. Then, in a quicksilver change of tone, he bore down upon the unfortunate Salupeto Pena, bellowing at the top of his not inconsiderable voice, 'I will not be treated like a DOG!' The habitual crowd of hangers-on around the bar was struck dumb, as was I. In the ensuing silence the Minister swept Salupeto Pena the length of the saloon to his usual corner. He did not actually have him by the ear, but one would not have been surprised to find that he did. It was an amazing sight to see the man who so often struck consternation in the CCPM, scurrying meekly behind the towering bulk of the Minister. Once they were seated the altercation continued. Engineer Salupeto Pena's replies were inaudible, but the Minister's repeated interjections – 'You have treated me shamefully', 'I will not stand for this', 'I am very hurt' – reverberated around the room, where everyone else tried to look as if nothing unusual was going on. I could not sit by and watch Salupeto Pena being humiliated, and asked Ambassador Gröbler to take me out on deck.

When Pik Botha came out to join us he was calm and smiling. The extraordinary bout of rage we had just witnessed had obviously been switched on for coolly calculated dramatic effect, and as quickly switched off. He told me that he was very angry with Salupeto Pena because it was he who had injected suspicion into

The Aftermath

Dr Savimbi's mind that the results circulated to the Council on the night of the 14th were not in fact final, perpetuating the misinterpretation of the NEC spokesman who had justified the further delay by injudiciously suggesting there might be further changes. It was this doubt sown by Salupeto Pena that had led Dr Savimbi to postpone his trip to Luanda. The Minister feared that UNITA might change its mind or commit some rash act during the weekend and this was why he had felt it necessary to treat Salupeto Pena roughly. 'It is the only way', he said.

The Minister would return to Pretoria but try to come back on Monday for the meeting, which he was still confident would take place; he thought things were on the right track – a view not shared by his aides, who privately expressed concern over very warlike talk on the part of Salupeto Pena. This was before the Minister virtually declared war on him.

Dr Savimbi had not been idle in Huambo. The leaders of seven opposition parties met there on 15 October (the same who had supported UNITA at the NEC meeting: UNITA, the FNLA, AD Coligacão, the PDP-ANA, the CNDA, the PSDA and the PDA) and they issued a communiqué that said, *inter alia*: 'The Angolan electoral process, in its entirety, was characterized by fraud and irregularities on a massive systematical and general scale, and therefore cannot be trusted. This fact is evidenced by the results of the investigations carried out by the commissions established by CCPM, NEC and UNAVEM II' (a patently untrue statement).

Other paragraphs said, more reassuringly, that war was not an option, and that it was imperative to find a solution to the present crisis that would foster 'national unity, democratization of society and the happiness of all Angolans'. In the last one the signatories (among them Savimbi) were pleased to note that the President of UNITA confirmed his readiness to meet President dos Santos, as soon as possible.

It was dismayingly clear that nothing whatever could be done to satisfy UNITA, short of a statement, against all the evidence, that the elections had been flawed by massive fraud and must be declared null and void.

* * *

The ceremony on Saturday morning, 17 October, to announce the official results was almost an anticlimax. It was well attended by party representatives and such dignitaries as Pik Botha; the diplomatic corps turned out in force, and frustrated journalists who had been picketing the NEC, waylaying all and sundry, had a field day. At last the NEC was able to say publicly what had been known for some time: that the MPLA had won 53.74 per cent of the votes in the legislative election, giving them 129 seats in the 223-seat parliament, compared with 34.10 per cent and 70 seats for UNITA; and that dos Santos had obtained 49.57 per cent of the votes for the presidency, compared with Savimbi's 40.07 per cent.

The results for the other parties and presidential candidates had little impact on the overall picture. The only real surprises were that Holden Roberto had gained only 2.11 per cent of the votes in the presidential race, while his party, the FNLA, had obtained only 2.40 per cent in the parliamentary elections. The party had at least scraped into third place, but Holden Roberto was denied even that satisfaction, the third place going to Alberto Neto, who had got 2.16 per cent of the votes, although his party, the PDA, had won only 0.20 per cent of the legislative vote, and thus gained no seat at all.

Most diplomats and observers heaved a sigh of relief that there had been no outright victor in the presidential race, and that there would be a second round, feeling this to be a further indication for any reasonable person that there had not been massive fraud. But such logical interpretations no longer had much validity: the process set in motion by Dr Savimbi on 3 October had acquired a momentum of its own, which had little to do with rationality and would be difficult to check.

* * *

This act of the Angolan drama could not be concluded without a pronouncement by the United Nations as to whether the elections had been free and fair. It fell to me, as the Secretary-General's Representative and head of UNAVEM II, to make that declaration, and although the judgement was a collegiate one, the cold fact remained that it would be personified in myself.

Contrary to some of the sweeping allegations aired later, I did not take this responsibility lightly. Nor was it the case – as the fevered imagination of one journalist, who was rallying to support UNITA's cause, rashly led her to claim – that the Secretary-General telephoned me during the night of 19 October to instruct me to reverse the judgement I had previously reached of stating that the elections were fraudulent. Headquarters had no say. This was a question that had to be settled on the spot with the information, evidence and observations that we had to hand. We reviewed not only the reports of the NEC, the Provincial Electoral Councils and the joint investigating commissions, but also the reports from UNAVEM Electoral Observers all over the country. Our analysis covered every stage and aspect of the process, from the setting up of the machinery and the procedures, through the three phases of registration, electoral campaigning and actual voting, right up to the counting and collection of ballots and the fraud investigations.

The conclusions were reached, and the declaration drafted, in joint consultation with my two most senior civilian aides (Ebrima Jobarteh, my executive director, who had overseen the electoral part of the UNAVEM operation, and Hugo Anson, my senior political adviser), plus Sammy Buo, the director of the

Electoral Division, and Dr Singela, the legal adviser. We worked for a large part of Friday night and Saturday morning to finalise it.

I made the declaration in the rec hall at 4.00 p.m. in English and Portuguese, before an audience comprising political parties, NEC officials (including Dr Caetano de Sousa and Dr Onofre dos Santos), Ambassadors and national and international journalists. Shortly before the meeting copies of the text were delivered, as a courtesy, to General N'dalu and Engineer Salupeto Pena.

The declaration analysed each one of the stages. On registration, while commending the remarkable number of voters registered, it noted our concern that not every voter in areas of difficult access might have had the opportunity to do so, and related my unsuccessful appeals to the NEC for a further extension beyond 10 August, concluding: 'While it would have been ideal to ensure that every eligible voter was registered, we nevertheless recognise that this process succeeded against many odds'.

The declaration stated that the electoral campaign had been conducted without major violent incidents, but noted some reports of intimidation and some difficulties of access, particularly in areas controlled by UNITA, as well as complaints about the continued existence of two armies and lack of access to government-controlled media. It paid tribute to the outstanding performance of all concerned on the two voting days. As for the fact that counting and compiling the votes had taken longer than the eight days stipulated by the Electoral Law, the declaration concluded that this was understandable, given the massive nature of the task and the many difficulties. It then described the actions taken by the NEC to investigate the allegations of fraud. The verdict came in the final two paragraphs:

In the light of the above-mentioned facts and observations, and after considering very carefully the concerns and views expressed by all the Angolan parties, as well as by other international observers, the United Nations considers that, while there were certainly some irregularities in the electoral process, these appear to have been mainly due to human error and inexperience. There was no conclusive evidence of major, systematic or widespread fraud, or that the irregularities were of a magnitude to have a significant effect on the results officially announced on 17 October. Nor, in view of their random nature, could it be determined that such irregularities had penalized or benefitted only one party or set of parties.

I therefore have the honour, in my capacity as Special Representative of the Secretary-General, to certify that, with all deficiencies taken into account, the elections held on 29/30 September can be considered to have been generally free and fair. The United Nations urges all Angolans and all Angolan political leaders, as well as the international community, to respect and support the results of this stage of the electoral process. A further certification will be made after the second round of the Presidential election.

Since I uttered those words there have been several attempts, instigated by UNITA, to induce me to modify that statement, or even to concede that I was totally mistaken. To this day I remain as convinced as I was in October 1992 that our judgement was the right one. The elections may not have been perfect, but I have yet to see elections that are, even in the most 'developed' countries. And such irregularities as did take place were not on one side only. The only blatant attempt to subvert the sovereign will of the Angolan people, as expressed through the ballot boxes, was that launched by UNITA three days after the elections and sustained for many long and tragic months afterwards.

16 The Débâcle

All hopes for a peaceful dénouement were now pinned on the summit between President dos Santos and Dr Savimbi. There were many intermediaries. Pik Botha, not a whit discouraged by the dismissive treatment he had received from both sides, was back in his floating headquarters off the Ilha on Monday, 19 October. The three members of the Troika had also flown into Luanda. The only mission that did not turn up was that from the Organisation of African Unity. Fortunately for me, the customary cordial and complementary relationship continued with the Troika, and Pik Botha had been sufficiently chastened by his experiences of the previous week to appreciate that it was useless to try and 'go it alone' as the sole arbiter.

His agenda and that of the Troika were not identical. Minister Botha still favoured what he called an 'African compromise', involving an interim government of national unity, while the Troika stood by strict compliance with the electoral process. On Monday 19 October the US State Department spokesman stated that the United States endorsed the elections as 'generally free and fair' and urged the competing parties to organise a run-off vote for the presidency as soon as possible. Hank Cohen was bringing urgent personal messages from President Bush for both President dos Santos and Dr Savimbi.

There was no time to lose. Over the weekend there had been a spate of incidents all over the country. After the announcement of the results on Saturday there had been shooting incidents between UNITA and MPLA supporters in Luanda and Huambo, in which several people had died, and a bomb had exploded in Kuito/Bié airport killing several policemen. Our UNAVEM military and police observers were busy counselling calm and patience, and intervening to resolve or, if possible, prevent disputes.

The meeting between the two leaders was now supposed to take place on Monday, 19 October. Pik Botha was so sure it would that he stationed himself at Luanda airport to greet Dr Savimbi on arrival and persuaded Hank Cohen to wait with him. The Minister's plane had again been despatched to Huambo to fetch the UNITA leader and General N'dalu, the only MPLA official whom Dr Savimbi appeared to respect and trust, had also gone there to escort him to the vital meeting.

Once again Dr Savimbi led everyone a merry dance. At the very last minute he imposed a new condition: he would not fly to Luanda unless the venue was changed from Futungo de Belas to Luanda airport, citing a likely threat to his life if he ventured within the portals of the Presidential palace. Negotiations went back and forth across the airwaves. I offered a cordon of 'Blue Berets' to surround the aircraft on Savimbi's arrival and escort him to the palace, or to the UNAVEM camp, which could provide a neutral, international venue. Pik Botha, still at the airport, was pulling out every stop to induce Savimbi to travel, and was becoming increasingly irascible as all his and our efforts proved of no avail. Dr Savimbi remained adamant, and there was no way in which President dos

Santos would accept a meeting at the airport (a calculation that Dr Savimbi may well have made before proposing it). Hank Cohen and Pik Botha spent about five hours in broiling heat waiting for the UNITA leader, who never came.

The most that could be achieved was an agreement between General N'dalu and Dr Savimbi that two joint commissions be set up immediately, one to deal with political, the other with military issues. Only when they had reached satisfactory conclusions would the summit meeting be held. The sceptics (and their number was growing daily) suspected a device for gaining more time for UNITA to prepare itself militarily. Those still clinging to the hope that peace might yet be saved consoled themselves that UNITA was still ready to engage in dialogue.

I met the Troika twice that day to discuss how to save the situation. We glumly concluded that a last appeal by them to Dr Savimbi was the only further step that could be taken on the spot, and it was a decidedly forlorn hope.

* * *

In New York, Ambassador Jesus was presenting an oral report to the Security Council (19 October) on behalf of the *ad hoc* Commission. In the five days since the Commission's departure, so much had happened that its message seemed to come from another world. The members of the Commission believed they had helped reduce the tension that had erupted after the elections by contributing to the dialogue between the two Angolan leaders and helping to put the political process back on track. They were happily unaware of how badly wrong things were going, even as Ambassador Jesus was speaking. He and his colleagues were generous in their praise of the work of UNAVEM and myself, giving a much-needed fillip to our spirits, which were now prey to mounting despondency. Their recommendations were also positive: there must be a much stronger UN presence and mandate for the second round.

The Security Council approved the text of a presidential statement that reiterated the by now monotonous appeal to both parties to abide scrupulously by their commitments. The Council also noted with satisfaction my public certification that the election had been 'generally free and fair', and that the two leaders accepted a dialogue aimed at the completion of the electoral process. The Council asked the Secretary-General to recommend how the UN could best contribute to the smooth operation of the second phase, and declared its readiness to act on them without delay.

* * *

UNITA's formidable propaganda machine was already cranking into action. Jonas Savimbi launched one of his mammoth messages to the people of Angola,

The Débâcle

datelined Jamba, 19 October, which raised speculation about whether he was physically there, though it seemed unlikely since General N'dalu had seen him in Huambo that day. The speech contained the usual accusations of fraud, as well as against the 'Communist regime of the MPLA-PT of Angola'. It also attacked 'international organisations'. The UN, though clearly targeted, was not once mentioned. The following extract is an English translation of a radio transcript:

> I wanted to tell all the governments that, if we could thank the international community for its cooperation, we have the right, as Angolans on our Angolan soil, to say that the behaviour of the international community in Angola was negative.... [Some Angolans] upon learning that the elections had been fraudulent, committed suicide, some had heart attacks, disappeared from this world. A significant sign that the process was neither clean nor transparent.... We have two societies here in Angola. One, watching the departure of the international organisations, will clap and give flowers to them. But a major part of society will consider the coming of those organisations to Angola was the worst disgrace for our nation.... Not wanting to waste your time with international organisations, I turn to the Angolans. Angolans, have hope. Angolans will be men and women who will rise ... to change history, will grow to attain honour and dignity. To attain justice, many of us are willing to make any kind of sacrifice.

The only small comfort to be gained from the speech was that the rest of it was predicated on a second round of presidential elections. It was a rallying call to UNITA supporters to ensure that this time UNITA carried off the victory that Savimbi maintained should rightfully have been UNITA's in the first round.

The UNITA public relations offensive was also coming nearer to me personally. In a press conference on 19 October the UNITA spokesman, Norberto de Castro, expressed surprise about my certification of the elections, alleging that only a few hours earlier I had said to Salupeto Pena that I had never in my life seen anything like the Angolan elections in any part of the world, not even Latin America 'where *coups d'état* were a daily event'; I was supposed to have added that it was pressure from above that had prevented me from acknowledging that fraud had taken place. Norberto de Castro challenged me to deny this.

I first heard of this barefaced lie in a question from the BBC, to which I replied with a categorical denial that I had made these remarks to Salupeto Pena (or indeed to anybody else). My denial figured large in the *Jornal de Angola* of 20 October. On Monday evening Victor Lima conveyed to Hugo Anson the President's concern about this attempt to undermine the validity of the elections, as well as the hope that I would issue a *démenti*. The next day I had the opportunity to reiterate my denial before Angolan television as I left Futungo de Belas after seeing the President, made it unnecessary. The matter was not to end there, however.

* * *

Early on Tuesday 20 October I met Pik Botha, who made no attempt to conceal the intense fury he had felt the previous day. He was plainly very surprised to have been stood up by Savimbi. His anger had cooled overnight and he was now calm, if resentful, and determined to have one last shot at bringing off a personal coup by engineering the meeting. He was going to Huambo that morning to meet Dr Savimbi, after which he would return to Luanda to meet the President. He hoped that the agreement to set up two commissions would enable an agenda to be agreed so that the two leaders could meet 'within three or four days'. In addition he confirmed our own observation that the atmosphere at Luanda airport on Monday had been very tense: at one point, heavily armed UNITA troops had almost taken over the airport.

Two of Mr Botha's aides reported that Salupeto Pena, completely beside himself, had shouted that if UNITA saw the slightest incident that might affect Savimbi's security 'we will not hesitate to order our penetration battalions to enter Luanda, take the airport, radio station, Futungo.... We would kill Anstee, we would kill Cohen, we would kill Durão Barroso, we would kill Millington, and we would stop Botha from going home'. The Russians were not included in these dire threats, perhaps because they were not considered sufficiently important!

The Minister said he would impress upon Dr Savimbi in the clearest terms that such statements were absolutely unacceptable, and that South Africa completely supported my statement concerning the elections (a welcome sea-change from his attitude during our first encounter only a week before). He would also suggest that Dr Savimbi should see me as soon as possible. He could not delay his departure to Pretoria beyond that evening, but wanted to see me again, after his meeting with President dos Santos. The Troika were also meeting the President that morning, and then going on to see Dr Savimbi – the same programme as Mr Botha, but in reverse.

And then I too received a call asking me to meet the President at 11 a.m. I was accompanied by Jobarteh, the President by an unusually large entourage: Foreign Minister 'Loy', General N'dalu, Vice Minister 'Nando' and Vice Minister Venâncio de Moura. The Troika were in the anteroom waiting to see the President, but he said he wished to see me alone first. The Troika had wanted me to be present at their meeting with him but the President did not think this was appropriate, since he felt (as I did myself) that it was important to keep the UN as a separate channel, representing the interests of the international community as a whole, rather than those of individual countries or group of countries.

The President then discussed the prospects for the meeting with Dr Savimbi. He welcomed the establishment of the two commissions as it must be well prepared: an inconclusive meeting would only aggravate a tense situation further. I gave the President the Security Council President's statement of the previous day, underlining that the *ad hoc* Commission had unanimously recommended the strengthening of the UN presence in Angola. The President expressed satisfaction, stressing the great responsibility of the international community for what was happening in Angola. The security situation within towns, much worse than at any time during the civil war because of the presence there of armed UNITA elements, had come about because of the international community's insistence on giving a special position to UNITA in the peace process.

'So we look now to the international community to defend us. But if they will not come to our defence, then we shall have to defend ourselves.'

* * *

At 6.30 that evening a huge cavalcade of police outriders on motorcycles and police vehicles with blaring sirens roared into Vila Espa past our startled guards at the gate. It ended up in front of my house, but before rumours of my imminent kidnap could circulate very far, Pik Botha and his advisers emerged from Government cars sandwiched in the midst of this cortege. Soon my front room was crammed full of very large men.

Pik Botha was like a man transformed, restored to his usual ebullient and confident self, and brimming over with optimism. His meeting with Dr Savimbi had gone very well and he had made some forceful points, taking Savimbi to task for the threatening language used by his associates; Savimbi had expressed shock and said he would ensure that such threats ceased. The Minister had also made clear that South Africa accepted my statement on the elections, which it considered balanced, and had advised Savimbi to do the same. Vice President Chitunda had asked, 'What about all the fraud?', but, according to Botha, Savimbi had cut him short and agreed with Botha's advice and his assertion that no major fraud could be proven. The Minister had also impressed upon Savimbi that war was out of the question, that he would receive no support whatsoever and that the best thing was to cooperate in a government of national unity, with a view to holding the second round in two or three months' time.

He said he had also received an assurance from Savimbi that he would meet the President within the next few days, and would be happy to see me. Botha was writing a personal letter to the Secretary-General urging that the UN should organise the next elections, as well as having a strong observer presence, and that 'Blue Helmets' were a must.

After he left I met the Troika, whose plane from Huambo landed just as Pik Botha's was taking off. Any encouragement from my meeting with the latter was quickly dispelled. All three were in deep depression, having been confronted with an impenetrably hardline stance. Secretary of State Durão Barroso thought the situation was very serious indeed and could see no solution. Assistant Secretary Cohen said that Dr Savimbi and UNITA clearly felt they were negotiating from a position of strength, feeling comfortable and secure in Huambo; he described it as the 'Charles Taylor syndrome'.

Savimbi had posed the question 'Who asked Pik Botha to come? Was it the Troika?' The Troika had promptly denied this and Savimbi had gone on to say that he felt that Botha's presence owed more to the interests of his own country than to those of Angola. UNITA had also been critical of the UN. In a private conversation with Savimbi, Hank Cohen had stressed that the United States would never deviate from the UN's opinion about the elections, but he described Savimbi and UNITA as 'very cocky' (UNITA's symbol is a black cockerel, but the pun, I am sure, was unintended). UNITA's attitude was ambiguous: on the one hand Savimbi had declared his intention to stick by the Bicesse Accords: on the other he had told the Troika that UNITA would never accept the election results (though he had assured the Secretary-General that he would).

Savimbi had mentioned Pik Botha's proposals for a government of national unity as an interim solution and said firmly 'we reject that'. He had seemed to accept the second round and thought it should take place in three to four months. Moreover he had insisted that the UN should run them, which, the Troika had pointed out, was a contradiction since he had strongly criticised the UN. Finally, Savimbi had said he accepted the proposal for two commissions to prepare the meeting between himself and President dos Santos and was ready to enter into dialogue.

In my notes at the time I commented: 'The Troika's mission has ended inconclusively, though with a sense of foreboding about the outcome and of impotence as regards finding solutions. As he left, Ambassador Cohen said, only half jokingly, that the observer countries should bow out and leave everything to the UN, which sounded ominously as if the UN was to rival Oxford as "the home of lost causes". Nonetheless we continue to soldier on in the hope that we are able to find a chink in the darkness'.

I did not even try to sum up Pik Botha's whirlwind appearance on the scene. It had been a lively, if confused interlude, during which I had revised my initial impression. There was something engaging about his personality, even if his way of going about diplomacy was reminiscent of a bull in a china shop, and I respected him for having recognised the error of his initial conclusions about UNITA's claims of fraud. I felt he had gone away a sadder and wiser man as regards his assessment of Dr Savimbi and UNITA. His visits had pointed up still further the apparent irrationalities in the UNITA leader's conduct, which were beginning to look ominously like a smoke screen for a more coherent strategy that did not bode well for peace in Angola.

* * *

The Big League of mediators flew off to the four corners of the globe simultaneously, leaving the Angolan crisis to rumble on, impervious to the pressures of the outside world. We lesser mortals on the ground continued to wrestle with an intractable situation that seemed to slip further from our grasp with every passing day.

Our central concern was the work of the two commissions. General N'dalu was to lead for the Government while Vice President Chitunda headed the UNITA team. On Wednesday afternoon (21 October) I met General N'dalu just before his first encounter with Dr Chitunda. I found him subdued. He commented that many people in the MPLA were coming to believe that war was inevitable, although the fact that Dr Chitunda, who was always cast as a 'hardliner', had come to Luanda was a relatively hopeful sign.

General N'dalu also threw new light on the non-appearance of Dr Savimbi for the meeting with President dos Santos on 19 October. The previous evening Pik Botha had given me Savimbi's version, as recounted to him: he had been ready to leave for Luanda at 11 a.m. but N'dalu had received a message from Futungo insisting on better preparation of the meeting and the setting up of two commissions. N'dalu said this was a complete travesty of the facts and an attempt to put the blame on the Government. He had arrived in Huambo at 9.00 a.m., but had had to cool his heels until 2 p.m. before Savimbi received him. In the meantime it was the latter and UNITA who had dreamed up the idea of the commissions and not, General N'dalu most emphatically said, the Government. Notwithstanding, the Government was pushing hard for the meeting to take place before the end of that week. N'dalu was a man whose word and sincerity I had come to trust. All these petty lies and subterfuges, by UNITA, like the fabricated conversation between myself and Salupeto Pena, were a sorry indication of the depths to which UNITA was prepared to sink in order to get its way, and made one despair of ever finding a way through the morass of tangled deception. Where did the truth lie? When could one believe UNITA, and when not?

General N'dalu's meeting with Dr Chitunda was to follow 15 minutes later, at 3.00 p.m. True to UNITA form, Chitunda did not turn up: he was 'too tired' after the one-and-a-half hour flight from Huambo. The meeting was rescheduled for 10.00 a.m. the next morning. This news was given to me by N'dalu that evening, at a farewell dinner for Jeff Millington, who could hardly suppress his joy at being released from this purgatory, or his despondency about what he thought lay ahead for Angola. It was a curious evening of camaraderie and nostalgia, with lots of jokes and repartee, a small island of apparent normality amid the stress and foreboding that marked all our days now. Jeff's successor, Ambassador Edmond De Jarnette, was introduced at the dinner. He was a career foreign service officer, until then US Ambassador to Tanzania. The UNITA delegation was conspicuous by its absence. No excuse or apology was sent. We waited a long time before sitting down to a very late dinner. Apart from the discourtesy, it seemed incredible that UNITA should not send a word of farewell or acknowledgement to the man who had helped it for so long. If this meant that UNITA was disappointed in him, it was plainly a reciprocated sentiment.

The meetings of the commissions were to be closed, and restricted to the two parties. Through our staff officer at the CCPM building, we learned that the first meeting between General N'dalu and Vice President Chitunda did take place on Thursday morning (22 October). The UNITA military representatives, including General 'Ben-Ben' and General Zacharias, had turned up once again attired in their new FAA uniforms, which caused us quite disproportionate joy. As I commented: 'We clutch at symbols, if not at straws, in our search for a positive outcome'.

The two chief negotiators decided to hold a briefing meeting with the CCPM every day. Unfortunately they forgot to inform me about the first one, which was held at 8.30 a.m. on the morning of Friday 23 October. Even Antonio Monteiro did not hear about it until 7.30 a.m. He told me that he had come away somewhat encouraged. Both delegation leaders were at pains to make clear that this bilateral dialogue was exclusively concerned with preparing the summit meeting and was being conducted within the framework of the Bicesse Accords. There was no intention to leave the observers and UNAVEM out, nor to deviate from the consultative mechanisms established under the Accords.

Dr Chitunda said that the first day had been very positive. They had agreed on the main points of the agenda: analysis of the political and military situation; analysis of the fulfilment of the Peace Accords (including the electoral process, internal security and the formation of the FAA); proposed solutions for the national crisis; the conditions for an eventual second round of Peace Accords; and a draft agenda for the summit meeting. Priority was to be given to diminishing military tension throughout the country, including the volatile situation around Dr Savimbi's residence in Miramar. (This had grown so intolerable that poor Antonio Monteiro had had to abandon his delightful residence, put his prized Portuguese furniture in store, and move to the Hotel Imperio, where he also had his office.) Dr Chitunda added that the solution most favoured by both sides was to go ahead with the second round and the two sides would try to agree mutually acceptable conditions.

The Débâcle

There was not a great deal to show by the end of that week, but at least the two sides were still talking.

* * *

On 22 October the EC and its member states issued a declaration (delayed by some bureaucratic mix-up) supporting my statement on the elections and expressing the hope that all who had competed in them would 'respect the choice of the Angolan people'. The member states looked forward to the second round of the presidential elections 'in a peaceful climate and without intimidation from any side', and urged compliance with the Bicesse Accords.

An even more significant corroboration came from Pik Botha in a statement issued in Gaberone on 23 October, in which he declared that the South African government accepted my findings and urged the UN to make additional personnel available for the second round. He also appealed to 'all political leaders in Angola' to respect the election results and renounce force, in favour of dialogue.

These welcome expressions of support were no match for the virulent attacks now being levelled at me by UNITA. I had requested an appointment with Dr Savimbi in Huambo, but had received no answer. Meanwhile Norberto de Castro had returned to the attack on Radio Vorgan on Tuesday evening (20 October), after my *démenti* of his earlier statement. He claimied that I was lying, that I was receiving money from the MPLA and was involved in smuggling mercury and diamonds. I sent our information assistant to Tierra Angolana to obtain a transcript. She was almost forcibly held there against her will by UNITA journalists, who gave her a message for me. The following are typical extracts:

> ...all the Angolan people hate you because you are a liar. They admitted to have felt admiration for you but that this had changed after you declared that the elections had been free and fair.
> ...you also lied when denying having said that you were pressed by higher instances to declare the elections free and fair. Neither Norberto de Castro nor Salupeto Pena lie. If she [you] did not say it, why does she not defend herself?
> ...the United Nations, namely UNAVEM II, supports Communism.
> ...If Namibia is such a small country compared to Angola, how is it that the UN sent 6000 observers there and only 400 here?
> ...Angola is a very rich country, and all the wealth is in the hands of the MPLA. Miss Anstee must have received something from them.
> They said that your salary was US$20 000 per month, all for nothing.

UNAVEM II will be a shameful chapter in the history of Angola. What did the UN know about Angola, what did Anstee know about Angola, how could they pretend to understand our people?

I expressed the hope to our information assistant that she had at least dispelled their inflated notions about my salary!

The next morning John Flynn telephoned to say that the previous evening he had heard another vicious attack on Radio Vorgan, which he described as 'Goebbels-like'. Among the more choice remarks were accusations that I was corrupt, in the pay of the 'Futungistas' (that is, the presidential entourage) and had betrayed my own country, Angola, and the trust of the United Nations. It was only through the help of the US Liaison Office and the British Embassy that we managed to get a full transcript of the broadcast, which UNITA had refused to give us. The following extracts give some idea of the venomous trash that was being poured out over the airwaves.

> Angolans invited international observers for the sole purpose of being neutral, but the neutrality of one observer has been corrupted by one of the parties. When a neutral element allows itself to be corrupted by one of the parties, it automatically stops being neutral and becomes allied with that party. This is what happened to Mrs Margaret Anstee and her UN team...
>
> ... irregularities occurred in the Angolan elections the knowledge or with the connivance of Margaret Anstee.
>
> With what moral force will the UN impose itself, demanding all Angolans to accept the elections results, in which the UN representative assisted in rigging? It is a mistake to think that Margaret Anstee holds the truth on whether there was fraud or not in the 29 and 30 September elections, because Anstee sold her honour and dignity for diamonds, industrial mercury, and for US dollars, which she received from Jose Eduardo dos Santos. Thus the referee became a player of one of the teams.
>
> This is the great democracy they came to teach us! If we are mistaken, may God Our Lord be equally corruptible so that Margaret Anstee will never again have a clear conscience because of her gross fault, as well as because of the sad and bitter fruits of her enormous lack of honesty, which her mission implied. Margaret Anstee has proved, by her own future unhappiness, the lack of competence and integrity for a duty of such great importance. It is not enough to be a UN official it is not enough to be European when carrying out a mission in Africa: it is not enough to be British to be able to say something with recognised authority in Angola.
>
> Mrs Anstee was always respected during her mission in Angola, because no one expected that she lacked the highest moral values to such an extent that she would sell herself to the Angolan communists in order to keep them in power. She was mistaken because her Futungo bosses, with all the contempt that this represents for the UN, and her country of origin, as we said, the com-

munists, her bosses, will not continue in power in Angola. Mrs Anstee, contrary to the request of Angolans and the good intentions of the UN, worked solely to push Angola into another well-foreseeable war and to discredit the UN. This applies to her: the smell of money had no regard for honour or dignity and even less for justice, for reason and for truth. Mrs Anstee has scored high on the scale of low morals.

The Angolans still hold their pride and for this reason they will prove to Mrs Anstee that her Futungo de Belas bosses in Luanda will not continue in power in Angola, because the Angolan people no longer want communist dictators in power. Even if for this reason we have to take up arms, or if it means the death of more sons of Angola. When she arrived in Angola on her mission, Mrs Anstee, with her age and apparent maturity, led us to believe that we were with a mother and all that this represents.

Allow us to tell you that the woman forgot the pains of birth, if she ever experienced this motherly pain, with all respect to decide to take wealth from our land and leave the children of other women in a war which will inevitably bring more deaths.

The devil may be deaf and dumb, but we need to close the exit doors of Angola on Mrs Anstee after she witnessed at least one month of war without a break, a war that she would leave in Angola due to her corrupt character.

Moreover, if Mrs Anstee does not have the moral character to understand the gravity of the situation that inevitably accompanies her, she will never be rid of it. Because the crime that Anstee committed in Angola will inevitably spill the blood of sons of other women, mothers like herself. The devil may be deaf or dumb.

Mig Goulding cabled to say that the Secretary General was 'disturbed at these totally unjustified attacks'. He was also losing patience with the Angolans. When the Permanent Representative to the UN, Ambassador 'Mbinda', had called to seek his advice Dr Boutros-Ghali had not minced his words. He would continue his efforts with Dr Savimbi, but the Angolans must first help themselves if they wanted the continuing involvement of the international community. Given the acute fatigue among contributing countries it was fanciful to think of UN peacekeeping forces being sent to Angola. The President must persevere in his efforts to get Savimbi to meet him. There must be dialogue and early agreement on the second round. If there was no visible progress, the world would quickly transfer its attention and resources to other situations, and Angola would be in danger of becoming another Lebanon. Ambassador 'Mbinda' undertook to report this, but I am sceptical of how clearly this very plain message was transmitted back to Luanda and Futungo.

The Secretary-General was trying to reach Dr Savimbi to tell him that the attacks on his Special Representative must stop, but was unable to get through. I myself called Savimbi's satellite telephone number to tell him that the Secretary-General was trying to reach him, but the man who answered, after some evasive exchanges, said it was the wrong number. Subsequently it was always engaged. It looked very much as if contact was being evaded, a favourite UNITA tactic (perhaps another taught by the CIA?) After having tried, equally unsuccessfully, to telephone Engineer Salupeto Pena by telephone, I sent a staff officer to the Hotel Turismo at midnight. He was told that Salupeto Pena was 'busy' but left my written message.

My offer to meet Dr Savimbi in Huambo was still pending. I had discussed this with Salupeto Pena on Tuesday 20 October, before the full force of Vorgan's malevolent fury had been unleashed, and he had said that he would take up the possibility with Dr Savimbi on Wednesday. It was now Friday. Normally I would have pursued the matter vigorously, but the circumstances had changed drastically. I decided to wait for UNITA to make the first move and then think very carefully before accepting any invitation. A number of people in Luanda, including Ambassadors with good sources of intelligence, were advising me that it would be imprudent for me to go to Huambo. At the very least, the Vorgan campaign should be stopped first and assurances given for my security (after all, Savimbi was hypersensitive about his own). Headquarters agreed that it would be unwise for me to visit Huambo until the Secretary-General had spoken to the UNITA leader.

The UNITA hate campaign showed no sign of abating. *Terra Angolana* contained two articles demonstrating that its capacity for virulently libellous invention was unlimited, with banner headlines to match. One read 'The Two Faces of Sra. Anstee'. This jolly publication came out, appropriately enough, on Saturday 24 October, United Nations Day (a UN holiday that UNAVEM had no time to observe). The director of *Terra Angolana* was that man of many parts, Norberto de Castro.

* * *

Despite all the imponderables, we still had to plan for the future. Before the elections the Government and UNITA had agreed in the CCPM that UNAVEM's mandate should be extended, in a modified form, until the end of the year. The official request was submitted to the Secretary-General in a letter of 28 September from President dos Santos. We had sent our corresponding plan to New York in the first week of October, based on a number of criteria that almost immediately became obsolete. The plan became out of date within a few days of its despatch to New York.

When the Security Council met to consider Angola in informal consultations on Monday 26 October, five days before UNAVEM's mandate was due to expire, the situation had become even more unpredictable. The Council decided to extend UNAVEM II's existing mandate for one month, pending clarification of the prospects for a second round. Some members felt that a strong message

The Débâcle

should be sent to Dr Savimbi about UNITA's attacks against me, and were very concerned that the Secretary-General could not reach him by telephone. The Secretary-General was asked to provide a written report for the next day. That evening the Ambassadors of the 'Permanent Five' (China, France, Russia, the UK and the United States) called on the Secretary-General to convey their anxiety about the worsening situation. Dr Boutros-Ghali expressed his outrage at the treatment I was receiving and stressed the need for the Angolan parties to work together to save the Peace Accords.

As requested, the next day (27 September) the Secretary-General wrote to the Council President summarising the situation, which he described as explosive. The letter contained the following paragraph:

> I am also concerned about the unwarranted and malicious campaign unleashed by UNITA-controlled mass media, namely by Vorgan radio and Tierra Angolana newspaper, against my Special Representative, Miss Anstee, and UNAVEM II. Death threats have been made against Miss Anstee and several disquieting incidents have occurred against UNAVEM in certain regions. This must stop immediately and the security and safety of all UNAVEM II personnel must be guaranteed. I have for several days attempted to reach Dr Savimbi to convey to him my outrage at these attacks and to urge him to travel to Luanda to meet President dos Santos as he had promised me on 15 October that he would do. However, it has proved impossible to make contact with him.

At a formal meeting of the Security Council on 27 October, the President read out a statement urging the two leaders to engage in dialogue without delay so that the second round could be held. There was a special plea, directed at UNITA and other parties, to respect the election results. The Council also strongly condemned the 'attack and baseless accusations made by Vorgan radio' against myself and UNAVEM II, calling for their immediate cessation and reiterating its full support for me and my staff.

UNAVEM II was extended, lock, stock and barrel, until 30 November 1992.

* * *

In Luanda on 26 October the mixed Government–UNITA commission reported some snail-like progress. A military commission had been set up, headed by Generals Alberto Neto and 'Ben-Ben', to verify and prevent all offensive movement of military forces, or their rearmament, and ensure their return to their respective areas, as well as reactivate the regional groups and subgroups with the corresponding elements of UNAVEM. On the electoral process, Engineer Salupeto Pena said that UNITA had not yet decided whether or not to go to the second round. If it did it would insist that the UN should organise it, but the Government was not equally keen on the UN being involved in the actual organisation. I expressed the hope that a clear determination would soon be made so that a firm, official request could go forward to the Secretary-General. A large exodus of military and police observers was taking place that same week and they were unlikely to be replaced until the situation became clearer.

After the briefing, Salupeto Pena told me that Chivukuvuku had a message for me from Dr Savimbi and wished me to go to the UNITA headquarters at three o'clock, a peremptory and discourteous request to the Special Representative of the Secretary-General. I preferred to meet him on my own ground, but was told that Chivukuvuku was 'far too busy' to come out to Vila Espa. As a diplomatic compromise the meeting took place in my downtown office. Chivukuvuku began by saying that Dr Savimbi would like to see me in Huambo the next day or the day after. He went on to describe UNITA's view of the present situation, with particular emphasis on the need for a much greater UN presence to organise the second round, which he said could not take place before April or May 1993, but gave no indication of whether the legislative elections would, in the meantime, be accepted by UNITA. He did refer to some kind of interim 'government of national reconciliation'. He also obliquely referred to the attacks on me, saying that, while UNITA disagreed with my declaration of 17 October, it wished to dissociate itself from the subsequent attacks on UNAVEM and on 'individual persons', for which he apologised.

I said that, while the scurrilous attacks on my person amounted to malicious libel, they were not confined to me. If there was to be an extended UNAVEM presence, it was imperative that the attacks cease forthwith and that UNITA make public the disclaimer that Dr Chivukuvuku had just given to me. My request to see Dr Savimbi had been made before the attacks started, and I did not feel it was appropriate for me to go until the Secretary-General had been able to speak to him and a public retraction had been made by UNITA. I also asked for assurance on my security, since death threats had been made and the kind of propaganda coming out of Vorgan and *Terra Angolana* might well be interpreted as incitement in certain quarters. Chivukuvuku said he would inform Dr Savimbi.

* * *

While the two sides indulged in an interminable fencing match, unrest was spreading like wildfire throughout the country, with accusations and counteraccusations of troop movements on both sides. As UNITA took over more towns and districts the Government administrators left, and the thin patchwork of central administration was unravelling before our eyes. Huambo had *de facto* become a UNITA garrison town, the black cockerel flag flying over the airport and heavily armed UNITA troops lining the streets, although the Governor was still in residence and Government police were still stationed there. People rarely ventured out at night, and did so at their peril. The particularly brutal killing, on the night of Tuesday 20 October, of a well-known and respected writer, Fernando Marcelino, and his wife and sister, who were gunned down in cold blood in their car, sent shock waves through Angola, particularly among the intelligentsia. The Government was moving FAA troops around to counter UNITA moves or anticipate real or rumoured advances. Reinforcements were being sent to Caxito, the capital of Bengo province, which lies just a few kilometres north of Luanda, and was strategically crucial to the city's defence. During the night of Thursday 22 October Luanda again reverberated to the thunder of a bomb explosion that destroyed the offices of the Banco de Comercio e Industria and shattered the windows of the Hotel Presidente.

Everyone who could was getting out of Angola. Most of the diplomats' families, and those of the few foreign businessmen, had left in July. Now the remaining few were leaving and well-to-do Angolan families were sending their women and children to Portugal. Less than a month earlier, every plane coming in to Luanda airport had been loaded with people eager to return for the elections. Now every departing plane was equally loaded with people scrambling to get out before the storm. Those who had no option but to stay – the vast majority – were involved in an equally desperate scramble to stock up supplies.

The siege mentality that had gripped the capital during 16 years of war was returning like some inadequately exorcised ghost. Supplies of basic goods dwindled, prices soared and inflation spiralled to new heights. The quiet passage of the election had caused an instantaneous strengthening of the 'new' kwanza; the exchange rate for one US dollar on the parallel (black) market slumping overnight from 3600 kwanza to 2800 kwanza. Now, a few weeks later, the reverse process was again in full swing, and the many poor could buy less and less. Strain and fear were visible on the faces of the people in the markets and in the streets, faces that had beamed with surprise and civic pride when they thought they had achieved the unattainable. The miracle had not happened after all. It seemed all too likely to prove a cruel mirage, like so much in their stunted lives, which up to now had known little but war. A cloud of foreboding hung over the city and its people as they waited for the storm to break, but hoped against hope that something would be done to avert it.

If this sensation of the need to take some drastic action to retrieve the situation was very strong as one moved about the city, you entered a different world inside the CCPM building. There were a lot of people hanging around – civilians, men in uniform, armed guards – but there was a desultory air about the place. Much time seemed to be spent waiting for meetings that were announced, but either did not happen at all or were postponed, sometimes several times. UNITA was reputed to be the side usually requesting more time, or not turning up at all. I was often there, anxiously seeking news, and whether there was anything that UNAVEM could do to hasten the process. The most frequent activity observed was trays bearing bottles of Chivas Regal whisky being carried upstairs; rumour had it that these were being delivered to the office of Salupeto Pena, who, it was said, was drinking heavily and was frequently subject to bouts of ungovernable rage. Some said afterwards that he had been taking drugs as well. General N'dalu, formerly irrepressible, became quieter and more morose with every passing day.

Late on 27 October, UNITA presented its proposals. It wanted the full involvement of the UN in the organisation of the second round, which should be 'jointly planned' by UNITA and the MPLA; impartial state mass media; immediate confinement to quarters and monitoring of the antiriot police; cessation of 'arbitrary arrests and persecutions' of UNITA militants; reinstallation of mechanisms for concerted action in provincial capitals; new electoral registration (it was claimed that many civilians had lost their cards); a new ballot; an electoral code of conduct; and definition of the period in which the second round should take place, taking into account all that needed to be done beforehand, as well as 'meteorological conditions'. UNITA's final demand was for 'the creation of an adequate governing mechanism for the transition period', to deal with pending issues of the Peace Accords, such as the formation of the FAA, carry out training programmes for demobilised troops, restore a climate conducive to economic reconstruction and foreign investment, and promote national reconciliation. What form this 'mechanism' was to take, and what part UNITA expected to play in it, was not specified.

General N'dalu asked Ambassador Monteiro if the observers could comment on these proposals. After a brainstorming session with his US and Russian colleagues and myself on 28 October, the Ambassador produced a 'non-paper'. Starting from the premise that the Bicesse Accords remained the legal framework and that its outstanding provisions should be completed, the paper made specific suggestions for solving the crisis. They covered the organisation of the second round of presidential elections; reduction of hostile propaganda; police and security forces; human rights; conflict situations; transition arrangements until the second round; the creation of a 'Council of the Republic', a purely consultative body composed of the cosignatories of the Peace Accords, the President of the National Assembly and the Supreme Court and other leading personalities to advise the President; extension of the central administration; and referral of any impasses in the CCPM to the 'Council of the Republic'. All these issues were hardy old favourites, debated *ad nauseam* in the CCPM before the elections, with the exception of the imaginative proposal for a Council of the Republic. General N'dalu liked some of the ideas and it was arranged that we should all see the President the next day.

The Government side now produced its own proposals, which bore a striking similarity to many points in UNITA's paper. The main differences lay firstly in the insistence in the first section on the cessation of all offensive and military occupation and the withdrawal from towns and villages of 'all forces displaced during this period' and the disarmament and control of 'military forces outside and inside the assembly areas' – both clear references to UNITA; and secondly, while both sides favoured a 'government of unity and reconciliation', much depended on their respective interpretations of how this would function. UNITA's proposal was vague while the Government's was spelt out in detail.

All three proposals were so close that, on the face of it, it should not have been impossible to achieve agreement.

At 6.00 p.m. on Wednesday 28 October an informal meeting was held in the CCPM building between UNITA, the three observers and myself to look at Antonio's 'non-paper'. UNITA was represented by Engineer Salupeto Pena, Fatima Roque, General 'Mackenzie' and my attacker, Norberto de Castro. The latter had the effrontery to proffer his hand, but his gaze studiously avoided my own. Antonio spoke beforehand to Fatima Roque and elicited an assurance from her that we would not be subjected to another diatribe on fraud or a harping on of old grievances, since the emphasis was on finding solutions. Nonetheless, hardly had we sat down before she unleashed a violent broadside about fraud, which became a frontal assault on me. From one moment to the next she had become a pocket virago, positively spitting accusations and wild claims as if someone had pushed a button that set the whole performance in motion. It was with difficulty that she could be silenced to permit discussion of the 'non-paper'.

In contrast to Fatima Roque (it was UNITA's habit to allow one of the lesser members to lead the attack in order to demonstrate the strength of feeling among its followers), Salupeto Pena was in an unusually conciliatory mood and stressed the importance that UNITA attached to close involvement of the international community and a larger role for the United Nations. He noted the common ideas in the three documents, which UNITA was going to study, and hoped it might be possible to reach agreement next day with the Government.

Afterwards he asked for my reaction to Dr Savimbi's invitation, to which I replied that I was awaiting a response to the two points I had made to Dr Chivukuvuku. Salupeto Pena said that he could offer all guarantees for my security; as to the public disclaimer of the attacks on me, there was no difficulty in principle but it would have to be agreed with the political committee – otherwise Dr Savimbi would be accused of acting without due consultation with the party. I said I felt confident that some way could be found around this difficulty and reiterated the importance of a public statement.

The next morning (Thursday 29 October), as foreseen, President dos Santos asked to meet the three observers and myself at 9.30 a.m. Ambassador Monteiro presented the 'non-paper' and described the informal meeting with UNITA representatives. I had to explain that I could not associate myself formally with the paper, because of my separate role and the prior procedures required for an extended and different mandate for UNAVEM. The main burden of my intervention related to the urgency of having a clear request for the future role of UNAVEM.

President dos Santos said he saw many ideas in the 'non-paper' that were in consonance with the Government paper. He reiterated his Government's keen interest in having a strengthened UNAVEM for the second round, adding that, in order to get a clear picture of what would be acceptable to the Secretary-General and the Security Council, he had sent the Prime Minister to New York that week.

The President spoke of the need to amend the Electoral Law, which specified that the second round should take place 30 days after the announcement of the initial results. The delay might be anything between two and six months, particularly since the rainy season would last until April, making vast areas of the country inaccessible. Such a delay posed problems, among them the status of the new parliament, which should start operating as soon as possible.

I had a few moments alone with the President, who enquired whether I would see Dr Savimbi soon. I explained the position and he agreed that there should be a public disclaimer of the accusations against me before I went to Huambo. When I asked about the possible timing of his own encounter with the UNITA leader, the President said that the legal position was difficult: UNITA was not only violating the Bicesse Accords, but also the laws of the country, which had been worked out jointly with them. If the President had a meeting with Savimbi before clear steps had been taken to reinstate the rule of law it would look as if he was condoning these violations and public opinion would react negatively.

I came away from Futungo de Belas with the disheartening impression that the meeting was not likely to take place very soon.

On Thursday evening (29 October) an emergency CCPM meeting was called at the request of the Government to discuss two points: the military situation throughout the national territory, and the CCPM's role in the post-electoral crisis. Engineer Salupeto Pena agreed to the agenda, but to very little else.

General N'dalu said that a very dangerous military situation now existed. Many FALA troops, wearing FALA uniforms and armed, had left their assembly areas. Government administrators were being forced to leave one place after another. So far the Government had not ordered any movement of troops, nor in any way retaliated. Today there was fighting in Huambo, Lobito and M'Banza Congo and he proposed that the CCPM should urgently visit the most affected areas, particularly Huambo, Benguela, and M'Banza Congo.

Engineer Salupeto Pena responded very angrily and aggressively, demanding the suspension of the meeting on the ground that no proper discussion could be held with such a one-sided attack. Had there, he demanded, been no violation of the Accords by FAPLA? What about the electoral fraud? The situation in Malange? The refusal to allow UNITA leaders to leave Luanda? The fact that two UNITA committees had been destroyed in Luanda? Why was it, he asked sarcastically, that the finger of blame was always pointed at UNITA, while if the Government committed violations, this was considered acceptable? N'dalu replied calmly but firmly: no one was trying to place the blame on one side but rather to seek immediate practical solutions to dangerous situations. If UNITA wanted to have more time to prepare its position, the meeting could be postponed. In the meantime he wanted to comment on the second point since the Government felt it important that the CCPM should resume its normal functions, with a regular plenary session every week. The mixed commission was no substitute for the CCPM, which must continue to deal with the fundamental issues. On this point also, Salupeto Pena said he needed more time.

The meeting broke up in some disarray, agreeing only to resume on the following day at 5.00 p.m.. The three observers and I agreed that it was one of the worst CCPM meetings we had ever attended. There was comment once again on the dangerously erratic swings in Salupeto Pena's moods and reactions, which were becoming daily more apparent.

Our gloom deepened when we learned that the discussion in the mixed commission on the Government and UNITA position papers had not gone well. As I had anticipated, the two sides meant very different things in talking of a government of national reconciliation. UNITA wanted joint government at all levels, from ministerial portfolios to posts throughout the civil service and this was not at all a palatable prospect to the Government. Things looked very bad.

* * *

I had something nearer home to worry about also. An urgent radio report had come in from our Regional Commander for the central region about an incident in Lobito. UNITA had organised a protest march, which our UNAVEM team had been monitoring when some UNITA supporters had physically attacked a UNAVEM car, shouting abuse and brandishing cutlasses and sticks:

'A highly placed individual among the UNITA ... threatened that since UNAVEM had taken sides with the Government, 'UNITA will soon descend on UNAVEM. If you don't leave Angola now we will kill you all'. A lot of uncomplimentary remarks were made about the Special Representative of the Secretary-General, and he said he will arrange her assassination when she next comes to Lobito'.

Before the CCPM meeting on Friday I pointed out to Engineer Salupeto Pena that this incident contradicted the assurances I had received from him the day before, and from Dr Chivukuvuku earlier, that UNITA had given instructions that all such threats and attacks must cease. Salupeto Pena appeared to take the matter very seriously and said he would immediately speak to Dr Savimbi 'to see what he could do'.

The safety of our staff was worrying contributing countries. The Brazilian Ambassador came to see me to express his anxiety about the safety of the Brazilian military and police contingents, because of the perception on UNITA's part that Brazil favoured the MPLA. He wondered whether we should not bring all the observers in from the regions and concentrate them in Luanda. I assured him that we were taking all possible steps to safeguard the security of all UN staff, but did not think it appropriate to bring outposted personnel back to Luanda, since there was still a considerable job of verification and monitoring, and to retreat would be seen as dereliction of duty.

Nonetheless Tom White had prepared a new evacuation plan, completely revised to meet the new circumstances. It was not easy. Our teams based in the north-eastern, eastern, south-eastern, southern and central regions were supposed to make a dash for the Namibian border, either by air or road. If those routes closed, they were to try to make their way across country to the seaports of Lobito and Namibe. UNAVEM would take care of other UN and Agency staff stationed in those areas. For everyone stationed in Luanda and the northern region, the best solution would be evacuation by air from Luanda airport. We had to recognise, however, that the airport would almost certainly close or be inaccessible, and our alternative plan was a road move or a helicopter lift to Cabo Ledo, a new airfield approximately 100 kilometres south of Luanda. We had a UNAVEM team there (it was a 'critical point') and could control the airfield and provide emergency lighting for night landings.

In the event that neither Luanda nor Cabo Ledo airports were functioning, the third possibility was evacuation by sea. Embassies were booking vessels on a contingency basis, but we did not think that the UN should do so since it could be misinterpreted politically. Much later, when things got even worse, we did arrange for a large barge, which would accommodate a large number of people in excruciatingly uncomfortable conditions for a journey of two or three days to the nearest port outside Angolan waters. Fortunately we never needed to use it. For the time being we limited our options to an evacuation by air, and on 27 October warned Headquarters to arrange aircraft to stand by to lift about 510 personnel from either Luanda or Cabo Ledo at very short notice.

As for myself, the death threats were increasing daily. I now went everywhere in a convoy of three vehicles, my official car sandwiched between two UNAVEM station wagons flying large UN flags. Sigi rode beside my driver, and each of the two escort cars carried a UN security guard and a UNAVEM police or military observer. Only the three security guards were armed – with pistols. My flak jacket (still borrowed) and what I called my 'running shoes' were always on the seat beside me.

That these precautions were not exaggerated is shown by the summary of our daily situation reports for 29 and 30 October 1992. In every region confrontation and outbreaks of fighting were multiplying, as was the number of locations taken over by UNITA.

In the very early hours of Friday 30 October there was heavy exchange of fire between UNITA forces and antiriot police at Luanda airport, as a result of which twelve civilians were killed, among them three young Portuguese men, accompanied by two Angolan girls. They were slaughtered in cold blood on their way back from a nightclub (the fact that anyone had gone to a nightclub at all caused general stupefaction but their insouciance had cost them dear). Rifles had been laid across the bodies in a crass attempt to make them look like mercenaries. Horrific pictures of the corpses still sprawled in the car were shown in the media, and the bodies, as well as those of others killed in that night's bloody events, were left where they fell for most of the following day, as we observed when driving into town in further last-ditch efforts to save the situation.

* * *

Last-ditch efforts were also going on in New York. The Security Council met three times. Ambassador M'binda made a statement expressing concern about 'information regarding the presence of South African fighting forces alongside UNITA'. The South African Ambassador categorically denied these 'mischievous' allegations.

The Council adopted Resolution 785, approving the extension of UNAVEM's existing mandate to 30 November 1992 and requesting recommendations for its future mandate and strength from the Secretary-General. It strongly condemned any resumption of hostilities, and called on all states to refrain from any action that could jeopardise the Peace Agreements directly or indirectly. It reiterated full support for myself and my staff and singled out UNITA's radio station Vorgan for 'strong condemnation' because of its 'attacks and baseless accusations'. The resolution also supported my statement on the elections and called upon UNITA and other parties to respect the results. The Council again urged the two leaders to engage in dialogue 'without delay, so as to enable the second round of the presidential elections to be held promptly', reaffirming that it would 'hold responsible' any party that refused to take part in such a dialogue, as well as its own readiness to consider 'all appropriate measures under the Charter of the United Nations to secure implementation of the "Acordos de Paz"'.

This was the Council's strongest resolution yet, but the Angolan situation was slipping further out of its control, if indeed it had ever been within it.

On 30 October Pik Botha telephoned the Secretary-General to say that he had appealed to both Angolan leaders to work together, and had tried to convince Dr Savimbi to avoid any use of force. He was under the impression that UNITA had been trying to control several major roads leading to Luanda. The Minister stressed that South Africa did not support what Savimbi was doing and had advised UNITA to stop the escalation.

* * *

On the same day, in Luanda, UNITA presented its counterproposals to the Government's position paper. These followed the same format as the latter, and mainly consisted of a routine meshing of two texts and a trifling scoring of points by drafting amendments. The most radical element was a new paragraph reading:

> Formation of the Government of National Unity and Reconciliation for the transition period which extends up to the conclusion of the electoral process. The joint management of the key ministries is essential for National Reconciliation and for the implementation of the Peace Accords. It should also include the participation of UNITA and other political party members in public offices, in the central and provincial Government, in local and public enterprises.

General N'dalu told me on Friday afternoon that this paragraph was the main sticking point. The description given resembled more a coalition government, which the Government could not accept, he said, especially as UNITA appeared to be insisting that the newly elected parliament should be held in abeyance. The Government wished to establish a new government as soon as possible, as well as the new Parliament. I subsequently met Engineer Salupeto Pena, who spoke of three critical points of difference: electoral structures for the second round; representation in the media; and representation in a government of national unity and reconciliation.

The CCPM was to meet immediately after the end of the meeting of the mixed commission, which started at 6.00 p.m.. We waited for what seemed an eternity. My tiny, insalubrious office had never seemed more oppressive. Little groups of people stood about in the spartan, chairless corridors and anterooms, dispiritedly exchanging views. Journalists and TV cameramen from Angola and other countries around the world thronged the foyer – almost baying for blood, it seemed to my tired mind. At last the observers and I were summoned into the main conference room. Salupeto Pena was not there. General 'Gato', was leading for UNITA, General N'dalu for the Government. The burden of the message was that the CCPM was to be postponed yet again until 10.00 a.m. the next morning (Saturday 31 October). Although all spoke of the military and security situation as acutely dangerous, and almost out of control, the atmosphere was reassuringly calm, General 'Gato's' utterances reasonable. As the brief meeting drew to a close and we filed out, a considerable commotion arose outside. Engineer Salupeto Pena and was being interviewed, declaiming at the top of his voice and uncontrollably releasing pent-up rage. His eyes had a wild look verging on madness. I did not stop to hear what he was saying but Sigi and another of my security guards, who had been waiting nearby, were in a state of shock, horrified to hear Salupeto Pena – speaking in English to foreign journalists – make what both described as an unequivocal declaration of war, quite at variance with the tenor of the meeting.

* * *

I sent two cables to New York. The first, on Friday night, was a laconic two lines about further postponement of the vital CCPM meeting. The second, despatched early on Saturday 31 October, was longer, a *cri de coeur*. My Beechcraft, most inconveniently, had had to leave that morning for Johannesburg for urgent technical repairs. Now we had suddenly been informed that the second Beechcraft, belonging to the WFP, had also left because Lloyd's of London had withdrawn its insurance on all UN aircraft in Angola after erroneous press reports that a UN Beechcraft had been hit by bullets during the shooting at Luanda airport. I begged New York to convince Lloyd's to renew the insurance or arrange for UN coverage.

The Beechcraft was the only rapid means of transport we had to all parts of the country, and was even more essential now. During the previous night a UN military observer, wounded in crossfire in Lobito, had had to be transported urgently to Luanda, and in the event of a general evacuation we needed every aircraft we could lay our hands on. I made a plea for all helicopters, including those brought in for the elections, to stay in the country, and for urgent attention to the matter that day, even though it was Saturday.

I was not to know that this was the last cable I would be able to send for some time.

Part VI
Over the Brink

17 The Bloodbath

About this time, one of the foreign newspaper articles about Angola – it was still considered newsworthy – began, '"I wake up each morning not knowing what is going to happen today", a frustrated senior United Nations official said'. The reference is clearly to me, and the remark a truism that could apply to every human being. What I was trying to express was the feeling of events spinning out of control and the sense of dread with which I began each day.

Saturday 31 October 1992 was no exception. After the previous night's performance in the CCPM the sinking feeling at the pit of my stomach was stronger than ever. It is hard to convey how lonely I felt under the weight of a responsibility that, considered rationally, was not mine alone to bear, and that I could not be expected to discharge with the paltry means at my disposal. The snag is that emotion overwhelms reason. I could not forget the blind faith that millions of ordinary Angolans had placed in the elections, and in the United Nations, to bring peace and prosperity to their stricken land, personified in the faces of the women who smiled at grief and suffering, and in the children playing in Luanda's seedy streets, who excitedly called their version of my name – 'Margareth, Margareth' – as I went by in the car because they had seen me on television. All these things forced me to go on trying to do something, against all the odds.

There were two engagements in my diary. The first was at 10.00 a.m., the postponed CCPM meeting. It was clearly going to be make-or-break, for the brink was now very near. Would the parties draw back as they had always done before? The second was an official luncheon at the British Embassy. In the light of the cataclysmic decline in the situation, John Flynn had decided to organise a 'reconciliation lunch', to which he had invited General N'dalu and Engineer Salupeto Pena, as well as myself and several Ambassadors. It was to be a social occasion but one that might allow the two sides to discuss their differences in a less confrontational atmosphere, and certainly more congenial surroundings.

The messages brought at breakfast time by the UNAVEM Chief of Staff did not bode well for either. Just after midnight a speeding truck, alleged to be carrying UNITA men, had fired on the airport. UNAVEM patrols, sent out very early, had failed to reach the centre of Luanda by either the airport route or the Samba road, which hugged the shoreline. There was a great deal of shooting along both; some road blocks; many armed, belligerent groups from the MPLA and UNITA; and the police were out in force. The camp was cut off from the city. At 9.30 there were reports of heavy fighting near Radio Nacional, the Government radio station. It looked as if the balloon was already going up, even before the CCPM made a last stab at avoiding catastrophe, and that the meeting might not even take place. There seemed little prospect of anyone from UNAVEM getting there, except by helicopter.

About the middle of the morning the message reached us that the CCPM was indeed convening, and that UNAVEM's presence was urgently required. In the meantime our patrols had radioed that the coast road was passable, although with some risk as marauding groups were still abroad. Normally UNAVEM was represented in the CCPM at the highest level, by the Chief Military Observer and myself, but on this occasion General Unimna decided, without explanation, to send Brigadier Nyambuya. We set off in convoy around 11.00 a.m. In a burst of misplaced optimism, or perhaps just a dogged attempt to defy the fates, I decided that John Flynn's lunch might just take place, and instead of wearing trousers, opted for a cotton dress and sandals. Prudently I also put my flak jacket and 'running shoes' in the car. The Samba road – usually milling with people and antediluvian vehicles swerving wildly to avoid the larger potholes – was eerily empty, except for a few police. We arrived at the CCPM building without incident. Perhaps everything was going to be 'normal' (whatever that meant) after all.

Any such illusions were soon shattered. The two sides went at it hammer and tongs, hurling accusations and counter accusations at one another over the recent surge in violent incidents. In the preceding weeks we had witnessed some vehement exchanges and fierce crossings of swords, but nothing had prepared us for this. Salupeto Pena was like a man possessed, incapable of controlling either his utterances or his temper. Gone was the studiedly mild and measured countenance with which he had previously kept the world at bay. Instead the volcano I had always suspected lay beneath the apparently unruffled surface was in full eruption. It was a frightening sight. He no longer appeared quite sane. The atmosphere was not helped by the fact that General N'dalu, always a firm but calming influence, was unaccountably absent. During most of the meeting 'Nando', the Vice Minister of the Interior, stood in for him. He was UNITA's *bête noire* at the best of times, and these were far from that.

The meeting was to discuss two points – the overall situation and the CCPM's role in the post-electoral crisis – but 'Nando' had a *ponto previo*, a 'prior point'. This was a ploy that was frequently resorted to by both sides and usually spelt trouble: meetings could get hung up on *pontos previos* to the extent that the agenda was never tackled at all. 'Nando's' *ponto previo* concerned Lunda Norte and Huambo. In Huambo, three Government officers had been taken prisoner by UNITA and he demanded their release. The hospitals were full and the wounded must be evacuated by common agreement. In Lunda Norte UNITA had attacked Cafunfo (the diamond mining centre), which was not a military objective and the Government people were *indignados* (indignant). There were many foreigners there, and they too must be evacuated.

Salupeto Pena growled ominously back that he too had a *ponto previo*. On Huambo, General N'dalu had contacted Dr Savimbi and the liberation of the captives was imminent. There was no problem over evacuating the wounded if the situation was calm. As for Cafunfo, FALA had not attacked an economic objective. He blamed the Government police. A plane was already on the ground to take out foreigners but there could be no safety for them as long as combat persisted. He then turned his attention to Luanda, where he claimed that UNITA had suffered two dead and two wounded, that UNITA's offices had been surrounded, and that the UNITA members of the joint CCPM group at the airport had been held prisoner since the day before. UNITA and FALA had had nothing to do with the major disturbances in the capital on Thursday. They would never take the initiative of opening fire.

He then tried to get back to the agenda but 'Nando' took him up on his remarks. Joint commissions must work on the evacuation. The captive officers had been seized when sitting at the meeting table, not in combat. In Luanda, people had seen UNITA GMC trucks open fire at the airport. The cause of the problem was the popular demonstration that UNITA had wanted to hold in Luanda and that the Government had refused to authorise (the demonstration was due to take place that Saturday afternoon). Salupeto Pena retorted that authorisation to hold the demonstration had been requested 15 days before, but that the negative reply had been received only at 6.00 p.m. the previous evening. People were already on the move, it was too late to stop them. 'Nando' said, couldn't UNITA use the radio and the TV to alert people that the demonstration was off? The Government's decision was a preventive measure to avoid further disturbances and heightened tension. And, anyway, what were they demonstrating about? 'Las urnas' (the polls), spat out Salupeto Pena, and launched into another homily about electoral fraud. 'Nando' replied, just as hotly.

Antonio Monteiro brought them to their senses with a jerk by demanding: 'Why don't you discuss whether outright war has been declared or not, not whether the CCPM can stop the fighting?' 'Nando' declared 'We are not at war. But we are beginning to get fed up.' Salupeto Pena said: 'We are not at war – only responding to attacks', and then went into another long harangue about the incidents at Cafunfo, M'Banza Congo and Huambo, saying that UNITA was the first to want peace in the latter place, since its President was there. Nevertheless he agreed to 'Nando's' proposal to resuscitate the joint military commission, and proposed a joint declaration. Antonio Monteiro interjected that such a declaration should cover not only the suspension of hostilities, but also respect for UNAVEM and the protection of its staff, as well as the role of the CCPM.

This started off a different discussion. Salupeto Pena said UNITA was trying to track down the man who had made the assassination threat against me in Lobito. There had been an even more serious incident two days previously, when a UNAVEM helicopter carrying a Russian crew and an electoral observer flying to Huambo had been hit by UNITA fire and forced to make an emergency landing in a minefield near the airport. The UNAVEM regional commander and his team had not been allowed to rescue them. The Russians had been badly beaten up by UNITA troops before being released. I had protested vigorously. Salupeto Pena now said that the helicopter had been camouflaged and had not been recognised as belonging to UNAVEM. It had also behaved suspiciously, he said, circling twice over Dr Savimbi's house while making its approach to the airport. There had been problems of information (this was true: that particular helicopter had not received a general warning, sent out by Colonel Mortlock, that no flights should go to Huambo that day). Salupeto Pena's view was that UNAVEM personnel should be withdrawn when fighting was going on. I said it was essential that a public declaration on respect for UNAVEM be issued by both sides forthwith, but did not accept Salupeto Pena's suggestion. Our people had to do their work. Antonio agreed: this would send quite the wrong signal, and UNAVEM had a duty to perform. 'Nando' suggested that separate declarations covering all these points should be made. This was agreed.

'Hoje' (Today!) stipulated Antonio sternly.

They were never to be issued.

When the two sides finally got down to the agenda, the debate was astonishingly cool and businesslike – another of those sudden reversals to which I never quite became accustomed in Angola. Salupeto Pena graciously said that he was in agreement with the reactivation of the CCPM (ironically, this was to be the last one ever held). Then the general military situation was discussed. 'Nando' said placatingly that *faits accomplis* must be avoided, and a global understanding reached to end all violence once and for all. The military commission must get back to work. There was surprisingly rapid agreement on what should have been the obvious course of action in the first place: military missions composed of senior officers from both sides, together with the military advisers of the three observer countries and UNAVEM military observers, would go forthwith to the areas where fighting had broken out – primarily Huambo, Benguela, M'Banza Congo, Lunda Norte, Malange. Each side was to send immediate orders to its followers to stop fighting and await the joint military groups. The CMVF would immediately draw up a plan of action to decide who should go where, when, and in what order and I gladly promised UNAVEM planes and helicopters to transport them.

All of this was settled in no more than 15 or 20 minutes, after an hour of fruitless mutual recrimination and denunciation. The meeting broke up at about 1.15 p.m. Just as it did so a message was brought in for 'Nando', who said there appeared to have been an incident at a downtown police station. The military men repaired to the next room to prepare their plan, which should go into operation that very day. The CCPM was to meet again very soon. Brigadier Nyambuya decided not to attend the planning group, arranging for Major Fritz, the US military adviser, to keep him informed while he went back to camp to alert our UNAVEM regional commands of the impending visits and see to the air transport needs.

None of us were under any illusion that a major breakthrough had been made. All we had achieved was a stay of execution, a remission in the relentless advance of the cancer of war and devastation threatening to engulf the country once more. But we had gained a little time in which to try to make more reasonable counsels prevail.

When the meeting had been at its most acrimonious I remember thinking that there would be no reconciliation lunch that day, and that my best bet would be to hasten back to the camp while the going was good. The sudden improved turn of events put a different complexion on matters. I decided to look in on the Embassy to see what was happening, and told Brigadier Nyambuya that I would be back in Vila Espa early in the afternoon. As I took my leave separately of General N'dalu, who had appeared towards the end of the meeting, and Engineer Salupeto Pena, I commented that I looked forward to seeing them at the British Ambassador's lunch shortly. Both appeared to assent, although both had a distracted air, which was not surprising in the circumstances.

I was not to get back to the UNAVEM camp for several days, and was never to see Salupeto Pena again.

* * *

An uneasy calm pervaded the city. The streets, which on Saturdays were usually thronged with lively crowds, were deserted. I put this down to the considerable scares of the morning. There were more police about, but there were no disturbances and all was quiet when we passed in front of the Hotel Turismo, where the bomb explosion had sparked off the violent confrontation of two weeks before.

The British Embassy Chancery and the Ambassador's residence were in an old part of the town, reached by a narrow, cobbled road winding steeply up from the quay and over a narrow bridge, spanning the cleft of a deep ravine. The Embassy was near the crest of the hill, surrounded by terraced gardens and commanding a splendid view of the ocean far below. It had been the British Consulate in the old days of colonial trade, going back some 150 years or more, and tradition has it that its commanding position was chosen initially to keep an eye out for illegal slaving ships at the time of the British embargo. Next door there was a Government police station cum army post, and several hundred yards further up the hill was the imposing rosy pink and white colonial building that housed the Angolan Ministry of Defence.

The picturesque facade of the residence was marred now by all the paraphernalia of modern security. There were Ghurka guards at the gate, who waved my car into the small courtyard. Inside I found that my host, John Flynn (Drina was back in England with the two children), and the Moroccan and Cape Verde Ambassadors were all avidly waiting to hear what had transpired at the CCPM.

'Good news' I cried, as a more than welcome gin and tonic was pressed into my hand, 'Well – better news than we feared', I quickly amended and launched into a detailed account of the morning.

It must have been about 1.40 p.m. when I arrived. I had just about got to the end of my story, with the encouraging news of the imminent despatch of the joint military missions, but not to the end of my gin and tonic, when my concluding theme was rudely contradicted by a monumental explosion, which appeared to come from the street outside. The shock wave reverberated around the hills and shook the house to its foundations. In the stunned silence that followed we all looked at our watches. It would have been around 2.00 p.m. The silence was in any case very brief. The first explosion, which had probably been caused by a mortar shell, was the signal for a cacophony of firing in all directions, mostly at the bottom of the hill below us, near the waterfront and not far from the Hotel Turismo, which was obscured from the Embassy's line of vision by the contours of the hill. We were not, in any case, inclined to look out of the windows. Nor were we any longer confident that the two main guests, General-N'dalu and Engineer Salupeto Pena, would now appear.

At the time the United Kingdom held the presidency of the EC, and John and his staff busied themselves by radio with all the Ambassadors to ascertain their safety and get their versions of what was going on. My priority was to get back to the UNAVEM camp just as soon as I could. My radio would only work outside, and since some bullets were landing in the Embassy grounds that made for brisk, short conversations. I could not reach General Unimna, Nyambuya or Jobarteh, but Tom White, ever dependable, answered with alacrity and I asked whether I could return by the coast road. The reply came back quickly. The shooting was spreading rapidly. Our patrols could not penetrate the perimeter of the town.

Tom suggested lifting me out by helicopter. This idea appealed to John Flynn, and to his military attaché, Colonel Bob Griffiths. The terrain adjacent to the residence was not suitable but a hill on the seaward side, the site of an old colonial fort, Fortaleza São Miguel, perhaps a quarter of a mile away, offered the right conditions. The problem was how to get there. It meant driving back down the cobbled lane towards the hub of the fighting, across the narrow bridge, and then up the hill itself. I called 'Petroff', the Vice Minister of the Interior, who had given me all his telephone numbers to use in case of emergency. Surprisingly I got through to him immediately, and asked for a police escort to enable me either to drive back to the UNAVEM camp or to make a dash to the hill-top.

His advice was crisp and immediate: 'Stay where you are. This is very serious. UNITA has attacked the police station opposite the Hotel Turismo. We are responding. Fighting is breaking out in many places. There is no way in which I can guarantee your safety in either of the plans you are proposing'. That was that.

Since the UNAVEM satellite phone was still working, on my next radio contact, I requested that New York be informed of what was happening and where I was, and that the UNAVEM staff be assured that I was 'somewhere in the town', actively monitoring the situation and trying to do something about it. On the radio we studiously avoided naming my location. We knew that our radio messages were monitored by others, including UNITA, and in view of the death threats it was imperative to keep my whereabouts a secret.

John Flynn and his staff were also anxious not to reveal my presence. They had enough trouble on their hands. UNITA was taking hostages in Miramar, where most Embassy residences were located. Among the first to be taken were the head of a major British company in Luanda, Hall Blyth, and his Bulgarian-born wife. Earlier, since they had radio contact with the Embassy, they had informed the Ambassador that, to avoid capture, they had climbed over the wall into the garden of the Swedish Embassy, which, like most others in that area, had been vacated earlier in the day. A little later it became clear that this ploy had been to no avail.

There was great anxiety over the US liaison mission. Their compound was uncomfortably close to the UNITA headquarters in Miramar and they radioed that they were surrounded by UNITA troops, with individual elements trying to force their way in. The new Ambassador, Edmond De Jarnette, who had only arrived the week before this baptism of fire, had been in the Hotel Presidente when the fighting broke out, but had been instructed by Washington to join his colleagues in the compound. Since Miramar was rapidly becoming the hub of the fighting we found this inexplicable. Later in that long, hot afternoon the Americans told us, in whispers over the radio, that Salupeto Pena had 'invited' them to join him in Dr Savimbi's house 'for their protection' and that the State Department had advised them to accept. John Flynn advised them most energetically to do no such thing, and spoke with some force to the State Department in Washington in the same vein. A code word – 'Zebra' – was agreed with the Americans in the event that they too were taken hostage. We already knew that the Zimbabwean Ambassador, Nevile Ndondo, was in UNITA's hands, and there were unconfirmed rumours that two or more unnamed Bulgarians had also been taken.

By now John was in touch with the Foreign Office in London and I – courtesy of the British Embassy satellite telephone – with New York. Perversely, but luckily, the Luanda telephone lines, so notoriously unreliable, were functioning as perfectly as they knew how, and John and I were in contact with Antonio Monteiro, who had a bird's eye view of one part of the action from the Hotel Imperio, very near the Hotel Tropico and the Hotel Tivoli, where a number of important UNITA figures were lodged, among them Fatima Roque. Neither Antonio nor I could get much news of Petukov, but we were able to contact Yuri Kapralov, the Russian Ambassador, who was sweating it out in precarious siege conditions in his residence in Miramar, close to the dividing line between UNITA and Government troops.

What had initially seemed to be a calamity – my being stranded in the Embassy – turned out to be a blessing in disguise. I was much nearer to the centre of the action, and much better placed to try to do something about it, not least because I had communications within the city centre that would have been denied me in Vila Espa, as well as all the information I would have had in my headquarters (they kept me informed by radio).

I had long ago changed into my 'running shoes' but was hampered by my long skirt. John gave me one of his shirts and the run of his wife's wardrobe, which yielded two pairs of comfortable trousers. Thus kitted out, I was better equipped to nip back and forth from the residence to the chancery, which involved running up and down a lot of stairs, through the bowels of the old building, and in and out to the car to use the radio. Sitting in a sweltering airless car, bundled up in a flak jacket, and with a lot of banging going on all around is not a recommended recreation for a Saturday afternoon.

The afternoon dissolved in a blur anyway. At some point pangs of hunger asserted themselves and the ill-fated 'reconciliation lunch' became a running buffet for anyone who could take a few minutes off. We were a fairly numerous bunch to feed: Andie Henderson (John's number two); Stephen Noakes (his First Secretary); Colonel Bob Griffiths; the latter's assistant; and the Vice Consul, Alan Marshall, as well as the two Ambassadors, my contingent of six, and all the guards on the gate. Luckily for us, though not for them and their families, the Flynn's cook, Antonio, and their maid, Maria da Luz, were also prisoners in the Embassy. They were quite remarkable, very calm, and ready to produce snacks at any hour. No doubt this admirably stoic reaction was the product of living through many years of war. Luckily too, Drina had stocked her freezers well before she left and I noted that, if we were really desperate, the cellar was equally well provided.

None of us had a very clear idea of what was going on, which side had the upper hand, or how long the grim battle for Luanda would last. Outside the horrendous racket of death and destruction thundered on. We were getting information every few minutes from radio and telephone contacts around the city, but could not yet compose the pieces of the jigsaw into a picture. I remember that it was a beautiful and sunny day, very hot. Through the windows that we dared not open the gardens shimmered in a haze of opulent colour, and in the far distance the ocean glistened, the sun marking out a gleaming path to the horizon and on towards a world of normality, where people were going about their weekend pursuits. Here the world of humans had gone mad. It was as if the pent-up hatred and frustrations of the last 16 months, and particularly the last few weeks, had boiled over and detonated the cacophony of sound that now engulfed the once beautiful city in its idyllic setting. The chattering of automatic fire crepitated about the streets, punctuated by the heavier bass thud of a mortar or an exploding bomb, the snarl of a Government jet fighter screaming across the rooftops, or the more ponderous, jarring rumble of a watching helicopter. The city shuddered and reverberated under the onslaught. Everyone who could do so was huddled indoors. Sometimes the explosions were very near: the police next door were firing down the narrow lane that led past the Embassy. But firing at whom? Were UNITA forces advancing up the hill towards the Ministry of Defence? Did UNITA know that I was in the Embassy? Were Government planes bombing Miramar?

From Miramar, Salupeto Pena was boasting of having in his power an unspecified number of 'white people', including six Ambassadors, all of whom he was threatening to kill. No mention was made of the one unfortunate black person, the Zimbabwean Ambassador. He had gone to the Hotel Presidente with other diplomats from Miramar, but, a diabetic, had gone back for his insulin and had been captured by UNITA.

There was little we could do on the spot. The best chance of obtaining a cessation of hostilities was through international intervention at the highest level: the Security Council, the UN Secretary-General, the Foreign Ministers of the great powers and of the architects of the Bicesse Peace Accords. Through the Foreign Office John was in touch with Douglas Hurd, I was in touch with the Secretary-General, Antonio Monteiro with Durão Barroso, and all of us at various times with Hank Cohen and Jeff Davidow in Washington. I was requesting that the Secretary-General speak urgently to both President dos Santos and Dr Savimbi. I was told that he was trying to do so, and meanwhile had issued a strong appeal asking them to withdraw their forces immediately, return them to barracks, and resume 'the constructive dialogue which has been promoted by my Special Representative'. He also appealed 'for the safety and security of all, including United Nations personnel and the expatriate community'.

The sudden tropical darkness fell without our noticing it or the blood-red sun sinking into the ocean. Ashore the bloody combat continued, only a little abated by the cover of night. I sat with John and his staff monitoring the crackling radios and the telephones. London, New York and Washington were still awake, but contact was less frequent; and in order not to endanger them further, so were the periodic checks on the Americans, who were hiding in the foundations of one of the buildings in their compound. Everyone took it in turns to snatch a little rest. At about 2.00 a.m. I went up to a bedroom and lay down fully dressed on cool white sheets under the mosquito net, while the guns roared and stuttered outside. Sigi was doing his best to accommodate his large form in an armchair in the hall below like a protective St. Bernard, but without the brandy. The four UNAVEM guards and police observers were spending the night in their vehicles, the residence being full to overflowing.

It was impossible to sleep. I remember feeling more exhausted than ever before in my life. I had been on the go since 5.00 a.m. the previous day, but that was not the real cause. It was as if the very springs of my energy had dried up. Every bone ached and my head throbbed with pain, as well as from the unremitting noise pounding the city. Each fresh salvo seemed to drum out the death-knell of everything we had been trying to do to help the Angolan people, to ram home, with scornful insistence, the futility of the UN's mission in this country. I suddenly realised, with considerable horror, that I was frightened. The revelation caused me almost more consternation than the sensation itself. With a shock and a vividness that even the most malicious death threats had never had, it came to me that I might very well not survive this weekend. What on earth was I doing here? I thought of the quiet gardens at Knill, slumbering under the age-old hills of the Welsh Marches, and of the little *adobe* house in Bolivia where I had never yet lived, with its view of the sacred lake of the Incas and the Royal Cordillera of the Andes, and wondered whether I would ever see them again. Worst of all was to understand that, if it happened, it would be a useless death, achieving nothing.

This sombre reverie was broken by a knocking at the door. John and Sigi stood there. There was a call from New York. It was 3.00 a.m. in Luanda, 10.00 p.m. the previous evening in New York. It was the Secretary-General to tell me he was trying to speak by satellite telephone to the two leaders.

I did not go to bed again. It was preferable to be in company and some calls were still coming through. At about that time, when the adrenalin was at its nadir, Bob Griffiths told me he wanted me to know the game plan if the worst came to the worst. He did not say so, but we both knew he meant if UNITA attacked the Embassy. He led me to the Ambassador's small office at the back of the Chancery, looking over the dark garden. 'This is the inner sanctum', he said 'where we make our last stand if necessary. The Ambassador has a pistol, I have a pistol, and so does your guard, Sigi.' I pointed out that my two other guards had side arms too. I could not believe we were saying these words. They seemed in any case pathetic, since we would presumably be facing men brandishing grenades and automatic rifles. Writing them now, looking out at the bird-loud garden in a summer dawn at Knill, they sound ridiculously melodramatic. After all, we survived to tell the tale, didn't we? And no one invaded the Embassy. All I can say is that, during the long hours of that interminable night, we did not know that this would be so, or indeed which way the battle outside was going. The words, which we strove to speak matter-of-factly, as if discussing arrangements for some official ceremony, had a horrible ring of probability. I cannot forget, either, that many in that frightened city were suffering the same premonitions, and for many they proved all too tragically prescient. All those Angolan deaths were senseless, and could have been avoided.

At 4.00 a.m., as we all huddled in the communications room, Bob Griffiths made scalding hot mugs of tea. I had never tasted better in my life and felt my strength surging back. With dawn came a faint glimmering of hope that negotiations might be possible, as my rough jottings at the time recorded.

6.00 a.m.   Antonio Monteiro telephones about the situation at the Hotel Turismo. There have been soundings from General Tadeu, the UNITA police chief, about the evacuation of 20 badly wounded men as well as 30 women and children; but Nicaud, the Red Cross representative, has lost contact.

8.20 a.m.   Chivukuvuku (as I recall, by now holed up in the empty French Embassy with Vice President Chitunda) telephones John Flynn. John urges an immediate truce. He explains that Washington is very worried about Salupeto Pena's attitude and intentions, and insists there must be no more threats and that safe conduct be provided for all the 'hostages'. Chivukuvuku agrees.

8.30 a.m.   UNITA is claiming that Government troops and police, disguised as civilians are advancing up the hill towards Miramar, but there is no indication that the Government is moving to take over UNITA-controlled points. There are no indications as to what UNITA is doing outside Luanda. The airport is closed.

8.35 a.m.   Antonio phones John. He has been able to talk by telephone to General N'dalu who informed him that UNITA has attacked N'dalatando, Lobito and Lubango. Salupeto Pena has also phoned Antonio. The Government is insisting that before any truce or ceasefire, there must be a formal commitment from Dr Savimbi that hostilities will stop everywhere. N'dalu and Salupeto Pena have also been talking by phone, and the latter is in touch with Savimbi in Huambo by satellite. Salupeto Pena wants the women and children to be evacuated from the Hotel Turismo but UNITA is not prepared to surrender there or anywhere else.

9.00 a.m.   Jeff Davidow speaks to me from Washington. He tells me that Savimbi has just called him by satellite telephone (it is the middle of the night for Jeff) and had a long and rambling conversation with him during much of which he was barely coherent. Savimbi said he had been under bombardment for 72 hours, that everyone would die, and that his people were not to be humiliated. He was willing that there should be a ceasefire, but only if the Government made a public statement first that it was ready to have a one. It is agreed that we would try to make a breakthrough at our end, and call Davidow back in 45 minutes time.

9.15 a.m.   Antonio calls again. N'dalu wants UNITA's answer – will they suspend hostilities all over the country, and will Savimbi put the seal of his personal commitment on this? John relays the gist of my conversation with Davidow. Antonio says the Government will not agree to take the initiative of requesting a ceasefire, even on humanitarian grounds. N'dalu himself might be prepared to do so, but others on the Government side don't trust UNITA. According to N'dalu, UNITA effectives in the Hotel Turismo have moved into the church next door, and are trying to disperse.

9.40 a.m.   An emergency message, very difficult to understand, crackles over the radio from the Americans. Someone is stealthily entering the compound, they tell us. It is a desperately tense moment. We all await anxiously by the radio. Someone thinks they hear the word 'Zebra' in the indistinct medley of sounds coming from it. I scribble this on a piece of paper for John, who is trying to telephone Savimbi. A few minutes later we learn that the intruders were armed civilians. They have left and the Americans remain undetected in their hiding places.

While these frenzied messages were going back and forth, the noise of shooting and heavier explosions was still resounding all over the city, and in the lane outside. Neither side was going to give an inch, unless there was agreement at the very highest level on a ceasefire. Our top priority, as agreed with Antonio, was to try to get Savimbi to see reason. Given the uncertainties of my own standing with him after the Vorgan attacks (though he himself had made no comment) and the need to keep my whereabouts secret, we agreed that John should be the negotiator. Speaking to Dr Savimbi was easier said than done. Time and again his satellite number was dialled, but his phone was either engaged or deliberately switched off. My notes go on:

11.00 a.m.   Still trying to get Savimbi.

11.30 a.m.   Kofi Annan phones from New York. He has received an urgent call from Marcos Samondo, whom Savimbi had telephoned at around 3.00 a.m. New York time. Savimbi is worried about the safety of his two nephews in Luanda, the brothers Engineer Salupeto Pena and General 'Ben-Ben'. If they were killed he had said, he would be killed, civil war would erupt, expatriates would be killed and UNAVEM staff 'may have difficulties'. We are given a different satellite telephone number, provided by Samondo, on which to call Dr Savimbi.

11.45–12.00 noon   Antonio calls again. Salupeto Pena has telephoned and seems really to have gone over the edge, screaming murderous insults about the Portuguese, the observers, the UN; ranting that he would go out into the streets and kill every Portuguese whom he met – women, children and men. Foreigners were 'killers and racists', supporters of mulattoes, only interested in stripping Angola of its diamonds and oil. They were only trying to call Savimbi now because white people were in danger. Black Angolans – the only true Angolans – were of no consequence to them. In a disconcerting change of tone he had then announced that this was merely his 'personal opinion'. UNITA's 'official opinion' was that they would accept the ceasefire and renew negotiations. He had called Dr Savimbi and had been told that this was the line he must take. Antonio says he sounded quite deranged.

12.15 p.m.   John finally gets through to Dr Savimbi.

This was to be a marathon conversation, lasting over an hour. I sat beside John taking notes. I could hear only his side of the conversation, which sounded unreal to the point of aberrancy. One needed only to hear one side of it to grasp that it kept wandering all over the place to subjects quite unrelated to the most gravely pressing need of the moment: a truce or ceasefire. John was superb, crystal clear in his propositions, patient in dealing with the long, meandering monologues of his interlocutor, whom he later described as being also 'very nearly over the edge', humouring his quaint philosophical digressions and his vanity and all the time gently but relentlessly coaxing him, in his persuasive Scottish burr, back to the central issue. It was without doubt a most delicate negotiation, a *tour de force* on John's part – one jarring note or false manoeuvre and the UNITA leader would have been pushed into a more intransigent position. I doubted whether I could have been as serene, finding it hard to take that someone so obsessed with saving his own life and that of his near relatives could prattle on inconsequentially, apparently oblivious to the fact that every moment lost in this self-regarding exercise meant the death of hundreds more of his fellow citizens fighting in the streets outside, and in other towns and cities all over the country.

Initial courtesies done, John succinctly presented the three points at issue: first, a simultaneous statement by both sides, declaring (the second point) a ceasefire that would, with immediate effect, cover the whole country, and, third, an immediate return to the negotiating table. There were then long silences while Jonas Savimbi held forth. My one-sided notes of John's remarks charted the course of the conversation. With his help I have reconstructed the main tenor of this extraordinary dialogue. Savimbi's first utterances certainly did not address John's proposals.

JS: 'I don't accept the result of the elections. I am not the only one. If I were alone no-one would have disturbed order and peace. Since I am not alone, as you can see the country has fallen apart. [Savimbi then went off on a sidetrack about the reasons why Brazilian nationals had not been able to leave Luzamba.] The last time we met and spoke you knew who would win the election but it was a fraud.'

JF: 'No, that is not correct I did not know who would win. Even during the election I said to everyone that I did not know.'

JS: 'We are the Ovimbundu. We have lived 300 years under the humiliation of the north, under Van Dunem and others. We have had enough. The Ovimbundu are 100 per cent behind me and I am prepared to die for them. When your leaders signed the Munich Agreement your most illustrious son – Churchill – cried shame and woe. I am his greatest admirer. You [in Britain] made a mistake then. His example is mine. Dos Santos is not even Angolan he is from São Tome. We cannot live under the mulattos and the Kimbundu.'

(12.30 p.m. I pass a note to John. Word has reached us that a UNITA officer wants to surrender. He has been put in touch with Colonel Higino Carneiro of the Government CCPM delegation.)

JF: 'No people should be under others. There must be equality for all people in a democratic country.'

JS: 'I am considering resignation but remember that if I do the war will become worse than that in Mozambique. I am waiting for Tuesday [the US election]. If Bush wins I will remain mild and stay. If Clinton wins I will resign. I am a Christian and when someone lies I know and he loses my love. This is not your problem [he again mentioned Munich and Churchill] and still you remain a man I appreciate. I know more about British history than I know about African history.'

JF: 'It would be unwise and unfair if you resigned. The people who voted for you will be disappointed. They continue to need you. Angola continues to need you. Does this consideration affect your views on a ceasefire? This is the *urgent* issue at this moment. Don't resign at this stage.'

JS: 'I am in Huambo for the safety of my life. The Government wants to kill me. Dos Santos is no match for me but I have to retreat to my own land. I am prepared to discuss peace.'

JF: 'It is exactly that that I wanted to talk to you about. The fighting must be stopped and both sides must get back to negotiations. Would you be ready to declare a ceasefire? It is desperately needed. You have women and children at risk and there is now fighting across the country. It must be stopped. The UN Secretary-General is urgently trying to contact both you and President dos Santos to appeal for a ceasefire.'

(12.45 p.m. Word reaches us that General 'Ben-Ben' and Colonel Higino Carneiro are in touch about a ceasefire, especially as regards Miramar. Chivukuvuku may also be involved in this negotiation without Salupeto Pena's knowledge. I scribble a note to John who is listening intently to another diatribe.)

JS: 'What are your terms? Please go ahead and tell me the terms. The Secretary-General is my friend. Boutros-Ghali is a good Secretary-General. There is only one difficulty. When I told Nasser to steal the Jewish territory I did not appreciate the problems that would cause with the Jewish people. We are like them. There have now been 70 hours of fighting which was started by the MPLA although everyone accuses UNITA. You want me not to resign. I am consulting with my wife. If Bush loses I will resign and UNITA will no longer be my business. I think I should resign and I will call all my people to observe a ceasefire but without my presence they would not accept it. [There was then a lot more about Churchill, his admiration for him and how he taught his children to love Churchill.] The last time we met I said there was something fishy about what was going on with the election. Nevertheless I love you [Britain] very much. If your Government wishes to talk to me I am prepared to do so but I will never come again to Luanda. Let us talk about the ceasefire. You can play a good role. Those other stupid leaders, Chiluba and the rest, I don't want to see them involved. [There was then an attack on the Brazilian Ambassador.] I told Salupeto Pena to leave foreigners out of it.'

JF: 'You admire Churchill greatly. Churchill was defeated in an election but regained power democratically later. Churchill personified a situation in which two peoples who had fought one another came together again in peace. His mother was American, his father English. I am Scottish. The Scots and the Irish fought the English for centuries but now we live together.'

JS: 'Ambassador, if you allow the MPLA to kill my nephew Salupeto Pena and Ben-Ben, Chitunda and the others, I will be forced to consider the whole position. I would never have a future afterwards. Don't try to expel my people from Luanda. The Americans have made a great mistake and the South Africans – they do not know me. In the 70 hours of fighting here we have put down 300 riot police, we have also arrested hundreds. We have generals of theirs under arrest. If I lose my people, Salupeto and Ben-Ben, then I would lose control of my people. My people cannot be expelled from Luanda.'

JF: 'The fighting must be stopped. Only then will you save the lives of your people and your senior officers. You cannot allow so many people to die. There are women and children in the Hotel Turismo who are in imminent danger of dying. The Government is prepared to get them out but you must tell Salupeto Pena to deal.'

JS: 'I want a ceasefire with dignity. My people must remain in Luanda. How would it be if I bombed Miramar the same way my house is being bombed? I want to find a solution. [There was then a diatribe against the Cardinal, whom he called 'a bastard' and accused of saying that, although Savimbi would have been a great leader, because he came from the south he could not.] I want you to come to Huambo when you want. You will be a bridge between the Government and my Ovimbundu people. I have seen a paper which says that if Chivukuvuku under Salupeto Pena appeals for a ceasefire I will go along with it. I will control my people. But if you kill Chivukuvuku, Chitunda and Salupeto, no one will control this area. I will remain here. If you come on Monday I will welcome you but you must not allow them to kill my nephew. [There was then a incoherent diatribe about how he would react to the Government having tried to kill him in Luanda. In Lubango he would behave "like a wolf ... in Lobito I swear I will kill them all whatever the price".] The sooner you come the better. Get my nephew and Chitunda out of jail. If you do not the worst will happen. I am restraining my people just now'.

JF: 'Do I understand correctly? You want a ceasefire with dignity, and which allows your people to stay in Luanda? Do you agree to a ceasefire and to make peace?'

JS: 'If you are going to come to Huambo I will issue a ceasefire declaration but not if they kill Salupeto Pena and the others. Then all is lost.'

JF: 'I will come to Huambo if there is a chance of making peace. But now the airport is closed. There is fighting all around and I cannot even leave my Embassy. Do you agree to a ceasefire?'

JS: 'Yes. I accept that you will negotiate in your capacity as Ambassador. (I loved very much N'dalu but he is now finished. He is a bandit. I have no more links with him. He is a Cape Verdean. I am a Bantu. He now says that if the MPLA does not win his race will be attacked.)'

JF: 'I would like to come to Huambo, but only if there is a ceasefire. No one can travel with fighting going on. If you agree to a ceasefire would you be prepared to make a declaration at the same time as the Government? Yes? Then I accept to come to Huambo. Can I tell the Government that you will issue a ceasefire statement provided there is no attempt on the lives of your people in Luanda?'

At this critical juncture, when everything seemed almost sewn up, my attention was again distracted by developments in Luanda, as my notes record:

1.05 p.m.   I receive a message that Salupeto Pena has approached the US, now very calm. I pass a note to John.

1.10 p.m.   I am called away to speak to Antonio. The Red Cross representative, M. Nicaud, and Salupeto Pena have talked by telephone. The situation of the women, children and wounded in the Hotel Turismo is desperate and UNITA wants them evacuated by the ICRC and UNAVEM. Antonio is awaiting the Government's reaction, but wants me to start organising UNAVEM. About 60 people are involved.

I returned to the communications room. During the ten minutes of my absence, Savimbi had wandered off the point again and was going on about his childhood. John was speaking soothingly.

JF: '...yes, my father was a railwayman too, but in Scotland, so we have a lot in common. But to get back to the present problem. What should I tell the Government about your position? May I say that you agree to the declaration of a ceasefire and that it should take place at the same time on both sides, on condition that the Government stops all attacks on your people; that it should cover the whole country; and that the negotiations should begin again forthwith?'

JS: 'Yes. But let my people come out first. I apologise for anything I have said to offend. You are the only one I have spoken to. Davidow does not know where I am. When I am wrong you tell me frankly. There is no way I wish to fight with you. I want to hear from you. You must call me later, at 5.00 p.m. I don't want any more war.'

JF: 'I am sure the Government will agree. The time is now 1.15. I will call you before 5 p.m. to tell you of their reaction. Then I hope to come and see you personally.'

He put down the phone and mopped his brow. It had been an exhausting hour. Savimbi had been hard to follow and sometimes incoherent. Some points – that his people, the Ovimbundu, must not be humiliated, and that he had been under bombardment in Huambo for 70 hours – he kept hammering over and over again, as well as making vicious attacks on his *bêtes noires*. In his constantly expressed concern about the fate of his nearest collaborators in Luanda, there had been one very odd omission – he did not mention his other nephew, General 'Ben-Ben'. Neither had he vented his wrath on me or the UN. On the contrary, he had taken the initiative of asking John (who had not revealed that I was sitting by his side), 'Tell Miss Anstee that I will apologise to her personally for the attacks on her. If you came to Huambo I will tell you personally that what Vorgan said did not have my approval. I repudiate it strongly. It is not in my education to say such things'. (There was then a long aside about Robert Williams, a Welshman not a Scotsman: 'My father taught us that these people were the greatest in the world. I do not think that now'.) 'I am very sorry. Those words upset me particularly for such a civilised lady. If she wants to call on me I will tell her.' These unsolicited comments reassured me that, if we ever got out of the Embassy, I could continue to mediate between the two leaders.

1.25 p.m.   I speak with one of Antonio's aides and tell him John needs to talk urgently to the Government about his conversation with Savimbi.

1.30 p.m.   N'dalu calls John, who relays Savimbi's agreement to a ceasefire and to a simultaneous declaration, which John urges should be agreed as soon as possible. I radio Tom White and alert him about possible UNAVEM involvement in the evacuation from the Hotel Turismo. The problem is to get safe passage for our unarmed observers as fighting continues on all the routes between the camp and the town.

1.45 p.m.   Antonio calls. There is tremendous shooting near his hotel, and the Hotels Tropico and Tivoli. Salupeto Pena claims that some leading UNITA members have been killed. The Government seems to be getting the upper hand in the battle for Luanda but the situation in the rest of the country is far from clear.

2.00 p.m.   Antonio again. N'dalu and Salupeto Pena are talking.

2.05 p.m.   Kofi Annan rings from New York. The Portuguese Permanent Representative has been in touch to say that the Prime Minister of Portugal, Cavaco Silva, has spoken to President dos Santos. The President and the Secretary-General are to talk at 10.00 a.m. New York time.

2.15 p.m.   Antonio talks to John. Salupeto Pena is still being a negative influence. General 'Ben-Ben' and Colonel Higino have met to discuss how to stop the fighting, but without result.

2.20 p.m.   Higino calls. The Government leaders seem to be in different places and not communicating with one another. He wants to know about the conversation with Savimbi, which John has just recounted to N'dalu. John repeats Savimbi's position, and that he needs confirmation before 5.00 p.m. of whether or not the Government will agree to a ceasefire.

We learn that General 'Ben-Ben' and Higino are to meet again shortly. The information is presumably needed in that connection. Our hopes rise slightly.

2.30 p.m.   Antonio again, relating another exchange with Salupeto Pena, who said that the meeting between 'Ben-Ben' and Higino came to nothing, and was again very negative. Antonio thinks things are 'not looking good'. Our hopes dwindle once more.

2.45 p.m.   Jobarteh and I speak. The prospects for the UNAVEM/ICRC rescue at the Hotel Turismo look bleak. All is quiet at the UNAVEM camp. They can only hear the distant boom of guns in the city. Yesterday was a different story. The Government attacked the motel between our camp and the President's palace, where some UNITA elements resided, blowing up part of it. This had been very noisy and uncomfortably close. Staff in residential complexes nearer town had had unnerving experiences but everyone was safe.

3.45 p.m. Antonio calls again, rather agitated. There has been much shooting at the Hotels Tivoli and Tropico and the UNITA people staying there are in great danger, among them Fatima Roque and my tormenter, Norberto de Castro. Fatima Roque has appealed for protection as a Portuguese national (Antonio took her into the Hotel Imperio a day or so later). The Government, he says, is likely to give its answer only by tomorrow. UNITA is said to be moving along, taking positions, as well as more hostages at Miramar and shooting everywhere. They have spread their people all over town and there is firing in all parts of the capital. There is certainly no ceasefire.

We too had had an experience bearing this out. As we sat over a late lunch at about three o'clock, discussing what we thought was the imminent prospect of a ceasefire, John even jocularly suggested that we might like to take a dip in the swimming pool (water had been a scarce commodity in the embassy). He was interrupted by a series of enormous explosions in the lane outside. Unperturbed, he continued 'Ah, our police friends next door are active again, firing on the city', only to be contradicted by Bob Griffiths bursting into the dining room with the urgent command: 'Keep away from the windows, everyone! These are incoming mortar shells'. UNITA, it seemed, was making a determined effort to take the little bridge just below the Embassy, and advance up the hill towards the Ministry of Defence. Despite John's conversation with Savimbi, we were a long way from a ceasefire.

Antonio told me that the Government Generals were meeting with President dos Santos to take a decision on what to do next. Hank Cohen had telephoned the President from Washington and requested that Ambassador De Jarnette and his staff be rescued from the US compound by 4.30 that afternoon, and the President had agreed. A partial truce was to be negotiated for that purpose. Jeffrey Davidow had spoken to General Bock of UNITA, who had given all the guarantees for the operation. But Bock was in Huambo, and it was far from certain how valid those guarantees would be in Miramar, especially given Salupeto Pena's unpredictable behaviour. N'dalu was talking to the President about how to do it. UNAVEM would have to be involved, and guarantees would have to be obtained from Salupeto Pena. We agreed that it would be a very risky operation indeed and John therefore relayed to Davidow in Washington our view that it would be safer to aim for the general ceasefire and build on Savimbi's agreement.

John and I then analysed the situation. According to Antonio, the President was taking the 'moral high ground': Luanda was not Angola, and whatever was done should protect the good of all Angolans. Savimbi was apparently ready to settle for anything that would lead to a solution: a ceasefire, provided it came into force at the same time on both sides, over the whole country, that the Government put a stop to attacks on UNITA people, and that the negotiations resumed. The problem was that the UNITA leadership had over-reached itself, and attacks were taking place in other parts of the country by men akin to warlords, who might not respond easily to commands for a ceasefire. We agreed that we must somehow avoid a human tragedy of immense proportions.

4.35 p.m.   Antonio calls again. Salupeto Pena 'can't reply' about the rescue operation for the Americans.

4.45 p.m.   Kofi Annan rings. President dos Santos did not speak to the Secretary-General at 10.00 a.m. as agreed. I stress the urgency of contact, the desperation of the present situation.

5.10 p.m.   N'dalu sends us a message via Antonio. UNITA is attacking Benguela and Lobito. He claims it is clear that they don't want a ceasefire, whatever Savimbi says. While this conversation is going on, John asks Higino to transmit an urgent message to President dos Santos about the need for a ceasefire, the deadline for our reply to Savimbi having elapsed.

6.00 p.m.   General Bock rings John from Huambo, worried about the delay. He says Savimbi is resting, having been under pressure from shellfire for four days since 29 October. UNITA will accept a ceasefire from midnight that night (Sunday). John explains that UNITA's reported attacks on Benguela and Lobito are probably the reasons for the delay in the Government's reply and urges UNITA to maintain proper control of its soldiers everywhere.

6.05 p.m.   Antonio rings with a message from his Prime Minister, who is also urging a ceasefire. He tells me that N'dalu will ring me at 6.15 p.m. about the Americans.

6.15 p.m.   Instead, Kofi Annan rings. The Secretary-General has at last been able to speak to President dos Santos. He pressed hard for a ceasefire but the President insisted he needed 10 to 12 hours or more in which to discuss the matter with his MPLA people. The Secretary-General told him firmly that this was unacceptable. The ceasefire must be agreed and announced rightaway. They agreed to speak again in one and a half hour's time, at 1.30 p.m. New York time.

6.30 p.m.   General Bock telephones John from Huambo and makes three points. First, he has spoken to Salupeto Pena, who will accept a ceasefire throughout the country starting at midnight (Sunday 1 November). Second, UNITA will hand over all the hostages (the foreigners that is) in the UNITA area in Miramar to the Red Cross and other organisations such as the UN at first light tomorrow (Monday 2 November). Third, the ceasefire declared in Huambo is holding. Both sides are cooperating, but if a general ceasefire is not in operation from midnight or word gets out about the losses in Luanda, UNITA may lose control of its soldiers. As for Benguela and Lobito, once there is a general ceasefire any problems there can be quickly solved.

6.40 p.m.   Antonio telephones. The Government wishes four conditions to be met before agreeing to a ceasefire. First, I personally and UNAVEM must accept responsibility for Savimbi's word, and his good faith. Second, no UNITA security forces must remain in Luanda, only the FAA. Third, all troops other than the FAA must be confined to the cantonment areas. Fourth there must be 'economic tranquillity'.

6.50 p.m.   Venâncio de Moura, the Vice Minister of Foreign Affairs, rings (I think from Futungo). John gives him Bock's message.

Approximately 7.30 p.m.   Jobarteh and I speak. He reports much movement of heavy tanks and artillery in the vicinity of the UNAVEM camp.

During what seemed to be an eternity we continued to wait for news of real progress. The suspense was heightened by more rumours, among them that the UNITA generals in the CCPM, Zacarias and 'Mackenzie', had surrendered to the government. Outside the guns continued to roar.

9.00 p.m.   Kofi Annan rings again. The Secretary-General and the President have had their second conversation (three hours after the first, rather than the one and a half agreed). Dr Boutros-Ghali got the President to agree to a midnight ceasefire, but only 'in principle'. I am warned that it is not a firm agreement. The Secretary-General will meet the Ambassadors of the 'Permanent Five' (China, France, Russia, the United States and the UK) at 9.30 a.m. tomorrow in New York, and wants to be able to advise them that all foreign hostages have been released, a ceasefire declared through the whole territory and modalities worked out between the generals from both sides as to how to maintain it. The President had insisted that I should personally be a party to this negotiation and wanted to delay a ceasefire until he and his generals could meet with me. The Secretary-General had again insisted that a statement must be made now. The President had also wanted to know if the UN could arrange safe conduct out of the city for the UNITA people and send more troops to maintain the ceasefire.

The ceasefire was still elusive, with midnight only two and a half hours away. If Savimbi was to be believed, UNITA was ready to accept a ceasefire. The Government clearly did *not* believe in his sincerity. We were thus in one of the familiar impasses created by mutual distrust and suspicion. But this time, with every minute of delay, more people were being killed.

9.30 p.m.   N'dalu rings, still with ceasefire conditions that the Government wants to be negotiated with UNITA: 'tranquillity' in the cities – only the FAA should be allowed to operate there; the cities should be protected by UN guards; the negotiations between the two sides should be put back on course.

9.35 p.m.   Bock and John speak. John tells him about the general lines of the agreement the Secretary-General discussed with President dos Santos. As insurance, there must be only one army. He stresses that the Secretary-General wants an unconditional ceasefire. Bock raises a question about the riot police. John firmly says 'no conditions' and emphasises that the Secretary-General did not accept any conditions during his conversation with the President. Bock goes on about UNITA's reasonableness while in

Lobito the Ovimbundu were being killed like dogs. He has heard that Salupeto Pena and Chivukuvuku have been arrested, along with Generals Zacarias and 'Mackenzie'. John says he has no firm information but will find out. Meanwhile, he enquires, how long will it take UNITA to get agreement? A new contact is arranged for 10.45 p.m.

John says that it is his firm impression that Savimbi was listening in on the conversation in the background and directing Bock both in this latest conversation and the earlier one. I call N'dalu to underline that the Secretary-General has stipulated an immediate ceasefire *without conditions*. He says he will consult the President.

10.50 p.m.   The US military adviser, Major Fritz, calls. He escaped the fate of his colleagues because he stayed behind in the CCPM on Saturday to plan the ill-fated 'pacification' mission. Since then he has been constantly with Higino Carneiro. He says Chivukuvuku and several other leading UNITA figures are in Government hands. Chivukuvuku 'may be injured in the foot'. No one knows the whereabouts of Salupeto Pena, or what may have happened to him. Nor about 'Ben-Ben'. This uncertainty about Savimbi's nearest and dearest could easily shatter the slender base upon which we are trying to get a ceasefire. We are astounded to learn there is a rumour that 'Ben-Ben' has sought refuge in the British Embassy. If so, we haven't seen him! Fritz has been travelling all over town with Higino and says that everyone wants blood and a lot of murder is going on in the streets.

We whiled away the seemingly interminable passage of time working out how to set up the ceasefire in Luanda. Bob Griffiths, with true military precision, jotted it all down: everyone should stop and identify themselves; a curfew should be announced over all forms of public media; people should be told to stay indoors; at dawn, having identified themselves, UNITA should be assembled under a white flag, to await instructions as to where to go; by midday, they should be transported to their destinations; all arms should be removed from them and from all unauthorised people in the day time. UNAVEM would play a key role in all of this, and provide at least symbolic guarantees by its presence. The snag was that our plan presupposed, first, a degree of rational organisation uncharacteristic at the best of times of Angolan undertakings, and second, a margin of time in which to get agreement on such moves, but time was running out fast. I also had to work out the details with my UNAVEM colleagues, but lengthy communication was difficult due to the precariousness of my radio calls from the car as the shooting still continued, although we could talk via New York. Furthermore, for reasons I could not fathom, I had been unable to speak even once to General Unimna since the fighting had started and it was he who had to give the military orders. He had simply disappeared off the radio waves and never answered any of my repeated calls during the whole weekend.

I was concerned about the morale of the UNAVEM staff and knew there must be speculation and concern as to where I was, and what I was doing, despite my brief radio message of Saturday afternoon. That proved to have been a wise move because, I later discovered, in my absence no one had gathered them together to inform them of what was going on, though many of them had monitored my laconic and infrequent radio exchanges with Tom White and Jobarteh. Fortunately the camp had not been in any real danger, the main scare having been on Saturday afternoon when Government troops and tanks had attacked the UNITA motel.

11.00 p.m.   Bock talks to John and demands a high-level delegation from the international community, which should first see President dos Santos in Luanda and then Dr Savimbi in Huambo.

11.15 p.m.   N'dalu calls back. He has spoken to the President. They agree on a ceasefire at midnight. We suggest a brief text. The modalities can be discussed tomorrow, Monday. A first priority will be to rescue the Americans. He warns that shooting is still going on in the streets (we can hear it). We discuss the possibility of arranging the immediate renewal of talks between the two sides in the UNAVEM camp as a neutral place.

11.20 p.m.   John conveys N'dalu's message to Bock. He insists on immediate action and emphasises the need for simplicity. A brief statement must be issued simultaneously in New York, on the radio in Luanda and on Vorgan. He repeats the text we have discussed with N'dalu. A fax must be sent to Samondo in New York, so that he knows what is happening. Bock appears to agree.

11.55 p.m.   Bock rings John again, with some last-minute quibbles and queries that could lead to more delays. John, for the first time abandoning persuasive and diplomatic language, says loudly and very firmly 'You *must* agree'. My notes just have the one word he uttered with such emphasis, *devem*.

12.00 p.m.   Midnight strikes. We all wait with bated breath. The next hour is a welter of calls back and forth, which seem to threaten the fragile web we have woven for the midnight ceasefire. At 12.10 N'dalu complains that UNITA is still firing. Five minutes afterwards Bock calls and wants to speak to Salupeto Pena and Tadeu. Savimbi says 'I will never come to Luanda again'.

The Portuguese inform us that hotels have been attacked, citing the Mondial and the Este, and quote threats by Salupeto Pena. N'dalu rings again to say the ceasefire is not working. At 12.50 John rings Bock to give him the numbers of the Tivoli and Tropico hotels so that he can check on the safety of UNITA colleagues there, and assures him that Fatima Roque and Norberto de Castro are alive and unharmed. He advises direct contact between him and N'dalu.

1.00 a.m. We hear broadcasts of the ceasefire over the Angolan radio. John calls London, and I call New York and say that a ceasefire of sorts is in place, which we will try to consolidate once daylight returns. London tells John that Vorgan has also broadcast the ceasefire declaration. I learn that, with a confidence that I would not have shared at that time, Headquarters had already issued a brief statement. It read:

1 November 1992

> The United Nations has just arranged for a ceasefire agreement between President Jose Eduardo dos Santos and Dr Jonas M. Savimbi. The ceasefire will go into effect on 2 November at 00:01 hours local time and will cover the entire territory of the country. It has also been agreed that all foreigners who are being held will be released and that movement of foreigners will be not impeded.
>
> The Special Representative of the Secretary General, Miss Margaret J. Anstee, has been instructed to work out the modalities of the ceasefire arrangements with the two parties.

Identical communiqués on the ceasefire are broadcast by Radio Nacional de Angola and Vorgan until 2.00 a.m.

By now the city seems quieter. We have achieved some kind of agreement, however tenuous. There will be hard and difficult work in the days ahead to try to make it stick. I get to bed at 3.00a.m. to snatch a couple of hours' sleep, but it is impossible. Sporadic firing and explosions continue during the night but much less than the night before.

* * *

Monday 2 November, 6.00 a.m.   I radio the camp and tell them to send a message to all UNAVEM Regional Commanders, informing them of the ceasefire and instructing them to urge all the parties to ensure it is maintained throughout the country.

8.10 a.m.   General N'dalu calls me. They will send an escort to take me back to the UNAVEM camp as soon as possible. The first priority is to rescue the Americans. Several UNITA generals are in Government hands, Salupeto Pena's whereabouts unknown.

9.00 a.m.   There is a lot of firing. We are assured that much of it is celebratory. Ambassador De Jarnette and his staff have been retrieved unharmed by a Government armoured escort. Looting is reported at Savimbi's residence, as well as in empty Embassies. The Government is trying to restore control and tanks surround Miramar. There have been many arrests, including people in civilian clothes. There was firing in the early hours of the morning at the Hotel Turismo but all the occupants have now surrendered. General Wambo is in Government hands. There is no trace of General 'Ben-Ben' or Vice President Chitunda.

Yesterday evening a six-vehicle convoy made a dash out of Savimbi's residence on Miramar with the top UNITA leaders together with guards, and using the two British hostages, Mr and Mrs Chambers, as human shields. They drove into a hail of bullets, said to have come from local militia. No one knows what has happened to Salupeto Pena and it is feared he is dead, but there is still no confirmation. Chivukuvuku is alive with a leg wound, and in Government hands. The Chambers miraculously survived with relatively minor injuries.

UNITA is said to be holding a senior government official, but there are no details of who or where. A Brazilian Hercules has landed at Luanda airport to evacuate nationals, so some air services may be expected to resume.

10.40 a.m.   Antonio and I have a long telephone conversation about the next steps. (It is still unsafe to move about the city.) N'dalu says it is essential to reinforce the police as many of the largely pro-MPLA population want revenge, and there is looting. People are being killed in the *musseques* (shantytowns). We agree the CCPM must meet urgently.

11.10 a.m.   Antonio rings again. The problem is who should represent UNITA. No one knows where their political leaders in Luanda are. We discuss whether General 'Gato' or Secretary-General Mango could represent them in a bilateral meeting, but no one knows where they are either. It has been agreed that there will be a meeting of military people from both sides in the CCPM building at 4.00 p.m. this afternoon, with UNAVEM military observers present. Later there will be a political meeting. There is another problem: N'dalu is unable to call Bock to make the arrangements. (Later it is learned that the Ministry of Defence's satellite is not working. For several days General N'dalu made and received all his calls with Savimbi and other UNITA leaders in Huambo from the British Embassy. It was the only neutral communications system that seemed to work in the centre of the city – UNAVEM's also did, but was 15 kilometres away. All other independent systems in Luanda itself, based on top of the Banco Popular, had been put out of action at the start of the fighting.)

The morning wears on without definite news about the general situation or when I can leave the Embassy. I send a cable to the Secretary-General through the good offices of the Embassy and the UK Permanent Mission to the UN in New York so that he has an update before he meets the 'Permanent Five'.

While relieved that the ceasefire seems to be taking hold, however imperfectly, we are all pessimistic about longer-term prospects. John is concerned about a possible UNITA counterattack on Luanda, where the utilities are particularly vulnerable. UNITA has blown them up many times before and the city could not survive long without water, or even power. Bob Griffiths gives us a military analysis, also full of foreboding. He thinks the nature of the conflict will change, strategic areas could be bombarded and lines of advance on the city could be through outlying areas such as Vila Espa, and so UNAVEM, he warns me, could find itself in danger. UNITA occupies well-defended positions at Viana and Catete, and dominates the causeway at Cacuaco. By reinforcing its support base at Viana, UNITA could cover the whole of Luanda and hold the city to ransom. It could advance from the east, through Viana. It could also advance from the north, having a strong force in N'dalatando, and this would allow access to fuel from the refineries. UNITA is estimated to have between 4–5000 troops in Quibaxe. We should also watch the Rio Cuanza bridge, he warns. In his view the northern and eastern approaches are the most probable but the southern one should also be watched. As a further disquieting piece of information, he thinks that UNITA has trained divers at Miramar.

11.50 a.m.   Higino calls me on behalf of N'dalu. The Government is taking preemptive action to prevent revenge killings, including through the media. There is no movement of UNITA troops to the north or the east.

12.05 p.m.   N'dalu calls. The convoy will pick me up soon. N'dalu sees no possibility for a CCPM meeting today after all. He has spoken with several senior UNITA generals in Luanda, but they cannot represent UNITA without consulting Huambo and communication with Savimbi's headquarters is difficult. Chivukuvuku is wounded, and in the military hospital, but may be fit enough to participate. We also discuss the advantages of holding the meeting in the UNAVEM camp rather than the CCPM building. I offer all facilities, including UNAVEM escorts for UNITA and a cordon of 'Blue Berets' at the site.

12.10 p.m.   Bock calls John, excited and perturbed about the incident at the Hotels Tivoli and Tropico and all the rumours and speculation. He has been told that the Government is looking for Salupeto Pena and his colleagues. He has spoken to N'dalu, who has promised to do his best to see they are not harmed. UNITA has been unable to make contact with Salupeto Pena, 'Ben-Ben' and Mango. There are rumours in the Western press that all are dead. This has caused the UNITA military to exert pressure on Savimbi; to retaliate on Luanda from the north (thus confirming some of Bob Griffiths' analysis). UNITA is holding back from making an offensive out of Huambo but the Lobito situation is very bad. The UNITA commander there approached his government and police contacts to negotiate the ceasefire, only to be told curtly that there was no ceasefire and they intended to liquidate UNITA. UNITA forces are ready to move west from Huambo in one hour. Bock alleges that the Government is using marines and MIGs, and firing rockets from Catumbela (the airport midway between Lobito and Benguela).

This is fighting talk once again. There are rumours that UNITA has control of two WFP Antonov cargo planes at Catumbela. I am chafing to get back to camp, have proper discussions with my staff and get some effective action underway.

1.00 p.m.   Davidow calls from Washington and I give him an update. Minutes later N'dalu calls again. Higino will collect me in half-an-hour and take me to the Ministry of Defence, where a military helicopter will be waiting to fly me back to Vila Espa. Travel by road is still unsafe, he says. He adds that the news circulating about the deaths of Salupeto Pena and 'Ben-Ben' is still unconfirmed.

* * *

At about 1.45 p.m. Higino appeared at the gates of the Embassy with two escort cars. I took an emotional farewell of the companions with whom I had shared those momentous events. Looking back, it seemed like a very long weekend indeed. It was just as well I was leaving as my bedroom was needed for the two injured British hostages. The two Ambassadors were to leave later in the day as their residences were nearby, but my security guards would have to spend another night in their vehicles as there were pockets of fighting on the way out to the camp.

The officers and men from the police post next door were also out in the lane. John took advantage of our first exodus from the compound to thank them for having protected the Embassy, but was more than a little miffed to learn that they had done so because they were under instructions from Vice Minister 'Petroff' to see that 'the lady comes to no harm'.

Colonel Griffiths accompanied us up the hill to the Ministry. The helicopter would only take two passengers, but in addition to Sigi I wanted to take Brito, my chauffeur, who was worried about his family. General N'dalu was waiting me in the open space in front of the Ministry of Defence, where a tiny military helicopter with two Angolan Air Force pilots in the front seat stood ready. All around armed soldiers were guarding strategic points, looking very much as if they meant business.

N'dalu and I had a brief exchange. I thanked him for the helicopter and we discussed what should be done next. I stressed – though I knew we were on the same wavelength and that his problem lay with the MPLA hardliners – the importance of somehow arranging a meeting as soon as possible with UNITA. I pledged UNAVEM's support, UNAVEM's facilities, and my own availability to talk at any hour of the day or night.

I clambered aboard the helicopter, a tight squeeze with Sigi and Brito. Sigi looked very odd – for some extraordinary reason he had got his UN cap on backwards, the peak jutting over his collar. It gave him a devil-may-care look, but I realised he was frightened, and afterwards he spontaneously admitted that he had found the flight back the worst moment of the whole adventure.

The helicopter lifted off, General N'dalu, Higino and Bob Griffiths becoming increasingly tiny figures below. Bob later told me that N'dalu had had to restrain one of the soldiers from shooting at us because he had thought I was Salupeto Pena trying to escape. This seemed totally unbelievable, and yet it took on an unnerving plausibility in the context of the bizarre unpredictability of Angola, and the vast array of rumour and suspicion.

The pilots took a circuitous route back to the UNAVEM camp, avoiding the main part of the city for security reasons. We flew over headlands, along marshy beaches, and then high above the run-down shanty towns on the outskirts of the city. It was all eerily quiet and motionless – no movement could be seen in the deserted streets below at the height of that Monday afternoon, no sound heard except the juddering roar of our craft, which filled the empty sky. Luanda seemed like the stricken body of a giant wounded animal, motionless, yet poised to spring in a last feral attack. We knew that what lay below us it was no void, that there were more than a million people lurking out of sight, prey also to strong emotion, most of them holding their breath in fear of what was to come next, some fired with thoughts of vengeance, some perhaps with guns pointed at us, a small wavering dot in the sky.

After a seeming eternity that must have lasted only a few minutes we swept back inland over the craggy, cove-jagged coastline near Futungo and I guided the pilots to a jerky, dust-enveloped landing on the road outside the UNAVEM camp, expertly pin-pointed right in front of the main gates. I had radioed beforehand to say that I would be coming, and how, but word had not, it seemed, reached everyone and the timing had been uncertain. The disconcerting sight of a camouflaged Air Force helicopter hovering over the camp and then diving to earth, contrary to reason, had everybody running towards the gate. I thanked the pilots and scrambled out, tousled and still clad in my ill-assorted outfit of borrowed shirt and trousers, and the inevitable flak jacket.

Jobarteh came to escort me in but General Unimna was nowhere to be seen. It was an intensely emotional moment for me. For the staff too it seemed. They lined up spontaneously on either side of the road inside the gates and a small ragged cheer went up as I entered. I knew what it meant – this was not just for me, but for all of us. They had not expected to survive either. Someone pressed flowers into my hands.

Sissy was standing a little way off, clutching Missy, who looked anything but welcoming. We went indoors and I had a nice cup of tea!

18 The Slide into the Abyss

That afternoon, Monday 2 November 1992, my first act was to send a cable to New York to inform them of my safe return and of my efforts to consolidate the tenuous ceasefire. My top priority was to organise an urgent, high-level meeting between the two sides.

At 4.00 p.m. I met General Unimna (who reappeared without explanation for his inaccessibility during the fighting), Jobarteh and other senior staff to work out a game plan. We agreed that I must speak personally to President dos Santos and Dr Savimbi as soon as possible. We also urgently needed to bring in armed UN guards, and possibly more police observers, to help provide guarantees if UNAVEM was to be the venue for talks between the two sides. The possibility of obtaining a contingent of 'Blue Helmets' quickly, on loan from the UN operations in Somalia or Lebanon, was discussed.

Security ranked high on the agenda and there was consensus that the UN offices in Angola should be advised to evacuate all dependants. Non-essential UNAVEM staff would also be invited to leave voluntarily. The updating of our evacuation plan, too, was urgent, including assured access to Cabo Ledo airport. Given the dangers at Luanda airport, as many of our helicopters as possible should be flown on to the small piece of wasteland adjoining my house. Water and diesel fuel were running out – the tankers could no longer transport it because the ceasefire was not yet fully secure. Both were severely rationed. As if to underline the gravity of these problems, a series of heavy explosions punctuated our meeting.

Our people in the field reported that the ceasefire in Lobito was holding but the situation in Viana and Caxito was dicey. I requested a military appreciation of the likelihood of a conventional attack on Luanda. The centre of the town was calmer. Nobody was out, except groups of drunken, armed civilians. The Samba route was better, but one of our patrols had been arrested – on the ground that UNAVEM was helping UNITA – but had been allowed to go on its way. Unsurprisingly the ceasefire was very brittle.

My various attempts to telephone President dos Santos were not helped by the fact that the ever temperamental telephone exchange had now been badly damaged. At my umpteenth try a voice came on the line, saying quietly: 'This is José Eduardo speaking'. I was so startled that for a moment or two I failed to realise that it was the President himself. I told him that, now back at my headquarters, I was working to strengthen the ceasefire and bring about an early joint meeting. I asked the President to appoint someone with whom I could liaise on the details. He at once named General N'dalu.

I strongly recommended that he make a statement to the nation on radio and television, enjoining everyone to cease hostilities, and assuring them that measures to consolidate the ceasefire and return to the negotiating table were underway. Cautious as always, the President said he was ready to do this once the fighting had stopped! I pointed out that this was a vicious circle and that such a statement, made rightaway, would help bring about full cessation of hostilities, adding that we were bringing all possible influence to bear to ensure that the same message went down the UNITA line. The President then said he agreed in principle to making the statement and would speak to General N'dalu (with whom I had raised the matter during our rapid exchange at the Defence Ministry).

General N'dalu called to tell me that, although the fate of Engineer Salupeto Pena and Vice-President Chitunda was unconfirmed, the Government was examining bodies that might be theirs. I stressed the need for the Government to tell Huambo urgently, as well as give lists of those who were safe in Luanda. He said the whereabouts of Generals 'Ben-Ben' and 'Gato', and of UNITA Secretary-General Mango, were still unknown. General N'dalu had visited Chivukuvuku in hospital, and the latter had asked to speak to me. As the road to the city was still impassable, I asked the Red Cross representative to visit him. The request was for his wife and family to be allowed to leave Jamba and join him.

Later that day I reestablished direct contact with Dr Savimbi's headquarters in Huambo, or its vicinity (his exact whereabouts were a well-kept secret). At 7.30 p.m. a voice claiming to belong to 'George' (pronounced in the English manner) came over the telephone wire from Huambo. 'George' said he was Dr Savimbi's private secretary, ringing up at his request to ask for what he termed the UN's 'official report' on their senior representatives in Luanda. I could only say that we had had no news but that I was stressing to General N'dalu the urgent need to ascertain and provide this information, as well as to guarantee the safety of those in Government hands. General Bock also spoke to assert that UNITA troops were not moving in on Luanda from Viana or in Caxito. According to him, it was the Government that was attacking *them*.

We had a much quieter night and for the first time for many days some much-needed sleep. A curfew greatly assisted in calming the city. Circulation improved on Tuesday, but utmost caution was still required. The Government was making strenuous efforts to restore law and order, but horrendous stories filtered in of continued slaughter in the *musseques*, of private vengeance killings by the population at large, and even of suspected UNITA sympathisers being defenestrated from high buildings and of trucks being loaded with bodies, thrown pell-mell on top of one another, the grisly cargo being carried to mass graves in the cemeteries. I spoke several times to General N'dalu and stressed the importance not only of regaining control of the populace, but also of getting out the top-level message I had proposed to the President.

Antonio Monteiro had phoned at 9.15 with the same anxieties that I was experiencing. There seemed no longer any doubt that Salupeto Pena was dead, killed while trying to escape from Miramar rather than surrender, though no announcement had yet been made. 'Ben-Ben', his brother, was reported to have been wounded, but was missing. Antonio confirmed that

Chivukuvuku was recovering from his wounds. Norberto de Castro (who was Portuguese) was to return to Portugal with the first special plane taking the many Portuguese now clamouring to leave (in the event he was recognised and made to return to the city, along with Dr Morgado). Fatima Roque had taken refuge in the Hotel Imperio, a humanitarian act on Antonio's part that was to cause him problems with the Angolan Government (he was nearly declared *persona non grata*) and bring him small thanks from the lady herself, once she was safe and sound in Portugal. He was concerned about Benguela, as was John Flynn, who rang a little later. Both sides had lost radio contact with their forces there during the night. General N'dalu claimed that UNITA was trying to take over Benguela and had said to John: 'If UNITA takes Benguela, it is all-out war'.

The reports from our Regional Commanders and observer teams gave the impression that the situation was calming down. There were two dangerous trouble areas: Benguela and Caxito.

In Caxito, General N'dalu claimed, UNITA was assembling its forces to attack the capital. There had been heavy gunfire the day before, but by 12.15 p.m. on Tuesday the UNAVEM teams had reported that the fighting was decreasing and they were negotiating a ceasefire. At 5.30 p.m. the news was less good: shooting was increasing, including crossfire over the UNAVEM camp. Our team thought that UNITA was gaining control. There were also problems in Malange.

During the day we evacuated to Windhoek 110 family dependants and non-essential staff from the UNDP and the specialised agencies. Rounding up the families and getting them safely to the airport was a major logistical exercise. The airport was not yet open and I had to request special permission for the three planes that carried them.

My main worry, as that Tuesday came to a close, was that it had still not been possible to arrange a meeting between the two sides. We still needed to establish who would represent UNITA, and late that afternoon the UNITA Generals Wambo and Andrade were escorted to the British Embassy so that they could speak to Dr Savimbi. They also had the unenviable task of telling him that the death of Engineer Salupeto Pena and Vice President Chitunda was now confirmed.

The morning of Wednesday 4 November brought two cables from Mig Goulding. The first was virtually a reprimand to General Unimna for inadequate reporting on the military and police situation since the fighting broke out. The international mass media (fortunately erroneously) had reported many UNAVEM casualties, and troop-contributing countries had been bombarding Headquarters for news.

The second was to me. The Secretary-General had asked Mig to come to Luanda so that we could jointly recommend a plan of action that, if agreed by the parties, he could submit to the Security Council, together with his proposals

1. A 'bairro popular' (shanty town) in Luanda (UN/DPI photo)

2. A view of the UNAVEM headquarters in Vila Espa, outside Luanda: 'container city' (UN/DPI photo)

3. The author inspecting FALA assembled troops with Major-General Unimna of Nigeria, February 1992 (UN helicopter in the foreground) (photo by Dmitry Titov)

4. Boy soldiers (UNITA) (photo by Marco Vercruysse)

5. The CCPM, photographed just before the elections in September 1992. Front row, left to right: Vladimir Perukov (Russian observer), Jeffrey Millington (US observer), Elias Salupeto Pena (Head of UNITA Delegation), the author, General N'dalu (Head of Government Delegation), Antonio Monteiro (Portuguese observer).

6. The author meeting with Jonas Savimbi (right) Head of UNITA in Uige on 25 September 1992. Also in attendance are Gilberto Rizzo (left), spokesman for the UNAVEM II and Ebrima Jobarteh (second from left), Director (UN/DPI photo)

7. The crucial meeting between President dos Santos and Dr Savimbi on 26 September 1992 three days before the elections (collage by kind courtesy of Professor Gerald Bender)

8. A Russian helicopter being unloaded from a giant Antonov cargo plane at Luanda Airport to join the makeshift airforce hurriedly assembled for the elections (UN/DPI photo)

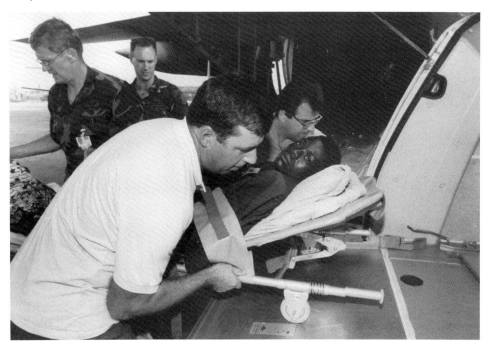

9. Francisco Domingo, the sole survivor of a UNAVEM II helicopter accident, in which 15 people died, including four Russian air crew, is carried off a rescue plane at Luanda Airport (UN/DPI photo)

10. Onofre dos Santos, Director General of the elections (standing), and Dr Holden Roberto, head of FNLA (seated with a white scarf) during electoral registration, 1992 (photo courtesy of Onofre dos Santos)

11. Angolan youth before the election, Luanda, September 1992 (collage by kind courtesy of Professor Gerald Bender)

12. Women waiting in line to cast their votes in the Sumbe hinterland on 30 September, 1992 (UN/DPI photo)

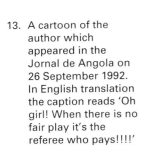

13. A cartoon of the author which appeared in the Jornal de Angola on 26 September 1992. In English translation the caption reads 'Oh girl! When there is no fair play it's the referee who pays!!!!'

14. A UN medals' parade at UNAVEM Headquarters

15. Refugees fleeing from the fighting which erupted after the elections (photo by kind permission of Marco Vercruysse)

16. Inauguration of Abidjan negotiations, April 1993. The author with Foreign Minister Essy of Côte d'Ivoire

for the future mandate and strength of UNAVEM. Mig and Dmitry Titov would arrive in Windhoek on Friday 6 November, and I was to send the Beechcraft (now restored to service) to fetch them.

At 12.30 on 4 November the three observers came to Vila Espa for our first meeting since the conflict broke out, to discuss how to bring the two sides together in a meeting and get optimum mileage out of Mig's visit. Hardly had we begun when Antonio Monteiro received a phone call to say that UNITA had taken over Capanda, where the Angolan Government, the Russians and the Brazilians, through the firm of Odebrecht, were building the huge dam that I had visited a few months earlier. They were reported to be holding 50 Russians and 30 Brazilians, and wanted to negotiate – exactly what was not clear.

The Brazilian and Russian Ambassadors and the firm of Odebrecht asked me to intervene urgently to ensure the safety and release of the hostages. As bad luck would have it, our two military observers in Capanda were out on patrol and out of radio contact, and the telephone lines were severed. I set about trying to contact UNITA and called General N'dalu, who was about to talk to Dr Savimbi. At my request he raised the question of Capanda, telling me afterwards that Savimbi had agreed to order the hostages' release. He would also instruct his commanders everywhere to restrain their troops and cease operations. Our two observers turned up unscathed in Dondo, much later, having been captured on their patrol by UNITA and held for several hours.

At 7.40 p.m. Dr Savimbi called me by satellite telephone. It was our first contact since the attack on me by Norberto de Castro and Vorgan radio. He treated me to another 'stream of consciousness' number, rambling and deeply concerned with his own predicament, but – as far as the vagaries and dramatic changes of his mood could be trusted – on the whole quite positive. The call lasted over half an hour. When I asked him how he was, he replied 'very bad'. He added that it was his duty to stop the war. He was very saddened by the deaths of Salupeto Pena and Chitunda and was trying to come to terms with it. He had been, as he termed it, 'in disarray' but was now managing to pull himself together. He was determined that there should be no revenge for these deaths. He wished to resume relations with me, the Secretary-General, General N'dalu and the leaders of the United States and South Africa so that we could work together to solve the crisis, which he considered 'very, very serious indeed'.

I expressed my deep condolences for the tragic loss of two of his closest collaborators, with whom I had also worked closely, particularly Engineer Salupeto Pena, and he thanked me. He then explained emotionally, and at great length, how, the previous Friday, he had tried to persuade both Chitunda and Salupeto Pena to go to Huambo the following day to discuss the progress of the negotiations. They had said, however, that there was to be an important meeting of the CCPM on Saturday, followed by the UNITA rally in the afternoon.

Dr Savimbi said 'I advised them strongly to stop the rally, if the Government had not authorised it. It was essential to stop firing in the country'. They had replied that it was impossible to stop the people. 'I told them I *know* the people; you *can* stop them. I offered to send them a plane on Saturday afternoon to give them time to go to the CCPM meeting and then to come to Huambo and to go back to Luanda on Sunday afternoon to complete the negotiations, but they refused.' This was clearly a great cause of grief to him.

At that point he embarked, equally emotionally, on recollections of the upbringing he had had from his father and the influence on him of a Catholic priest. He went on to say: 'I am well-educated, I apologise from the bottom of my heart for the insults that were made to you by the radio of my party. I don't control the radio, I don't write the editorials. I don't even listen to the radio and I had to ask my wife if she could confirm what was said. When she did, I called Valentim and ordered him to stop immediately these "faithless, baseless and undiplomatic attacks on a lady and the Special Representative of the Secretary-General".'

During our long conversation he apologised to me at least four times. 'My people', he said, 'had no reason to insult you. This was done without my knowledge. I want you to know that you have my total confidence. I may disagree with you, for instance about the election, but this does not in any way affect my respect for your integrity and your moral authority. Those who say that if you appear in Huambo, we would kill you, are saying something which is totally without foundation.'

Dr Savimbi said he had told General N'dalu that afternoon that the Government must help him restore his authority over his troops. The Government television and radio were not helping by their 'euphoric approach', and by heaping all the blame on UNITA. He had instructed his commanders in Capanda, Caxito and N'Dalatando to stop fighting – he had been unaware that they were until N'dalu told him. He repeated that the problem was that many of his men had had no education and had known only fighting for 16 years. They felt that they had nothing to look forward to in peace – they expected to be dropped. They resorted to arms again out of frustration, because, by making explosions, they felt 'they were chiefs again'.

He referred to his two colleagues as his best negotiators, saying that the balance between them had made the Bicesse Accords possible. Chitunda had been more to the centre and Salupeto Pena more to the left. The agreements of 15 May 1991 had been brought about by Chitunda. Angola, and not only UNITA, had suffered a severe blow. Now the essential thing was to end the fighting and start a dialogue, in which he asked for my full collaboration. This I naturally promised and explained that my first priority was to help consolidate the ceasefire and facilitate the resumed negotiations. Dr Savimbi said he was meeting his people in Huambo that night to decide on the new team. His people in Luanda would not do because they were in virtual custody.

It was essential that his own security should be assured and that there should be no threats: 'Last night, I was exhausted and deeply distressed by the deaths of my collaborators but I was forced to change my sleeping place three times because I was warned that there could be shooting there. I cannot be chased like a dog in a town'. I reiterated that we would do everything we could to restore confidence. UNAVEM teams all over the country were working actively to support the ceasefire and foment dialogue. Dr Savimbi thanked me and restated his high esteem for me and his apologies: in the African tradition, a lady should always enjoy respect because 'she is a potential mother, daughter and sister'.

He requested that I speak to no one in UNITA but himself and asked me to call him the next day at 9.00 a.m.

* * *

Communications were not on our side. I could not get through to Dr Savimbi the next morning (Thursday 5 November) as a thunderstorm in Huambo had put his satellite out of action. I managed to get through to his number on the land-line but he was willing to speak only on the satellite phone 'for security reasons' (I suspect he was a long way away from the land-line). I left a message stressing the adverse international repercussions if UNITA did not release the foreign hostages at Capanda. The Brazilian Ambassador had a C130 standing by to collect them but I still awaited confirmation that it would be safe to do so. The Russian Ambassador had transmitted a personal message to me from President Boris Yeltsin urging me to rescue his 55 compatriots. There were also 18 Brazilians and 17 Angolans.

During the night we had had alarms over Caxito, now controlled by UNITA. Towards midnight it was reported that Government forces were advancing on the town, and a major battle seemed imminent. The UNITA commander offered to escort our UNAVEM teams 'for their own security' to Quibaxe, a UNITA stronghold, but we thought it prudent to refuse this invitation. Eventually the teams moved to a safer location with a Danish non-governmental organisation outside Caxito.

Meanwhile General Unimna and Brigadier Nyambuya arranged for two Government representatives and two UNITA generals to use our radio facilities in the UNAVEM camp to instruct their respective commanders in Caxito (UNITA) and Funda (Government) to desist from what could only be a collision course. After much perseverance, General Faisca in Funda and General Bula Matadi in Caxito were put in contact with one another and agreed a ceasefire from 6.00 p.m. that day, to be consolidated at a meeting at noon the next day in a neutral place, supervised by UNAVEM. The two generals were to contact one another again through UNAVEM channels at 5.30 p.m. to confirm the arrangements. This was a potentially important breakthrough, given the rumours that UNITA was planning retaliatory action on Luanda from the north and the danger that preemptive action by the Government could cause a bloody battle and put the ceasefire in danger everywhere.

* * *

At 7.00 p.m. hours Dr Savimbi telephoned: he too had been trying to make contact throughout the day. The conversation was rather reassuring. Some progress had been made towards the reopening of formal negotiations. General-N'dalu had proposed four points for discussion: a general declaration covering the ceasefire, his agreement to a dialogue and renunciation of violence; observation of the principles of the Bicesse Accords; acceptance of the election results; and a commitment to get the UN more closely involved in the presidential run-off election, as well as in helping to bring about the formation of a new government and National Assembly. President dos Santos had appointed General N'dalu to head the Government's negotiating team and he and Dr Savimbi had agreed to stay in daily contact. Dr Savimbi hoped to be able to tell us the names of his new delegates within the next two days.

On Capanda, Savimbi told me that he had instructed his commander there not to destroy the infrastructure and to let the rescue plane go in: I had his guarantee that the plane could bring out all foreign personnel the next day. He had also told his commander in Caxito, General Numa, not to destroy the infrastructure and to agree an early ceasefire. I told him what UNAVEM was doing to expedite this process. Savimbi said he would like to see me soon and asked that we keep in regular touch.

* * *

My day was still far from over. An urgent invitation came from General N'dalu to a working dinner downtown with the observers. As the curfew was still strictly enforced and the streets particularly dangerous at night, he was sending a police escort. This cortege of heavily armoured jeeps, each carrying several police toting automatic rifles, caused quite a stir when it arrived in the camp. My car and the two vehicles carrying my security guards were wedged in between the armed jeeps and this bizarre cavalcade then made a roundabout way to the city, circling across the bare, rocky plain to the south, and then down to the coast and along the Samba road. There was no sign of life in the dark streets, except an occasional group of police, dark faces glimpsed in the shadows only because of the glow of their cigarettes. It was as if everyone had abandoned the condemned city to escape the very horror of all that had happened. This impression of silent and all-pervading menace was abruptly replaced by one verging on farce when our lugubrious procession ground to a sudden halt. It turned out that my escort had no idea of where they were escorting me to. It was of no help when I ventured the thought that our destination might be the Hotel Imperio, because my police guardians did not know where that was either, and I hadn't a clue as to our present whereabouts. Nor, apparently, did my escort have any means of communicating with General N'dalu (one wondered how they would have coped had we run into trouble). There was something almost hilariously ludicrous in the unlikely spectacle of all those policemen, loaded down with lethal weapons, charging round an empty square looking for a passer-by to tell them the way. Predictably there weren't any, because of the curfew, and anyone tempted to flout the curfew would have given our ferocious-looking contingent a wide berth. Eventually it was all sorted out and I arrived. The others present besides General N'dalu and myself were Vice-Minister 'Petroff', Antonio Monteiro and Ambassador De Jarnette. Vladimir Petukov was reportedly unable to attend because of illness. (He never did recover from the shock of the previous weekend. Shortly afterwards he returned to Moscow and never came back. Ambassador Kapralov took over his functions.)

General N'dalu wished to inform us about his two long telephone conversations with Dr Savimbi, the second one two hours before Savimbi's last call to me. They had discussed much the same things, and it was encouraging to find that Savimbi had given the same assurances about Capanda and Caxito to both of us and that his comments on the resumption of negotiation had been consistent. Another welcome signal was that he had ordered the release of the FAA officers and other military personnel whom UNITA had seized during the initial conflict in Huambo ('Nando's' *ponto previo* at Saturday's CCPM), which the Government had made a precondition for further negotiations.

We agreed to send a plane to Capanda the next day to rescue the hostages, once proper communication had been reestablished with the UNITA people at Capanda airport, and then discussed the top priority issue: a meeting between President dos Santos and Dr Savimbi. There was consensus that it could not take place in Luanda: the two Generals said that the Government could not guarantee Savimbi's safety there, because of popular ire. Some venues outside Angola were discussed but a site within the country was generally preferred. N'dalu suggested Namibe.

As for Savimbi's security, the Government representatives said that the heavily armed guards that had hitherto surrounded UNITA and terrorised people living nearby could no longer be tolerated. The idea of international protection through the United Nations was mooted and I said I would discuss the possibilities with Mig Goulding. General N'dalu's next telephone assignation with DrSavimbi was to be at 3.00 p.m. the next day, when the latter was to give his reaction to N'dalu's four points.

In the dingy street below my posse of guards awaited, smoking and fiddling nervously with their guns. Generals N'dalu and 'Petroff' took me down and got the macabre convoy organised. Then we were off, speeding back again through the unlighted streets, where the stale, heat-laden air seemed to pulse with danger, and monstrous secrets to lurk at every corner. Out in the open countryside the dark shapes of the jeeps ahead, with their crouching figures and silhouetted guns, looked like a massive porcupine against the faintly paler dome of the African night sky, tinselled with stars.

I was especially glad to see the lights of the camp that night. It was just midnight when I was finally decanted, an unlikely Cinderella, at my door. Inside the telephone was ringing. It was Kofi Annan. The South African Government wanted to evacuate 300 people from Luanda early next morning. Two planes were to pick them up, but formal Government authorisation to land had not been received. Could I help? This was a tall order at midnight, in a city under curfew, and without a telephone system, where nothing functioned very well at the best of times. In any crisis of this kind everyone not only expects the UN to deal with – and solve – the main problem, but also to sort out everyone else's as well. Wearily I woke up Tom White and by radio got Major Strilchuk out of his spartan bunk in the UNAVEM hangar. The major and I spoke again at 5.30 a.m. At 7.00 he confirmed to me that the two planes had landed and were loading the passengers. They left without incident. At least one job had been completed satisfactorily.

* * *

The plight of the people at the Capanda dam was not so easily resolved. More negotiations followed, frustrated by difficulties of radio communication with the people on the ground and the lack of UNAVEM presence. Eventually a cargo plane was sent in, and brought out a lot of the hostages, although it was shot at by the occupying UNITA forces. UNAVEM observers were on board. They reported that UNITA had wrecked the huge, sophisticated installation, which had been one of the main prides and hopes for Angola's future. It was a scene of mindless destruction: the modern hospital had been totally ravaged, engineering equipment and computers had been smashed, torn from their moorings or simply carried away – to where, in that terrain, was a mystery. Worse still, it had not been possible to pick up all of the hostages, because not all of them had been assembled when the plane had landed. More flights were made under equally hazardous conditions.

By this time both the negotiations and the flying were being undertaken by UNAVEM, though the task was beyond our mandate and our resources. Most of the stragglers were rescued in this manner, but a small group of Russians, including one woman, and several Angolans remained unaccounted for. It seemed the Russians had hidden in a ditch and tried to escape on foot. With difficulty we persuaded the local UNITA force to let our helicopters reconnoitre the savagely inhospitable scrub country surrounding Capanda for any signs of the fleeing fugitives. For weeks Ambassador Kapralov and I snatched at straws, following up tenuous leads that a group of white people had been spotted, or even grimmer reports of discovering white corpses that could have been theirs, but we never found them. To my knowledge no one knows even today what fate befell the little group, or in what circumstances, or at whose hands they almost certainly died.

* * *

There were also problems over Mig Goulding's arrival. The Beechcraft, which I had sent to collect him and Dmitry Titov early on Friday 6 November, developed engine trouble on the homeward flight and had to return to Windhoek. They thus did not reach Luanda until late in the day.

Mig Goulding was staying at my house and over dinner I briefed him and Titov on the latest developments. Sissy excelled herself with whatever food was available, but other normal amenities of hospitality, notably light and water, were sadly lacking. We were rationed to very small amounts of water for an hour or two a day, and so there was a mere trickle for our respective showers the next morning. Sissy had arranged a delightful breakfast table on my tiny verandah, which was hung with creepers and bougainvillaea. More flowers from the garden adorned the table itself. It was all very civilised and elegant. Alas no one had warned me that one of the helicopters, all now parked hard by the house, since the airport was unsafe, was about to take off. We were engulfed in a cloud of stinging red dust, and dignity was thrown to the winds in a wild scramble to get ourselves and our breakfast into the house.

Our game plan was simple. We wanted first to get the views of the President and other prominent members of the Government's negotiating team, and then those of Dr Savimbi, so that we could send the Secretary-General our recommendations on the immediate steps needed to consolidate the ceasefire, get a negotiating process started and determine the future role of the United Nations.

The first part began well. On Saturday 7 November we had a long, free-ranging meeting with President dos Santos, and another meeting later with General N'dalu and Vice-Minister de Moura. We also had a working lunch with the three observers. Dr Savimbi, however, suddenly became *incomunicado*. We were able to talk to his staff in Huambo on Saturday and a meeting was provisionally arranged for Sunday morning, but just as we were about to fly to Huambo the ineffable 'George' rang to say they were 'out of contact' with their leader and we should not travel.

All day we waited in vain for news. Meanwhile a constant stream of Ambassadors was calling on us. (The French Ambassador arrived unannounced at breakfast time on Sunday and found us consuming porridge in the torrid tropical heat. 'Très britannique' he commented drily but promised me that, though sorely tempted, he would not include this piece of local colour in his cable to the Quai d'Orsay.) There were various lines of speculation about the reasons for Savimbi's non-availability: he might be making his way from Huambo, where he felt threatened, to his base at Jamba; he might not yet have decided what position to take and so wanted time to think; he might be in a state of psychological shock; or he might be planning some major military move. Whatever it was, we had to cool our heels and wait.

President dos Santos had stated his position very clearly. For him the way forward involved four things: reconfirmation by both sides of the validity of the Bicesse Accords; acceptance by UNITA of the election results and the holding of the second round of presidential elections, when adequate conditions had been established, especially as regards demilitarisation and the restoration of the Government's authority; an enlarged role for the UN, both as mediator and guarantor of adequate security conditions for the second round; and the return of UNITA to legality. The first three were points that General N'dalu had proposed to Dr Savimbi.

The President gave us a fascinating insight, from his viewpoint, into the background leading up to the tragic events of the previous weekend, tracing the origins back to UNITA's precipitate departure from the FAA on 3 October and its refusal to accept the election results. He revealed that the Government had since found, in its searches of UNITA premises, documents in the handwriting of Salupeto Pena, Chitunda and Chivukuvuku, which the Government had interpreted as indicating that UNITA had had a well-developed plan to take over Luanda as part of a broader, nationwide strategy comprising the takeover of municipalities and communes all over the country. In the Government's view, this strategy had been prepared as a fall-back position prior to the elections and had been put into effect when it had become clear that UNITA had not won. UNITA's demobilisation policy had been a mirage: armed FALA forces had been quickly reconstituted and deployed, often under the guise of security forces guarding UNITA leaders and installations. The President listed various locations throughout Luanda that had been occupied and equipped with heavy arms, including one (very near the UNAVEM camp) from which mortars had been trained on the Presidential palace. He also described the immediate events leading up to the weekend confrontation, beginning with allegations on Thursday and Friday (29–30 October) from populations in certain quarters (especially Samba) that they had heard of orders to UNITA supporters to attack Futungo, and culminating early Saturday afternoon with UNITA's alleged attack against the police general command.

The President's conclusion was that all UNITA's acts had been informed by a single objective: to take power at any cost – if possible through the ballot box, but if that was not attainable, then through armed force. All UNITA's acts, beginning with the departure from the FAA, had been illegal. The Government's policy was to avoid being dragged into the situation of illegality that UNITA was trying to force upon it, for example by rescinding the elections, and to work out solutions from the *de jure* constitutional position established in the Electoral Law and the new constitution.

The President elaborated on his four points, going over well-worn ground. Most striking was his emphasis on a greatly expanded role for the UN, which signified a remarkable *volte-face* in the Government's policy at Bicesse to limit UNAVEM to a marginal role of verification. Now he wished the UN to take on tasks not only of verification, but also of mediation, establishing adequate conditions of security and defending legality. He particularly wanted a more active mandate and much greater numerical involvement in the second round of presidential elections, though he stopped short of suggesting that the UN should actually organise them, citing instead the Namibian model of supervision. On the military side, he said the government was convinced that nothing short of a sizeable contingent of armed 'Blue Helmets' would be adequate to the task. This again marked an astonishing change in position.

Mig Goulding, while responding sympathetically to the Government's views, pointed out two difficulties: the financial constraints arising from the growing concern of the Security Council and contributing countries over the escalating number, size and cost of UN peacekeeping operations; and juridical restrictions on the UN, for example in providing armed protection to political leaders. It would be essential to put forward a very well-documented case demonstrating that the plan was a viable one and would produce the results desired.

The President reiterated that the Government now wished the UN to take the leading role. He summarily dismissed any idea of further mediation by South Africa and implied a considerable diminution of the Troika's role.

It was generally agreed that none of this could be achieved without the immediate renewal of dialogue, and the President welcomed our proposed visit to Huambo. It was further agreed that the objective should not be shuttle diplomacy, but rather 'face-to-face' diplomacy between the two sides, since this was a matter between Angolans. An early meeting between the two leaders continued to be of utmost urgency. In order to facilitate constructive dialogue we tried to persuade the Government to make some gesture towards compromise, such as releasing the high-level UNITA officers and civilians held in Luanda or allowing one or two to accompany us to Huambo, but were unsuccessful.

One half of the equation was now clear, the other still awaited. Our patience was sorely tried when Monday morning came and we were still being fobbed off about the meeting with Dr Savimbi. We visited the UNITA generals and political leaders, who were living in the Ministry of Defence (including my erstwhile 'admirer', Norberto de Castro, now very chastened, bowing ingratiatingly – though not meeting my eye – and exuding sweetness and light and all manner of reasonableness, in striking contrast to his earlier intemperate and slanderous imprecations over Vorgan's airwaves). General N'dalu escorted us in, and then left us alone with them for a discussion that lasted over an hour. All seemed in good health, and were actively interested and involved in bringing about a ceasefire.

On the general situation there were contradictory signals. Luanda was calm, the airport had been open again and the curfew was lifted on Saturday 7 November. But the danger of a military confrontation continued at Caxito: General Numa of UNITA, like his leader, had disappeared. His presence had now been promised for Monday 9 November. Elsewhere in the country UNITA continued to take over rural municipalities, driving out and sometimes killing Government police and administrators. In some Government-held towns, gangs of demobilised soldiers had turned themselves into Somali-type looters and murderers. In other places, extraordinarily, the joint Government–UNITA CCPM machinery continued to operate. The country was disintegrating into something akin to anarchy. Dialogue was imperative.

* * *

On Monday morning we were promised that Dr Savimbi would call us at 3.00 p.m. This time he did, but with no indication of an early appointment, saying that two questions had to be sorted out first. He had just discussed these with General N'dalu, who was to consult the President and call him back that night.

The first question required clarification of the government's thinking on the recent events in Luanda. Did they consider them an attempted *coup d'état* – the version they were putting out officially – or simply another example of the hostilities that had recently been erupting all over the country? If the former then the Government was virtually outlawing UNITA, and the security risk for UNITA's leaders would be very high indeed. The second issue was a request for two or three of UNITA's high-ranking officers and political cadres in Luanda to travel to Huambo to explain what had happened in the capital. Relations were very strained within UNITA because of the death of Salupeto Pena and Chitunda, and it was essential to clear up the uncertainties in the minds of his followers.

Mig replied that we understood the importance of these concerns and had ourselves asked the Government to allow some senior UNITA representatives to accompany us to Huambo, but we suggested that it was not necessary to await the Government's response before he saw us. Indeed our visit might be helpful in bringing about their resolution. Moreover the mission with which the Secretary-General had charged us was extremely urgent and Mig's many other responsibilities would not allow him to stay in Angola much longer. (The Angolans' conviction, and in particular UNITA's, that the world was prepared to wait indefinitely on their will never ceased to amaze.) Dr Savimbi remained adamant that he wished to hear from General N'dalu first. He would call us again that night.

Characteristically, Savimbi had neatly lobbed the ball back into the Government's court. We tried to contact N'dalu, but he was at the President's office. We were not sanguine that the Government would give up its *coup d'état* theory since it had made much of it in public, but hoped we might get the Government to reconsider its refusal to let us take UNITA representatives with us by regarding it as a response to a request from the UN, rather than from Savimbi. Such a move would be welcomed internationally, as the horrendous wave of killings by both sides in Luanda and all over the country had caused widespread revulsion and concern was building up about the welfare of UNITA people in Luanda, not a little fuelled by UNITA's formidable propaganda machine and worldwide network of contacts.

Special interest focused on Dr Chivukuvuku. UNITA lobbyists and right-wing groups in the United States were bombarding the UN, as well as the US Administration, with requests that he be allowed to go abroad for treatment, since there was speculation that gangrene was probable and that his life was in danger, or at the very least, his leg. General N'dalu had told me that the President could not agree to this because of the supposedly incriminating evidence in Chivukuvuku's handwriting about UNITA's premeditated strategy. The only acceptable ground would be that his life was in danger, and the General asked me to send one of the UNAVEM military doctors to give an objective view. Dr Waldecir visited Chivukuvuku, but after discussing his case with the Portuguese-trained specialist dealing with it, for whose professional capacity he had the highest regard, he concluded that neither Chivukuvuku's life nor his leg were in danger.

Jobarteh and I had visited Abel Chivukuvuku on 5 November and found him in reasonably good spirits, with no complaints about his medical or general treatment. He had told us an interesting story about the last moments at Miramar. He and Dr Chitunda had been hiding in the deserted French Embassy, but in touch by radio with Salupeto Pena. When Salupeto had given the order to bolt from Miramar, Chivukuvuku had demurred. He told had Chitunda that, with Miramar surrounded, to try to escape was suicidal and that it was better to stay where they were and surrender. Chitunda had insisted that it was their duty to follow the others. And so they had, and ran into an annihilating hail of bullets. Within minutes of the conversation Chitunda was dead. Chivukuvuku, like the English couple, survived only by a miracle.

* * *

Tuesday 10 November dawned and we were still without confirmation of an appointment with Dr Savimbi. 'George' of Huambo had been constantly on the satellite telephone, reiterating Savimbi's eagerness to see us, but evading any commitment as to time and day. Savimbi's security, his constant and secret movements about the countryside to protect himself from attack, the

Government's attitude and lack of response – each time a lengthening list of 'why-nots' was trotted out.

Mig was becoming very restive, and with good reason. We knew our Secretary-General was not a very patient man. Mig had to return to New York soon and could not do so empty-handed. And UNITA could not be allowed to go on stringing everyone along. In the middle of Tuesday morning we decided that we should go anyway, with or without an invitation. 'George' was appalled when we broke the news and stammered and stuttered in his efforts to make us reconsider. He was clearly under very strict orders, poor young man, but his pretexts were wearing thin. He was firmly told that our Beechcraft would arrive at 1.00 p.m. and that we expected our safety and that of our aircraft to be assured. We also informed the UNAVEM Regional Commander in Huambo, Colonel Mortlock.

Flying into Huambo at that time was very hazardous and the UNITA troops extremely jittery, but we landed safely and were met by Colonel Mortlock and by Brigadier Wanda from UNITA. Our party consisted of Mig, myself, General Unimna and an interpreter for the latter. Brigadier Wanda asked us to wait at the UNAVEM camp, where word would be brought to us as to where, when and even – it was distinctly inferred – *whether* Dr Savimbi would meet us. A long afternoon of waiting and speculation ensued, punctuated by unsatisfactory telephone conversations with 'George'.

The suspense and the oppressive heat and humidity inevitably affected our mood, leading to ominous speculation. Why this delay, and the constant prevarication? Was it because of genuine concerns of security? (Given the strength of UNITA's forces and weapons in the streets of Huambo and at the airport, this appeared an increasingly untenable supposition.) Was it simply to put us off our balance – a well-known UNITA negotiating ploy? Or was something more sinister being planned? Might we be taken hostage, as bargaining pawns in the tug-of-war with the Government? Might there even be an ambush in preparation, for which blame could then be attributed to the Government, or to an unfortunate 'accident', or even to one of the 'breakdowns' in UNITA's famed and hitherto almost infallible system of communications that were suddenly becoming so frequent?

Wild as such surmises must appear, they seemed all too credible in the cloak-and-dagger atmosphere created by the mysterious and contradictory messages we were receiving, and in a situation in which reason and logic no longer seemed to have any role. Late in the afternoon Mig took me aside to say that General Unimna and Colonel Mortlock considered, as military men, that the situation was so dangerous that I should return at once to Luanda while there was still enough light for the Beechcraft to take off. My immediate reaction was 'Why me?' though the answer was obvious. No rationalisation that we should not put so many senior staff at risk simultaneously could conceal the fact that the real issue they had in mind was gender. So it goes without saying that I replied stoutly (though feeling anything but stout inside) that such a course was unthinkable. If anyone was to go back to Luanda to reduce exposure, then perhaps it should be General Unimna, since Mig and I had been instructed by the Secretary-General to carry out a mission on his behalf. We all stayed.

The rapid descent of nightfall soon put paid to any ideas of returning to Luanda in any case. Instead we decided on a plan of 'collective security': every available UNAVEM vehicle would accompany us to the meeting place, each with a large UN flag flying. While none of us thought this would deter any dastardly act, we hoped it might at least give pause for thought. Having no arms, we could rely only on safety in numbers.

We had been waiting for over six hours when the summons at last came. It was almost an anticlimax. At around 7.45 p.m. a dilapidated American sedan chugged up to the camp gates and disgorged General 'Wiyo', well-known to us from the CCPM, and Brigadier Wanda. We were told nothing more than that we should follow them. This did little to dissipate the lingering suspicions in our minds as our long convoy straggled out of the camp. The main thoroughfares of Huambo were lampless and deserted, though there must have been many watching eyes and listening ears. Soon it became clear that we were heading for the open countryside. Our ungainly cavalcade bumped its way along winding, rutted streets, bordered by squat, shuttered houses that became fewer and further between. It was a night of full moon and its ashen light lent a spectral quality to this eerily unpeopled scene, deepening the sense of melodrama.

As signs of habitation began to disappear, one of the UNAVEM team conjectured that we might be bound for an agricultural school lying some way out. But hardly had he voiced this thought than we swung abruptly to the right and drew up before a very small house, its windows boarded up as if uninhabited. Many people emerged suddenly from the shadows – the familiar panoply of stern-faced UNITA guards, laden down with arms and ammunition. The four of us from Luanda, plus Colonel Mortlock, were bundled into the house without ceremony. The rest of our cortege remained outside in the moonlight with the vehicles.

We found ourselves in a poorly lit room, small, shabby and distinctly malodorous. Paint was peeling off the grubby walls, the floor was bare and there was a clutter of cheap furniture: a sofa and chairs stood at one end, a large wooden table surrounded by more chairs could be glimpsed in the darker depths at the back of the room. The disagreeable smell that hung over this unappetising scene was unmistakeably of poor drains and stale urine.

The room was already crammed with people, all men, several of them conspicuously armed. Dr Savimbi, who was not armed, greeted us cordially. He looked in good shape, so far as one could see in the dim light. With him were Dr Valentim, General Bock, whose fiery telephone rhetoric and belligerent utterances were belied by his tiny stature (though not by his flashing eyes, while one missing arm indicated that his combative spirit was not confined to words alone); General Manuvakola (then Deputy-Secretary General of UNITA), General 'Wiyo' and one other adviser. Greetings over, we squeezed into a tight circle. There was no room for General 'Wiyo' and the adviser, who sat at the table in the penumbra. Room was made for guards, however. One stood ramrod straight beside Dr Savimbi's chair during the nearly four hours that the meeting lasted, clutching a Kalashnikov in one hand and, incongruously, a briefcase in the other. I could not help wondering what was in the briefcase, which must be precious, or what he would do if required to use the rifle suddenly; clearly he could not manage both simultaneously. But perhaps he was there just for show. He might almost have been a statue of black alabaster, for he never seemed to blink or move a muscle, nor for one second did he relax the unrelievedly grim and disapproving gaze that he levelled at us, plainly convinced that we were up to no good. For good measure another similarly armed (but briefcase-less) guard glowered at us from the narrow passage leading to the front door. (Much later Colonel Mortlock told me that this man's hands had flown to his gun when I had opened my shoulderbag and that he had looked positively disappointed when I had extracted a handkerchief and blown my nose. Fortunately for my composure I had not noticed the incident, although I had been acutely aware of other dark shadows lurking in the background.) While Dr Savimbi's manner was welcoming, the atmosphere was certainly not.

As my eyes grew accustomed to the gloom I noticed an even stranger feature of our meeting place. High shelves running round the walls were piled with shiny cellophane boxes, each containing a pink-cheeked plastic doll with piercing blue eyes and tinselly golden hair. They were not simply white; they were aggressively blonde. In bizarre contrast to the surly demeanour of the guards and the pervading grimness of the scene before them, they beamed benignly down on us, like a galaxy of misplaced cherubs. I racked my brain for an explanation. Was this sordid little dwelling sometimes a shop? – though in view of Salupeto Pena's expostulations it seemed odd that a UNITA supporter should be selling such blatantly white dolls.

While the surroundings highlighted Dr Savimbi's obsession with security, he himself appeared fairly relaxed. He again apologised handsomely for UNITA's earlier attacks on me, as did Jorge Valentim, but his discourse was very rambling and often inconsistent; he was clearly not yet able, or perhaps not willing, to discuss the issues in an orderly fashion.

As in the case of the marathon telephone calls during and after the recent conflict in Luanda, we had the impression that Dr Savimbi was presenting 'a stream of consciousness' and obtaining psychological relief by pouring forth his grief and grievances. He ranged widely, dipping at times into ancient history – of the Roman, Persian and Bantu Empires – while at other times Churchill and De Gaulle were given an airing. There was much agonising and speculation over what had happened in Luanda and on the death of his closest collaborators ('You never kill an envoy; you send him back and then the envoy may be changed or the message may be changed.') It seemed significant that he dwelt on Chitunda at some length but barely mentioned his nephew, Salupeto Pena; perhaps he realised what a negative and dangerous role the latter had played at the end. Nor did he mention General 'Ben-Ben', who at that point seemed almost certain to have been killed as well. (In retrospect the omission no doubt indicated that he already knew that he was still alive). He complained that the Government was delaying the return of the bodies of those killed. While expressing a willingness to intercede, we had to remind him that UNITA had never responded when we intervened similarly about the bodies of the Government policemen killed in Miramar.

There were several recurrent themes, the main one being concern for his own safety. He bemoaned the fact that, after our meeting, he would have to flee to another place to spend the night, and referred to himself and UNITA as 'being hunted – outlaws in our own country'. His remarks were laced with a great deal of bitterness and suspicion about the Government's attitudes and motives, and he described the reported widespread killings of Ovimbundu people in Luanda and other places as 'genocide'.

The familiar claims of electoral fraud loomed large among his concerns, and the general sense of theatre was heightened by a flurry in the back room heralding the entry of several men staggering under the weight of large cardboard boxes containing allegedly stolen ballot papers favouring UNITA, which, it was claimed, had been found that very day in Huila province (I was later able to produce official records to show that UNITA had won hands down in the areas mentioned). Dr Savimbi also kept insisting that deep dissension existed within UNITA ranks between hardliners (mostly his generals, he said, and here, as if on cue, General Bock obliged by making a warlike speech) and the group (very small, according to Savimbi) that favoured peace.

He complained that it was very difficult to control his followers and guide them along the path of peace. This led him to proclaim dramatically: 'I have no further role to play – I intend to resign and retire from the political scene to make way for a younger man'.

One could not help speculating 'methinks he doth protest too much', and that he was looking to be dissuaded from resigning and flattered into recognition of his important role in history and for the future. Both Mig and I obligingly urged him not to abandon his people and Angola at this critical time.

At times there were disconcerting flashes of clarity, a kind of pithy brilliance, as when he suddenly said 'It needs *more* authority to say "We have lost but it is not the end"', or 'I may be a bad loser, but the MPLA is a bad winner'.

He was not the only one to be inconsistent. At one point Jorge Valentim urged the UN to help create an environment that would be favourable to a meeting between the two leaders, but almost in the next breath said 'Don't press the President to meet with President dos Santos; if he does, he will lose the leadership of UNITA'.

Other phrases stay indelibly in my mind. Trying to make Dr Savimbi see the contradiction between his repeated assertions of his commitment to peace and to dialogue rather than violence and his clear reluctance to enter into dialogue and negotiation with President dos Santos, Mig said bluntly: 'You have two choices: war or dialogue'.

Savimbi replied: 'I will never lead a war. I prefer to retire'.

His very last words to us when we finally left at midnight were that 'war solves nothing'. Recalled after over two years of senseless slaughter, they echo in my mind with a distinctly hollow ring.

* * *

When comparing our impressions of this marathon and labyrinthine session later, Mig and I had reluctantly to agree that, although there were positive signs – notably Dr Savimbi's reiterated commitment to peace and negotiation (not always echoed by his followers, in what was clearly an orchestrated presentation) and agreement on the need for stronger UN involvement – they were outweighed by the disquieting elements. Chief among these were the high level of suspicion, mistrust and bitterness epitomised in Savimbi's marked reluctance to enter into dialogue with the Government, despite protestations of his predilection for peace and negotiation; and particularly to meet face-to-face with President dos Santos, for whom he made no secret of his personal antipathy and distrust, and whom he held responsible for all that had happened. It was also disturbing that no mention had been made of the points put forward by General N'dalu as a basis for negotiation, and that UNITA threatened to boycott the National Assembly and any government of reconciliation. Deadlock also seemed to threaten because of the Government's refusal to budge from its position that the recent events in Luanda had been an attempted *coup d'état* by UNITA, or to allow some of the UNITA generals detained in Luanda to travel to Huambo. UNITA was proving equally obdurate with its continual harping on about electoral fraud and a consequently ambiguous attitude to the second presidential round, with some of Savimbi's colleagues insisting on the cancellation of the elections and seeking an ill-defined 'political solution'. Another cause for concern were the claimed dissensions within senior ranks of UNITA and the erosion of Savimbi's authority, though we agreed that these could well be more apparent than real, our encounter having borne all the signs of a carefully rehearsed piece of theatre.

We conveyed this assessment to the Secretary-General on our return to Luanda the next day, and sent with it a paper outlining the form that an enlarged UN role might take. But we warned that the proposal would have considerable resource implications, which could only be defended in the Security Council if both sides could be shown to have a genuine desire for peace and negotiation. Here we had to say that most local observers of the Angolan scene were not at all sanguine about the prospects for continuing the Bicesse process, and that we shared those doubts.

* * *

The night was far from over in Huambo. During our long verbal duel we had been aware of a considerable commotion outside, confused shouting and chanting, and the impression of a sizeable crowd advancing on the little house. Mig and I exchanged glances but no reference was made to the disturbance. When we emerged our colleagues outside told us that an angry mob had approached, dragging some unfortunate man who was then tied to a nearby tree. It was not clear what his crime was supposed to be or what summary justice was meted out to him. More upsetting news had come over the UNAVEM radio: a Belgian doctor working for Médecins Sans Frontières had been seriously wounded by an unknown assailant, to whom he had unsuspectingly opened the door.

Our return cavalcade to the town and the UNAVEM camp, guided by General 'Wiyo's' battered sedan, passed off without incident but the dark ambiguities of our talk with Savimbi and these new examples of all-pervading violence cast a pall over all our spirits.

It was now past midnight, the moon had disappeared and there was no question of flying to Luanda. Accommodation was found for us in the Weatherhaven camp but little sleep was to be had. There were many comings and goings during what remained of the night, bangings on doors, and urgent voices asking for volunteers to give blood for the wounded MSF doctor. But although the UNAVEM team, one by one, gave blood as requested, and although the victim was later evacuated, he died a few days later. As far as I know, no one ever found the unknown assailant who perpetrated this senseless and indiscriminate killing, but the finger of suspicion pointed at UNITA.

* * *

Early next morning, we went back to Luanda. Our spirits were further dampened by our second meeting on 12 November with President dos Santos to tell him about our Huambo visit. We came away sobered by a further hardening of the Government's line. This was in keeping with what we had heard earlier that day from Foreign Minister 'Loy', who had peddled his usual line and delivered his punchline with all the satisfaction of one whose prophecies in the wilderness had at long last borne fruit: 'Savimbi means war' he said.

The President thanked us for our efforts but underlined that no progress could be made until there was prior agreement on the four principles the Government had presented to Dr Savimbi. He insisted that it was 'a question of life and death' that UNITA should give a clear and unequivocal acceptance of the first round of elections, including the legislative elections; this commitment could take the form either of a public declaration, or if that were too difficult, a letter addressed either to the Secretary-General, Mig or myself.

The President also made clear that the Government required a reversion to the *status quo* that prevailed before the election: all the conditions of the Bicesse Accords should be observed, including the restoration of central administration in all the municipalities and communes as of that date. It was the Government's intention to proceed to the election of local administrators so that UNITA would receive due representation at the provincial level. We reiterated to the need for some gesture to Dr Savimbi and UNITA, stressing that it might serve both as a test of UNITA's sincerity and an exchange for concessions. The President recognised that this was necessary and various possibilities were discussed, including the return of the bodies of the slain UNITA leaders and the despatch to Huambo of a delegation of the UNITA generals in the Ministry of Defence, which the President said would be the subject of further consultation. (General N'dalu intimated that the UNITA generals were not at all keen to go to Huambo, in case they were punished for having surrendered.)

Regarding Dr Savimbi's fears for his safety, the President said he would consider sending a letter giving him guarantees on this score and reaffirmed his willingness for the UN to provide security for him, though the legal limitations on the UN side were again explained. The security arrangements for a personal meeting between the two leaders were also discussed. The President was adamant that, on grounds of sovereignty, he would meet Dr Savimbi nowhere but in his office in Futungo. Mig having mentioned that the UN might provide a contingent of 'Blue Helmets' for the meeting, I asked whether this would be acceptable in Futungo. The President said he would consider this possibility. He had no objection to any preparatory meetings, at a lower level, taking place outside Luanda, with UN security of the type envisaged.

The obvious next step was to obtain Dr Savimbi's formal acceptance of the results of the first round of elections. This was easier said than done.

Immediately after that meeting we tried to contact Dr Savimbi on his elusive satellite phone, but were only able to leave a message with 'George'. His leader rang back at 3.00 p.m. on a very bad line, just as we were about to begin a press conference. During a 25-minute conversation Savimbi wandered verbally all over the place, and only with difficulty could he be brought back to the main issue at hand. When he said he had spoken to the Secretary-General since, to tell him that our meeting had gone very well and that he would accept everything that we had put to him, Mig seized this opening to tell him of our meeting with President dos Santos and of the need for his explicit acceptance of the legislative elections. This produced a long, convoluted monologue, beginning with another string of apologies, and the now familiar piece about his mother having been born in Huambo and his father in Bié, and yet he was now a hunted outlaw in his own country. He had told the Secretary-General that no one should choose violence, and in a few moments Vorgan radio would issue a statement that he agreed fully with the 'programme' put to him in our meeting. But the UN must defend his life so that he could play a role. He had gathered from his conversation with the Secretary-General that we had told him that he (Savimbi) was not very enthusiastic about playing a role (which he had, in fact, repeatedly said). That was a mistake and the only bad thing about our conversation. He had assured the Secretary-General that he *was* ready to play a role, but the UN must ensure that no more UNITA leaders were killed. These points were repeated three times.

Brought back with difficulty to the election results, he said that his tribe formed 45 per cent of the electorate and he had never expected to be defeated in a free election. He did not agree with me on the results and was not persuaded by the 'Quick Count'. But he had apologised to me and had accepted the defeat which he had not anticipated. 'They said that "Savimbi is the master" but they were wrong; I did not succeed'.

Reminded yet again by Mig about the purpose of the conversation, he said that *personally* (a word he kept emphasising) he was 'swallowing defeat', but needed a few more days in which to create a good atmosphere with his people and give them hope that he would win the second round. He also explained his apology to me. He did not want 'her career to end with the outbreak of fighting and the dissolution of the country into five Angolas'.

Again, Mig posed the vital question, pointing out that we were now 20 minutes late for the press conference. To this Savimbi at last replied 'You can tell dos Santos that Savimbi accepts UNITA's defeat in the parliamentary elections. Savimbi also asks that the second round should be organised by the UN. There must also be freedom of movement in Huambo and a much larger UN presence there so that Savimbi is not killed'. He added that the new parliament could meet 'as a provisional arrangement' until the second round took place, but it must be made clear that no president had yet been elected.

Since Savimbi's acceptance of the election results was so crucial, the line so bad and his remarks so ambiguous, Mig proposed sending him a letter conveying his understanding of what he had said so that he could confirm that we had got it right. Savimbi agreed, and ended the conversation by saying that he had made a commitment himself to the Secretary-General, to Mig and to me that he would not resume the war. What he needed from us was a 'recipe' so that he could tell his people that they could hope for victory and peace.

Before he left Luanda three hours later, Mig signed the letter, which I was to deliver personally. I managed to convey my request to 'George' that same evening, but he rang back the next day at lunchtime to say that Dr Savimbi had 'flu and a high temperature and therefore could not receive me. The alternative proposed was that General Manuvakola, the Deputy Secretary-General of the party, should meet me in Huambo later that day to receive the letter. I therefore sent Jobarteh to Huambo, where he duly delivered the letter and emphasised that I would like an early appointment with Savimbi.

'George' telephoned me on Friday evening (13 November) to assure me that the letter was in Savimbi's hands and that he was discussing his reply with his closest collaborators. I reminded 'George' that I also wanted to see Savimbi, and was told that I would be contacted 'soon'. Notwithstanding, there ensued a repetition of the pantomime of the previous weekend: numerous telephone conversations with different people over several days, and conflicting information. A recurrent theme was Savimbi's 'flu and high temperature, accompanied by the assurance that he was bravely struggling to overcome his indisposition and answer the letter.

On Monday afternoon 'George' told Elizabeth Pantaleón that the meeting would take place the following day. By lunchtime on Tuesday, however, no confirmation had been received and Savimbi's satellite was switched off. Interestingly the *Jornal de Angola* announced that Savimbi had visited Zaire the previous Friday (when he had been too ill to talk to me), in an attempt to obtain military support, and had then tried to get into Brazzaville, where his plane had been denied permission to land.

At 4.45 p.m. I finally succeeded in speaking to 'George'. Despite an abysmally bad line, I managed to make out that Savimbi's reply to Mig's letter was 'in the computer' and that it confirmed acceptance of the election results. Savimbi had just spoken to General N'dalu to inform him of this and discuss 'the next steps'. Finally 'George' said that Savimbi was 'examining his programme' with a view to receiving me towards the end of the week. Clearly UNITA was playing for time. I therefore stressed to 'George' that I must be sent Savimbi's letter immediately and we agreed that it would be handed over to Colonel Mortlock.

Hardly had I put the phone down when General N'dalu appeared, unannounced, to tell me about his conversation with Dr Savimbi, who had said that, after much debate and with great difficulty, 'all my people now agree that we should accept the results of the legislative elections'. N'dalu had stressed that there must also be a commitment to dialogue, to the Bicesse Accords and to greater involvement of the UN. Savimbi confirmed that his reply to Mig's letter would be despatched urgently, adding that he was asking me to show it to the President.

I asked General N'dalu about Dr Savimbi's alleged movements during the past few days. He said that the Government had firm information that he had been in Zaire on Sunday and Monday and had returned to the Huambo area only at midnight the previous night (Monday). So much for 'flu and high temperatures!

Nor had these indispositions prevented Savimbi from giving a very long interview (in Portuguese) to the Voice of America on Monday 16 November. The interview was another tangled skein of ambiguities, threaded with inconsequential and irrelevant remarks, but every so often dangling a strand of apparent reasonableness that might portend renewed commitment to the peace process. He implied that UNITA would attend the multiparty conference being convened in a few days' time, only to qualify his position evasively later. A similar ambivalence shrouded his remarks as to whether the election results should be accepted: 'We', he said (it was unclear whether he was using the royal plural or referring to UNITA) 'and the people' do not think they should be. But since the UN has said that they were free and fair, this is an axiom which must be accepted' (though he went on to question it later).

There were the usual trades against the MPLA, the Government and President dos Santos, as well as about the deaths of Salupeto Pena and Chitunda and the other killings in Luanda. The interviewer took him up about alleged atrocities by UNITA in other parts of the country, whereupon Savimbi replied that there had been no killings in Huambo, and indicated that he could not be held responsible for what happened elsewhere. His last words were ominous – the effects of the first of November in Luanda would 'last many years'.

It was hard to deduce whether these were just the inchoate and impromptu remarks of someone who (as he constantly claimed) was still in the throes of deep psychological shock or whether they were a cunning and elaborate smoke screen thrown up to hide his real, and very well-defined, intentions.

Also on 16 November the Voice of America ran an interview with Jeffrey Davidow. Jeff tried to pour oil on troubled waters by urging both sides to seek a political solution: renewed war would devastate Angola. Asked what the United States would do now that the UN was 'getting ready to assume a position of mediation of the crisis', he said: 'The US would be supportive of the UN. We have great faith in Miss Anstee and in Mr Goulding'. He categorically stated that it was out of the question for the United States to provide military aid to any party in Angola.

* * *

Colonel Mortlock called at 1.30 p.m. on Wednesday to say that Dr Savimbi's reply had just been handed over by a UNITA representative, who had said that Savimbi would be pleased to see me on Saturday afternoon, 21 November. I immediately informed General N'dalu and we agreed that, as soon as the original came, an audience would be arranged with President dos Santos.

Dr Savimbi's reply to Mig Goulding, dated 17 November, said, in English translation:

Excellency,

Please accept my warm regards.

I inform Your Excellency that the Permanent Committee of UNITA's Political Commission met in Huambo on 15 and 16 November 1992 and reached the following conclusions:

1. UNITA accepts the results of the – admittedly fraudulent and irregular – legislative elections of 29 and 30 September 1992, to allow for the implementation of the peace process as agreed in Bicesse on 31 May 1991.
2. UNITA believes it is of utmost importance that the United Nations be increasingly involved in the peace and democracy process in Angola, and that the United Nations adopt the following positions:
   a. Effective participation in the consolidation of the ceasefire and the maintenance of peace, through the dispatch of Blue Helmets to Angola as soon as possible.
   b. Greater involvement of the United Nations in the organisation and verification of the second round of the presidential elections.
   c. To ensure immediately that all UNITA leaders in the organisation and sympathisers held captive in Luanda be set free, as UNITA has done in other provinces.
   d. To guarantee the physical integrity of UNITA's leaders, militants and sympathisers, and that of its installations, in order to avoid a repetition of purely genocidal acts as occurred in Luanda, Malange, Benguela, Lobito and Huila.

I reiterate my warm regards.
With high consideration.
(*Signed*)
Dr Jonas Malheiro Savimbi
President of UNITA.

UN headquarters reacted quickly and I was asked to transmit urgently to Dr Savimbi a further letter from Mig, dated 18 November. After expressing his gratification that the permanent committee of the Political Commission of UNITA had accepted the results of the legislative elections, Mig said that he was 'obliged to observe that the Permanent Committee's characterization of those elections as "reconhecidamente fraudulentas e irregulares" is not accepted by the United Nations, which regards it as a unilateral expression of UNITA's views. Miss Anstee will, of course, make this clear to President dos Santos'. With regard to the second paragraph of Savimbi's letter, Mig said that I would discuss these matters when I saw Savimbi on Saturday. He merely recalled that, as indicated in our meeting on 10 November, it was 'not possible for the United Nations to assume responsibility for guaranteeing the physical security of yourself or other members or supporters of UNITA'. He acknowledged that this was a problem and referred to his earlier suggestions of various arrangements that had been successfully applied to similar situations elsewhere.

General N'dalu made another unannounced call on me at 7.00 p.m. on Wednesday evening to tell me that the President would see me the next morning.

The Slide into the Abyss

He himself had had a further telephone conversation that afternoon with Dr Savimbi, who had asked him to meet him on Saturday 21 November and said that UNITA was interested in attending the multiparty meeting, the Government was convening in Luanda, also on Saturday 21 November. This raised the question of security. Now that he had accepted the election results, Savimbi had said, his generals could return to the new Angolan armed forces (FAA), and he had also promised his collaboration on the extension of the central administration. In addition there had been some progress on Caxito and in settling incidents in other places.

All of this looked promising, but at the end of our meeting General N'dalu informed me in confidence that the Government had evidence that Savimbi's visit to Zaire a few days earlier had been primarily to contact the FLEC, the armed rebels fighting the Government in Cabinda. If this was true, then clearly UNITA had a double agenda.

* * *

Early next morning, 19 November, I sent Mig's reply to Colonel Mortlock for delivery to Dr Savimbi, together with a personal invitation from President dos Santos to Savimbi to send UNITA representatives to the multiparty meeting on 21 November.

When I saw President dos Santos, he predictably reacted to the offending phrase 'admittedly fraudulent and irregular' in Savimbi's letter and I told him we had taken this up. I stressed that the important thing was that we now had in writing Savimbi's acceptance of the election results, an observation with which the President agreed.

We also discussed how to provide security for UNITA. The President repeated his view that he would prefer the UN to provide this, as UNITA had no confidence in the Government. I had perforce to rehearse once more the UN position on this and the legal constraints. Informally, New York had responded rather more flexibly to my request for 'Blue Helmets' to provide security at important forthcoming meetings between the two sides, which I had reiterated as soon as I had received Savimbi's letter. I explained to the President that they might perform this function, if requested by the Government and approved by the Security Council, but could not, of course, be available for Saturday's multiparty meeting. We discussed the possibility of UNAVEM providing such security – including during travel from and to Huambo – with its existing resources.

The President welcomed my forthcoming meeting with Dr Savimbi, adding that the Government was anxious to have bilateral meetings with him. A meeting between a Government delegation and Savimbi was being proposed for

Saturday, but he preferred to let my meeting with him take place first, so it could be postponed until Sunday. It was not clear whether General N'dalu, or someone else, would lead the Government delegation.

* * *

Had the stakes not been so high the confusion over my visit to Huambo would almost have been comical. On Friday 20 November I sent an urgent letter to Jonas Savimbi telling him that I would be seeing President dos Santos on Saturday 21 November before flying to Huambo to keep our appointment, which had been agreed for 2.00 p.m. That same afternoon I received a message that he wished to postpone the appointment until Monday or Tuesday, because he wanted first to see General N'dalu and the Government delegation, who were not due until those days. I pointed out that the latter timing was almost certainly due to the President's preference that my meeting with Dr Savimbi should take place first! I did not think that the timing of my meeting with him, to which the Secretary-General attached great importance and urgency, needed to be contingent upon bilateral discussions between UNITA and the Government, though I naturally hoped these would resume as soon as possible. I also expressed the hope that Dr Savimbi would accept President dos Santos' invitation and send UNITA representatives to the multiparty meeting. Anticipating his concern about security, I offered to bring the UNITA delegation to Luanda in a UNAVEM plane and to deploy military and police observers to accompany them.

Notwithstanding, UNITA decided not to attend, citing its concern about security. UNITA's absence raised the question of my own attendance, but during a late-night telephone conversation with Mig in New York we both agreed that, since this was all part of the legitimate democratic process, I should go to the opening. I tried to call Savimbi to inform him of this decision and to make a last-ditch attempt to get him to change his mind about UNITA representation, but the satellite was once more switched off.

The initial ceremony was brief, consisting of a speech by President dos Santos followed by a half-hour interlude, during which the President mingled with participants and guests. After that the meeting was closed to all but participants. UNITA's absence was most unfortunate from many points of view. President dos Santos, in his speech, spoke at some length about the need for a spirit of national unity, mutual tolerance and respect, and the participation of all Angolans, as well as rejection of tribalism and regionalism: all Angolans had the same rights and responsibilities and there could be no distinction such as 'first-and second-class citizens'. The President likewise reiterated his intention to establish a government of national unity and reconciliation based on 'universal democratic principles'. Sadly, these admirable and conciliatory sentiments were rendered hollow by the invective against UNITA that preceded them. The President accused UNITA of unleashing a new war and of violating the Bicesse Accords, making no mention of the fact that, through the efforts of the United Nations, UNITA had, however grudgingly, conveyed its acceptance of the results of the legislative elections. Towards the end of the speech, he stressed that all who had seats in the parliament must assume their responsibilities, indicating that all would be invited to participate in the new government.

General N'dalu told me that the UNITA representative in Portugal had given reasons other than security for UNITA's non-participation: Savimbi's preconditions that his people in Luanda should be released and the antiriot police disbanded. UNITA's representative in Washington had said that UNITA had wished to be represented by some of its people in Luanda, but that the Government had refused UNITA's request that thay be sent to Huambo for briefing. Neither General N'dalu nor I knew of any UNITA requests in this sense.

To judge by what was said on Government television on Sunday 21 November, and in the *Jornal de Angola* on the 2nd, the closed meeting of the multiparty conference had turned into a 'ganging-up' exercise on UNITA. None of this was likely to make UNITA any more amenable to dialogue, much less to participating in the new Parliament or the new Government, but in a sense UNITA had asked for it by deciding at the last moment not to go to the meeting. Its absence fuelled anew all the fears of other parties about its real intentions and gave the Government (which had behaved correctly in issuing a personal invitation signed by the President) a pretext to vent its pent-up spleen, however ill-advised this might be in the interests of working out a joint solution.

* * *

I did not receive confirmation of my meeting with Dr Savimbi until Monday morning (23 November). It was to be at 1.00 p.m. the next day at his 'White House' in Huambo. I at once tried to inform General N'dalu, but learned to my dismay that he had left the country for Europe the day before for medical treatment. This was very strange, as when I had seen him on Saturday at the multiparty conference he had not mentioned any such possibility, but spoke rather of the imminent return of his family from Portugal. I was told that General N'dalu would be away for at least 12 to 15 days, and that in the meantime Vice Minister of Interior 'Nando' would take over his responsibilities for negotiating with UNITA.

This was a disquieting development: N'dalu was the only MPLA member that Savimbi seemed to trust. In contrast 'Nando' was a hardliner, and UNITA's *bête noire* as it believed he was the main instigator of the hated 'antiriot' police.

Meanwhile the Government had sent Lopo de Nascimento – a moderate of similar cast of mind to N'dalu – on a diplomatic mission to make their case known abroad. He saw the Secretary-General in New York on Monday 23 November, and while conceding that it was up to the two parties to show willingness to find a solution, he also pleaded that Angola should not be abandoned by the United Nations. The Secretary-General replied very frankly: although he had told President dos Santos on 1 November that electoral victory would turn into defeat unless early concessions were made to UNITA, three weeks had passed without progress. The Angolan Government, on whom greater responsibility lay as the winner, should beware the fatigue of the international community, and while the Secretary-General wanted to help, he could not ignore the impatience of that community. He was also surprised that General N'dalu should have left Angola at this crucial time.

Separate conversations between Mig and Lopo increased our disquiet about General N'dalu's position. Lopo said the Government had decided that one person could not combine the roles of principal negotiator and Chief of General Staff of the Angolan armed forces, to which Mig replied that, in our view, N'dalu was more valuable in the first role than in the second. Lopo seemed to be unaware of any health factor, which also opened up troubling speculations. What was the FAA Chief of General Staff doing in Europe?

Mig wished me the best of luck for the next day's meeting: 'At least the "White House" is a step up from the boarded-up dolls' house' he quipped.

* * *

Rather than see me before I went to Huambo, the President – or perhaps his advisers – decided to set down his views on Dr Savimbi's letter in a letter of his own to the Secretary-General, dated 24 November. It began by saying that 'the reluctant acceptance of the results of the elections makes UNITA's position all the more ambiguous'. In the Government's view the solution of the Angolan crisis required not only UNITA's *unequivocal* acceptance of the election results but also fulfilment of other conditions, such as respect for the Bicesse Accords and strengthening the role of the UN. It considered that the tasks of the three observer countries were complementary and useful, and should continue, although the modalities should be adapted to the new institutional framework. Finally the President asked the UN to participate in the protection of UNITA leaders since this aspect could constitute a pretext for their non-participation in activities that were indispensable to the functioning of the country's institutions and the Bicesse Accords.

The final paragraph dealt with 'UNITA members who are in Luanda under Government custody'. It was not encouraging: their situation had to be dealt with 'within the framework of the overall solution to the crisis, since, in the areas occupied by UNITA, there are Government officials being retained by that organization'.

* * *

Events began to move rather swiftly. On Tuesday morning (25 November), as I was leaving for Huambo, Vice Minister de Moura called to convey a Government proposal that delegations from the two sides should meet, in a place other than Luanda or Huambo, with neither side having any security other than that provided by UNAVEM II. Wednesday or Thursday had been suggested, with Namibe as the location.

Luanda airport was the scene of an unprecedentedly high level of military air activity and was closed to civil aircraft. Something was clearly afoot. Luckily I was bound on an errand of interest to the government and special authorisation to take off was soon forthcoming (once they had kept me waiting for four hours in broiling heat). Our pilot was a former RAF officer who had flown Spitfires during the Battle of Britain. That had required great skill and courage, but it had been a very long time ago, and he was the oldest resident in the camp. He soon put any doubts to shame. We were flying from one uncertain situation into another. Instead of circling Huambo airport he made a combat landing, diving straight down from about 20 000 feet so that, as Colonel Mortlock later told us, no one saw us descend until suddenly there was a little silver flash hurtling towards the runway. UNITA had seized control over the airport weeks before, but this time both the MPLA and the UNITA flags were flying over the control tower. The town was still split between the two sides, but heavily armed UNITA soldiers were in much greater evidence on the streets than those of the Government.

Although we had been courteously received at Huambo airport by Brigadier Wenda and at the UNAVEM camp by General 'Wiyo', there was the usual long wait before being summoned into Dr Savimbi's presence, and the usual suspense, real or engineered, as to where the meeting would take place. In the end it was not the 'White House' after all, but the local UNITA headquarters.

The meeting was a great improvement on that of 10 November with Mig. It was more structured and more positive in tone. At the end Savimbi kept saying to me: 'You see, I am a different man from last time. I no longer talk of resigning. You can count on me. I am constructive'. And it was true: he was a different man – calm and in control of himself, coherent, and to all appearances the epitome of sweet reasonableness. But, as always, some of his colleagues, especially Manuvakola, a fiery and dyspeptic young man, were less than forthcoming. As usual, too, the leader left the hard running to them. Audiences with Savimbi were always like carefully rehearsed theatrical productions.

I suggested that we should discuss four issues: consolidation of the ceasefire; negotiations between UNITA and the Government; UNITA's participation in the next stages of the electoral process and the transitional government of national unity and reconciliation; and the future role of UNAVEM. UNITA wanted to add the liberation of prisoners, the return of the remains of dead UNITA members and the need for Dr Savimbi to have a meeting with all the UNITA senior officials, members of its permanent and political commissions, now scattered round the country.

The most positive development was UNITA's readiness to accept the Government's proposal for a meeting in the next day or two. Savimbi suggested Thursday 26 November, to give more time for preparation, and Lubango instead of Namibe as the location. The prospect of direct face-to-face dialogue marked a real breakthrough and much of the rest of the discussion turned on items for the agenda.

The discussion on the consolidation of the ceasefire was less encouraging. Savimbi said that the country was effectively in a state of war, a judgement with which we had perforce to agree. We also had another inquest on the events of 31 October and 1 November. Here Savimbi repeated several times that 'something went seriously wrong in Luanda'. He said that he had called in the survivors of UNITA's security forces in Luanda and told them they were 'cowards, and no longer soldiers, because they were sent to Luanda to protect their leaders and they failed.... Instead they picked little fights with the antiriot police, before the major fighting, and said: "We've won here, we've won there" instead of carrying out their mission'. He conceded that his nephews might have been rather 'nervous' and headstrong. These comments were the nearest I ever heard him get to admitting that provocation by UNITA had escalated the tensions that eventually erupted into the terror of that dreadful weekend and of its aftermath.

More positively, Dr Savimbi asserted his firm conviction that UNITA must participate in the Parliament, provided the problem of security could be solved. He was greatly put out by the statement in Mig Goulding's letter of 18 November that the UN could not guarantee his physical security or that of his followers. In vain I rehearsed again all the alternative arrangements. He would have none of them. It was the UN or nothing – curiously enough, the same position as in that President dos Santos' letter of 24 November.

Another prerequisite for UNITA's participation in Parliament was for him to have a meeting with senior UNITA members from all over the country, to convince them of the rightness of this decision and about his own participation in the second round, to which he seemed personally committed. He realised that the Government might suspect that the purpose was to gain time for war preparations, and he therefore proposed that the UN should monitor the proceedings as well as provide security.

Dr Savimbi's position on the future UNAVEM role was consistent with that at our last meeting. I pointed out that the Security Council could not approve any increased UN presence until there was a detailed request, and the two sides convinced the international community that this time they really meant business. It was agreed that a consensus on this must be reached at Thursday's meeting, as a basis on which we could work out a detailed proposal.

We left Huambo airport just before nightfall. As we flew over the darkening landscape, relieved only by the fitful flares of occasional campfires, my colleagues and I agreed that there were some encouraging signs, but that security was a very central problem, a rock on which the whole process could founder. I warned New York that we would have to do some very creative thinking. The traditional UN approaches were not sufficient.

* * *

I saw President dos Santos on the next afternoon to tell him about my meeting with Dr Savimbi. The only other person present was Victor Lima. I stressed the positive aspects such as UNITA's agreement to a meeting with the Government, as well as Savimbi's willingness to take part in the second round and to send UNITA members to the new Parliament. I also relayed his wish to have a meeting with his own people and for some concessions on the return of the slain leaders, as well as his concern about the situation of his people in Luanda.

The President was also positive, saying he considered that useful progress had been made and that the Namibe meeting was of considerable significance. The Government favoured, in principle, the return to UNITA of its dead leaders, but the timing had to be carefully considered: the funerals might become political events resulting in dangerous explosions of violence. He concurred that a detailed request for the extension and enlargement of UNAVEM must rank high on the Namibe agenda and spoke with some force about security, expressing a strong wish for the UN to find a solution, even if this meant breaking with past practice.

* * *

Back at the camp everyone was feverishly preparing for the next day's meeting. The bland assumption of the Angolans that UNAVEM would be able to perform virtual miracles at the drop of a hat was something we had come to expect. This was a particularly tall order and the lead time only 24 hours. From our point of view, as the providers of logistics and security, UNITA's suggestion of Lubango would have been much easier as our Southern Regional Command was based there. The Government, however, insisted on Namibe, where we had only three or four people and two vehicles. We could fly our six UN security guards from Luanda, as well as some military and police observers, but Lubango would have to bear the brunt of the effort and transfer personnel and vehicles by road. Huambo would have the job of coordinating the departure of the UNITA delegation, which had announced it would travel on a special South African plane. The Government delegation and the observers would fly in a Government plane.

General Unimna and Ebrima Jobarteh inexplicably elected not to go, so I set out early on 26 November accompanied only by Brigadier Michael Nyambuya of Zimbabwe at the senior level. As it was my father's birthday, I felt this bestowed a certain positive augury on the day, but I was nonetheless highly nervous as to how events might turn out, not least the logistical arrangements.

Initial fears on this score dissipated as the Beechcraft swooped in over the ocean, circled the bleached desert and rocky outcrops that make Namibe a small southern oasis, and came in to land: an imposing array of gleaming white 4 × 4 vehicles was drawn up in perfect formation, each bearing the UN emblem in large black letters, and flying outsize UN flags. Beside them stood Colonel Jamwal, the Indian commander of our southern region, and an equally impressive array of 'Blue Berets' – all the military and police observers he could muster from Lubango, and all smartly saluting as we alighted. It was a most heartwarming sight. In addition my plane was packed with as many observers and security guards as it could carry and a further plane load was to follow. UNAVEM might not have guns, or many people, but we were certainly putting up a good showing, and image is important. Colonel Jamwal had performed a virtual miracle in transporting so many men and vehicles across the mountains of southern Angola during the night.

The UNAVEM headquarters, in a rather primitive hotel compound on the beach, was not suitable for the meeting and the team had set up arrangements in a house tucked away in a cove beyond the tiny port, accomodation that had originally been rented for our electoral team. Security arrangements had also been made, including surveillance of the cliffs behind. The Vice Governor of the province, however, found it totally unsuitable for such an auspicious occasion: the provincial administration could provide much better accommodation. I told him I did not doubt it, but UNITA had insisted on a *neutral* venue where the only security would be provided by UNAVEM, and a Government building hardly met these criteria. Nonetheless, at his insistence we went to see the alternative accommodation he was offering in the Governor's office, an erstwhile palatial but now rather dilapidated relic of Portuguese colonial times. The room was a vast, cavernous salon on the first floor, reached by an outside stone staircase. One side consisted of floor-to-ceiling windows leading out on to a wide balustraded terrace running round three sides of a courtyard, of which the fourth side was the street. The tiled roofs of the building sloped low to within easy reach of the terrace. My security chaps groaned aloud.

My main concern, however, was that UNITA would refuse to accept this venue because it was under a Government roof, so that we would have an impasse from the start. My pleading was in vain. By this time the Government delegation had arrived, led by Vice Minister 'Nando', who was much less pragmatic than General N'dalu. He insisted that we must meet in the Governor's palace and there was no gainsaying him.

In any case this worry was soon supplanted by an even greater one. As time went by our team at the airport could report no news of any incoming aircraft from Huambo – was the UNITA delegation going to turn up? Then came the disquieting news that the South African plane had been refused clearance to land in Huambo to collect them. Was this a Government plot to prevent them from coming? Or a pretext dreamt up by UNITA? Or, even more Machiavellian, had UNITA foreseen that the Government would not allow the passage of a South-African flight, and so put the onus of the failure of the talks on the Government, while running small risk of having to honour its own commitment to attend the meeting? There was no lack of conspiracy theories as the observers, Mike and I paced up and down the balcony during the long hours of suspense.

Fortunately we had a back-up position. Colonel Mortlock had been told to have two helicopters on standby, but we could communicate with him only through Luanda, a process complicated by the fact that neither Jobarteh nor my special Assistant (at that time Gaby Muranaka), could be located there. It was my secretary, Elizabeth Pantaleón, who saved the day and got the message through to Huambo. There were still problems: the helicopters were much slower and would take two and a half hours to reach Namibe. They could not fly back to Huambo by night, and one of UNITA's stipulations had been that its delegation would not spend a night in Namibe for security reasons. Colonel Mortlock had to apply all his diplomatic skills to persuade them to do so, on the understanding that I would arrange for UNAVEM observers and security officers to watch over them. In the light of what happened later it was remarkable that UNITA agreed, but at last we got the glad news that the helicopters had set off. Even the elements seemed to be against us, for they were further delayed by a storm. Thus it was that the meeting did not begin until 4.30 in the afternoon.

My spirits revived when the two sides met. They fell on one another with cries of joy, warm embraces and enquiries about mutual friends and relations, like brothers after a long separation rather than men who only a short while before had been once more fighting to the death. Months later, after several reencounters of this kind, I was driven to the conclusion that the family reunion act didn't mean a thing.

The meeting itself was not only cordial but more businesslike than the general run of CCPM sessions. It lasted over four hours, during which our Blue Berets and blue-uniformed security guards patrolled the conference room, paraded up and down the terrace outside and blocked the street to the exiguous traffic of Namibe. A large blue UN flag fluttered over the building. The meeting ended with an upbeat joint 'Declaration of Namibe', which read, in translation, as follows:

> The delegation of the Government and UNITA, in the presence of the Special Representative of the Secretary-General of the United Nations, Miss

Margaret Anstee and the observers of the Comissao Conjunta Politica-Militar, meet in the city of Namibe on 26 November 1992, within the framework of reactivating the negotiating process conducive to the complete application of the Angolan Peace Accords, formally and solemnly declare the following before the Angolan people and the international community:

1. The full acceptance of the validity of the Angolan Peace Accords as the only means of solving the Angolan problem.
2. To reiterate and effectively apply the ceasefire throughout the whole national territory and the immediate cessation of all offensive movements.
3. To solicit the extension of UNAVEM II's mandate in Angola and call for its larger quantitative and qualitative involvement. The two parties commit themselves to present their specific requirements for this new mandate promptly.

There had been some differences about the expanded role of UNAVEM which had been discussed in a separate sub-committee. UNITA wanted to spell out what it would entail, while the Government wanted to discuss the details later. I had to insist strongly that this was not good enough and that they must come to an agreement on the *specific* functions they wanted the UN to undertake. Both sides promised to give me their agreed list of tasks by Sunday evening, 29 November.

The late start of the meeting did not permit discussion of four other items included in the jointly agreed agenda: the modification of the CCPM; UNITA's participation in the new Parliament and the government of national unity and reconciliation; the release of the UNITA 'prisoners' in Luanda and the return of its slain leaders; and UNITA's desire to hold a meeting of its political committee. They were to be discussed at the next meeting, which would take place the following week, at a time and place to be decided later.

It seemed that we were at last embarked on a new process of continuing mutual consultations and dialogue. As I reported to the Secretary-General, the meeting could be considered a significant breakthrough. It must be followed up by concrete actions and concessions on both sides but it was no mean achievement that they had at last sat down around the same table again, exchanged views in a remarkably relaxed and low-key fashion, and agreed to return to the path of peace.

The meeting ended in a final series of bear hugs and a generally jokey atmosphere, with both sides cheerily looking forward to meeting again in a few days' time. The members of the UNITA delegation were installed in various small hostelries and UNAVEM personnel were allocated to watch outside their doors during the night. Some of my people complained bitterly that these establishments were insalubrious and cockroach-infested, but no doubt the UNITA delegates had slept in worse places during their long years of bush warfare. The most important thing was that next morning we flew them safely back over the mountains to Huambo.

Namibe being an air force base for the Government, there was no problem about taking off in the dark. Mike and I had had no food since a very early breakfast. We had had no time even to be hungry, but suddenly were ravenous. We were also feeling relieved and rather pleased with ourselves, as well as proud of the splendid way in which our UNAVEM colleagues had responded to a very considerable challenge. The staff officer rummaged in the back of the plane and produced some sandwiches. With remarkable foresight, and complete disregard for regulations, he also produced a small bottle of whisky: normally there was no alcohol on board the Beechcraft except, occasionally, beer. On this occasion we had two whiskies apiece which, combined with the euphoria of having pulled off the almost impossible achievement of a successful face-to-face meeting between the Government and UNITA, meant that we were feeling no pain by the time we landed in Luanda around midnight.

We leapt lightly from the plane ready to have a for once upbeat encounter with the gaggle of journalists and TV cameramen still hanging around the UNAVEM hangar, only to be intercepted by Major Dennis Strilchuk. He wore, as usual, a greasy blue UN cap back to front and what the Spanish so aptly call a *cara de circunstancia* – a face bursting with news. Dennis prided himself on having a background in military intelligence and loved to purvey news, preferably bad news. He constantly appeared in my house or office, saluting and saying 'I hate to be the bearer of bad tidings, Ma'am' in a mournful tone completely at odds with the deep satisfaction evident in every other aspect of his demeanour.

This occasion was no exception. With skill born of long practice he pre-empted the goods news on the tip of our tongues by saying with his own peculiar mixture of gloomy pleasure 'Bad news, I'm afraid, Ma'am. Heavy fighting in Malange'. Instantly sobered, we could hardly believe it. We drove back to Vila Espa in stunned silence. No one in the radio room there could tell us anything about Malange, but our sense of having successfully surmounted the obstacles put in our path had totally evaporated.

The next day Major Strilchuk's news about Malange was completely discounted: for once everything was quiet in that most turbulent town. But our spirits did not quite recover as we busied ourselves preparing for the follow-up meeting in Namibe.

Perhaps that was just as well. On Sunday 29 November, just over two days after the 'Declaration of Namibe', UNITA forces attacked and captured Uige and Negage, important towns in Uige province to the north of Luanda. There was heavy fighting, in the course of which a grenade landed in the UNAVEM camp and a young UN police observer, Sergeant Adilson Costa of Brazil, was killed.

19 Cry Havoc...

In one of those ironic turns that became par for the chequered course of our operation in Angola, this devastating news coincided with a breakthrough on the vital question of security for Dr Savimbi and his cohorts. In response to my pleas, Mig Goulding had engaged the legal counsel and the military adviser in New York in some creative thinking.

The results had reached me just as I was leaving for Namibe early on 26 November. There was a possibility of seeking Security Council approval to send us a specialist armed unit, probably a police detachment trained in VIP protection. This proposal had been advanced with evident reluctance, because there would be dire political consequences if anything happened to Savimbi while he was perceived to be under UN protection (the memory of the Lumumba incident in the Congo 30 years before was still very much alive in Headquarters) and a possibility that UNAVEM might appear to be siding with UNITA if Savimbi was accompanied by 'Blue Helmets' wherever he went (though President dos Santos had stressed the Government's interest in obtaining UN protection for him). Mig had also confirmed an understanding we had reached earlier by telephone, whereby the Secretary-General would recommend the provision of a self-contained company of infantry, initially borrowed from another peacekeeping mission, to provide security at agreed meeting places, where the two parties could meet under UN auspices. Contingency plans had already been made and a unit identified.

On 27 November I had cabled back that now that Namibe was to be followed by other joint meetings and should culminate in a summit between the two-leaders, the infantry company was needed urgently. Could an *ad hoc* request be put to the Security Council without waiting for the broader request for an extension and expansion of UNAVEM II's mandate, which was going to take more time to prepare? His prompt and affirmative reply had arrived on Saturday, but before I could take any action UNITA had occupied Uige and Negage.

* * *

All our energies were now directed at getting UNITA to withdraw from Uige and Negage. Heavy fighting had broken out simultaneously in both towns at 4.00 a.m. on Sunday 29 November, and had continued throughout the day. At lunchtime a scrawled message from our team in Uige was delivered to my house, laconically informing us that the Brazilian police observer, Sergeant-Costa had been killed by a grenade that had hit the Weatherhaven camp. Two military and two police observers were still there. The message went on: 'At the moment the team is in container and are safe. Several bullet holes in car and Weatherhaven Camp. Cannot go to base radio as it is dangerous. Political people are not in control of their military people in Uige'. At 6.30 p.m. they reported: 'Mortar firing stopped. UNITA moving freely in town. Some firing heard from Médecins Sans Frontières house. Body of deceased UNPO has been wrapped in plastic as it was beginning to smell'.

At this point four UNITA soldiers walked into the UNAVEM camp in Urge and communication abruptly stopped, giving rise to even more concern to those of us huddled round the receiver in the tiny radio hut in Vila Espa. Renewed contact later brought confirmation that UNITA now controlled the town. Darkness had fallen, and I could only too well imagine the trauma of the four men left in the macabre company of their slain comrade rolled up in plastic.

We had been in urgent touch with UNITA through our own channels but it was not until 3.30 p.m. the next day (Monday 30 November) that we were at last able to obtain clearance to send in a C130 to evacuate our men, alive and dead. Once again I had a sad journey to the airport to receive the bedraggled little group that stumbled out of the bowels of the huge aircraft. The body was reverently carried out, still rolled in plastic, which somehow added to the pathos and tragedy. The four survivors were visibly exhausted after their physical and emotional ordeal.

At 3.00 p.m. on Wednesday 2 December we held a memorial service on the tennis court for Sergeant Adilson Barboza Costa. There was a large attendance from the diplomatic corps and the Government – Foreign Minister 'Loy' came personally – other UN organisations and the UNAVEM personnel. A Roman Catholic priest officiated, the Brazilian Ambassador spoke and I gave a eulogy in Portuguese, at the close of which I posthumously conferred the UN service medal on Sergeant Costa. The hot season was nearing its peak and a scorching sun beat down on the molten asphalt. In the middle of the moving ceremony the New Zealand Major standing stiffly to attention with the large UN standard, suddenly swayed and collapsed, bringing our hard-pressed medical team rushing on to the scene once more.

The Brazilian Government sent a special plane to carry the remains of the dead policeman back to his family, and a day or two later the coffin, draped in the UN flag, was sent off with full honours. None of it, however, compensated for the loss of a young life – Sergeant Costa was in his early twenties and had arrived only a short while before.

* * *

The situation was deteriorating everywhere. By 23 November UNITA had occupied 50 of Angola's 164 municipalities, and 40 more were reported to be so occupied, though not yet confirmed. All this had happened in less than two months since the elections. Now UNITA's net was widening. The Government claimed that UNITA was attacking outlying villages near Malange in preparation for an assault on that city also. A bridge on the road between Dondo and N'dalatando had been blown up by UNITA forces and violence had broken out in M'banza Congo, Cabinda and Lubango. We had had to evacuate our team from Cafunfo, the diamond-producing region, where there had been violent fighting between Government and UNITA troops. From virtually all our 68 posts reports were pouring in of renewed disturbances and potential clashes, which our tiny teams were trying to contain with reason and negotiation, in many cases with success. But the rot was spreading fast.

On the political front I had been doing my utmost to contact the two leaders, but it was proving difficult to reach senior Government officials, who seemed to be closeted in permanent meetings. Victor Lima called me, concerned about a speech made on Vorgan radio by Dr Savimbi on Saturday 28 November, which he claimed amounted to a 'declaration of war' – similar to his notorious speech of 3 October. It was not, in fact, though the tone could have been more conciliatory, especially coming just two days after the Namibe meeting, which the UNITA leader at least hailed as a positive development. The usual well-worn themes reappeared, but he abjured war once again, called on his followers to 'protect and love the UN' (which made hollow reading in the wake of Sergeant-Costa's death) and support UNAVEM. He even apologised publicly to me, in his and Valentim's name, for the attacks on me by Vorgan radio and expressed 'complete confidence' in Mig Goulding and myself.

Immediately after my conversation with Victor Lima, Dr Savimbi called me to convey his condolences about the death of Sergeant Costa and his 'shock and dismay' over what had happened in Uige. I made no bones of the fact that this was a disastrous development for which responsibility lay squarely with UNITA, however it had come about. According to Savimbi, Generals 'Ben-Ben' and Numa had told him two weeks before that they were planning to march on Uige, and he had instructed them to desist immediately; the present attack must have been the initiative of a local commander. He had asked Generals 'Ben-Ben' and Numa to ascertain urgently what had happened. Savimbi went on to say that this demonstrated the urgent need for his scattered leaders and members of the political commission to meet. I pointed out that it was now even more difficult to obtain the Government's agreement, since recent events could only reinforce their conviction that such a gathering would cloak warlike purposes. The UNITA forces must withdraw forthwith from Negage and Uige. Savimbi agreed that some dramatic gesture on UNITA's part was necessary and said he would 'try' to make the troops withdraw, claiming that he did not have control of his men on the ground.

I also raised the Government's concern about his speech. Savimbi claimed that it was the most moderate statement he had ever made. In it he had said that UNITA must accept the elections (even if they considered them fraudulent) and participate in the Government and parliament. To those who said that 'Savimbi is becoming weak, he no longer wants to fight', Dr Savimbi said he had stressed that UNITA should not fight any more, not because he was becoming weak but because 'war does not pay'. He had also said that the negotiations must go on.

The crux of the matter was to what extent Savimbi was sincere when he said he did not control his troops on the ground – a major admission for one who had always been famed for the iron-handed, centralised control he wielded over his supporters. I had another major concern: all the indications were that the Government would now be gearing up to 'contain' UNITA, which in practical terms meant a counteroffensive with incalculable consequences and the danger of escalation. I conveyed my fears to NewYork, and asked the Secretary-General to call both President dos Santos and Dr Savimbi, which he subsequently did.

On 30 November UNAVEM's mandate ran out again, with no prospect of the Secretary-General being able to recommend the expanded role agreed with the two parties, as we had hoped. By its Resolution 793 of that date the Security Council simply extended the existing mandate (*de facto* now quite irrelevant) to 31 January 1993, and expressed the same concerns and appeals in what was virtually a rehash of earlier resolutions, apart from welcoming the Namibe Declaration, which had already been overtaken by events. A faint shaft of hope flickered on 1 December with the arrival of a fax from Jorge Valentim and General Demostenes Chilingutila to Vice Foreign Minister Venâncio de Moura and General Higino Carneiro, sent through our channels. The operative paragraphs relayed the following outcome from a meeting with Dr Savimbi:

1. We reiterate to you our confirmation that the attacks on Uige and Negage were not ordered, nor were they known to the Directorate of UNITA. They were the initiative of troops coming from Luanda, with which the Directorate at present has communication problems.
2. UNITA is prepared to bring about the immediate return of Uige and Negage so that the Government can reinstall its administration.

Armed with this apparently conciliatory message I sped off to hand it to Venâncio de Moura at a previously arranged meeting with him, which I had been requesting since UNITA's invasion of Uige and Negage. When I arrived at the ministry I found Minister 'Loy' himself awaiting me. Vice Minister de Moura and General Higino joined us later.

UNITA's willingness to hand back Uige and Negage was clearly unexpected and my interlocutors looked distinctly taken aback. I could not help feeling that the surprise was perhaps not entirely welcome, that it did not fit in with the Government's latest game plan. The initial response was very hardline and laced with much scepticism. Minister 'Loy' pointed out the contradiction between UNITA's assertion that it had known nothing of the attacks because of poor communications, and its offer to withdraw its troops. Anyway, he went on, this was not nearly enough. What about the 96 municipalities and three other provincial capitals now controlled by UNITA? I argued that the message was a significant initial step towards enabling the Namibe talks to resume. The Government's scepticism was understandable, but in my view that made it all the more important to test wether the words would be followed by actions. In the end the Minister and his colleagues admitted that it was an important gesture, and would be followed up in a telephone conversation later that evening by de Moura and Higino.

Outside, the usual huddle of reporters lurked in wait. With the Minister's agreement I deliberately informed them of the content of the UNITA fax, adding that now words must be translated into deeds, in order to put some pressure on Dr Savimbi to go ahead.

Very late that night I had another conversation with that gentleman himself, in which I told him about my conversation with Minister'Loy'. He assured me he had already managed to get messages to his ground forces saying he was totally opposed to their move and instructing them to withdraw. This withdrawal should take place within the next 24 hours, and he proposed that a joint delegation of the Government, UNITA and UNAVEM should be sent to ensure that this happened.

Late as it was, I called Venâncio de Moura. The next morning he consulted the President, who said the Government would not agree to send FAA officers to take part in the joint mission. The Government remained extremely sceptical about UNITA's sincerity and I was told in no uncertain terms that it expected UNAVEM to verify that the with drawal was actually taking place. As if that was not enough of a facer, de Moura added that the Government wanted UNITA to do the same with regard to Caxito, N'dalatando and M'banza Congo. I again took the position that Uige was an essential stepping stone towards getting back to the negotiating table, where all these issues could be discussed. De Moura, whose discourse often vacillated like a weather vane, conceded that the position was an extreme one and that there was room for a more pragmatic approach. The trouble was that one never knew whether he was just expressing his view or one with a wider following at the top level of Government.

Whatever that view might be, the message was dispiriting: it was now the Government that was playing hard to get. Although I could well understand – and indeed, to a considerable extent, shared – the Government's scepticism about UNITA's motives and intentions, it hardly made the task of mediation and reconciliation any easier: In this lethal game of hide and seek you got one side in line only to find that the other was dragging its feet. The Government's latest position posed two problems. The first was technical: under our mandate UNAVEM was only allowed to work through the joint mechanisms set up under the Bicesse Accords and involving both sides. The second consideration was more serious: the Government's attitude jibed uncomfortably with information I was receiving from Ambassador De Jarnette, who had access to intelligence unavailable to us, that the Government, exasperated by UNITA's constant encroachments, was preparing for an all-out offensive and had no interest in further talks just now – rather the reverse. After his baptism of fire on arrival,

Ed De Jarnette had quickly integrated himself into the group of observers. He was a team player, and an objective and intelligent analyst whose advice I had come to value.

As if this was not enough, all communications with Dr Savimbi's headquarters had broken down again. I therefore had to send the Government's unpromising reaction to him in a letter, transmitted through Colonel Mortlock, using the most neutral language I could muster. It produced a telephone call the next day (3 December) from Dr Valentim and General Chilingutila, who had received much the same message by telephone from General Higino. Chilingutila proposed that he should travel to Uige that day and he requested that General Unimna accompany him. A flurry of exchanges between Huambo and Vila Espa followed about the conditions under which UNAVEM would participate.

We too had grave doubts about UNITA's sincerity. At the same time, it was undoubtedly extremely anxious to get the Uige–Negage situation resolved. This, I speculated, could well be related to concern about UNITA's place in the new administration, which the Government was quickly pushing ahead. The United States had also sent a strong message to Dr Savimbi, and the three observers in Luanda issued a joint statement demanding UNITA's withdrawal. Whatever motivations lay behind their words, the UNITA leadership had never before been so assiduous in getting in touch with me, nor had the satellite and landline telephones, so often accident-prone, ever worked so well. This reinforced my conviction that we should do everything possible to facilitate a negotiated outcome before further steps were taken by either side that would intensity the crisis. A related development was a report that a Government emissary, General Alexandre Rodríguez 'Kito', had visited President Mugabe of Zimbabwe on 2 December and asked him to call an urgent summit meeting of the Front Line States to dicuss Angola, warning him that, whereas the Government had so far adopted a 'defensive' attitude, it could soon launch an offensive against UNITA.

The Government was already engaged in an all-out diplomatic offensive to make its grievances known to the world and prepare the ground for any retaliatory actions. On 30 November Minister 'Loy' had addressed a letter to me, which I received on 2 December. He also sent a copy to the Secretary-General, requesting him to circulate it to the Security Council. It was essentially a rehearsal of the points he had made to me during our meeting of 1 December, when, curiously enough, he had made no reference to this letter, which he had signed the day before.

* * *

On 2 December President dos Santos nominated the first Government of the Second Republic, describing it as a 'government of national unity'. The new Prime Minister was Dr Marcolino José Carlos Moco, who had been Secretary-

General of the MPLA. It was a very canny political appointment in that Marcolino Moco was an Ovimbundu, though this was hardly likely to impress the UNITA leadership. Only one Ministerial post (the scarcely luminary Ministry of Cultural Affairs) and four Vice-Ministerial posts (defence, agriculture, public works and social assistance) had been reserved for UNITA. Dr Savimbi had said that UNITA would not be interested in a few minor positions, but when the offer of the five posts was made in writing by President dos Santos, he accepted and gave the names of his nominees.

Some familiar faces remained: Venâncio de Moura was rewarded by being appointed Foreign Minister; General André Pitra 'Petroff' became Minister of the Interior, while retaining his post as Chief of Police; and 'Nando' remained as a Vice Minister of the Interior. There were some disquieting omissions: no post was assigned to Lopo de Nascimento, or to General N'dalu, hitherto Vice-Minister of Defence and Chief of the Government delegation to the CCPM, as well as the appointed Government negotiator with UNITA. This did not bode well for the 'moderate line', especially as he was the only senior MPLA person in whom Savimbi appeared to maintain confidence. The omission of Lopo de Nascimento marked a further blow to the moderate cause. General N'dalu also lost his post as Chief of General Staff of the FAA, being replaced by General João de Matos. The posts of Deputy Chief of General Staff and Army Chief of Staff were reserved for UNITA, if and when it returned.

Six positions (one Minister, four Vice-Ministers and one Secretary of State) were given to other political parties, but in essence the MPLA retained control over all key posts in all the key ministries.

* * *

On 4 December, after further complicated negotiations with the Government and with the UNITA leadership in Huambo, a UNAVEM Antonov left at 7.00 a.m. for Huambo with a UNAVEM team on board, led by the Chief Operations Officer, Colonel Egar, who took General Chilingutila to Uige and then back to Huambo by nightfall. On his return to camp that evening, Colonel Egar told us that UNITA did indeed appear to have withdrawn from the two towns, leaving only about 20 soldiers in Uige and 15 in Negage for the security of UNITA officials. Chilingutila had emphasised three points: UNITA did not want war; the Government administration could return to Uige and Negage, but the Government must guarantee the security of UNITA delegates there.

Any hope that this might help to break the deadlock was short-lived. The Government side dug in its heels and refused to take part in the planned follow-up joint visit to Uige and Negage, insisting that they would not do so until UNAVEM gave an unequivocal guarantee that all UNITA troops had effectively withdrawn. Not only was this contrary to the principles of joint action established by the Peace Accords, upon which UNAVEM's own mandate was predicated, but it confronted us with a very real dilemma of a practical nature. There was no way in which we could prove beyond all possible doubt that all UNITA military personnel had left. To do that we would need many more military observers. Furthermore there was the perennial problem of identifying UNITA military men. As a long-standing guerilla force they were past masters at slipping from military to civilian guise and *vice versa*. The weight of responsibility being laid upon us was made crystal clear to me in a disagreeable meeting with General Higino, usually a blandly affable young man (he had risen from Colonel to general in the few short months that I had been in Angola and was feeling his oats). He insisted that the onus was on UNAVEM to provide a cast-iron guarantee of UNITA's retreat and virtually threatened that, should anything go wrong, the entire blame would lie with us. This was rich, coming from the side that had always wanted UN power curtailed, but reason and scruples were hardly the order of the day. The Government had us over a barrel and knew it. Higino and his colleagues were well aware that there was no way in which we could obtain the requested guarantee without their cooperation in a joint tripartite mission, and despite their public insistence that the problem must be solved urgently, they were privately quite happy to bide their time in order to further their own ploys.

* * *

One of the most important of these ploys was the formation of the new administration. On 4 December, President dos Santos officially swore in the new authorities in a grand formal ceremony at Futungo de Belas. As usual the Diplomatic Corps and other dignitaries were summoned to appear well before the scheduled hour, and as usual the latter proved a purely academic point of reference. So, on a blisteringly hot morning, with the palace air-conditioning – true to form – on the blink, we stood around in the crowded anteroom for an unconscionable time before at long last being ushered into the vast marbled hall where the ceremony was to take place. Even when we had been marshalled into our places another long wait ensued. Now I am a pretty good walker, but I am hopeless at standing still for long periods, even less so in high heat and humidity. So I cannot claim to have paid a very attentive ear to the speech of the new Prime Minister, which laid out, at considerable length and with a wealth of supporting detail, the programme of his Government. By the time the President had launched into his equally diffuse peroration I could feel myself swaying, the room going round at an increasingly vertiginous rate. With what clarity of mind I could still summon up, I realised that I was faced with a political as well as a physical and protocol dilemma. I was in the front row, in full view of the television cameras. If I walked out in the middle of the President's speech, political implications could be drawn. If I fainted on the marble floor, then I not only risked creating a highly visible diversion, not to mention doing myself some damage, but also giving ammunition to an ever less than charitable Government press to speculate on the effects of strain, fitness to carry on and – who knows? – even on feminine frailty. In the end, with as much dignity and serenity as I could muster, I got myself out on to the terrace, where I managed to recover before the assembled multitude surged out to enjoy the sumptuous reception laid out there, with Angolan drummers and dancers for entertainment.

Not that there was much to rejoice about. I had captured enough of the two speeches to deduce that the references to UNITA were hardly charitable. The political temperature was rising as rapidly as the sweltering seasonal heat and nothing that either of the two orators said seemed directed at cooling it. Both had insisted, among many other conditions, that UNITA must accept the elections without 'circumvention' and had warned that the war option remained very much open and imminent if UNITA did not forthwith withdraw from the places it had occupied. Neither condition was unreasonable. What worried me was the hardline context and obdurate tone in which they had been presented. The speeches were directed at the general public, to dispel any impression that the Government was weak, and putty in UNITA's hands. That too was understandable. But none of it made the task of bringing the two sides together any less formidable.

During the reception the President asked eagerly for news of the mission, which had left for Uige and Negage that day, describing it as 'a very significant and important step'. That gave me grounds for hope that, if the mission was successful, then the drums of war might beat more faintly, but it was snuffed out by the Government's subsequent refusal to cooperate in any follow-up actions.

* * *

Headquarters was also exercised about the *impasse*. On 3 December I received a message from the Secretary-General that he wanted me to return to NewYork for consultations. He thoughtfully suggested that I might like to take a few days' break in Britain on the way back. After four and a half months of intense daily strain, during which I had not been able to leave Angola or even my office for so much as a day, this was a welcome prospect indeed. As the Secretary-General was to be away on 11 December, I had to leave as soon as possible, flying out from Luanda on the night plane to Europe on 7 December, and going straight through to New York in time to report, somewhat jet-lagged, first thing on 9 December.

During this period of flux and uncertainty UNAVEM's presence on the ground, though numerically the same on paper, was gradually dwindling. As military contingents completed their tours of duty, there was increasing reluctance on the part of contributing countries to replace them until the future became clearer, the more so since threats and attacks against our personnel had become prevalent. There was also to be a change at the apex of the military structure: it had been agreed during Mig Goulding's visit that the Chief Military Observer, Major General Unimna, would relinquish his post and return to Nigeria in December. This was a relief all round, including, I suspect, to him himself. The matter had to be handled very delicately because Nigeria was an important African member state and a very sensitive one at that. The deal was that he would be succeeded by another Nigerian Major General and that, in the meantime, his command would be handed over to Brigadier Nyambuya. I had excellent relations with the latter, who was intelligent, competent and pleasant to work with, and enjoyed the liking and respect of the whole mission. Moreover, having been a guerrilla fighter himself, he could 'talk turkey' with both sides, particularly UNITA, about how the warring sides in Zimbabwe had buried the hatchet and set up a unified state and armed forces. I thought it a mistake to bring someone new in when the future of UNAVEM was itself in doubt, nor was I anxious, at this difficult stage, to have to incorporate an unknown personality into a team that had been riven by differences in the past. I asked Headquarters to delay the arrival of Unimna's replacement until it was clear whether there was going to be a ceasefire and an expanded UNAVEM or not. A main concern in Headquarters had been hierarchical: the CMO must be a Major General – but I managed to get over my view that experience, familiarity with the problem and compatibility were as important as rank.

Mike Nyambuya and I worked on together until we both left Angola in the middle of 1993. In January 1994 I met him in Harare: he had just had an accelerated promotion to Major General and was off to be Deputy Field Commander of the large UN military contingent in Somalia: I had first known him two years earlier as a Colonel!

* * *

Immediately after my departure the military and security situation appeared to calm down, but both sides were increasing their readiness to conduct further hostilities, belying their intermittent public declarations of willingness to negotiate. UNITA had withdrawn most of its forces from Uige and Negage, but was occupying scores of other municipalities, including two more provincial capitals, Caxito and N'dalatando. The Government continued to arm civilians and to send soldiers and police in civilian clothes to the main cities under threat. The situation was particularly tense in Malange, Benguela, Kuito/Bié, Huambo, Luena and Lubango. On 8 December the new Deputy Foreign Minister, Jorge Chicoty, said that the international community must 'begin to take clear positions and recognise UNITA as a terrorist organisation... UNITA can no longer be recognised by the international community as a normal political party'.

The increasing Government pressure for international condemnation of UNITA spilled over into attempts to cast UNAVEM's leadership in doubt: 'UNAVEM leadership could undergo changes in the coming days ... with the replacement of General Unimna as CMO.... Margaret Anstee could also eventually be replaced, according to the same sources, as a result of the present "erosion"' asserted the Government newspaper *Jornal de Angola.*

There were still some chinks of light. UNITA announced the names of those who were to fill posts allotted to it in the new Government, Parliament and armed forces. Interestingly, two of them were among the UNITA elements in Luanda under government 'protection': Victor Hossi, to be Minister of Culture and Dr Carlos Morgado, to be Vice-Minister of Social Assistance and integration. This announcement briefly boosted hopes for a peaceful, political solution, but they were swiftly dashed by the new Prime Minister's statement on 10 December that UNITA could take up its government positions only 'when the Peace Accords have been fulfilled'.

Another noteworthy happening was a press conference given on 9 December by Norberto de Castro, formerly the vituperative voice of UNITA on Radio Vorgan but now applying his accomplished viper tongue to lash out against the UNITA leadership. This was no great surprise, since de Castro had always been seen as an opportunist, but his statement was nonetheless a propaganda coup for the government.

The Government was maintaining its hard line on every possible occasion. At the swearing-in ceremony for officers of the FAA general staff, on 10 December, General João de Matos said that 'faced with the intransigence of the UNITA leadership, which wants to continue the war, there will be no alternative to general mobilisation of the population to defend the country'. Similarly uncompromising positions were being consistently taken up by other hardline members of the government, including Prime Minister Marcolino Moco, Foreign Minister de Moura and Vice Interior Minister 'Nando'.

In this new constellation, the stars of respected former Government moderates such as General N'dalu and Lopo de Nascimento seemed to be in complete eclipse.

* * *

In NewYork we were trying to sort through the rubble of the peace process and find some way of reconstructing it. The first and obvious step was to rekindle high-level political dialogue, but in the present stalemate – with each side accusing the other, probably with good reason, of not being interested in serious negotiation, and of using the relative calm then prevailing to prepare for worse hostilities – nothing less than some dramatic new initiative seemed likely to do the trick. All informed observers considered it highly unlikely that either side could win a war quickly or decisively, yet both sides seemed hell-bent in that direction. The grim prospect was for another long-drawn-out and bloody slogging match, which must at all costs be prevented.

On 12 December the Secretary-General telephoned President dos Santos and Dr Savimbi and asked them to meet together, under his auspices, in Geneva, in the last week of December. Savimbi accepted, while dos Santos said he was willing to meet Savimbi but only in Luanda. The Secretary-General urged President dos Santos to take into account the critical situation and the danger that, unless the two sides produced early evidence of their willingness and ability to work together to implement the Bicesse Accords, the international community would no longer feel justified in committing scarce resources to the UN operation in Angola on its present scale.

In a conversation with Hugo Anson in Luanda on 16 December, Victor Lima took a very hard line. The Government would react very strongly to any attempts to negotiate with the President and Dr Savimbi as if they were equal partners. UNITA had violated the Peace Accords and was behaving like 'a terrorist organisation'. In his view there was a real danger that the international community now saw the government as legitimate but weak and UNITA as increasingly illegitimate but strong, and that therefore a 'deal' would have to be worked out to satisfy UNITA's ambition for power. Such an approach was unprincipled and a delusion, because the Government had the means to fulfil its obligations and defend the Angolan people against UNITA. The Government had been led by the international community and the United Nations to take the path of multiparty democracy. It now looked urgently to the international community and the UN to assist it.

When Hugo pointed out that this would mean giving the UN a clearly defined, larger and more central role, as well as the necessary staff and resources, including 'Blue Helmets', to carry it out, Lima said he agreed. Nonetheless Hugo had the impression that the Government's main concern was to get a strong resolution from the Security Council condemning UNITA, recommending assistance to the Government and possibly imposing sanctions on UNITA, rather than a major strengthened role for UNAVEM. This impression was borne out in a press conference given that same day by Foreign Minister de Moura, in which he not only rejected the 'eleven points for establishment of peace' that had been presented by UNITA via the US Defence Department, but also insisted on the observance of the principle of non-interference in the internal affairs of Angola by foreign governments and organisations, and rejected any idea of the United Nations sending 'Blue Helmets' to Angola. This last statement was in complete contradiction of everything we had been discussing with both sides, and on which we had obtained agreement in principle, including from President dos Santos, and made a complete nonsense of any notion that a stronger UN role could provide the chance to make a new peace process stick. It was an all too familiar example of the Angolan Government wanting it both ways – a minimal UN presence, with maximum responsibility, thus making it a toothless but handy scapegoat (the Uige–Negage situation was a prime example). For their part the UN and UNAVEM were placed in a 'no win' situation.

* * *

The Secretary-General was becoming increasingly concerned at the lack of headway on his own proposal. On 18 December he addressed a long letter to the President of the Security Council, then Ambassador Gharekhan of India, saying he felt it incumbent on him to report the lack of progress and the generally worrying situation. In particular, he would 'value any support which the Council might wish to give to my efforts, perhaps in the form of an appeal to both leaders to accept my invitation to a joint meeting in Geneva or, if this were preferred, in another UN location such as Addis Ababa' (where the Secretary-General was himself due to go after Christmas).

On 22 December, on behalf of the Council the President made a statement that could only be described as anodyne, repeating all the old appeals, by now distinctly shopsoiled. The one innovative paragraph considered it essential that 'both parties agree without delay on security and other arrangements which would allow all ministers and other high-ranking officials to occupy the posts which have been offered by the Government and for all deputies to assume their functions in the National Assembly'. This was in response to a reference in the Secretary-General's letter to UNITA's security concern. He had gone on to say that, if certain conditions were fulfilled, he would be ready to 'seek the Council's authority to make some UN military personnel available, on a temporary basis, to facilitate the return to Luanda of Dr Savimbi, the UNITA members of the new Government and ... of the elected Assembly'. He had accordingly instructed me to 'try to engage the two sides in discussions of practical arrangements which would be acceptable to both of them and which I could recommend to the Council'. The Council's paragraph in response was so sibylline as to be not only meaningless but also distinctly less than helpful, with its inference that the two sides must work this key issue out alone.

The next paragraph contained a veiled but diplomatically worded threat that, if the two sides did not get their act together soon, the international community would not feel 'encouraged to continue to commit its scarce resources to the continuation of the UN operation in Angola on its present scale'. The last paragraph of all appealed to both President dos Santos and Dr Savimbi to accept the Secretary-General's invitation 'to attend, under his auspices, a joint meeting at an agreed location'.

Even allowing for diplomatic niceties this was hardly soul-stirring stuff. But I expect by then most people had their minds on Christmas with their families.

* * *

I too had nurtured hopes of spending Christmas with all that remained of my family, my much-loved aunt, Christina Mills, but others of my senior staff had prior claim. I did, however, have my promised few days in the tranquillity of Knill. On a brilliant December day, with the merest hint of snow glistening on the distant hills and the wayside trees and grasses laced with frost, I took Christina for her birthday lunch to a splendid pub just over the Welsh border. Ancient beams, a blazing log fire and the pre-Christmas conviviality of the other guests made Angola and the spectre of imminent war seem an unreal nightmare.

She wanted to know when I would leave Angola – a question to which I myself would have liked to have known the answer. From the word go I had said that I only wanted to be committed up to the date of the elections. Later there had been some question of my going on to Mozambique to head the operation there, and that did have some appeal, provided that the basic errors that had so seriously undermined the Angolan peace process were remedied. I was interested enough to provide Headquarters with specific suggestions of what these were and how to avoid repeating them in Mozambique. When Angola went wrong, however, I was honour bound to soldier on and try to get things back on track. During Mig Goulding's visit I had told him of my readiness to do this, but also of my wish that some term be set on the endeavour. He suggested that I stay on until the end of 1992, and that in the interim a suitable successor would be sought. When I met the Secretary-General in December, however, he said he wanted me to stay on for another year. I thanked him for his confidence and explained the personal and family reasons why it was not possible for me to accept such a long commitment. At the same time I assured him I would not leave him in the lurch but would stay on until someone had been found to replace me and, if possible, until I had got the peace process back on track, something about which I felt a strong moral and personal obligation. We agreed that 28 February should be the target date for my release.

* * *

Comforted by this assurance of relief in sight, and braced by a few wintry walks over the hills of the Welsh Marches, I landed in Luanda in the suffocating dawn of 21 December, fired with new energy.

That day our military people made their third wearying trip to Uige with UNITA, but once again the Government refused to go. A resident UNAVEM team had returned to Uige and was living in the Bishop's palace, our earlier camp having been destroyed. In these unlikely surroundings the UNAVEM and UNITA visitors met both them and our team from Negage. General Chilingutila said that General Dembo, now Vice-President of UNITA, would stay in Uige to ensure the full withdrawal of UNITA's troops from the two towns, while he himself would be telephoning General Higino Carneiro that evening with a strong recommendation that the Government should send representatives to Uige to monitor UNITA's withdrawal. This was all well and good, as far as it went, but we could not get much further without a change of attitude on the government's part. To that end I asked for an early appointment with Foreign Minister de Moura and this was granted the next day, 22 December. I explained that my purpose was to discuss my conversations in New York and request a meeting with President dos Santos, if possible the next day, so that I could see him before going to Huambo to talk to Dr Savimbi, which I wanted to do before Christmas.

The exchange that followed was one of the most disagreeable I was ever to have with the normally ebullient and affable Venâncio de Moura, and became downright acrimonious in parts. I suppose I set the tone by being extremely forthright in conveying the message that the Secretary-General would recommend an extension and enlargement of the UN mandate only if the peace process resumed and the two sides agreed on the specific tasks to be undertaken. I was under instructions to produce a realistic joint plan by the first week of January, and within the next two days I would present to both sides a compromise proposal based on the separate submissions I had received from them after Namibe. To discuss it, however, meant returning to the negotiating table. Uige and Negage were central to this, and I gave a copy of our report of the latest visit, expressing concern that yet again the Government had refused to take part. I insisted that unless Government representatives participated, no progress could be made.

Minister de Moura said he would inform the MPLA's political committee later that day about the Secretary-General's views and would ensure that I saw the President as soon as possible. Many members of the Government and the MPLA considered that UNITA should first withdraw from *all* its illegal positions, but as proof of its moderation the Government was insisting only on the vacating of Uige and Negage before restarting the stalled Namibe talks. The Government insisted, however, that there should be a clear statement by UNAVEM that UNITA had withdrawn all its forces. If it proved inaccurate then the Government would make that very clear to the international community and the media. To underline this barely concealed threat the Minister added, rather aggressively, that I should realise that the reputation of both the UN and myself, as its highest representative in Angola, were at stake. I had perforce to point out with some vigour that we could not perform miracles if the political will and good faith necessary to reach agreement did not exist. Moreover UNAVEM's mandate and resources permitted us only to verify what *both* parties *jointly* verified themselves. Minister de Moura retorted that UNAVEM's role should be one of *arbitration*. This preposterous and disingenuous piece of sophistry was obviously meant to goad but I replied, as coolly as I could, that such a role would indeed be desirable but was not possible since, as the Minister might recall, our role had been deliberately limited to mere verification under the Bicesse Accords at the Government's request, to satisfy its concern about infringements of sovereignty. We were already exceeding our mandate, especially in assuming the function of mediator, but there were practical as well as legal limits to what we could do. Arbitration was to be a key role in the *new* mandate under discussion, but even then we would need to have the right quantity and type of resources. His own public statement a few days earlier, that 'Blue Helmets' would not be acceptable, had thrown us into complete confusion. The Government could not have it both ways. If it wanted the UN to take a strong stand and larger responsibilities then it must allow it to be equipped to do so. We seemed to be back at the centre of a vicious circle, which could only be broken if the two sides returned to the negotiating table and came to agreement.

The Minister suddenly reverted to his normally courteous self, assuring me that the Government still wanted a pacific solution, and was willing to return to face-to-face negotiations if the Uige and Negage issue could be resolved. I had the impression of someone who had geared himself up to shoot a tough party line, agreed on in the heart of Government, but had then lapsed back into his own *persona*. But while I detected some flexibility in his own position about sending Government representatives to Uige, I sensed that other hardline elements in the Government were digging their toes in.

* * *

Mulling over this afterwards I concluded that there was one practical way in which the UN could break the deadlock. I found that Mike Nyambuya had been thinking along the same lines and so we jointly put the proposal to Mig Goulding. The idea went back to our earlier discussion of the need for a contingent of 'Blue Helmets' to address UNITA's security concerns. Mig had told me that a company of 'Blue Helmets' from Ghana was already being held in readiness, awaiting the two sides' agreement on new joint meetings, and could be available, *in situ*, at a week's notice. Mike and I now recommended that they be sent immediately, initially for a somewhat different purpose: to verify once and for all the withdrawal of UNITA troops from Uige and Negage. This would call the Government's bluff on two issues – the 'failure' of UNAVEM to give categorical assurances of UNITA's withdrawal and their own recent *volte-face* in saying publicly that 'Blue Helmets' were not necessary. It would test whether UNITA's intentions were genuine and might at the same time serve a secondary but useful purpose by providing security to enable UNITA's nominees for ministerial and vice-ministerial positions to take up their posts. I conceded that the proposal was unorthodox and involved some risks, but added our conviction that unless we took some drastic action we would not be able to extricate the process from the present morass.

Mig responded by return, on 22 December, that Headquarters could not put our proposal forward. It would have to convince the Security Council and the troop-contributing countries that there was a militarily and politically realistic task for the unit to perform, and that it was accepted by both sides. The Military Adviser considered that the tasks envisaged required the skills of military observers and that infantry would not be appropriate. (I was wryly amused that the judgement of a military adviser sitting in an office in New York all those thousands of miles away could be considered superior to that of my own experienced force commander on the ground.) Needless to say the reply depressed us. It was all very sensible and logical, but it missed the point: we wanted to have some new leverage to deal with Uige and Negage, which was the main stumbling block to a return to dialogue.

* * *

A more immediate snag was that my request for an urgent meeting with the President was getting nowhere. Venâncio de Moura suddenly became totally *incomunicado* and remained so until after Christmas. On 24 December I was informed by his secretary that we should 'go through protocol at Futungo'. This we proceeded to do, but as the Angolan administration folded up like a flower at sundown at noon on Christmas Eve, we did not get very far. I was receiving the message, loud and clear, that no one was particularly anxious to meet me. The same was not true of UNITA and, in embarrassing contrast, I was getting daily calls from Huambo, urging an early visit to Dr Savimbi. Unless a response come from Futungo soon it would be difficult to adhere to my plan to see the President first. Yet it made no sense to see Savimbi without having seen the President, and if I did the Government would, no doubt, perversely attack me for it.

The surmise that something was afoot was reinforced by a campaign in the Government media against any summit meeting outside Angola, laced with perceptibly xenophobic undertones. I asked for urgent advice as to whether the Secretary-General would contemplate holding the meeting somewhere on Angolan soil. The reply came that he would be delighted if the two leaders could agree to meet in Angola, but it was unlikely that he would be able to attend personally. 'Under his auspices' could be satisfied by my presence, as his Special Representative, plus a message from him and perhaps some UN troops to ensure security. If it proved impossible to agree on a meeting in Angola, the Secretary-General remained strongly in favour of a meeting in Geneva or Addis Ababa in the next two weeks, which he could himself attend. Mig spoke on these lines to Ambassador M'binda in New York on 23 December and got the usual reaction, but even more narrowly focussed: the meeting would have to be in Luanda and UNITA would first have to withdraw completely from Uige and Negage.

On Christmas Eve a new gloss was put on the possible location when John Flynn told me of a conversation he had had with Victor Lima. The latter had given him to understand that the Government might be ready to consider New York. The idea first put forward by Lima had been that the Government could be represented by Prime Minister Marcolino Moco. When the Ambassador had pointed out that this would not be acceptable, Lima had then suggested that the President might consider going to New York in the last third of January. It was inferred that his travel would be contingent upon his being able to combine the meeting with a visit to President Bush or President Clinton, depending on the exact date. This raised many other considerations, not least the fact that the United States had not yet recognised the Angolan government.

There were also some faintly encouraging signs on Uige and Negage. General Higino had talked from our radio room to General Dembo in Uige the previous day. They had agreed to speak again on 26 December. If – as all too rarely happened – things went according to plan, there appeared at last to be some prospect of a Government delegation visiting Uige a day or two later. We all had our fingers crossed.

* * *

Typically, while both sides were playing for time in one way or another, both were also urging that I give them, before Christmas, my compromise draft on the future role of UNAVEM. I prepared a draft immediately on my return and sent it for Headquarters' comments. It sought to remedy the deficiencies and limitations of the mandate of UNAVEM II by going beyond mere verification. Both the Government and UNITA had suggested it should cover mediation, supervision and arbitration, and I was a little dashed when Headquarters replaced 'arbitration' (the function that Minister de Moura had been so keen on) by the much fuzzier function of 'technical assistance'. In its modified draft form the paper said that both sides should formally accept 'United Nations mediation and supervision and technical assistance' in the completion by them of nine basic tasks:

1. Implementation of the ceasefire.
2. The assembly and demobilisation of both sides' troops.
3. Collection, storage and custody of weapons, including those in civilian hands.
4. Formation of the new, unified armed forces.
5. Formation and supervision of a neutral, unified police force.
6. Extension of the central administration to the entire country and assurance of the free circulation of people and goods.
7. Release and exchange of prisoners (principally supervised by the ICRC).

8. Security for UNITA leaders and installations.
9. Second round of presidential elections.

The role of the UN was not only to be much stronger but would also encompass areas previously outside its mandate, notably the formation of the new armed forces, extension of the central administration and security for UNITA leaders. On the last point the paper presented an array of options that could be applied, singly or in combination, including the provision by the UN of a specialist armed unit, if the Security Council agreed. Options were also presented for the UN's role in the second round of the presidential elections. UNITA wanted the UN to organise the whole operation, while the Government favoured a more limited role, but with a larger number of UN observers than in September 1992. I proposed three possibilities: observation and verification on the same lines as for the first round, but with a far larger number of observers, and with UNAVEM possibly becoming a full member of the National Electoral Council; supervision and control of the elections, as in Namibia; and full responsibility for the organisation and conduct of the elections, as in Cambodia. The last two options would involve amendments to the Electoral Law, as well as a large increase in resources. It was suggested that the Government should contribute financially to the electoral part of the mission.

The revised draft was sent to Minister de Moura and Dr Savimbi on Christmas Eve – I could only hope that they appreciated the timing of this unusual Christmas gift! I expressed the wish that it would be possible to arrange a tripartite meeting very soon to reach agreement, so that the Secretary-General could make his recommendations to the Security Council early in the NewYear, as required by the Council.

* * *

Luanda, always a-buzz with rumour, was full of foreboding as the season of supposed peace and goodwill approached. UNITA now occupied nearly two thirds of all the municipalities, the number having almost doubled in the month since Namibe. The most doom-laden presentiments centred on Christmas Day itself. December 25 being a special anniversary in the history of UNITA, some great offensive was anticipated, though exactly who was going to start it – the Government or UNITA – depended on whom you were talking to. In the event Christmas Day passed off uneventfully.

There were not many people in camp over Christmas. The contingents were all being run down by a process of attrition, until UNAVEM's future became clearer. Those still in the mission who could go on leave, had gone on leave. Of the senior staff besides myself, only Mike Nyambuya and Colonel Egar, the Chief Operations Officer, remained. On Christmas Eve a marvellous outdoor party was organised on the baseball court, with music and dancing until after midnight, though there was a lamentable shortage of female partners. On Christmas Day the cafeteria put on special Christmas fare and I organised a lunch in my house for some of my closest collaborators. We had managed to get a large frozen turkey from Windhoek, and Sissy presented it, sizzling hot, with all the trimmings, to the assembled company on the terrace, also sizzling hot in the mid-day tropical heat. Dessert presented more of a problem as I had only one small Christmas pudding, but Colonel Egar, as a good Chief Operations Officer should, carved it up meticulously in enough tiny pieces for everyone, and there were plenty of mince pies. We all enjoyed ourselves determinedly – conscious, though no one spoiled the fun by saying it, that things were likely to get worse rather than better.

On New Year's Eve there was another big party on the baseball court, but my most indelible memory of that evening is of an earlier hour spent sitting on the sand on the Ilha, watching the sun sink into the ocean and then, as the shadows deepened, a night heron fishing in the wavelets lapping the shore.

* * *

Real life had begun again in earnest immediately after Christmas, though there were some bright spots. There was some tenuous progress on Uige and Negage: on 27 December we managed to take two FAA officers to Uige and became hopeful that the Government would immediately send much-needed supplies of food and medicine there, to be followed by Government administrators. On the gloomier side, UNITA was alleging government attacks on N'dalatando and Caxito. Our aim was to try to get the restoration of Government administration in all these places by negotiation rather than force of arms, and that meant getting back to the negotiating table.

The OAU delegation, earlier postponed at the Government's request, visited on 27–28 December, headed by President Robert Mugabe of Zimbabwe, and further comprising President Antonio Mascarenhas Monteiro of Cape Verde and OAU Secretary-General Salim Salim. Mike Nyambuya and I briefed them. They met President dos Santos but were unable to see Dr Savimbi. He would not come to Luanda, nor would he accept another venue in southern Africa, since UNITA had reservations about the affiliations of the Front Line States. The Government raised no objection to their going to Huambo, but it had been agreed at the recent meeting of Front Line States that the delegation should not see the UNITA President. Thus there was a total impasse. We did not get the impression that any spectacular initiatives were likely to emerge from this mission.

My efforts to see President dos Santos were not making headway. New Year's Eve arrived, but despite repeated telephone calls and two official notes there was still no word. Even the normally accessible Venâncio de Moura was proving elusive, to the extent that a promise to telephone, extracted by a messenger who waylaid him en route to a New Year's Day reception at Futungo, had not been honoured. Ed De Jarnette told me he was having the same difficulty in contacting anyone in the Government. According to our Portuguese colleagues, this was due to Christmas and New Year inertia, but even allowing for yuletide jollities we felt the silence was ominous. It was possible that the Government did not wish to see me on account of the Secretary-General's recent letter and the Security Council statement, but we were beginning to fear that the real reason was that it wanted to strengthen its position before returning to the negotiating table, through what they hoped (almost certainly vainly) would be 'limited' military action. On 30 and 31 December the air force undertook strafing attacks on N'dalatando, and two UNAVEM helicopters, due to fly to Negage to count UNITA troops in the assembly areas of Bungo and Quipedro, were refused permission to fly; UNITA, as a *quid pro quo*, subsequently refused to allow those troops to be counted. And then General Higino inexplicably failed to turn up at Vila Espa on 30 December for the scheduled radio contact with General Dembo; he did come the next day, but then General Dembo was 'unavailable'. All these were straws in a wind that bode no good. Each side was 'upping the ante' in a lethally childish game of tit-for-tat.

* * *

If the Luanda media were anything to go by – and they were often the channel for revealing the Government's innermost feelings – the UN was still in very bad odour, blamed for everything that had gone wrong.

Sometimes, the comments were directed at me personally but were often so bizarre as to lose all credibility, and interesting only in that they were usually related in some way to my gender. In the last *Jornal de Angola* of 1992 my photograph appeared in the list of Top Ten Personalities of the Year. Nice, you would think, until you read the caption carefully. In the midst of some generally complimentary remarks of the role I had played lurked a little bracket: 'although it was rumoured that she was the mistress of Salupeto Pena.' Concurrently a *canard* was spreading rapidly through Luanda about my recent visit to New York. The purpose was not, it was alleged, to brief the Security Council and the Secretary-General, but to have an abortion, the progenitor of the baby, it was whispered, being none other than Dr Savimbi. It was difficult to know whether to attribute this absurd slander to lack of knowledge of biological realities, or to feel flattered that one was still considered young enough. Elizabeth, my wonderful Filipino secretary, rolled her eyes in mock admiration and said: 'Miss Anstee, we are all wondering, how *do* you find the time for so many things?'

* * *

Meanwhile 'George' was calling incessantly from Huambo. Dr Savimbi was extremely anxious to see me and considerably put out by the repeated postponements. I could not wait about for the Government any longer. I arranged to go to Huambo on Saturday 2 January1993, and wrote another Note to Minister de Moura to inform him.

Unlike previous encounters this one went off like clockwork – no delays or waiting around for last-minute news of where to go. This time we were bidden to drive straight from the airport to the White House, which was barricaded like a fortress, with the road outside blocked off and armed guards everywhere. The meeting did run true to form in that it lasted two hours and wandered all over the place. But basically it revolved around three subjects: my visit to NewYork; the present situation and ways out of the impasse; and UNAVEM's future mandate.

At every turn I emphasised that it was UNITA's actions since the elections that had precipitated the crisis and therefore its responsibility to take the lead in resolving it. In response, Dr Savimbi reiterated his commitment to a negotiated solution and, with his customary unrivalled showmanship, described how he had finally managed to win over his hardline followers to that view at a meeting held in Huambo some 10 days previously. He complained that the present upsurge of fighting in Lucala, Caxito and N'dalatando (which he attributed to the Government) did not help him in maintaining his position with his hardliners, or in getting UNITA troops to complete the withdrawal from Uige and Negage. Again I pointed out that all the provincial capitals mentioned should be in the hands of the democratically elected government and that it was UNITA that had started the aggression. Undeterred, Savimbi went on to criticise the President's New Year message as 'warlike' (a favourite epithet for each of them in describing the other's oratory). I said that UNITA had to understand that the Uige–Negage incident, coming so quickly after the Namibe meeting, had created far wider problems, reinforcing those voices on the Government side that claimed that UNITA never kept its word and could not be trusted; and discrediting the moderates who favoured negotiation. The Government was now itself adopting what it had deduced UNITA's strategy to be: showing military strength to secure better bargaining power. Brigadier Nyambuya argued that military action would not get either side anywhere; sooner or later they would have to return to negotiations and meanwhile the suffering of the Angolan people would worsen. Savimbi concurred with this judgement.

The obvious conclusions were drawn: the fighting must be stopped immediately, before it got out of hand; Namibe II, and a summit between the two leaders must take place urgently; and UNAVEM's future mandate must be decided. Dr Savimbi reiterated that he was ready to go anywhere in the world for the summit meeting proposed by the Secretary-General, except Luanda. As for stopping the fighting, the most promising point to come out of the meeting was a proposal (news to us), apparently made a few days previously by General Matos, that he was ready to travel to Huambo, and to allow three or more of the UNITA hierarchy 'under protective custody' in Luanda to do so also. General Chilingutila quoted him as saying 'The politicians will take a long time to sort things out, so we military men had better get together'. I encouraged Savimbi to pursue this possibility with vigour and urgency and promised to urge early action by the Government.

Savimbi also said that the UNITA generals were ready to go back to the FAA, but 'were afraid because their colleagues are in protective custody'. The same was true of the UNITA ministerial appointees and the 70 UNITA MPs. I reiterated our offer of limited security arrangements, expressing the hope that at least the question of the FAA generals might be settled if General Matos' visit materialised. I also urged Savimbi to make a clear public statement of UNITA's firm intention to relinquish control of all the municipalities it occupied as soon as possible, and he appeared to agree. We did not get very far on UNAVEM's mandate because UNITA, with an inefficiency so uncharacteristic as to give pause for thought, had failed to distribute the document I had faxed on Christmas Eve.

I had seldom seen Dr Savimbi and his colleagues in a more amenable mood, or so anxious to cooperate, which again caused me to speculate about the underlying motives. In addition to encouraging General Matos' proposed visit to Huambo; they agreed that a joint commission should be set up in Uige; that UNITA would facilitate troop counts in Bungo and Quipedro; and that there should be a return to Namibe in the very near future.

Even so I cannot say I felt very optimistic on the flight back to Luanda that all of this would happen soon. It was possible that UNITA might, tardily, have seen the light, as well as the error of its ways. But it was all too clear (presumably to UNITA, as well as to me) that the initiative at that moment was with the Government, and that the Government had the bit very firmly between its teeth. I could only hope I would be able to see the President early the next week.

* * *

When we got back to the camp, the tropical dusk was gathering and the baobab tree stood sentinel against the fading crimson glory of the sunset. We repaired to my house to brief our senior military colleagues, but had hardly settled ourselves when a messenger came with the news that General Higino was in the camp, in radio communication with UNITA in Uige, and wanted to see me urgently.

Mike Nyambuya and I received him together. First there were some exchanges about the situation in Uige, where the Government had now sent some 200 troops to support the two FAA officers, as well as some civilian administrators. Then General Higino said that Venâncio de Moura wanted to see me – and me alone – as soon as possible. Without more ado he bore me off, still in my dusty and travel-stained field gear, to the Minister's elegant residence.

There I was greeted with fulsome apologies by the host for his inability to respond to my various messages. The President had been greatly put out, and annoyed with his colleagues, when he found out that I had been kept waiting for an audience, but had thought it better not to have a hurried encounter over the holiday period. I was promised that it would almost certainly take place on Monday 4 January. The Minister repeated several times that the Government did not want anyone to think that there had been any reticence in seeing me. I replied, a little coolly, that, this having indeed been the impression at UN Headquarters, I was doubly glad to have these assurances. Perhaps to reinforce the latter, as well as to celebrate the New Year, the Minister plied me with champagne (French, and pink to boot) and together with General Higino, the only other person present, we drank to peace for Angola. The atmosphere could not have been more different from that of our last acrimonious encounter.

They were both palpably anxious to hear about the meeting with Dr Savimbi. I gave them a brief rundown, but omitted any reference to General Matos' proposed visit to Huambo, since I was not sure how far he might have consulted others and I did not want to upset the applecart. They made no mention of any such idea.

I received categorical assurances from both gentlemen that it was the Government's firm intention to proceed to Namibe II, just as soon as the UNITA troops had been verified as having returned from Uige and Negage to their assembly areas in Bungo and Quipedro, and had been counted there. I said I was relieved to hear this as I had been concerned by recent high-level statements indicating that the Government was increasing its conditions, by insisting that UNITA must leave *all* occupied municipalities before the talks could recommence. Venâncio de Moura said this was not the case; the Government merely wished to go back to the situation prevailing before 29 November. I was careful to establish that he did mean 29 November, and not 29 *September*. The Minister said the Government wanted Namibe II to take place as soon as possible and even inferred that it might be during the coming week. (I reflected, but silently, that no doubt UNAVEM would be given the usual last-minute notice to perform herculean logistical miracles, if and when it did happen!) General Higino said, mysteriously, that a date had been chosen but 'was locked in his heart'. I replied that I did not want to pry into state secrets; my concern was that it must be very soon, otherwise the situation would deteriorate beyond repair. (According to Ed De Jarnette, he had been told some days before that the date would be 8 or

10 January; his supposition was that it was predicated on the prior attack on N'dalatando.)

We also spoke of the Secretary-General's invitation. The Minister was adamant that a summit meeting could not take place outside Angola. When I tested the waters about a possible encounter in New York in late January, as mooted by Victor Lima to the British Ambassador, he summarily dismissed any such notion, but I did not detect the same insistence as previously on Luanda. I also mentioned the Secretary-General's willingness to try to arrange the presence of some UN troops for security, of which the Minister took note with interest (despite his declared public aversion to 'Blue Helmets'). He emphasised the Government's view that the Secretary-General's long-promised visit to Angola was essential to ensure the success of the meeting. I was non-committal, merely voicing a warning about his overloaded schedule.

As I thought over the events of the day, it seemed not unreasonable to conclude that the Minister's sudden enthusiasm to see me had been triggered off by my visit to Dr Savimbi. But this new glimmer of light was still a very flickering one and I was not sure to what degree Minister de Moura and General Higino represented the mainstream of Government thinking. Both had told me, ruefully, that they had had to endure a barrage of criticism from their peers after the débâcle following the Namibe meeting, at which they had been among the principal negotiators. All in all, however, the outlook on this second day of 1993 offered a little more hope than gloom.

* * *

Early next morning (Sunday 3 January) I decided to consult General N'dalu, whose views and judgement I had sorely missed since his abrupt departure from the scene, and who had returned from abroad a couple of days previously. (When I enquired of my companions of the previous evening what his role was likely to be, I was told rather enigmatically 'There will always be a role here for General N'dalu. He is one of those lucky people who can always choose what they want to do'.)

General N'dalu sounded in fine fettle on the phone but we did not get very far with the items I had sought to discuss. Something very strange had happened, he said. He had received a call from Lubango that morning at about 9 o'clock when the caller (I think it was his brother) suddenly said that heavy firing had just broken out nearby and the call was interrupted. N'dalu feared something serious was going on.

I felt dazed and appalled. I called Mike Nyambuya to get an immediate report and I tried to call Minister de Moura but he was out. Soon the awful news began to trickle in from the radio room. Without warning, Government forces had attacked UNITA areas in Lubango, including UNITA's command headquarters. Fierce fighting continued throughout the day.

It was not until evening that I was at last able to locate Minister de Moura. Wherever he had been all day, he had clearly not had his ear to the ground, or else he put on a very convincing act. When I told him the news he professed to know nothing and emitted a long wail of dismay, which was only a fraction of the despair I was feeling. It did, however, occur to me to wonder silently about a government system that could allow its Foreign Minister go in ignorance for 12 hours of an incident that was bound to have serious international repercussions and news of which was already reverberating around the world's airwaves.

The next day, in retaliation, UNITA took captive the two FAA officers and the 200 FAA troops whom the Government, at our urgent behest, had sent to Uige. We were back to square one with a vengeance.

Part VII
Conflagration and Mediation

20 ...And Let Slip the Dogs of War

The Government attack on UNITA in Lubango came like a bolt from the blue. We had all feared some kind of Government offensive, but not in Lubango, of all places. Lubango was the one provincial capital in which the joint commission was working best. The UNITA and Government counterparts treated one another almost as friends and frequent meetings of the local Joint Military Verification Team (CMVF) were held in the UNAVEM compound.

True to form, each side blamed the other. Colonel Jamwal, our regional commander, reported clear indications that this was a planned offensive by the Government to flush out UNITA strongholds in Lubango. It seemed all too likely that it was also the beginning of the expected Government riposte to curb the spread of UNITA's tentacles across the country. By 3 January UNITA had occupied 104 of the 164 municipalities.

The first radio message from our team reached us at 10.59 a.m. that Sunday morning, reporting that heavy firing had broken out at 9.00 a.m. and that Colonel Jamwal was trying to restore the situation by contacting the military commanders of both sides. Meanwhile the chief of the FALA component of the CMVF, with two of his colleagues, took refuge in the UNAVEM complex. The Hotel Imperio, where UNITA had its command headquarters, was under attack, including by a tank and an armoured vehicle. A UNAVEM vehicle patrol flying large UN flags was sent to try to stop the fighting, but was forcibly stopped by Government police. At 11.00 a.m. intense shooting by Government forces was still continuing, and MIG aircraft were seen flying over Lubango and known UNITA areas.

Silence followed. At 1.00 p.m. the UNAVEM radio in Lubango failed to answer our routine call. The reason became clear when, to our enormous relief, a second message came through at 4.33 p.m. At 12.30 a shot had been deliberately aimed at the UNAVEM duty room in Lubango. The bullet had pierced the wall and hit the telefax machine. No one had been hurt but several UN military observers had had a miraculous escape. At 1.00 p.m. armed Government police had entered the UNAVEM complex and forcibly captured the three UNITA men, who were legitimate members of the joint monitoring mechanism, the CMVF. They had killed one of them on the spot, before the horrified eyes of the Regional Commander and despite his vehement protests. The only concession that had been made as a result of UNAVEM's intervention was that the other two would not be killed. They had been led away to an unknown destination and an even more uncertain fate. They were never heard of again. A week or two later when I visited Lubango, Colonel Jamwal gave me a chillingly vivid account of this scene. As the two men were being taken away, one of them, whom he had known well from daily contact, had called out desperately to him to save him. He had known there was nothing more he could do and was now haunted by this terrible memory.

At 3.00 p.m. armed Government policemen had come again, claiming that more UNITA people were hiding in the camp, but they had found none. They had taken the dead body away and prevented UNAVEM patrols from leaving the complex to verify what was happening in the city, where explosions and firing were continuing. Later still, the police again visited the UNAVEM camp and informed Colonel Jamwal that the Government had decided 'once and for all to finish off UNITA in the area in order to ensure a lasting peace'. Fighting continued sporadically throughout the night. At 8.30 the next morning UNAVEM was able to patrol the city without hindrance. A large number of UNITA houses, as well as the Hotel Imperio and surrounding buildings had been damaged, some totally destroyed and looted. The number of casualties was not known but the patrols saw many dead lying on the streets of this normally tranquil city, better known for the scent of its thousands of flowering trees than for the stench of death.

Snug in the hollow of its surrounding hills, basking in a temperate, balmy climate that was the nearest Angola knew to eternal spring, it had seemed a haven of peace. But now the war was reaching places that had remained virtually untouched during the earlier long years of strife.

In Luanda on Monday 4 January news reached us from Uige that UNITA's commander there, Brigadier General Apollo, had seized the two FAA officers, General Nzele and Colonel Domingos. They were being held in his house and would only be released when UNITA personnel in Lubango were released. Our UNAVEM people on the spot sought to resolve the issue with Brigadier Apollo but he was 'not available for comment'.

In my telephone conversation the previous evening with Minister de Moura I had protested vigorously about the shocking happenings in the UNAVEM camp in Lubango, and Brigadier Nyambuya had done the same to the FAA Chief of General Staff, General João de Matos, and General Higino Carneiro when they had turned up unannounced on Sunday evening. They had not, however, come to discuss Lubango, which appeared to figure very low on their agenda, but to ask UNAVEM to facilitate a meeting between General de Matos and General Chilingutila of UNITA, in either Benguela, Lubango or Namibe, to discuss a cessation of hostilities. This was obviously the same initiative about which Dr Savimbi had informed me, with the difference that General de Matos was not prepared to go to Huambo. But the whole situation and climate for negotiation had been changed totally by the events in Lubango. It seemed incredible that these two senior military leaders could believe that this initiative was still on; and to include among the potential meeting places Lubango, where UNITA dead lay strewn in the streets, was positively surreal.

On Monday I forwarded two draft notes of protest to New York for review by the legal counsel – one to the Government about Lubango, the other to UNITA about an incident in N'dalatando. I added that I would also take up the Lubango incident in strong terms with President dos Santos, with whom I now had a confirmed audience the following day. The Security Council must be seized of the latest developments at its meeting on Monday afternoon, so I also cabled suggestions for a statement on Angola.

To add to all the bitter ironies of these days, on 5 January I received from the Foreign Ministry the text of the message the Minister and General Higino had sent to Dr Valentim in Huambo on New Year's Eve. Its opening words and general message beggared credulity in the light of what had happened three days later. 'We sincerely reciprocate your season's greetings', it began, and went on to reiterate the Government's well-known prerequisites for the resumption of dialogue and its 'longing for peace'. The message ended 'We reiterate our best wishes for a Happy New Year', a valedictory phrase that, in retrospect, sounded distinctly sarcastic.

On 5 January I had my long-awaited meeting with President dos Santos. The President was accompanied by Minister de Moura and Victor Lima, and I by Brigadier Nyambuya. We too exchanged, rather sombrely, the compliments of the season. Although it was water under the bridge now, I summarised my conversation in New York, and the main points of my meeting three days before with Dr Savimbi. I deplored the events of the last few days in Lubango, and now the retaliation in Uige and Negage, which made it even more difficult to restore peace, but stressed that our objective remained the same – to bring about a rapid cessation of hostilities, to return to the negotiating table and to obtain speedy agreement for an extended and expanded UNAVEM mandate. I suggested three stages: at the military level, the proposed meeting between the Chief of General Staff, General de Matos, and General Chilingutila of UNITA to stop the fighting; a return to Namibe to continue discussions at the political level; and, ultimately, a summit between the President and Dr Savimbi.

The President painted a grim picture in reply: the country was already at war. He accepted that no one could win, but added that it was much easier to start a war than to stop it. Peace negotiations took an inordinate amount of time: he had tried to initiate peace negotiations in 1982, but in the end it had taken two years, from 1989 to 1991, to bring about the Bicesse Accords. He was not ready to predict how long it would take this time but we were in for a very long haul. Events since have proved him all too right. He also referred to the recent new outbreaks of violence in the country, including in Lubango, the responsibility for which he placed squarely at UNITA's door: it had deliberately provoked the Government forces as part of a predetermined plan to take over the town. The President himself took the initiative to apologise profusely for the incursion of the police into the UNAVEM camp, which he described as a grave error and totally unacceptable – as an Angolan, he was deeply embarrassed that people from other countries who came to help should be treated in this way. He went on to express outrage at UNITA's action in seizing their delegation in Uige, at which point I observed that this was an example of the negative effects of retaliation and counterretaliation.

As for ways out of the situation, the President listed three conditions: UNITA's withdrawal from Uige and Negage; the reinstatement there of government administration; and resumption of the talks at Namibe II. A message had just been sent to Huambo by Minister de Moura reiterating the Government's willingness to return to the Namibe negotiations, on those terms, and General Higino was trying to speak by radio to General Dembo of UNITA in Uige to get them to release the FAA personnel. The President was none too confident that a meeting could be arranged between General de Matos and General Chilingutila, citing the high degree of mistrust between the military people. He believed it would be easier to bring the two sides together at the political level.

In the course of this exchange I said that the President's statesmanlike stance and tolerance over several months of great provocation had been widely admired. Now was the time to exercise those qualities of restraint even more; it would be a tragedy if the sympathy engendered among the international community became dissipated by what might be perceived as precipitate action on the Government's part. The President took this point, but added that he was under tremendous pressure from the people to demonstrate that the Government was in control and exercising its legal authority.

The President then turned to UNAVEM's future mandate, saying he realised the situation was very difficult, since it was necessary to reactivate the Namibe talks before a recommendation could be made. We discussed the subject of 'Blue Helmets', and Brigadier Nyambuya and I tried to dispel the reticence felt about them in certain quarters (not least by the Foreign Minister!). We stressed that, if they came, they would be used only for very specific and limited functions that could not be adequately carried out without armed troops (such as the collection, storage and custody of weapons, and the security of UNITA personnel), and that this would most certainly not be a Somalia-type operation, nor would there be any interference in sovereignty (in the first place, because they would be requested by a sovereign country). The President confirmed that reservations existed, though he acknowledged that, in the meeting with Mig Goulding and myself in November, he had spoken of such troops being used for specific tasks and said he would give careful thought to what we had said.

At the end I reverted to the question of a summit meeting. The President said he fully understood the good intentions of the Secretary-General, but added, somewhat chillingly, that he did not consider this an opportune moment to meet Dr Savimbi anywhere, under any circumstances. Savimbi was a rebel, and after the latest events in Uige and Negage, he, as legal President, could not submit himself to such an encounter; nor could he do so as an individual and live with his conscience thereafter. After further discussion the President conceded that he still subscribed to a process of negotiation that might eventually culminate in a meeting between the two, but he left us in no doubt that this would take a long time and that a very great deal would have to be accomplished before he would agree.

* * *

I could see no way forward except to try to prevail upon Dr Savimbi to release the FAA personnel in Uige. Various attempts to reach him only produced vague promises that he would speak to me 'within a few hours', and it was not until 9.00 p.m. on 6 January that he eventually called me. In the interim our radio room was inundated with messages about new outbreaks of fighting: in Lobito, Benguela, Kuito/Bié, Ondjiva, Cuito Cuanavale and elsewhere. Telephone contact between the Government and General Chilingutila had so far not proved possible, nor between General Higino Carneiro and General Dembo in Uige. General Higino had, however, spoken on our radio to Brigadier Apollo in Uige that morning, and afterwards Higino had told Mike Nyambuya that he had threatened to kill two of the UNITA generals held in Government custody in Luanda if the FAA general and colonel taken captive by UNITA in Uige proved to be dead.

I waded straight in when the UNITA leader called, rehearsing what had happened in the four days since we had met in Huambo. Only some dramatic gesture, I said, could save Angola and I appealed to Dr Savimbi, as a patriot and statesman, to make that gesture. I suggested that it was incumbent on him to do so since, as he himself had recognised in previous conversations with me, all the problems since the Namibe meeting had been started by the UNITA takeover of Uige and Negage. Moreover President dos Santos had assured me that, if things could be sorted out in these two places, the Government was ready to return to Namibe. Accordingly I urged him to release the FAA hostages forthwith.

Savimbi went on again about his difficulties with his hardliners: he had had to exert much pressure to get his commanders to leave Uige and Negage, the taking of which he again acknowledged to have been a cardinal error on UNITA's part. When he had finally persuaded them, the Government had dragged its feet about returning and had then attacked N'dalatando and Caxito. Now UNITA personnel were being driven out of Cunene, Namibe and Lubango and the Government radio was constantly emitting declarations of 'victory'. In the face of all these provocations UNITA had lost control over its commanders, and their soldiers were even less inclined to negotiation. He personally was still fully committed to peaceful negotiation, but 'I am now alone'. He added 'I do not believe anything that the President says' (exactly what the President had said of him) and foresaw that the next attack would be on Huambo. A leader of an opposition party had called him that day to say 'Be careful, they want to kill you'. He concluded 'Uige and Negage are over. There is no word I could tell my soldiers which they would believe'.

I replied that it was absolutely imperative that something should be done. If we could not resolve Uige and Negage, then we could not get back to Namibe. The sole remaining alternative was to arrange, on a most urgent basis, the proposed meeting between General de Matos and General Chilingutila in order to produce a ceasefire and an end to the bloodshed, so that we could then proceed to political negotiations. Savimbi said he agreed, but General Chilingutila was so cast down by recent events that he was no longer ready to meet at all. Later he modified this remark, saying that Chilingutila *was* still ready to meet but not in Lubango. I pointed out that two other places had been suggested: Namibe and Benguela. Savimbi immediately excluded Namibe, rather surprisingly preferring Benguela, 'if a ceasefire can be arranged' (but next morning's news reported that UNITA had been driven out of that city altogether) or Sumbe.

At the close of our conversation I warned Dr Savimbi that if the relentless slide into war continued unabated, then we would have to consider withdrawing UNAVEM teams from a number of places, both because they could no longer perform their mandate and on account of fears for their safety. Savimbi launched into an impassioned appeal against UNAVEM's withdrawal. This included an emotional passage in which, 'speaking as an African', he implored me to consider myself as a 'mother' who should not abandon her children or become frustrated with them, 'even when they break plates' (a somewhat odd analogy for hundreds, or perhaps thousands of deaths). He urged me to carry on my efforts and to find a place where, within 24 or 48 hours, the military leaders could meet.

That same night Mike Nyambuya and I made parallel efforts, through military and political channels respectively, to get Government agreement on the meeting and on a suitable venue. Next morning he got General de Matos to agree to meet General Chilingutila, either that day or the following, in Sumbe. I conveyed this message to Huambo and was promised a reply by 1.00 p.m. In the meantime we got on with contingency planning to provide the necessary support arrangements, including strengthening our presence in Sumbe.

The next hours were fraught with frustration. We worked non-stop for the rest of the afternoon and night to try to bring about the meeting in Sumbe. There was much to-ing and fro-ing with the various military and political dignitaries involved, bedevilled by the usual Angolan phenomena of satellites struck by lightening or phones not working in Huambo and a different variety of crossed wires on the Government side. We had anticipated agreement on Sumbe, because that was one of the places suggested by Dr Savimbi. But then General Chilingutila sent a message indicating that, while open to other suggestions, UNITA really preferred Huambo since General de Matos had suggested it in the first place. To this General Higino replied that this was indeed the case, but in a different context, and now they proposed Sumbe. Very late on 7 January,

Colonel Mortlock informed us that Sumbe was not acceptable and that General Chilingutila was considering other venues. The next morning Mike Nyambuya and I studied the map of Angola and came up with the idea of Menongue: one of the few places left where conflagration was neither actual nor obviously imminent. We put this new idea to both sides and urged that the meeting should take place there the following day.

It was somehow typical of the bizarre square dance of communications in which we were enmeshed that it was Marcos Samondo who, late on 8 January, rang me from New York with a message from 'George' in Huambo, to the effect that UNITA agreed that the meeting place should be Menongue, on condition that they received assurances that neither Huambo nor Menongue would be attacked during the meeting. I made the obvious point that UNAVEM would need to have the same assurances (but then no one ever seemed to worry about the safety of *our* personnel!) But I still had no answer about the Menongue proposal from the Government side, who remained closeted with the President at Futungo de Belas.

To Headquarters I expressed my concern that the Security Council did not seem to have discussed Angola during the course of that week (it was now Friday), as well as my hope that they would do so before the weekend and urge both parties, in no uncertain terms, to ensure that their respective military leaders met, under UNAVEM auspices, within the next 24 hours. As a result the Secretary-General sent a letter to the President of the Security Council that same day, 8 January. In it he painted a dark picture of the severe deterioration of the situation in the one short week since the beginning of the year. There had been outbreaks of fighting in 10 of the 18 provincial capitals, as well as in other centres of population; with each side accusing the other of starting the hostilities. UNITA premises had been destroyed, and its personnel captured or killed in many places. The Government had been unable to reestablish its administration in many rural areas and two thirds of the municipalities in Angola remained in UNITA hands. UNAVEM personnel had been exposed to great danger and in one case had had to spend three days consecutively in slit trenches. It had been necessary to evacuate UNAVEM teams from two capitals. The letter went on to describe my efforts to restore the ceasefire and relaunch the political dialogue begun at Namibe, and informed the Council that I had secured an agreement for Generals de Matos and Chilingutila to meet, but not yet on the meeting place, Menongue being my latest proposal. In these 'grave circumstances', said the Secretary-General, he believed it would be useful if the Security Council could endorse the efforts of his Special Representative and make a strong appeal to the two sides to agree to a meeting in Menongue at the earliest possibly opportunity.

Mig told me that the letter reached the Council when the agenda was already overloaded with Iraqi and Yugoslav items. The President had therefore simply made an unscripted statement to the media on the lines of the Secretary-General's letter. It sank without trace. Angola was slipping farther and farther down the long international agenda and everyone was becoming out of patience with the antics of the two sides.

* * *

The Secretary-General's concern over the safety of our staff was by no means exaggerated. Unarmed and scattered in minuscule units in 68 different places, they could hardly be more vulnerable. Parallel with our attempts to get the two sides to talk again, we were having to draw up more elaborate plans for their security and possible evacuation. As a first step, until the situation became clear I stopped the return of all civilian staff who were out of the country on leave. We had a small, closely knit team in Luanda, which worked on the upgraded security and evacuation programme. Orders had earlier been sent out to all stations to dig slit trenches and some were now in use. They were also being excavated in Vila Espa, reminding me of wartime schooldays. Rumours of an impending all-out attack on the capital were once more gaining credence with the upsurge of bellicose activity around Caxito and N'dalatando.

The Chief of Staff, now Colonel Ross, masterminded the contingency plans. The basic principle was that everyone had to stick to their posts for as long as humanly possible. UNAVEM could not be seen to be quitting when the going got tough: its credibility would suffer even further if we did not stick to our (non-existent!) guns. At the same time we were responsible for the safety of our personnel, and the death or serious injury of any of them would create an adverse reaction internationally, and particularly in the countries on whom we relied to provide troops. Several Ambassadors from those countries had been making increasingly worried representations since October. The Brazilian Ambassador had been particularly vociferous about the need to do more to protect the Brazilian troops, while at the same time criticising us for not being tougher on UNITA, apparently blissfully unaware of the inherent contradiction in what he was saying. UN Headquarters was also receiving similar démarches and had asked me to take all possible safeguards, and to err on the side of safety.

After the outbreak of fighting on 31 October, all non-essential international personnel of the UNDP and other agencies had been evacuated by UNAVEM. On 8 January there were only two international UN-system staff members other than UNAVEM outside Luanda and 60 in the capital itself. In contrast UNAVEM still had 295 staff in locations all over the country, mainly in troop assembly areas and critical points in remote border regions. Most of them were living in exposed and defenceless Weatherhaven sites, and many had already been caught in cross fire or other decidedly disagreeable situations. Nonetheless we had so far evacuated only two teams: one from N'dalatando and the other from Kuito/Bié.

Wherever possible we also tried to take care of non-governmental organisations (NGOs) and other foreign nationals stranded by the fighting. We had rescued Portuguese from Caxito and Uige, as well as Brazilians and Russians from Capanda, among other examples, and there were heart-warming stories of individual acts of bravery. One of the most striking was carried out by a young officer in the Egyptian contingent, Captain Essam, in Kuito Bié. He had already received a shrapnel wound when the team was ordered to evacuate that town. Nonetheless when safely en route to the airport, he turned back into the fighting and, under direct fire, which penetrated the windscreen of his vehicle, rescued two representatives of Médecins Sans Frontières (MSF). The Regional Commander, Colonel Mortlock, sent me a full report, which I recommended that Headquarters should use in a noon press briefing as an antidote to all the negative news about the UN. I also sent an official commendatory note to the Egyptian Ambassador for transmission to his government. To my knowledge the story was never used by UN headquarters, nor did Captain Essam receive official commendation from anyone higher than myself.

We came up with a four-phase plan. The first phase envisaged immediate withdrawal of our personnel from two types of area: those where UNAVEM had no further role (for example critical points or troop assembly areas where there were no soldiers left, either because of demobilisation or because they had gone back to fight); and those where the excessive danger to UNAVEM personnel outweighed the effective contribution they could make to peace (the case of N'dalatando and Kuito/Bié). Measures were taken to reduce moveable equipment to a bare minimum and, where possible, to dismantle and remove the Weatherhavens.

The second phase embraced stations whose area of operations could be covered by other stations, or whose ability to influence the current situation had diminished. These would be closed gradually as UNAVEM's overall personnel strength declined. Phase three included stations that still had the potential of positively influencing the conflict and must remain manned as long as possible. Stations that were absolutely essential, such as all Regional Command headquarters, fell into the fourth and final phase and would be closed only as a last resort. The plan included elaborate arrangements to withdraw and save the maximum amount of equipment as well as people. We felt that we had on hand a rational, logical strategy that would allow us to react calmly and in an orderly fashion to events as they developed.

Alas, the 'best-laid plans of mice and men...'! Fighting spread like wildfire through the country, engulfing one area after another so rapidly that, only a few days after its completion on 7 January, our four-phase plan had to be rolled into one. Virtually all our field stations and regional headquarters were in grave danger, and intimidation and deliberate attacks against our personnel were increasing from both sides, though mainly from UNITA. Vila Espa, the operations and radio rooms, and our hangar at the airport were hives of activity day and night, planes and helicopters going off in all directions to ferry teams back, often in the most hazardous of circumstances. The speed of our withdrawal from the areas overrun by fighting meant that in many cases we were unable to retrieve equipment as well as people.

* * *

Our compromise proposal of Menongue as the site for the ceasefire meeting between the military leaders was still on the table, but although UNITA had accepted it the Government, infuriatingly, was now playing hard to get. We could not locate anyone on their side throughout Saturday 9 January. I finally ran Minister de Moura to earth early on Sunday morning and there followed four days of unremitting activity and increasing frustration, during which I acted as a go-between in a cat-and-mouse game between the two sides. This involved countless hours of trying to telephone Huambo, often in the middle of the night, or chase Government contacts who were either closeted in Futungo or had simply vanished from circulation. Dr Savimbi had some excuse since fierce fighting had broken out in Huambo on Sunday 10 January, and that afternoon 'George' told me I could not speak to him as 'we are rather scattered just now'. On Monday night he told me they 'were trying to survive'. Savimbi, with whom I had, after midnight, another of those marathon conversations (or monologues) at which he was so adept, said that two bombs had been directed at his White House and it sounded as if part of it might have been hit. On Tuesday afternoon 'George' told me that they had been subjected to two terrible bombardments, which could only mean that the Government wanted to kill his 'President'. Savimbi himself was back in his 'stream of consciousness' mode, his speech slow and slurred. Not to be outdone, Minister de Moura blew up in a violent tirade against UNITA at 2 a.m. one morning.

The exchange was enough to fray anyone's nerves. First the Government said it had not yet made up its mind about Menongue, and then, before it did, fighting broke out there also. It then suggested Luanda as its preference (which UNITA predictably rejected out of hand) or Sumbe. UNITA made the counterproposal of Geneva, which, equally predictably, the Government rejected (this was the cause of Venâncio de Moura's irate explosion in the middle of the night). The Government, while still insisting on Luanda as its first choice suggested some other location in Africa, preferably in a neighbouring country, but this was not accepted by Dr Savimbi, who considered the 'Front Line States' to be biased against UNITA. Addis Ababa was suggested as a compromise. UNITA came back with Nigeria, Morocco or Côte d'Ivoire, all countries traditionally favourable to UNITA and therefore not pleasing to the Government. UNITA likewise objected to Ethiopia as unfriendly to it, at which point, my patience wearing thin, I pointed out that the meeting would be under *United Nations* auspices, not Ethiopian and that we had an infrastructure there for the meeting (in the Economic Commission for Africa) which did not exist in the other countries. It was only on Wednesday 13 January that I was able to inform Mig Goulding that I had the oral agreement of both sides to Addis Ababa.

While this leisurely academic game of battledore and shuttlecock was going on, Huambo was going up in flames, with many hundreds of casualties and much destruction. Our UNAVEM camp was caught in the middle of the battle, in cross fire, and our personnel were taking cover in their slit trenches. The one UNAVEM helicopter parked by the camp had been put out of action by gunfire and an Argentinean police officer had been struck by a bullet in his left side, dangerously near his heart and lungs, and needed urgent evacuation. I was trying to get both sides to agree to this and declare at least a temporary ceasefire, while conducting what was becoming more and more like a geographical quiz on Angola and Africa rather than a serious peace negotiation.

My notes of some of Dr Savimbi's comments during the marathon midnight monologue give some idea of the breathless drama of the situation.

– He was still at the White House, miraculously unhurt, despite the bombing, and was personally conducting the operations at the front and commanding the resistance.
– The attack had been started by the Government on the pretext of one dead man. On average, three to four people were killed in Huambo every day but did not produce a reaction by 30 tanks.
– Dr Savimbi had called General 'Ben-Ben' from Kuito/Bié to Huambo and told him not to allow a repetition of what happened in Luanda. He himself had instructed his commanders in Huambo not to retaliate, but when the attack had become violent, it became impossible to hold them back.
– He had never known such an intensity of fire before, tanks and artillery were being used and the town was being destroyed.
– The MPLA and Soukissa (the Huambo police chief) had committed a serious error and a miscalculation. Huambo was the homeland of Ovimbundu and there would be stiff resistance – it would take the Government at least two weeks to take Huambo. The Ovimbundu were prepared to die there.
– He himself was still on the side of negotiations and peace, but had no majority in this view; when we saw him on 2 January, 60 per cent had agreed with him, now only 40 per cent. His military commanders, except General 'Wiyo', were all out for war. Only the politicians – Valentim, Manuvakola, Jaka Jamba, etc. – wanted peace.
– My intervention (he used the term 'Mama' again) was the only hope and the matter was urgent.

This emotional appeal culminated with the words: 'The elections have weakened my position. The death of Salupeto Pena has weakened my position. Yet if I can strike a deal, my people will still accept. But unless Madame can help us, there is no hope for this country'.

Madame was getting thoroughly exasperated with her wilful charges, but once the green light was given on Addis Ababa we all worked with a will on the difficult logistics for the meeting, which the Government wanted to start that weekend (16 January).

On Thursday 14 January at 3.30 p.m. I received a call from 'George'. I expected to be given practical details such as the names of the UNITA delegates, their date and mode of travel, their needs for assistance and so on. Instead I was flabbergasted to receive a long rigmarole telling me that UNITA's political commission had met throughout the previous night and had agreed to propose five points for 'the integral application of the Bicesse Accords'. These were of a high level of generality. They embraced:

1. UN mediation.
2. The need for an interposing force ('Blue Helmets') to maintain the ceasefire.
3. A guarantee of the absolute security of the negotiators by the UN.
4. The reestablishment of 'peace corridors' for humanitarian assistance to civilian populations.
5. A meeting at the highest level between President dos Santos and Dr Savimbi.

His monologue finished, George waited expectantly. This seemed to be the sum total of the message. Bemused, I enquired what relevance it had to the military meeting on the ceasefire in Addis Ababa and the urgent practical questions I had put to him the day before. To my consternation 'George' replied that UNITA now wanted to have a broader 'Namibe-type' meeting, encompassing both political and military matters. I told him categorically that this was just not on, reminding him of the tortuous negotiations that had led to the present proposal for a purely military meeting. When Dr Savimbi had made clear to me, on 6 January, that it was now impossible for UNITA to withdraw from Uige and Negage and release the FAA hostages, we had fallen back on the *only* possible alternative: a ceasefire meeting between military representatives. All arrangements were underway for the Addis Ababa meeting to start in two days' time, and if UNITA posed new conditions now, this would be interpreted – not only by the Government, but by the international community at large – as lack of good faith and genuine intention to reach a settlement. If I was to believe Dr Savimbi's many assurances to me, this did not appear to be what he wanted and I insisted that he should speak to me personally. If UNITA reneged on our agreement at this time, then there would be nothing further I could do as a valid mediator.

This at least silenced 'George' and he said he would pass on my message and call back later that day. In the meantime I advised Mig Goulding that we should firmly call this bluff and, in our public statements, proceed on the basis that we had the agreement of both sides to Addis Ababa and were simply working out the practical modalities. The Secretary-General should also talk to Dr Savimbi personally. I added that this really did seem to me to be the moment at which our patience with UNITA should come to an end, and that we should point unequivocally to it as the side responsible for extinguishing this last hope of reconciliation, unless UNITA changed its position.

* * *

A concurrent nightmare had been the evacuation of our regional command from Huambo. There was no way they could get to the airport, or we fly in a plane to collect them, since the airport itself and the ground between it and the camp were being fought over. Our one helicopter there was no longer airworthy. Our wounded Argentinean had still received no proper medical attention other than first aid more than two days after being hit, and was having to lie in an open slit trench, made even more uncomfortable by torrential seasonal rains. So did everyone else, except when engaged in the hazardous business of trying to get messages back and forth, when they were exposed to cross fire. Particular courage was shown by the two Bulgarian pilots who, oblivious of their own safety, sat in the exposed helicopter receiving and transmitting radio messages. Another member of the Huambo team was injured by falling structures when the camp was hit and Colonel Mortlock had a miraculous escape. I still use as a paperweight a fearsomely jagged piece of shrapnel that hit his cot seconds after he had left it, and which he later ceremoniously presented to me.

We had been working for days to get a temporary ceasefire while the evacuation took place. In this regard UNITA proved more accommodating than the Government. Neither Mike nor I could get any firm response from the latter, despite repeated entreaties. In the end it was decided to go ahead without them, and to proceed with a plan worked out on the ground by Colonel Mortlock, whose unwavering courage and calm leadership during those dark days of dread were the admiration of us all. This entailed travelling by back roads from Huambo to Bailundo, a place under UNITA control where our evacuees from Kuito/Bié were now located, and from where we could lift them all out by air. It was a bold plan, fraught with risks, and reliant on some rather frail assurances given to Colonel Mortlock by local UNITA commanders, but the perils of inaction were greater.

On the morning of 14 January a convoy of some 29 UN 4×4 vehicles, decked with large blue UN flags and carrying all the UNAVEM personnel, as well as a number of staff from NGOs in Huambo, left the Weatherhaven camp for the last time. Whatever equipment could not be accommodated in the vehicles had to be left. The mournful cavalcade was seen off on the outskirts of the town by a little huddle of Angolans who had gathered to say goodbye. They were not merely being friendly – they were distraught to see the UN leaving. Colonel Mortlock told me afterwards that he would never forget a small, weather-beaten old lady who embraced him and, with tears in her eyes, said 'Now our troubles will really begin'.

There followed several hours of tension while the convoy wended its way through UNITA lines and checkpoints. It was almost more unbearable for us in Luanda, since for long periods the convoy was out of radio contact. When the confirmation came that the group had arrived safely in Bailundo, joy and relief knew no bounds. A series of shuttle flights by helicopter carried them to Benguela, whence we flew them, still dirty and bedraggled, to Luanda. Colonel Mortlock looked thin and totally exhausted. We kept our debriefing sessions very short: all he wanted to do was to have a shower and a long, long sleep.

Once again our tiny sick bay was full of patients. The bullet was at last successfully removed from the wounded Argentinean, whom I found in extraordinarily good spirits. Curiously he was less affected psychologically than one of his compatriots, a military observer who, along with a Slovakian comrade, had been beaten up by a hostile crowd in their camp in the remote Sambo assembly area. It was perhaps easier to be philosophical about a stray bullet, an impersonal but lethal object that comes your way by accident, than about being beaten up, without apparent reason, by people who until yesterday had been your friends and neighbours and for whom you had come so far from home and family to help.

* * *

The media, both national and international, were beginning to smell a rat about the Addis Ababa meeting and were bombarding my minuscule press office. In order to avoid having to answer leading questions, I issued a brief press communiqué in Luanda on Friday 15 January, wording it in a way intended to put pressure on Dr Savimbi. It stated that the only thing holding things up were the practical details needed from UNITA about its attendance, and that I had had no official information to indicate that UNITA was no longer willing to attend the meeting, as suggested in some media reports. I pointed out that it was Dr Savimbi himself who had personally appealed to me, in three separate conversations, to arrange the meeting.

There was still no word from him. My numerous attempts to telephone him were unsuccessful. The next day 'George' faxed an identical letter to Minister de Moura and myself, conveying the decisions of UNITA's permanent committee. They were agreeable to a meeting in Geneva, or in any African country, except one of the Front Line States, but it must be a 'Namibe-type' meeting. It was as if my conversation of the day before with 'George' had never taken place.

Immediately afterwards I had to go to Futungo de Belas to attend the annual New Year diplomatic greeting ceremony, traditionally held on 15 January. Later

I was able to have quite a long chat with the President, who confirmed that the Government was still ready to go to Addis Ababa. While I was talking to the President my bodyguard ran up with a radio message from the camp that Dr Savimbi was telephoning me there. It was 1.00 p.m. With the President's blessing I rushed back to Vila Espa, to receive a message that the UNITA leader would call back at 3.00 p.m.

At 3.10 p.m. the phone duly rang, but it was 'George'. Dr Savimbi was in a meeting, he told me, but would telephone me 'within the hour'. Four hours later I got through to 'George' and asked what had happened. He told me that the meeting was about to finish, and they would be calling me back 'within a few minutes'. That was the last I was to hear from UNITA for a week. Savimbi did not call; nor did George.

I spent a wretched weekend glued to the telephone, cancelling engagements that would have taken me out of the camp. Our switchboard was constantly dialling Savimbi's numbers for some 18 hours each day, but we failed to get through, either because the UNITA satellite was switched off or because, when the phone did ring, no one answered. In despair I rang Marcos Samondo in New York late on Sunday to enlist his help, and complained about the lack of promised follow-up. He said that he was having communications difficulties too but would try to arrange something. Monday morning came and he had not got back to me either.

UNITA had certainly kept the communications lines buzzing to other places the day before and its worldwide propaganda machine was swinging into gear. The Secretary-General received a letter from Dr Savimbi, identical to the ones he had sent to Minister de Moura and myself. Marcos Samondo too wrote to the Secretary-General, a kilometric letter in which he defended UNITA, attacked the Government and toed the latest party line on the Addis Ababa meeting. Early on Sunday morning I heard him beating the same drum in a very smooth and plausible performance on the BBC World Service.

By Monday morning it was clear that UNITA did not want to talk to me, and that its strategy was to postpone the Addis Ababa meeting so that it could consolidate its military advantage before sitting down to talk. This was borne out by what Samondo was reported to have said when he handed over his 'clarifying' letter in New York. While this letter complained piously that the Angolan Government had launched 'systematic and unprovoked attacks' on 'UNITA positions', he boasted that UNITA was doing well on the battlefront and claimed that from now on the Government would have to take UNITA's position seriously.

Ambassador M'binda was a frequent visitor to the UN Secretariat building in New York, presenting the Government's side of the story, though his instructions sometimes seemed to be out of date, or otherwise out of kilter with what I was being told in Luanda, which added to the confusion of an already dangerously muddled situation. When he called on 15 January to enquire what the Secretary-General's views were on UNITA's latest position, Mig suggested they should consider accepting that political matters could be discussed in Addis Ababa, but should insist that this could happen only *after* discussion of the military questions, as a second stage.

In Luanda, the Government was playing a very discreet hand. General Higino came to see me on Saturday 16 January. He was in an uncharacteristically subdued mood. Their delegation was ready to leave and was patently anxious to have the talks. The Government was even withholding publication of Dr Savimbi's letter of 14 January (insisting that the talks should extend to political issues) because it did not want to jeopardise my negotiations with UNITA – an unusual display of restraint and sensitivity. It was plain that things were not going well for the Government side at the battlefront, and that, in taking that precipitate action on 3 January, it had not only obstructed the slow progress towards dialogue but had bitten off more than it could chew. Alarmed by UNITA's steady encroachment, it had allowed itself to be provoked into trying to teach UNITA a lesson. But both the method and the timing had been ill-judged. True, it had ejected UNITA from some of the important cities, but in so doing it had earned itself a great deal of opprobrium – losing some of the sympathy earned at the time of the elections – and had set off an even more violent riposte by UNITA, for which it was, at that time, no match militarily.

General Higino was on his way to see the President and I gained the impression that the Government was likely to be a little more pragmatic about the meeting. Nonetheless I advised Mig that I did not think it wise for us to press the Government to allow political matters to be discussed in Addis Ababa. UNITA had behaved in blatant bad faith and I did not think we should let it off the hook, for two reasons. First, and most importantly, to turn a blind eye would merely reinforce UNITA's evident belief that it play with us at will; and, secondly, this would fuel new criticisms that we were too lenient on UNITA. The matter should be left to the Government to determine. If it decided to make some conciliatory gesture, then that was another matter, but we should not intervene.

Events over the next few days bore out the pessimism of my analysis. On Monday 18 January General 'Ben-Ben' issued a communiqué that was very belligerent and triumphalist in tone and implicitly conditioned negotiations on further military advances.

My daily notes for 19 January bear out the gravity of the situation:

UNITA appears to be making rapid advances, despite what were always considered to be over-extended supply lines. There is speculation that they are receiving reinforcements of men and arms from abroad. If, as seems possible, they take Soyo (an important port and oil-producing area on the coast north of Luanda), they will then have control of all major towns in the northern region, except Malange, which may well be the next target, as well, perhaps, as Cabinda. With control of revenue from oil and diamonds, there will be ample funds for financing additional support from abroad, through mercenaries and black market arms. If the present trend continues, it no longer seems quite so implausible that the hitherto unthinkable might occur and Luanda itself be besieged.

The rumours about illicit arms supplies were by no means new, nor were they confined to one side. There were persistent rumours about supplies to UNITA from private sources in South Africa, and possibly China, none of which could be proved. On the Government side there were reports of suspicious-looking cargo being unloaded from Russian planes at Luanda airport. Speculation that Russia would not be averse to selling arms for financial reasons, given its parlous economic situation, combined with its increasingly overt pro-Government stance, lent credence to such reports. The Interior Minister 'Petroff', left for Europe in the first week of January to visit Portugal and Spain, *inter alia*, according to press reports, to improve the capability and equipment of the police.

Much of our assumption that the two sides must come to terms sooner or later, because neither side could win a war, was based on the premise that the 'triple zero' provision in the Bicesse Accords (precluding the provision of arms from any source) was being scrupulously observed and that neither wide was receiving outside military support. In the new circumstances, this might no longer be the case. Moreover both sides still had the huge quantities of arms supplied earlier by their allies – mainly the two superpowers – during the Cold War and now back in circulation after the collapse of the peace process; these arms were still capable of killing people, however obsolete some of them might be by Western standards. What could the UN do about preventing new supplies, given the lack of proof and the possibility of plausible circumventions? The only suggestion I could come up with was that a suitably stern reminder of the 'triple zero' obligation should be included in the next resolution of the Security Council, though I realised only too well that this might well fall into the category of 'sound and fury, signifying nothing'.

* * *

During that lost weekend I had plenty to occupy my mind besides the wearying business of waiting for UNITA to call, like some adolescent wallflower waiting to be asked to dance. The Secretary-General had to present a progress report to the Security Council the following week, with his recommendations of what should be done with UNAVEM. I had delayed drafting it in the hope of having something positive to report, but now it could be put off no longer.

When it was eventually issued, the report[1] recognised the force of the argument that, by its actions, UNITA had removed itself from the Bicesse process and should be obliged, by force if necessary, to accept the authority of a duly elected government. But it stated, as the Secretary-General's view, that, while in no way condoning UNITA's defiance of the agreements it had signed, he could not support such a position; early peace would not be achieved in Angola by simply allowing the two sides to fight an inevitable, prolonged and bloody war. The report therefore recommended that the international community persist in trying to bring the two sides together and help them to reach and implement an agreement. Three options were put forward for the Council's consideration. Under the first, UNAVEM would maintain the same strength (350 military observers, 126 police observers, 83 international civilian staff and 155 local staff) and try to reestablish deployment in 67 different locations. We calculated that this option would cost around US$5.6 million per month. The second option would reduce UNAVEM's deployment outside Luanda to about six locations, but with some flexibility to ensure it facilitated the Special Representative's peacemaking efforts. This option would need 75 military observers, 30 police observers and 49 international civilian staff, and would cost US$1.8 million per month. In the third option, UNAVEM's deployment would be restricted to Luanda, but with the capability to deploy one or two outstations if required and if security permitted. For this only 30 military observers, six police observers and 28 international civilian staff would be needed, and the monthly cost would go down to US$1.1 million.

Under each option there would be a Special Representative, whose mandate would cover the kind of things that I had been doing since the elections, namely providing the good offices of the UN to bring the two sides together and help them to reach agreement, and meanwhile to broker and – 'within the resources available' – help implement national or local ceasefires. It had been agreed with Headquarters that, under the last two options, the next Special Representative should be at a lower level than Under-Secretary-General (my own rank) and that the Chief Military Observer should likewise no longer be at the Major-General level.

The report came down against the first option, because of the prevailing uncertainties, and hovered between the last two before finally inclining towards the third, and most limited, proposal, with the proviso that sufficient equipment would be retained to permit a rapid upgrading to the second option if things improved. I suggested that the Council be asked to establish a deadline of one month, up to 28 February 1993, after which the choice would be between expansion of the UN presence or its total withdrawal. The text I proposed was intended to offer both a carrot and a stick, which would put pressure on both sides to come to their senses. If, within that one-month period, they did declare a ceasefire and resumed negotiations within the Peace Accords, then the Council should indicate its readiness to consider a very significant expansion of UNAVEM, along the lines of my proposal of 24 December, annexed to the report. Mig Goulding felt that one month was not enough. A deadline was introduced into the report but it was for three months, until 30 April 1993, and the carrot was omitted: only the threat of total withdrawal was left.

This last section of the report also contained two very direct observations. The first was intended as an initial response to the insidious wave of criticism placing all the blame for what had happened on the UN, with scant regard for facts or circumstances. It was epitomised in a *Times* leader of 9 January and in my sessions with the shoals of journalists who had again flocked to Luanda. After one of these I wrote: 'I have a dispiriting feeling of taking part in a wake in which everyone is picking over the life of the dear (or not so dear!) departed'.

In the report the Secretary-General promised that he would, with his Special Representative, be examining 'how far this tragic breakdown of the peace process in Angola was due to shortcomings in the mandate given to, or in the performance of, the United Nations'.[2] It went on to express the Secretary-General's present view that the fundamental cause of the breakdown had been 'the failure, often deliberate, of both parties to implement in full the provisions of the Peace Accords relating to political, military and police matters or to make the necessary efforts to promote national reconciliation'.[3] The point was also made, a little further on that

> the deliberately limited role assigned by the two parties and the observers in the Peace Accords to UNAVEM II in military matters, which was only to verify the efficient working of joint monitoring mechanisms to be established and chaired by the parties themselves, hampered its ability to correct the drift towards non-compliance, which had already become apparent by late 1991.[4]

Few people seemed to take this message on board, however, and sweeping criticisms, unfounded in fact, continued unabated, and indeed do so to this day.

The second observation, couched in unwontedly strong terms, complained of the

> outrageous harassment and physical abuse to which UNAVEM II personnel have been subjected, together with the theft and looting of United Nations property, by officials and supporters of both sides, but especially UNITA. When protests are made about such incidents, the leadership of both sides says that they result from unauthorized actions by uncontrolled elements. But the fact is that both parties, or media under their control, have at one time or another in recent months, meticulously criticised UNAVEM II's performance and accused it of bias in favour of the other side. Such statements increase the likelihood that, when the situation deteriorates 'uncontrolled elements' will use violence against United Nations personnel.[5]

* * *

The Secretary-General spoke to Dr Savimbi for one hour on 19 January and put pressure on him to send General Chilingutila to Addis Ababa for a ceasefire meeting. Savimbi undertook to 'consult his colleagues' and to call the Secretary-General the next day. Once more the promised call did not materialise. I was anxious to know whether Savimbi had indicated why his negotiations with me were interrupted so abruptly when he failed to make a telephone call to me on 15 January that had been announced several times by his colleagues. I asked this because of a BBC interview of 20 January, in which Savimbi was said to have referred very derogatorily to my trustworthiness as a negotiator – this in striking contrast to his last conversation with me, when he had been full of flattery and again kept referring to me, embarrassingly, as the 'mother' of the process. No one could reply: the conversation had been personal and no record had been kept. I was left in limbo, now knowing whether I had again dropped out of favour with UNITA and its leader, and if so, why. Could it have been the tough talking to 'George', or perhaps his retelling of it? Or was UNITA's behaviour simply a standard example of its accomplished art of getting its own way through delaying tactics and generally being awkward, which had nothing to do with me personally?

On 20 January the Secretary-General was visited by Ambassador M'binda who, on instruction, said that the Government was not against political negotiations, but these must follow the military question. Nor did the Government reject the idea of a summit meeting, but it had to be prepared by meetings at lower levels. The Government urged the Secretary-General and the Security Council to maintain the UNAVEM presence. The Secretary-General said, as he had already said to Dr Savimbi the previous day, that there would be no basis for him to recommend maintenance of UNAVEM at its present strength unless the two sides showed a minimum of readiness to negotiate a ceasefire and restart a dialogue.

At a dinner in Luanda that evening General Higino casually handed over to our Colonel Egar a copy of a letter, dated 19 January, from Foreign Minister de Moura to Dr Savimbi. Somewhat surprisingly (though we were beyond surprise by then) this letter conveyed the exact opposite of what Ambassador M'binda had been instructed to say one day later to the Secretary-General. I began to feel quite sorry for him for, whether by accident or design, the poor man always seemed to be out of step. The letter accepted UNITA's proposal for a joint political and military meeting in Addis Ababa, to take place on 23 January, and proposed several 'basic premises': reaffirmation of adherence to the Bicesse Accords and of the clear will to restore the ceasefire throughout the country; unqualified acceptance of the results of the elections, and recognition of the legitimacy of the democratic legality thus established; free movement of persons and goods throughout the national territory; and respect for the United Nations and a strengthening of its role. Mediation in the meeting was to be undertaken by the UN, in the presence of the three observer countries; and last but by no means least, 'absolute guarantees of security for the negotiators' were to be provided by, naturally, the United Nations.

All of this was quite helpful, but the letter had to reach Dr Savimbi. By 21 January the Government had still not been able to get the fax through and once more turned to us. Miraculously our fax worked. Even more miraculously 'George', who had not been heard from for a week, spoke to Elizabeth Pantaleón. He claimed that they had had to close down the satellite 'for security reasons'. He was reminded (since he did not seem to have it on his mind as an urgent priority, or indeed at all) that I had been waiting since the previous Friday to receive the promised call from his boss and that the ceasefire was of the utmost urgency.

* * *

The deadline of 31 January for UNAVEM's mandate was fast approaching, and I continued to put forward to Headquarters the common view of myself and my senior colleagues in Luanda that only very decisive positions and actions by the UN could prevent an even worse war in Angola. Up to now the Security Council's resolutions had been very evenhanded, though the tone of the more recent ones had been stronger. In my opinion this was due in part to the fact that sinning was not the monopoly of any one side, in part to the desire not to rock the boat unduly while the process remained broadly on track, and in part to the inherent and generalised difficulty of getting the diverse opinions and interests of the members of the Security Council to coalesce in strong condemnation – compromise (often unworkable in practice) being the course normally chosen. In the case of Angola the voice of the United States was key in regard to UNITA. After the election the situation was changed drastically by UNITA's actions, but the first Security Council Resolution thereafter (Resolution 785) remained circumspect in its language; there was still the hope that the process could be put back on track. The next Resolution (793) was adopted on 30 November, in the wake of the successful meeting in Namibe and when the full impact of UNITA's incursions into Uige and Negage the day before had not yet filtered through to New York. Moreover considerable ambiguity surrounded how the tragic confrontations of 31 October and 1 November were sparked off; and UNITA, however grudgingly, had accepted the election results. Once again the Security Council hedged its bets and came down on the side of impartial expressions of concern, appeals, demands and urgings to the two sides.

In Luanda there was growing restiveness over this approach among the representatives of the three observer countries, especially on the part of Ambassador De Jarnette (there was, moreover, a new Democratic administration in Washington with different views on the issue), the Ambassadors of other influential countries, and the international and national media. Pressure was growing for the United Nations to 'come off the fence' – to condemn UNITA clearly, and express support for the Government while still censuring the latter for its own faults. (Lubango and its sequels elsewhere could not be swept under the rug.) In UNAVEM we also believed that the time had come for straight talking, but we could not suppress some wry amusement that most of those who buttonholed us to press this view came from countries that were either permanent or elected members of the Security Council. It was the Council, not the Secretariat, that would decide the wording of the resolution and adopt it.

I recommended to Mig Goulding that the following elements should be included in their next resolution:

- Condemnation of UNITA for its three major violations of the Peace Accords: initial rejection of the election results and continued rejection of the United Nations' certification that the elections were generally free and fair; abandonment of the new Angolan armed forces; and seizure of at least four provincial capitals and 105 out of 164 municipalities (the state of play on 20 January).
- Support for the new Government, within the Peace Accords and the democratic process.
- Censure of human rights abuses by both parties, including the extensive killings carried out by civilians armed by the Government.
- A request to all governments to respect the 'triple zero' provision concerning deliveries of lethal equipment to Angola.

* * *

When, in December, I had acceded to the Secretary-General's request that I stay longer in Angola, it had been agreed that I could fulfil two engagements I had accepted when I had expected to be a 'free woman' by the end of 1992: to speak at a conference on preventive conflict management in Vienna on 25–27 January, organised by the Austrian government, and to deliver the annual Sigwick Memorial Lecture at Newnham, my old college in Cambridge on 5 February. There was still no indication of when, or even whether, the Addis Ababa meeting would take place, Dr Savimbi having failed to return the Secretary-General's call on 20 January, and the evacuation of UNAVEM personnel from dangerous outstations had been completed. Headquarters therefore agreed that I could go ahead with these engagements and take some of my forfeited Christmas leave at the same time. I would be in constant communication by telephone and could easily be recalled, if required.

I left Luanda for Lisbon on Friday 22 January, on a flight combination that would get me to London late that night. It was not to be: TAP, the Portuguese airline, left Luanda about an hour and a half late, I missed the connection in Lisbon and had to spend the night there.

My few hours of sleep in the comfortable hotel room, after the unimaginable luxury of a hot bath, were rudely cut short by the telephone. It was Mr Jaka Jamba of UNITA. It was also the first time anyone from UNITA had spoken to me since communication between us had been so unexpectedly broken. The time was between half-past one and two o'clock in the morning. As I was beginning, ruefully, to discover, UNITA was a past master at calling you up in the small hours when your vital spark was flickering at its lowest. Only later did I wonder how, from some unknown location in the vicinity of Huambo and in the middle of a battle, they had managed to trace me to Lisbon where no one, including myself, knew I was going to spend the night, much less where I would be staying.

Bashfulness was not a notable UNITA characteristic nor did embarrassment come easily to its members. With no excuse or apology for the long silence, Jaka Jamba, who was one of the softer-spoken members of UNITA's tough leadership, put the proposition to me in terms that brooked no argument or delay: UNITA wanted the meeting – now to cover political as well as military matters – to be held in Addis Ababa from 27 to 30 January. I agreed without further ado.

21 Peace Talks in Ethiopia

It was late on Saturday 23 January when I reached the Welsh border, and I left again at midday on Sunday to catch the last plane to Vienna. There was no point in my returning to Luanda, since I could more easily reach Addis Ababa from Frankfurt, allowing me to take part in the Vienna meeting for the first of the three days and say my piece about Angola.

There was a very pleasant surprise: the Austrian Government bestowed on me its highest award for foreign diplomats – Das Grosse Goldene Ehrenzeichen am Bande – in recognition of my five years' service as Director-General of the United Nations office at Vienna. I had for so many months been subjected to verbal and other aggression that this civilised occasion, marked by appreciative words, champagne and the presence of friends and former colleagues, seemed something out of a dream world.

Early on Tuesday 26 January I set off for Addis Ababa in the company of Mr Layashi Yaker, the Executive Secretary of the UN Economic Commission for Africa and doyen of Africa Hall, who had been attending the same meeting as myself. I had been Resident Representative of the UN Development Programme in Ethiopia in the mid-1960s, and for a time had had my office in Africa Hall, where the peace talks were now being held. On my previous return visits, huge portraits of Marx, Lenin and Engels had dominated great tracts of the city, and my oldest Ethiopian friend, Princess Aida Desta, whom I had known at Cambridge, had been languishing for long years in prison with her mother and sisters. Now the portraits had been swept away, Aida was free and Ethiopia too was in transition. Much had changed since my first stay there nearly 30 years before. But it still smelled the same as we drove that night from the airport – the pungent mixture of eucalyptus smoke and dark, rich earth that was unmistakeably Addis Ababa, and unmistakeably Africa.

My UNAVEM colleagues arrived the next morning, wearied by the long night flight from Luanda, a milk-run calling at various places across Africa *en route*. It would have been less tiring to have come with the Government delegation on their special jet, but we had opted for independent means to avoid any accusations that UNAVEM owed favours to the Government. By Wednesday morning everyone had arrived but the bulk of the UNITA delegation. Besides myself, the UNAVEM team consisted of Mike Nyambuya and Bill Egar on the military side, Ebrima Jobarteh, and two interpreters, Afonso Almeida and Christian Prat-Vincent.

The Government had brought a large delegation of 15 people, headed, rather surprisingly, by Dr Fernando Faustino Muteka – who had not played any preeminent role in the CCPM and was chiefly noted for having been Secretary of State for Coffee: he had been at Namibe, but simply as one of the delegation, in his capacity as political adviser in the presidency. He was thus rather an unknown quantity. The choice was significant in that he was an Ovimbundu, the first person of that ethnic origin to have been appointed to the MPLA Government's Council of Ministers in January 1978. The Government's political team included three Ministers or Vice-Ministers: General Higino Carneiro headed the military part of the delegation, which included three other generals. The Angolan Ambassador to Ethiopia, Dr Almeida, was also attached to the delegation, as were representatives of three parties–the FNLA, the PLD and the PRS. Two members of UNITA's delegation – Brigadier Samakuva, the UNITA representative in London, and Marcos Samondo from New York – had arrived directly. But the time and mode of arrival of the main UNITA delegation, headed by General Eugenio Manuvakola, now Secretary-General, was a well-kept secret.

I had planned to leave Wednesday morning free so I could have a meeting with the two delegation heads to agree on procedure, which assumes an almost disproportionate importance in delicate negotiations of this kind. The morning wore on and there was still no news of UNITA's arrival. Everyone stood around talking desultorily and tension rose by the minute. My spirits were again at rock bottom. My whole life seemed to be spent waiting in vain for UNITA.

Colonel Ross and Hugo Anson plied us with daily updates from Luanda. Their messages were not encouraging. Fighting was continuing everywhere and there was a growing perception that UNITA was gaining the upper hand, and might shortly attack Cabinda, Malange and even Luanda, as well as Saurimo and Luena. A few days earlier it had taken Soyo, the north-western oil port, without evidence of serious resistance. It had destroyed much of Luanda's water supply at Quifangongo during the weekend: depriving the capital of electricity and water was as likely a way of bringing Luanda to its knees as direct assault, and far less risky. An outright push to take Luanda could not be discounted.

The general view was that UNITA still had a larger number of better led, trained, equipped and motivated troops than the Government, and some observers were beginning to warn against assuming too easily that the war would be inconclusive. Early on 26 January there were reports of fighting in Menongue and of UNITA concentrating troops at Catengue for an assault on Benguela. Cabinda was also expecting an attack, but a strong warning by the United States that its oil interests in the enclave should not be harmed appeared to be having an effect. A fierce battle was still going on in Huambo. The information available to UNAVEM was, however, sporadic and in many cases unverifiable, since we had had to reduce our presence in Angola from 67 to just six locations along the Atlantic coastline: Luanda, Cabinda, Sumbe, Benguela, Lubango and Namibe. We had lost our 'eyes and ears' in the interior, and with them our capacity for on-the-spot verification and mediation.

The Government, suffering on the battlefield, was maintaining a strong propaganda offensive through the media. Every day brought fresh allegations that Zairean troops, white mercenaries and South African aircraft were assisting UNITA. On 24 January President dos Santos had addressed an unusually short, sharp note to the Secretary-General, beginning with the words 'It is with profound indignation', and making similar allegations about foreign incursions. He said that a South African aircraft had been shot down during the fighting, but no firm evidence was forthcoming. UNAVEM also continued to be under attack by the media, as well as the object of derogatory remarks by some members of the Government. On 24 January the *Jornal de Angola* referred to 'UNAVEM's collaboration with UNITA' and our colleagues feared that further hostile actions against UNAVEM personnel and installations might be incited by what was obviously an orchestrated campaign.

* * *

In the afternoon, to our great relief, the UNITA delegation turned up. But to our dismay, and contrary to earlier information from UNITA, the pivotal person for the discussion of the ceasefire, General Chilingutila, was not in their midst. They numbered six in all: General Manuvakola, the two representatives from London and New York, General 'Gato' (still nursing a wounded arm, the price of his miraculous escape from Luanda on 1 November) General Jerónimo Ukuma and Brigadier Paulo Sachiambo.

Mystery shrouded the manner of their exit from Angola and Huambo (if indeed that was where they had come from). It was assumed that they had made their way by minor roads and tracks and small, light planes to Kinshasa, from where a jet aircraft of the Côte d'Ivoire Government had flown them to Ethiopia. Much was made of the group having emerged from the bush and the heat of the battle for Huambo. Their appearance belied this, for they were clad not in battle-stained fatigues, but in natty suits, collars and ties, impeccably colour-coordinated. Brigadier Samakuva, it was explained, had purchased all this gear in London, hoping, as he told me jokingly, that he had hit on the right sizes and colours acceptable to the wearers. General Manuvakola was the epitome of sartorial elegance in a tasteful shade of green, with tie and socks to tone. UNITA thought of everything.

The delegation did not show the same readiness to meet forthwith. Since we only had until Saturday, I was anxious to launch the encounter before we all repaired to our beds, and at least establish the agenda. The UNITA delegation pleaded extreme fatigue, though they could hardly have been more exhausted than my own people, who had flown all night. This was to become an all too familiar ploy over the coming months. For relatively young and vigorous men, inured to the rigours of bush fighting over many years, the UNITA team was remarkably prone to bouts of insuperable exhaustion at critical points in our negotiations. Jeffrey Davidow advanced the plausible theory that this was the result of US assistance, which had included the despatch of two American consultants to Jamba to indoctrinate UNITA in the gentle art of negotiation. One of the main messages, according to Jeff, had been 'Never be in a hurry. Always keep the other side waiting'. UNITA had certainly taken it to heart. On this occasion I managed to jolly them along into accepting an initial meeting at 9.30 p.m. that evening, before which I met privately with both leaders to agree on procedures.

Much had happened since the two sides last faced one another in Namibe two months before, none of it good. Their comrades were locked in ferocious combat in dozens of locations away on the other side of the continent. And yet, bewilderingly, the atmosphere was as robustly genial as it had been in Namibe. Once again great shouts of greeting and enveloping bear hugs seemed to signify a joyful reencounter between friends too long parted, rather than of warring parties seeking to end a bloody internecine war. This time round I was less inclined to reap encouragement that these outward signs of brotherly love betokened an early end to fratricidal fighting on the ground.

I opened the meeting with a brief statement of what I hoped we would get out of it – at least agreement on a ceasefire, and a definition of the main political issues that would, together, lay firm groundwork for continuing negotiations, with an agreed timetable and location, which could proceed in an atmosphere uncomplicated by a simultaneous prosecution of hostilities.

Dr Muteka and General Manuvakola both reiterated their unflagging commitment to peace and a return to negotiation. The Government delegation proposed two items for the agenda: reestablishment of the ceasefire and completion of the fulfilment of the Peace Accords. UNITA agreed in principle, stressing that the ceasefire must be supported by effective mechanisms and guarantees. The meeting came to an end at 11 o'clock.

* * *

The next morning, as the first light began to seep over the dusky blue hills surrounding Addis Ababa, I swam in the warm, thermal waters of the Hilton swimming pool. Steam spiralled gently into the chilly morning air, carrying with it more than a whiff of sulphur to mingle with the tang of burning eucalyptus drifting in from the clusters of ramshackle huts crouched in the lee of the hotel, where townsfolk were setting about their chores, dogs were barking, cocks crowing and children shouting. I knew from experience that the swimming pool was a social and business meeting place for its habitués, mainly rather large Ethiopian gentlemen; there was only ever a smattering of ladies, usually equally generously proportioned, sedately swimming up and down, their unhurried breaststroke providing ample opportunity for conversation, while a babble of Amharic rose from the ends of the pool where whole groups, immersed to the neck, their faces blurred in a cloud of vapour, engaged in animated conversation. It was a timely reminder that other things continued serenely on their way outside the closed, obsessional world of Angola.

Soon I was back in that almost stiflingly unreal atmosphere. By the end of the morning all we had to show for our efforts was agreement on four agenda items: reestablishment of the ceasefire; completion of the implementation of the Peace Accords; the role of the UN in the first two areas and in the electoral process (the second presidential round); and the release of prisoners.

Even then it was not simple. The UNITA delegation set off an incredible wrangle about the *ordering* of the items, arguing that it was not fair for the two items proposed by the Government to take precedence over those they had put forward. I argued with all the patience and diplomacy I could muster that it was not a case of fairness, but of logic: you could not deal with the role of the UN, or the release of prisoners, until you had settled the terms of the ceasefire and what remained to be done on the Peace Accords. General Manuvakola remained irritatingly obdurate, simply repeating woodenly the same arguments over and over again, like a spoilt child deprived of a coveted but useless toy. There were only two conclusions to draw – either he was impenetrably thick or he was deliberately spinning out the debate on whatever pretext came to hand, however specious.

The afternoon's events bore out the latter hypothesis. The meagre harvest of the morning had included the establishment of two commissions – one military, the other political – but once again a logical plan was foiled by Manuvakola's insistence that there should first be a 'general debate about the underlying causes of the renewed conflict in Angola' in plenary session. The Government delegation did not want this and it was hard to see where a time-consuming reprise of mutual grievances would get us other than precipitating an unhelpfully acrimonious exchange.

After two meetings with the delegation heads I managed to get a compromise agreed: a plenary session would be held at which UNITA could make a general statement. This consisted of the familiar complaints about the 'antiriot' police, armed civilian groups and breach of the 'triple zero' provision of the Peace Accords through the supply of lethal equipment to the police. Fortunately my fear that this would spark off a fruitless and interminable exchange of recriminations proved groundless: when I gave the floor to Dr Muteka, he wisely forbore to comment. This calm demonstration of maturity and restraint and an all-too-rare injection of common sense, in the face of considerable provocation, was refreshing. If the UNITA team's intention had been to filibuster, his refusal to be roused by their jibes stopped them dead in their tracks and enabled us to get on with the business in hand.

Even so the commissions did not begin work until 5 p.m. and made little progress before the 'working reception' I gave later in Africa Hall, to which we had invited the Ethiopian Foreign Minister and other dignitaries of the Ethiopian Government, the Secretary-General of the Organization of African Unity (OAU), Ambassador Salim Salim and some of his senior colleagues, and Ambassadors of African countries and of those that were members of the Security Council. The OAU was specially important since it had its headquarters in Addis Ababa and could, we hoped, be helpful in bringing to bear on both sides the full weight of African opinion in support of a peaceful negotiated solution. Here, at least, they could talk to UNITA, as President Mugabe and his group had been unable to do during their brief mission to Luanda at Christmas. Mr Yaker and I had gone to visit Ambassador Salim Salim on arrival and we had also paid a protocol call on the Ethiopian President, whom I found to be impressively pragmatic, given his youth and his long background of guerrilla warfare rather than statesmanship.

Ever an optimist, I had pushed for the commissions to reassemble after the reception. The Government delegates were willing to do so, but those of UNITA would have none of it, insisting they must have a delegation meeting instead. Again this looked like a deliberate stalling tactic, though they may have found themselves in genuine difficulties, being relatively low-level, with uncertain mandate and authority. The absence of General Chilingutila still seemed ominous. The emphasis was clearly political rather than military. None of this boded well for a ceasefire; though it remained our top priority as the quintessential first step for political negotiations, all the signs were that it did not figure high on UNITA's agenda.

* * *

UNAVEM's mandate was fast running out again and the Security Council was due to debate its future before it expired on 31 January (which happened to fall on a Sunday), on the basis of the Secretary-General's report of 21 January.[1] It seemed more sensible for the Council to consider these matters *after* the Addis Ababa meeting and I pleaded for the debate to be delayed until Monday 1 February, but it seemed that the timetable for such matters was cast in iron, irrespective of contingent events. Hence the Council discussed Angola on Friday 29 January, when we were still in the throes of our meeting. It adopted Resolution 804, which was couched in much stronger language than its predecessors. The preamble employed such phrases as 'gravely disturbed' and 'gravely concerned' to describe its reaction to the various worsening aspects of the situation, while the operative part of the resolution actually used the words 'strongly condemns' for the 'persistent violations of the main purposes of the Acordos de Paz'. Here, in keeping with our recommendation made from Luanda, UNITA was singled out for its triple layer of sins: initial rejection of the election results, withdrawal from the new Angolan armed forces, and seizure by force of provincial capitals and municipalities, as well as the resumption of hostilities. The Council 'demanded' that 'the two parties cease fire immediately, restore, at their meeting in Addis Ababa, continued and meaningful dialogue, and agree on a clear time-table for the full implementation of the Acordos de Paz'. It also 'urged' them, and particularly UNITA, to 'produce early evidence of their adherence to and fulfilment without exception of the Acordos de Paz'. There was a parallel series of appeals to member states to support these efforts, as well as to 'take all necessary steps to stop immediately and effectively any direct or indirect military or paramilitary interference from their territories and to respect scrupulously the provisions of the "Acordos de Paz"; concerning the cessation of supply of lethal material to any Angolan party'. Hence my request that the Council address the illegal supply of arms was also met.

Some of the other 19 operative paragraphs supported the efforts of the Secretary-General and myself 'under extremely difficult circumstances', 'strongly condemned' attacks against UNAVEM personnel and 'demanded' that both sides ensure our safety and security, and expressed the Council's condolences to the family of the Brazilian police observer who lost his life. It also 'strongly condemned' violations of international humanitarian law, in particular 'the attacks against the civilian population, including the extensive killings carried out by armed civilians', calling upon both parties to abide by their obligations under that law and under the Peace Accords. A separate paragraph 'demanded' that 'UNITA immediately release foreign nationals taken hostage'.

Thus far most of my recommendations had been taken into account, but the nub of the resolution – the future mandate and disposition of UNAVEM – was much more wishy-washy. It plumped for the third and most limited of the Secretary-General's three options: approving his recommendation to 'maintain a Special Representative in Angola based in Luanda, with the necessary civilian, military and police staff' (that is, 30 military observers, six police observers and 28 international civilian staff). UNAVEM's mandate was extended for three months, up to 30 April 1993, but without any deadline or explicit stick or carrot provision that might goad the parties into early agreement. Operative paragraph 15 simply added 'the proviso that, as a provisional measure, based on security considerations, the Secretary-General is authorised to concentrate UNAVEM II in Luanda, and at his discretion, in other provincial locations, with the levels of equipment and personnel he deems appropriate to be retained in order to allow the subsequent expeditious redeployment of UNAVEM II as soon as this becomes feasible, with a view to the resumption of its functions in accordance with the "Acordos de Paz" and previous resolutions on this matter'.

The most one could deduce from this convoluted language was that the Council was ready to expand UNAVEM, if circumstances permitted and this was made clearer by a subsequent paragraph, which stressed its 'readiness to take action promptly, at any time within the period of the mandate authorized by this resolution, on the recommendation of the Secretary-General, to expand substantially the United Nations presence in Angola in the event of significant progress in the peace process'. This was hardly a clarion call to the two sides to sort themselves out once and for all.

Despite the exhortations to both sides in Resolution 804 to cease hostilities against UNAVEM, the likelihood of such attacks was increased by that very resolution. There had already been strong reactions when the recommendations in the Secretary-General's report for scaling down UNAVEM became known in Luanda. The Governor of Luanda criticised UNAVEM in a television interview on 25 January, and hostile actions by the local population increased because we had not prevented the resumption of war. The situation was aggravated by a marked decrease in law and order in Luanda. A particularly nasty incident over the weekend of 23–24 January had resulted in the killing of a number of people from Zaire, and some expatriates had been killed within 500 metres of the UNAVEM camp.

Of parallel concern were UNITA's intentions. Its act of sabotage on 25 January had led to severe water rationing. Despite the purges of early November, UNITA still had a secret following in the city, especially in the poorer suburbs. Luanda was thus extremely vulnerable to guerrilla attacks and there was no reason to suppose that UNITA's participation in the Addis Ababa talks would deflect any plans it might have to conduct attacks against strategically vital public utilities. Action against the airport was also possible. Vila Espa was extremely vulnerable to infiltration by crowds of protestors bent on violence, being protected only by a wire fence and a few Ghurka guards, armed only with kukris, their traditional knives. Before coming to Addis Ababa, Brigadier Nyambuya had recommended to New York, with my backing, the deployment of an infantry company of 100 armed troops from UNIFIL, in Lebanon, to undertake a temporary mission in Angola to provide security at the airport and for Vila Espa.

Nor did Security Council Resolution 804 inspire confidence among the world at large, particularly international journalists who knew the country well. Some of them – quoting the increasing mutual distrust between the Government and UNITA, as well as the ferocity of the resumed civil war, in which at least 10 000 Angolans had been killed in three months – insisted a ceasefire could not work without many thousands of armed UN troops. I shared this appreciation, but had no option – given the very narrow room for manoeuvre afforded me – but to proceed on a stage-by-stage approach. To paraphrase Mrs Beaton's profoundly practical culinary instruction, it was a case of 'First get your ceasefire'!

* * *

That was proving no easy pursuit. During the whole of Friday 29 January the military and political commissions droned on in their separate meeting rooms. The Americans became so impatient that, with the aid of the Portuguese, they had come up with a document of their own. Well-meaning enough, this initiative simply muddied the waters. There was no alternative but to let the two sides feel out one another's positions, and then try to speed the process. There was no point in coming up with an instant solution if it did not engage the commitment of the parties to the conflict.

It quickly became clear that the 'antiriot' police force was the nub of UNITA's negotiating strategy. UNITA demanded that it should be 'extinguished' (to use a literal English translation of a very forceful Portuguese verb) as a prerequisite for a new ceasefire and for reverting to the implementation of the Peace Accords. It wanted the members of the antiriot police to be placed in assembly areas, like FAPLA soldiers; their equipment to be placed under custody; and a neutral security or public order police to be created, in which UNITA would be integrated. The Government could not accept the abolition of the emergency police, arguing that – under its authority as Government, which UNITA had recognised at Bicesse, and which had since been ratified by the elections – it had the obligation to maintain law and order and ensure security and public tranquillity. It was however amenable to the monitoring of the emergency police by UNAVEM, within its new mandate, and accepted that any equipment considered inappropriate should be transferred to the new Angolan armed forces (the FAA).

While there was agreement on other key points, the debate on the antiriot police raged back and forth with few signs of progress. A complete breakdown began to look alarmingly probable, and so, some time after midnight, I called in Dr Muteka and General Manuvakola and leant on them hard to find some accommodation, reminding them of the compromise we had proposed earlier (to confine the emergency police to barracks, except when a riot or an emergency required their presence; and to incorporate UNITA elements as soon as possible). I stressed the human urgency of getting a ceasefire quickly: while we were weaving circles around the same old issues in Addis Ababa, the battles raged on in Angola, claiming even more innocent lives and maiming countless others. Such was my exasperation that I ended up saying: 'It is a pity that neither of your delegations includes a woman, for if there were a few women here then we might have a better chance of finding a quick practical solution to bring to an end the senseless killing and the human suffering'. Both Dr Muteka and General Manuvakola appeared to take this unaccustomed tirade quite meekly and promised to try to find a way out.

I had hoped that, in a plenary session on Saturday, we might be able to bring the two sides closer to agreement on the outstanding issues, but although some progress was made, the main bone of contention remained. The timetable was complicated on this last day by a lunch hosted by Ambassador Almeida. I was determined to finish working through the documents presented by the commissions before letting the meeting break up, knowing full well that, if I let them go, I would never get them back to the table. Dalliance by the delegations had lost us much time at the beginning of the morning – UNITA, as usual, turning up late. So I remained impervious to the beseeching glances Ambassador Almeida kept bestowing in my direction, and to the increasingly indignant notes to which he eventually resorted when even baleful looks failed to have any effect.

It was late afternoon before I was satisfied that we had got as far as we could: if we could not get a ceasefire my more limited aim was to obtain written agreement on as many issues as possible, and acceptance of an early date for a follow-up meeting that would concentrate only on the areas of disagreement. After considerable demur by UNITA, which seemed to delight in putting things off, the Government, in contrast, was anxious to have the next meeting even earlier – we agreed to meet again in Addis Ababa barely ten days later, on Wednesday 10 February.

The lunch was an elegant and sumptuous affair: long tables decked in flowers and snowy linen set out on the lawn; buffets loaded with exquisite dishes of French and Angolan cuisine; a separate barbecue; and every conceivable form of aperitifs and prelunch drinks, wines to accompany the food and French champagne to celebrate. Celebrate what? I asked myself. And to crown it all, Addis Ababa had produced one of those champagne-like days that are one of the splendours of the high plateau in Eastern Africa: brilliant sunshine, the cloudless sky a robin's-egg-blue, and the diamantine quality of the air given that extra indefinable edge by the sharp fragrance of eucalyptus borne faintly on the breeze. The Ambassador's wife, to whom I felt it doubly incumbent on me to apologise, as a woman and as the Chairman, for the tardiness of our arrival, seemed to bear no ill-will and took everything in her stride. Among the Government and UNITA delegations an atmosphere of holiday outing began to take over, with much back-slapping, gales of laughter, and regaling of jokes.

At the end of the meal I found myself in a group comprising the two delegation leaders and some of their colleagues. More quips and anecdotes were exchanged between them, along with family news, and reminiscences of earlier days before they were separated by the deep fault-line dividing Angolan society and even families. Individual toasts were drunk in champagne, but there was hesitation about what more general object of blessing might be honoured, since they could hardly drink to their respective causes. My suggestion that 'Peace' could well fill the bill was enthusiastically seized and acted upon.

Everyone seemed to be enjoying themselves hugely. I was not, haunted by the knowledge that while we stood in this idyllic setting of flowers and verdant beauty, well-fed and wined, the grim, dark battle for Huambo was pounding brutally on, and the fighting, killing and dying were continuing all over Angola. I was glad to have the pretext of seeing to the papers for the final meeting to slip away early from a celebration I could no longer stomach.

* * *

The meeting got underway at 9 o'clock. We approved the final reports of the political and military mommissions, which recorded the areas of agreement and, where none had been reached, spelt out the positions of each side.

The areas of agreement covered broad issues such as commitment to the validity of the Peace Accords and recognition of the electoral results. The main area of disagreement remained the disposition of the antiriot police, in which connection UNITA resuscitated its old accusations that the Government had violated the 'triple-zero clause' by importing lethal equipment from Spain, a charge the Government equally vehemently rejected. UNITA also demanded the abolition of the so-called 'auxiliary forces' (the ODP – the People's Vigilance Brigades – and the BPV – the People's Defence Organisation), while the Government denied the existence of institutionalised forces of this nature, claiming that armed civilian groups were simply the result of military escalation provoked by UNITA's rejection of the election results. There were similar discrepancies over the FAA, UNITA promising to return once there was a settlement of the conflict but demanding the removal of military personnel incorporated since their withdrawal, which the Government did not accept. The last area of difference related to the exchange of prisoners, notably the UNITA people held in Luanda since November and the Government people detained in Uige and Kwanza Norte.

Both sides agreed on the urgent need for a ceasefire, but whereas the Government was ready to put it into effect immediately, UNITA made its acceptance contingent on several conditions that were not acceptable to the Government, among them the abolition of the antiriot police.

It was nearly midnight before we had tied all this up and the two leaders and I could go into a crowded press conference of impatient journalists who had been waiting all evening for news. The most important part of our final communiqué read, in English translation, as follows:

> After three days of direct conversations on political and military questions relevant to the solution of the post-electoral crises in Angola, the Government of the Republic of Angola and UNITA have reaffirmed the validity of the Peace Accords for Angola and their will to conclude their full implementation.
>
> The two Angolan delegations have examined in detail, in an atmosphere of frankness and openness, the underlying problems of the present crisis, and have reiterated their commitment to find, as soon as possible, lasting solutions for the consolidation of peace and democracy in Angola.
>
> The Government of the Republic of Angola and UNITA therefore express their objective to maintain and strengthen a direct political dialogue which will lead once again to the respect of the ceasefire throughout the national territory, allowing the normal development of the democratic institutions resulting from the elections of September 1992. To this end, and in order to allow the resumption of the functioning of the structures provided for in the Peace Accords, the two delegations agreed to meet again in Addis Ababa on 10 February 1993.

Not surprisingly this was found to be pretty thin gruel by a hungry pack of tired journalists ravenous for meat, and some of them were determined to extract some blood. There was some hostile questioning, especially, but not only, from the large crowd of Angolan journalists the Government delegation had brought on their plane. 'How can you just go on talking', went up the outraged cry, 'while so much blood is being shed all over Angola?'

It was a sentiment I shared, having been consumed by similar feelings of anguish during the past few frustrating days. But I restrained myself, simply pointing out that it was better to talk than not at all, and that although we had not obtained the ceasefire, a failure I deplored, we had managed to whittle down the areas of disagreement to just a few items, and had agreed to meet again on 10 February to discuss these in a much more tightly focused meeting. I could not add that even this outcome was very much better than had appeared possible 24 hours earlier, at 1 a.m. on Saturday morning. Total breakdown had then seemed imminent until I had had my straight talk with the two leaders.

At one o'clock in the morning we held a brief, formal session in which Dr Muteka, General Manuvakola and I signed all the reports. I begged both sides to agree to a ceasefire for the 10 days between then and our next meeting on 10 February, so that the bloodshed could cease while we went on with the talking. But I was not able to obtain such a concession and could only appeal to them to use those 10 days to resolve the major issue of the antiriot police through some of the various alternative approaches exhaustively discussed in Addis Ababa.

For my part, I determined to speak directly to Dr Savimbi to try to get him to agree to the confinement of the emergency or antiriot police to barracks under UN verification, including arms control, coupled with a genuine programme for incorporating UNITA, and other non-MPLA and non-FAPLA elements, into all branches of the police, including the anti-riot police.

* * *

I arrived in Knill in the small hours of Monday morning, 1 February. There were only four days left of my ill-fated 'rest and recuperation'. One evening was taken up giving an after-dinner talk on Angola to an agricultural society in Powys, in the same splendid pub to which I had taken my aunt for her birthday lunch. Conviviality was running high by the time I spoke, but to my delighted surprise the questions denoted not only much interest, but also great indignation about the inadequate international response to Angola. There was even vigorous support for sending 'Blue Helmets' to ensure a ceasefire, an unexpected view coming from a normally conservative group of men, immersed in farming among rolling Welsh hills a lifetime away.

My efforts to contact Dr Savimbi to seek a compromise on the antiriot police were to no avail; the satellite telephone was hermetically closed. I was in daily contact by telephone with Luanda and New York, and they were having no greater luck in reaching UNITA.

And then, with the eerily accurate timing to which I was becoming accustomed, Mr Jaka Jamba phoned me on Friday 5 February – at the precise moment I was leaving Knill to drive to Cambridge – to tell me, on behalf of Dr Savimbi, that UNITA could not get back to the Ethiopian capital by 10 February, owing to 'logistical problems'. The UNITA delegation had still not managed to return to Huambo and had not been able to brief Dr Savimbi in whatever mysterious secret headquarters he was now occupying, nor obtain instructions for the next round. I forbore to ask the obvious question as to how the delegation had managed to reach Addis Ababa in a couple of days, but were now, according to him, bumping endlessly through the bush. I restrained myself to an expression of profound disappointment and a sharp reminder that time was of the essence. Jaka Jamba assured me that they shared this sense of urgency, and would telephone me at the UNAVEM camp on Monday 8 February. I asked him to convey to Dr Savimbi my compromise proposal for handling the emergency police.

That evening I gave my lecture in Cambridge, perhaps aptly titled 'What Price Peace?' I used my experiences in Angola as a springboard for examining the major problems facing UN peacekeeping. At the dinner afterwards in Newnham, a banner from the women's suffragette movement had been hung for the occasion, blazoning the splendidly appropriate device 'Better is wisdom than weapons of war'.

When I got back to Vila Espa at breakfast time on Monday I found that the Government had made hay with UNITA's last-minute request for a delay, portraying it as proof of UNITA's bad faith and unwillingness to talk. I waited in vain all that day for Mr Jaka Jamba's promised telephone call. Repeated attempts to telephone him or Dr Savimbi proved fruitless. The satellite had been switched off. Once again we were in the tedious position of waiting for UNITA to drop the other shoe.

* * *

The impasse at Addis Ababa, though hardly our fault, had not improved the popularity of UNAVEM in Luanda. Rocks were now being thrown at UNAVEM vehicles when they went downtown and the camp was vulnerable. We were also concerned about fulfilling the UN commitment to provide security at the site of high-level negotiations between the Government and UNITA. After the second round in Addis Ababa, I intended subsequent meetings to take place in Angola and therefore had to be able to assure UNITA of sufficient UN troops to keep them safe. I cabled New York, strongly supporting Brigadier Nyambuya's plea for the earliest possible provision of a 100-man infantry company. I suggested that this company could also be responsible for the security of Vila Espa – which I hoped could be a 'neutral ground' for the detailed negotiations that would follow a ceasefire – and our installations at the airport. The proposed company could also be of inestimable value in securing the humanitarian relief channels we were hoping to open up. We did not want to have a repetition of Somalia and stand accused of providing 'too little, too late' to alleviate terrible human suffering.

Mig told me that there were good prospects of an infantry company being provided from Ghana, but that it could not be used for the day-to-day security of the UNAVEM camp *per se*, as opposed to security for special high-level meetings. Headquarters made an initial *démarche* to Ghana on 12 February. Paradoxically, our normal complement of UNAVEM personnel was simultaneously being drastically reduced in response to Security Council Resolution 804. By 13 February we were down to 75 military observers and 30 police observers, many of them, together with equipment we had been able to salvage from the outposts, having been transferred to Mozambique.

* * *

Now that the second meeting in Addis Ababa was postponed *sine die*, it was even more urgent to stop the fighting, in the face of a growing humanitarian disaster of immense proportions. At least 10 000 people had been killed since hostilities broke out again and a further million rendered homeless. Now horrific reports were seeping out of Huambo, where street-to-street fighting had been going on for a month. My attempt in Addis Ababa to get the two sides to declare a temporary ceasefire during the interlude between the first and second meetings in Addis Ababa having failed, the only alternative was a truce for humanitarian purposes, and on 10 February I addressed identical, personal letters to President dos Santos and Dr Savimbi enclosing an appeal that read as follows:

> In the light of reports of great suffering and destruction in Huambo and other areas of Angola, the Special Representative of the Secretary-General, Miss Margaret Anstee, appeals to President José Eduardo Dos Santos and to Dr Jonas Savimbi to agree to a truce so that humanitarian aid can be given immediately, particularly to the people of Huambo, where Government and UNITA forces have been engaged in battle for more than one month.
>
> Thousands of people are reported to be wounded in Huambo, without any proper medical assistance. Food and water are reported to be scarce. A truce is vital to permit help to be brought to the wounded and to suffering civilians.
>
> The Special Representative appeals for orders to be given urgently so that the practical aspects of such a truce can be implemented immediately.

The truce appeal was given the widest possible publicity in Luanda and New York in order to build up public support, nationally and internationally, as well as draw attention to the tragedy. UNITA's fax machine was as inaccessible as its satellite telephone, and I eventually resorted to the good offices of Marcos Samondo in New York to get my message through to Dr Savimbi.

Contact with the Government was easier. I met Foreign Minister de Moura on Tuesday evening, 9 February, and the following morning I saw the President to explore the lie of the land for the next Addis Ababa meeting.

The meeting with the Foreign Minister followed a familiar pattern, wandering all over the place. It was difficult to have a structured discussion for his mind tended to flit, bird-like, between all the subjects at hand, alighting only to deliver some fierce pecks here and there with a razor-sharp beak. On Addis Ababa, the Minister proclaimed himself optimistic, counselled me to be patient, and stressed the Government's willingness to consider an acceptable compromise on the central issue of the emergency police. He underlined the key role of the UN, describing the Secretary-General's last report to the Security Council as 'very bad indeed', criticising especially his recommendation to withdraw from Angola, if matters had not sorted themselves out by 30 April. Rather the UN should immediately and greatly increase its presence in Angola. I could not refrain from pointing out that, in the absence of a ceasefire, the only way would be to bring in a large force of 'Blue Helmets' to interpose themselves between the two sides and act as a buffer to stop the fighting, a possibility he had repeatedly ruled out publicly as unacceptable to the Government; apart from quietly trying to get negotiations moving again, no other role was possible.

The Minister also criticised UNAVEM for withdrawing from the areas where fighting had broken out. When I reminded him that we were there to verify the peace process, not all-out war, and stressed the need to avoid unnecessary loss of human life in a situation where we could do nothing, the Minister retorted that the UN had lost far fewer people in Angola than in other peacekeeping missions. This callous comment made me so angry that I found it difficult to restrain myself from walking out, but I managed to react calmly, forcefully rejecting it as totally unacceptable.

A third crossing of swords took place when the Minister averred that the Government had been forced by the Secretary-General's report to take the hardline position with UNITA that, if there was no *prior* commitment to sign a ceasefire at the next Addis Ababa meeting, the Government was not prepared to engage in further dialogue. When I pointed out the illogicality of this, he conceded that it was a negotiating ploy designed to bring pressure on UNITA. He also admitted that he personally was against such tactics, but that there were still many hardliners in the top levels of Government whose opinion had to be humoured.

The meeting with the President was much more consistent and unreservedly cordial. The only other person present was the saturnine Victor Lima. The President was at pains to say that much more had been achieved at the Addis Ababa meeting than he had thought possible; he had never expected a ceasefire at the first encounter. Like all of us, he was sceptical about UNITA's reasons for being unable to return to Addis Ababa on 10 February, believing that Dr Savimbi wanted first to secure more gains on the battlefield. Despite the sterner stand being taken by the international community towards Dr Savimbi (which he welcomed), the latter had still not come to terms with the fact that he could not win through warlike means, but the President was optimistic that this reality must dawn on the UNITA leader eventually; we would all have to be patient for some time, maybe a month, maybe more. A central consideration in UNITA's mind seemed to be control of Huambo; he could not understand how Dr Savimbi could continue attacking an area where the majority of the population were his own supporters. The President regretted that I had been unable to obtain UNITA's agreement to a temporary ceasefire in Addis Ababa and urged me to continue to press for this. I told him that both leaders would be receiving an appeal for an immediate humanitarian truce later in the day, expressing the hope that he would take the initiative of accepting the proposal, rather than waiting for UNITA.

As for the next Addis Ababa meeting, the President promised me that the Government would be flexible in seeking viable compromises on the 'antiriot' police and the armed civilian auxiliaries. He thought that Dr Savimbi's main preoccupation was security, and welcomed my plans to bring the negotiations back to Angola, assuring me that there would be no problem with bringing in 'Blue Helmets' for this purpose. Even Foreign Minister de Moura had agreed.

We discussed the role to be assigned to Dr Savimbi if or when the situation was normalised. Ambassador De Jarnette had proposed to me, and to Victor Lima, that the post of leader of the opposition (that is Savimbi) should be institutionalised, with the rank of Minister of State, plus attendant privileges and a seat in the Assembly. The President did not seem to think that this was viable (although Ambassador De Jarnette had received encouraging reactions from other high-level Government officials). He would prefer Dr Savimbi to take a seat in the Assembly as leader of the opposition; but his name had not been included in the list of UNITA candidates and this could only be corrected by a decision of the tribunal. We also discussed Pik Botha's idea that Dr Savimbi might head an organisation charged with reconstruction. I suggested that it would be useful if his undoubted organisational capacities could be directed into constructive channels. The President agreed, albeit somewhat sceptically.

The President emphasised that US recognition of the Angolan Government, though it would have been more helpful earlier, was still desirable, not least as a further signal to Dr Savimbi. I knew that Ambassador De Jarnette had been pushing this very hard with the State Department and that he was leaving for Washington the following day. In reporting this conversation to New York, I asked the Secretary-General to try to help these efforts. Recognition was not to come until several months later, however, and then at a moment that could hardly have been less propitious.

At the close of our conversation the President emphasised the importance of the UN role in Angola, expressed his appreciation of our efforts and counselled me personally to have 'courage and patience'. In a curious parallel to my relations with UN Headquarters, I felt that our work was better understood and supported at the pinnacle than lower down.

* * *

Patience was a virtue I had to cultivate assiduously, not having been unduly blessed with it by natural temperament.

On 11 February, three days late, Mr Jaka Jamba called me, claiming that the Government's bombardment of Huambo had rendered UNITA's communications inoperable. I resisted the temptation to ask why they were working now, though privately wondering whether this confirmed the rumours circulating through Luanda that day that Huambo had fallen to UNITA. He went on to say that the UNITA delegation had still not arrived back in Huambo, 11 days after the Addis Ababa meeting had ended, and that UNITA could not suggest a new date for the second meeting until they did arrive. Again he blamed the delay on the Government bombardment and also on an incident in Uige airport on 7 February, when, according to a communiqué issued by General 'Ben-Ben', the Government had deliberately bombed the airport just as UNITA was releasing foreign oil workers from Soyo – because of this all pilots were refusing to fly in UNITA areas for fear of Government attack. I expressed some puzzlement about this, since Mr Samondo had told me only two nights before that the delegation was already on Angolan territory, travelling by land. 'Which is the correct version?' I enquired, but got no reply.

Mr Jaka Jamba said that my compromise solution on the antiriot police had been conveyed to Dr Savimbi, who was 'reserving judgement until he could get a full report from the delegation on the Addis Ababa meeting'. It transpired that neither my letter transmitting the official report of the meeting, nor my appeal for a humanitarian truce had reached him. Jaka Jamba gave me a new fax number in Abidjan, to which we retransmitted all this correspondence without difficulty.

None of this got us much farther, except to lend credence to speculation that Dr Savimbi and his senior colleagues were not in or near Huambo, or even in Angola at all, and that all the palaver about the difficulties and hardships suffered by the delegation was just a lot of eyewash to allow UNITA to play for time, presumably to gain complete control of Huambo as an additional bargaining chip. Evidently this objective was taking longer to achieve than calculated, and meanwhile UNITA's excuses for the delay were wearing increasingly thin. These views were shared by Foreign Minister de Moura and General Higino Carneiro, whom I met on 12 February. General Higino said the Government's information was that the UNITA delegation was now in Kinshasa, while Dr Savimbi was in Abidjan. I pressed my appeal for a humanitarian truce, noting that the President had seemed favourable to the idea. Minister de Moura said

Peace Talks in Ethiopia

that he was going at once to the President and would let me have a formal acceptance of the proposal as soon as possible.

The observers were also stepping up pressure. They had issued a joint statement on 11 February exhorting the UNITA leadership to make the follow-up meeting possible 'without delay', and they now advised me that they intended to issue an even stronger one on 13 February, setting a deadline of Wednesday 17 February for Dr Savimbi to accept a date. If he did not the observers would declare UNITA to be outside the law and would call for support for the Government; the 'triple zero' provisions of the Peace Accords concerning arms supplies would be declared null and void. The observers wanted UNAVEM to offer to ferry the UNITA delegation from wherever they were now back to their base in Angola (wherever that was). I saw no objection but suspected that the UNITA leadership would be reluctant to accept, as they presumably did not want their whereabouts to be known, much less have their excuses rumbled.

Mr Metelits of the US Liaison Office came on Saturday 13 February to explain further what he termed 'a completely new ball game'. When I asked about the practical effect of declaring the 'triple zero' provisions of the Peace Accords null and void, he said, after some pressing, that the three countries would then provide arms and military expertise to the government. I warned that ultimatums boomerang, if not backed up by convincing measures, and expressed the hope that the ultimate consequences had been thought through in Washington (at whose insistence, according to Metelits, the original statement was being toughened up and the deadline imposed). Supposing that, in spite of outside help for the Government, UNITA still managed to win? Would the observer countries, particularly the United States, be prepared to take even more drastic action, and if so, by what means and through what channels? Mr Metelits did not answer my question but said, first, that the US administration's tougher stand was due to a recent bipartisan letter from both houses of Congress expressing dismay over the turn of events in Angola and urging both US recognition of the Government and much stronger US action; and second, advantage would be taken of Ambassador De Jarnette's presence in Washington to have high-level discussions on Tuesday 16 February, which would probe into all eventualities and risks. I pointed out that this would be *after* the observers' ultimatum had been issued. Metelits added that US recognition would be part of the package of measures to be applied if Dr Savimbi did not observe the deadline. This did not appear very logical either since it was something that should be done anyway, and should have been done earlier.

I hastened to convey to New York my concern that the observers, by launching an initiative without apparently thinking through the ultimate implications, might inadvertently leave us without any framework (the Peace Accords) within which to work and the UN with no recognisable *raison d'être*, and probably in the midst of outright war. What would be the Security Council's attitude if the Peace Accords, which had been our 'Bible', were cast aside and the three observer countries (two of which – Russia and the United States – were permanent members of the Council), who were the main architects of those Accords, were to adopt a position in support of one of the parties? What should the Secretary-General recommend in such circumstances? I asked Headquarters to try to find out from Washington their precise intentions as to the follow-up of the new statement.

That statement duly appeared. After suggesting that the provision of transport by UNAVEM should resolve UNITA's difficulties, it went on:

> In view of the persistent situation of armed hostilities which is contrary to the Cease-Fire Agreement, the Observers inform the UNITA Leadership that they will wait until 22.00 hours on 17 February (next Wednesday) for UNITA to communicate its decision about the date of the meeting in question.
>
> The Observers will certainly draw the conclusions which they deem appropriate if the UNITA Leadership fails to respond.

The sting in the tail of this statement came over clearly enough, but it was not at all clear what practical form it would take if UNITA failed to oblige.

To judge by an interview with Dr Jorge Valentim, broadcast on the same day on Vorgan radio, UNITA was feeling anything but obliging. Delivered in his usual bombastic style, the message was triumphalist, arrogant and bellicose: UNITA was winning hands down, especially in Huambo, supported everywhere by a grateful populace, which well understood that the Government and the MPLA were to blame for everything, including the delay in holding the second Addis Ababa meeting by closing the frontiers and preventing the UNITA delegation from returning to their base. He contemptuously rejected the 'MPLA's request for a humanitarian truce', a clear misrepresentation of the fact that the appeal had been made by the United Nations, but which enabled him to argue that the MPLA wanted the truce so that it could reinforce its garrisons, which were completely surrounded by UNITA troops, and because the MPLA was losing the war. This remarkable display of sophistry hardly suggested a party preparing to return to the conference table to negotiate peace and reconciliation.

UNITA at last made contact again at 3.15 p.m. on Tuesday 16 February. Mr Jaka Jamba told me that General Manuvakola and his companions had arrived back in Huambo only at 3.00 p.m. that day after a peripatetic and often perilous journey (if what he said was true, it had taken 16 days). Dr Savimbi was 'very anxious' to meet me at some appropriate time, but the present moment was not propitious. He was elusive about my appeal for a humanitarian truce, saying that the first step must be to return to Addis Ababa and find general solutions. General Manuvakola came on the line to say that he and the delegation were exhausted but were contacting their colleagues, not all of whom were in the same place, and hoped to get back to me within 'three or four days'. I made a very strong plea for a date for the meeting to be established there and then, but he would only promise that we would speak again on Friday.

I had another go at Mr Jaka Jamba, pushing hard for an immediate answer on my humanitarian truce appeal so that, while we were awaiting for UNITA to make up its mind about a date, there could be a pause in the killing. I argued that unless there was some positive gesture, no one would believe UNITA's assertions that it sincerely wanted peace and an early meeting in Addis Ababa; its international credibility had already sunk very low. Jaka Jamba promised that the matter would be seriously considered in the light of my clarification that the appeal was from me and not the Government (something that was obvious from the text of the appeal), but he evaded commitment, grudgingly saying that he would try to call me about the truce before Friday.

Meanwhile the observers' deadline of Wednesday 17 February passed without any clearer indication of what their countries would do if UNITA ignored their ultimatum. In a conversation with Dmitry Titov, Ambassador Davidow denied any possibility of providing military support to the Government or making of the Peace Accords null and void, and he took a similar position publicly in an interview with the BBC. The Prime Minister of Portugal, Dr Cavaco Silva, was evasive when questioned on sanctions for non-compliance with the deadline. With this confirmation that nothing would happen if it did not respond, I felt sure that UNITA, which had publicly rejected and ridiculed the ultimatum, must by now be laughing all the way to somewhere, but not necessarily Addis Ababa! One could not help wondering what purpose was served by establishing a deadline if non-compliance would bring no retribution, and indeed whether the communiqué had not made matters worse rather than better. It was a classic example of a constant phenomenon in peacekeeping: the temptation, in the face of frustrating and exasperating circumstances, to take strong initiatives without thinking through all the consequences, or providing proper back-up, and then finding that the sword has broken in one's hand.

Nor were matters helped by a statement made to Kofi Annan (Mig's former deputy, who had just replaced him, while Mig became Under-Secretary-General for Political Affairs) by Ambassador Walker, US Deputy Permanent Representative to the UN, that the United States had 'no plans to recognise any party at this stage'. This ambiguous remark sounded ominously as if the United States was waiting to see which side would gain victory! One could hardly imagine that it was considering 'recognising' UNITA, but if this formulation simply meant that it did not intend to recognise the *Government* officially, then this was news that was not likely to help the UN in finding a solution. US recognition of the Government, once it had been democratically elected in September 1992, was long overdue. Late as it was now, it would still have been helpful in establishing legitimacy and could have been a more effective message to UNITA than empty blusterings about deadlines.

In view of UNITA's telephone conversation with me on 16 February, the observers extended their deadline until 19 February. High-level representatives of the Troika were to meet in Lisbon on Tuesday 23 February. Antonio

Monteiro told me that, if by then UNITA had not yet indicated a date for Addis Ababa, they would discuss what measures they should take.

* * *

As UNITA was not to make contact again until 19 February, I spent Wednesday 17 February 'visiting the troops' in Namibe and Lubango, and also called on the provincial authorities. Both towns conserved a remarkable aura of tranquillity and normality, while the rest of the country was consumed in war and destruction. The influx of people fleeing westwards was, however, making itself felt, most particularly in Benguela.

News trickling out of the beleaguered city of Huambo indicated that thousands of people had been killed in the battle that had been raging for nearly six weeks. The Government estimated 10 000 dead and 15 000 wounded in that one place alone. Food, water and medicines were virtually exhausted. On 18 February I reiterated my appeal for a humanitarian truce. So far neither side had given a formal reply. My appeal had by now been echoed by the ICRC as well as by the Roman Catholic Bishops of Angola. With the responsible UN agencies, especially UNDP, UNICEF, WFP and the UNHCR, we were working hard on contingency plans and strategic stockpiling of food, medicines and other emergency supplies, so that they could be rushed to Huambo and other badly affected areas as soon as the flag of truce was raised. We were hampered by the lack of first-hand information and it was going to be necessary to conduct a rapid needs assessment as soon as access was possible, not least as the basis for an international appeal. Our initial response could be met from emergency supplies in the country, but they would quickly be exhausted once they could be freely distributed.

Some insights into the military situation, as seen by the Government, were provided on 18 February, when General João de Matos, Chief of General Staff of the FAA asked to see me and Colonel Cameron Ross, our Chief of Staff (Brigadier Nyambuya was on leave). I had had little previous contact with General Matos, who cut an imposing figure – tall, good-looking and emanating a sense of military briskness and efficiency. It is fascinating to recall the conversation that followed, in the light of General Matos' subsequent success in turning the balance of military advantage round, in spite of what then seemed overwhelming odds. He waded straight in, saying he wanted to ask me three questions. Did I really have hope that peace would be restored? What was the present disposition of the UNAVEM teams in the field? Were there any UNAVEM personnel in areas controlled by UNITA?

Most of the discussion revolved around the first question. I said that, although very frustrated, I had to persevere with the negotiations since the alternative – continued internecine war – would simply result in a prolongation of human suffering, in which neither side could gain victory. Hope should be the last thing to die. General Matos was very sceptical: 'You have known Savimbi and UNITA for only a short time' he said, 'we have known him for over 25 years. We know from bitter experience that he cannot be trusted and that the only thing that interests him is to gain power by military force. He will go on stringing out the peace negotiations but will always come back to fighting. Hence, he must be resisted'.

But the General was equally categorical that military victory was impossible for either side. Since he had discounted both the peace process and the military option, I enquired what he saw as the solution. He replied that violent war at the present level of intensity could not be sustained for more than one or two months. But a stand-off situation involving guerilla harassment and terrorism could go on for a very long time, even without outside help, because of the enormous quantity of arms and ammunition available throughout the country. After a lengthy discussion he appeared to concede that there was no alternative but to attempt to renew the discussions in Addis Ababa and arrive at a ceasefire; his thinking was not entirely consistent. He was not hopeful about the possibility of organising the humanitarian truce.

On the military situation, General Matos said that the Government had begun at a serious disadvantage since it had demobilised virtually the whole of FAPLA and the FAA was still in embryonic form, whereas UNITA had not demobilised and had a hidden army spread over various regions. The Government had had to rely initially on the police. A big effort was now being made to build up the FAA, which was becoming a more effective fighting force. But once the FAA was fully engaged in war, it would be very difficult for it to stop. This sounded ominously as if the Government might refuse to go back to Addis Ababa if it acquired sufficient military strength before UNITA replied (another repetition of the 'tragic seesaw' we had been experiencing all along). Since General Matos seemed to accept the inevitability of peace negotiations, I took his comment as a signal that we had better not dilly-dally in getting the second round of meetings in place – that, of course, did not depend on us but on UNITA. He was at pains to stress that he was speaking as an individual and from a military standpoint, and not as a political representative of the Government.

General Matos revealed that the Government had actually considered withdrawing from Huambo, in order to reduce the terrible casualty rate, but had concluded that this would only incite what they considered to be Dr Savimbi's insatiable appetite to advance further. He told us that Dr Savimbi had recently been heard assuring his supporters, foreign as well as Angolan, that by March UNITA would have overrun the whole country, including Luanda. General Matos dismissed this as totally impossible. Interestingly he affirmed that Dr Savimbi was now in Jamba – 'at least, he was as of 18.00 hours last night'. While the situation in Huambo remained critical and UNITA had considerably superior strength, he gave the impression of confidence that the Government could somehow hold out. Nor did he think that Menongue, also under siege, was in danger of falling.

On his other two questions, we informed him that we aimed to reestablish small UNAVEM teams in Luena (Government-held) and Uige (UNITA-held), the only places where we could plug into UNITA's military command chain and obtain clearance and guarantees for flights, including humanitarian missions. General Matos welcomed this possibility and promised full cooperation.

General Matos showed an understanding of the limitations of our mandate, which he said was not fully comprehended in Angola, even among intellectuals. He agreed that the CCPM had not acted on our frequent warnings of the discrepancies between the rate of FAPLA demobilisation compared with FALA, and had not made full use of UNAVEM's air support in the search for the supposed UNITA 'hidden army', conceding also that the Government had been satisfied that no proof of the existence of such troops had been found.

Given that UNAVEM served as a useful whipping-boy for both sides whenever things went wrong, it was comforting to find someone who took a more dispassionate view. Militarily, not much more could go wrong for the Government. A rough map prepared by Colonel Ross revealed just how precarious a toehold the Government retained. Even along the coast UNITA dominated the area from the Zairean border to a point only a few kilometres north of Luanda, as well as stretches between Sumbe and Lobito and to the south of Benguela. Inland the Government controlled only a few tiny islands around the provincial capitals of Malange, Huambo, Kuito/Bié, Menongue, Luena, Saurimo and Dundo, all surrounded by large tracts of UNITA-held territory and under siege, or even themselves battlegrounds. With a few more tenuous enclaves in the diamond-mining areas in the province of Lunda Norte, this was the sum total of the territory where the legitimately elected Government could have a presence, and some of those did not look likely to hold out for long. One look at this map made it easy to explain UNITA's reluctance to return to the negotiating table.

* * *

On Friday 19 February, UNITA called at 3.00 p.m. to announce I would receive its definitive reply at 9.00 p.m. General Manuvakola telephoned considerably later than that and we had another of those kilometric and repetitive conversations at which UNITA seemed to excel and which, by enmeshing the subject at hand in a welter of different nuances, unerringly managed, perhaps intentionally, to sow more confusion than clarity. (I suspected that all UNITA leaders had to undergo a special course to perfect this bewildering technique!) The gist did seem to be clear, however: the UNITA delegation was ready to return to Addis Ababa, provided UNAVEM could transport them and guarantee their security, for which they stipulated complicated conditions. If UNAVEM came up with an acceptable proposal, they would be ready to travel the 'next day'. If they travelled by their own means there would be a much longer delay – at least seven days. General Manuvakola said he would contact me again on Saturday.

Colonel Ross and Tom White immediately began work on the plan. Since the Beechcraft had limited seating capacity and range, it might be necessary to hire a larger, faster aircraft – a considerable additional cost for which we had no budget. When the observers had put the onus on UNAVEM to solve UNITA's logistical problems by transporting them, Mr Metelits had assured me that the United States would pick up any additional tab involved; now, after telephone conversations with Washington, he told me that the best that could be done would be for the three observer countries to 'support most strongly' any request we made to UN Headquarters for additions to our budget! Budgetary processes being notoriously long and difficult, I was worried that we would lose this last-ditch opportunity for peace for want of a relatively small amount of money – the story of the Angolan operation from start to finish.

Early next morning I sent a fax to General Manuvakola, confirming that we would undertake the delegates' transport and could meet their security requirements. I requested information in order to draw up a detailed plan: from which airport would the delegation be leaving and how many passengers would be travelling? I assured him that, if refuelling stops were necessary, either Bujumbura in Burundi or Mbuki Mayi in Zaire would be used (UNITA had listed countries where it was not prepared to set foot, even for a refuelling stop). Lastly, I told him that we were tentatively scheduling the flight for Tuesday night, so that the meeting could start on Wednesday 24 February, and I looked forward to his promised call at 3.00 p.m. to finalise the details.

We also needed to make progress on the substantive issues before we got to Addis Ababa. I was deeply worried about public statements UNITA had made in Washington and New York, which showed that UNITA still sustained a totally intransigent position on the antiriot police, in spite of all my suggestions for compromise. I therefore asked Kofi Annan to convey to Marcos Samondo the same points that I would be emphasizing to UNITA in my renewed local contact with them. If we could get acceptance of the basic premises I had so often enunciated, then it should not be difficult to reach agreement on certain indispensable actions. The alternative on which we had most nearly obtained acceptance in Addis Ababa envisaged the following steps, all under UNAVEM's verification and supervision:

– Immediately after the ceasefire came into effect, the Government would confine the antiriot police to barracks.
– All their armament would be verified by UNAVEM, which would decide which elements could be retained and which exceeded their requirement either in type or quantity; the latter either to be destroyed or handed over to the FAA.
– The incorporation and training of sufficient elements drawn from UNITA and other non-MPLA sources to ensure a balanced and neutral composition.

>This might entail demobilising some ex-FAPLA elements previously enrolled in the antiriot police, to make room for these new entrants.

Such on operation would require urgent strengthening of UNAVEM's capacity but I pinned my faith on the last Security Council Resolution and Headquarters' commitment to me to have a company of 'Blue Helmets' on call at 48 hours' notice, though I knew from sobering past experience that I might well be whistling in the wind.

Everything now depended on finalising the transport arrangements for the UNITA delegation. Exasperatingly, UNITA once again went to ground over another frustrating weekend. When the silence continued throughout Sunday, I contacted the UNITA representatives in London and New York. I did not mince my words to Samondo and Samakuva: further silence and delay by UNITA would look very much like prevarication, in which case, given the intense media interest and speculation, I would be obliged to say something publicly on Monday morning. Whether as a result of these tactics or not, I received a fax at 7.00 a.m. on Monday, promising telephone contact at 10.00 a.m., which this time actually took place. It was agreed that the UNITA delegation would be transported overnight on Thursday 25 February, and that the meeting would start on Friday 26 February. The Government agreed to this plan, I informed the observers and Mr Yaker and we seemed to be in business.

* * *

On Monday 22 February I wrote to Dr Muteka and General Manuvakola proposing the following agenda:

1. Reestablishment of the ceasefire.
2. Conclusion of the implementation of the Peace Accords:
   – the antiriot police;
   – the 'triple-zero' provision.
3. Role of the UN.
4. Release of prisoners.
5. Humanitarian assistance.

The first four items stemmed from the first meeting and I had added humanitarian assistance because of the rapidly deteriorating situation and the need to obtain the cooperation of both sides if we were not successful in obtaining a truce or, better still, a ceasefire.

In New York, Kofi Annan's department had urged Marcos Samondo to impress on his leadership the need for flexibility, especially with regard to the antiriot police, and had outlined my proposed compromise. Samondo had apparently listened carefully, but had not made any comment, merely undertaking to convey the appeal to his leadership.

The Troika's meeting in Lisbon was now geared to ensuring a successful outcome in Addis Ababa. To prepare the ground, on 18 February Ambassador Davidow had separate meetings in Washington with the Angolan Ambassador and the UNITA representative, urging them to develop realistic proposals for a negotiated settlement and to consider some additional elements, such as power-sharing, for the interim period before the second presidential round. The Angolan Government was asked to send its delegation to London before the Addis Ababa meeting, to discuss that very issue with Hank Cohen.

Despite US pressure, UNITA was now posing additional conditions. When General Manuvakola finally spoke to me on Monday 22 February, he linked the Addis Ababa meeting to the health of Chivukuvuku, alleging that he was in imminent danger of losing his leg or even his life and threatening to 'hold UNAVEM responsible'. A veritable blitz, UNITA-style, followed. Marcos Samondo sent me a copy of a letter from Manuvakola to the Foreign Minister, demanding that Chivukuvuku be sent abroad for treatment on the grounds that gangrene was setting in and New York was again besieged with enquiries about his health. The ICRC and ourselves had been monitoring his progress, and on 23 February I sent two of my senior colleagues to see him. No Government representative was present, the only other person being General Wambu, chief of UNITA's military intelligence. They found Chivukuvuku in good health and spirits with his leg on the mend. The Red Cross also confirmed that there was no danger to life and limb, and I sent a reassuring report to General Manuvakola.

* * *

The human disaster worsened every day that passed without truce or ceasefire and I still had no formal response from either side to my appeal. On 19 February I cabled the Secretary-General to suggest a number of actions, among them that he should issue a public appeal for an early cease-fire on the eve of the renewed talks in Addis Ababa. This was done on 25 February.

I also called for the preparation of contingency plans both in New York and Luanda, for a much larger operation than was possible with our current resources, and which should address two aspects: the terrible suffering in the battle zones (notably, but not exclusively, in Huambo); and the wider, longer-term problems caused by the conflict. Jan Eliasson, then the Under-Secretary-General for humanitarian affairs, decided to send out a mission to make an urgent on-the-spot review. I had been in some doubt about the need for such a mission, especially as it would come during my absence in Addis Ababa. We agreed that the leader of the team would fly to Ethiopia afterwards to brief me and hear my views.

* * *

A further drama occurred on 23 February, when one of our military observers, Captain Shaidaft Feyez of Jordan was kidnapped by some unidentified elements in the enclave of Cabinda. 'Never a dull moment' could well have been UNAVEM's motto! There were so many warring factions in Cabinda that he could have been in any number of hands. The Angolan Government sent out police and military patrols, and we contacted the UNITA, FLEC and UNDP offices in Kinshasa and Brazzaville since he could easily have been taken over the border. This was to be a continuing saga while we were in Addis Ababa, involving the assistance of UN colleagues in Zaire and Congo before we secured his release several weeks later.

* * *

The two-day delay requested by UNITA meant that we could no longer make use of the once-weekly commercial flight to Addis Ababa, while our knowledge of UNITA's sensitivities and capacity to make propaganda from the flimsiest evidence made it impossible to travel in the Government's official jet. Since we has no budget for any faster mode of transport, we were reduced to a long and tortuous two and a half day journey, flying to Harare in the Beechcraft on Wednesday afternoon, 24 February, and continuing the next day by commercial flights, involving a second overnight stay in Nairobi. The Beechcraft would return to Luanda to transport the UNITA delegation, who would be picked up from an as yet unspecified spot in the interior by helicopters and transported to an airstrip other than Luanda, but still not yet agreed, where the Beechcraft could operate. The Government had assured us of full safety guarantees for these flights and UNAVEM personnel would accompany the UNITA delegation. Given these complications, I told everyone that the first meeting would take place after lunch on Friday 26 February.

By Wednesday morning all was in order, except for the time and place of the UNITA pick-up, information that UNITA wished to give us only at the very last moment for security reasons. We were due to leave at 1.00 p.m. Everyone else left for the airport but I stayed behind until the last moment to handle some urgent matters, not least the problem of the kidnapped military observer. I was walking out of the door to get in the car, when the phone rang. It was General Manuvakola.

Once again UNITA was demonstrating in the split-second timing that gave me the eerie sensation that my every move was being watched. Nor did General Manuvakola have good news. He launched into the long-winded discourse that seemed to be UNITA's preferred mode of communication over the satellite telephone, the burden of which was that UNITA was not happy with our security and transport arrangements. The delegates were convinced that the Government was out to get them and that it would be sheer lunacy to give us information about when and where they could be picked up. Appalled, I argued that we had been meticulous in obtaining all possible assurances from the Government, which was keen to have the second round of talks; it was not in its interests to make any attempt against the lives of the UNITA delegation, and those of the accompanying UNAVEM officers to boot – it would be outright folly and would bring the full opprobrium of the international community down on the Government. Moreover UNITA would be held responsible for the talks not taking place if the delegates did not turn up when every facility and guarantee had been provided for them.

But Manuvakola simply resorted to another familiar UNITA ploy, repeating the same arguments, almost parrot-fashion, and with distinctly paranoid overtones, as if one had said absolutely nothing in between that even merited acknowledgement, much less any modification of position. The conversation fluctuated back and forth for an hour. If UNITA's aim was to sow confusion it was a brilliantly executed operation. General Manuvakola insisted that he was not saying that UNITA would not attend, but simply questioning the arrangements. The not very satisfactory outcome was an agreement to go on working on a more acceptable solution.

This placed us in an almost insoluble dilemma, as was no doubt intended. It was difficult to suspend the meeting at this late stage and we could not do so unilaterally. I telephoned Dr Muteka, and after some hurried consultations he told me that the Government wished to keep to the agreed timetable. The Government was clearly anxious to have the talks and, if they did not take place, to ensure that the blame lay squarely on UNITA. He also reiterated the Government's guarantee of safe passage for our aircraft. The observers were of the same view. So we set out, much later than intended and with greatly reduced expectations. Colonel Ross and Hugo Anson remained behind to mastermind the negotiations with UNITA. Lieutenant Colonel Bill Egar, the Chief of Operations, was to accompany the UNITA delegation.

The journey to Harare was a nightmare. Our spirits were low, the physical discomfort great. The Beechcraft proved intolerably cramped for a journey that took over five hours. Most of us had long legs, and could not stretch or move. There were no toilet facilities and although a thoughtful staff officer had rigged up a temporary arrangement and makeshift curtain in the tail of the aircraft, everyone went to great lengths to avoid having to use it, touching no liquid or other refreshment, not even water!

It was very late when we reached Harare, where Brigadier Nyambuya joined us. I had been expected to dinner by my old friends Bernard Chidzero, the Minister of Finance, and his wife, Micheline, but the hour had passed and we were only able to speak by telephone. Very early the next morning, as we flew over the heart of Africa – with its endlessly varied succession of jungles, bush and open plains, mountains, lakes and scattered, brown-thatched villages spread below us – I worked on the notes for my opening remarks at the meeting. When we at last reached our destination on Friday 26 February we found that the Government delegation and the observers had already arrived, as well as Marcos Samondo and Brigadier Samakuva for UNITA.

From Harare and Nairobi I had talked by satellite phone to Colonel Ross. He and his military team had come up with an impressive array of alternatives to meet the UNITA delegates' objections and allay their fears. Thier arrival would be delayed, but the journey now seemed to be on. At 11.00 a.m. on Thursday 25 February General Manuvakola had promised to call back with final details for the pick-up.

The all-too-familiar ritual of waiting for UNITA began once more. This time I had been given the largest suite in the Hilton Hotel, a huge conglomeration of intersecting reception and dining rooms, bedrooms and bathrooms, in which I regularly got lost and which was certainly beyond my UN *per diem*. Though hardly cosy, it provided a suitable venue for the marathon of meetings, often very large, that would take place over the next few days at all hours of the day and night. During the first afternoon I spoke to Dr Muteka and General Higino, the observers, and Marcos Samondo and Brigadier Samakuva, who purported to be as much in the dark about the whereabouts of the rest of the UNITA delegation as we were. Not much light – indeed a considerable degree of gloom – was shed by a cable from Hugo Anson at the end of the afternoon saying that, General Manuvakola had not made the promised contact; there was now no possibility of transporting the UNITA delegation to Addis Ababa until the morrow, Saturday, for reasons of aircraft safety.

I was in a deep sleep when the telephone rang in my cavernous bedroom at about 1 a.m. It was, of course, General Manuvakola. He said that the dangers resulting from the fighting continued to be too great to allow the delegation to leave. Once again I recounted all the steps taken by UNAVEM to make sure that nothing could go wrong, including the renewed assurances I had received from the Government to respect our planes and the UN flag. I asked him to wait until Saturday, when I could explore further measures to assuage their concerns.

I roused my own team from their slumber to discuss this latest turn of events, and spoke to Colonel Ross in Luanda. Throughout Saturday morning I had intensive consultations with the representatives of all parties to the Peace Accords. I saw Samondo and Samakuva first. I confirmed that UNAVEM was prepared to send two helicopters to a place of UNITA's choosing, with the UNAVEM Chief of Staff, Colonel Ross, on one and the Chief of Operations, Lieutenant Colonel Egar, on the other, to transport the delegation to an airstrip where the UNAVEM Beechcraft could land and take them, the UNAVEM Chief of Operations and two UNAVEM security guards to Kinshasa, where a Gulfstream aircraft was on call to bring them to Addis Ababa. (The latter was a desperate but essential gamble on our part as we did not have the money to pay for the Gulfstream. I had felt encouraged to take this risk by a message from Kofi Annan that an adviser to the US mission in New York had called on 25 February to say that if the UN had to bear 'extra expenses' to transport the UNITA delegation, the United States would be prepared to 'think how to help'.)

I asked Samondo and Samakuva to ensure that this information got through and to impress upon their leader that every precaution had been taken and that the delegation must come. Looking increasingly uncomfortable, they promised to do so. We ourselves were having the usual difficulties in getting back to UNITA. Colonel Ross had been trying for hours to apprise them of these latest arrangements. Our telephone operator in Vila Espa finally succeeded in getting through to our old friend 'George' at 10.53 a.m. on Saturday morning (it was reported to me with military precision), but during the 30 seconds it took Cam Ross to get to the nearest telephone, 'George' hung up, and yet again pulled the plug on the line. Exactly the same thing happened a little later. UNITA clearly did not *want* to know what had been arranged for them.

The signs were too clear to ignore. The UNITA men were accomplished guerrilla fighters, their skills well honed over 16 years in the bush. They had told us that their delegation was in the Huambo area. By their own public announcements their forces not only occupied a large part of the city but controlled the countryside around. It simply was not credible that the delegates could not get to an airstrip 'for security reasons', especially when Colonel Ross had offered to send helicopters anywhere, even into Huambo town itself, to collect them. The only explanation must be the one we had long suspected: that all the delays – the initial request for a postponement beyond 10 February, the long periods of silence and 'playing hard to get', and now this increasingly arcane debate about travel – were due to the UNITA leadership's determination to win the battle for Huambo before engaging in further talks. They had miscalculated, and it was taking longer than they thought. It was remarkable that the Government forces were still holding out after seven weeks of ferocious fighting and artillery bombardment. They were completely cut off and since neither side was taking prisoners, the terrible carnage must have made them aware that they were involved in a fight to the death, in itself often a spur to almost miraculous feats of resistance.

During the dramatic negotiations of that day I played the final card, which I had thought out during what remained of the night after Manuvakola's interruption. My proposal was for an immediate truce, to come into effect at midnight that night, cover all Angola and last for the duration of the Addis Ababa meeting, including the time necessary for the UNITA delegation to return. This would not only provide a guarantee for the safety of the UNITA delegation, and enable this critical meeting to take place, but would stop the continued hostilities and allow desperately needed humanitarian assistance to be delivered. If the

Addis Ababa meeting was successful, then the temporary truce could merge into a ceasefire.

I tried out this proposal on the three observers and they assured me of their fullest support. I put it to Dr Muteka and General Higino, and I also asked Mr Samondo and Brigadier Samakuva to transmit it to their leadership. I told them all that I intended to have a press conference that afternoon (Saturday 27 February) at 5 o'clock, and hoped that I could make a public statement about the truce then. I did not have high expectations of a positive answer from UNITA, if only on account of the communications problems, but I did hope that the Government would consent and say so publicly. This would sweep away any genuine safety concerns impeding the UNITA delegation's travel, as well as boost the Government's international image. Dr Muteka and General Higino certainly saw it like this and waxed as enthusiastic as the circumstances would allow. They went off to make a strong recommendation to President dos Santos, who was sitting with his closest advisers in almost permanent session in Futungo de Belas, waiting for news from Addis Ababa.

Muteka and Higino were so optimistic that a favourable reply would be forthcoming that we agreed that I would include a paragraph to this effect in my statement to the press, thus putting the onus on UNITA to agree also, if it was sincere. Minutes before the conference, Muteka and Higino came to tell me that they had had no green light from Luanda. I thus hurriedly had to water down this part, simply expressing the hope that both sides would urgently indicate to me their acceptance of the truce proposal before midnight. I added for good measure 'since both leaderships have repeatedly reaffirmed to me their commitment to a return to negotiations leading to a ceasefire and a peaceful solution, I cannot conceive that they could, in good faith, refuse the arrangement proposed'.

These words exuded a confidence I no longer felt – if indeed I ever had. After my press conference the Government representatives gave one of their own: Dr Muteka afterwards handed me a courteously worded letter, promising, on behalf of his Government, that he would 'do everything she wants to support her so that it will be possible for the martyred people of Angola to find peace' and enclosing the communiqué issued in Luanda that afternoon and given out at his press conference. Unfortunately 'everything she wants' did not apparently include agreeing to a truce, and there was not even a mention of my proposal in the communiqué.

The communiqué accused UNITA of 'confounding national and international opinion to justify its absence' and avowed that the Government was not 'indiscriminately bombing and shelling' Huambo airport; that since the runway was not operational due to intense shelling by UNITA, it had authorised an UNAVEM aircraft to pick up the UNITA delegation on 'an airfield somewhere in Angola'; and that it guaranteed 'all security conditions so that UNAVEM II can pick up the UNITA delegation from the runway of the airfield of N'gove – the locality where the headquarters of the FALA/UNITA troops, carrying out military actions against Huambo City, is established'.

I told the Government delegation in unequivocal terms how disappointed I was that the communiqué omitted all reference to a nationwide truce. This not only diminished the last faint hopes of making the meeting happen, but the Government had also missed an important trick. Acceptance of the truce would have put the onus squarely on UNITA and might have swung the balance in favour of their travel. Dr Muteka and General Higino explained that the Government had had a long and bitter experience of UNITA's taking advantage of ceasefires simply to improve its military position. I pointed out that no truce would go into effect unless UNITA also agreed, that the UN would oversee it and would, I hoped, send in urgent reinforcements. The most I could wring from them was a verbal assurance that the Government accepted the idea of the truce 'provided UNITA also agreed'. That left us in the 'no go' situation of who would make the first move.

I went to bed resigned to the fact that, although we had pulled out all the stops, the Addis Ababa talks were doomed to failure. Very early on Sunday morning Brigadier Samakuva and Mr Samondo asked to see me. General Manuvakola had called them at 4.30 a.m. and told them to convey to me the message that the UNITA leadership greatly appreciated all UNAVEM's efforts, but for reasons of safety could not reveal in advance where the pick-up point was to be. UNITA preferred to use its own means of transport (a decision that would have saved us all much time and money had it been reached earlier); this would involve a delay of an unspecified number of days and UNITA requested a postponement of the meeting. The inference seemed to be that the rest of us should hang about indefinitely in Addis Ababa until the delegation turned up. My colleagues and I explained why a postponement *sine die* was totally unacceptable and would simply fuel the growing conviction that UNITA was playing for time in order to obtain military gain, especially total control of Huambo, before returning to the talks.

It appeared that the two hapless UNITA representatives also realised that UNITA stood much to lose by its stance and had tried, without success, to convey this to their leadership. Marcos Samondo had never struck me as a dove – quite the contrary – but on this occasion he seemed genuinely upset at his comrades' refusal to come and for once was stumped for words. Brigadier Samakuva, who seemed to me a level-headed, straightforward character – he spoke rarely, but when he did he was concise and to the point, rather than engaging in the lengthy circumambulation beloved of UNITA – was also clearly perturbed.

We enquired about UNITA's reaction to my request for a truce. They told us that their leadership had discussed this and was 'favourably inclined to the idea' but wanted to know more about possible mechanisms of enforcement. Cursing inwardly that I did not have more people on the ground, I replied that I thought there would be a good chance of getting UN reinforcements in quickly, if there was genuine agreement, and referred to Security Council resolution 804. I emphasised that UNITA could make a diplomatic coup and recover a lot of its lost respect internationally by coming out first with a formal acceptance, adding that the Government was ready to accept, provided UNITA agreed. The UNITA representatives undertook to return to the charge with their leadership.

Once again we were bedeviled by communications problems. Manuvakola refused to open the satellite telephone even to the two UNITA representatives, except very late at night or in the early morning hours, and so it would not be possible to obtain their reaction before the next day, Monday. A more worrying aspect still was that neither of these two senior leaders had been able to speak directly to Dr Savimbi, though we were told that all their messages, as well as my own, had been relayed to him. Both UNITA men were concerned that the full strength of the swing of international opinion against UNITA, even in quarters formerly sympathetic towards Dr Savimbi, was not getting through to their leader.

Pessimism notwithstanding, we still tried to salvage the meeting. We persuaded the two UNITA representatives to meet on Sunday afternoon with the Government delegation in the faint, and ultimately vain, hope that, without outsiders present, they could hammer out some new proposal. I then had separate meetings with the Government delegation and the observers and it was agreed to present UNITA with what amounted to an ultimatum.

Late on Sunday I told the two UNITA representatives that the UN wished to have, by 9 a.m. on Monday morning, a clear indication from the UNITA leadership that their delegation would arrive in time to permit the talks to start on Tuesday 2 March. In the event of a negative response the meeting would be cancelled, and the delegations of the Government, the three observer countries and UNAVEM would return to Luanda. I made plain the serious implications of such an outcome and that UNITA would be universally held responsible for the breakdown. After my detailed explanation, during Saturday's press conference, of the elaborate planning that had gone into the transport arrangements, further protestations by UNITA that they were inadequate would cut no ice; who would believe that I would risk the lives of the senior UNAVEM personnel and UN pilots accompanying the delegates by sending them out without guarantees from the Government that satisfied me?

Samondo and Samakuva came back next morning, even more crestfallen, to tell me that their leadership still deemed the dangers too great to use the UNAVEM aircraft. Although their own arrangements were in hand, they could not be in Addis Ababa in time to start the meeting by Tuesday or even Wednesday. Indeed they could not give any day at all. They therefore maintained their request that the meeting be postponed until such time as they could confirm their definite availability.

What happened next is perhaps best described in the words I used at the further press conference I gave later that day, of which the following are extracts:

> These developments have left me with no alternative but to cancel this second round of peace talks in Addis Ababa. It is a decision I have taken with the

Peace Talks in Ethiopia

greatest regret. This outcome is a bitter disappointment to all of us who are engaged in the Angolan process, particularly the Angolan people, who continue to be the victims of this savage war.

In my statement of Saturday I outlined in detail the meticulous arrangements the UN had organised in order to ensure the safe transport of the UNITA delegation here. These had, moreover, been under discussion with UNITA for over a week before the scheduled opening of the meeting. While I can understand UNITA's concern for the safety of its leaders, I cannot find justification in their refusal to accept the guarantees provided by UNAVEM, particularly when senior military observers and other UN personnel were to accompany them.

Given the collapse of the arrangements for this meeting a ceasefire seems more remote than ever. I have, however, enjoined both parties to respond favourably to my appeal of 28 February for a truce, in particular to enable delivery of desperately needed humanitarian assistance.

As to the next steps, I am reporting what has happened to the Secretary-General, and he, in turn, must report to the Security Council, which will then decide on the measures to be taken in the context of its resolution 804 adopted on 29 January 1993.

It must be clear to everyone, both inside and outside Angola, that continued military action can bring no victory for anyone, but only more death and destruction to a people who have already suffered beyond human endurance. Unless this cycle of violence, revenge and retribution can be broken the Angolans face an even more desolate future. A humanitarian disaster of incalculable proportions is already only too poignantly evident.

Despite this grievous setback in Addis Ababa both the Angolans and the international community must redouble their efforts to find an early solution. It is never too late for peace.

On the same day, 1 March, the three observers issued a communiqué in which they too laid the blame for the meeting not taking place squarely on 'UNITA's failure to fulfil its commitment to come to Addis Ababa'.

* * *

The Government delegation and the observers flew back to Luanda in their special plane later that Monday night. My colleagues and I had to wait until the next day to catch the only direct commercial flight.

On the Monday evening I was invited to dinner by the Algerian Ambassador. What I had expected to be a social occasion turned out to be a briefing session for the Acting OAU Secretary-General and a number of African Ambassadors: Cameroon, Côte d'Ivoire, Mozambique, Nigeria, Sierra Leone, Tanzania and Zambia. The Executive Secretary of ECA, Layashi Yaker, was also there.

For two or three hours I was bombarded with questions. All the Ambassadors were gravely concerned about the turn of events in Angola, and after all the recent buffetings it was a pleasant change to find them appreciative of the role played by the UN. They particularly like our idea of establishing a group of 'Friends of the Secretary-General', made up of prominent leaders, who could be brought into play at critical moments under the umbrella of the UN. With one exception, they all came down heavily against Dr Savimbi and UNITA. The exception was the Côte d'Ivoire Ambassador who held his peace – in contrast to his colleague in Luanda, who constantly came out in support of Dr Savimbi, protesting electoral fraud. Côte d'Ivoire was maintaining its traditional stance of backing Savimbi and UNITA.

* * *

All of this, however, represented no more than clutching at straws. As we hedge-hopped our way back across Africa to Luanda, it was difficult to see any way forward. I could wash my hands and walk away, for the positively last extension of my mission, which I had reluctantly accepted, had expired two days earlier, on 28 February. Ostensibly I was now a 'free woman' but there had been no word from New York about my successor; there seemed to be a bland assumption that I would simply soldier on. Bleak as the prospects now was of obtaining a ceasefire, that very realisation meant that the tragedy of human suffering would grow even worse, and one could not leave a vacuum.

22 From Addis Ababa to Abidjan

I had plenty of time to think on the long journey back from our ill-starred excursion to Addis Ababa. The next day, Wednesday 3 March, I met Foreign Minister de Moura and General Higino, who seemed to be at a loss to know what to do next. I suggested that one way forward would be for the Government to accept, explicitly and formally, my reiterated appeal for a truce. My reasoning was that, since there was no longer any immediate prospect of the meeting that, up to now, we had envisaged as a means of agreeing a ceasefire, we should perhaps reverse the process and try to bring about a truce as a *prelude* to talks, which could then lead to a more permanent ceasefire. If the Government took the initiative, it would reinforce its claim to the 'moral high ground' and give the Security Council and the international community cogent reasons to put pressure on UNITA to follow suit. The Government would, of course, wish its commitment to be subject to certain conditions, for example that UNITA too should formally commit itself to the truce, and that the UN should provide sufficient troops to monitor the ceasefire and ensure its observance.

Both the Minister and General Higino grasped eagerly at this idea, and said they would discuss it with the President. General Higino waxed quite enthusiastic, saying he thought that about 8000 UN troops would be needed, and the Minister, who had so stoutly and so often proclaimed that the Government would *never* accept 'Blue Helmets', even suggested that the Government might request the United Nations to send in armed troops to help them defeat UNITA militarily! I hastily disabused him of any notion that the Security Council would ever consider such an extreme action.

I had made my proposal in full realisation that, even if the Security Council agreed, there would be a time lag before such a force could arrive. My thought, which I communicated to Kofi Annan, was that, since the three observer countries had publicly hinted at their intention to take decisive action, they could be asked to provide a bridging operation under the UN flag, if not with their own troops (since there could be a problem of nationality) then by facilitating, with money or other means (aircraft, ships, equipment), the urgent despatch of troops from other countries. I felt strongly that such a contribution would be infinitely preferable to the proposals they appeared to be considering – declaring the Peace Accords officially defunct, eliminating the 'triple zero' proviso on supplies of armaments and providing military support to the Government – all of which could only prolong the fighting indefinitely.

It would also be essential for the Security Council and other influential parties to exert pressure on Dr Savimbi to accept such a proposal. For that reason I suggested to Venâncio de Moura that it should go hand-in-hand with the bilateral *démarches* by President Houphoüet-Boigny of Côte d'Ivoire and King Hassan of Morocco, both long-term supporters of UNITA, which had been under consideration for some time.

The next day, 4 March, I won the support of the Minister for Social Affairs, Mr Norberto dos Santos, for the idea, pointing out that, if the truce worked along the lines I had proposed, then the way would be open to provide succour to the thousands already suffering the effects of the fighting. Thus it could simultaneously serve political, military and humanitarian objectives. The Minister reacted enthusiastically and said he would immediately contact the Prime Minister, to whom he was very close.

Headquarters had agreed that I should go to New York for consultation, along with Brigadier Nyambuya and Jobarteh. A few hours before I left on 4 March I was received by the Prime Minister, Marcolino Moco, and immediately afterwards by President dos Santos. The Social Security Minister had obviously briefed the Prime Minister about my proposals, and he was extremely receptive. But when I saw the President it was clear that the hardliners had the upper hand. Although he was very cordial, expressing warm appreciation of our efforts to bring off the Addis Ababa meeting, he made no bones of the fact that the Government had had enough: its delegation had turned up in Addis Ababa in good faith, but UNITA had not deigned to appear. They felt they were being led by the nose. If the Government made the first move on a truce, it would be interpreted as another sign of weakness. UNITA's behaviour at Addis Ababa showed that it had no intention of accepting a ceasefire and it was still less likely that it would accept a truce. The Government wanted a full ceasefire, not just a truce, and every possible means should be employed to bring it about.

The President did not discount the possibility of total military victory over UNITA but conceded that it would take a very long time. This was why he favoured a return to the negotiating table and all possible forces should be mustered to maintain a dialogue. What had happened over apartheid in South Africa demonstrated the force of international opinion when properly applied. It should be mobilised now. The Government was the legally elected Government and should not be treated as equal to UNITA. Angola, a member state of the United Nations, was being defied and challenged by an armed party that the international community was treating with excessive tolerance. The last declaration of the Troika, he said, should form the basis for action. He was sending an urgent letter to the Secretary-General invoking Article 51 of the United Nations Charter,[1] and he insisted that the Security Council must condemn UNITA, 'disqualify' it for rebellion, and impose sanctions. When I suggested that sanctions were often ineffective, especially against a guerilla force in a country as large as Angola, with long, immensely permeable borders, he said that a good deal could be done to stop UNITA's gallop if the many countries through which they operated refused them travel permits and froze their assets and bank accounts.

I had a very clear message to take to New York.

* * *

My colleagues and I reported to headquarters on Monday 8 March to find that the Security Council had had informal consultations about Angola the previous Friday. They recognised the need for action, but decided to await my arrival so that I could give them a full briefing. This would not take place until Thursday 11 March, thus giving us time for brainstorming sessions with the task force on Angola, set up in the Secretary-General's office.

* * *

Events in Angola were taking a dramatic turn that could not fail to affect our thinking. On Sunday 7 March, General João de Matos confirmed the fall of Huambo to UNITA. Vorgan radio announced that FALA forces had taken total control of Huambo city, and at 12 noon on 6 March had hoisted UNITA's black cockerel flag over the Provincial Governor's palace and the Interior Ministry building.

The fall of Huambo was hardly unexpected. The miracle was that the Government forces had held out so long, given that UNITA had surrounded Huambo, as well as occupying parts of the city itself, and had subjected it to intense attacks and bombardment for eight weeks. The relief column from Benguela had not managed to fight its way through to Huambo in time, but General Sukissa (the police chief commanding the Government force) and what remained of his troops managed to make their way back to the coast along the same route. Thousands of refugees from the blood-soaked and stricken city attempted to do the same, often with tragic results.

An immense humanitarian challenge now arose, both as regards the decimated civilian population remaining in Huambo and those fleeing westwards. Together with the UN organisations concerned I had for weeks been working on contingency plans against the day when access to Huambo again became possible, and was now in daily consultation with Luanda from New York about its implementation.

UNITA – now very much in the ascendancy, militarily speaking – was posing conditions for ceasefire talks: they must be held in Geneva; the agenda would have to be different (a somewhat obscure requirement since the issues remained the same); and the Government must stop its air attacks on Huambo.

Conversely the major setback in Huambo had not made the Government more amenable to peace talks, but rather the reverse. Now the talk was of war – a word that up to now had been used sparingly. On 8 March General de Matos declared on state television that 'the country must prepare itself psychologically for a long war ... during which there will be high casualties, because this time the war will be carried out in urban centres, including provincial capitals and municipalities, and will therefore hit a large part of the population'. The battle for Huambo had been lost, but this was only one battle in what would be a protracted war and he promised that there would soon be a radical change. The armed forces now had greater potential and the majority of the military units that had been demobilised had been reconstituted. As evidence of this the Government had launched a military operation to retake the oil port of Soyo.

Monday 8 March was also International Women's Day. It was celebrated in Luanda by a march of some two thousand women dressed in black, demonstrating in favour of peace and denouncing UNITA. Whether by accident or intent (and the evidence seemed to point to the latter) the march got out of hand, converged on the building housing the UNDP, and staged a noisy protest in which the horde of women demonstrators denounced the UN as well as UNITA, and unleashed a vicious attack on me personally, baying for my blood. They chanted slogans: 'We want peace, we don't want UNITA' and 'Margaret, you are a *bandida* [bandit], you are a criminal'. My crime, it transpired, was that I had not prevented the two sides from resorting to war again. The authorities did nothing to disperse the unruly crowd. When I got back to Luanda Minister Norberto dos Santos apologised to me and confided that the whole thing had been organised by 'elements' in the Government, but he never divulged their identity. My overwhelming feeling was of intense frustration that I had been far away and hence unable to confront the crowd in person.

More in the same vein was to come. On 9 March Jonas Savimbi made an 'Address to the Nation'. It lasted 68 minutes and was a mixture of bombastic oratory, sounding like a prepared text, interspersed with jumbled digressions, bewilderingly mingling protestations of commitment to peace and unity with threats of prolonged, all-out war. The tone was distinctly triumphalist. The people of Huambo, he said 'have paid dearly with their flesh the 55 days and 55 nights of violent clashes, the likes of which have never been seen before in African military theatres. The battle of Mavinga (in 1988) was ten times less violent than what happened in Huambo. We have won. Those with strength are the ones with reason'. He was at pains, perhaps excessive pains, to assure all Angolans that victory in Huambo did not mean secession. Rather he extolled Huambo's advantages as a centre of unity for all Angolan peoples, compared with Luanda, which he ridiculed as 'Luandalandia'. 'Luanda has inherited values extraneous to Africa', he proclaimed. He appealed to other political leaders and parties to join in this search for unity and reconciliation. In a phrase somewhat at variance with the flowery rhetoric of the rest, he promised them 'I shall be the first to look for you and those who know my telephone number; please call me' (a hollow promise indeed to anyone who, like us, had tried to call that elusive telephone number when he did not want to answer!)

There were virulent attacks on a number of individuals, including Cardinal Nascimento. One of the more vicious was reserved for me:

> We do not want the talks to be held in Addis Ababa anymore. We shall only attend the talks if they are held in Geneva. First of all, we want to see the restructuring of the UN mediation so that we do not talk as if we were children. UNITA requests the withdrawal of Miss Margaret Anstee as the Representative of the Secretary-General. [This from the man who had entreated me to be 'the mother of the process'!] As long as she is here there will be no negotiations, because she has no experience in African affairs [conveniently forgetting my curriculum vitae, which had been sent to him when I was appointed]. She should leave. On the side of UNITA, she has no backing. She has never had it, even diplomatically, when we wanted to speak to her.
>
> Now we hear from Luanda, from a communist regime, that ladies like her are on the streets, so much so that even UNAVEM II [sic] tells me that Miss Anstee is a bandit. I am not the one saying it, I am just repeating what happened in Luanda two days ago. By the way, whom does she serve most here in Angola? It is Luanda where she has all her friends. It is in Luanda where she favoured rigging the elections. It is in Luanda where she is fêted here and there. Now she is considered a bandit there. Now, why should we need Anstee?
>
> We want a well-structured UN mediation. We therefore feel that Miss Anstee is no longer useful. She has lost prestige. We want a person of prestige and, if possible, an African. During the Bicesse negotiations we insisted a great deal that the verification forces should be led by an African.

Much later this last statement gave me cause for wry amusement. On 2 December 1994, in the wake of the signing of the new Peace Accords in Lusaka on 20 November, the French periodical *Libération* published an interview with Jonas Savimbi. Skulking in the bush after the poor, battered city of Huambo had fallen a second time, this time to Government forces, Savimbi criticised the lack of speedy despatch of 'Blue Helmets' to monitor the Lusaka agreement. He quoted me almost approvingly, recalling my quip about being given a Boeing 747 to fly but the fuel for only a DC3. In the same breath he went on to criticise my successor, Maître Beye – an African – and said he would never receive him again. Plus ça change...!

Despite the decidedly Africanist tone, the Front Line States, and especially Namibia ('slaves of the MPLA'), came in for their share of Dr Savimbi's verbal thrashing in his 'Address to the Nation' in March 1993. So did Portugal and the Portuguese, though in a more nuanced fashion.

Dr Savimbi described UNITA's programme as envisaging 'the establishment of a provisional government and a government of national unity which will last for at least two years ... and a major administrative decentralisation that would serve the interests of all the people of Angola'. He announced the departure, on 13 March, of a UNITA delegation which would visit 'Lisbon, Paris, London, Bonn, Munich, Rome, Brussels, Abidjan, Nigeria, Rabat, New York and Washington', and highlighted the positive role that could be played by Nigeria and President Babangida, by King Hassan II and by President Felix Houphoüet-Boigny.

These intimations of peace and reconciliation were overshadowed by the undisguised vein of intimidation running throughout his ranting discourse. The Black Cockerel was crowing victory and military might. 'With Huambo we have demonstrated... that we have military strength. We have seized tons and tons of weapons, guns and tanks that will allow us to continue with the war for the up coming years, if that is necessary'. 'Wars are bad and destructive but often they are worth it so that, once peace is established, it will be a lasting peace...' 'The war will not end soon, because we will go much further. The war was started by the MPLA assassinating our men in Luanda, while they were on a peace mission. Our troops will not accept being disarmed. We will not remain here in Huambo. We will go to Bié, Benguela and Cabinda'.

The bellicose tone reached a crescendo in his closing words, which could only be described as a clarion call to arms:

> I am launching a general appeal to all UNITA armed forces, wherever they might be, in order to gather together in their old areas. We have uniforms, arms, ammunition, bombs and food. Come but do not go to the assembly areas. You should leave for your old areas and we will immediately organise to collect you. We will immediately order the reorganisation of your units in order to continue with the battles for the sake of bringing dignity to the Bantu people in their land of origin. Come quickly. I know that you will trust my word.[2]

Not to be outdone, President dos Santos gave an equally mettlesome speech at the swearing-in of newly appointed members of the Government on 9 March. He rejected UNITA's conditions for peace talks; the Government now had war as its top priority. The economy would be directed accordingly and the Government would increase defence spending, diverting resources from other sectors. The same day Parliament approved the Law on Obligatory Military Service for all male Angolan citizens between 20 and 45 years old. The President called on the international community to abandon its ambiguous position and give clear support to the Government of Angola in the defence of its sovereignty and of the democracy defined in the Peace Accords, including the lifting of the 'triple zero' provisions.

Foreign Minister de Moura and General Higino were despatched with messages to the Heads of State of Gabon, Senegal, Côte d'Ivoire and Morocco, countries long associated with support for UNITA. Government forces were also regrouping along the Benguela–Huambo road in preparation for a fresh battle for control of the central highlands.

All the signs pointed inexorably to a recrudescence of even fiercer hostilities, unless something dramatic could be done to avert the tragedy.

* * *

These developments were being followed with growing concern in New York. A great furore arose over Savimbi's demand for my withdrawal. It was no secret that for some time I had wanted to be relieved of my post, as soon as I could hand over to a successor and could leave without impairing the process. On 11 March several members of the Security Council sought me out to convey their commiseration, not so much because of the aspersions cast on my character and professional capacity, but because I was now well and truly stuck with the post. As one of them said, 'If Savimbi had desperately wanted you to stay on he could not have found a better way of ensuring that you do'.

Asked to comment at the noon briefing on Savimbi's demands, the Secretary-General's spokesman, Joe Sills, said succinctly, 'she has the full support and confidence of the Secretary-General. Period'. And that was that. Dr Boutros-Ghali asked me to go and see him, to tell me the same thing in person and express his disgust and indignation at Dr Savimbi's remarks. 'Now I'm afraid you have no choice but to stay on for some time longer. I will not be dictated to', he said.

I offered to resign, drawing public attention to the many difficulties and basic flaws in the UN operation in Angola, from its inadequate original mandate and resources, to the constantly low priority accorded to it by member states, compared with other peacekeeping operations, and to do so in a way that would not cause problems for the Secretary-General but perhaps even strengthen his hand with the Security Council. But Dr Boutros-Ghali would have none of it. He could not, he insisted, countenance anything that might be exploited by UNITA, however devious the argument, as indicating that it was Dr Savimbi who was calling the shots.

The Secretary-General revealed that he wanted to appoint as my successor Sergio Vieira de Melo, a Brazilian and an outstanding UN career official with the UN High Commission for Refugees. I applauded this choice. Since now it could not happen for several months because of Dr Savimbi's intemperate remarks, we agreed that his identity must be kept completely secret between us and not divulged even within the Secretariat, which I warned the Secretary-General was a very leaky ship indeed. And the dangers were great: the slightest whisper that a new name was under consideration would be interpreted as a concession to Dr Savimbi's demands, and would make my task even more difficult since I would be seen as a lame duck. It was only after I received a firm commitment on this vital point that I agreed to soldier on.

* * *

The informal consultations of the Security Council lasted many hours. The Angolan Government had gone to town to present its case. In the end it had not been President dos Santos but his Foreign Minister, Venâncio de Moura, who had written to the Secretary-General on 5 March, and the letter and its annexes were circulated as official Security Council documents. The letter placed the blame for the débâcle at Addis Ababa squarely at UNITA's door, and assured the Council of its full cooperation in implementing the Peace Accords and observing Resolution 804. It requested the Council to make UNITA respect the electoral results, return to the Angolan armed forces, vacate all the provincial towns occupied by force, and put an end to the hostilities it had unleashed even before my confirmation of the electoral results on 17 October 1992. Significantly the Minister did not invoke Article 51 of the Charter.

The Council also received a message from the new National Assembly of Angola (in which a number of UNITA deputies, who had been in Luanda when the hostilities broke out, had incorporated themselves – including my erstwhile tormenter and rabid UNITA propagandist, Norberto de Castro, now singing a very different tune). The Assembly appealed to the Security Council to condemn UNITA as the aggressor, release the Government from the 'triple zero' option and impose sanctions on UNITA.

Invited by the Security Council to give a very full briefing, I described the present situation and the events leading up to it (making no bones about the extreme gravity of the crisis) and some of the underlying factors that had allowed it to develop, among them the total inadequacy of the UN mandate and the resources assigned to it. I also described the horrors of the human tragedy engulfing Angola.

Both in meetings with the Secretariat and the Secretary-General, I took a consistent approach to what should be done. After intensive brainstorming sessions within UNAVEM we had come up with five possible options for action:

1. Sending in a major *peacemaking force* of armed UN troops ('Blue Helmets') to enforce a ceasefire.
2. Obtaining a truce, to be monitored and enforced by a smaller *peacemaking mission* of armed UN troops as a basis for getting back to the negotiating table, resumed implementation of the Bicesse Accords and agreement on a new and expanded role for UNAVEM.

3. Coordination and supervision of *humanitarian relief only*, under a Special Representative of the Secretary-General, supported by a limited number of staff.
4. Maintaining the *status quo*, that is, the current authorised strength and mandate of UNAVEM II (verification, mediation).
5. A *mediation* role, pure and simple, involving only a small 'good offices' mission, consisting of a Special Representative at a lower level, assisted by a few military and political advisers.

We had concluded that options 1 and 4 were neither realistic nor acceptable and that the best way forward would be through combinations of options 2, 3 and 5, which could be mutually supportive, I emphasised that it was imperative to revise UNAVEM's mandate, which had been completely overtaken by events. On paper, we were being asked to observe and verify the implementation of a peace process that had broken down, through the medium of a mechanism (the CCPM) that no longer existed *de facto*. While we were unable, by force of circumstance, to do any of these things, we were nonetheless performing a central mediating role in the negotiations to get the process back on track, a role that had never been given legitimacy by the Security Council.

Not for the first time I found that, while both delegations and the Secretariat were extremely exercised about the situation, their inclination tended towards fudging the issues rather than taking the kind of clear-cut stand that I was advocating. No one wanted to hear of any solution that involved stepping up activities in Angola, and the mere mention of 'Blue Helmets' was anathema. The meeting with the Secretary-General, prior to my session with the Security Council, itself the culminating point of various discussions in the Secretariat, favoured a two-pronged approach: renewed efforts to promote dialogue, and an all-out campaign to alleviate the humanitarian problems. On the first, the Secretary-General's old idea of getting the two leaders to meet surfaced again, this time in New York, with the thought that the Security Council might make this an offer that neither leader could refuse by itself issuing the invitation. I accordingly included this proposal in my briefing.

The Council members asked many searching questions, which I tried to answer very frankly. They gave every sign of welcoming this approach, and in the course of a long career I had always found it paid dividends to tell member states exactly what it was like on the ground. Apart from anything else, it opened their eyes to the practical realities of problems and made them less likely to come up with directives unsuitable to the situation. I heard afterwards that my presentation had not met with the approval of those senior headquarters colleagues who belonged to the traditional school of Secretariat thought that the least said the better – 'keep 'em guessing' seemed to be the motto, an attitude that always seemed to me not only shortsighted, but contrary to what I deemed to be a basic principle of the United Nations. The Secretary-General had not been present, but shortly afterwards directed that his Special Representatives should no longer brief the Council. Only two designated senior officers in his 'cabinet' would in future be entrusted with this task. Rumour had it that it was my briefing of the Council on 11 March that led to this decision.

I was greatly encouraged by the forceful tenor of the Council's discussions, but it was not maintained to the same degree at the formal meeting on the evening of Friday 12 March. Difficulties arose over the draft resolution, in particular as regards the degree of condemnation to be meted out to UNITA and the manner in which these strictures should be given practical application, for example through sanctions. The United States, despite having been party to those tough communiqués in Luanda and Addis Ababa, which had hinted darkly at greater retribution to come, favoured a less strongly worded resolution than would have been preferred by others, notably Brazil, Spain and the Russian Federation.

Resolution 811 of 12 March was certainly stronger than any that had gone before and pointed the finger unequivocally at UNITA, but I for one had become sceptical as to whether the Council's resolutions, so carefully worded and negotiated, had any more effect on UNITA than water had on a duck's back. Dr Savimbi simply pressed ahead with his agenda, undeterred by the increasing international obloquy directed against him and his movement. I believed that he was encouraged in this stance by the concurrent incapacity of UN member states to get the Serbs in Bosnia to heed their admonitions, and no doubt the converse was also true. In peacekeeping situations it was now becoming the done thing among rebels against authority and the established order to 'cock a snook' at the UN, and not at all far-fetched to detect a 'copy-cat' phenomenon.

In its preambular paragraphs, Resolution 811 proclaimed the Council to be 'gravely disturbed' and 'gravely concerned' by the latest turn of events, with emphasis on UNITA's responsibility for the collapse of the Addis Ababa talks, and on the humanitarian tragedy 'of grave proportions'. Fourteen operative paragraphs followed. The first and second did not mince words, but 'strongly condemned the persistent violations by UNITA of the Peace Accords', going on to 'demand(s) that UNITA accept unreservedly the results of the democratic elections of 1992 and abide fully by the "Acordos de Paz"', and that the two parties 'and particularly UNITA' produce early evidence, not later than 30 March 1993, that real progress had been made. The third paragraph 'strongly' demanded an immediate ceasefire and the immediate and unconditional resumption of dialogue.

The members of the Security Council had been incensed by Dr Savimbi's unbridled and ill-judged attack on me, as evidenced by their many angry comments on the subject and their defence of me in their meetings. Operative paragraph five of Resolution 811 '*strongly condemns* verbal and physical attacks against the Special Representative of the Secretary-General and UNAVEM II personnel in Angola, and *demands* that these attacks cease forthwith'. The next paragraph condemned the kidnapping of the UNAVEM II military observer in Cabinda on 23 February and demanded that he be released 'unharmed and unconditionally and without further delay'. Another paragraph invited the Secretary-General to organise a meeting between the Angolan Government and

UNITA 'at the highest possible level', to take place in good time before 30 April 1993 (this fell short of our proposal in that the Council invited the Secretary-General to take action, rather than issuing the invitation itself, and refrained from identifying the two leaders as the object of the invitation).

Two other paragraphs dealt with the humanitarian problem, one calling on all 'Member States, United Nation Agencies, and non-governmental organizations to accord or increase humanitarian relief assistance to Angola and encourages the Special Representative of the Secretary-General, with *the resources at her disposal*, to co-ordinate the provision of humanitarian assistance to the population in need'. (my emphasis) The second 'strongly' appealed to both parties 'strictly to abide by applicable rules of international humanitarian law, including unimpeded access for humanitarian assistance to the civilian population in need'.

Other paragraphs ploughed familiar furrows, holding 'responsible' any party that refused to take part in dialogue, reiterating dark but unspecified threats that they would 'consider all appropriate measures under the Charter of the United Nations' if they did not, and supporting the Secretary-General and myself fully in our 'continuing efforts to restore the peace process and to carry out the mandate of UNAVEM II under extremely difficult conditions'. The Secretary-General was to report our progress and present his recommendations for the further role of the United Nations as soon as possible, and the Council itself decided 'to remain seized of the matter'.

In short, while the language was more forceful than ever before, the resolution was again a mixed bag of pious hopes rather than a harbinger of decisive action.

* * *

That same evening UNITA's Washington office issued a sharp riposte, bristling with righteous indignation. UNITA's non-attendance in Addis Ababa was 'based solely on concerns for the security of its negotiating team'; they had not found the UN security guarantees sufficient, since Vice President Chitunda, Engineer Salupeto Pena and thousands of UNITA supporters had been killed in Luanda at the end of October 'while under a UN security guarantee'.

This was not the first time, nor would it be the last, that UNITA trotted out this bare-faced lie. At no time had the UNITA functionaries in Luanda, or their supporters, been given security guarantees by the United Nations, nor did our mandate permit this, much less our pathetically small resources. The Bicesse Accords stipulated that UNITA was to be responsible for its own security, and UNITA had amassed a small army in Luanda; especially around Miramar, all armed to the teeth. I advised my colleagues at Headquarters to dispel this dangerous misrepresentation. They protested to Marcos Samondo verbally about this and other distortions in the press release but did not feel a public denial would put this campaign at an end. Neither did I, but it would have been good, in my view, to have a statement of the true facts on record. UNITA simply went on peddling this falsehood and, lacking any public contradiction by the UN, it gained credence among the gullible and the ill-intentioned. As late as October 1993, more than three months after I had left Angola, when visiting Lisbon I was bombarded by 'hate mail' from UNITA supporters in Portugal, accusing me, among other things, of being personally responsible for Salupeto Pena's death while he was 'under my protection'!

* * *

I left New York on Saturday 13 March, and spent a couple of days in the UK to arrange yet another hurried postponement of some personal and family commitments. On a sparkling spring day I snatched a couple of hours to climb Herrock, one of the chain of hills encircling the Hindwell valley and in whose lee the tiny hamlet of Knill lies enfolded. From its crest skylarks were flinging themselves into the air in dizzying spirals of song. In counterpoint to these ecstatic melodies there came from the next hill-top the keening of buzzards as they floated in effortless circles, high above Knill Garraway, scanning the wild landscape below for their prey. As always I drew strength from these hills, yet this second, melancholy image seemed more in keeping with my anticipation of what was likely to lie ahead.

* * *

I received the Government's reaction to Resolution 811 on 17 March from Acting Foreign Minister João de Miranda. He referred to Dr Savimbi's attack and said that the Government was anxious for me to stay on in Angola, as there was 'difficult and sensitive work' to do, adding 'we have full confidence in you as the Special Representative of the Secretary-General'. This was in comforting contrast to the demonstrations against me in Luanda 10 days earlier, though I could not help wondering whether Dr Savimbi's public declaration of animosity had not suddenly endeared me to the Government. One lived on a perpetual seesaw.

Most of our discussions around the paragraph in Resolution 811 which invited the Secretary-General to organise a meeting between the two parties at the 'highest possible level'. Dr Miranda repeated the Government's conditions for a meeting between President dos Santos and Dr Savimbi but did not preclude one in which the Government could be represented by the Foreign Minister, though he voiced the usual doubts as to who could represent Dr Savimbi with adequate delegation of authority.

I also sounded out the Foreign Ministry's views about our proposal to create a group of 'Friends of the Secretary-General', made up of African 'elder statesmen'. I had discussed this with the Secretary-General and a number of African Ambassadors, and had mooted the idea in my briefing of the Security Council. Like most of my interlocutors in New York, Dr Miranda welcomed the idea as a potentially promising new approach, in line with the Government's own démarches to key countries in the region.

* * *

One of the reasons given by the United States Permanent Mission in New York for watering down the Security Council Resolution was its desire to avoid alienating UNITA too much, in order to maintain the leverage the US government considered it still had over Dr Savimbi. This it now strove to exercise. In New York, Jeffrey Davidow had told me that the United States – having been foiled by UNITA's non-appearance in its intention of presenting to the Addis Ababa meeting a 'US package', based on the assurances on power-sharing it had extracted from the Government delegation in Lisbon – now intended to engage Dr Savimbi in direct dialogue, and arrange a bilateral meeting with UNITA. On 18 March I learned from the acting UN liaison officer in Luanda that, as a result of a very forthright letter from Secretary of State Christopher to Dr Savimbi, the meeting would take place in Rabat during the coming weekend. The Americans stressed that they were not talking about a substitute for the Bicesse process, but simply of trying to find a 'proper place' for UNITA, so that its representation in a national reconciliation Government would be consistent with the election results. Any meeting between the two sides that might eventuate from this initiative would have to be under the auspices of the United Nations. This was reassuring, since these moves had a close bearing on the Secretary-General's own efforts to bring about a 'high-level meeting', and it was important to avoid appearing to be in competition.

* * *

As for my own efforts, I met Prime Minister Marcolino Moco on 18 March and received a promise that the Government would give careful consideration to an invitation to a 'high-level' meeting. I also requested an audience with the President. The usual difficulties surrounded my efforts to contact Dr Savimbi but we managed to contact 'George', who, with his customary air of mystery, said that none of the leaders were in the same place as himself, but that he would ask them to call back.

On Friday afternoon (19 March) the Secretary-General's office asked me to arrange for him to speak directly to President dos Santos. He was afterwards to talk to Dr Savimbi. The latter was more complicated, since 'George' did not follow up our call of Thursday and the satellite was switched off again over the weekend. I was having communication difficulties in another quarter too: since Mig Goulding's transfer I was not getting the same meticulous systematic and prompt feedback from New York. This seemed to be due to several factors, among them greater preoccupation with Yugoslavia and Somalia; a different style of management; and a new organisational structure whereby peacekeeping responsibilities were divided between two Under Secretaries-General – Kofi Annan and James Jonah – one dealing with 'operational' the other with 'policy' aspects, matters difficult to separate from one another in practice – which was leading to 'turf' battles. Thus it was not until 26 March – a week later, and after many reminders – that I was told what had transpired between the Secretary-General and President dos Santos, information that was vital to my own handling of negotiations on the ground. It seemed that President dos Santos remained adamant that he could not have a meeting with Dr Savimbi, but was ready to accept preparatory talks at a lower level. The Secretary-General had said he would only reluctantly agree to a lower-level meeting and suggested that the two leaders might meet in Morocco, without a third-party presence. He continued to have difficulty in reaching Dr Savimbi, but it was hard to envisage how such a conversation could be productive, in the light of President dos Santos' reactions.

The Secretary-General had, however, talked to President Houphoüet-Boigny about the role he might play, while King Hassan II had called him to indicate his willingness to host meetings between the two sides. It also transpired that, at a meeting of the Headquarters task force on Angola on 15 March, the Secretary-General had decided that further action to organise the 'high-level' meeting should be halted until there was a clearer picture of the initiatives being undertaken by other interested parties. Again this vital information was not sent to me until 26 March, eleven days later! Apart from the resultant lack of coordination between efforts at Headquarters and in the field, this lack of communication placed me in an exceedingly embarrassing situation at a time when I was being besieged by the media about progress on the high-level meeting. Worse still, diplomatic missions in Luanda purported to know what had been said during the Secretary-General's conversation with the President and wanted to check their understanding. As I could only hedge, the impression was gaining ground that UNAVEM was 'out of the loop', which reinforced the view of those who claimed we were 'lame ducks' and made the task of negotiation even more formidable.

* * *

On 23 March Ambassador De Jarnette came to lunch and told me that the venue of the bilateral meeting had now been changed, at UNITA's request, to Abidjan and would start on Thursday 25 March. The Government would have a representative in the wings, but wished this to be an extremely discreet arrangement. The UNITA delegation already in Abidjan was virtually the same as that at Addis Ababa, but was headed by Dr Jorge Valentim (later there was speculation that this was due to Dr Savimbi's dissatisfaction with the performance in Addis Ababa of General Manuvakola, whom he considered to have been too malleable and accommodating).

For a few days the centre of action moved away from the UN and Angola to the United States and Abidjan. On 29 March Ambassador De Jarnette brought me the statement made by the US delegation at the close of the meeting the previous day. This affirmed, with due caution, that the two sides 'seem prepared to meet under UN auspices by 12 April'. After rehearsing the areas of agreement between them, and describing the humanitarian crisis as critical, the statement went on:

> We believe that there are a series of interrelated issues which should be discussed by the parties at the next round of direct talks. Without prejudice to the order in which these issues are discussed, we believe that their eventual implementation should be considered as an integral package. These issues include: (a) a cease-fire, (b) completion of the Bicesse Accords, (c) national reconciliation, to include broadened participation by UNITA at the national, provincial, and local levels, (d) role and size of UNAVEM, (e) release of all prisoners/detainees through the ICRC, (f) creation of the necessary conditions to permit emergency, humanitarian assistance to all Angolans, (g) definition of the powers of provisional administration, (h) guarantees of the security of people and property, and freedom of the press.

The statement gave a much more upbeat impression than Ed's personal account to me. According to him, the US representatives had had four days of exceedingly difficult discussions with the UNITA delegation, punctuated with parallel consultations with that of the Government; on no occasion did the two sides meet. For the first three days the talks, in his words, 'went backwards', with the UNITA delegates insisting on their own agenda, which was unacceptable to the United States and would most certainly be rejected by the Government, because it entailed dismantling parts of the Bicesse Accords and delegitimising the government and the election results. They also wanted equal status for the two presidential candidates and a transitional government for two years.

On the third day the UNITA delegates – having told the Côte d'Ivoire Foreign Minister that they agreed with all the critical issues proposed for discussion by the United States – reasserted their original proposals unchanged from the first day, when they met the US delegation afterwards. This tried the patience even of the Ivoreans, who compared UNITA's behaviour to that of 'a group of small boys'. President Houphoüet-Boigny picked up the telephone and called Dr Savimbi, his long-time protégé, to say that this just would not do. He left the UNITA leader in no doubt that he would cut off his financial support and stressed that opposition to President dos Santos was no longer justified. This did the trick. The UNITA delegation received new and more amenable instructions. Even so, they did not formally agree to the US formulation until late on the Sunday night.

Meanwhile the Government too had to be reckoned with. Its delegation was given the US proposals on the Saturday night and faxed them back to Luanda. Their official reaction the next day was distinctly cool. The US delegates redrafted their text to try to take account of these views, but the Government said that the proposals were 'an adulteration of Bicesse' and that it would repudiate them. The Americans had modified the language of their proposal still further, but by this time the Government delegation had been ordered back to Luanda. This explained the very tentative wording of the US public statement. For its part, the UNITA delegation had cancelled its public relations tour on the orders of Dr Savimbi, no doubt as a consequence of President Houphoüet-Boigny's little homily over the telephone.

Ed had sent the new version of the proposals to Futungo de Belas, along with a request for an urgent meeting with President dos Santos. He confided to me that the prospects for the further, broader meeting to take place 'under UN auspices by 12 April' seemed quite uncertain; if it did eventuate, the Government had informed the US delegation that it favoured Angola or Addis Ababa as the site, whereas UNITA preferred it to be elsewhere, and had mentioned Geneva or Abidjan. The Moroccan Government was offering Rabat.

The main problem was to get the Government to accept the proposed resumption of joint talks, to which UNITA had agreed. The shoe was now on the other foot. On 31 March, Ambassador De Jarnette had still not been received by President dos Santos, and I myself had been waiting for an appointment with the President since my return from NewYork a fortnight earlier. Both Ed and I were concerned that the Government might make a wrong move before we could speak to him. Meanwhile UNITA was going great guns, in every sense of the word. It was forging ahead with plans for a meeting, part of its eagerness deriving from expectations that the key towns of Kuito/Bié and Menongue would shortly fall into its hands. It was also going all out to redeem its sadly tarnished image by demonstrating that it was the party most amenable to the resumation of negotiations. There was a real danger of the Government finding itself 'wrong-footed' by taking a negative stance on the Abidjan proposals – or simply ignoring them altogether – in a situation in which UNITA embraced them and could present itself as the only party to be complying with the demands of the Security Council.

Then on 1 April General Higino informed Brigadier Nyambuya that there had been some shift in Government thinking. It was now willing to meet UNITA by 12 April 1993, at a venue decided by the UN, but the following principles must be observed: respect for the Bicesse Accords and their ongoing validity, for the results of the elections and the legitimacy of the government, and for all relevant Security Council resolutions, particularly 801 and 811. In the discussion he clarified that these were 'presumptions', or 'assumptions', and not 'preconditions'. Ed De Jarnette received the same message.

On Saturday 3 April General Higino came to see me, on the President's instructions, to confirm this position. He also said that the Government would insist that the talks took place under my chairmanship; that the Government deplored Dr Savimbi's attack on me and considered that any submission to his demands would seriously undercut the UN's influence. April 12 was suggested as the date, and after some discussion of the government's expressed preference for Angola or Addis Ababa, the General hinted strongly that it might accept Abidjan after all. I gathered that considerable pressure had been put on the Government by the 'Troika', on the grounds that President Houphoüet-Boigny's influence would be critical, and that Abidjan was a major UNITA communication centre, permitting speedy communication with Dr Savimbi. We agreed that it would be better to agree the agenda at the meeting itself and that we must, this time, come to a favourable outcome and cover all aspects thoroughly, however long that might take. General Higino estimated around 10–15 days – a hopelessly optimistic guess as it turned out.

On Saturday evening, unable to contact the UNITA leadership directly, I asked Mr Samondo to convey the information that we were tentatively proceeding on the basis of Abidjan and 12 April. I added that I would be asking both sides to agree to a cessation of hostilities before the meeting started, with two objectives: to create a more auspicious atmosphere for the discussions; and to enable better access for humanitarian assistance.

On Sunday morning Ambassador De Jarnette told me that he was trying to get the United States to make a declaration in advance of the meeting and was continuing to push for early US recognition of the Government. It was debatable whether such a move, which would almost certainly have been beneficial some months before, might not prove actively counterproductive at this critical juncture. Ed confirmed my view that UNITA, negotiating from a position of military strength, would demand devolution of power to a degree unlikely to be acceptable to the Government. In his opinion Dr Savimbi was bunkered up somewhere in southern Angola, obsessed with his military campaign and totally oblivious of the significant move of international opinion against him, about which none of his advisers had dared to tell him openly. Ed considered it essential that, somehow, Dr Savimbi should be got out of Angola for a while, so that he could see the reality of the situation for himself.

On 6 April I wrote to President dos Santos and Dr Savimbi to ask them to nominate their delegations. That letter officially transmitted my new appeal that hostilities should cease before the meeting began, and throughout its duration. I was also constantly in touch with the Foreign Minister of Côte d'Ivoire about the logistical arrangements, which posed considerable headaches since Abidjan was not the site of a large UN office with conference facilities, as in Addis Ababa. At one point the Ivoreans had even thought of siting the meeting in Yamoussoukro (the extraordinary city created by President Houphoüet-Boigny away in the bush), where there were magnificent conference facilities, but had apparently abandoned the idea because of its remoteness and the fact that there was only one hotel – a large affair but, it was said, in need of repair. (Later, I privately thought, that it might have been more productive of speedier, and perhaps more positive results, had the two sides been isolated, far away from anywhere, under the same roof, and with no distractions from the task in hand.)

With its usual exquisite sense of timing, UNITA's official voicepiece, Vorgan radio, launched another vicious attack on me. The first news broadcast took place on 5 April, followed by a longer editorial on 6 April, but because of the difficulty of receiving Vorgan broadcasts UNAVEM did not learn of these attacks until 7 April. The initial attack denounced my alleged partiality in not sending aid to Huambo (this was ironic as I had spent a great deal of time trying to get the two sides to agree to its delivery) and claimed that I was providing food to Government troops, which was equally untrue. The summary transcript in English that we received read:

A ... complaint was broadcast in terms that UNAVEM is sending no help to Huambo and denouncing Miss Anstee as she is responsible for doing nothing (not only UNITA is asking for it, also CARITAS and the Assembly of Churches of Huambo) once UNITA has given clearance for the flight, meanwhile she authorises the help to government troops.

The editorial the next night embroidered this theme, not only spewing out venomous personal insults, but going so far as to make a direct threat against my life, which could only be interpreted as an invitation to some trigger-happy soldier. This is what it said:

The hypocrisy of Ms Anstee is becoming more and more obvious at every occasion. The Angolan populations are the coins to play with to get prestige and reputation for certain individuals. During the war for Huambo there were many requests to reach a truce and to send supplies to help the populations of Huambo, now the war is over, there is peace, and surprisingly no humanitarian help is arriving.

The insincerity of Ms Anstee, who pretends to be the mediator in the conflict, is evident. She promised to bring some aid to Huambo on the 23rd March and none arrived: she argued that she would send it only if Kuito/Bié and Menongue were also allowed to receive aid supplies, this was a plot arranged with the government to resupply the exhausted FAPLA troops.

Ms Anstee went recently to Caimbambo.... What for? She knows that Caimbambo is a war zone and that there is no civilian population there. Why she does not come to Huambo?

Whose friend is she? Certainly not of the Angolans. She is the friend of those that stole votes and of those that gave her diamonds and mercury. How can the people be confident in her if she does not provide any aid to Huambo?

She has discredited herself since a long time ago; she came here looking for riches; she arrived poor and she will depart rich.

The Angolans will not forget the attitude of Ms Anstee, which is not impartial. She is accomplice of all the crimes done in Angola. If she insists on remaining here one lost bullet can hit her, as it happened to so many members of UNITA, to make her pay for the riches she has received.

If the international community insist on keeping her at her post ... [not recorded] ... she is a prostitute and a corrupt, who does not inspire any confidence.

This attack reiterated many of the old accusations of the previous October, namely allegations of diamond and mercury smuggling – UNITA's standard charge against anyone who dared to criticise it or find its conduct less than vestal pure – and of accepting bribes from the MPLA and the Government, to which multifarious activities was now added, for good measure, nothing less than prostitution! It was in clear contravention of Security Council Resolution 811, which demanded that such attacks cease 'forthwith'. Even more seriously, the onslaught was deliberately timed in relation to the renewal of talks in Abidjan, due to start less than a week later, under my chairmanship, and picked up the theme of Dr Savimbi's visceral outburst of 9 March, that UNITA would never participate in negotiations conducted by me.

Naturally the broadcast was seized upon by the media, merited headlines in the *Jornal de Angola* and was given prominence by the BBC World Service. I immediately telephoned my aunt, who often listened to the World Service very early in the morning. Her reaction was typically debonair: 'I don't mind about your morals, darling – though a prostitute might be a first in the family – but *do* be careful about that stray bullet'.

* * *

Leaving aside the more sinister threats against my physical safety, the Vorgan attack was a blatant example of bad faith on the part of UNITA, and particularly of Dr Jorge Valentim who, as 'Minister for Information', controlled everything that Vorgan put out and knew, better than anyone else in UNITA, the herculean efforts we had all been exerting to bring help to civilian populations in the areas where fighting raged, including Huambo. My appeals for a 'humanitarian truce' during the Addis Ababa talks having fallen on deaf ears, we had resorted to an *ad hoc* approach, while striving to maintain the essential basic principles that all such aid must be non-political, must go to civilians and not to military personnel, and must be even-handed that is, it must go all over Angola, whichever side controlled the area. These principles are self-evident, but far from easy to apply in an all-out war situation. Neither side was slow to make political and propaganda capital out of aid, nor to pose conditions, demands and counterdemands that were almost impossible to meet or to reconcile and frequently brought the whole operation to a grinding full stop.

The terrible events of the previous few months meant that humanitarian relief had become a central part of our role. Before Security Council Resolution 811, that aspect had not been within UNAVEM's mandate, but it had always been a part of my own remit as Special Representative to coordinate all humanitarian aid related to the peace process. Earlier, there had been other 'normal' humanitarian activities carried out by various organisations in the UN system. Now the overriding need was to alleviate the cruel ravages of war and everything was related to the 'peace process', if such it could now be called. My own remit had, therefore, widened accordingly.

Two main tasks occupied a good deal of my attention during those early months of 1993: setting up a coordinated UN operation capable of undertaking the massive humanitarian challenge now facing it, in cooperation with the community of non-governmental organisations (NGOs) and raising the voluntary resources needed to fund it; and simultaneously organising the immediate distribution of the aid we already had to hand, which involved complex negotiations with the two parties. Neither was easy.

On the organisational side there were the well-known and all-too-well-documented interagency rivalries in the UN system to deal with. Angola confirmed my earlier experience that coordination works much better on the ground than one would ever imagine possible from the tortuous exchanges between the various headquarters and the excessively bureaucratic directives and divisions of responsibility in which they result, so long as two provisos are met: one, the situation is really fraught; and two, you have reasonable personalities on the spot, genuinely dedicated to helping people in desperate straits. If that happens, then everyone simply knuckles down and gets on with the job. The first condition was more than met in Angola; one could hardly imagine a more harrowing situation. Moreover the constantly difficult and disagreeable – often dangerous – conditions had never been such as to attract types more interested in protocol or personal or organisational aggrandizement than in working together to find solutions. Thus there was a good basis for minimal friction at the local level. That fortunately proved to be the case, with the exception of one or two minor incidents.

A considerable effort was made to involve NGOs. We recognised the special contribution that they could make, and the additional resources they could mobilise. There were a goodly number working in Angola, with significant variations in size, delivery capacity and special interests. Most of them were very keen to do their own thing, and to be seen doing it. This was understandable: in the main they were staffed by energetically keen and highly motivated people, and they too had to raise their funds, and so needed public relations prominence. There were some limiting factors to total liberty of action, however. One of them was the need to coordinate the overall relief effort, so as to ensure the most effective use of scarce resources. Another was that only the UN had the air capacity to reach remote destinations; and only UNAVEM could communicate on a systematic basis with both sides, to obtain the necessary clearances for aircraft and truck convoys to travel. This dependency inevitably led to strains, and sometimes complaints. Our policy of 'safety first' – that is, not undertaking any flights or supplies by land to combat areas unless these were first cleared explicitly by both the Government and UNITA – was not always understood. The shots most difficult to call ended up on my desk, and involved some agonising choices. Usually they were balanced on a knife edge and one was torn between the overwhelming human needs, on the one hand, and on the other the knowledge that a downed plane, or a mined convoy, and the death of people involved in the exercise could, in addition to the personal tragedy, place the whole humanitarian operation in jeopardy. Misjudgements that gave either side the slightest excuse to challenge the UN's impartiality could prejudice the overall negotiations to restore the peace process, on the success of which depended the long-term welfare of the population. Whichever way you looked at it, it was a no-win situation, which nevertheless you somehow had to win.

We also had to deal with our various headquarters in the UN system, some of whose reactions fuelled our uncharitable conviction that too many staff there had had no field experience except that gleaned from whistle-stop tours, and no understanding of the grim realities with which we daily had to cope. What the NGOs sometimes considered to be excessive caution on our part, these desk-bound observers often construed as recklessness. Notable among such reactions was a letter sent to Jan Eliasson on 12 March by the Executive Director of the World Food Programme. This letter proposed that Eliasson's office in New York should make all the arrangements with the Government and UNITA for flight clearances, and obtain them *thirty days in advance* to facilitate WFP's planning procedure! I had to point out that this might not only be unhelpful, but could prove dangerously counterproductive; it would also pose insurmountable practical problems since the situation changed daily, and sometimes hourly. I also had to dispel the erroneous premise upon which this bizarre proposal was based – that we had no systematic arrangements for obtaining clearances. UNAVEM had daily contact not only with the Government, but also with UNITA, through its military commanders in Uige, including General Dembo, UNITA's Vice-President; this channel having been requested by UNITA because of communication problems with Huambo. Arrangements often had to be of a last-minute, *ad hoc* character because of the changing operational situation and the exceedingly fluid front line between the two warring sides. We overcame these difficulties by close day-to-day, and sometimes hour-to-hour, liaison with our agency counterparts in Luanda. All of this, I pointed out, as gently as I could, made total nonsense of any suggestion of obtaining clearances thirty days in advance, in a fluctuating situation of all-out war.

As an additional guarantee I had given orders that UNAVEM military and police observers should accompany all relief flights. They were unarmed, but we all felt that the presence of 'Blue Berets' would underline the international character of the mission and provide at least some symbolic degree of protection. Even this was not without its difficulties. While others clamoured for more security, the local UNHCR representative, a lady of many commendable qualities but with a distinct predilection for 'going it alone', did not want to have anyone on board from any other organisation, even though she was using UNAVEM and WFP planes. On top of this, on 19 March General Dembo actually had the nerve to send a message that UNAVEM observers would not be 'allowed' on flights carrying relief provided by WPF, UNICEF or UNHCR! He got a very strong message back that this was unacceptable and contrary to Security Council Resolution 811.[3] No doubt UNITA's objections were partly due to concern that our UNAVEM personnel would observe (as they did) that military elements were bearing off some of the aid (UNITA claimed that they were merely unloading the planes). My energetic intervention paid off – General Dembo withdrew his objections.

Sometimes there were problems with the observers themselves. One or two were reluctant to embark on journeys that, despite advance security guarantees, inevitably retained a significant degree of danger, and which, they claimed, were not within their mandate. Early one morning, when I was at the airport to see off a bevy of planes carrying supplies to various destinations, I had to intervene personally with some UNMOs. I fear that, in addition to telling them bluntly that it was their duty to go, I also used blatantly sexist arguments, pointing out that while they, military men, were demurring, a number of civilian officials, including two very young women, were embarking without hesitation. They went. More importantly, they came back. There were to be other occasions when our relief planes and vehicles came under attack and some did not return. One of the early incidents occurred on 8 April, when a WFP Antonov, delivering emergency aid to Uige, was greeted by UNITA machine-gun fire as it landed, despite the fact that UNITA had given clearance. One crew member was badly injured in the leg, and the aircraft's fuselage sustained 45 bullet holes. On this occasion the plane managed to limp back to Luanda. Others, later, were not so lucky.

Another organisational problem related to the strengthening of our capacity to manage this greatly increased relief operation. A small coordination unit was to be set up and there was the customary to-ing and fro-ing between the various UN organisations about its composition and location. The Department of Humanitarian Affairs even attempted to dictate to me the geographical location, within Luanda, of the unit that was supposed to be under my command (that at least had been established, although not without some initial semantic hedging!) I took the strongest exception to such decisions being made in New York, when they should be taken on the ground by the person responsible, in consultation with the operational agencies involved and with the aim of achieving maximum operational flexibility and efficiency. Having dealt with major disaster operations for over 20 years, I recognised the tell-tale signs of Headquarters seeking to strike a compromise that would, in theory, keep everybody happy, but would, in practice, undermine efficient management of the operation by fudging lines of command and end up making everyone unhappy.

There was a parallel argument going on about staffing the unit. Time being of the essence, I had suggested that we use two or three of my UNAVEM civilian staff who, with the reduction of UNAVEM, were now due to leave the country. Objections were immediately raised in New York – we must have people with direct operational experience of disaster relief. This response caused a chuckle or two in Vila Espa, since similar criteria did not appear to apply when it came to staffing Headquarters. I replied, rather tartly, that if such people could be provided without delay then I would be very content. Bitter experience had shown me, however, that delays of weeks, sometimes months, were involved in fielding staff; so for the time being I preferred to make do with people whose skills I knew, and who had considerable knowledge of local conditions and were acquainted with key authorities throughout Angola. Some of them, moreover, had worked on operational programmes and humanitarian relief.

A philosophical argument had also arisen in New York, which culminated in a proposal that UNAVEM should be divorced altogether from the humanitarian activities. Many pros and cons could be adduced for this thesis but, while agreeing that we should minimise the association in public, I had no patience with any suggestion that we should put it into practice, considering it to be academic and counterproductive in the situation with which we were faced. Whether we liked it or not, UNAVEM resources were central to the humanitarian effort: our military personnel were heavily engaged in the clearance procedures (for which only we had all the contacts), in air logistical planning, and in the provision of essential communications. UNAVEM planes, and sometimes our vehicles and other equipment, were being pressed into service. While there was no need to formalise the arrangement in a bureaucratic organisational structure, this was surely a case, if ever there was one, where *all* UN resources on the spot should be harnessed to respond to a desperate human tragedy. In support of this argument I quoted Security Council Resolution 811, which stipulated that the Special Representative of the Secretary-General should coordinate humanitarian assistance 'with the resources at her disposal'.[4] 'What other resources did I have to hand other than those of UNAVEM?' I asked. If UNAVEM ceased to provide support the current humanitarian operation, insufficient as it was in relation to needs, would have to be cut back, and very considerable additional resources found to fill the gap.

In the end I won out on all three issues – the location of the office, its staffing, and the key, if discreet, role of UNAVEM – but it took a lot of scarce time and energy that could have been better employed.

Despite these distractions, we were getting on with the delivery of relief supplies wherever we could. Our major preoccupation was to get to the main fighting areas where the suffering was greatest, especially Huambo, where it was reputed that hardly a building had been left intact, food supplies were precarious and medicinal drugs non-existent, while many of the population had either fled to the surrounding bush or undertaken the perilous journey to the coast. I had wanted to discuss the practical arrangements with both President dos Santos and Dr Savimbi immediately on my return from New York, but had not been able to talk personally to either. Then, late on Friday 26 March, none other than Jorge Valentim telephoned me to request urgent assistance, particularly with food and medical supplies, for the civilian population of Huambo. I said we would do our best and asked him to provide information about the size of the population in need. The next morning (Saturday) I hurriedly convened a meeting of representatives of UNDP, WFP, UNICEF and UNHCR. It was a long, hot and difficult meeting. The pitfalls – logistical and political – were all too obvious. Bearing these in mind, we drew up a plan involving three stages: an initial flight on Monday 29 March to make contact and organise distribution arrangements, to be followed, if all was in order, by other flights carrying food and medicine over the succeeding days, and a road convoy of 70 trucks to start from Benguela on 3 or 4 April.

I immediately despatched this proposal to Dr Valentim, making clear that its implementation would depend on our getting the necessary flight clearances and security guarantees from both UNITA and the Government, and reminding him to telephone me later that day to give me the vital details on the requirements. On the Government side, I telephoned the Minister for Social Affairs, Norberto dos Santos, and Foreign Minister de Moura, and the latter said he would refer the matter to the President urgently. The answer was not long in coming. Norberto dos Santos called me on Sunday evening, 28 March, to tell me that the Government's policy was that humanitarian assistance in Angola had to be 'global' and available to all Angolans, in the wake of a truce, and not concentrated in individual areas such as Huambo. I replied that aid must, of course, go indiscriminately to all civilians in need but that there were practical difficulties. For a start, a truce was nowhere in sight, neither side having taken up my repeated appeals. In the meantime (as he and I had agreed only four days earlier) it was necessary to proceed on an *ad hoc* basis wherever we could obtain access. Moreover, application of the policy he had outlined would mean *stopping* the supplies now being delivered to many areas, most of which, by force of circumstance, were in Government-controlled zones, since these were ones we could safely reach. In other words, strict observance of the policy would hit the Government side as much, and probably more, than UNITA. I also recalled Security Council Resolution 811, which strongly appealed 'to both parties strictly to abide by applicable rules of international humanitarian law, including unimpeded access for humanitarian assistance for the civilian population in need'.[5]

It was no good. The Minister, clearly discomfitted, was obviously under strict instructions. He claimed that virtually no civilians remained in Huambo and that the supplies would go to UNITA troops. I explained that this was precisely why the initial mission would comprise people qualified to assess the number of civilians and make arrangements to ensure distribution to them only. The

Minister then enquired why we were not sending food to Kuito/Bié and Menongue, Government towns under fierce seige by UNITA. I replied that we were attempting to do so, but that severe fighting was impeding our efforts.

Dr Valentim did not get back to me during the weekend, so that the flights planned for Monday had to be put on hold. I agreed with the UN Agency heads that since a truce seemed highly unlikely, we should attempt to make a trade-off of between Huambo and Kuito/Bié. Accordingly I sent a carefully worded letter to Dr Valentim, asking UNITA to cooperate in our plan to airlift food, medicine and other emergency assistance to civilian populations in Kuito/Bié and Menongue. I did not feel very sanguine as I sent it off. The only reply we received from the UNITA leadership, after many difficulties of communication, simply said that they were prepared to receive the first flight in Huambo on Wednesday 31 March, instead of 29 March.

Since the Government would not give clearance for this flight unless UNITA allowed relief flights to go into Kuito/Bié and Menongue, and since UNITA had not agreed to the latter, the Huambo flight was not able to leave on 31 March either.

* * *

While these exchanges were going on, another way of helping some of the civilians from Huambo emerged. On 30 March the Governor of Huambo, Mr Manuel Baltazar, appealed to me to provide urgent assistance to help evacuate to Benguela refugees from Huambo, mostly women and children, who had reached the small town of Caimbambo on a horrendous journey of escape. They had struggled long miles through bush, mountains and torrential rivers, not daring to use the road, which was being fought over at various points, with villages and towns changing hands in bewildering succession. The several thousands who had taken this perilous route had suffered terrible privation and many had not survived to tell the tale. Heart-rending stories had been reaching Luanda of exhausted refugees often with children on their backs, drowning while trying to cross the turbulent rivers that surge down from the central highlands towards to the sea. There were even rumours of their being ambushed or pitilessly shot down by UNITA troops while in full flight. Now, after weeks of hardship, they were straggling down from the hills and nearing the coast. Those that we were asked to help were the weakest and most vulnerable, many of them sick with malaria or diarrhoeal illnesses, or injured during the long trek.

I conferred with Brigadier Nyambuya and we sent four helicopters from Luanda and Lubango. These together with two helicopters from the Ministry of Territorial Administration, began the shuttle evacuation the following day, 31 March. The refugees were taken from Caimbambo to Benguela and Lobito, where makeshift shelters had been set up and emergency relief was being provided by WFP and UNICEF. The operation was fraught with difficulties: there was no airstrip in Caimbambo for larger planes and the helicopters' capacity was severely limited. There was a frantic scramble for each flight, which we tried to control with a few UNAVEM military observers and some Angolan soldiers from the FAA. Inevitably there were incidents. On the first day a soldier, firing into the air to disperse the crowd, hit one of our helicopters; it was patched up and back in service the next day. In another incident a 14-year-old boy was accidentally wounded and died during the flight to safety. To cap it all the weather was atrocious, with torrential rain falling in an area that had been drought-stricken for years and frequent electric storms that made low-altitude flying hazardous.

As the negotiations over fresh peace talks were in a state of suspended animation, I flew down to see the operation at first hand on Friday 2 April, accompanied by some UNAVEM and agency colleagues. We transferred to one of the UNAVEM helicopters and juddered our way eastwards to Caimbambo over a series of hills thickly covered with scrub and dense, low forest.

The visit is not one I shall easily forget. Caimbambo must once have been a quiet rural town, unpretentious but snug in its bowl of surrounding hills. Now it was anything but snug. Occupied by UNITA for several months, and only recently recaptured by Government forces, it presented a doleful sight. Its modest buildings were reduced to empty shells; the small hospital and the school had been thoroughly looted by the UNITA soldiers before they left. Nor was it safe from further devastation. Fighting was still going on only a few miles up the road towards Huambo, around Cubal, and there were nightly skirmishes in the vicinity of Caimbambo itself. This sad, derelict place – without food, medical supplies or any kind of infrastructure – had become the unlikely haven for thousands of exhausted refugees, who stumbled in, ragged and starving from their long ordeal of flight from Huambo and villages along the line of conflict.

The helicopter lift was in full swing in a small patch of open land, almost reduced to swamp by the rain. The little settlement was scattered over a wide area, with no set pattern of streets, but criss-crossed with tracks, now ankle-deep in mud. In the school hundreds of bedraggled refugees were patiently waiting for meagre emergency rations. In many cases they had lost touch with their families and did not know whether they had survived. They told appalling stories of the long battle in Huambo and the suffering they had endured during their flight, yet their spirit seemed indomitable. Conditions in what was euphemistically still referred to as the hospital were even worse. I doubt if it had ever been able to provide more than the most frugal of comforts to the sick, but now it had nothing at all to offer. Doorways and windows gaped emptily, there was not a single item of equipment or a single bed. The walls were ingrained with dirt and on the filthy floor a few sick people sprawled, cocooned in bundles of stinking rags. The stench of human excreta was overpowering. Most pathetically of all, in one corner lay a very young girl, barely 15 years old. The young Angolan doctor, who was desperately trying to cope with the impossible challenge of bringing succour to the sick and injured without drugs or equipment, told me the girl had staggered into the village the night before and that morning had given birth to a seven-month baby, born prematurely as a consequence of the privations she had suffered. The tiny brown morsel of humanity was clutched to her side. Both were crawling with flies. Yet the girl smiled at me when I knelt beside her, and clasped my hand. I suppose it meant something that both were alive – just.

As if all this human degradation and suffering were not misery enough, the heavens opened. Thunder reverberated around the hills, lightning flashed as if the devil himself was about to appear (and really one could hardly imagine a more convincing image of Hell) followed by a deluge of rain, beating down like stair-rods, that drenched everyone to the skin in seconds. We were hurried across a grassy square, now a squelching quagmire, to a building that seemed to be some kind of decayed municipal office, where the local authorities – for Caimbambo *did* have its elected officials, striving valiantly to cope as wave after wave of destitute human beings poured in – spoke to us of their needs. There were several moments during the day when I was moved almost to tears, and one occurred here, when these men and women of Caimbambo produced food for us, a few bits of dried meat arranged on a platter. I ate a little, to avoid offending their hospitality, and asked for the rest to go to the refugees. Rain was still pelting down from a leaden sky when, some time later, we made a dash back to the helicopter. Incredibly, a large crowd of refugees had left the scant shelter of the school to see us off, the rain and wind plastering their sodden garments against their bodies. As the helicopter clumsily lifted off, fresh gusts of wind and scouring spray from the whirling blades whipped them with even greater force, but they stood their ground, impervious to the elements, cheering and waving, haggard faces actually wreathed in smiles. I suppose that if you had been through what they had, the prospect of imminent rescue would have made even these appalling conditions seem tolerable. That rousing send-off was another vivid reminder of the irrepressible spirit of ordinary Angolans that shamed one into forgetting one's own fatigue and scepticism and try once more to get their leaders to talk peace, however hopeless it seemed.

Our own immediate troubles were by no means over. Because of the storm the helicopter operation had had to be suspended for the day. Ours was the last to leave Caimbambo. The clouds hung low and menacing over the crests of the tangled hills that lay between us and the ocean, and fog obscured the deep valleys below. The elderly, battered helicopter bounced and shuddered as it strained to reach an unaccustomedly high altitude, our Russian pilots having decided that this was the best hope of survival. Outside all one could see were swirling dark vapours rushing past the portholes, on which scudding bursts of rain and hail beat out a tattoo like intermittent machine-gun fire, the thick veil of cloud rent asunder from time to time by blinding blue flashes of lightning. Several months later the chief Russian pilot, who had been our captain on that occasion, confessed at my farewell party that he himself had thought it was touch and go whether we would make it to Catumbela airport that wild evening. Fortunately he had kept his thoughts to himself at the time. It was perhaps also fortunate that I not only had immense faith in the skills of our Russian pilots and their helicopters, which seemed to fly in blatant defiance of the laws of aerodynamics, but, being wet through and shivering, was much more concerned that my chronically temperamental back would collapse at a time when I could not afford to lose even a second to illness.

Catumbela airport was awash with water. We had still to make a visit to Lobito to see the reception facilities for the refugees. But we had not gone very far along the low-lying causeway that connects Benguela and Lobito, when we ran into water, which very soon was gushing past us, axle high and rising. The rain was still hurtling down, as if in penance for all those years it had withheld its blessings from these parched lands. It was all too evident that the Catumbela river had burst its banks and that the flood was rising rapidly. We were advised that we could perhaps battle our way through to Lobito but would be stranded there for the night, or even longer. That, with the Abidjan negotiations at hand, I couldn't afford to risk and so we turned round in mid-water and splashed our way back to the airfield. But when we clambered aboard the Beechcraft, and the engines were started up, the chief pilot told us ruefully that he was getting warning signals that something was wrong. Once again an overnight stopover seemed unavoidable, but luckily it proved possible to radio Luanda to get a WFP plane to come and pick us up. It was a very cold, tired and dishevelled (though by this time *dry*) little group that ultimately reached Luanda late that night.

Our operation to rescue the refugees from Caimbambo lasted five days – 30 March to 4 April. UNAVEM helicopters made 116 flights, on which over 4000 civilians, mostly women, children and old people, were flown to safety. The same helicopters carried in 163 tons of food, provided by WFP, and three tons of blankets and medicines, supplied by UNICEF. In addition, WFP was able to send a convoy of trucks carrying 300 more tons of food through to Caimbambo, despite heavily mined roads, and on the return journey evacuated a further 1700 refugees, too exhausted, sick or injured to walk further.

* * *

That, then, was the saga of our foiled attempts to send humanitarian aid to Huambo and of our successful evacuation of several thousand refugees from Caimbambo, the two events that sparked UNITA's latest venomous attack on me and that it cited as proof of my perfidy and corruption. Nor was this the only example of UNITA's cleverness in manipulating the truth, for it had also engaged in a complicated propaganda ploy in late March, announcing to the BBC that Huambo was open for international humanitarian aid, and claiming that the UN was not responding, when in fact UNITA had not only not contacted any of us but had also made it impossible for us to contact them by switching off their satellite.

The only gratifying aspect of this whole sorry business was the number of people who rushed to defend my virtue. Both the Secretary-General and the Security Council issued statements publicly deploring Vorgan's attacks, particularly denouncing the threats against my life. The Secretary-General's statement was given out at the noon press briefing on 7 April. The UN spokesman, Joe Sills, said that Dr Boutros-Ghali was trying to contact Dr Savimbi to protest to him personally. The three observer countries also issued a denunciation on 7 April while Ed De Jarnette told me that the State Department had read the riot act to the acting UNITA representative in Washington. This gentleman's defence was that the attack had probably been put out on the Government's imitation of Vorgan radio, in order to discredit UNITA! I was assured that this had been received with the incredulity it deserved, but it was nonetheless another dismaying demonstration of UNITA's cavalier disregard for truth and for other people's intelligence.

Typically also, UNITA was quite unabashed by all these recriminations, and on 7 April Vorgan rebroadcast its editorial of the previous evening and declared that UNITA would not accept my mediation. All this, coming as it did just five days before the new talks were due to open in Abidjan, caused wider concerns that went beyond solicitude for my safety and personal dignity. President Houphoüet-Boigny had a considerable political investment in ensuring that the negotiations culminated in success, and he too entered the fray. Once again he personally telephoned his long-time protégé, Jonas Savimbi, and upbraided him severely for the attack, saying (according to what his Foreign Minister, Amara Essy, told me) that this was 'no way to treat a lady' and demanding that he make a personal apology to me before the talks began.

* * *

I was to leave for Abidjan on Easter Saturday, together with my senior UNAVEM colleagues. On Good Friday (9 April) President dos Santos received me at mid-day. We had over an hour of relaxed and open conversation. I was alone, but he had Foreign Minister de Moura with him, as well as Victor Lima.

The President wanted me to know how distressed he had been by UNITA's renewed attacks. He wished formally to reaffirm the Government's complete confidence in me, its satisfaction with the mediation role being undertaken by the UN, and its wish that I should continue to be the mediator. He said that the he recognised, and sympathised with, the difficulty of my task and the inevitability of my becoming the 'scapegoat'.

Cautious as ever, he nonetheless conveyed a relatively upbeat impression about the prospects for a settlement and a successful outcome in Abidjan, and reaffirmed the Government's own determination to do everything possible to bring about peace. He was aware that the international community might be suffering from 'Angola fatigue', but still hoped that, if a turnaround was achieved in Abidjan, it would step in swiftly, since, without such outside support, any settlement to be unsustainable. He also expressed the hope that President Houphoüet-Boigny would play an active part in making UNITA see reason; it was on account of the Ivorean leader's long acquaintance and influence with Dr Savimbi that the Government had reluctantly accepted Abidjan as the site of the talks. As for the agenda, the Government was prepared to work on the basis of the eight points set out in the US statement after its bilateral meeting with UNITA in Abidjan. (This was reassuring, but there were worrying indications that UNITA, which had accepted these points at the end of that meeting, would revert to its earlier, much wider demands.)

The President said that the ceasefire must be the first item to be dealt with, but regretted that he could not agree to my reiterated appeal that the two sides stop fighting *before* the meeting started, because he did not think that the other side would keep its word. He was also concerned about the means of monitoring the ceasefire. He clearly had a significant number of armed UN troops in mind, which I found reassuring in the light of the Government's earlier ambiguity on this point, and since I wholeheartedly shared his view. I was, however, obliged to warn him (as advised in New York) that it might take six months to assemble them, at which news he looked considerably taken aback. He then raised the possibility of advance troops being made available quickly under the UN banner by the Troika governments (the US alone would cause him political problems, he confided), Brazil, and perhaps some African countries with US financial support.

We agreed that power-sharing was the key item on which all else depended and that, within it, the crucial issue was to find a role for Dr Savimbi. The President inferred that if the Government only knew what Savimbi wanted, it was ready to consider it (short of his becoming Head of State, he added jocularly). We concluded that it might be a good idea for President Houphoüet-Boigny, since he knew Dr Savimbi so well, to put the question to him bluntly. On UNITA's participation in the new FAA, the President envisaged some practical difficulties in forming a unified force of 50 000 men now, since many demobilised soldiers had joined up again. Government soldiers alone numbered perhaps 30 – 40 000. UNITA's regular forces too were probably of the order of 30 000. Perhaps the best solution, he suggested, was simply to join the two together, under one command, and then reduce the number to the stipulated 50 000 over a period of time, which would also allow for proper vocational retraining and counselling for reentry into civilian life. I thought this a sensible idea, pragmatic and practical. As for UNITA's participation in civilian government at all levels, the President displayed an open mind. Two principles, he insisted, must be observed: that the Government, elected by popular vote, must carry out its mandated programme, to which everyone in high Government posts must subscribe; and that participation must be of the widest nature, embracing other parties and civil groupings besides UNITA. He recognised there could be a contradiction between them.

We then turned to the humanitarian situation. The President expressed gratitude for the assistance granted so far, particularly the UN airlift out of Caimbambo, which he said had 'captured Angolans' hearts'. As for the broader issues, he restated the policy that humanitarian aid must be provided globally to all Angolans, and that this required a ceasefire. Meanwhile he had decided to permit religious organisations and NGOs to provide limited assistance in areas where the Government was not in control. I pleaded that the UN should also be allowed to send an exploratory mission to Huambo in order to ascertain how many of civilians were there, their needs, and the availability of distribution networks and safeguards to ensure the aid got to the right people. This, I argued, would not only be a magnanimous gesture but would allow us to put further pressure on UNITA for similar access to Kuito/Bié and Menongue. To my happy surprise, the President agreed to this proposition with alacrity and instructed his Foreign Minister to take the necessary measures.

At the end of our conversation the President shook my hand warmly and, with evident sincerity, wished me well for the Abidjan meeting. He recognised, he said, that it would be very complex and difficult, adding, rather dismayingly, that Angola was relying on the UN, and on myself in particular, to ensure its successful outcome.

* * *

Be that as it may, I thought to myself, as I hurried back to the camp, let me at least get this initial mission underway to Huambo. I instructed all concerned to set up this limited but important operation for early the following week. No food or medical assistance was to be sent in on this initial mission, but it could be a spearhead for subsequent flights carrying such aid.

UNITA had, of course, to be informed. Because of the usual communication difficulties, this could not be done until I met Dr Valentim in Abidjan on Easter Monday. This time there was no *quid pro quo*, even veiled, on the Government's side. Any expectation that UNITA too might regard this as modest progress was doomed to be short-lived, however. Dr Valentim retorted, almost petulantly, that no such mission was necessary as Huambo's needs were well known. UNITA, with customary contrariness, refused to give clearance for the flight.

Thus on the very eve of the crucial Abidjan talks I was being given yet another sharp lesson – if indeed one were needed – that in Angola it was difficult not only to get the two sides to tango but even to persuade them to step on to the same dance floor at the same time. It was hardly an auspicious omen.

23 The Abidjan Marathon

The journey from Luanda to Abidjan on Easter Saturday was accomplished much more comfortably than that to Addis Ababa. This time President Houphoüet-Boigny sent one of his executive jets to fetch me and my entourage. The Côte d'Ivoire Government also took care of transporting the UNITA delegation – I think from Kinshasa, a point they reached by their own means from Angola, their travel no doubt facilitated this time by their control of Huambo and large tracts of the Angolan countryside.

Already from the air the verdant lushness of the environs of Abidjan had captured our imagination, its bosky bays and inlets almost a visual shock to eyes so long accustomed to the harsh red contours that girded Luanda like a halter of blood. That first image of softness and luxuriance grew more vivid as we sped round the curving shoreline of the lagoons that tempered the onslaught of the Atlantic rollers, along roads whose steep verges were wreathed in tumbling vines, a tangle of exuberant tropical foliage and huge waxy blossoms in psychedelic colours. Yet there was nothing unkempt about this fecund profusion of nature's bounty; the opulent gardens of the large mansions that bordered our route were carefully manicured. As the centre of the city came into view, I remembered how it had often been described to me as an offshoot of Paris, transplanted to the west coast of Africa. No doubt Luanda, in some distant heyday when its buildings had been cared for and its streets kept clean, had seemed like a Portuguese city, wafted across the ocean to perch, incongruous, on an alien shore. Here there could be no greater contrast to the slovenly, decayed grandeur of present-day Luanda than this slick, sleek white city, its towers of glistening glass and marble shimmering like a mirage of crystal and ivory between the ocean and the sky. It boasted the self-assurance that comes from success, with perhaps more than a hint of the brashness of the *nouveau riche*, and yet also a certain veneer of sophistication that could only have its origins in France.

We were bound for the Hotel d'Ivoire, which the Government had chosen as the site of our meeting. It was a vast mausoleum of a place, surrounded by lawns, studded with flowering tropical trees and small enclaves of cultivated gardens that swept down to the shore of the lagoon. I was given a small suite in the tower block overlooking a huge ornamental lake, part of which served as a swimming pool. Amara Essy was very much a 'hands on' Foreign Minister, and in the evening he came to show me the various meeting facilities. I had been acquainted with him, though not well, when he was Permanent Representative of the Côte d'Ivoire to the United Nations, where he had made a very good name for himself. Over the next few weeks we were to get to know one another very well. He was not very tall, and still absurdly young-looking for a Foreign Minister, but he exuded a formidable presence, with his lively, outgoing personality and most engaging manner, which one felt to be capable of charming even the most truculent of war-makers into acquiescence. He had one of the nicest smiles I have ever seen and an infectious optimism, of which I was to have very great need in the days to come.

The Hotel d'Ivoire boasted several very large conference rooms but we opted for a smaller room on the top floor of the tower block. Although it had several disadvantages, it provided a certain intimacy that was most necessary for forthright dialogue. Physical surroundings can often have an appreciable influence on negotiation. Offices for myself and my staff, as well as for the delegations of the two sides and of the three observers, were provided in scattered locations around the hotel. In practice I found it more convenient to use my suite as my office, and it was in my small sitting room that I met with the delegations and with my colleagues.

The next morning I decided to try out the swimming pool. I was stopped dead in my tracks when I opened my door and found three rather menacing-looking men standing right outside. This was certainly surprising at 5.45 a.m. on a Sunday morning and my first thought was 'UNITA!', for Minister Essy had confided to me the Ivorean Government's fears for my safety in the light of UNITA's repeated threats against my life. The second thought that flashed through my mind was that my personal bodyguard was presumably still asleep some doors away and that I had no means of communicating with him. People have often asked me what it feels like to be the object of death threats. All I can say is that it is not very pleasant. You shrug it off as a cynical attempt at intimidation or a crass bluff that must be resisted, but at the same time you cannot quite quell the niggling feeling than in a movement as fanatical and authoritarian as UNITA, some overzealous follower might take the law into his own hands, thinking to acquire fame and kudos from the leadership. So I admit to a certain 'frisson' on finding myself confronted by three burly Africans (being scantily clad, I have discovered, does not add to one's store of self-confidence).

All this took only a moment, however, and then they introduced themselves as the round-the-clock bodyguard put in place by the Ivorean Government. It was another example of the care with which the Government had prepared the meeting, but I wished that someone had warned me. They were under instructions not even to let me swim alone. I felt somewhat ridiculous every morning, plodding up and down, without a soul in sight except one armed man sitting on the edge of the pool. As time went by they became visibly more relaxed, and the bodyguard on duty more often than not caught up on some sleep on one of the loungers. I reckon that they, like myself, had come to the conclusion that if someone was absolutely determined to bump me off, there was little that they or anyone else could do about it.

Later that Sunday Minister Essy gave a buffet lunch for all the participants at his not inconsiderable mansion, set in a garden full of riotous colour, where peacocks paraded the neatly tended lawns. There were additional guests – former President Canaan Banana of Zimbabwe, on his way through Abidjan to try to mediate the Liberian conflict on behalf of the OAU, and the British Ambassador to Côte d'Ivoire, Margaret Rothwell. The notable absence was that of the main part of the UNITA delegation, which once again had us all on tenterhooks by not turning up on time.

UNITA's repeated attacks on me also posed a diplomatic predicament. Everyone, from the Secretary-General and President Houphoüet-Boigny to the three observer countries, was insisting that a formal apology and personal guarantees for my safety should be forthcoming from the UNITA leadership before the talks began and the first two had made this clear to Dr Savimbi personally. During the weekend John Marques Kakumba, the local UNITA representative in Abidjan, asked to meet me urgently with a message from Dr Savimbi. A good-looking, smooth and very well-heeled young man, reputedly highly successful in business, Mr Marques was patently ill at ease and his discomfiture mounted when I insisted on having Brigadier Nyambuya and Jobarteh present. He would undoubtedly have preferred a more intimate *tête-à-tête* but we all felt it necessary that there should be witnesses. In addition, my two African colleagues argued strongly that it was not safe to leave me alone with someone from UNITA. To me this seemed exaggerated, though when one reflected on how many things had happened without rhyme or reason, and with little respect for human life, it was perhaps not an unreasonable precaution.

The apology transmitted through this second-hand intermediary was a sorry, hangdog affair and the assurance that it would not happen again had a hollow ring, it having already happened twice, despite protestations that it was all a dreadful mistake that would not recur. It was clear that UNITA, feeling its oats in the wake of all its victories, had been convinced that it could get away with murder (at least figuratively, and, who knows, maybe even literally). The leadership had been taken aback by the intensity of the international reaction and now, under duress because they wanted the talks, were 'going through the motions' of repentance. I fear I gave Mr Marques a hard time, along with a piece of my mind, while inwardly upbraiding myself for venting my outrage on the messenger rather than his master.

* * *

I had a potential domestic disaster on my mind as well, albeit at a great distance. When I telephoned my aunt to ensure that all was well, her wail of despair indicated that it most definitely was not: one of our two beautiful white cats was 40 feet up a tree, and she was keeping vigil at its foot, armed with tempting plates of food in fickle spring weather. For the first two or three days in Abidjan I dashed to my room after every meeting to get the latest news on that 'stand-off' saga by telephone. All the well-meaning efforts of helpers to go up ladders, or lash bamboo canes together to encourage descent proved counterproductive, merely driving the cat even further up the tree. It sounded like an all too familiar pattern. On the third day we held a council of war at long distance and agreed that there was no help but to call in the fire brigade. And then, when my aunt was looking for the telephone number to summon them, the little cat suddenly appeared, ravenously hungry, on the doorstep. I could only hope that this was an omen for the Angolan peace talks.

* * *

I was painfully aware that these talks had a 'now or never' quality, certainly for me, and perhaps also for Angola. I knew that, if this last-ditch effort failed, many months, and perhaps even years, would pass before there was another chance of peace. Everything would depend on the intentions of both sides: if one or both of them was simply playing along, with no real commitment, then there was little anyone could do. At the same time, in any situation falling short of that absolute negative, the role and skills of the mediator in bringing about mutual understanding and compromise, and eventually a solution, could be crucial; a false step could spell the death of many hopes and many people.

President Houphoüet-Boigny too was also taking the meeting very seriously. I was summoned to his private residence on Monday morning (12 April). Although there was no pomp and circumstance, the protocol was rigidly formal. The Chief of Protocol, a tall, debonair Lebanese, seated me in the corner of a large reception room, to the right of a chair clearly reserved for the Head of State. I had not long to wait before the Life President entered from some inner sanctum, flanked by the tall Lebanese and Minister Essy. They did not escort him so much as give the impression that they were there to catch him if he fell or stumbled, for he shuffled in, a tiny, myopic old man, steeped in time and wrinkles and wearing a beautifully cut European suit. After we had shaken hands his two courtiers – for such, with their deferential care, they seemed – guided him to his appointed place. Once seated, he turned his almost sightless gaze on me and warmly bade me welcome.

We talked for nearly two hours. This was due in large measure to the President's tendency, in the middle of our discussion of the present situation, to digress into a lengthy soliloquy on his first acquaintance with Dr Savimbi and his unsuccessful attempts to get the latter and the then President Agostinho Neto together after the breakdown that followed hard on the heels of independence in 1975, and later to arrange a meeting between President dos Santos and Dr Savimbi. It was a fascinating tale, full of not-so-promising analogies to the present. I was to hear it time and again in the frequent visits I was to make to the President; it was a standard piece of the agenda. Minister Essy listened also, with a rapt smile on his face, as if absorbing the story for the first time, though he must have heard it hundreds of times; indeed he chipped in from time to time to supply a missing name or date that slipped the fading presidential memory.

These were the musings of a very old man, who admitted to 87 years of age but was popularly rumoured to be well over 90. It was not that he was in the least 'gaga' – his acute comments on some of the present-day issues, to which he would disconcertingly return suddenly, like a ghost reemerging from the past, proved that this man, who had been a formidable politician, both in colonial France, where he, a black African, had held ministerial positions (I heard about *them* at some length, too) as well as holding indomitable sway in his own country during the three decades since independence, still retained much of his former acumen. Rather his meandering discourse reflected a mind that loved to revisit bygone times, not simply to dwell on former triumphs, although there was more than a hint of vainglory in all of this, but also to draw on the lessons of the past.

Despite the European trappings of mind and body there was still much about him of the traditional 'African tribal chief'. Most of all he conveyed to me the impression that this Angolan affair, which trailed such long filaments of memory in its wake, was 'unfinished business' that he wanted to have done with and to set aside, duly completed, in the little time left to him. He was also clearly convinced – with the almost unconscious arrogance of one who had wielded great power (a concept not easy to grasp, as one contemplated his shrunken little frame, which could never have been imposing, even at the height of its physical powers) – that he alone could bring about this final miracle, which would contribute so much to peace in southern Africa, on account of the unparalleled influence he could exert on Jonas Savimbi, about which he gently boasted. He described to me, almost with glee, the indignant rebuke he had delivered to his protégé for the way he had treated me, rather as a stern parent would tick off an obstreperous and ill-mannered child. In fact he was every inch – few of them as there were – the father figure and clearly saw himself as such, not only for his own country but for the whole of Africa.

These impressions are the conglomerate of perceptions registered on a number of different occasions, for my visitations to the President became almost a daily event. If I did not see him, then we spoke by telephone. Margaret Rothwell told me that, in two years as British Ambassador, she had twice been received by the President, which demonstrates the exceptional intensity of the treatment accorded to Angola. From the very first encounter President Houphoüet-Boigny demonstrated his readiness to intervene whenever his personal voice might help to sway the course of events towards peace. He also met separately with both delegations and, with the observers as a group. For a frail, elderly man whose health was clearly failing fast, this meant a draining expenditure of energy and willpower.

Foreign Minister Essy had obviously been given instructions to make the Angolan talks his number one priority. In contrast to his President he was young, blessed with great stores of energy and an immense capacity for hard work, but he spent so many hours with us that I began to wonder how on earth he found time for all the myriad other issues that must engage a Foreign Minister's attention in a country as important as Côte d'Ivoire is in the African context. Moreover the country was itself going through the upheavals that accompany a transformation from a one-party state, headed by a relatively benign but despotic patriarch, to a multiparty democracy, a process from which he, as a senior Cabinet Minister, could not long remain aloof. For a few weeks it seemed that resolution of the Angolan issue became the cornerstone of Ivorean foreign policy. When the going got rough the Minister even moved himself and his office into the Hotel d'Ivoire so that he could be on call night and day for consultations with me, the two delegations and the observers.

* * *

To our relief the UNITA delegation turned up during the course of Monday 12 April, a day late. They always seemed to take a particular pleasure in keeping everyone waiting, on the pretext of the perils of their travels, although these must have been much less on this occasion. Once more they had to be leant on to allow at least the opening session to be held that day (the UNITA delegation was perennially 'fatigued'), but both Minister Essy and I were determined that the meeting should be inaugurated on schedule. Disgruntled journalists and cameramen were already encamped in the hotel's reception area and the last thing we wanted were despatches going out to the world at large, hinting that the meeting had had to be delayed because of differences emerging before discussions had even begun.

On this occasion we prevailed, and the opening ceremony took place at five o'clock in the afternoon. The press were allowed in to take pictures and hear the formal opening speeches. I opened the meeting with a few words of welcome, also expressing gratitude to the Côte d'Ivoire, and briefly outlining the objective of the talks. Minister Essy then delivered a set speech, the main theme of which was peace, which he described as the 'second religion' of Côte d'Ivoire. Dialogue was their 'privileged weapon'. He reiterated President Houphoüet-Boigny's doctrine, enunciated twenty years earlier, that peace in Africa required peace inside each African state, peace between African states, and peace between Africa and the rest of the world. His President would remain at the disposal of the participants for 'as long as the meeting will last. He will not run out of breath since, as he likes to say, "when one runs after peace one has no right to run out of breath".'

I then read a message from the Secretary-General, which urged everyone to 'approach these negotiations with a genuine desire and firm determination to achieve a successful outcome'. He stressed the need for the two sides to 'show a spirit of mutual accommodation and respect for each other's concerns', and urged them to agree to 'an immediate cessation of hostilities throughout Angola in order to create favourable conditions ... conducive to finishing the dialogue, and also allow the provision of humanitarian assistance to alleviate the suffering of millions of Angolans who are innocent victims of this senseless war'. There was a sting in the tail of this message: the outcome of the meeting would be 'a major determinant of whether I can recommend to the Security Council a continuing role for the United Nations in the consolidation and maintenance of peace in Angola'.

Finally the heads of the two delegations spoke, Dr Faustino Muteka for the Government and Dr Valentim for UNITA. Both were bland statements, high on commitment to peace. The real business was yet to come.

* * *

My team from Luanda was a very small group. Substantively, we were only four: besides myself there was Brigadier Nyambuya, Jobarteh, and the Chief Operations Officer, now Major Stephen Honest, an UNMO from Nigeria. My spokesman, João Linō Albuquerque, was with us to deal with the public information side. The remaining four persons from Luanda provided support services: two interpreters-cum-translators, Elizabeth Pantaleón, Deolinda Leitão-Greene (a bilingual Portuguese/English secretary), and my personal bodyguard Antonio Moreira de Barros (Sigi had returned to New York some time earlier).

The UN Economic Commission for Africa had also provided a conference officer and two assistants from Addis Ababa, but we sorely missed the Commission's supporting services. NewYork had sent a political affairs officer, José Campino. It was a meeting run on a shoestring, and no mistake.

The Angolan Government, as usual, had the largest delegation, some twenty-five in all, headed by Dr Muteka, for whose moderation and negotiating skills I had formed such great respect in Addis Ababa, with the more mercurial General Higino as his number two. Another prominent member was Dr Pitra Neto, the Minister of Trade. He did not speak often but when he did he was brilliant, convincing and reasonable. For my money he outshone everyone else in either delegation, both intellectually and diplomatically, but he was called back to Addis Ababa soon after the talks started. Another member was General 'Gato', but his star seemed to be in decline and, although handsome and elegant as ever, he cut a rather sad figure. The lawyer, General Rasoilo, in contrast, clearly exerted a good deal of influence and was a tough hardliner.

There were only nine members of the UNITA delegation. Secretary-General Manuvakola, who had headed their team in Addis Ababa, was now relegated to playing second fiddle to the loquacious Dr Jorge Valentim, lending credence to the rumour that he was in the doghouse for having been too 'soft' in Addis Ababa. UNITA's General 'Gato' proved to be one of the more active and certainly one of the most vehement pleaders of the rebel cause. This time Marcos

Samondo was not present, and Brigadier Samukova left half-way through, an absence to be regretted as I always felt he inclined towards moderation and good sense. Jardo Muekalia, the representative in Washington, was a valuable addition in this regard. In contrast João Vaikeni, the representative in Geneva, was pugnacious and opinionated, often aggressively arguing positions that could not stand up to reasoned analysis, throwing the whole debate off course. The smooth-tongued Marques Kakumba seemed to be little more than an elegant go-between, his main contribution being his excellent contacts with the Ivorean Government. General Paulo Sachiambo played a low-key, generally constructive role.

In demonstration of the importance it attached to this negotiation, the United States had a comparatively large presence at the meeting, including three people from Washington. The Deputy Assistant Secretary of State for African Affairs, Ambassador Jeffrey Davidow, headed the delegation. When, after some days, he had to return Washington, Ambassador De Jarnette took over. The other two from Washington were Robert Cabelly and Richard Roth, Director and Assistant Director respectively for Southern African Affairs in the State Department. Both were 'old hands' in the long-drawn-out Angolan game and knew the main cast of characters, especially on the UNITA side, very well indeed. Cabelly had been special assistant to Chester Crocker and he spent long hours closeted with the UNITA delegates, trying to make them modify their position – ultimately without success, despite what should have been, from their viewpoint, his impeccable credentials. The fifth member was Major Fritz, the military attaché in Luanda.

The four-strong Portuguese delegation, too, was composed of men well-versed in the tortuous history of Angola's search for peace. Ambassador Monteiro was at their head, and frequently acted as spokesman for the three observers. Supporting him were Dr Antonio Franco, Paulo João Lopes Pinheiro and Pedro Santis Fontes Machado.

Ambassador Yuri Kapralov led the Russian delegation, but when the meeting dragged on he had to leave. His number two was nominally the Ambassador in Côte d'Ivoire, Mikhail Mairov, but he had little knowledge of the subject and Yuri's place *de facto* was taken, by Sergei Kossikov, who had long experience with the CCPM. In Abidjan we again observed the declining interest and influence of the Russian Federation in the Angolan peace process, especially after Ambassador Kapralov left.

The OAU also sent an observer to the meeting, the Senegalese Ambassador to Gabon, who did not attend the sessions but was kept fully briefed.

* * *

At the first working meeting, immediately after the opening ceremony, I summarised the steps taken since November 1992 to get the peace process back on track, urging that we should not reopen issues upon which agreement had been reached in Addis Ababa in January, but concentrate on resolving the principle obstacles to agreement. We then adopted an agenda based on the points proposed by the United Sates after its bilateral meeting with UNITA, on which I had obtained informal agreement in separate meetings with each delegation beforehand. Having anticipated a possibly lengthy wrangle, I hoped this was an augury of still better things to come.

The agenda was nonetheless formidable, comprising nine items:

- A ceasefire.
- Completion of the Bicesse Accords.
- National reconciliation, to include broadened participation by UNITA at the national, provincial and local levels.
- Role and size of UNAVEM.
- Release of all prisoners/detainees through the ICRC.
- Creation of the necessary conditions to permit emergency humanitarian assistance to all Angolans.
- Definition of the powers of provincial administration.
- Guarantees of the security of people and property.
- Freedom of the press.

In spite of our auspicious start, we got bogged down in the very first item. The Government's declared aim was a lasting ceasefire, for which the meeting should draw up a phased plan and timetable encompassing all the necessary actions. UNITA insisted that a suspension of hostilities throughout the country must precede negotiations on a ceasefire, and wanted UNAVEM II to be strengthened and to act as an interposition force. Thus we from the outset had to contend with a fundamental difference in approach, veiled in what at first sight appeared to be a semantic difference. The Government conceived of the ceasefire, as a package, of which all aspects, from the initial stopping of the fighting – *cessation* of hostilities – to the consolidation of the ceasefire, must be agreed at the outset. UNITA, while agreeing that a ceasefire might be the ultimate objective, at that stage did not wish to move beyond a *suspension* of hostilities. If the UNITA view prevailed, then the meeting in Abidjan would not achieve much beyond a breathing space, to be followed by discussions on a permanent ceasefire and on the political issues at some later date. UNITA clearly wanted to play it long. In an effort to break the logjam I proposed a technical subcommission to consider these issues in detail, but Dr Valentim was adamant that they must be discussed exclusively in the plenary, irrespective of how much time it took. This was reminiscent of General Manuvakola's tactic at the first Addis Ababa meeting. UNITA never seemed to have any sense of urgency about reaching an agreement that might bring an end to the killing more speedily.

I had agreed with the heads of both delegations that press conferences would only take place when there were concrete results to report; in the interim the UNAVEM spokesman would give a daily statement, the contents of which would be previously agreed by the two delegations, and adhered to by them in any observations they themselves made. The first such statement merely indicated that the agenda had been agreed and discussion begun on the first item. I was therefore not best pleased to hear on the radio an almost a blow-by-blow account of the debate. UPI, under the heading 'Angolan peace talks fail to make progress', datelined Lisbon, 13 April, quoted, with evident satisfaction, a report from Portuguese radio that the talks had 'stumbled at the first hurdle on Tuesday'. After seven hours of negotiations 'the two delegations revealed they had reached stalemate', the report went on. This was exactly the kind of negotiation through the media and the process of self-fulfilling prophecy that I had hoped to avoid, but from the very first day neither side honoured their agreement to keep their mouths shut. General Higino and Dr Valentim were constantly to be seen in the midst of a mob of journalists that were ravenous for whatever morsel of information was thrown in their direction.

At the same meeting on 13 April Dr Valentim expressed regret for the incident at Uige on 8 April (when a WFP plane delivering food had been shot at by UNITA), saying that it had been an unfortunate accident, because the plane had arrived an hour earlier than expected and a 'confused' UNITA soldier had reacted by pressing the trigger. This version did not correspond with our understanding of the facts, and any comfort to be gained from Valentim's strong assurances that UNITA was taking all necessary steps to avoid a recurrence of such incidents was short-lived: only a day later, on 14 April, another WFP aircraft at Luena airport, bearing UN markings, was fired at by UNITA's long-range artillery. Though hit, it managed to limp back to Luanda but all WFP food and flights to Luena had to be suspended. I had the unpleasant job of making a strong protest to Valentim about this latest deplorable incident. As usual there was a glib 'explanation' – the WFP aircraft had not been fired upon deliberately but had come accidentally into the line of UNITA mortar fire directed against the airfield.

In the same meeting Dr Valentim referred to the Vorgan radio attacks and said that 'UNITA had no animosity towards the Special Representative of the Secretary-General in Angola'. This was not only far from an apology, but excruciatingly condescending. No doubt I was meant to feel gratitude for this gracious dispensation! I may say, however, that in Abidjan (as indeed on every other occasion when we had met) Valentim's manner to me in both public and private, was unfailingly courteous, to the point of unctuousness. On no occasion did UNITA question the fact that I was chairing the meeting and acting as mediator in Abidjan. Since the earlier comments could not have been made without Valentim's knowledge and acquiescence (or even direct orders), I was hardly likely to set much store by his sincerity and reliability. But he was the leader of the UNITA delegation, and I had somehow to work with him if I was to have any chance of brokering peace. I could not let my own injured dignity or personal sensibilities stand in the way.

* * *

We still seemed to be talking in circles on our first agenda item, and I therefore persuaded the two sides that, since the ceasefire was related to all the other issues, we should go through the other items on the agenda, registering points of agreement.

During our discussion on the second item – completion of unfinished business under the Bicesse Accords – the Government side needled the UNITA delegates to say clearly whether they stood by the documents both sides had signed at the first round of talks in Addis Ababa in January, which registered their agreement on many of the points included in the Abidjan agenda. Dr Valentim, a past master at avoiding unequivocal commitments by talking around the point in the cascading phrases of grandiloquent, flowery rhetoric to which the Portuguese language so accommodatingly lends itself, managed to spin out the exchange for an hour or so before being pinned down to reluctant confirmation of UNITA's adherence to the agreement it had signed in Addis Ababa.

The curious thing, once again, was that the atmosphere between the two delegations was generally good. My main problem, as mediator, was how to advance the debate from general principles (on which there was almost always agreement) to concrete steps translating them into effective action. Here the Government delegates were more down to earth, while those of UNITA tended to remain on a high conceptual plane. This was possibly because Dr Savimbi had them on a very short leash. More sombrely, it could also be because UNITA regarded the Abidjan enterprise as an elaborate charade to be played out as long as possible, while back in Angola it concentrated on remorselessly advancing its territorial gains until it conquered the whole country.

It was agreed that the third item – national reconciliation and UNITA's participation in all levels of government – would be best addressed by a bilateral meeting between the two delegations, without the presence of the UN or the observers. This meeting lasted all day on Thursday 15 April. The press made a great song and dance about it, adducing all sorts of interpretations, mostly negative. In fact this was the most sensible way of going about things. Carving up the spoils of government involved many delicate issues internal to Angola and the striking of bargains between people who were not just fighting one another, but also knew one another very well, had in some cases been to school together and were even related to one another. The basic issue was power, and how to share it. They were much more likely to get down to the 'nitty-gritty' on their own, face to face, than under the prying eyes of foreigners, however well-intentioned.

None of the rest of us ever knew exactly what went on behind those closed doors. What was clear was that it took place in a highly cordial atmosphere for gales of laughter were frequently to be heard. Both sides also told us that many very specific points, including those relating to posts for UNITA and the status of Dr Savimbi, had been discussed. But the joint paper they presented to the plenary was disappointingly general, merely registering agreement on certain points of principle relating to UNITA's participation in government, and even these were hedged about with carefully conditional language.

* * *

My aim was to get through a first reading of the agenda by the end of the first week. On Thursday 15 April I set up a small subgroup to work on the fourth item: 'Role and size of UNAVEM'. Here the matter was pretty straightforward, since they had, as a basis, my comprehensive paper of 24 December 1992, which attempted to reconcile the positions of the Government and UNITA as presented to me after the Namibe meeting.

By Friday afternoon we had only got to item 6 in the plenary and it was obvious that the first reading would not be completed on time, unless we continued during the weekend. There were difficulties: on Saturday afternoon Dr Muteka and General Higino wanted to make a lightning visit to Luanda to brief President dos Santos, but they were ready to meet on Sunday morning. The UNITA delegates were more difficult, accepting with bad grace a meeting on Saturday morning, while the prospect of a Sunday session brought forth an impassioned homily from Dr Valentim that this would conflict with their religious obligations. When I pointed out that it could be timed so as to allow everyone to attend their respective church services, he intervened again, and very grumpily said that I was working them too hard; they were all quite worn out and needed rest.

Privately exasperated by this show of religious fervour on the part of people who thought nothing of killing one another or lying through their back teeth, I held on to my fast-flagging patience and suggested that it was hard to think of a better way of spending the Sabbath than trying to speed the end of war and suffering in Angola. As for fatigue, people genuinely in search of peace could not afford to be tired. We had lost a lot of time (most sessions were delayed because UNITA turned up late; the Government delegation was amazingly punctual) and had not even completed a first reading. Since I also tried to lace our meetings with some humour, I added, by way of further argument, that they were younger than myself and (resorting, I regret, to blatant sexism in jollying them along) belonged to the so-called 'stronger sex'.

I got my way, and we completed our first reading. But the observers were increasingly convinced by this episode, and the extraordinarily childish arguments advanced by UNITA, that they were simply stringing everyone along. I could not but share this view, and tried to get matters moving through other channels: President Houphoüet-Boigny and the Secretary-General. A good opportunity presented itself when the President invited me and the heads of the three observer delegations to meet him on Saturday 17 April to review the events of the week.

The audience with the President afforded an unexpected moment of almost slapstick comedy. We were seated in the familiar semicircle of armchairs to await the President, myself next to the President's own seat and the other three to my right, the farthest away being Yuri Kapralov. The majestic Chief of Protocol (no other adjective will suffice) duly ushered in the tottering head of state. An Ivorean interpreter had been brought along, a rather large gentleman, now perched on a smaller chair between me and the President. It transpired that no one needed interpretation except Yuri Kapralov. The interpreter rose to sit by the Russian Ambassador, who simultaneously motioned that it was not necessary for him to move. This gesture was unfortunately missed by the Chief of Protocol who, with the acute sense of anticipation that had no doubt assured his rise to his present lofty function, withdrew the interpreter's chair to facilitate his move. This was done skilfully and silently, albeit with a fine diplomatic flourish, as befitted a master of his craft, so that it passed unnoticed by the ill-fated interpreter, who was lowering his considerable bulk with care – meeting no resistance, he subsided, at speed, to meet the unyielding marble floor with a reverberating crash. I am ashamed to say that this regrettable incident sent us all off into gales of hysterical laughter, though being the nearest – and the Chief of Protocol so dumbfounded that he simply stood clutching the chair in a kind of trance – I did at least help the poor man to his feet and dusted him off. The only person not party to this cruel joke was the President, who had certainly heard the crash but who, as Minister Essy told me afterwards, was too blind to see exactly what had happened and so merely contemplated us with a pained and puzzled smile.

The analysis that I presented to him, when we had all composed ourselves, made the same points that I later cabled to the Secretary-General. There had been no major setbacks, but nor had we made any major breakthroughs and progress was painfully slow. I pointed to two problems. The first was the marked tendency of the two sides to deal with one another only at the level of general principles and to shy away from discussing specific measures. It was therefore now my aim to concentrate on these practical aspects. The second concern was that argument tended to become circular. Thus when the delegations could not agree on the procedures leading to a ceasefire, we had moved on to other items, but it had become equally clear that no progress could be made on them unless there was agreement on a ceasefire. The nub of the question was how far either of them was genuinely committed to peace, and a ceasefire, and not just using rhetorical declarations to mask their desire to go on fighting, while paying lip-service to the international community's desire that they negotiate.

The crux of the negotiations resided in two issues: the ceasefire and national reconciliation, including much greater participation by UNITA at all levels of government. The Government was keener on the former, UNITA on the latter. Mutual concessions were essential. What we were talking about, in essence, was that the Government must make political concessions in exchange for military concessions by UNITA, and *vice versa*. The Government would have to be very specific, and generous, about the posts it intended to offer UNITA, including some special status for Dr Savimbi and I had urged Dr Muteka and General Higino to try to bring back concrete proposals from President dos Santos. UNITA must be prepared to move on from a mere 'suspension of hostilities' to acceptance of a package that would embrace an agreed list and timetable of detailed measures leading to a consolidated ceasefire. That would entail ceding their military gains on the ground. I had made these points very strongly to Dr Valentim and Brigadier Samukova, further pointing out that their desire for a strengthened UN presence would come to naught unless there was agreement on a ceasefire.

I asked both President Houphoüet-Boigny and the Secretary-General to contact both leaders personally and use their considerable personal influence to obtain these concessions.

* * *

The second week in Abidjan was devoted to trying to bring the two sides closer together by refining and reconciling positions on the key issues, particularly the vital one of stopping the fighting and consolidating a ceasefire.

This process was done through a series of separate meetings. With a great deal of patience and prodding we did seem to make some progress in narrowing the gap. The Government accepted, for the first time, that the process must embrace two phases: in the first, all fighting should stop and a number of measures be taken, including verification that both side were honouring the agreement; the second, the ceasefire would be consolidated and all unfulfilled aspects of the Bicesse Accords completed. To facilitate our thinking I drew up a detailed outline of how this might work:

Our discussions with the UNITA delegates on 21 April made it plain that their willingness to agree to the kind of approach set out in my outline depended on their receiving military guarantees in the shape of a greatly strengthened UN presence to verify the first phase, and in the second phase to take a more active role of *supervision* and *arbitration*, a major change from the existing role of mere *observation* and *verification*. They even argued that agreement on the future role of the UN should precede agreement on the ceasefire! I pointed out that this would be putting the cart before the horse: as Resolution 811 made clear, the Security Council would do nothing unless there was a clear and detailed agreement between the two sides on both phases, that is to say, on a consolidated ceasefire, as well as an immediate cessation of hostilities.

President Houphoüet-Boigny was again proving active and helpful. He saw the UNITA delegation on 21 April and pressed home the message that nothing less than agreement on a ceasefire would do. In the afternoon he saw the Government delegation at 5.30 p.m. and asked me and the three observers to come to him at 6.30 p.m. – a very heavy day for a visibly frail and elderly man. The President told us that he had been encouraged to receive a personal letter from President dos Santos, containing what he described as a 'generous offer' of ministerial portfolios to UNITA. He had also talked to President dos Santos, and had been trying, so far unsuccessfully, to speak to Dr Savimbi to urge him to accept both President dos Santos' offer of posts and a ceasefire. He was anxiously awaiting a call from the latter (the first disquieting sign that Dr Savimbi's 'don't call me, I'll call you when it suits me' dictum was even being applied to his oldest and staunchest benefactor). While hoping that Dr Savimbi would call him by the next day, Thursday 22 April, he asked us to allow him three or four days, in which time he was confident that he could work out an agreement between the two sides.

The observers and I were not as sanguine as the President that this could be done in three or four days, though we did not say so to his face. They had had a discouraging meeting with the UNITA delegation, which continued to insist that armed UN forces ('Blue Helmets') must be in place *before* the two sides could meet to define the implementation of the ceasefire. My efforts to persuade UNITA not to put the cart before the horse had failed miserably.

I conveyed my preoccupation to New York that the question now looming ever larger was how to ensure, in the event that we did hammer out an agreement, that the UN could respond swiftly and adequately to support it. I shared UNITA's concern that, without verification of the first phase and supervision and direct participation in the second phase, any agreement might quickly crumble and warned that, even for the verification function foreseen for the first phase, it would be necessary to beef up UNAVEM's resources very considerably and pretty smartly. The current strength of 75 military observers and 30 police observers would be a drop in the ocean. For the second phase an even more significant build-up would be needed, including sizable numbers of armed troops ('Blue Helmets'), which both sides had agreed were essential. I appreciated that no decisions could be taken until we had an agreement in Abidjan that could be acted upon by the Security Council, but I urged Headquarters to begin some contingency planning, with a view to locating sources from which troops could be rapidly made available and, if possible, put on standby. I appealed for urgent reactions from my colleagues in New York.

* * *

One of the ironies in Abidjan, as in Namibe and Addis Ababa, was that the one area in which both sides were almost totally in agreement was on the future expanded role and size of UNAVEM. The working group, chaired by UNAVEM, had very quickly come to an agreement on the basis of my compromise paper of 24 December, leaving only one or two points to be sorted out in plenary. The UN was to be entrusted with eleven very important tasks:

- Mediation, arbitration and good offices.
- Implementation of the ceasefire.
- Assembly and demobilisation of troops.
- The collection, storage and custody of weapons, including those in civilian hands.
- The formation of the unified Angolan Armed Forces. (FAA)
- The development of a neutral police force (UNITA wanted the UN to be responsible for 'the formation and supervision of a neutral, unified police force', while the Government wanted that responsibility limited to 'the verification and monitoring of the neutrality of the police').
- Extension of the central administration to the entire country and assurance of the free circulation of people and goods.
- The release and exchange of prisoners (principally supervised by the ICRC).
- Security for UNITA's leaders and institutions.
- The second round of presidential elections.
- Verification of observance of the 'triple zero option'.

Everything was in that list that had been omitted from the limited role given to the UN the first time round at Bicesse, and the specific inclusion of the words 'mediation', and 'arbitration' was significant, in contrast to the earlier 'observation' and 'verification'. The paper went on to detail exactly what was entailed under each of the headings. For the two areas where divergence had always been greatest – the manner of providing security to UNITA, and the second round of presidential elections (where UNITA wanted the UN to assume total responsibility for the organisation of the elections, whereas the Government wanted only significant strengthening of the observation and verification role) – a series of options were presented.

The outstanding issues could only be resolved in the context of the overall agreement, and it was agreed that the two sides should have another face-to-face meeting, with no outsiders present, to discuss the ceasefire and the UN mandate.

* * *

The second 'face-to-face' meeting took place on the afternoon of Thursday 22 April. Afterwards Dr Muteka and Dr Valentim jointly presented me with documents that represented the respective points of view of their delegations, and requested that the observers make a synthesis that could bring the two positions closer together and be discussed at a plenary session the following day. By working almost through the night, this was done but then UNITA, which always wanted all the time in the world, insisted that the plenary should be postponed until Saturday.

During that second weekend in Abidjan we worked intensively to flesh out the synthesis into the first draft of what was now termed for the first time 'The Protocol of Abidjan', albeit still in very embryonic form. Its basic principle was strict adherence to elements that were either included in the Bicesse Accords or subsequently agreed by both parties.

As we toiled through different versions of the text in a series of plenary sessions inter-mingled with separate meetings with each delegation, I was worried that we were not making progress on some basic problems. The Government had made only a small number of adjustments to the text and raised three issues of principle. UNITA, however, had made much more extensive changes and fundamentally stuck to its original formula.

In our bilateral meeting with the UNITA delegates on Sunday, Ed De Jarnette took them severely to task since their latest modifications enshrined exactly the same approach as the one they had presented on the first day. He said bluntly that the United States was running out of patience with UNITA. He emphasised the difficulties of persuading the United States, and indeed the whole international community, to contribute to the despatch of significant additional UN forces to Angola. The State Department in Washington, to whom he had spoken the previous day, felt that even the observers' document represented 'a difficult sell'. He also pointed out that there were certain elements in the document with which the Government was not in agreement, so it was not only UNITA that was being asked to make concessions. Ed could not have been more forthright, but admonitions of this kind simply ran off UNITA like water off a duck's back, even when they came from the United States. Dr Valentim just smiled blandly and launched into yet another circumambulatory oration in which his listeners, and I suspect he himself, soon lost their way. Perhaps this was one of the negotiating tactics imparted by the US advisers about whom Jeff Davidow had told me, in which case the Americans were being paid back in their own coin. Allied to Valentim's natural aptitude for aimless rhetoric, it proved highly effective in blocking progress.

* * *

It was evident that we were not going to get much further with our discussions without new instructions coming to the UNITA delegation from Dr Savimbi himself. I was in frequent touch with Minister Essy, who had by now moved into the hotel to follow matters more closely. He had told me that President Houphoüet-Boigny had finally reached Dr Savimbi on Friday 23 April, when they had spoken twice, and when the President had urged the UNITA leader, in the strongest terms, to accept a ceasefire.

The Ivorean Government proposed, and I agreed, that in view of the impasse Minister Essy should fly to Huambo on Monday 26 April, together with some of the UNITA delegation, to take the latest version of the 'Protocol of Abidjan' personally to Dr Savimbi and try to obtain his approval. The Government delegation left for Luanda on Sunday afternoon (25 April) to take the Protocol to President dos Santos and the Angolan Cabinet. The idea was that Minister Essy would also see President dos Santos in Luanda on his way to Huambo. It was, in any case, considered diplomatically incorrect for the Foreign Minister to go straight to Dr Savimbi's rebel headquarters in Huambo without first stopping in the capital of Angola, with whose Government the Côte d'Ivoire had full diplomatic relations.

Minister Essy got back to Abidjan very late on Monday night and immediately spoke me. The poor man had had an exhausting and at times frustrating day. Dr Valentim and the other UNITA members had insisted that their lives would be in danger if they so much as landed in Luanda – the plane would be shot at or stormed, highly unlikely as this seemed when the aircraft was an official Ivorean Government plane, with its Foreign Minister on board, and the Angolan Government was in the middle of peace negotiations with UNITA in the full glare of international publicity. In the end the Minister had gone without them, but there had been innumerable difficulties about UNITA clearance for his plane to land in Huambo. Finally the Minister had simply insisted by radio that he was going to land, and had done so. Thus the journey was not without danger – perhaps even more than we realised at the time: much later Minister Essy told me that he had learned afterwards that UNITA had given his pilot incorrect coordinates for landing, in his view deliberately. Despite all these fatigues and hazards, and a scarcely veiled irritation with UNITA, Minister Essy sounded positively jubilant. He told me that he had obtained Dr Savimbi's agreement to the outline 'Protocol of Abidjan', and President dos Santos' agreement to the inclusion in it of observance of the 'triple zero' clause, which the Government delegation had wanted to have deleted.

Despite this good news, there was still a lot of very hard work to be done to put flesh on the skeleton and get the document signed. The Abidjan talks were already taking longer than expected – we were now in the third week – and the deadline of 30 April, by which date the Secretary-General had to present his recommendations to the Security Council, was virtually upon us. Early on 27 April I rashly advised New York that, in the light of Minister Essy's information, it might just be possible to reach agreement and get the Protocol signed by Thursday 29 April.

I had invited Minister Essy to report on his mission to a plenary session that same day. UNITA asked for a postponement and when I reminded him of the Security Council's deadline of 30 April, Dr Valentim treated me to another long monologue, this time on the theme that peace could not be hurried and the international community must wait on UNITA's pleasure.

The plenary finally got underway that afternoon. To the dismay of myself and the observers, despite Minister Essy's optimistic report on his mission we had one of the most dispiriting sessions since the talks had begun. Apart from minor accommodations, both sides still seemed as far apart as ever on the major issues.

* * *

While all this shilly-shallying was going on, the spectre of mass death was stalking the war-shattered countryside of Angola. The human disaster was multiplying daily as more and more people fled, or were displaced from areas of battle, or were trapped in cities under siege, where there were no basic necessities or even the most rudimentary medical services to care for the sick and wounded.

WFP had sent a mission to Angola to size up its food needs before I had left for Abidjan. A broader needs assessment mission from the Department of Humanitarian Affairs went to Angola from 17–30 April, by which time I was embroiled in the Abidjan talks. I thus had to run a daily operation in Angola as well as handle the negotiations in Abidjan. To make matters worse, communications between Abidjan and Luanda left a great deal to be desired, and we had no code arrangement or any form of secure communication.

One very positive development was that the coordination unit was taking shape, and an excellent person had been appointed to head it. This was Manuel Aranda da Silva, a Mozambican national (Portuguese by birth), who had held ministerial rank in post-independent Mozambique and, more recently, had been directing WFP's operations in the Sudan. He came through Abidjan *en route* to Luanda so that I could brief him, and I liked him immediately. He was eminently suited to the challenge: totally dedicated, operationally efficient and able to get on with other people, being modest and unassuming, and intent only on getting the job done.

He had a dual task ahead: a pivotal role in relation to the mission undertaking the assessment and preparing the initial appeal to be launched by the Secretary-General, and, in the meantime, the daunting challenge of distributing the food and medical resources already available as equitably as possible. Manuel and I were in daily contact as far as the erratic telephone system would allow, as I was with Colonel Ross and Peter Scott-Bowden, my Special Assistant, who had stayed behind in Luanda for just this kind of critical liaison work.

On Monday 26 April another even more serious incident occurred with one of our relief planes. A WFP Antonov 12, with UN markings and carrying a Russian pilot and crew of five, as well as an Angolan employee, delivered a cargo of emergency food supplies to the besieged town of Luena. It was about 50 kilometres into its return flight to Catumbela when it was hit by a ground-to-air missile. Though his craft was badly damaged, the pilot managed to turn back, but crash-landed just short of the airstrip. The plane burst into flames on impact and the occupants had to jump clear. The providence that had kept them from serious harm until then deserted them: they landed in a minefield. All were injured in the blast, two very seriously. They needed urgent medical attention but there was no longer any qualified doctor or any medical supplies. UNAVEM tried desperately to mount a rescue operation from Luanda, but Luena was two and a half hours flying time away and no planes could land after dark. Early next morning the evacuation operation was effected, but it was too late to save one of the wounded, who had died during the night, while another was in danger of losing his legs.

We were all appalled by this latest tragedy, with its toll of dead and injured. Furthermore the spate of incidents during one month made it difficult to dispel the suspicion that UNITA was hell-bent on stopping humanitarian aid reaching people under siege, however much they resorted each time to the by now tarnished excuse that it was 'a regrettable accident'.

To cap it all, the incident coincided with the most crucial juncture yet in the Abidjan talks, when we were trying to get UNITA to 'bite the bullet' (perhaps an unfortunate analogy) and agree to the Protocol of Abidjan. At the same time a severe protest had to be registered. I duly did so, and wearily listened again to Dr Valentim's explanations, apologies and renewed assurances, which by now had lost all shred of plausibility, for all his winning ways.

* * *

My hopes of an agreement on the Protocol by the Security Council deadline of 30 April having been foiled, the Council adopted, on that date, Resolution 823, extending UNAVEM's mandate until 31 May 1993 and requesting the Secretary-General to submit recommendations as soon as possible. It stressed its readiness 'to expand substantially the United Nations presence in Angola in the event of significant progress in the peace process'. The Resolution expressed the Council's support for the Abidjan talks and its hope that they would result in an immediate ceasefire and the full implementation of the Bicesse Accords, and demanded that the attacks against aid flights cease.

With the passing of this Resolution I no longer had a deadline to wield as a lever over the two delegations, the new one of 31 May being too far off to carry any weight. All our efforts were now concentrated on getting agreement on a 'Memorandum of Understanding', consisting of 38 paragraphs that interpreted the measures envisaged in the Protocol and elaborated what they meant in more detail. But the discussion was going in circles, around the same issues.

Time was becoming critical: we were now in our fourth week. At the same time I found myself in a cleft stick, since to push the delegations too hard could be counterproductive, especially with UNITA. The Government side was ready to move much faster, and I suspected was under pressure from Luanda to do so. The UNITA delegates invariably preferred to play things out, usually required more time to study, and refused to work more than a limited number of hours a day (they would have done well in a radical trade union!) The Ivorean Government was also running into difficulties as a result of the protracted duration of the talks. It was playing host to a large African Development Bank meeting on 10 May, which would need our meeting rooms. More importantly, Minister Essy stressed President Houphoüet-Boigny's desire to be present at the signing of the Abidjan Protocol, as an additional guarantor, but that he would be leaving for France on about 15 May.

We again resorted to the technique of 'face-to-face' meetings and the two delegations remained closeted together for nearly three days. By their own accounts, these talks were going well and permitting a thorough ventilation of all the issues.

The session on Wednesday 5 May, at which they were to present their joint position, began splendidly. Dr Valentim, who had been chosen as rapporteur, assured the assembled company that complete agreement had been reached, with only one or two small differences, waxing lyrical in the process, even by his flowery standards. There was, however, he went on, a small difficulty over paragraphs 4 (the timing of the expansion of UNAVEM's presence and mandate) and 11 (the withdrawal and quartering of UNITA troops). While we were digesting this, and after a few more verbal gymnastics on his part, we learned that there were also 'some points' on paragraphs 12, 13 and 16 to boot (the first two related to the quartering, verification and monitoring of the rapid reaction/antiriot police and the last to security arrangements for UNITA personnel and installations). In the midst of this peroration I was suddenly visited by a recollection of the old French song that begins cheerfully 'Tout va très bien, Madame la Marquise' and then proceeds, verse by verse, to relate a succession of disasters, culminating in the news that the poor lady's 'château' has burnt to the ground, together with everyone and everything in it.

What all this amounted to was that, despite the herculean efforts the observers and ourselves had made to meet UNITA's concerns, it still insisted there were not enough guarantees to justify the withdrawal of its troops. We were right back in the old vicious circle, in which UNITA maintained that it could not withdraw from its positions, or accept a ceasefire, until *after* the 'Blue Helmets' were in place, whereas the Security Council required a ceasefire and some demonstration of good faith *before* it would authorise more UN troops. Supported by the observers, I tried to assuage UNITA's fears once more by pointing out that, immediately on the signing of the Protocol, the Secretary-General would recommend to the Security Council both the reinforcement of UNAVEM II and an extended and expanded UNAVEM III; that UNAVEM II would merge into UNAVEM III; and that the UN would do its utmost to get in an initial contingent of armed troops at the earliest possible moment (I sounded more confident than I felt, for New York had been stonily silent on this point, which I had raised repeatedly by cable from Abidjan).

We seemed to be making progress until General Manuvakola took the floor and launched into a diatribe about the 'lack of symmetry' in the Memorandum of Understanding. Aghast, we heard him pounding out the arguments that had dominated the first week in Abidjan. It was a performance reminiscent of his intemperate outbursts in that strange house full of dolls, where Mig Goulding and I had met Dr Savimbi at dead of night on 10 November. He had been more reasonable in Addis Ababa, and almost subdued in the present meeting, but now he seemed to have reverted to type. Or was he simply trying to reinstate himself in UNITA and recapture his laurels as a hardliner? I sharply intervened that we should not go back over arguments that we had had *ad infinitum* four weeks previously.

But it was too late. The Government delegates, who had looked irritated and then indignant as Dr Valentim droned on, were now infuriated. As usually happened when verbal assault was the order of the day, it was General Higino who now leaped into the fray and let fly at the UNITA team, accusing them of bad faith, of wanting to reopen absolutely everything and of reneging on the joint discussions of the previous three days. It was indeed hard to fathom what, if anything, had been achieved during the time they had spent closeted together. No doubt the Government side had deliberately acquiesced to Dr Valentim acting as their joint spokesman at the plenary as a good way of flushing him out. If so, they had succeeded beyond their wildest nightmares. A verbal duel across the table followed. The Government argued that it accepted the whole of the revised Memorandum of Understanding as it stood. Dr Valentim claimed, contrary to everyone else's view, that no impasse had been reached and asked the observers to try their hand yet again at some new language, which they agreed to do the next day. But then another bombshell dropped. Dr Muteka announced crisply that the Government delegation was leaving that very evening to confer with President dos Santos and would not be available for another plenary until Saturday, 8 May. I hurriedly called a recess, during which the observers and I pleaded with them to delay their departure until lunchtime on Thursday, by which time we might have reached an accommodation and they could take an agreed text. Moreover their departure could be interpreted by the media as tantamount to their walking out of the talks. Both Dr Muteka (usually a phenomenally patient man) and the more volatile General Higino were fed up and immovable. They steadfastly maintained their position, including resistance to any further modification being made to the paper, which they accepted as it was. We were really and truly very near breaking point, just when the prospect of agreement had seemed brighter.

In reporting this discouraging turn of events to New York on Thursday 6 May, I said that if there was no flicker of light by the weekend I would be left with no alternative but to suspend the talks. I also conveyed my view that it would be counterproductive for the Security Council to give further *ad hoc* extensions of UNAVEM II. Indeed I thought it might prove helpful, if we got irretrievably stuck, for the Council to state publicly that unless something came out of Abidjan, UNAVEM II would come to an end on 31 May.

The only real possibility that I could see of breaking the present deadlock was for me to give a clear commitment that at least a token force of armed UN troops ('Blue Helmets') would arrive in Angola *immediately* the Protocol was signed. This, I felt, would give a much needed boost to confidence, the lack of which was a major stumbling block. I appreciated how difficult a proposition this was, but urged that it be seriously considered since – if UNITA's concerns were genuine, rather than a pretext for stalling and continuing the war – then such a commitment would be a vital key to the success of the Abidjan talks. I asked for an urgent reply by the weekend at the latest. There was no reaction.

During the rest of Thursday we and the American delegation worked on UNITA in separate meetings. I felt I was making some headway in making them understand that the 'Blue Helmets' could not come first, but that I was doing my utmost to ensure that some would be *in situ* just as soon as the Protocol was signed. We had less success on the other main stumbling block – UNITA's insistence on 'symmetry' and 'parity', that is not withdrawing its troops unless the Government did likewise – despite our combined efforts to overcome it by explaining that the Government was making its own concessions, such as the simultaneous confinement to barracks of the antiriot police.

In a surprise development, Dr Valentim and General Manuvakola told me early next morning that it was imperative for them to go back to Huambo to consult Dr Savimbi, and asked for my assistance with the Ivorean Government to obtain a plane. The timing was unfortunate in that the Government delegation was due back the next day, Saturday, and this would mean a further delay. Valentim promised that they would be back in three days if they had a plane (ten, they said, if they had to go 'the long way'). I immediately contacted Minister Essy.

A night and morning of suspense followed. President Houphoüet-Boigny talked very seriously to the UNITA delegation, insisting that this time a firm agreement to the text of the draft Protocol must be brought back from Dr Savimbi. To further that end it was agreed that Minister Essy would accompany them, as well as someone from UNAVEM. The President provided the plane, which was to leave at 4 a.m. on Saturday morning. Then it transpired that Savimbi was not in Huambo and so departure was delayed. Savimbi was to call President Houphoüet-Boigny at 10 a.m., which would allow the President to convey his uncompromising message directly. But the call did not come.

At last a message was received that Dr Savimbi was 'somewhere at the front, near the frontier' and unable to communicate. It seemed also that the place had only primitive air facilities so that the President's plane could not land there. Even more disconcertingly, Dr Valentim made clear that the delegation wished to go on their own, without Minister Essy or anyone from UNAVEM. This meant that there would be no one to exert pressure on the spot, nor to apprise Savimbi of what was going on in the real world and how low UNITA's credibility and his own image as an icon of democracy had fallen, even among his most ardent erstwhile supporters. (The Americans were convinced that Savimbi was totally cut off from what was going on outside and that his own followers were too terrified to give him news he would not welcome.) Minister Essy was thoroughly disgruntled by UNITA's cavalier behaviour in saying 'We want your plane, but please don't burden us with your company', but we concluded that it was better to facilitate the encounter between Savimbi and his delegation, even in these least favourable circumstances. Because of the alleged landing difficulties the Ivorean plane could only take the UNITA delegation to Kinshasa, whence a small plane would ferry them to wherever Savimbi was. All of this, of course, was an elaborate charade to avoid revealing his whereabouts and prevent anyone else from conveying their views to him.

The plane left for Kinshasa on Saturday afternoon. The UNITA delegation promised President Houphoüet-Boigny and myself that they would be back 'without fail' by Tuesday 11 May. The observers and I had agreed that, if the UNITA delegates did not fulfil their promise, then I would seriously have to consider suspending the talks.

Meanwhile the Government delegates, true to their word, had returned to Abidjan at 4 a.m. on Saturday morning and told us that, after meetings with the President, the Council of Ministers and the Political Bureau of the MPLA, the delegation had been authorised to initial the Protocol. General Higino then proceeded to raise objections to parts of the text, but after more discussion Dr Muteka said that they could initial the document as it was. Our surmise was that they had had a difficult time with the hardliners in the Government, and even President dos Santos himself, and so had to go through these motions before acquiescing. Indeed both Muteka and Higino argued that, had they not gone to Luanda, the Protocol would, in all likelihood, have been rejected. Now we had to wait for UNITA.

* * *

Those long days of suspense could hardly be described as congenial. The Hotel Ivoire was a very plush hotel, but was built on such a grandiose scale that it lacked all charm and intimacy. Much of the time its labyrinthine halls and corridors echoed with emptiness. At weekends and on holidays, in contrast, it became a place of pilgrimage for large numbers of the inhabitants of Abidjan, who flocked to it as if to some arcane temple. Then its vast lobbies and vestibules were crammed with families on a Sunday outing: children in brightly coloured clothes scampering down the lawns to the lake, or sucking ice-creams and eating sticky cakes, pop music thundering out remorselessly, and young lovers entwined under the vaults of flowering trees.

For us the hotel became a sort of gilded cage in which we fretted for freedom. My most precious moments were at dawn, when everything was deserted, and I swam among the tropical flowers and watched the crows sweeping and gliding against the towering white cliff-face of the hotel above me like black rags blown aimlessly about by the capricious morning breeze. Otherwise my waking hours were spent between my suite and the meeting room. To venture out from the lift to the lobby meant, for me, running the gauntlet of a clamouring phalanx of journalists, whose frustration was even greater than my own, if that were possible, because the process was so slow and news so scant. Once, in the mad charge to encircle me, a large glass showcase was smashed by a TV camera that barely missed my head. Often I ate in my room. Before long I had made my way several times through the whole room service menu and those of the two or three restaurants in the hotel. The cuisine was most certainly not French. Chips seemed to be served with everything.

Soon my UNAVEM colleagues and I were actually homesick for Luanda and the familiar, unpretentious frugality of the camp. Apart from anything else, Abidjan is one of the most expensive cities in the world. This not only limited our sorties into the city for a change of ambience, in the rare moments when there was time to do so, but also, as the days and weeks wore by, added to our official worries a nagging concern of a more personal nature – would we be able to pay our hotel bills? The standard UN *per diem* covered barely half the daily cost of the Hotel d'Ivoire, however one tried to pare the cost. Telephone calls were astronomic in price. Only near the end of our long vigil did the UN relent and give us a rate that came nearer the basic, irreducible cost. The observers had similar problems. Only the two delegations of the Government and UNITA had not a care in the world as regards paying their bills. Both had been seen wielding large rolls of banknotes and were also known to enjoy the night life of Abidjan, frequenting the best restaurants and night clubs until the wee small hours, sometimes finding themselves at the same place, or even going there together.

The most difficult time was experienced by our tiny secretariat staff servicing the meeting, especially my two secretaries, Elizabeth and Deolinda. Abidjan was not an easy town for unaccompanied women to visit at night. They worked incredibly long hours, seven days a week, and the lack of recreation or change of scene was a great strain. I myself went out seldom – partly because of work, but also because it was a bore, with my posse of bodyguards and the inevitable scrum with the journalists.

An occasional, most agreeable refuge was offered to me by Margaret Rothwell, the British Ambassador. There I could curl up on the sofa and talk of everything under the sun except Angola. There was only one snag – she had a dog that its previous owners had chained in a yard as a guard dog, and he had not quite absorbed the cultural shock of being transported to an ambassadorial drawing room. Large, of mixed origin, he nonetheless bore unmistakeable signs of some pedigree of an aggressive nature, manifested most evidently and alarmingly in an enormous set of fangs, which he displayed menacingly on the merest occasion. After a couple of visits he seemed to grow accustomed to me, to the point of resting his head on my knee and allowing me to pat him. The Ambassador kindly organised a dinner for those of my staff who spent their time 'confined to barracks'. So, on a Sunday night, I duly turned up with my two secretaries to a most enjoyable, relaxed evening, for which the Ambassador had cooked, with her own hands, a superb steak and kidney pie. When we left my various guards were waiting at the door. I turned to say a last farewell, at the same time patting the dog on the head. In a trice he had sunk those redoubtable fangs into my left wrist! Our departure became something of a rout, with crest-fallen guards rushing tardily forward to staunch the blood. It just went to prove the old adage that, no matter how many guards you have, someone will get you if they are really hell-bent on doing so! News soon spread among the coterie attending the talks that I had been 'attacked', but it was something of an anticlimax when it was revealed that the aggressor against my 'physical integrity' had not been some zealous UNITA henchman, loyally carrying out his organisation's deaththreats, but the British Ambassador's dog!

Sometimes, when we were waiting for one or other side to respond, brief half-day excursions could be snatched. On one of these we drove to the ancient capital of Côte d'Ivoire; on another I spent a few hours at a pleasant beach resort as the guest of the UNDP Resident Representative and his wife; and once I paid a fleeting visit to a colourful market in the heart of Abidjan.

One day, when the Government delegation was away in Luanda, the Ivorean Government organised for the rest of us a visit to Yamoussoukro, the phantasmagoric city built by President Houphoüet-Boigny in the middle of the jungle, in the area where he was born. We took the hour-long flight in the President's own plane, a magnificent affair in which we sank into deep fauteuils. Yamoussoukro comprises the President's own palace, the 'Palais des Hôtes', a vast international conference centre and offices for the President's Foundation, many other administrative buildings, schools of higher learning in various disciplines, and a luxury hotel, now slightly decaying. The *pièce de résistance,* overshadowing all else, is the huge basilica, exceeding St Peter's in Rome in size, and conceived and adorned in a suitably monumental and ostentatious style. Its cost must have been equally phenomenal but is a well-kept state secret. The anomalous and artificial character of the whole enterprise was perhaps best illustrated when I enquired about the music. Clearly such a magnificently conceived temple required an outstanding choir, but how could one be kept going in the heart of the African bush? Simple, I was assured, and someone scurried away. Within seconds, celestial music enveloped us and soared up into the great dome above us – at the mere press of an electric button in the basement.

Our guide was the President's own elegant Chief of Protocol (he of the chair), aided by a French couple who ran the whole vast agglomeration of palaces and gardens. We were shepherded into the no less munificent guest palace before going on to luncheon in the President's own palace. There I was whisked away by the admirably competent French lady to 'wash my hands' in the elaborately appointed main apartments, where, as was painstakingly pointed out, various kings and princes and their consorts had slept (everyone else used humbler, but no doubt luxurious, toilets on the ground floor). When we came at last to the main bedroom for heads of state, I was ushered into a large bathroom, positively aglow with dazzling gold taps and appurtenances. There was only one snag – no toilet paper, no soap, no towels. A minion was sent scurrying off to rectify the omission, returning, breathless, with the necessities some fifteen minutes later, after traversing endless salons and staircases. I hadn't the heart to say to the gracious chatelaine that, as an experienced field person, I always carried the basic wherewithal on my person.

Then we walked to the presidential palace for lunch, before which French champagne was served in a salon whose walls were crowded with portraits of courtly French ladies of another age. The staff had had less than 24 hours' notice of our visit and, with journalists and local dignitaries, we numbered nearly a hundred, yet we sat down to a superb four-course lunch that was worthy of the most élite of Paris restaurants. It was a *tour de force*, but totally anachronistic. The President's palace was even more sumptuous than that for his illustrious guests, but one wondered how on earth it was possible to live in it. There was a sort of child-like pride in all of this magnificence, so clearly inspired by France of *la belle époque*. When the tour was over, Minister Essy told me that President Houphoüet-Boigny was waiting by the telephone in Abidjan to hear my impressions, which I duly gave in suitable hyperbole.

As we left the palace, and as if to underline the bewildering clashes of culture at every turn during this bizarre experience, live ducks were thrown to the crocodiles in the moat for our entertainment. Diplomacy deserted me, and I turned away. I learned from Antonio Monteiro that his President, Mario Soares, had done likewise and caused quite a diplomatic stir, as well as headlines in the Portuguese press. My other diplomatic gaffe occurred during the last item on the agenda, a tour of the higher educational institutions, when I was rash enough to enquire about the proportion of women students. This caused general consternation, except among the tiny huddle of girls who seemed almost exclusively to be there to acquire secretarial skills.

This sortie was an exception. Most of the days were a long, hard grind, wrestling with the same issues, trying to find new wording or approaches that would break one deadlock only to find that a new one, just as intractable, had emerged. It was like an endless modern play in which the characters aimlessly prattle on, oblivious of the big issues of life and death that eventually overwhelm them. The American delegation whiled away the time casting stars to play the key roles in a 'film version of Abidjan'. They told me they had picked Emma Thompson to play me.

As for my own state of mind, I can hardly recall a period in my life when I was more despondent. The nervous strain of these interminable days and weeks was arguably worse for the observers and the UNAVEM staff – and particularly for me, as mediator – than for the two delegations. They presumably knew what they were up to, whereas the rest of us could only guess at their intentions and try to avoid the various hidden shoals flung suddenly in our course as we tried to steer this volatile ship to safe harbour.

I found myself sleeping less and less and finding it difficult to relax. Reading was perhaps the best medium for that. Savouring the delicate psychological subtleties of the relationships in *The Golden Bowl* provided total distraction from the text of the Abidjan Protocol, though Henry James' masterly analysis of the deviousness and duplicity of his characters was perhaps no bad training for dealing with the innumerable hidden agenda of the protagonists in our own real-life drama. My other main reading was more directly relevant: I was rereading Basil Davidson's *In the Eye of the Storm*: his account of the anticolonial struggle in Angola some twenty-five years earlier, written before independence unleashed the civil war whose aftermath we were trying to sort out. His remarkable insights into the root causes of the present tragedy, and the extraordinary close analogies with the situation with which I was wrestling (even though, at that time, neither UNITA nor Jonas Savimbi had achieved any real significance, meriting only a paragraph or two) did not make comfortable reading, or bode well for our negotiations.

* * *

In contrast UNITA was now very much calling the shots. Its delegation did not, of course, return to Abidjan by Tuesday 11 May. This put me in the dilemma of deciding whether or not to apply the guillotine and suspend the talks. So much was at stake that all my instincts conspired to make me hang on, in the hope that they would come back with something positive; there could be genuine logistical reasons for the delay. At the same time continued waiting would only sharpen the voices of those critics who accused us of being too lenient with UNITA, but the possibility, however frail, of a ceasefire and of saving lives left us with no alternative but to wait.

After several false alarms, Dr Valentim and his companions finally returned to Abidjan at 11.00 p.m. on Thursday 13 May. They had been away for six days, instead of the promised three, without any valid explanation and despite having an Ivorean Government plane at their disposal. I convened a night session just as soon as they arrived, among other reasons so that Minister Essy could pass on the news, preferably good, to his President, who was now definitely leaving for France early the following morning. The UNITA delegation felt no similar sense of urgency. On 'grounds of fatigue' Dr Valentim and his colleagues refused to attend the meeting, at which the rest of us had been prepared to sit throughout the night if necessary. Everyone else was incensed. It was hard to allay the suspicion that UNITA's delayed return and its rejection of the night session were designed to prevent any further negotiations taking place while President Houphoüet-Boigny was still in the country, and so remove one factor of pressure.

In this they were successful. A very disappointed and disillusioned Minister Essy invited me to accompany him to the airport on Friday morning to bid farewell to the ailing President. President Mitterand had sent an Air France Concorde to fetch him and the gleaming white streak was already drawn up at the end of a broad avenue of red carpet. The Prime Minister, the Cabinet, the Diplomatic Corps – everyone who was anyone was there to see the President off. Guards resplendent in scarlet, bedecked with gold tassels and braid and tossing white plumes, lined the approach to the airport and the pathway to the plane. When the President arrived, a tiny shrunken figure, walking with difficulty, it was almost an anticlimax. Farewells and formalities were kept to a minimum, no doubt out of concern for his visibly failing strength. He spoke briefly to me, expressed his hope that the Protocol would soon be signed, and asked me to keep him informed by telephone. Then he walked slowly and uncertainly towards the plane. A truly daunting flight of steep steps led up, high as a house, to the door of the great white machine. How ever was the ascent to be made with dignity? Two of the guards of honour grasped him firmly by each elbow and piloted him up, but it was clear that his feet were not touching the staircase and that they were really carrying him. The small black-clad figure swung between them like a broken doll, in pathetic contrast to all the pomp and circumstance of which he was the object.

President Houphoüet-Boigny was never to return alive to Abidjan. He died of cancer in France only a few months later. Nor was he to achieve his cherished goal of seeing peace restored in Angola during his lifetime.

* * *

My own position continued to be very complicated, although in some respects it was easier. Not only had UNITA's attacks on me ceased, but throughout the negotiations Dr Valentim treated me with an exaggerated courtesy that almost amounted to obsequiousness..

Public criticism had also died down on the Government side and there had even been recantation. One of the few agreeable surprises in Abidjan was to learn that Lázaro Dias, a former Justice Minister and now Vice-President of the National Assembly, had publicly apologised for a vitriolic column he had written against me in early March in the *Jornal de Angola*. In it he had thrown on me the entire blame for the renewal of war, and urged me to go away and 'finish growing old in a rocking chair, lulled by the wails, sobs and tears of the Angolan children whose deaths she has made no effort to prevent'. His handsome apology in the same newspaper on 14 April was entitled 'Senhora Anstee, desculpe-me' – 'Miss Anstee, forgive me'. Whether this was because the Abidjan talks had just started, because Cardenal do Nascimento had given him a good ticking-off, or because UNITA had threatened to kill me, I do not know. I wrote to assure him that I forgave him, but this did not prevent him from violently attacking me again on a later occasion (on what grounds I no longer remember).

In contrast to these various olive branches, real or apparent, quite a flutter was caused by the appearance of the May 1993 issue of *Africa International*, a francophone monthly. This contained a full-page photograph of myself with a headline straddling it in red: 'L'Ennemi Publique No. 1' ('Public Enemy No. 1'). The accompanying article, by Grégoire Ndaki, was in fact sympathetic, concluding that I was a mere 'scapegoat', being made unjustly to bear alone the blame for the failure of the UN mission in Angola, which was really due to totally inadequate resources. The snag was that most readers would not get beyond the headline (untempered even by a question mark) and the long list of attacks and criticisms recorded by the author as having been made against me by both sides. There were also some new ones – that my 'British origins' had created suspicions, including that I was a stooge of the Americans and did not know Portuguese. There was no mention of the peace talks even then going on in Abidjan, under my chairmanship (accepted by both sides) and in Portuguese!

While that article did, in the end, try to be fair, it was yet another example of the journalism that seeks sensationalist news by dwelling on negative allegations and accentuating the 'smear' factor. If you are a mediator, caught in a prominent position between two warring sides, each of whom wants to exploit you for their own ends, this is par for the course and you just have to learn to live with it.

Harder to cope with was the growing feeling that I was getting less and less backing from my own Headquarters. When one is ploughing a lonely furrow with much at stake, as I was in Angola itself and particularly in Abidjan, it is all too easy to become paranoid. At no point, however, then or ever, did I feel that this neglect was in any way personal. Even when in the thick of the fray I recognised that there were a number of quite objective factors at work: the sheer weight of the rapid explosion of new – and different – peacekeeping operations in a bureaucracy that was neither staffed nor geared procedurally to cope with it; the low priority given to Angola, partly as a result of the overwhelming demands of former Yugoslavia and Somalia, which now occupied the forefront of public attention owing to the prominence afforded them by the media; and the bizarre division of responsibility for backstopping peacekeeping operations in UN Headquarters between two Under Secretaries-General (an arrangement that, happily, has been modified since). The difficulty of separating 'operations' from 'policy' presented itself in a particularly acute form during the Abidjan talks, since the 39 articles of the Protocol inextricably intertwined both, from military to political matters, civil administration and humanitarian affairs.

Initially I addressed my daily cables to whichever of the two Under Secretaries-General (both of whom I considered as good friends) seemed to be most concerned by the main thrust of the subject matter. When complaints reaching me about inadequate reporting revealed that there was less than optimum communication between their respective staffs in New York, I changed my tactics and sent my cables to *both*. While this solved one problem – ensuring that everyone who should know in Headquarters did know – it simply created another: my cables fell between two stools and either got no reply or else did so with such delay that it was no longer relevant.

This was particularly unnerving with regard to the Protocol of Abidjan itself. This highly complex and key document was being worked out on the spot and embraced a wide spectrum of immensely technical issues on which our UNAVEM negotiating team, consisting of only two people on the civilian/political side and two on the military, was far from claiming omniscience. Daily we churned out a new version, which we then sent, also daily, to Headquarters in the original Portuguese, followed as soon as possible by an English translation (since Portuguese is not an official UN language, translation could not be done in New York). The observers were also sending the various versions to their capitals and Ed De Jarnette and Antonio Monteiro were constantly observing to me 'Washington/Lisbon thinks this and that about the latest draft. What is the view in New York?' (I cannot say that the Russians did the same, but then Moscow was occupied with problems nearer home.) To such enquiries I had to resist the obvious reply 'I only wish I knew', and hedge. At one point I was goaded into drafting a terse, coded cable to New York that simply asked 'Is there anyone there?', but was dissuaded by my UNAVEM colleagues from sending it. In six weeks of negotiations in Côte d'Ivoire the only cable I received from Headquarters specifically referring to the Protocol merely asked, in a patently irritated tone, what was holding up the English translation of the latest version. Again I was restrained from sending an intemperate reply querying the reason for the urgency since we never got a reaction anyway!

Something much worse was to happen, however, which made me reflect that inaction by Headquarters was perhaps preferable to action. On the evening of Friday, 7 May, Under-Secretary-General James Jonah called with a personal request from the Secretary-General that I agree to yet another extension of my tenure (I had hoped to step down after the Abidjan talks) as Dr Savimbi had rejected Sergio de Melo on the ground of his Brazilian nationality (UNITA considered that Brazil favoured the Government). I was appalled, not so much by the extension, though it was the last thing I wanted, as by Headquarters yielding to pressure that for me ran contrary to the basic principles of the UN (de Melo was not a political appointee but a respected international civil servant with a proven record of competence and objectivity), and even more so that Dr Savimbi should have been consulted at all at that stage, as I had an agreement with the Secretary-General that the name of my replacement would remain under wraps while I was involved in delicate negotiations. For UNITA to be made aware, so soon, that moves were afoot to appoint a successor would not only look like yielding to Savimbi's pressure for my removal, but could colour UNITA's attitude, and its strategy, at the Abidjan talks.

Ironically, just one day after I had been asked to 'soldier on' against my wishes because Sergio de Melo could not be appointed news broke in the media that I was to be replaced immediately by the self-same person and journalists had a field day speculating about the reasons, mostly derogatory to me. Although I tried to put the record straight I knew that no one would believe what I said, as an interested party, unless an unequivocal statement was put out by Headquarters. Once again my plea to New York fell on deaf ears for several days. The observers were deeply concerned about the negative impact these rumours were having on the talks (they thought that expectation of my early replacement was another factor determining UNITA's delay in returning to Abidjan). Ambassador De Jarnette told me that UNITA already knew of Sergio de Melo's candidature at the time of the bilateral meeting with the Americans on 25 March (that is, barely two weeks after the Secretary-General and I had agreed that this information must be kept secret), and thought that even then it might already have been submitted to Dr Savimbi by New York for consultation!

New York's continued silence, and my knowledge of the lack of coordination and cooperation there, made me doubt even the validity of the information that de Melo's candidature had been withdrawn, and this view was bolstered by news that UNITA was launching a campaign against the Brazilian candidate. On Thursday 13 May (the day of UNITA's delayed return to Abidjan) I appealed again to New York that urgent public clarification be made, as the escalating rumours in Abidjan, Angola and Portugal risked undermining the Abidjan negotiations, now at their most sensitive stage. It was imperative, I urged, that the new appointment should either be confirmed – in which case much care would be needed in indicating dates, since the ongoing negotiations must be concluded first – or officially denied.

On 14 May Abidjan's main daily newspaper actually claimed that de Melo's appointment had been officially announced in New York two days earlier (12 May) by UN Headquarters. I again stressed that it was imperative to scotch the rumours one way or the other before the weekend, during which vital meetings would be taking place in Abidjan; otherwise there was a great danger that my authority as Chairman would be irretrievably eroded and the outcome of the talks jeopardised.

This at last produced a reaction. On the afternoon of Friday 14 May Mr Gharekhan, when making a statement on Angola at informal consultations of the Security Council, on behalf of the Secretary-General, added a paragraph, evidently as an afterthought, and that was subsequently read out by the Secretary-General's spokesman. It stated:

During the last few days, there have been press reports regarding the status of the Special Representative of the Secretary-General for Angola. I wish to clarify that Miss Margaret J. Anstee expressed the wish some time ago to be released from her responsibilities. The Secretary-General is giving consideration to this matter and will take a decision shortly. In the meantime, he wishes to stress that he continues to have full confidence in her. The Secretary-General is convinced that her deep knowledge of the Angolan situation, her competence and professionalism remain a valuable asset in this crucial phase of the ongoing negotiating process in Abidjan. He earnestly hopes that the parties will redouble their efforts to reach agreement without further delay and urges them to extend their full cooperation to his Special Representative.

Unfortunately this statement merely fuelled more speculation and uncertainty since, contrary to my very specific indications, it said nothing to dispel the notion that the Brazilian candidate was to be appointed shortly. It was immediately misinterpreted by the media, even by such usually reliable sources as the BBC. On the same day, the BBC Africa Service stated that an official announcement had been made in New York that 'Margaret Anstee' *had been asked to* step down'. (My emphasis.) Later that evening the BBC World Service ('News Hour') called me in Abidjan to get my reaction and I tried to put the record straight. Notwithstanding, on Saturday night the BBC stringer in Luanda, who was following the talks in Abidjan, stated on 'Focus Africa' that it was not clear whether Margaret Anstee was 'being given the push' or merely wished to 'stand down of her own accord'. I was fairly irritated by this, coming after my clarifying interview, and without checking with me. On Sunday the BBC correspondent in West Africa apologised, but the damage was done. I also cabled Joe Sills, the spokesman, and asked him to clarify the matter at Headquarters, and particularly with the BBC correspondent to the UN, pointing out that this constant and unfounded speculation was having a most injurious effect at a crucial moment when I was fighting to save the peace talks from complete collapse. I never heard whether action was taken or not.

It is impossible to say whether this unfortunate and eminently avoidable incident made any real difference to the ultimate outcome of the Abidjan talks. There were many other factors at work, most notably the true intentions of both sides, particularly UNITA's. But it certainly did not help, took up much time and effort and was scarcely likely to improve my own already pretty dejected spirits.

* * *

The main cause for despondency was the plenary meeting I had at last been able to hold on Friday 14 May. As so often, it began quite promisingly. I asked both delegations to present the results of their consultations with their respective leaderships. Dr Muteka took the floor first and said, with his customary brevity, that while the Government did have some observations, it was nonetheless ready to initial the Protocol. Dr Valentim put the proposition the other way round: UNITA found the Protocol 'generally acceptable', but had 'some observations'.

This sounded hopeful, but not for long. Dr Valentim proceeded to go once more through the whole text of the Protocol, point by point. His observations were the familiar objections that UNITA had been putting forward since the very first week. It was as if none of the lengthy subsequent debates during our long sojourn in Abidjan had ever occurred. And what the delegates had been doing during their six days' absence in consultations with Dr Savimbi was a mystery, since their position had not changed one iota.

There was general consternation and I decided that I had to bring matters to a head. I recalled that the Government side had agreed to initial the document, even though they had observations. Those representing UNITA had also said they found the document 'generally acceptable', though they too had observations. Could I take it that they were prepared to adopt the same position as the Government and initial the Protocol, on the understanding that all observations would be included in the summary records? Dr Valentim wriggled in his seat, and hedged very uncomfortably for one who could usually talk his way out of any corner. When I insisted on a straight answer he would only say that they were prepared to initial a document, but not this one in its present form. I then asked the UNITA delegates to meet separately with me and produce written amendments. When they gave the amendments to me in the afternoon most of them were totally unacceptable, and undermined the basic concept of the Protocol that political concessions by the Government would be matched by military concessions from UNITA. UNITA wanted to have the former without the latter. Its position had not only not changed for the better, but in some respects had hardened even further.

There was no alternative but to convene a plenary meeting for Saturday morning, at which the talks would almost certainly break down. That night, I tried to warn the Secretary-General, and suggest that he contact Dr Savimbi, but was unable to reach him or anyone else at Headquarters.

Early on Saturday morning Dr Valentim and General Manuvakola asked to see me. They seemed at last to have taken on board that this time the talks really were on the verge of collapse, and that UNITA was the cause. Hitherto, Valentim had taken the irritatingly complacent attitude that 'we are here to negotiate peace and we must all stay here for as long as it takes to secure peace', blissfully – or wilfully – overlooking the fact that there was absolutely no point in going on day after day if UNITA was not prepared to budge a single inch. I think he would happily have sat in Abidjan, filibustering as only he knew how, for a year or more, while battles continued to rage all over Angola. The strong Messianic streak with which Jonas Savimbi had infused his UNITA follwers seemed to convince them that, if they just held out long enough, other people would be forced to come round to their point of view – a kind of Chinese water torture. The Maoist background of the movement was often evident. I found it deeply ironic that the only people applying Marxist–Leninist techniques of negotiation were these self-declared archenemies of Communism and supporters of democracy, the UNITA delegation. The Government delegation, supposedly still died-in-the-wool Communists, according to Savimbi's scourging rhetoric, were totally pragmatic. This time, however, Valentim was visibly shaken by the prospect of breakdown. I also sensed that there were divided opinions undermining the normally monolithic stand of the UNITA representatives. General Manuvakola, Jardo Muekalia and John Marqués Kakumba gave signs of recognising the need for UNITA to make some move.

To explore these possibilities the plenary was postponed and the morning spent in an intensive round of informal consultations. At the end of it we were no nearer to breaking the impasse. At noon Dr Muteka and Dr Valentim came to see me jointly, and said they could see no alternative to holding the plenary, which was then rescheduled for 4.00 p.m. that Saturday afternoon. The writing was on the wall: a plenary in the present circumstances could have only one outcome – breakdown.

* * *

Acting on sudden impulse, I asked Dr Valentim to stay behind alone. I think he was taken by surprise. It was the first and only time that I was to see him on his own. There were usually at least two UNITA people present, presumably to make sure everyone toed the party line. I made an impassioned appeal for one more effort to be made to avoid a breakdown, which would have terrible consequences for the Angolan people that could only be attributed to UNITA's intransigence. In the long run it was UNITA that would suffer most, and it would be well-advised to think again about the Protocol, which in my view provided the best deal UNITA could expect, and moreover represented significant political concessions by the Government. Inevitably our talk revolved once again around the immediate availability of 'Blue Helmets' to protect UNITA's withdrawal. Here I could do no more than reiterate that the Security Council stood ready to act, but the Protocol must be signed first. Valentim seemed to be moved by my argument – or perhaps by my emotion – and promised to try to do something.

This time he was as good as his word. That afternoon John Marques Kakumba telephoned with the proposal that Dr Savimbi should call the Secretary-General and President Houphoüet-Boigny (now in Paris), and asked me to facilitate the contact with the Secretary-General. I waited until it was 10 a.m. in New York, and then rang Dr Boutros-Ghali at his residence to alert him to the expected call and brief him about the situation. As was always the case when I had direct contact with the Secretary-General, he was courteous and businesslike. He took a pencil and paper and asked me to dictate to him notes on what he might say to Dr Savimbi, which I did. He promised to call me back as soon as the conversation had taken place. As usual, that part was not to be so easy.

I postponed the fatal plenary session once again, until Sunday morning. During Saturday afternoon and evening I was in constant contact with both delegations, the observers and Minister Essy, and did not move from my suite. At ten o'clock that night John Kakumba called to say that Dr Savimbi had had difficulty calling the Secretary-General as he was 'at the front'. I was always deeply suspicious about these supposed communication difficulties. Kakumba went on to convey a request from Dr Valentim that I arrange for a personal message to be sent from the Secretary-General through them. I got the impression that this initiative was being taken by the UNITA representatives in Abidjan in a desperate attempt to save the talks and get their leader to see reason.

I again telephoned the Secretary-General. Together we drafted the following brief message:

> On the basis of our old friendship, I appeal to you to accept and sign the Protocol of Abidjan, in order to avoid further deterioration of the tragic situation being endured by the people of Angola and to prevent a worsening of the situation at the international level, where I fear you would find yourself totally isolated.
>
> I also ask you to trust me, as Secretary-General, and as your old friend, to do all I can to help you when the Protocol is signed.

The last sentence was a coded message to reassure Savimbi that the Secretary-General would spare no effort to bring in adequate international support, including 'Blue Helmets', to help consolidate the ceasefire. The Secretary-General could make no outright commitment without the authorisation of the Security Council, but he hoped that this expression of his own strong personal support would prove sufficiently persuasive.

At 11.00 p.m. I telephoned Dr Boutros-Ghali's message to Dr Valentim, who said it would be immediately transmitted to Dr Savimbi (I forbore to ask by what means, since communication was so difficult).

Minister Essy called at midnight to say that he thought he had persuaded the UNITA delegation to accept the Protocol of Abidjan. Cheering as this news was, I felt bound to express scepticism that they would do so without orders from Dr Savimbi. This assumption was confirmed on Sunday morning, when Dr Valentim requested another postponement of the plenary session until a reply was received from Savimbi to the Secretary-General's message. I agreed, but insisted that it could not be delayed much longer, since everyone now feared that UNITA was up to its well-known filibustering tactics again, and both the Government and the observers had accepted the further postponement with marked reluctance. At 11.45 a.m. Valentim called me again to say that Savimbi had received the message and would try to telephone the Secretary-General that day. I had fixed the plenary session for 10.00 a.m. on Monday morning, and made clear to all concerned that it must be held then and must be definitive – that is, either UNITA would accept the Protocol, or it would refuse to do so, in which case I would suspend the talks.

Dr Savimbi's call to the Secretary-General did not take place until just before 10.00 p.m. (New York time) on the night of Sunday 16 May. In Abidjan it was already 2.00 a.m. in the morning of Monday and in Angola 3.00 a.m., so Savimbi was following his usual custom of using his satellite telephone only in the wee small hours. Just after 2.30 a.m., my time, Dr Boutros-Ghali called to tell me that he had had a very long conversation with Savimbi, lasting over half an hour, during which, he confessed, he had at times found it hard to follow the UNITA leader's repetitive and wandering train of thought. The Secretary-General was concerned about the change he had detected in the man he had known for so many years, particularly his lack of coherence. It was clear that he had been treated to one of Savimbi's 'stream of consciousness' performances.

The gist of this rambling conversation had been that Savimbi wanted the talks to be extended for another week. The Secretary-General told him that this was too long, and proposed 'two or three days' I queried whether there should be any extension at all and argued that we should bring the matter to a head during Monday morning's plenary session. I could not see what could be achieved by further delay, unless some new element had entered the picture. There seemed to be none and we had exhausted all possible avenues of compromise. The Secretary-General insisted that peace was so important that we must give the talks another try, however hopeless it seemed, and I had to agree that we should leave no stone unturned in our search for a solution. Savimbi had told the Secretary-General that he would call him again on Monday night, and we could only hope that this conversation might break new ground on the substance of the negotiations.

At 3.00 a.m. Minister Essy called to tell me that Dr Savimbi had spoken in the same vein to President Houphoüet-Boigny. Fortuitously, the President had had the same reaction as the Secretary-General and opted for the compromise of a shorter time.

* * *

We spent Monday trying to find ways of bringing the two sides closer together on the main issues of contention, but without success. The impression, both of the observers and ourselves, was that UNITA's position had, if anything, hardened since the extension of time was agreed. Dr Valentim even referred to the time limit on the extension as an ultimatum, an impression we had studiously avoided.

Such hopes as I had were pinned on the further telephone conversation the Secretary-General was to have with Dr Savimbi on Monday night. Savimbi did not, however, make that call. Meanwhile an unexpected development had intervened: the Government delegation suddenly left for Luanda on Monday afternoon for consultation with President dos Santos.

Their visit was truly a lightning one, for they returned to Abidjan during the same night, having had a three-hour conversation with their President. They met me early the next morning and authorised me to convey the following four points to UNITA:

- The Government was ready to accept a specific reference in the Protocol, envisaging the simultaneous appointment of provisional and local authorities from among UNITA ranks as soon as UNITA troops had, under UN supervision, evacuated occupied towns and Government central administration had been restored (this met one of UNITA's demands; the draft Protocol contemplated the incorporation of UNITA elements at a much later stage).
- Once the central administration was in place, UNITA deputies could be appointed. (I was doubtful whether this would be attractive to UNITA.)
- The President had instructed the delegation to engage in bilateral talks with UNITA, if the latter so desired. (This was welcome. During the weekend I had obtained UNITA's agreement to face-to-face talks, but not the Government's.)
- If UNITA became flexible, the Government would become flexible.

The last point was perhaps the most important of all, since it was open-ended. The whole burden of the message was that the Government was exceedingly anxious to reach an agreement, in contrast to the hardline stance taken by Dr Muteka and General Higino during the weekend.

On Tuesday afternoon I met the UNITA delegation. Dr Valentim had spoken to Dr Savimbi and now gave an account of the latter's conversation with the Secretary-General, which was a complete tergiversation of the exchange recounted to me by Dr Boutros-Ghali. Among other things, I had to disabuse him of the notion that an open-ended extension of 'at least seven days' had been agreed. The explanation given for Savimbi's failure to make the second promised phone call was that he did not wish to give the impression that he 'doubted the Secretary-General's word', to which I had to point out that Dr Boutros-Ghali had not been looking for a reconfirmation of what had already been said, but a substantive proposal from Dr Savimbi that would move things forward. The only crumb of comfort was that he had instructed his delegation 'to be expeditious and to do all possible to ensure that the talks were successful'. It was no more than a crumb, for Savimbi did not seem to have given them any ingredients to ensure that success.

At least the UNITA delegates were pleased about the four new points put forward by the Government. They said that they too were ready to be 'flexible' and to meet bilaterally. They still stubbornly persisted, however, in their position that paragraph 11 of the Protocol (on the withdrawal of UNITA from occupied towns) must be reformulated.

I arranged the bilateral meeting for Wednesday morning, 19 May, but that foundered on misunderstandings between the two delegations. In the afternoon, I called a plenary meeting to enable both delegations to restate their positions in the light of the Government delegation's meeting with President dos Santos and Dr Valentim's telephone conversation with Dr Savimbi. My aim was no more than to avoid any further misunderstandings and to ascertain to what extent there was room for further manoeuvre. The Government side reiterated the offers they had made through me the previous day, and reiterated also that they accepted the latest version of the draft Protocol *in toto* and would not brook changes in the principles enshrined in it.

Dr Valentim began with another of his long disquisitions on generalities, of which we had had such a surfeit during the past six weeks. He even embarked on a lengthy discussion as to whether the extension of the talks was for five or seven days, a very academic question since, no matter how many days we stayed there, UNITA never brought anything new to the table. When I pressed him to descend from the lofty heights of the general to the more immediate and relevant particular, and to make some specific proposals, he simply trotted out once again the far-reaching amendments he had proposed the previous Friday (14 May). To no avail I reminded Valentim that the whole point of the extension had been to allow us to move forward from the positions of 14 May, these positions having caused the impasse in the first place.

The Government delegation was furious and the observers open-mouthed with astonishment that Dr Valentim had had the gall to hark back to their earlier amendments. Dr Muteka made short shrift of UNITA's proposals in his usual incisive way, reiterating crisply that the Government accepted the Protocol and would not accept any amendments of principle, and certainly not a modification of point 11, concerning the withdrawal of UNITA's forces. (This had been the main thrust of Valentim's presentation, using the argument that Government troops should be treated on a par with those of UNITA and hence withdrawn from the cities, thus refusing to recognise that the situation was no longer the same as at Bicesse in May 1991. Now there was a legally formed Government and a legally formed FAA, from which UNITA had decided of its own volition to withdraw, and UNITA was in the position of a rebel.)

In the face of this total block I resorted to informal consultations again, reminding everyone that we had very little time left. This produced a ranting intervention from Dr Valentim, who insisted that the talks could not be concluded until there was agreement. I replied that we could not endlessly go on debating the same issues unless there was some palpable movement. So far only the Government had come up with modifications of its earlier position while UNITA remained immovable. If we made a breakthrough by Friday, then we could continue for the time necessary to finalise the Protocol and its annexes; but if there was still no progress by then, there was no point in continuing the present round of talks.

Dr Valentim rounded on me and said it was the job of the mediator to find solutions, conveniently ignoring that no mediation is possible if one side to a conflict refuses to make even the smallest concession. It was plain that he was preparing the ground for blaming the failure of the talks squarely on the mediator, ascribing the customary scapegoat role to the UN. No one else who was a party to the negotiations could be taken in by this spurious argument.

* * *

There had, in truth, been a dramatic, and extraneous development that day that could well have irritated Dr Valentim and made him want to do the same to everyone else.

I had been visited very early that morning by Ed De Jarnette and Robert Cabelly, who advised me that the Clinton Administration intended to announce, later that same day, its formal recognition of the Government of President dos Santos and the opening-up of full diplomatic relations with the Government they had blackballed for two and a half decades. This move had been expected, and confidently predicted, at various times after the elections of September 1992 had been declared 'generally free and fair' and recognised as such by the US Government, but had been so long in coming that it was by now the dampest of squibs. The mystery was, in fact, why *now*, at the nether end of talks sinking into failure, instead of either much earlier, or later? Whichever way you looked at it, the timing was weird.

The media certainly thought so, and it provided another opportunity for them to plunge into happy speculation. My own view was the more mundane and perhaps cynical one that there was no rhyme or reason about the timing of this announcement. Once the Clinton Administration had embarked on the process, certain formalities had to be gone through. This particular train had left the station on a particular date, and arrived at its destination on another, having duly covered the track in between. No one had thought about the timing: once the procedures had been completed, the announcement was made, with the haphazardness that sometimes seems to inform US foreign policy.

I have often been asked, then and since, whether I thought that this strangely timed announcement hastened the demise of the Abidjan talks. My considered view is that it really made little impact at all. The Government delegation was pleased of course, and UNITA irritated, but they shrugged it off. They had been expecting it for a long time, and by now the fate of the Abidjan talks hung on quite other issues. At most, it added another element that UNITA could include in its well-honed campaign to present itself as the wronged and aggrieved party.

* * *

I believed then, and I believe now, that the only thing that might have tipped the balance in favour of an agreement was if I, as the UN mediator, had been able to offer even a token contingent of 'Blue Helmets', to arrive immediately and provide a symbolic international presence to monitor the initial stages of a ceasefire and act as a moral safeguard for the withdrawal of UNITA troops from the localities they had occupied and in which they would leave behind many civilian supporters. If things went well, then they should be supplemented as soon as possible by the full complement of troops and other staff required to support the implementation of the Protocol. Early in May, Brigadier Nyambuya had prepared a full plan for the total troops required, in consultation with our military staff in Luanda and the military advisers in New York. The estimate was between 12 000 and 15 000 troops.

It will be clear from this narrative that I had several times urged Headquarters to authorise me to make a commitment that such an advance battalion would be dispatched, as soon as the Protocol was agreed. Not only UNITA had asked me to do this. The Government delegation had made the same request, which they saw as the only means of obtaining a softening of UNITA's obdurate position on point 11. A long, late-night conversation with Kofi Annan had revealed that we were in an impossible 'chicken-and-egg' situation. He had told me that the Security Council would not authorise the despatch of even a symbolic battalion of 'Blue Helmets' unless the Protocol was signed first and a ceasefire already in place. I had argued, in vain, that I could not obtain either of these unless I could promise the battalion, and that we must find some way to break the vicious circle.

Even worse was to follow: Kofi told me that, apart from these political and diplomatic considerations, there were acute logistical and financial problems, owing to the increasing number of peacekeeping operations and the reluctance of member states to provide sufficient troops and the money to support them. I should therefore warn both sides that, even if they signed the Protocol and achieved a ceasefire, it would be *six to nine months* before the international community could send the troops necessary to monitor and oversee the operation! This was so patently ludicrous that I flatly refused to do so, since it would have destroyed any shred of credibility still remaining to me as mediator. A mediator must have some leverage to be successful – especially when one of the parties to a conflict is intransigent – and I was being left with none.

There were, naturally, risks in the course of action that I was proposing, but the stakes involved were even greater. It could also be argued, as I had done to myself, that UNITA's demand for the immediate arrival of these troops was a pretext, put forward precisely because it knew I would never be authorised to make such a commitment, and thus serving as a smokescreen for its real intentions, which might be to avoid signing anything in Abidjan and just go on fighting, while blaming the UN for the failure of the talks. Such a speculation, in my view, only reinforced the argument in favour of my proposal: while it would not have achieved the main objective of securing peace, it would at least have called UNITA's bluff, if that is what it was, and unequivocally identified the real culprits responsible for the breakdown.

During our last days in Abidjan my renewed efforts days to obtain a change of mind in Headquarters were, predictably, as unsuccessful as the previous ones. It may well have been too late by then; UNITA was becoming hourly more entrenched in its legalistic demand for equal status. Throughout Thursday 20 May, innumerable meetings and contacts took place at all levels and through all channels, in a desperate last-ditch effort to find a way out. With UNITA doggedly clinging to the same position it had held before the extension, unwilling to make even the slightest concession in response to those made by the Government, and with myself deprived of any new element that might break the deadlock, the collapse of the talks was now a foregone conclusion.

* * *

I convened the final plenary session for 3.00 p.m. on Friday 21 May. It was somehow fitting that it was once again delayed, until 6.30 p.m.. The meeting did not last long. There was no longer very much to say. I began by asking whether either side had any new element to put on the table that might yet render possible an agreement on the Abidjan Protocol, but I already knew the answer. If not, I said, everyone must be aware that I would be obliged to 'interrupt' the talks. I carefully avoided using a more definitive word, such as 'close', 'terminate' or even 'suspend', as I firmly believed – and emphasised in my remarks – that we had done much solid work, which must provide the foundation for progress towards peace at some more propitious time.

There were speeches from the heads of the two delegations, from Foreign Minister Essy and from the observers, They were all short and they were all sad in tone, with one exception: Dr Valentim regaled us with another display of his rhetorical skills and command of the more recondite and baroque flourishes of the Portuguese language. Not only was his oration excessively lengthy, as usual, but it was extraordinarily triumphalist in tone, not just for UNITA, but for everyone present. He congratulated all of us fulsomely, as if we had engineered some stupendous achievement, rather than having failed miserably in an endeavour on which hung the lives and well-being of millions of his fellow Angolans. Not for the first time I wondered about his grasp on reality – certainly he moved in a very different world from most of the rest of us. And if all this bombast was deliberately devised to beguile us, then he had made a very wrong judgement indeed about our gullibility and our sense of occasion. For six weeks I had carefully schooled my feelings in order to maintain my impartiality as chairperson and mediator, sorely tried as my patience had been on innumerable occasions. At this very emotional moment, when all was lost, I felt very like hitting Dr Valentim – not so much for having led UNITA's obstruction, which had caused the downfall of the talks, but for his blatant indifference to the tragedy that would inexorably follow from their failure.

In contrast I was deeply touched by Minister Essy's words. I knew that he cared as keenly about our lost labour as I did, and not simply because the Angolan crisis was an important element of his country's foreign policy. He had striven for peace in Angola with total dedication, day and night during these long weeks, even at the risk of his own life. I could not have wished for a better, more dependable or more honest partner with whom to work. He had also always been a determinedly positive thinker but even his cheery smile was dimmed. His final words affected me almost to tears. Turning to me, he said, in a scarcely veiled rebuke to UNITA, that many cruel attacks and criticisms had been made against me but that after working closely with me for all these weeks he could only say 'C'est une grande dame'. Such an accolade, coming from him, made a great many things worthwhile.

At the end I expressed the fervent hope that the talks would very soon be resumed and that they would take the Protocol of Abidjan, on which we had reached agreement on virtually all but one of its 39 comprehensive articles, as a foundation for further progress, rather than going back once again to square one.

Then the time for farewells came. This was another extraordinary scene. The two delegations – who had been trading angry words, accusations and counter accusations, and even insults – were mingling chummily together, for all the world as if they were at some social gathering, or fraternising after a friendly football match ('my brother' was a usual form of address between them). There were the ritual bear hugs and a great deal of jolly banter, interspersed with greetings and messages for friends and even relatives who happened to be 'on the other side'. Soon they would go their separate ways to continue to wage the war, though, as I reflected rather bitterly, none of these men would be on the front line, where the fighting, the killing and the maiming had gone on unabated while we had been talking in Abidjan.

Outside the conference room there were still the jostling crowds of journalists and cameramen to be faced. My own emotions can be imagined. *Le Monde* described me as having emerged with 'les traits tirés' (drawn features) after so many weeks of hard and fruitless negotiations. The outcome had been so predictable for some days that comment was superfluous, except to underline how very near we had come to success, only to be foiled at the last moment by UNITA's intransigence and the international community's inability to provide the mediator with even a modest lever that might just have broken the deadlock.

Then Minister Essy and I had the unappealing task of telephoning an ailing old man in France, President Houphoüet-Boigny, to break the news that his dream of bringing about peace in Angola, to which he had dedicated so much of his personal effort and prestige, was not to be realised. It was a grievous personal and political defeat for him also.

My last official act there was to send a cable to the Secretary-General, telling him that all was over. The extension of five days had achieved nothing except to salve our consciences with the knowledge that we had tried to the bitter end.

* * *

Headquarters had authorised me to go from Abidjan to New York, rather than back to Luanda, so that I could report personally to the Secretary-General and to the Security Council, and I was leaving that very night for London, just before midnight. I had despatched my draft report for the Security Council to New York earlier that day.

Back in the hotel I finished my packing, and then my staff and I gathered in my suite for the last time. The observers and Minister Essy joined us. I had organised champagne, despite the failure, because I felt that the tremendous efforts and devotion of the tiny UNAVEM support group, of the observers, and of Minister Essy himself, all of whom who had worked so tirelessly, were worthy of celebration.

Minister Essy took me to the airport, and, punch-drunk as we were, we mulled over what had happened. If we had any consolation at all, it was that there was nothing more that either of us could have done, with what we had to hand, to bring the two sides to agreement, but that was not enough to assuage our bitter disappointment and dejection.

Minister Essy reiterated a theme that had been emerging more and more in his private conversations with me: President Houphoüet-Boigny and the Ivorean Government were now completely disillusioned with Dr Savimbi and UNITA. Savimbi's cavalier treatment of the President was considered intolerable, his failure to heed his advice, or even to extend the minimal courtesy of being available when the man to whom he and his movement owed so much wanted to speak to him, as little short of the basest ingratitude. The discontent, the Minister told me, had extended to the Ivoreans in general, and had now produced political repercussions. The burgeoning opposition parties were using UNITA's behaviour as a political weapon against the Ivorean President and the Government, questioning the wisdom of their long-standing support of Savimbi and his organisation.

The big lesson to be derived from Abidjan, as both Minister Essy and I agreed in that farewell talk, was that Savimbi was now no longer ready to listen to anyone, even his old supporters and allies. He now felt himself to be strong enough to 'cock a snook' at the world at large, secure in his military gains and, even more importantly, in the conviction that the international community, represented by the collectivity of member states of the United Nations and by the Security Council, was too weak, or too disinterested, to constitute a threat to his ambitions.

Part VIII
My Farewell to Arms

24 Going the Last Mile ... and the End of the Road

I rarely sleep on planes, and was scarcely likely to do so on that night flight to London. I felt tired beyond belief and my thoughts were of unrelieved gloom. From that very first telephone call late at night in Vienna, sixteen months earlier, I had known that to accept the Angolan assignment was a massive gamble, in which the odds were stacked against me. For that very reason I had thrown into it everything I could. Hardest to bear was the fact that, on a number of occasions, we had to come so tantalisingly near success: I thought particularly of the triumph of the elections in the face of daunting obstacles. Even the Abidjan negotiations had come within a hair's breadth of total agreement on the 38 points of the draft Protocol.

But that hair's breadth had proved unbridgeable and I had to come to terms with the bleak fact that, for whatever reasons, we had failed and this time I would not have another chance. Failure is never easy to face, but it becomes almost intolerable when you know that the price is not just loss of money, but the destruction of hundreds of thousands of lives, through death and maiming, and the prolongation of bitter suffering and hardship for the millions who only wanted peace, and had demonstrated this through the democratic medium of the ballot box. Even the knowledge that many factors outside my control had dictated this outcome – the intransigence of UNITA, and the indifference of the international community figuring large among them – could not assuage the personal weight of the tragedy.

It was early Saturday afternoon when I reached Knill. I had just over a day there before I left for New York. I wandered like a zombie through gardens decked out in the full glory of their spring flowering, feeling as if I had come from another planet, or as a prisoner long captive in a dark cell who cannot bear the sunlight. Reality still seemed remote when I landed in New York on Monday afternoon.

***

I was not the only one to be concerned. Late on Friday 21 May the three observers had issued a strongly worded statement, that deplored the consequences of the collapse of the talks, which they described as a tragedy for the Angolan people and for which they laid the blame squarely on UNITA. They urged the two sides to reconvene negotiations as soon as possible, but there seemed little hope of this.

On 24 May UNITA issued a communiqué claiming that 'significant progress was made' in Abidjan. Only two of the 38 points 'presented by the observers' (no mention of the UN) remained unagreed: and here it confirmed that it would only withdraw its troops to barracks if armed UN troops were already in place, and insisted that Government troops, as well as UNITA forces, should be quartered and demobilised, side-stepping once again the inconvenient fact that the two armies were no longer poised against one another on an equal footing legally, as FAPLA and FALA had been at the time of the Bicesse negotiations. UNITA was 'committed to the path of negotiation' and ready to resume talks within the next two or three weeks, and to work 'with the Government and the observers' (again no mention of the UN) to resolve the 'two remaining security concerns'. The final sentence praised the Protocol which, with its 'emphasis on national reconciliation and devolution of power', UNITA considered could 'create a climate in which the nation can heal and rebuild'.

The omission of any reference to the UN, except as regards the need for 'Blue Helmets', was striking and could only have been deliberate. Anyone reading the communiqué, without knowing the background, would have concluded that only the two delegations and the observers had been present in Abidjan.

If the purpose of this communiqué was to convince all and sundry that UNITA was on the side of the angels and more sinned against than sinning, it was singularly ineffective in New York, where I found the tide of opinion against UNITA running higher than ever before, even among countries that had been long-time supporters – perhaps even more strongly in their case because they felt they had been taken advantage of and let down.

* * *

My own concern focused more on how to move forward and stop the killing, rather than apportioning blame. Although I had failed to get agreement from Abidjan on the despatch of an advance contingent of 'Blue Helmets' in support of a ceasefire, I remained convinced that only through some such tangible demonstration of international commitment to Angola, and its readiness to act, could we avert a long-drawn-out struggle that could only deepen the human catastrophe. Paradoxically, it seemed to me that the very magnitude of that disaster could provide a key to finding a solution that could hasten agreement on a ceasefire and a return to the peace process, as well as improve the impact and rapid delivery of humanitarian aid.

As has been recounted in these pages, one of the recurring obstacles to providing assistance to the needy had been the constant attacks on UN flights and convoys. The core of my idea was that a modest contingent of 'Blue Helmets' should be provided, in the first instance, primarily to provide protection to the aid flights, but with the thought that, should talks resume, then this time there would be 'Blue Helmets' *in situ*, whose functions could, by an additional, rapid decision of the Security Council, be switched or expanded to monitoring and overseeing the withdrawal of UNITA troops, immediately an agreement between the two sides was reached, and so satisfy UNITA's concern that there could be retaliation on the populations they left behind.

It was premature to envisage any rapid return to peace talks, but I wanted the Secretary-General to have a longer-term strategy so that, when that day arrived, the UN would be better prepared. It was with all this in mind that I had drafted the 'Observations and Recommendations' section of the Secretary-General's report during the last days in Abidjan. In it, I argued that the collapse of the talks made it imperative to rethink the UN's role in Angola. It was impossible to recommend the greatly enlarged mandate and scope of the UN presence, for which we had drawn up detailed plans in the hope that the Abidjan talks would be successful; nor was it desirable that UNAVEM II, successively extended month by month since October 1992, be further prolonged in its present form: its limited mandate of rectification and observation, through joint monitoring mechanisms that had themselves collapsed, along with the peace process, had long ceased to be relevant to the new situation of open and escalating war, and merely gave rise to misunderstanding and criticism of the UN's inability to stop the conflict. At the same time it was unthinkable that the UN should abandon Angola. A new chapter needed to be opened, with fresh and clearly defined guidelines. Recalling the various options I had outlined to the Security Council when I briefed them in Munich, my draft went on:

> ... the best approach would be to combine an expanded and strengthened emergency humanitarian operation with a small 'good offices' mission, with a new, clearly defined mandate, which can keep in touch with the evolution of both the military and political situation, and be on hand to assist and promote any openings for restoring a cease-fire and restarting the peace process, as well as help mediate between the two sides, should the opportunity arise.... In the case of the humanitarian operation, and given the extremely difficult war situation in which it will have to work, consideration might be given to providing a certain number of armed UN troops to ensure the security of the relief personnel and that aid goes to the civilian population in need, for which it is intended. This was one of the roles that the UN was to undertake under the expanded mandate being considered at Abidjan, and it becomes even more important now that the wider mandate and larger UN presence are no longer possible.

When I got to New York I discovered that this part of the text had been fudged. The 'good offices' part had been singled out and presented first, as the primary recommendation. A separate paragraph underlined the importance of devoting increased resources to the 'coordination' of humanitarian operations throughout Angola, but made no reference to the need for 'Blue Helmets'.

The report had to be finalised for submission to the Council within a day of my arrival. At an inconclusive early morning meeting, at which Kofi Annan and James Jonah were also present, as well as Ambassador Gharekhan (who now seemed to act as the Secretary-General's *alter ego* in these matters), the Secretary-General instructed the four of us to come up with recommendations and present them to him at the end of the day.

We met in James Jonah's office and under his chairmanship. It was an exceedingly difficult meeting. James himself favoured my strategy but it was given short shrift by Gharekhan, and, to a lesser extent, initially by Kofi also. The usual arguments were put forward: member states would not 'wear' this; it would cost too much; troops would not be forthcoming; the UN was over-stretched, there were risks involved, look at Bosnia and Somalia... My riposte was along well-used lines too: we should not allow our recommendations to be swayed by 'what the traffic will bear'; the Secretary-General's responsibility was not to give contributory countries and members of the Security Council what they wanted to hear ('small is beautiful') but to state squarely what was needed to do the job properly; if member states decided they could not, or would not, foot the bill then lesser alternatives, including complete abandonment of the mission, would have to be considered, but at the outset the needs must be frankly addressed. I was not naive enough to suggest that the presence of 'Blue Helmets' would solve the situation, but I did contend that, without some dramatic gesture by the international community, the Angolan conflict would fester on for a very long time. I argued that Angola was forgotten, relegated to second or third place behind Yugoslavia and Somalia, and regarded as a benighted African country to which no priority was accorded by influential member states.

Another of Ambassador Gharekhan's objections, which Kofi shared, was that you could not send in 'Blue Helmets' under a humanitarian mandate, authorised by the Security Council, and then switch their function to that of monitoring a ceasefire if the situation changed. I replied that I well understood this. Clearly, if the 'Blue Helmets' were suddenly required to do other things, in a different situation, then the Secretary-General would have to go back to the Security Council to request authorisation to modify their mandate. I was not trying to circumvent the Council's authority but to ensure prompt action at the appropriate time. If the 'Blue Helmets' were on the spot, the necessary legal authority could be arranged swiftly while the long logistical delays in starting from scratch, which could all too easily scupper any new opportunity, would be averted.

We discussed all these issues against time, since everyone else was hurrying away to other meetings on other fraught problems. Before we finished, however, I had won Kofi over to my side to the extent that he agreed, as did James Jonah, that my proposition should be put forward to the Secretary-General. As chairman, James asked Ambassador Gharekhan to prepare a brief minute of the meeting and our conclusions.

When we gathered round the Secretary-General's conference table once again, Dr Boutros-Ghali had a piece of paper before him. As we were settling down, Kofi leaned over to Gharekhan and asked for a copy of the minute of our earlier meeting, which was presumably what the Secretary-General had in front of him. Gharekhan, looking embarrassed, said 'But it's confidential'. Kofi expostulated 'How can it be confidential for us, when it is a minute of a meeting at which we were present?'

Gharekhan could find no argument to counter that, and grudgingly passed over the note. Kofi and I read it quickly and wondered if we had been at the same meeting. As Gharekhan immediately took the paper back, I can only recall its general thrust. In a nutshell – and allowing for a little, perhaps understandable exaggeration on my part – its burden was 'This poor benighted female came in from the field with all these wild ideas of despatching "Blue Helmets" to Angola but we have, after some discussion, managed to bring her back to the real world and to accept that it just is not a viable option'.

In short, it was made to appear that I was standing alone, and that the proposition had been killed before it even reached the table. Kofi was as scandalised as I, pointing out that the minute did not reflect the tenor of the meeting. But that was the brief that had been laid before the Secretary-General and which he took as a premise for the meeting. Since he presumably assumed that it represented the general view of his Headquarters colleagues, he stated it at the outset as if it was his own. None of them dared contradict him; my own solitary attempts to put my point of view therefore got nowhere and the meeting was soon concluded. It was a brilliant bureaucratic coup, worthy of Sir Humphrey (of 'Yes Minister' fame) at his most manipulative.

I was not disposed to leave matters there. The next morning I had a personal meeting with the Secretary-General and seized the opportunity to explain my concerns again. As always I found it much easier to have a meeting of minds when there were no intermediaries. He agreed to the inclusion in the report to the Security Council of an oblique reference to the need for protection for the humanitarian operation. A hurried last-minute amendment was made. The reference, in the 'Observations and Recommendations' section, ran as follows:

> With the humanitarian situation deteriorating daily, it would be important during this interim period to devote increasing resources to co-ordination of that area of activity throughout the country, in support of the Emergency Humanitarian Programme being put into effect from 1 May 1993 to 30 April 1994, *including the provision of adequate protection to ensure the security of the relief personnel and that aid goes only to the civilian population in need for which it is intended. This was one of the roles that the United Nations was to carry out under the expanded mandate which was considered in Abidjan.* (Report no. S/25840, para. 38. The italics are mine, denoting the addition).

I had already been warned that this time I would not be allowed to brief the Security Council at its informal consultations on Angola, which were to be held on Thursday afternoon, 27 May. Instead Ambassador Gharekhan would read out a written brief on behalf of the Secretary-General, in accordance with the procedure now in force.

I spent the two intervening days visiting as many members of the Security Council as possible, especially those with special interest in Angola, to make sure that they understood that the passage quoted above was a coded reference to the despatch of 'Blue Helmets' and to brief them about the longer-term strategy I had in mind, as well as my conviction that my inability to bring in 'Blue Helmets' quickly had been a key factor in the failure of the Abidjan talks that I did not want to see repeated. If I was not to be allowed to brief them collectively, I was determined to do so individually, though I recognised that this was less effective. I spoke to the Permanent Representatives of the United States, Russia, Cape Verde, Spain, Brazil and Morocco, and to the Deputy Representative of the UK. I also saw the Portuguese Permanent Representative, since Portugal, although not a current member of the Security Council, was one of the three observer countries and could exert an important influence. Ambassador Madeleine Albright, who had always been friendly towards me personally (once describing us as 'sisters' when we were the only women present in a Security Council consultation) seemed very favourable to my ideas. At her request I had two meetings with her, the second attended also by some of her senior colleagues; they, however, would have to consult Washington before taking a position. As always, Ambassador Jesus of Cape Verde and I saw things very much from the same perspective. Brazil too was very receptive. Even the cautious British did not discount the idea. In fact no one to whom I spoke seemed to be opposed to it; everyone recognised that something decisive and effective must be done and there did not seem to be many other ideas around.

* * *

The Security Council consultations on Thursday 27 May proved highly embarrassing for me. The President, Ambassador Vorontsov of the Russian Federation, an old friend, came across the crowded little room and invited me to sit at his side, as I had done with the previous President on the last occasion. I had to explain, to his evident dismay, that I was not permitted to do so, or to brief the Council, and that Ambassador Gharekhan would be reading out a statement. I was not even to answer questions. In fact it was not clear whether I was really supposed to be there at all.

After Ambassador Vorontsov had called the meeting to order, the Brazilian Permanent Representative proposed that I give them a full briefing, as on the last occasion. Ambassador Vorontsov then had to say that this was not possible and that he 'understood' that, instead, a statement would be made by Ambassador Gharekhan. It was all very awkward. In any case Gharekhan did not turn up, and the statement was read by Alvaro de Soto, another of the senior advisers to the Secretary-General, a very able man but one who had had nothing to do with Angola. The statement was predictably anodyne. No questions were asked because, with myself committed to silence, no one else present on the Secretariat side was qualified to answer. By this time the situation was not only awkward, it was absurd; and hardly the best way of bringing Council and Secretariat closer together or of fostering a common understanding of the realities on the ground on which to base decisions.

The discussion immediately turned to the draft resolution, to which Brazil proposed some amendments. Ambassador Jesus made a spirited intervention, supporting the revised text and requesting two more amendments. The first proposed the inclusion of a reference to the establishment of corridors for the delivery of humanitarian aid, for which the UN would provide protection in the form of 'Blue Helmets' – in other words, my own proposal. He asked the UN Secretariat to propose the wording. The other was to stress the importance, in any future negotiations, of building on the draft Protocol of Abidjan and the many agreements obtained in that context. The Spanish Ambassador followed suit, supporting the amendments proposed by Brazil and Cape Verde. The United States also spoke, but to say that it considered that the strengthening of the criticism of UNITA (proposed by Brazil) was too sweeping and would make it difficult to deal with UNITA. They made no reference to the proposal for protecting the humanitarian operation. Nor did the UK or France, who said they also preferred the less stringent wording as regards UNITA. In response, Brazil strongly argued that UNITA's intransigence should not be rewarded, and complained that Angola had had less attention from the Security Council than most other troubled areas. Brazil also proposed that the UN's mandate in Angola should be extended for only 45 days – that is, up to 15 July – instead of two months – up to 31 July – in order to break the logjam that occurred in the Council at the end of every month. Brazil did not mention UN protection for the humanitarian operation, which I concluded at the time was due to an oversight, and preoccupation with other aspects of the long draft resolution, rather than deliberate.

Angola was certainly the victim of the logjam of peacekeeping issues confronting the Security Council in the last days of May 1993. At the end of that consultation the drafters were sent back to the drawing board and a new round of consultations. No agreement was reached on Friday 28 May either, and Monday 31 May being Memorial Day, a US public holiday, it was not until Tuesday 1 June that the Council met in formal session and adopted Resolution 834. By that time I was back in Europe, where I was to launch the humanitarian appeal for Angola. I left, pretty dispirited, on Saturday 29 May. There was nothing more I could do, single-handedly, to influence the course of events in the UN, which had now acquired their usual momentum of compromise.

* * *

Judged by verbs and adverbs, Resolution 834 used the strongest language yet on the Angolan situation but it was short on decisive action as to what to do about it. The preambular part, in addition to the 'grave concern' that had now extended to the failure of both the Abidjan talks and the establishment of a ceasefire, this time went one step further and noted *with consternation*, the further deterioration of an already grave humanitarian situation' (my emphasis). The preamble also emphasised the importance of 'a continued and effective United Nations presence' and reaffirmed the Council's commitment to 'preserve the unity and territorial integrity of Angola'.

In the operative part, the only clear directive was that the 'existing mandate' (that is, no change) of UNAVEM II should be extended until 15 July 1993. For the rest it was a mixture of wringing of hands and pious hopes. The 'importance' of the good offices and mediation functions of UNAVEM II and of the Special Representative was stressed.

Despite the US concerns, the tone was more antagonistic to UNITA than before, though not as much as Brazil and others would have wished. The oft-repeated demand that UNITA accept unreservedly the results of the democratic elections of 1992, and abide fully by the 'Acordos de Paz', was reiterated. UNITA was 'condemned' for 'its actions and armed attacks, which have resulted in increased hostilities and which endanger the peace process', and the Council 'demanded' that they should immediately cease. UNITA's refusal at the Abidjan talks to agree to the withdrawal of its troops was 'deeply regretted' and the Council 'demanded' that it did so. The Council's strong appeal to the two parties to 'reinitiate as soon as possible the interrupted peace talks under United Nations auspices' was particularly directed at UNITA, whom it unequivocally held 'responsible for the breakdown of the talks and for thereby jeopardizing the peace process' – à propos of which it reaffirmed, yet again, that it would 'consider all appropriate measures under the Charter of the United Nations to advance the implementation of the "Acordos de Paz"' (though by this time UNITA, along with the rest of us, must have tumbled to the fact that this favourite phrase did not seem to mean anything at all!)

In contrast, the Government of Angola was given a pat on the back for its 'disposition ... to reach a peaceful settlement of the conflict in conformity with the "Acordos de Paz"'. The Council also urged that new talks should aim towards 'the earliest establishment of a ceasefire' and should take due account of 'what was achieved during the discussions of the Abidjan draft Protocol'. There were kind words and 'full support' for the efforts of the Secretary-General and myself 'under extremely difficult conditions'. The Resolution called on all states to refrain from 'any action which directly or indirectly could jeopardize the implementation of the "Acordos de Paz"', and from 'providing any form of direct or indirect military assistance or other support of UNITA inconsistent with the peace process'.

Four operative paragraphs were devoted to the humanitarian situation, but they did not include any reference to the provision of protection by the UN. The Council merely 'welcomed' the strengthening of humanitarian activities being undertaken 'under the overall co-ordination of the Special Representative'. It strongly appealed to the two parties to cooperate fully, and called on all member states, UN agencies and NGOs to do likewise. The Council reiterated its appeal to both sides to abide strictly by international humanitarian law, and to guarantee 'unimpeded access' for the delivery of assistance to the civilian population in need. It also 'commended' our efforts to establish 'agreed humanitarian relief corridors'. This was part of the addition requested by Ambassador Jesus of Cape Verde, but the other part about the provision of UN protection had been dropped. Instead the Council lamely reiterated 'its appeal to both parties to take all necessary measures to ensure the security and the safety of the personnel involved in humanitarian relief operations'.

My last-ditch effort in New York had foundered. But then I had known all along that it was another 'mission impossible', almost certainly doomed to come to naught.

* * *

Another issue that concerned me directly had also to be resolved in New York – the question of my successor, and how long I would be required to carry on in Angola. In my personal meeting with the Secretary-General, Dr Boutros-Ghali came straight to the point. After thanking me for all I had done, he said: 'You'll be delighted to know that I have found a replacement for you. I want you to meet him and tell me what you think about him'.

The person he had in mind was an Maître Alioune Blondin Beye, a former Foreign Minister of Mali, now occupying a senior position in the African Development Bank in Abidjan. Dr Boutros-Ghali had first met him, he said, when he (the Secretary-General) was Vice Minister of Foreign Affairs in Egypt at the time of the Camp David settlement. Maître Beye, then Foreign Minister of Mali, went to Cairo as the spokesman for a number of Moslem countries opposing the agreement. Dr Boutros-Ghali, with a reminiscent smile, remarked that Maître Beye had been a very clever negotiator, a lawyer by profession and a formidable adversary.

I welcomed the news and, recalling an earlier conversation with the Secretary-General about the qualifications required, asked whether he spoke Portuguese or Spanish. Dr Boutros-Ghali responded with alacrity: 'I really don't know. Highly unlikely, I should think. I *do* know he speaks no English, only French'. At this startling announcement I nearly fell off the sofa on which we were both sitting. Not speaking either of the two languages that would permit direct understanding of what was being said – rather than getting it second-hand through interpreters – was one thing but having no English would add a further complication when communicating with Headquarters and preparing reports. While it is true that English and French are the two working languages of the UN (a subject on which the Quai d'Orsay never tires of making démarches), the reality is that more people in UN Headquarters, whatever their nationality, command English rather than French.

The next surprise was that Maître Beye was already in New York. Things had obviously moved with a speed and degree of secrecy unheard of in the UN. How I wished that the same strict confidentiality had been exercised earlier! The reason, undoubtedly, was that the selection was made personally by the Secretary-General, whose parting request was that I see Maître Beye as soon as possible and let him have my reactions.

I met Maître Beye for the first time the next day, Thursday 27 May. He was extremely amiable, almost effervescent, and clearly possessed of a quick intelligence. We spoke in French and he cheerfully confessed that he had no Spanish or Portuguese, and only a rudimentary smattering of English. He was already familiar with the broad evolution of the Angolan situation, and the general framework of the Abidjan negotiations, which, being stationed in the Ivorean capital, he had followed from the sidelines. I rapidly filled in the details, dwelling particularly on my immediate concerns as to the best way forward, and my conviction that commitment to the rapid deployment of 'Blue Helmets' might just have saved the Abidjan Protocol, and could still hasten a return to the negotiating table and a ceasefire. I was naturally pleased to find that Maître Beye appeared to share these views.

I liked him and felt that he was well suited to handle the next phase of the mission, which would centre on mediation and negotiation, with the management and operational responsibilities of the Special Representative greatly reduced. It turned out that he had already signed a contract and that this was supposed to be a briefing meeting. As such it was far too short to cover the many complexities. Unfortunately Maître Beye had no time available for another session before I left. We agreed that we must meet again, either in Angola or outside, to bring him up to date on any further developments before I finally handed over the reins to him in early July.

I left New York well pleased about my imminent release, in contrast to my anxiety about the future prospects for a solution, given the Council's reluctance to abandon its 'wait-and-see' or 'show us first' attitude in circumstances in which the two sides seemed unlikely to reach agreement on their own.

* * *

I left New York for London on Saturday 29 May. The intergovernmental meeting in Geneva to launch the Secretary-General's humanitarian appeal was to be on Thursday 3 June. There was little time, and no need, to go back to Luanda; and moreover I was required in England for a literally more down-to-earth purpose – to help with the garden at Knill in preparation for the annual open weekend to raise funds for Knill's ancient little church. With my unexpectedly protracted absence in Angola, my contribution, always sporadic, had been nil that year, so I threw myself into three days of all-out gardening. Apart from other considerations, it proved marvellous therapy, despite lengthy daily telephone contacts with Luanda.

By Tuesday evening I was feeling quite human again, firmly back in the real world, and with my sense of perspective restored. I had still to prepare my notes for the launch of the Angola Appeal, before leaving for Geneva early next morning. As dusk was about to fall on a beautiful spring evening (summer comes late to this valley in the lee of the Welsh mountains), my aunt Christine and I took a walk around the whole garden – about four acres in all. We agreed, immodestly, that it was looking pretty good, and that there was not so much left to do before the open weekend, with ten days still to go. My experiences in Angola really should have taught me better than to indulge in rash prognostications.

I retired to concentrate on Angola again, but had barely written a few lines when I heard a strangled cry from my aunt. Looking out of the window I saw why. A large herd of over 50 cows was surging into the garden, tearing at every bit of greenery in sight. Although we rushed out immediately and eventually mustered help, it took an hour to get them out, at the end of which about a third of the garden had been reduced to something more akin to a roughly ploughed field.

My notes on Angola did not get written that night, but in the car and on the plane to Geneva the following day. I also took with me a strong and uncomfortable feeling that whatever I turned my hand to seemed fated to fall to pieces. I felt more like Sisyphus than ever.

* * *

Our humanitarian activities in Angola had perforce been of an *ad hoc* nature, unsatisfactory to ourselves and inadequate in relation to the human devastation spreading throughout the country. There were many reasons: the failure to agree on a ceasefire; the reluctance of both parties to agree to an interim arrangement that would allow the safe delivery of food and medicine to both sides of the constantly fluctuating battle lines; and the difficulty of even getting commitments on the safe passage of individual convoys and flights honoured, particularly by UNITA.

Every flight was a gamble with the lives of the UN and NGO staff who accompanied them. The tragic incident that had occurred in Luena had sent shock waves through the UN system, and understandably produced urgent messages of concern and caution from the headquarters most involved, particularly that of WFP. Moreover the humanitarian appeal would be unlikely to receive as generous a response as it deserved if these indefensible attacks continued.

My staff had made repeated attempts to sort out the business of clearances and security assurances, including two major meetings in Uige with General

Dembo. Both seemed to produce satisfactory conclusions but each was immediately followed by serious incidents. Restricting aid flights to those places where we could still travel to with safety meant concentrating on the coastal areas, which were under Government control, and we could therefore be accused of a less than impartial approach. WFP headquarters seemed to be reluctant for us to undertake any flights at all, given the deplorable record of attacks and broken commitments. But to suspend all assistance would be unacceptable from a moral viewpoint, and would lay us open to the kind of opprobrium that had been heaped on the Somalian operation, because the UN would be seen as not making a maximum endeavour to help desperately needy people. Worse still, it would have political connotations by implying that attacks could force the whole humanitarian operation to stop.

We were in the unhappy, but familiar, position of being damned if we did and damned if we didn't. It was clear all along that we would never be able to get a satisfactory and even-handed arrangement without a genuine ceasefire. When hopes of this faded as the month of May wore on, it was plain that some more effective strategy must be devised.

We adopted a two-fold approach. The first took the form of a one-month pilot emergency plan, based on 'humanitarian corridors' to named destinations, agreed with the two parties, which would be used, on selected days of the week, to transport specified quantities of food and non-food aid. The second was a longer-term, one-year plan, to extend from May 1993 to April 1994, which was to provide the basis for the UN consolidated interagency appeal. The one-day conference launching the appeal in Geneva had been delayed until after the end of the Abidjan talks since, if these reached a satisfactory conclusion, the prospects for effective humanitarian relief would be very much brighter.

With the failure to reach agreement in Abidjan, the need to press ahead with a more comprehensive pilot emergency plan became all the more urgent. On 26 May, from New York, I addressed personal letters to President dos Santos and Dr Savimbi, enclosing the emergency plan and requesting their immediate agreement so that I could make an announcement to this effect at the Geneva appeal meeting on 3 June, which would most certainly improve the prospects for a generous international response. To underline the urgency of taking action I included the recent estimates by our humanitarian team that at least one thousand people were dying every day in Angola, for reasons directly or indirectly connected to the war.

The plan envisaged that, between 7 June and 10 July 1993, 9000 metric tons of food and non-food items, would be delivered to a network of destinations reached by four road and ten air corridors, which would be used exclusively for that purpose on specified days of the week. Any violations would be communicated to the Secretary-General and the Security Council, and made public. I did not receive the green light from either leader before the Geneva meeting, and was thus deprived of an important argument to deflect the concerns of many would-be donors.

The basis of the appeal was a document projecting the needs over a period of twelve months, together with a summary of the various projects through which they would be addressed. It bore on its cover, not the usual UN hieroglyphics of numbers and references, but the photograph of a desolate and destitute little girl, perhaps two or three years old, sitting alone on the bare ground, with abandoned guns and spent ammunition scattered around her, in the midst of a scene of destruction. I had personally chosen it because it seemed to me to epitomise, in a symbolic and poignant manner, the terrible tragedy engulfing Angola and its people. For the same reason that picture now appears on the jacket of this book.

The situation described in the document did indeed reveal a human tragedy of incalculable dimensions. In my initial presentation I singled out some of the grimmer facts: that, for instance, some two million Angolans – one fifth of the total population – were suffering severely as a result of the war. Again I cited the horrific figure of at least one thousand people dying daily – silently and unnoticed by the rest of the world, even though the number was far greater than those dying in Sarajevo, which were always given headline billing. It is invidious, and certainly not my intention, to try to compare human suffering. I find it equally intolerable, however, that death in one part of the world should be considered more newsworthy, and the lost lives presumably more valuable, than death in another. In illustration of the horrors being endured I referred to the weeks of violent house-to-house fighting that had preceded the fall of Huambo, causing the deaths of at least ten thousand people and the flight of thousands more, while those survivors who remained in or near the city could not be reached with aid because we could not get agreement between the two sides.

I spoke also of the continuing agony of Kuito/Bié and Malange, both cities under siege for months, isolated and cut off from supplies from outside. In Malange desperate, starving folk crept out through UNITA lines at night to seek some sustenance from their fields outside the town, all too often losing life or limb to the antipersonnel mines that peppered the environs, or falling prey to ambush or a sniper's bullet. In Kuito/Bié the situation was even more horrendous. The population was under continuous daily shelling, which began in January 1993 and was to go on until October. The airstrip was in Government hands but the road to the town was occupied by UNITA, and so no supplies could get in. Dreadful stories reached us, through local radio operators working for the WFP, of starvation and deprivation; only the dogs were well nourished, feeding on the corpses that were left to rot on the streets because it was unsafe for the living to venture out to bury their dead. Later there were even tales of cannibalism. Not a building had been left undamaged, and there were no drugs or anaesthetics to relieve the suffering of the wounded.

Throughout the country hunger, malnutrition and disease were rife, and affected most severely the vulnerable groups – women, children and the elderly. As if all this were not enough, there had been persistent drought in the southern region. With the onset of renewed fighting, health services and social support networks had virtually collapsed, as had market and distribution structures and food production. The situation was likely to worsen with the further destruction and mining of main road arteries and devastation of the country's already shattered infrastructure as the battles continued. This could only lead to even more widespread displacement of the population, as well as to a probable harvest failure and a reduction in sowing and planting for the next season, because of the disruption of agricultural activities.

The plan was a multisectoral one, aimed not only at sustaining life but also at fomenting the revival of individual and community activities in productive sectors, so that the destitute could contribute to their own rehabilitation. Total emergency food aid requirements were estimated at some 350 141 metric tons. Since around 73 939 metric tons were in the pipeline for 1994, the gap to be filled was 276 202 metric tons. External funding came to US$226 054 100. Apart from food and medical assistance, the projects to be financed covered provision of safe water, sanitation and environmental health, agricultural production, improvement of rural infrastructure (including demining), the protection and relief of refugees and repatriates, shelter, and relief and survival kits. Some money was also needed for operational support, including logistical and air support, and radio communications. NGO activities and requirements, as far as we had been able to ascertain, would require additional external funding of some US$6 939 422.

After my presentation, the representatives of 15 governments spoke, from both developed and developing countries. The first was Minister Norberto dos Santos of Angola. His brief speech was constructive, reiterating his Government's commitment to cooperating fully by ensuring the efficient and safe delivery of the assistance provided. All the countries spoke positively although, as always happens on these occasions, some spoke more of what they had already done than of fresh money or aid in kind, while others deferred specific pledges until later. Predictably, some donors were concerned about whether, with the question of security unresolved, their contribution would reach the needy population.

UNITA was represented by its man in Geneva, Mr Vahekeni. This man, who had often been a thorn in my side in Abidjan, made a surprisingly positive speech and even 'applauded' the efforts of the UN and of 'Her Excellency Margaret J. Anstee, the UN Special Representative in Angola'! He also contributed one of the more memorable expressions voiced on that occasion: 'a hungry child knows no politics'. He said that UNITA could 'do its utmost to make the programme a success', but made no mention of my request for agreement to the initial one-month emergency plan.

The meeting took all day, and at the end of it I was able to say that a rough estimate of the pledges made indicated that the appeal had already produced promises of about US$70 million in 'fresh money' and additional contributions in kind, representing just under a third of the total required, while several countries had promised to make a commitment later. Later the DHA office in Geneva informed me that, as of 16 June, US$92 599 480 had been pledged in kind and in cash.

But most donors were slow to honour their commitments. Four months after the meeting only 27 per cent of the pledges had been confirmed and a reminder had had to be sent. By February 1994, moreover, when a revised appeal was issued, the situation in Angola had deteriorated even further. The number in need of emergency assistance had risen to a staggering 3.3 million (that is, one in every three Angolans) and the amount needed for February to July 1994 was US$179 million.

* * *

I returned to the UK and the day after the 'open weekend' flew back to Luanda, arriving at dawn on Tuesday 15 June for a hectic final two weeks, plunging immediately into meetings with Ministers, Ambassadors and officials. Apart from the demands of farewell protocol and packing, I had two key issues in mind – the humanitarian programme and, on the political front, the follow-up and consolidation of what we had achieved in Abidjan.

On the humanitarian side we at last seemed to be making some progress. President dos Santos sent me a formal note on 16 June, accepting my proposal of 26 May for four road corridors and ten air corridors. Through various contacts we also obtained UNITA's agreement in principle. Now the idea had to be put to the test in practice. On 17 June I again wrote to both leaders indicating that we proposed to begin the operation on Monday 21 June to Huambo, Kuito/Bié, Luena and Saurimo, with other destinations programmed later in the week. One encouraging sign was that both the Government and UNITA agreed that an initial 'assessment flight' should go to Huambo on Saturday 19 June, a very necessary step since no one had been there since the battle for the city began in January.

Manuel da Silva led this little delegation, which included Philippe Borel, the outstanding WFP representative, and members of other agencies. He brought back an astonishing story, describing a city struggling to get back on its feet. In some respects, he told me, there was almost normality: markets were functioning and locally-produced food was coming in for sale from surrounding areas. Salt and oil were the main basic items that were lacking. There was no dearth of consumer goods either – television sets, refrigerators and the like, looted from homes destroyed in the fighting. Money to buy them and power to make them function were in shorter supply. Education was starting up again, albeit on a very precarious basis, since school buildings had been destroyed and many teachers were either dead or had fled. Health care was the greatest need, and there were dire shortages of drugs and medical equipment.

The news on the general outlook for our operation did not bode so well. The group had been told that UNITA would not be able to approve flights to Kuito/Bié, Malange and Menongue for 'technical reasons' (they cited imperfections in airport landing strips) and security difficulties arising from the ongoing hostilities. All three towns were under intense siege by UNITA and contained beleaguered populations loyal to the Government. To deny access to them was to strike at the very heart of our proposal, based on even-handed delivery to civilian populations in need, wherever they were situated and irrespective of their political affiliations. Manuel and his colleagues had suggested various alternatives, including airdrops, but without being able to reach any conclusion.

This meant that we could not send the planned flight to Kuito/Bié on Monday 21 June, but we managed to persuade the Government to allow the other three flights – to Huambo, Luena and Saurimo – on the understanding that discussions with UNITA would continue. UNITA also cleared these three flights. Manuel da Silva accompanied the flight to Huambo and had another long discussion with UNITA about flights to Kuito/Bié, Malange and Menongue, including the possibility of airdrops. The UNITA people said they needed five or six days in which to consider these proposals. The Government clearly considered that UNITA was once again prevaricating and opted for the temporary suspension of all UN humanitarian assistance flights, citing security concerns.

Without common agreement and fair play on both sides the bottom fell out of our plan. The tragic losers were the people so desperately in need of help. We continued by every means possible to seek solutions. But the frustrating and heartless game of cat-and-mouse continued, and although it was possible to reinitiate some flights on a sporadic, *ad hoc* basis, as previously, my dream of leaving behind a well-organised and smoothly functioning operation was not to be realised.

The stop–go phenomenon was to continue for many months after my departure. It was not until mid-October that UN aid officials were able to reach Kuito/Bié – the first to get there – to find thousands of people dying of starvation and disease. No one will ever know exactly how many people perished during the ten months of fierce fighting in that small and once pleasant town, but the figure is calculated to have reached at least 25 000. From October 1993 the delivery and distribution of humanitarian aid was to become somewhat easier, but it still remained inadequate and subject to disruption as hostilities continued to wage back and forth over wide areas of Angolan territory.

* * *

Parallel to these intense negotiations I was also engaged in a round of meetings with senior Government officials, and ultimately President dos Santos himself, in a last attempt to get the political and peace negotiations back on course. I was also in touch, by correspondence and telephone, with UNITA and on 16 June sent a personal letter to Dr Savimbi, *inter alia* requesting a farewell audience in which to discuss these matters.

In the three weeks or so that had elapsed since the collapse of the Abidjan talks, both the Government and UNITA had repeatedly announced their desire to return to the negotiating table, but all the Ministers and other Government officials to whom I spoke maintained that there was no point in doing so unless some new element could be detected that would permit a shift in UNITA's hitherto unyielding stance. Otherwise they envisaged a repetition of the Abidjan impasse, with UNITA stonewalling and stalling indefinitely. On 16 June the Government went so far as to say publicly that it would not return to the negotiating table unless there was clear indication *beforehand* that Dr Savimbi accepted *all* the principles set out in the Abidjan Protocol, including the controversial point 11 on the withdrawal of UNITA troops. In my opinion this was an excessive demand, but I shared the view that it was pointless to reconvene the negotiations unless some new factor was introduced.

As for what that factor could be, the only idea emerging from discussions with my colleagues was the proposal I had made in NewYork of a symbolic UN 'Blue Helmet' presence. I did not pretend that this would necessarily change UNITA's position but felt it would at least flush out its real intentions.

The Government leaders were patently disillusioned by Security Council Resolution 834 and by a subsequent declaration from the three observer countries in Washington on 8 June, which reiterated much of what they had said before. They were frustrated with what they saw as a further repetition of strong words and condemnations that had no visible effect and no supporting action. Prime Minister Marcolino Moco went as far as to say to me that the international community now had the choice of watching democracy in Angola go down the drain or using force to stop UNITA. I had to tell him that the Security Council and the international community were highly unlikely to send in troops for combat purposes.

The Government told me that it was working on a strategy for the renewal of negotiations and on the role of the UN and the international community, which it intended to present to the Security Council before 15 July, and, in preparation for that, to make important *démarches* at the OAU summit at the end of June and to the Troika before their next meeting, to be held in Moscow on 8 July. It was the Government's hope that the African leaders and the three observer countries (which included two permanent members of the Security Council) would strongly support that strategy.

It was evident that this uncharacteristic burst of energy stemmed from concern about the military situation, which was very serious. In addition to the recent loss of the oil-producing town, Soyo (for the second time), and the diamond-producing town, Cafunfu, other UNITA advances and victories appeared to be imminent. It might well not be possible for the hard-pressed garrisons and populations in the encircled towns of Kuito/Bié, Menongue and Malange to hold out much longer. UNITA was intensifying its attacks on Caxito, and there was a widespread fear that this key town so near Luanda could again fall into UNITA's hands. General Matos, the FAA Chief of General Staff and other senior generals had been conspicuous by their lengthy absence in Europe at this crucial time. There were indications that frantic arms buying was going on, the impression being that the Government's weaknesses lay rather in the area of logistics and supplies, rather than in that of manpower.

Ambassador George Moose, who had been appointed US Assistant Secretary of State for Africa in the Clinton Administration a few months earlier, visited Luanda from 21 to 23 June. A main purpose of his visit was to formalise the opening of official diplomatic relations. This was done with a good deal of pomp and circumstance: an exchange of agreements in the Foreign Ministry on 21 June and a flag-raising ceremony at the modest, prefabricated US liaison office. We were all invited to attend this long-awaited occasion, which involved a good deal of standing about and getting very hot in the process. Mr Moose met President dos Santos but not, as it had been rumoured he might, Dr Savimbi. I was given to understand that he had indicated to Savimbi his desire to have such a meeting, but was not ready to go to Huambo. On his departure Ambassador Moose told journalists that he was still very ready to meet Savimbi 'in appropriate circumstances'.

I myself had several meetings with Ambassador Moose. They included a long working lunch in my house, on Monday 21 June, also attended by Ed De Jarnette and Robert Cabelly. The Assistant Secretary had just come from his first audience with President dos Santos who, he said, had indicated the Government's interest in getting a limited number of 'Blue Helmets' to Angola as soon as possible, initially to provide protection for the emergency humanitarian programme, but also to be on hand to monitor any ceasefire and facilitate further negotiations towards an agreement on the Abidjan Protocol by meeting one of UNITA's main concerns. Mr Moose recounted all this to me as a new initiative coming from the Government, and I was delighted to see that my idea, insistently plugged to everyone whom I had met, had not only percolated up to the President, with whom I had not yet had an opportunity to discuss it, but had been adopted as his own. I was even more delighted when Ed strongly supported it as the only immediately visible way out of the impasse. I reminded Mr Moose that Ambassador Albright had warmly welcomed the idea and had undertaken to follow it up with Washington. Mr Moose questioned both Ed and myself closely about the practical aspects, and while he was non-committal, I could see that he deemed it worthy of serious consideration. He warned, however, that opinions on what to do were very divided in Washington.

Ed later confided to me that Ambassador Moose had been much more forthcoming with the Angolans than his conversation with me would seem to indicate. In his final meeting with President dos Santos and Foreign Minister de Moura (that is, *after* the lunch in my house), he had actively supported the proposal, urging the President to put it forward at the forthcoming OAU summit in Cairo at the end of June. He had strongly advised the Government to promote the idea by getting it included in any resolution on Angola adopted by the African Heads of State, as a starting point for taking it thereafter to the Troika meeting in Moscow, and thence to the Security Council, when it resumed consideration of Angola on 15 July. The Foreign Minister had said that he would actively pursue this idea on his arrival in Cairo so that the President could take the matter up formally at the highest level.

Brigadier Nyambuya, who also regarded the proposal as the best hope for curtailing further bloodshed, conveyed the idea to his own national authorities, while I called Foreign Minister Essy. As a result we had good indications that both Zimbabwe and Côte d'Ivoire would support the proposal if the Angolans put it forward. I too urged the President to adopt the three-pronged strategy – OAU, Troika and Security Council – for the 'Blue Helmets' proposal when he received me on Wednesday 23 June. The issue was broached in the context of a much wider review. There was also a valedictory air about the occasion, for it might not be possible to have another meeting before he travelled to Cairo and I left Angola for good, and the President made some very kind and generous remarks about my mission. It was, indeed, to be the last time we sat and talked together.

The President was in a sombre but determined mood. He did not mince his words about the latest Security Council resolution and the Troika's declaration in Washington, recalling with some bitterness that both bodies had repeatedly stated in various earlier pronouncements that they were contemplating 'appropriate measures' to deal with the situation; instead the same words and phrases were being repeated and had now become meaningless. Always prone to scepticism, the President left me in no doubt that he expected no better from the Troika meeting on 8 July or from the Security Council on 15 July. From the time of negotiating the Bicesse Accords, the international community, especially the United States, had emphasised that the main responsibility for resolving the situation lay with the Angolans, he reminded me. He had accepted this but had hoped for more of a helping hand to save the democratic process in Angola. The message that he must now give to his people was that they should not count on the international community at all but rely only on their own combined efforts to defend democracy in Angola. He was not sanguine about further negotiations: Dr Savimbi had very clear objectives and would stop at nothing to achieve them. Nor did he seem to expect anything very concrete as a result of Ambassador Moose's visit.

The President then gave me his own personal, and distinctly disturbing, analysis of United States strategy towards Angola. He said that the message he had received from Ambassador Moose was that the United States 'wished to give Savimbi another chance'. This meant getting Dr Savimbi to meet Mr Moose (in some place other than Huambo) and agree to return to negotiations. If Dr Savimbi did not react before the Troika met in Moscow on 8 July, this would influence their decisions. Notwithstanding, the President was extremely sceptical that the United States was prepared to take concrete action about Angola. He believed the United States had a double-headed approach: it assumed that the UNITA forces had reserves for only six months more and would do everything possible to ensure that they got no fresh supplies (the flaw in this, as I pointed out to the President, was that the illegal arms market provided many loopholes, and Angola's frontiers were very long); at the same time it would interpret the 'triple zero' option in the Bicesse Accords flexibly towards the Government, in order to improve its military capability (it was not clear whether this would be hardware or merely know-how). I had expected the President to say that the intention was to give the Government some military leverage over UNITA but he defined the goal rather as bringing about a 'draw'. This led to the worrying, though unspoken, conclusion that the Government's present military situation must be parlous indeed.

We agreed that the grim prospect the President painted would involve many more Angolan deaths and much suffering before negotiations could start again. In the final analysis, the President considered that the United States would not allow democracy to be overthrown by force in Angola, because of the repercussions on such processes elsewhere, but would, if circumstances demanded it, be prepared to intervene by force at the last moment to save the day. I expressed the fear that this could be too little too late, and the cost too high, and therefore we should spare no efforts to try to bring about a more immediate solution. It was in this context that I referred to the 'Blue Helmets' idea and the three-pronged strategy for securing its acceptance. While the President said he supported the idea as rational, and the best chance of moving forward, my instinct warned me that his deep scepticism about the international community might deflect him from taking the initiative to pursue the proposed strategy officially, and with the vigour that the circumstances required.

The Secretary-General too was going to Cairo to attend the OAU Summit, where he would be meeting President dos Santos privately. I sent him a personal message recounting this conversation and the outcome of my other contacts, expressing the earnest hope that he would exert his influence to encourage the President to launch the three-pronged strategy in Cairo. If the Angolan Government did not take the initiative there, and mobilise the support of the other countries in the region, there was little that the rest of us could do.

I did not tell Dr Boutros-Ghali that the President had also complained to me confidentially, in the manner of a friend speaking more in sorrow than than in anger, about the way in which my successor had been appointed. The Angolan Government had been very happy when Sergio Vieira de Melos had been proposed, and had all along made clear, said the President, that the Government would prefer the Special Representative to come from a continent other than Africa, whose countries they felt were too deeply involved with the conflict in one way or another. They had been dismayed when de Melo's name was withdrawn because Dr Savimbi had objected to his Brazilian nationality, and that dismay had deepened when an African candidate was proposed instead. He stressed that this was not on account of the qualifications of the individual, but because they interpreted the whole unhappy episode as a further instance of the international community's excessive tolerance towards Savimbi: everyone pandered to his likes and dislikes and tried to placate him because they were afraid of his reactions, while the Angolan Government was given much shorter shrift. The conversation with the President confirmed what I had heard from several official quarters: that it had been touch and go whether the Government would accept the candidature of Maître Beye. Happily they had decided to do so, but I felt sorry for Maître Beye, who would have to overcome this reticence to his appointment, as well as tackle the almost insuperable problems inherent in the conflict.

* * *

My days in Luanda were fast evaporating. There simply were not enough hours to deal with the myriad things claiming my attention. My farewells involved not only calls on officials, Ambassadors and various dignitaries in Luanda, but visits to the remaining field sites still manned by UNAVEM. Although these were now few in number, it still needed two days of flights in the Beechcraft to see them all. But it was worthwhile, because everywhere I was greeted with warmth and affection.

I also used these trips to take my leave of provincial authorities. In Benguela I called on the Governor, Paulo Jorge, a staunch and long-standing MPLA member with whom I had had some verbal sparring matches in the past. He was gracious enough to say, with evident sincerity, that although he had disagreed with some of my actions, he understood that, as an impartial mediator, I had had no alternative, and that he was sorry to see me go. The latter sentiment was echoed in Luanda in an almost emotional parting with Cardenal do Nascimento. In those last, dark days, when I was weighed down by a sense of failure, it was a comfort to know that there were at least some who understood the immensity of the difficulties and constraints with which I had been faced, and recognised that I had done my best.

Other more mundane tasks were piling up on me. Packing was a nightmare. A million bureaucratic matters had to be attended to in the office. The list seemed to grow longer with every passing day. Even the Secretary-General's next report to the Security Council had to be drafted to cover events up until the end of June. And then there were TV and press interviews – the media, too, had suddenly begun to appreciate my efforts – and, even in socially deprived Luanda, some farewell lunches, dinners and receptions. I was getting only a few hours of sleep every night, but still enjoying my dawn swim and etching on my memory the sight of the camp garden awakening to a new day. It was the season of the *cazimbo* and so the water was briskly cold at that hour and the sky a leaden grey, but the ibis still flew over in V-formation to their feeding grounds; the egrets descended in white clouds on the rough grass that passed for a lawn; the lone kingfisher maintained his hunched vigil on the wire fence round the basketball court; bushes of hibiscus and bougainvillaea, brightly spangled with flowers, were thronged with tiny 'cordon bleu' finches, flashing their UN blue; and in the palms above the noisome, garishly yellow weaver birds swung on their nests, chattering and squabbling.

There was no doubt in my mind that it was time for me to go, for all sorts of reasons, professional and personal. But I knew that, perversely, despite all the frustrations, deprivations and even dangers, I was going to miss all this. That brief space for tranquil reflection every morning was also a reminder that there were some eternal, unchanging verities in Angola that transcended the sordid realities of every day and the whole miserable mess that human beings (and not only Angolans, by a long chalk) had managed to make of this superbly beautiful country through avarice and an inane, insane battle for power at any cost, waged not only between the confines of its frontiers, or even of Africa, but as part of the wider net of sinister conspiracies and international intrigues woven by the Cold War.

* * *

There was one farewell call that I did not make, although not for want of trying. On my birthday, 25 June, a fax came through from Dr Savimbi in reply to my request for an appointment, sent nine days earlier. In contrast to the usual business-like format of UNITA's communications it was rather tastefully set out, in a decorative typescript resembling handwriting. The text deserves to be quoted in full:

> *Dear Miss M. Anstee*
> *Special Representative of the*
> *S.G. of UN in Angola*
>
> *It was extremely kind of you to take up your time and write to me.*
> *I thank you for that. I profoundly regret that my time did not allow me to meet with you.*
> *I and all my colleagues share with you all the desappointments but also hopes for Angola.*
> *May the Almighty God be with you and family*
>
> *Sincerely*
>
> *Jonas M. Savimbi*

I had not expected him to receive me but protocol had demanded that I at least try to see him before relinquishing my mission. I had not even expected to receive a reply, given all that had gone before. But here it was, and it was courteous.

* * *

I had originally been told that Maître Beye would officially assume his functions on 28 June, so that he could accompany the Secretary-General to Cairo as the new Special Representative. I had been given various dates between 2 and 7 July for his arrival in Luanda. I had therefore arranged to leave Luanda on 30 June 1993. There was also to be a debriefing visit to Headquarters, which would cover not only my mission in Angola but also all the myriad administrative arrangements attendant upon my retirement from the organisation after 41 years of service. I had had no real holiday for many years, the Angolan experience had left me feeling drained emotionally as well as physically and I needed a brief cooling-off period to myself before returning to the 'real' world. I arranged to spend a week in Namibia, where I had never been, followed by a few days in Zimbabwe, and than to attend a workshop on Angola in Johannesburg, where Nelson Mandela was also expected. I would arrive in New York on 26 July.

On Saturday 19 June Maître Alioune Blondin Beye called from Abidjan to tell me he planned to arrive in Luanda early on Wednesday 30 June, the day on which I was leaving. He asked whether I could delay my departure by a day or two to bring him up to date on events and on my latest negotiations. This seemed to me an eminently sensible idea and on Monday 21 June I cabled New York to indicate that I was prepared to change my plans if Maître Beye's proposal was accepted. I asked for an early reply so that I could finalise my plans. The days went by and no reply came, but I thought nothing of it, this being par for the course.

Friday 25 June was to be a special day. It was my birthday but it was also the occasion for the farewell party given to me by the whole of UNAVEM and everyone who lived and worked in the camp, including the military, the civilians, the police, the local Angolan employees, the Skylink air contractors, and the Russian pilots and aircrews. It was a splendid, unforgettable evening. The shabby recreation hall had been specially decorated for the occasion. There was a well-stocked bar and buffet, no less than three heart-shaped birthday cakes decorated in the UN colours of blue and white, speeches galore, well-spiced with jokes and irreverent reminiscences, many touching gifts, and music and dancing. The main offering from the whole of UNAVEM was a 'Commander's Flag', a UN flag, fringed and embroidered with '09' – since my radio call signal as head of mission had been 'zero-niner' – set in a magnificent wooden frame, with a brass plaque commemorating the mission and the occasion. There were many other gifts from individual contingents, usually something typical of their culture. The chief Russian pilot pressed flowers and a miniature blue and white samovar into my hands, while the Ghurka guards presented me with a Ghurka knife – a rare honour, I was told. One of the most touching moments of all came when three local staff sang and recited a poem that one of them had specially written for the occasion. Then the dancing started and went on until well after midnight.

I retired at last in a warm haze of mingled sadness and happiness. The next morning, at breakfast time, a young woman appeared from the communications room bearing a cable from New York. 'This cable marked "immediate" came in from Mr Annan late last night', she said 'but I thought it would spoil your party, so I held it back until this morning. I know I shouldn't have, but I hope I did the right thing'.

Having quickly scanned the cable I told her that she most certainly had. It was the answer to the cable I had sent five days earlier about Maître Beye's request that I brief him. It was couched in terms more appropriate to a reprimand to a delinquent subordinate than to a message between two Under Secretaries-General, particularly when the recipient was the more senior. It curtly told me to get out on 28 June, report to New York on 1 July, and complete debriefing and administrative matters relating to my retirement on 3 July – a Saturday. Apparently no one had even consulted a calendar. Someone had, however, discovered that it was my birthday, for the last words were 'warmest regards and Happy Birthday'. Tacked on to the end of this extraordinary message the phrase sounded almost sarcastic. The rationale was that 28 June was the day on which Maître Beye assumed his functions (he was not due in Luanda until two days later) and there could not be two Special Representatives even in different parts of the world, though I was happy to relinquish the title immediately. Apparently protocol was more important than proper briefing of my successor and smooth continuity for the mission. I felt some anger but most of all I felt bitterly hurt. I replied, tersely, that because their cable had come so late I could not leave on 28 June, when I was giving a farewell reception for the authorities and the Diplomatic Corps. I advanced my departure to 29 June, asking the observers and the Government to cancel the farewell reception and dinner they had organised for that day (they were dumbfounded at the reason). I was certainly not going to cancel the leave I had been promised (though I eliminated Zimbabwe and South Africa), and I told Headquarters that the earliest I could arrive in New York was 14 July.

I left Luanda before they could answer. That glacial cable was the last official communication that I was ever to receive from UN Headquarters, a strange epitaph to 41 years of service.

* * *

Monday came and with it the bedlam of the packers. Their enthusiasm was more evident than their skill, so it was not surprising to find, months later, that parts of the same object had ended up in different parts of the globe, or that the breakage rate was phenomenal.

My farewell 'diplomatic' reception took place on the basketball court, whose harsh contours my dear Mr Andrade had softened with masses of bougainvillaea and frangipani. It was a lovely, balmy evening and a stiffish breeze fluttered the huge UN flag behind the reception line. As the guests began to arrive the sun gave a last flamboyant performance, plunging below the hazy horizon in a blaze of vermilion, against which my old friend the baobab tree stood silhouetted, stalwart and reassuring. Many people came and it, too, was a happy as well as a nostalgic occasion.

At noon, the next day, my immediate staff came to the little house where so many momentous things had happened and we had a *coupe de champagne*. When Tom White asked me to walk to the front gate, instead of getting into the car in front of the house. I was mystified but understood once we emerged. All the staff of UNAVEM, the whole camp, was lined along the road leading to the gate to see me off. Some of them pressed flowers into my hands. This spontaneous show of affection brought tears to my eyes and more than made up for the bitterness of rejection I had felt with that the last message from Headquarters. These were the people who mattered most to me. We had lived and worked closely together, every day of the week, in our cramped little camp; we had, on occasion, almost died together. Angola would always be a secret bond between us that on one else could share.

At the airport there were various friends and well-wishers to see me off, with many of whom that same bond had been forged during our long months of struggle: Antonio Monteiro, Yuri Kapralov, Ed De Jarnette, Dr Muteka, General Higino. There were also other Ambassadors and officials. I had friends among UNITA too, and was sad that the circumstances of war and Dr Savimbi's refusal to see me prevented me from saying goodbye.

Sissy travelled with me and my Special Assistant, Peter Scott-Bowden, was to accompany us to Namibia and returning the next day. As soon as the Beechcraft took off the new reality began to emerge.

'How about a little lunch?' asked Peter. That seemed an excellent idea, after consuming champagne on an empty stomach. Then the awful truth dawned – CASO (the Chief of Air Support Operations), a normally very efficient Argentinean officer, had forgotten to put the lunch on board. If one wanted an unequivocal sign that one was no longer the boss, it could hardly have been conveyed in a more telling way! Rummaging around the Beechcraft we eventually came on some rather ancient MREs ('Meals Ready to Eat' being the euphemistic title given to these emergency rations) which had been provided by the United States during the elections. I think they were left over from the Gulf War but we fell on them with gusto.

I spent much of the flight in the cockpit with the two pilots, looking my last on the coastal plains of Angola spread far below us, verdant at first but then, as we moved steadily southwards and vegetation grew sparser, turning to mingling shades of brown, russet and grey until they tapered into the palely shimmering haze of the desert; the Cunene river gleamed like a snake sunning itself in the sands and we slipped over the border into Namibia. I was persuaded to take over the controls for a bit – my first attempt at piloting. It was exhilarating, up there in the lonely sky with the empty spaces and misty blue horizons of Africa seeming to stretch ahead like eternity itself.

The desert changed back to scrubby bush, and just after sunset we dropped down into Windhoek, that delightfully anachronistic city, so clean and spruce, like a German provincial town transferred lock, stock and barrel to Africa. People from the Ministry of Foreign Affairs were there and we were whisked away to the hotel. The Namibian Government, in its generosity, had wanted to organise a two-week safari for me – all this, they kindly said, to mark their appreciation for what I had tried to do for Angola. I had declined, wanting most of all to go somewhere quiet, to rest and lick my wounds. I planned to do this privately, but they had insisted on organising a stay at a game farm at Ongavi, not far from the Etosha saltpan in the north.

We flew up early next morning, locating the nearest airstrip with some difficulty, where a solitary jeep stood waiting among the thorny scrub. There I said goodbye to the pilots and Peter and the Beechcraft flew on north, back to Angola. That really did feel like the final farewell, the breaking of the last link, in the middle of a desolately empty landscape in northern Namibia, as the engines of the little Beechcraft roared again into life and it soon became a tiny silver spot, growing ever smaller in the vast dome of the sky as it sped northwards.

We spent four nights at Ongavi, a huddle of grass-thatched bungalows, clinging to a rocky hillside above a valley that could almost be described as well-wooded for this barren part of the world. The décor was rustic, but there were all the creature comforts that one had lacked in Luanda. Above all it was quiet. Most of the time Sissy and I had the place practically to ourselves. The bar and kitchen staff were Angolan, so there was plenty of talk of 'home'. The weather was superb – clear sunny days and cool, almost cold nights. Our guide was Patrick, a South African of Irish descent, who combined an acting career with long stints of bush tracking, in which he was very knowledgeable. We did not spot much game at Ongavi, but we saw a lot of bird life, and had exhilarating, dusty rides in the jeep, bouncing along the red dirt tracks through the bush. One day we took a picnic and drove to the Etosha saltpan, where there was a great variety of game to be seen, but too many vehicles and people. What I most appreciated in Ongavi was the peace and tranquillity. I read, and sat in the sun, revelling in the wild beauty of the view from my balcony. I rested and slept and I unwound.

The most memorable night of all was spent under the stars, in a clearing in the bush. It was cold and we built a fire for warmth as well as for a barbecue, well-lubricated with wine. Afterwards I lay awake for a long time. I did not want to sleep but to savour to the utmost the sights and sounds of the African night. The night was cold and clear, the dark vault of the sky a blazing, jewelled canopy. Later, moonlight filtered between the surrounding trees. At times the silence was broken by the shriek of some night bird, or by rustling in the undergrowth. But if any animals came to inspect us, I did not see them. In the morning, when the sun was barely up, I took a long, solitary walk through the bush, watching the birdlife, before returning to our makeshift camp for hot tea and breakfast.

* * *

On Monday 5 July I was to be received by the Prime Minister and the Foreign Minister, and by President Sam Nujoma, and so on Sunday we made the long drive south to Windhoek. President Nujoma gave a working lunch at which his Prime Minister and Foreign Minister were present, as well as other senior members of his government. I was asked to give my analysis of what had gone wrong in Angola and, when I mentioned the drawbacks of the 'winner takes all' approach to the elections, which left no consolation prize for the loser, the Prime Minister reacted vigorously: 'Then you want second-class democracy for Africa! In the UK one party wins and governs, the others lose and don't and that is the way it should be. That is the way it was here'. I hastened to assure Dr Geingob that it was far from my thoughts to propound 'second-class democracy' for Africa. But might it not be the case that, in some instances, it could be difficult to go the whole hog at once? And if the choice lay between a return to all-out war – if one forced the 'winner takes all' concept, with all the terrible destruction and human suffering that that entailed – and a more pragmatic approach, through a government of 'national reconciliation', would it not be better to adopt the latter course and a phased approach towards the attainment of full democracy? Namibia, I pointed out, had enjoyed special circumstances, as well as a portion of luck, but many other countries were less fortunate. We debated the matter at some length, but came to no agreed conclusion.

At the lunch I was dismayed – though not totally surprised – to learn from the Foreign Minister that President dos Santos had not appealed in Cairo for African leaders' support in requesting an early dispatch of a small contingent of 'Blue Helmets' to Angola. Accordingly the OAU summit had not taken any stance on the matter either.

President Nujoma was plainly exercised by this last exchange, and after lunch took me back into his office so that I could explain in more detail. He then said he agreed that the strategy I had presented was the best – and perhaps the only – way forward if peace was to return to Angola soon, and himself suggested that he might call President dos Santos personally to recommend it. I welcomed the proposal: there was time – just – to do something before the Troika meeting in Moscow three days later, on 8 July, and the Security Council debate on 15 July, even though the OAU opportunity had been lost. Inwardly, however, I was not sanguine. Sadly, events were to prove me right.

* * *

The Troika, after their meeting in Moscow on 8 July, issued another strongly worded communiqué, reiterating much of what they had said in Washington on 8 June and on many previous occasions. They agreed that the UN should continue its role in the search for a peaceful solution in Angola, but did not define what this should be, or how the stated objectives could be attained. The one new departure was that the observers' statement opened the way to the waiving of the 'triple zero' proviso in the Bicesse Accords by suggesting that aid should now be provided to the Angolan Government in support of the democratic process.

* * *

Our last day in Windhoek was spent on a long drive through the desert to the coast and Walvis Bay. On Wednesday night (7 July) Sissy and I flew back to Europe. We parted in Frankfurt, she Vienna-bound, while I went on to London. After a long weekend in Knill, I flew to New York on 14 July.

By coincidence I reached New York when the Security Council was considering Angola. I attended both the informal consultations and the formal session of the Council on 15 July. The formal meeting was the longest and most comprehensive meeting the Security Council had ever had on Angola, lasting from 11.30 a.m. to 5.15 p.m. Sir David Hannay, the British Permanent Representative, presided over the session, which was also attended by the Secretary-General and Foreign Minister de Moura.

In his report to the Council,[1] the Secretary-General informed the members that he had 'agreed reluctantly to accede to the wish expressed by my Special Representative for Angola, Miss Margaret Joan Anstee, to be released from her responsibilities',[2] and had appointed Maître Beye. It was a satisfaction that the record had at last been put publicly straight about the circumstances leading up to my relinquishment of the Angolan mission, but the rest of the report made sombre reading, with its chronicling of new hostilities breaking out, or old ones rekindling and of many diplomatic initiatives from various quarters to stop the conflict, all predestined to futility in my view, because they were not backed up by effective action. Maître Beye had been received in Huambo by Dr Savimbi (I learned that he had been given the full gala treatment by the dancing, chanting and eminently mobile 'Rent-a-crowd' that I had encountered in Jamba a year or so earlier) as well as by President dos Santos, and as a result had reported to the

Secretary-General on 9 July, 'that the atmosphere might be right for some optimism for relaunching the peace negotiations'.³

This carefully recondite phrase was nonetheless the basis for continued scaling down and 'wait-and-see'. Brigadier Nyambuya had been replaced by Major General Garuba of Nigeria, but for the rest UNAVEM had been reduced to its lowest level yet: 50 military observers, 18 police observers, 11 military paramedics, 43 international civilian staff, plus local staff. The Secretary-General recommended that this small presence should be kept in place for another three months, to facilitate the new Special Representative's efforts to advance the peace process, support the humanitarian operation, and act as a 'preventive measure to check escalation of the conflict'⁴ – quite how, was not clear – and as a channel of communications between the parties.

The meeting opened with a long speech by Venâncio de Moura in which he demanded a firmer approach by the international community and restrictive measures against UNITA, such as freezing UNITA's bank accounts abroad; restricting the movement of UNITA-affiliated people across borders; closing its offices in other countries; and banning its use of propaganda facilities afforded by the media in UN member states.

No less than 21 speakers took the floor. The presence of two African Foreign Ministers (Zimbabwe and Namibia) plus two representatives of the Front Line States (Zambia and Tanzania) and of Egypt, currently holding the OAU chairmanship, meant that for the first time Africa was there in force. The tenor of the debate demonstrated, beyond a shadow of doubt, the surge in the tide of international opinion against UNITA, with only the United States being more muted in its expression, simply calling on UNITA 'to refrain from military action and return to the peace process'. In contrast, virtually all the other speakers were vehement in their condemnation of UNITA's actions and intransigence, and in urging effective action to make it come to heel. Feelings towards UNITA were scarcely improved by the receipt of news, during the debate, that yet another UN aircraft had been fired on by UNITA while trying to deliver humanitarian assistance to M'banza Congo on a flight plan cleared with UNITA in advance. Once again UNITA's sense of timing and occasion – and bare effrontery – beggared description.

Resolution 851 was adopted in the middle of the debate. It extended UNAVEM's mandate for two months, again saying that it was ready to take prompt action to expand the UN presence 'substantially' in the event of 'significant progress in the peace process'. There were 23 operative paragraphs and the words 'condemn' and 'demand' in relation to UNITA appeared more often than ever before. The Government, in contrast, was commended for its 'continued disposition ... to reach a peaceful settlement of the conflict in conformity with the Accords de Paz and relevant resolutions of the Security Council'.

Other more general paragraphs underlined the need to reinitiate the peace talks under UN auspices without delay, as well as the need to strengthen and fund the humanitarian operation. The main new elements came in operative paragraphs 12 and 13:

> 12. *Expresses its readiness* to consider the imposition of measures under the Charter of the United Nations, including a mandatory embargo on the sale or supply to UNITA of arms and related *matériel* and other military assistance, to prevent UNITA from pursuing its military actions, unless by 15 September 1993 the Secretary-General has reported that an effective cease-fire has been established and that agreement has been reached on the full implementation of the 'Accordos de Paz' and relevant resolutions of the Security Council;
> 13. *Recognizes* the legitimate rights of the Government of Angola and in this regards *welcomes* the provision of assistance to the Government of Angola in support of the democratic process;

Thus the Council edged up for the first time to the possibility of applying sanctions and an arms embargo on UNITA, but gave the rebels a breathing space in which to comply with its conditions. It also gave the nod, in suitably coded language, to those who wished to supply arms to the Government. The 'triple zero' proviso, if not officially dead, was in abeyance. A number of states would have liked to see sanctions imposed immediately, while Tanzania argued strongly for a larger UN presence without delay, expressing the view that had UNAVEM II had more people on the ground many of the problems would have been averted.

At the other end of the spectrum, Ambassador Albright's intervention was curiously nuanced. She warned that the eventual expansion of UNAVEM could not be taken for granted as far as the United States was concerned. Not only must 'conditions have been established that will make exercise of its mandate feasible' but 'before agreeing to additional commitments, we shall need to have the Secretariat's clear advice on the costs involved and their duration'. 'United Nations peacekeeping has become a growth industry', she went on, more ominously, 'but before we can effectively meet the increased demand, we must understand the needs of those demanding our services and how our scarce resources are being employed. Our goal is to retool the peacekeeping machinery so as to meet the new demand. Until then, we must ensure that our limited supply is used to best effect'. This was a far cry from her eager reaction to the idea of an immediate small detachment of 'Blue Helmets' when I had spoken to her six weeks earlier, and from my conversations with Ambassador Moose in Luanda only three weeks before.

What troubled me more about the Security Council position was the emphasis on sanctions alone, rather than in parallel with the possibility of an immediate strengthening of the UN presence on the ground. Sanctions have so often proved an ineffective and even totally useless tool. They would be almost impossible to apply and monitor where frontiers were so long, and stretched across such wild and uninhabited places as in Angola. More importantly still, from the time I had first put my idea forward after the failure of the Abidjan talks, my argument all along had been that we must offer UNITA 'carrots' as well as 'sticks' to have any chance of success, and the carrots were represented by the small contingent of 'Blue Helmets', which would meet one of UNITA's basic concerns. Resolution 851 was all sticks and no carrots so far as UNITA was concerned. And, to judge by Ambassador Albright's statement, cost and frugality were influential in producing this outcome and could well weigh more in reaching a decision than a rational analysis of what the Angolan situation required in order to assist a return to peace. History seemed in grave danger of repeating the errors of Bicesse.

* * *

From a personal point of view there was a more pleasing aspect of the debate. Almost everyone who spoke had some kind words for what I had tried to do. Some moved me greatly because they were so personally phrased that they were evidently no mere formality or cliché. That was particularly the case in the remarks of Ambassador Jesus of Cape Verde, Ambassador Marker of Pakistan and Sir David Hannay. All of this naturally left me with a warm glow, especially as the Secretary-General was present. The next day I received a formal note from Sir David Hannay, as President of the Council, thanking me on behalf of all its members.

No similar letter came to me from the Secretariat. Apart from a cordial farewell visit to the Secretary-General, I was left with the overwhelming impression that no one was interested in Angola or in what I had to say about it. The man and the place of the moment were General Morillon and Bosnia, where the charismatic French General had become an international celebrity and where his mission too was ending. It was only as an afterthought that I was asked to brief Kofi Annan's daily meeting and invited, at the last moment, to the farewell party for the General.

* * *

Pleasanter things were happening to me outside the UN, reassuring me that there was a life beyond. Once again the Centre for Strategic and International Studies (CSIS) invited me to Washington to speak. I went there on 21 July, and stayed two days.

The pattern was much as the previous year, though the circumstances were now very different. I addressed the Strategic Group on Angola, under the chairmanship of Professor Gerald Bender, who had become a valued friend and supporter during my time in Angola, and later gave a more public presentation. This time my theme was a summing-up of all that had happened in Angola and the lessons to be learned. But I also looked to the future, to what should be done to deflect Angola from the tragic road to hell on which it seemed inexorably bound. Once again I banged my drum about the urgent need for the international community to act rather than adopt a 'wait-and-see' attitude until the two sides got their act together on their own. This was not, I stressed, to take the main responsibility for finding a solution away from the Angolans – without political will on both sides, none was possible. But they could and should be given a helping hand, and here I expounded my proposal for the small detachment of 'Blue Helmets'.

I continued to peddle this throughout the visits Shawn McCormick had again organised with influential people in the White House, on Capitol Hill, and in the Departments of State and Defence, with the private sector and with the media, including many individuals who still remained obstinately pro-UNITA. There were radio and television interviews, even one on the White House lawn with Portuguese television. I had a long talk with Jardo Muekalia, the UNITA representative in Washington, finding him still anxious for peace negotiations to restart, and hopeful that UNITA could more readily agree to the Abidjan Protocol if the 'Blue Helmets' proposal were put into effect. I lunched with the Angolan Ambassador, who was also receptive to the idea, promising to take it up with Luanda again. With every passing week the likely impact of such a move was becoming less effective, but I still felt that it was not too late, if only someone would take action.

In the Administration there were a number of new faces. One old Angolan hand – Jim Woods of the Pentagon – was still very much there, and very positive towards my proposal. In contrast I found Assistant Secretary of State Moose, in the State Department, curiously unforthcoming; it was difficult to imagine that this was the same man who had lunched at my house in Vila Espa only a few weeks earlier. Once again the Pentagon was much more amenable to the prospect of the United States taking an active role in finding a solution for Angola, and more concerned about the need to do so. There was also a good reception in the National Security Council in the White House, where Shawn took me to see Nancy Soderberg, who was accompanied by Ambassador Jennifer Ward. I reflected that women seemed to be more sensitive to the need to do something to halt the terrible suffering in Angola, rather than simply watching from the side lines, wringing their hands and mouthing platitudes.

Best of all was Congress, where I spoke to several senators and congressmen who afterwards prepared a bipartisan appeal from both Houses of Congress to President Clinton and Secretary of State Warren Christopher, referring to my visit and urging the administration to give more attention to Angola, as well as lending support to the immediate despatch of a contingent of 'Blue Helmets' to carry out the functions I had described. Shawn McCormick read the text over the telephone to me in New York a day or two later. I was overjoyed. Perhaps, after all, something would now happen, since both US parties were behind the idea.

But a day or two later Shawn rang me again with more sobering news. The letter had been signed and sent, but at the last moment the reference to the 'Blue Helmets' proposal had been dropped because it would cost money. It was helpful in keeping the issue alive in the US Government, but it was not going to make any real difference because, like so many other well-meaning interventions, post Cold War, in the Angolan situation, it was long on words and short on action, especially if the dread words 'financial implications' were heard. Angola was well and truly an orphan of the Cold War.

* * *

My last day as an official of the United Nations was 31 July 1993. I had joined the organisation in the Philippines on 26 July 1952, so my service had encompassed 41 years. During those four decades I had risen from being a local staff member to the highest level – Under Secretary-General – below the post of Secretary-General. I had served in eleven different countries, in all the regions of the world, participated in virtually every aspect of the organisation's work, from economic and social development to narcotic drug control and disaster relief, and had undertaken official missions of one kind or another to more than one hundred member states. Privileged to have pioneered many new paths previously untrodden by women, I was the senior woman in the organisation. In fact I believe I was at that time the longest serving official of the UN of either sex at any level.

So 31 July should have been a momentous day in my life. The only official acknowledgement of the occasion from the Secretariat was a formal communication about pension and medical benefits after retirement. I left the tall building on First Avenue as I might have done on any other day during the preceding four decades.

It was a strange feeling of anticlimax. For years I had dreaded the idea of leaving the organisation that had been virtually my whole life for so long. Latterly I had found the prospect less daunting. The UN was now a very different organisation from the one I had joined, full of ideals, in my youth – better in some ways, but worse in others, notably in the human environment and treatment of staff. No doubt that was to an extent inevitable in an organisation that has become so vast, and on which so many demands are now being made without giving it the wherewithal to meet them, on which so much criticism is conveniently heaped by member states for shortcomings that more often than not stem from their own actions, or lack of action, and where senior staff are subject to constant strain and overwork. But it does not make for a happy ship, especially at Headquarters, and morale takes on even greater importance when struggling against overwhelming odds, which the UN has invariably had to do on virtually every front.

I was not sad for myself. I had been extraordinarily lucky, and had had an exceptionally interesting life. I still believed – and believe – in the ideals and aims of the United Nations and in the indispensable need for the organisation. There is no other. But I could not help mourning for earlier days when the personal touch and personal consideration had been the hallmark.

In a way that made it easier. It was time to go, and not just from Angola.

25 Lessons of the Forgotten Tragedy of Angola

I am often asked, both in public interviews and privately: 'Is there anything you would have done differently?'

I have given a lot of thought to this but each time I have arrived at the same answer: the only thing I could have done differently would have been not to accept the Angolan posting in the first place. By this I am not claiming that there were no mistakes along the way – we are all human – or that particular aspects of the mission might have been handled in another fashion. What I am saying is that, once I had taken the plunge, I found I had little room for manoeuvre. That was not apparent to me when I took the decision to accept what later turned out to be an almost impossible challenge. It soon became very plain on my initial visit to Luanda in February 1992 and during the first weeks of my mission proper in March. Then the full limitations of the 'small and manageable operation' hit me squarely in the face. But by then it was too late to retreat.

The obvious next question is: 'Do you regret having gone to Angola?' The answer is 'no'. It was a traumatic and often cruel experience that will haunt me for the rest of my life. In this I am by no means unique. Former UN colleagues from Angola have told me that they have been permanently affected by their time there – not in a negative way, but in the sense of feeling committed to the country and its people and being unable to put them out of mind until peace and reconciliation are won.

For myself, as for them, the mortification that we did not succeed cuts very deep. It is all the harder to bear because we came so tantalisingly close to success. None of us, if we were frank, had dared believe that the elections could be carried off successfully, given all the political and logistical problems, although everyone gave of their utmost to try to ensure that they were. When those efforts, and the efforts of countless Angolans, paid off, against all the odds, it was a savage blow indeed to have the fruits of fulfilment almost immediately swept away. None of us was naive enough to believe that the mere fact of over 90 per cent of the electorate turning out to vote calmly and *en masse*, was enough to consolidate peace or democracy, but it seemed such a promising step, and one that we had so much feared would not be taken, that its mere accomplishment seemed to hold forth prospects that equally rational steps would follow.

The onus of responsibility falls very heavily on the person who heads a peace-keeping operation, however great the outside constraints. I know that I felt it to be so. I have several times described in this book how desperately lonely I felt at times of great crisis, with few means at hand to combat it, and seldom anyone nearby to whom I could confidently turn for advice. Special Representatives of the Secretary-General, having to deal with highly sensitive and delicate matters, need to have in their immediate entourage one or two professionals well known to them and in whom they have very great confidence, both as regards their professional competence and, even more importantly, their unshakeable loyalty. Although I developed great regard for some of my nearest colleagues on both these counts, many strains and stresses might have been avoided had I been given more freedom in the choice of my closest collaborators.

In Angola I felt the need of such immediate support more than ever before in my four decades of international service. During that time I had held complicated positions, with a great deal of responsibility attached to them, and often with a large staff under my command. The yawning difference was that, whereas before mistakes or failure might signify waste of money and the collapse of a programme, which could adversely affect the people supposed to benefit from it, in Angola one was agonisingly conscious that they meant suffering, and perhaps death, for thousands and thousands of innocent human beings. Perhaps I had an exaggerated sense of responsibility, for it was the interaction of many players and circumstances, and not my actions alone, that would determine success or failure. Perhaps it was a kind of arrogance that made me feel the weight of responsibility so keenly. Whatever it was, I defy anyone who nurtures a reasonable concern for the welfare of their fellow beings, and found themselves in my position, to say that they would have been able to cloak themselves in detachment or indifference by accepting that the aim of the mission was almost impossible to achieve and that the main responsibility lay with others, notably the two main parties to the conflict.

Certainly, people on both sides found no difficulty in holding me personally and solely accountable for everything that went wrong – the traditional scapegoat role of the UN, personified in its senior representative on the ground. Slings and arrows showered on me from all sides, and were not confined to the highly publicised and virulent attacks launched against me by UNITA. There were many unpleasant jibes by the Government – veiled and unveiled, usually through its mouthpiece, the *Jornal de Angola* – which were then disavowed, disingenuously, by senior Government officials on the ground that they could not control the 'liberty of the press'. Criticism coming from both sides had the advantage of making me feel that I must be doing something right in my role as impartial arbiter!

There were some journalists, international as well as Angolan, who always seemed to know, infallibly, what ought to have been done, *ex post facto*, though, as I reminded myself, none of them had ever had to run an operation like this, or knew from personal experience what it was like to be perpetually in the 'hot seat' with little room for manoeuvre. Quite a lot of the international journalists were, however, very fair in their comments and gave full due to the limitations imposed on UNAVEM.

One of the main criticisms was that I had not understood the 'hidden agendas' of both sides, another that I was 'naive', which I suppose amounted to the same thing. That in itself is naive comment for the main thrust, or strategies, of the hidden agendas were not hard to discern: both parties wanted power at the expense of the other. What was not always apparent were the tactics that might be being used at any moment to achieve that end. Usually one had a pretty shrewd idea but what the critics forgot was that, even when we had divined that some skulduggery was going on, neither the Bicesse Accords nor UNAVEM's mandate, as established by the Security Council, afforded us any means of direct intervention. All we could do, along with the observers, was to try to steer things in the right direction by getting the CCPM to take action, as long as that body survived, and talking severely in private to whichever side was being more devious at a given moment. As for my naivety, one or two international journalists were kind enough to defend me against this claim, pointing out that it was hardly likely that I could have survived so long and carried out so many difficult assignments yet still remain totally simpleminded.

Some of this was due to the perception that, every time one detected knavish tricks on the part of either signatory of the Peace Accords, the news should be shouted from the rooftops. NGOs concerned with human rights complained that UNAVEM had not been vociferous enough on such issues. Unfortunately human rights were not part of our mandate, and there were therefore no monitors included in the team. This was a serious omission but once again it stemmed from the Bicesse Accords, which gave only cursory attention to this subject. Even so it was not true that we neglected human rights completely, despite our lack of qualified personnel. It was another area in which we went beyond our mandate, working through our police teams to deal with incidents on the spot or, if that did not work, taking them up in the CCPM or in direct interventions with either or both sides. We also organised the first human rights seminar ever held in Angola. But there is no doubt that monitoring of human rights must be given a prominent place in the mandate and staffing of UN peacekeeping missions.

The accusation of not speaking out sufficiently has not been limited to matters of human rights but extends to all breaches of the Peace Accords. This raises a fundamental question of judgement, and of style. I am convinced that, while it is perfectly right and proper for NGOs, particularly those involved in human rights, to speak out plainly against abuses – indeed it is their duty and their *raison d'être* to do so – the position of the United Nations, when it is functioning as a mediator, is necessarily more nuanced. This by no means entails turning a blind eye to wrongdoing, but rather dealing with it in a less public manner that will not put the negotiations at risk – that is, in direct talks, or by raising the matter through whatever monitoring mechanism may have been set up (in this case the CCPM). This does not mean that public disavowal or criticism will never be resorted to, but that they will be used sparingly, in carefully selected cases. A careful balance has to be maintained between avoiding ructions that could imperil the whole delicate negotiation and allowing offenders to go scotfree. It is almost invariably the case that both parties to a conflict transgress – there are no pure innocents in situations of this kind – even though one may be worse than the other, and it is therefore of the utmost importance to apportion blame scrupulously between them, according to their relative degrees of non-compliance.

In considering the pros and cons of 'quiet diplomacy' it is salutary to recall what happened when I made public statements that UNITA regarded as inimical to it – my declaration, on 17 October 1992, that the elections had been 'generally free and fair' and my press conference in February 1993, blaming UNITA for the collapse of the Addis Ababa negotiations. Both instances sparked off violent recriminations against me and led to a break in my direct communications with Dr Savimbi. In the first case, the direct personal channel was opened up again a few weeks later, after the battle for Luanda, but in the second I never did speak directly to Savimbi after my meeting with him in Huambo on 2 January 1993. I was not alone in this exclusion – he cloaked himself in silence and for many months saw no one from outside, but previously I had been given privileged access. These two public statements had to be made – there is no question of that – but there was a price to be paid as regards my capacity to mediate effectively at the top level, which illustrates the need to make such public utterances sparingly and only on the most important issues.

* * *

The question inevitably arises: 'Did gender have anything to do with the outcome?' I am probably not best qualified to answer, being the person involved. Nevertheless – having explained earlier that the fact that leadership of a peacekeeping mission was to be another 'first' for women in the UN was a factor spurring me to accept a mission for which I knew the prospects of success were, at best, marginal – I think it behoves me to give some personal views on the subject.

Predictably, the appointment of a woman caused surprise in some quarters. Predictably too, there was no lack of onlookers who, when the mission ran into difficulties, hinted darkly, or not so darkly, that this was what came of sending a woman to what they considered a particularly 'macho'–dominated area of black Africa. In this there was much simplistic thinking, as in the pontifications about 'tribalism'. As in most parts of Africa, women play a powerful, though usually unobtrusive role in Angolan life, and do a great deal of the work, especially in food production, and 30 years of war have meant that the womenfolk have been left at home to fend for themselves and their families while their men were away at the front. While women have been less to the fore in the senior ranks of UNITA – with the exception of the egregious Fatima Roque – they have acquitted themselves well in some key ministerial posts in the Government.

Contrary to conventional thinking, many of the people with whom I had to deal on both sides of the conflict seemed spontaneously to welcome the fact that

I was a woman. They told me they hoped that a woman would bring more sensitive insights to bear. They referred to qualities of compassion and understanding, as well as of empathy for the anguish of wives and mothers who had for so long suffered the consequences of a war in which they had little or no direct say. How far such qualities, real or imagined, were likely to influence negotiations with hard-bitten warriors on either side is a matter for conjecture. I mention this aspect here simply because it responded to a widely held perception of some special contribution that I might bring to the role of Special Representative. Even Jonas Savimbi frequently referred to me as 'mother' and appealed to me to apply the attributes associated with that function to the peace process.

For myself, I harboured no illusions that my gender would influence the outcome either way, nor did I credit myself with any exclusively feminine insights, but rather applied myself to doing the best job possible that my training and experience had fitted me to do. This was by no means the first time that I had pioneered a new area for women – there had been a string of such examples in my life, going back to the 1940s – and in some respects it was no different from the others. There was the same need to work exceedingly hard – much harder than a man would have to have done – to prove from the outset that I was up to the job, and to demonstrate that I could put up with just as much physical hardship and stress as a man. There was also the feeling – never allowed to lapse into complacency – that, once that first test had been passed, there were some ways in which it could be an advantage to be a woman: for instance, in the manner in which a particularly delicate, or even potentially abrasive, message might be transmitted.

The downside was that excessive expectations on the part of those who thought a woman could somehow work miracles by the mere fact of her gender bred, in turn, excessive disappointment and commensurate reactions when they were not fulfilled. It is interesting to note that these reactions were sexually charged. Accusations of diamond smuggling, even of mercury smuggling, and of obtaining illicit gains through bribery were par for the course for anyone, male or female, who transgressed in UNITA's book. They had become such run-of-the-mill insults that no one took them seriously. In my case a new element was added – Savimbi's 'mother' became 'a prostitute'.

Sexual slur also became a weapon in the Government's armoury when discontented: an extraordinarily varied and active sex life was attributed to me in gossip around Luanda, linking my name intimately with UNITA leaders. And then, on Women's Day, the official women's movement was deliberately mobilised to demonstrate against me as if I had somehow failed in my womanhood by not managing, single-handed, to still the reawakened guns of two adversaries determined to fight one another – an event that Dr Savimbi was quick to seize on to assert that I was totally discredited. Lázaro Diaz used, in the attack on me which he later retracted, a savage feminine image, virtually accusing me of infanticide. In the Government press I was often referred to as 'Doña Guida', an epithet that, as an article published in a Portuguese review in May 1993 recorded, was sometimes used affectionately, and sometimes quite the reverse, according to the author and the circumstances.

The same article mentioned that fun was often made of my manner of dress, about which I always tried to be meticulous, whether in an office or a field setting. When an article in the Government press claimed, with malicious intent, that I had 'fraternised' with UNITA soldiers in Jamba (when in fact I had visited them in a perfectly legitimate assembly area near Mavinga, accompanied by Government television), the writer referred sneeringly to my 'elegant safari suit'. I had had two or three field outfits made by our local dressmaker in the Welsh hills, since I had to address assembled troops as a representative of authority but, rather than elegant, (though I am delighted if they appeared so) they were intended to be comfortable and functional. By the end of a long day they were more often than not crumpled and travel-stained, as was observed by a more genial Angolan journalist – and I am sure it was no coincidence that she was a woman – who wrote sympathetically, at the height of my shuttle diplomacy between Huambo and Luanda, that she had felt encouraged on seeing me emerge, dusty and tired from the Beechcraft 'in her working clothes', after another trip to see Dr Savimbi in the central highlands.

I have no reason to believe that I received more or fewer attacks than would have been the lot of a man occupying my post in the same circumstances. One of the lessons of almost all peacekeeping operations is that, if you truly strive to be impartial, you must expect to be reviled, at various times, by both sides. An ultra-thick skin is an essential item of equipment for such assignments. What I *am* saying is that my own experience demonstrates that, if you are a woman, the attacks are likely to try to make capital out of that fact, perhaps in the hope of showing that female skin is thinner. You just have to try to prove that it is even tougher than any male counterpart's, even though that may not be true – many of these highly personalised jibes can be deeply hurtful.

On the more general issue of whether a woman is more or less qualified than a man to lead a peacekeeping operation, simply by virtue of gender, I believe that a great deal of bunkum is talked on both sides of the argument. The essential qualities are the professional attributes, experience and personality of the individual, whether male or female. If these are right for the job then I have no reason to believe that a woman will do better or worse than a man, though she may have to try harder. The imponderables are prejudice and perception.

* * *

Many of the problems encountered in Angola were rooted in the nature of the Bicesse Accords, in the negotiation of which the UN played no role. The thesis that the main responsibility for implementing the Accords must be vested in the two parties to the conflict presupposed a Boy Scouts' code of honour in circumstances hardly conducive to the evolution of the Boy Scout spirit. This principle was threaded throughout the key elements of the peace process, which then became defective in practice: for example in the very limited 'bystander' mandate and even more exiguous resources accorded to the UN, and in the institutional arrangements set up to monitor the Accords, whereby the two parties alternated in the chairmanship of the CCPM and took consensual decisions that often remained on paper, with no one to act as arbiter or enforce follow-up.

As always, none of this was as simple as it seemed on the surface. At one level the onus was placed on the two parties, on the reasonable argument that, to have peace, there must be a genuine political will to bring it about, and that without this no amount of outside intervention could be effective. But that in turn reflected another consideration that was equally strong: the countries most closely concerned with Angola genuinely wanted peace to be restored, but they wanted 'a quick fix', particularly the two superpowers, the main protagonists of the Cold War. Their priorities had shifted on to other matters – in the case of the then Soviet Union to an understandably tense preoccupation with its own new, and chaotic, reality. The result was an agreement flawed from the start, and a marginal role for the UN that was doomed to be ineffectual. In the end it was the UN (meaning UNAVEM, and not the Security Council, which had taken its cue of 'small and manageable' from the Bicesse negotiations) that was blamed for the breakdown, at which point everyone credited it with having a much larger mandate, room for manoeuvre and resources than it had ever been endowed with.

The dual lesson for peacekeeping operations is plain. The UN – and here I mean the Secretary-General, as the head of the Secretariat – should never accept any role in the implementation of a peace accord unless the organisation has been fully involved in the negotiation of its terms and its mandate. By the same token – and this is the second lesson – the UN Secretariat should always request resources for individual peacekeeping operations that reflect a realistic estimate – a conservative estimate, not an exaggerated one, but a realistic one – of what is needed to do the job properly, rather than a perception of 'what the traffic will bear', a concept that up to now has seemed to prevail in almost all instances. There should be two distinct functions in the process: that of the Secretariat, which has the responsibility of indicating clearly the mandate and resource requirements for conducting an effective peacekeeping operation in a given situation; and the policy and funding role of the member states, who must determine whether or not the operation should be undertaken, and with what resources. If the Security Council jibbed at the suggested budget, any significant reduction should be matched by a commensurate reduction in mandate. In extreme cases the Secretary-General should be ready to say 'no', and to refuse to handle inadequately funded programmes, or those where the UN was being asked to undertake a mandate inadequate to the size and complexity of the problem. What usually happens now is that the Secretariat tries to anticipate what the Security Council – which itself works on the basis of compromise – may be disposed to allow and the result is a fudged and, all too often, flawed outcome.

Another shortcoming of the Bicesse Accords was the inelastic timetable for the holding of the elections, which was more or less engraved in stone. The underlying supposition was that a series of crucial steps to stabilise the situation and reduce the potential for renewed conflict were to be taken before the elections, but no provision was made for the eventuality if they were not – for example by postponing the elections until they were. The lack of any conditionality, or any flexibility for the election date beyond the stipulated term, 'between September and November 1992', was to have dire consequences. The problem was exacerbated by the sequential, phased approach foreseen in the Accords for the accomplishment of certain key steps – the prime example was the provision that demobilisation would only start once the cantonment of troops was completed.

Nor was the 'winner takes all' concept helpful in consolidating the smooth transition to democratic government – quite the reverse. The shocked comments that greeted my remarks on this at my lunch with President Nujomo and his Ministers in Namibia in July 1993 and the fear of the 'second-class' democracy that inspired their reaction were, in my view, based on a misconception. It is not a question of applying solutions of differing degrees or 'classes' of excellence, but rather of recognising that there is no unique model of democracy that can be universally applied, like a rubber stamp, and that democracy depends on more than the mere act of elections and voting. It is what comes afterwards that matters, and determines whether democracy will be consolidated and strong institutions built up to sustain it. Circumstances vary immensely from country to country and from one culture to another. In a country like Angola, staggering from long years of war and not yet having made the transition from a state-run economy to a marketing economy with a growing indigenous private sector, then the 'State' is the only prize. Anyone unsuccessful in winning an election, by definition, loses everything and is left out in the cold, with no alternatives on which to fall back – hardly a sound recipe for reconciliation and stability, especially if the losers are guerillas who have been fighting out in the bush, with no homes or even modest employment to return to, and indeed no concept of civilian life but only of waging war. Some who took part in the negotiations at Bicesse told me that a valiant attempt was made to make some accommodation for the losers in the elections, but neither of the combatants wished to hear of it; each was bent on nothing less than total victory. A corollary of this is that demobilisation programmes must be accompanied by intensive vocational training, so that long-time fighters may feel confident of finding a productive place in civil society. Some external finance was available for such undertakings in Angola but they never got off the ground.

Fortunately most of these lessons were learnt in time to prevent a repetition of the same mistakes in Mozambique – there the UN was given an adequate mandate and resources, including several thousand 'Blue Helmets' with a supervisory role. Equally importantly, the UN was assigned the chairmanship of the institutional body set up to monitor the implementation of the peace agreements;

the timing of the election was flexible and made conditional on the prior fulfilment of key provisions of the agreement; and early steps were taken to accommodate the losers in the election within a new framework of national reconciliation. I had some hand in this for, having been warned that the Secretary-General might ask me to go on to Mozambique after Angola, I was determined not to face the same situation again; in the event, the renewed outbreak of war made my transfer impossible. Even allowing for differing circumstances and personalities, the more successful experience in Mozambique gives grounds for arguing that, had similar precepts been applied in Angola, there would have been a good chance that disaster could have been avoided. Indeed, all the same lessons were incorporated into the draft Protocol of Abidjan, and spelt out step by step for UNAVEM III. Unfortunately, neither became a reality at that time.

In similar realms of speculation, liberally laced with hindsight, it has occurred to me to wonder what would have happened had I not gone out on a limb, in the pre-electoral period, to mobilise essential logistical support for the elections – air and road transport, communications, air-traffic control, food supplies and so on, for which UNAVEM had neither mandate nor budget. Without that massive effort, the elections could not have taken place in anything remotely approaching free and fair conditions, for the simple reason that it would have been impossible to enable the participation of thousands and thousands of citizens in many remote areas of the country (mostly those controlled by UNITA). In such circumstances I would have had to declare, well before voting day, that the electoral arrangements did not meet the required standards. What would have happened then? Would the elections have had to be postponed, whatever the Bicesse Accords said, until such time as proper logistical arrangements were in place? If so, would that have permitted more progress in areas such as demobilisation, disarmament, the formation of the new armed forces and the extension of central administration before voting took place? Or would it simply have provoked an earlier return to war, as an expression of outrage at the poor organisation of the elections by UNITA, which would almost certainly have construed this as a blatant and deliberate demonstration of the Government's bad faith?

Probably the latter was the more likely hypothetical outcome. In any event, although it is intellectually intriguing to ponder whether my zeal in overcoming a major obstacle may not have been as productive of desired results as masterly inaction, it is not a speculation that keeps me awake at night. I thought then, and still think now, that it was my duty to do my utmost to make the peace and electoral processes function properly, whatever the external constraints upon UNAVEM.

* * *

The more I reflect upon it, the more it seems to me that the real nail in the Angolan coffin was that the solution of the conflict never enjoyed high priority on the agenda of the countries that mattered (in the sense of being able to drive through policy decisions and provide adequate resources to support them). Angola was well and truly an orphan of the Cold War, its civil war an anachronism left over from another time, which everyone hoped would somehow sort itself out and, as soon as possible, go away altogether. I have suggested that such sentiments may have prompted certain shortcuts in the Bicesse Accords, but their impact should not be exaggerated. Other factors were undoubtedly present: in any negotiations the desire, and the need, for compromise play a large role, not seldom inimical to effective implementation later. It must not be forgotten, either, that the Angolan Government's jealousy of its sovereignty played a large part in limiting the UN's role, a position I have often felt it must have regretted later, sovereignty becoming a somewhat hollow concept if you lose control of a large part of your territory.

Be that as it may, by the time the situation had again deteriorated into open warfare the decline in international interest was unmistakable. This was partly due to symptoms of 'Angola fatigue', a weariness that, in spite of the success of the elections, deepened when it became clear that some elements were still determined to fight. It may even be that this weariness increased *because* the elections were successful, the optimism initially engendered by that unexpected outcome being swiftly succeeded by exasperation when its fruits were so casually thrown away. In addition, Angola – never a major item in international news headlines – was now totally eclipsed by other peacekeeping operations – Bosnia principally, but also Somalia. Angola had lost its 'window of opportunity', such as it had been. This was particularly evident during the Abidjan negotiations. I have recorded my frustration at the unwillingness of the international community to send even a token force of 'Blue Helmets' to Angola in May 1993 to resolve the one outstanding issue preventing agreement on the 38-point Abidjan Protocol, which was a *sine qua non* for the rest to fall into place.

Again it is a matter of conjecture whether, had we been able to break this 'chicken-and-egg' situation, UNITA would have kept its word and withdrawn its troops. So much was at stake, however, in terms of human lives, and success so near, that I still believe that the international community should have taken a chance on peace. Instead it maintained its 'wait and see' and 'show us first' attitude, which anyone close to the negotiations could see was doomed to failure. The risks involved in the modest operation that I proposed were small, but by then, in addition to the disenchantment with Angola, the whole international climate with regard to peacekeeping had changed for the worse.

In a more personal and selfish way, this decision let me off the hook. After the débâcle over Sergio Vieira de Melo, no successor was in sight and I had had some qualms of conscience as to whether I was abandoning the struggle prematurely and should offer to stay on indefinitely. With the negative decision on the 'Blue Helmets', it became crystal clear to me that there was nothing further I could do. Not only had I not been given the mandate and resources adequate for the job in the first place, but now I had been left, as the principal mediator, with nothing in my hands with which to negotiate. One of the great lessons of Angola is that UN mediators must be provided with some leverage with which to exert pressure, or provide incentives, as circumstances require. My constant message at that time was that we must offer carrots as well as sticks to UNITA, but it went unheard. It was perhaps a forlorn chance, but to me it still seems tragic that it was not even tried. Two more long years of war might have been avoided.

* * *

Some salutary lessons are also to be learned from the Angolan experience for the internal operation of the UN.

There is an unfortunate tendency to make sweeping judgements about UN missions and either dismiss them as total failures or, more rarely, herald them as successes. The truth usually lies somewhere between the two, and so it was with Angola. Despite its limited resources in relation to the vast size and minimal infrastructure of Angola, UNAVEM had considerable operational successes to its credit. It was, by any standards, an outstanding logistical feat to deploy teams to 68 self-supporting sites all over the country within two or three months, together with communications and supply lines. For some eighteen months only the UNAVEM network could provide coverage of the whole territory.

A favourite criticism of UNAVEM is that it had no 'intelligence'. That is perfectly true, in the military sense of undercover information gathering. It does not seem to be well known, or understood, that the UN is not allowed to gather intelligence in that sense. In 1987, when I was responsible for coordinating major reforms in the Secretariat called for by the General Assembly, we proposed the creation of a small unit that would give the Secretary-General advance warning of likely trouble spots before they erupted into problems, in the functions of which the word 'intelligence', used quite innocently, was included. The outcry was immediate and vociferous: Moscow accused us of setting up an international CIA, Washington of creating a KGB! So it causes me some wry amusement nowadays when the UN is blamed for having 'poor intelligence' This lack of the military variety marks a major difference with conventional military operations or exercises such as the Gulf War.

In Angola, some countries with well-organised intelligence services had access to undercover information about secret activities of one or other side that impinged on the peace process. This was not available to us (though sometimes they were kind enough to tip us off), but I believe no one was better informed than UNAVEM about the overall day-to-day situation prevailing in the country. Daily information came in from all our teams, was sifted and analysed, used in briefings, sent in summary to New York and formed the basis for our actions and for positions that the Chief Military Observer and I took in the CCPM, or in talks with both sides. The information covered every aspect, from troop movements and police matters to political analysis of local developments, the progress of the electoral process and humanitarian needs. Whether this was enough, or whether UN peacekeeping should be equipped to extend to obtaining 'intelligence' in the undercover sense, raises political issues that I fear will not be resolved easily or soon.

There was, certainly, a serious gap in another area of information – the public kind. I had only one professional public information officer, supported by one very willing but inexperienced assistant. While UNAVEM was particularly meagrely staffed, the problem is common to all UN peacekeeping operations. Member governments, especially the major contributors, persist in the belief that public information and public relations are an unnecessary expense that should be reduced to a minimum in any budget. That has proved time and again to be a false economy that has cost the organisation dear. It is, moreover, not only the quantity, but the *quality* of public information that has to be changed. Nor is it simply a question of ensuring that the activities of the UN operation itself are promptly, objectively and accurately reported, and misrepresentations corrected. It is also essential, particularly during an election, to counteract the hostile propaganda of opposing sides with a balanced view of the situation that can reach the population at large. A UN radio in Angola, such as that which operated so successfully in Cambodia, would have been of inestimable benefit.

External difficulties, deriving from a UN apparatus no longer equipped to cope with the swift expansion of peacekeeping operations, also played their part in Angola, among them constraints in the rapid deployment of UN peacekeeping troops. Here member states must accept their share of responsibility, particularly in the tardy and inadequate response to the Secretary-General's proposals for strengthening operational aspects of UN peacekeeping in his *Agenda for Peace*, first published in June 1992, including suggestions for stand-by forces that could be made available at very short notice. The general reluctance of member states to provide adequate funding to implement missions agreed by the Security Council, and delays in paying their contributions, even when the budget has been adopted, are also major obstacles to well-managed and effective peacekeeping operations.

* * *

Angola highlighted the need for extensive streamlining of UN internal structures, procedures and policies to adjust to the new challenges. The increasing burden of peacekeeping responsibilities, worldwide, affected the backstopping – both political and administrative – of UNAVEM. Overworked Headquarters staff did their best to respond to UNAVEM's needs, but delays sometimes occurred in providing replies on urgent policy and operational matters, and the strain on the Headquarters operation visibly mounted during the latter part of my time as Special Representative. Some of the more glaring defects that exacerbated these problems have since been addressed. Now there is only one Under Secretary General dealing with all aspects of operational peacekeeping missions and the Department for Peacekeeping Operations includes the Field Operations Division. This makes for a unity of purpose and direction at Headquarters that was often lacking when I was in Angola. The military advisory capability and response to emergency situations have also been significantly strengthened.

A major requirement that has still not been sufficiently addressed is a greater *rapprochement* between Headquarters and field perspectives through systematic interchange of staff. In any organisation with a far-flung field operation there is tension between headquarters and field staff, but this can be stretched to intolerable lengths if the operational arm – the people at the front, as it were – come to feel that back at base there is a lack of understanding for their efforts and problems. In my view this can never be adequately resolved unless it becomes the norm for all persons occupying key positions at Headquarters dealing with peacekeeping and humanitarian operations to have had a corresponding experience of field missions – preferably some of the more difficult ones. It is no coincidence that the people whom I found the most responsive in New York were those who had themselves been in similar predicaments. They were also the ones most likely to come up with sound practical advice, rather than the theoretical second-guessing that still hampers UN field operations and usually come from those who have never been, even metaphorically, in the 'firing line'.

This dichotomy is nowhere so starkly etched as in the matter of administrative and financial procedures. Many long-established financial rules and regulations and auditing practices are quite unsuited to the present-day realities of UN peacekeeping in the field. There were several instances in Angola where patently unreasonable demands or criticisms were made, without any regard for the emergency and often life-threatening situations in which split-second decisions were having to be taken. Reproofs delivered to the UNAVEM Chief Administrative Officer about the adequacy of financial management in the mission were blatantly unfair in circumstances where Headquarters had been unable, over a period of many months, to respond to our repeated pleas for a fully-qualified Chief of Finance. No doubt there were reasons for the failure to fill this key post, but it was hardly reasonable to throw the blame for the result on overworked field staff doing their best to cope. In contrast, scant recognition was given to the exceptional logistical achievements of the same staff in establishing a network of staff, supplies and communications covering the whole country, or, in later stages, putting into effect, with the military, prompt evacuation measures that undoubtedly saved the lives of staff at great risk. The main official comment on the latter was an auditors' report that severely criticised UNAVEM for failing to save all the equipment as well! This was an instance where I felt it might have been salutary for them to have had to write their report while cowering in slit trenches, under crossfire, rather than comfortably doing so long after the shooting was over. It is certainly not my suggestion that financial, administrative and auditing controls be waived, but rather that they be better adapted to the present requirements, and often stark realities, of peacekeeping operations.

Member states must also recognise their own share of responsibility in the matter of financial and administrative procedures. Many are often scathing about the slowness and cumbersomeness of UN responses to emergency operational requirements. They are frequently right. But the loudest critics of UN lethargy are usually in the forefront of those demanding stricter controls and alleging widespread corruption. The plain truth is that UN procedures, built up over many years to control an organisation formerly only marginally involved in field operations (I speak only of the UN 'proper', and not of organisations such as the UN Development Programme and UNICEF, which have greater flexibility), are so all-entangling that it has been impossible to carry out efficient peacekeeping operations, responding promptly to emergency situations, without cutting corners in the established regulations and procedures. This has brought swift retribution in the form of stern disciplinary measures and the slapping-on of even tighter controls. It is of course essential that UN staff should be, and be seen to be, both efficient and scrupulously honest. Unfortunately some of the measures taken and the manner of them have served only to damage staff morale, stifle initiative and compel blind adherence to procedures that in significant respects are obsolete and certainly not conducive to expeditious action. Member states cannot have it both ways: if they want rapid-response peacekeeping they must be more flexible in their procedural demands. They must also restrain themselves from becoming involved in 'micro-management'. Probity and open procedures can be safeguarded by other means than stranglehold day-to-day regulations or interventions. Reform proposals for the UN usually emphasise structural reorganisation, but a major exercise to streamline and update procedures would have more effect.

A fundamental problem in the UN is a failure to recognise that its most vital resource is its people, and that that resource must be developed and nurtured. This embraces many facets. At one level, the selection, briefing and administration of peacekeeping personnel need improvement, although the short notice with which many large and complex operations have to be mounted these days makes this difficult. Some civilian and military personnel sent to Angola proved unsuited to the difficult conditions and a few had to be repatriated or sent back to Headquarters. In the case of the military, the responsibility lay with the troop-contributing countries. Civilian personnel were directly recruited by the UN, in the first instance from the Secretariat itself. For this latter category the briefing of what they should expect was woefully inadequate. More attention was also needed to the prior substantive briefing of electoral observers: I was momentarily dumbfounded when, in a briefing on the eve of the elections, a lady nonchalantly put up her hand and asked 'Would you mind repeating the names of the two main presidential candidates?'

This was an isolated incident, however, and, in welcome contrast there were many people who not only adapted fast but fulfilled a potential that had never been tapped within the bureaucratic constraints of Headquarters. This was especially the case with women who, although often professionally qualified, had never been able, because of constraints of the system, to occupy professional posts at Headquarters. For years they had conscientiously carried out administrative tasks, often making possible the success of their male bosses. Let loose in the field, with a wide range of responsibilities, the majority of them responded magnificently, to the credit of the organisation, as well as achieving a measure of self-fulfilment they had not previously experienced. Nonetheless, inspired amateurism is no longer sufficient, and it is high time that a Staff College was set up to train field personnel in the rudiments of various aspects of peacekeeping, electoral observation and running humanitarian operations. There should also be a more systematic mechanism for keeping track of experienced civilian peacekeeping personnel (both UN career staff and outsiders) who have performed well and can be called upon at short notice when new missions arise.

Much more should be done to improve the incentives and rewards for those who acquit themselves well and accept harsh living conditions. There is a public misconception, often fanned by the media, that UN field personnel bask in some kind of paradise, doing very little. That was not the case in Angola. Many people in UNAVEM put up with very inadequate living conditions, worked horrendously long hours, were frequently exposed to high risk, and had little in the way of distraction or relaxation. Exigencies of the service often required them to postpone sorely needed leave. Yet while much was demanded of those prepared to work with dedication for the cause of peace, narrow implementation of the organisation's rules and regulations often penalised them in return. It is essential for the maintenance of high morale in adverse circumstances that devotion to duty should be recognised. One of my recommendations to the Secretary-General on relinquishing my mission, was that a special UN gallantry award or medal should be introduced for military and civilian staff who perform outstanding deeds of valour. I was thinking of the young Egyptian captain who risked his life in Kuito/Bié but received no recognition – not even a letter of commendation – from anyone outside Angola, but others would also have qualified. At medals paradesI had doled out dozens of UN medals to departing contingents of 'Blue Berets', but these were merely for having served in Angola and were restricted to the military: civilian service went unremarked. I had in mind something more special, to be handed out sparingly, and to be highly prized. I was told that the idea was 'under consideration', and so it remains to this day.

* * *

My own memories of Angola remain very fresh, and the lessons I learned there still run very deep. The hardest one of all to assimilate is my conviction – for such it remains – that, had there truly been an international resolve to do so, then peace could have been brought to Angola and its people. It was not that member governments did not wish that to happen, but simply that they had fish to fry elsewhere, and they wanted 'a quick fix'. When that was not forthcoming, their attention lapsed into a knee-jerk reaction to the succeeding phases of the tragedy that inexorably engulfed Angola. Had there been an outraged public outcry, as in the case of Rwanda or Somalia, or intense media coverage, as in former Yugoslavia, perhaps something might have been done. Ironically, had that happened, in 1991–2 or even, I believe, in May 1993, Angola would almost certainly have precipitated more decisive international action than any of these.

But it did not happen. The peoples of the world remained silent, and the people of Angola continued to suffer, in silence, one of the greatest human tragedies of our time. It is they, above all, who deserve an award for gallantry. Angola was truly 'an orphan of the Cold War'.

Epilogue

Nearly two years have passed since I left Luanda. I write the last words of this long odyssey my the little adobe house overlooking Lake Titicaca and the Royal Cordillera of the Andes, which I had so often dreamed of in Luanda and feared I might never see again. My hillside is flowering, even at this great altitude. Sometimes, as in Angola, there is no water, sometimes no electricity. Sometimes I am even awakened at dawn by the crackle of machine-gun fire, and reach automatically for a non-existent radio. But it is only the Bolivian navy, practising on the shores of the lake. There is peace here.

I had hoped that, by now, there would also be peace in Angola. My successor, Maître Alioune Blondin Beye and his UNAVEM colleagues, together with the representatives of the three observer countries, have continued to labour unceasingly towards that end. I have followed their efforts from afar, and their perseverance has won my admiration. I know just how much patience and tenacity it takes to go on negotiating the same issues day after day.

On 20 November 1994 I rejoiced with them when a breakthrough at last appeared to be at hand, the signing of a new ceasefire and peace agreement in Zambia – the Lusaka Protocol, largely based on the Abidjan Protocol, on which we had so nearly reached agreement nearly a year and a half earlier. The ceremony was dignified by the presence of several African Heads of State, including President José Eduardo dos Santos of Angola, but not by that of Dr Savimbi, who failed to turn up at the last moment. Consequently the agreement was signed not by the leaders, but by Foreign Minister Venâncio de Moura and General Eugenio Manuvakola, then Secretary-General of UNITA. This time the United Nations was was to have a central role and UNAVEM III was to be blessed with the strong mandate and adequate resources, (including 'Blue Helmets) that had been denied to me in 1992.

Once again, though this time with an unofficial voice and from a distant mountain top, I urged that the only chance of consolidating the Lusaka agreement was to send a symbolic presence of 'Blue Helmets' forthwith. Once again, however, the counsellors of 'wait-and-see' and 'show us you mean business' prevailed. The despatch of the main body of troops was made conditional on the ceasefire holding and it took many months to assemble.

Sadly, and perhaps predictably, the ceasefire has proves precavious and the killing and the suffering have continued. Angola has not been able to get on with the urgent business of repairing the physical ravages of 30 years of war, of clearing the horrendous harvest of mines (one at least for every inhabitant) which daily claim more lives and limbs), of reopening roads, of planting crops and restoring the trappings of normal life that have been denied the country for so long. Much less has it been able to heal those deeper, intangible wounds of mistrust and hatred, inflicted by civil strife.

Yet, as I write, there are at last some signs that the warlords may after all give peace a chance. Those of us who carry the tragedy of Angola in our hearts pray that it may be so, that the Angolan people will at last come into the prosperous heritage that is rightfully theirs and that their country will no longer be forgotten, war-torn lands at the end of the world – 'as terras do fim mundo'.

Villa Margarita
Lake Titicaca   *May 1995*

Notes and References

2 The Background

1. S/22627 of 20 May 1991, paragraph 3.
2. S/22627.

3 First Mission to Angola

1. Ryszand Kapuscinski, *Another Day of Life*, Harcourt Brace Jovanovich Inc. 1987. (originally published in Polish, 1976)
2. Report of the Secretary-General to Security Council on the Question of South Africa, para. 86, p. 23, A/48/845, S/1994/66 of 10 January1994.

4 A Small and Manageable Operation

1. S/23671.
2. S/23671, para. 9.
3. Ibid., para. 31.
4. S/23671/Add. 1.

5 The Military Conundrum

1. S/23191.
2. *Ibid.*, para. 16.
3. S/24145.
4. S/24245, para. 19.
5. S/24249.

6 The Formation of the New Angolan Armed Forces

1. S/23556.

7 The Police Imbroglio

1. S/24556.

8 Alarms and Excursions

1. In a paper prepared for the Catholic Institute for International Relations in June 1993 ('One Hand Tied: Angola and the UN'), Alex Vines writes that 'Fubo' was composed of units of government special forces, transferred to Malange to prevent UNITA from infiltrating the city, and according to the same source they were under orders to encourage anti-UN sentiment in an attempt to depict the UN as pro-UNITA: 'This involved shouting anti-UN slogans during the day and firing gunshots at night. Most of the shots were exchanges between UNITA and MPLA supporters but some

were directed towards the UN compound. If the MPLA fared badly in the elections it intended to blame the UN for helping UNITA.'

10 The Registration of Voters and the Electoral Campaign

1. S/24145 of 24 June.
2. S/24556.

11 Politics, Pride and Personalities

1. Ryszard Kapuscinski, *Another Day of Life*.
2. S/24556.

12 Life in Luanda

1. Ryszard Kapuscinski, *Another Day of Life*, op. cit.

15 The Aftermath

1. Later Mr Hossi was among those UNITA members of parliament caught in Luanda when hostilities erupted. I hear he is now a highly successful and properous businessman there.

20 ...And Let Slip the Dogs of War

1. S/25140 of 21 January 1993.
2. S/25140 para. 33, 21 January 1993.
3. Ibid.
4. Ibid.
5. Ibid. (para. 34).

21 Peace Talks in Ethiopia

1. S/25140.

22 From Addis Ababa to Abidjan

1. Article 51 states 'Nothing in the present Charter shall impair the inherent right of individual or collective defence if an armed attack occurs against a Member of the United Nations, until the Security Council has taken measures necessary to maintain peace and security. Measures taken by Members in the exercise of this right of self-defence shall be immediately reported to the Security Council and shall not in any way affect the authority and responsibility of the Security Council under the present Charter to take at any time such action as it seems necessary in order to maintain or restore international peace and security'.
2. These extracts are taken from an English translation of a transcript of the Vorgan broadcast.
3. Paragraphs 10 and 11.

4. Operative paragraph 10.
5. Paragraph 11.

24 Going the Last Mile

1. S/26060 of 12 July 1993.
2. Ibid., paragraph 2.
3. Ibid., paragraph 8.
4. Ibid., paragraph 18.

Index

Note: MJA is used as an abbreviation for Margaret Joan Anstee.

Abidjan
   description 447
   living conditions 470–4
Abidjan meeting 427–32, 443–5, 447–65, 466–70, 474–90, 536
AD Coligacão 235
administration
   Angola 134–6, 252
   UN 539–40
Africa: condemnation of UNITA 521
   see also specific countries
Africa International 476
African National Council (ANC) 95–6
aid, humanitarian 433–9, 445–6, 465, 508–9
   Angola Appeal 503, 504–7
   mission 405–6, 425
   support of UN troops 494–8, 500–1, 510–11, 524–5
Aida Desta, Princess 380
air traffic controllers 191
aircraft
   crashes 188–90
   election support 39, 42, 188, 190–2
   for Ethiopia peace talks 403, 406
   supplied by US 52, 56–7, 61–2, 403
   UNAVEM 18, 261
Albright, Madeleine 498, 522, 523
Albuquerque, Joâo Lino 453
Almeida, Afonso 380
Almeida, Dr 117, 118, 187, 200, 381, 388
Almeyda, Lucinda Matos de 90
Alvor agreement (1975) 8
Aly, Hussein 15
Andrade, General 294
Andrade, Senhor (gardener) 171–2, 517
Angola
   background 7–14
   countryside 174–5
   military situation 47–63

   people 163
   plight of 505–6, 507
   police situation 69–77
   politics 127–34
   recognition by US 395, 399, 486, 510
   see also specific names and subjects e.g. Huambo; UNITA
Angola Appeal 503, 504–7
Annan, Kofi 300, 399, 428, 516
   Ethiopia peace talks 403, 404, 409
   Luanda fighting 276, 281, 283, 284
   meetings in New York 428, 487, 496–7
Anson, Hugo 15, 22, 224, 236, 241, 381
   election aftermath 213
   Ethiopia peace talks 407, 408
   summit meetings 339
Anstee, Margaret J.
   official assumption of duties 34–44
   preliminary mission to Angola 15–29
   recreations 170–2
   replacement rumours 477–9
   successor 501–2, 512–13
antiriot police *see* police
Apollo, Brigadier General 358, 361
Argentina: election support 191
arms supplies: illicit 373
   see also triple zero option

Baltazar, Manuel 439
Banana, Canaan 448–9
barracks: FAA 65
Barros, Antonio Moreira de 453
BBC 170, 433, 479
'Ben-Ben' General 372, 396
   appointed Joint Chief of General Staff 67
   ceasefire 278, 281
   death feared 289, 290
   description 179

disappearance 154, 155, 209, 285, 293, 309
  fighting in Huambo 367
  leaves FAA 207
  summit meeting commission 246, 251
  Uige and Negage problem 330
Bender, Gerald xiii, 523–4
Benguela 176, 513
  description 175
  fighting 283, 294
Bereuter, Doug 113–14
Beye, Maître 419, 543
  as MJA's successor 501–2, 512–13, 520–1
  request for briefing 515–16
Bicesse Peace Accords 4, 20, 22, 128
  Abidjan meeting 457
  dealing with breaches of 529–30
  effects of 532–5
  police 69
  provisions 10–14
  triple zero provision 10–11, 373, 522
  troop assembly 47
birds 166, 167, 513–14
Blue Helmets *see* UN troops
Blyth, Hall 271
Bock, General 282, 293
  ceasefire 283, 284–5, 286, 288, 289
  Goulding's visit 307, 309
Boneo, Horacio 16, 33
  election organization 25, 38–9, 91–2, 94
Borel, Philippe 507
Botha, Pik 95, 151, 233, 259
  description 224
  on elections 247
  encounter with Salupeto Pena 234–5
  future role of Savimbi 395
  intervention 221, 224–7, 229–30, 232, 244–7
  relations with Savimbi 239–40, 242, 243–4
Boutros-Ghali, Boutros
  Abidjan meeting 452–3, 459–60, 481–3, 484
  Angolan criticisms of UNAVEM 143–4
  ceasefire 283, 284–5
  ceasefire consolidation attempts 320
  central administration 135
  demobilization 49–51, 56, 59–61
  election support 102, 113
  electoral campaigns 125
  Ethiopia peace talks 376, 405
  FAA formation 65, 67
  Luanda fighting 273, 274
  police 69–70, 76
  proposed visit 140–1
  relations with Dos Santos; letters 50–1, 320–1
  talks 427–8
  relations with MJA 30–1;
    appointment 3–4, 5, 22;
    reactions to attacks on 249, 251, 421, 443; resignation 520–1
  relations with Savimbi: letters 50–1, 208–9, 210, 211–12, 213–14;
    phone calls 156–7, 230–1, 232, 249–50, 313; talks 427–8
  summit meetings 339, 340, 344, 352
  troop assembly 48–9
  Uige and Negage problem 336, 342
  UNAVEM funding 37–8, 40, 41–2
  UNAVEM mandate 13–14, 31–4
  use of UN troops 512
BPV (People's Defence Organization) 390
Brazil: UNAVEM safety 257–8
Brazzaville 314
British Embassy: Luanda fighting 269–90
Brito (chauffeur) 290
Bula Matadi, General 297
Buo, Sammy 194, 236–7
  appointed Chief Electoral Officer 106
Bush, George 111, 113–14, 239

Cabelly, Robert 486, 510
  Abidjan meeting 454
Cabinda 7–8, 51, 60
  issue of 145–6
  military observer kidnapped 406, 424

Caetano de Sousa, Antonio 101, 117, 118, 197–8
  appointment to National Electoral Council 97, 98
  election aftermath 206, 207
  election results 200, 230
Cafunfo 330
Cahama 183
Caimbambo: refugees 439–42, 445
Campino, José 453
Canada
  on election 205
  election support 103
cantonment *see* troop assembly
Capanda
  dam 83–4
  fighting 295, 296
  hostages 295, 297, 298, 299, 300–1
Castro, Norberto de 250, 255, 282, 286, 294, 303
  attacks on MJA 241–2, 247
  criticises UNITA leaders 338
  National Assembly of Angola 422
cats 166, 449
Catumbo, Alfonso 78–9
Cavaco Silva, Prime Minister Anibal 212, 281, 399
Caxito 182, 296, 304
  ceasefire 292
  fighting 294, 298, 347, 509
  UNITA occupation 297, 332, 337
CCFA (Joint Commission for the Formation of Angolan Armed Forces) 12, 19, 64–5
CCPM (Joint Political Military Commission) 529
  buildings 21
  Cabinda 145
  chairmanship 533
  custody of weapons 49, 55–6
  demobilization 35–7, 49, 51–2, 55–6, 61, 62–3
  election aftermath 202–3, 208, 209, 256–7
  election fraud 217–19, 222
  elections 87, 92–4, 96–7
  FALA hidden army 52–4

  government administration 134–5
  Holden, Roberto on 131
  incidents 78–84, 124–5
  Jamba issue 136–7
  loan of US aircraft 56–7
  meetings 19, 28–9, 34, 51–2, 265–9
  police 71–2, 73, 77
  registration of voters 117.
  release of prisoners 134
  role of 12–13
  second election proposals 255, 260
  soldier retraining schemes 54–5
  summit meeting 253–4
  summit meeting commission 246
  UNAVEM's budget 37
ceasefires
  Abidjan meeting 455, 457, 459–61
  attempts to consolidate 292–327
  Luanda 275–91
Centre for Strategic and International Studies (CSIS) 111–13, 523–4
Chicoty, Jorge 99, 131, 337–8
Chilingutila, General Demostenes 207
  meeting with Matos 358, 359, 360, 362–3
  not in Ethiopian peace talks 382, 385
  Uige and Negage problem 331, 333, 334, 341–2
China: support for Roberto Holden 130
Chingunji, Tito 132–3
Chipenda, Daniel 99
  as presidential candidate 131
Chitunda, Jeremiah 23, 147, 148
  death 293, 294, 305
  election aftermath 216
  election fraud 243
  Savimbi on 295–6, 308
  summit meeting 245–6
  at Uige 153, 155, 156
  UNITA plan of attack 302–3
Chivukuvuku, Abel 23
  appointed 'Foreign Minister' of UNITA 35, 133
  ceasefire 278
  election aftermath 200, 206, 207, 210, 211–13, 214–15
  elections 88
  Luanda fighting 274

UNITA plan of attack 302–3
  wounded 288, 293–4, 305, 405
Christiano, Senhor 121
Christopher, Warren 427, 524
'Clark Amendment' 9
Clinton, Bill 524
CMVF (Joint Ceasefire Verification and Monitoring Commission) 12, 13, 19, 174, 178, 268
  custody of weapons 55–6
  demobilization figures 51
  hidden army of UNITA 52, 53
  incidents 79
  Lubango 357
  police 74
  troop monitoring 48
CNDA 99, 132, 235
coalition government: rejection of 149
Cohen, Herman (Hank) 41, 57, 59, 116
  air support 39, 52
  description 137
  election aid 94–5, 96
  on elections 205, 212
  Ethiopia peace talks 405
  FAA 64
  Luanda fighting 273, 282
  meeting with Savimbi 239–40, 244
  police 74
  see also Troika
communications: IMMARSAT sets 188
Conrad, Joseph
  Heart of Darkness 171
  Nostromo 171
Convenção Nacional Democratica de Angola 99, 132, 235
Costa, Adilson: death 327, 328–9
Côte d'Ivoire 215, 414, 415
  UN troops 511
  see also Abidjan; Houphoüet-Boigny
Coulson, Anita 193
Council of Social Communication 124
Council of the Republic 254
crime: in Luanda 163
Crocker, Chester 9, 112, 137
CSIS 111–13, 523–4
Cuba: support for MPLA 8, 9–10, 127

da Silva, Manuel 465, 507, 508

Daily Mail 169
Davidow, Jeffrey 115, 282, 315, 382–3, 399
  Abidjan meeting 427, 454
  on elections 205
  Ethiopia peace talks 405
  Luanda fighting 273, 275
Davidson, Basil: *In the Eye of the Storm* 474
Dayal, Virenda 3
De Jarnette, Edmond 282, 377, 478, 486
  Abidjan meeting 428–9, 430, 431, 454, 463
  appointment 246
  attacks on MJA 443
  ceasefire consolidation attempts 298
  future role of Savimbi 395
  government offensive 332–3
  humanitarian aid 510
  Namibe II 351–2
  'Protocol of Abidjan' 477
De Klerk, F.W. 151
De Melo, Sergio Vieira 421, 477, 478, 536
  as MJA's proposed successor 512–13
De Moura, Venâncio 35, 96, 116, 203, 284, 359
  appointed Foreign Minister 334
  and UN 422, 520, 521
  ceasefire consolidation attempts 321
  Ethiopia peace talks 394
  humanitarian truce 396–7
  Lubango fighting 353, 358
  Lusaka Protocol 543
  Menongue meeting 366
  Namibe II 351–2, 360
  reluctance to meet MJA 348
  South African aircraft 109–10
  truce 415–16
  Uige and Negage problem 331, 332, 342–3
Dembo, General 348
  FAA hostages 360
  humanitarian aid 435, 436
  security 503–4

Dembo, General *continued*
  Uige and Negage problem 341–2, 345
demobilization process 35–7, 49–63, 155, 534
democracy 127–8
  second class 519, 534
Denmark: election support 100, 101
diamond mining 181–2
Dias, Lázaro 122, 475–6, 531
Domingo, Francisco 190
Domingos, Colonel 358
donors
  election support 39–42, 92–4, 99–103, 535
  humanitarian aid 506–7
  soldier retraining schemes 54–5
Dos Passos, Luis 99
  as presidential candidate 131–2
dos Reis, Jose Julio 90
Dos Santos, José Eduardo 35, 133
  Abidjan meeting 443–5, 464
  Angola Appeal 504
  Cabinda 145–6
  ceasefire 283, 284, 286
  ceasefire consolidation attempts 292–3, 311–12, 317–18, 323
  criticisms of UNAVEM 142, 144
  demobilization 57, 63
  description 50
  election aftermath 215, 221, 222–3, 230, 231–2
  elections 87–9
  electoral campaign 123
  Ethiopia peace talks 371, 394–5
  FAA formation 65, 66, 67
  FALA troop movements 58–60
  Goulding's visit 301, 302–3
  Lusaka Protocol 543
  MJA's first meeting with 22, 49–50
  MJA's last meeting with 511–13
  and MJA's successor 512–13, 520–1
  peace process 10
  police 70
  Pope's visit 139
  propaganda 381–2
  registration of voters 119, 120

  relations with Boutros-Ghali
    letters 50–1, 320–1; talks 427–8
  relations with Savimbi 146–8; *see also* summit meetings
  second election proposals 255–6
  spread of fighting 359–61
  truce 416
  Uige and Negage problem 336
  UN troops 510–11, 512, 519–20
  UNAVEM's role 360
  on UNITA 318–19
  US visit 345
  war 420–1
dos Santos, Norberto
  Angola Appeal 506
  humanitarian aid 438–9
  and proposed truce 416
Dos Santos, Onofre 103–4
  appointment as Director-General 97–8
  description 98
  election fraud 221
  election results 200
  meeting with Botha 224
  registration of voters 107–8, 117–19
  voter education 122
dos Santos, Wilson 132–3
double key system 49
Driggers, Mr 103, 114
Dundo 181
Durão, Barroso José 10, 13, 59, 273
  description 137
  election aftermath 227
  meeting with Savimbi 244
  UNAVEM funding 37, 38

EC
  election support 95, 100, 101, 111
  on elections 204–5, 247
Egar, Bill 83, 334, 346–7
  Ethiopia peace talks 376, 380, 407, 408–9
Egypt: election support 101
election fraud
  alleged by UNITA 201–38
  investigations 209, 217–18, 227; results 233–4

election results 205, 222, 227–8, 230, 233
  announcement 227–8, 235–6
  delays 199, 213, 214, 215
  'Quick Count' 192, 205, 313
elections 527
  aftermath 199–238
  Bicesse Peace Accords provisions 11
  budget 90
  campaigns 122–6
  declared 'generally free and fair' 236–8
  donor support for 39–42, 92–4, 99–103, 535
  logistics 24–5, 91–2
  organisation 187–98
  prelude 87–98
  registration of voters 99–121
  role of UNAVEM 24–5
  second round 254–6, 346
  staff training 96
  timetable 90–1, 534
  UNAVEM mandate 31–4, 90
Electoral Code of Conduct 121–2
Electoral Law 89
Eliasson, Jan 405, 435
Essam, Captain 365
Essy, Amara 443
  Abidjan meeting 451–2, 463–5, 469–70, 482, 489–90
  description 447–8
  and Houphoüet-Boigny 450–1, 474–5
  UN troops 511
Ethiopia peace talks 366–7, 368, 375–7, 378–9, 380–414
evacuation
  plans for UN staff 258, 292, 294
  UNAVEM camps 364, 369–70

FAA 353
  Bicesse Peace Accord provisions 11–12
  build up 401
  custody of weapons 56
  departure of FALA 207, 225–6
  Ethiopia peace talks 390
  formation 57, 59, 62, 63, 64–8

  hostages 353, 358, 359–60, 361
  return of UNITA 350
  UNITA participation in 444
Faisca, General 297
FALA 230
  Catumbo incident 78–9
  component in FAA 11
  demobilization 35–7, 47–8, 51–7, 63, 155
  delays 57–60
  disbandment 66–8
  field teams' relationship with 178
  hidden army 52–4
  leaves FAA 207, 225–6
  Quilenges incident 49
  troop assembly 18–19, 25, 26–7, 47–8, 178–9
  troop movements 203–4, 256
FAPLA 163
  Catumbo incident 78–9
  component in FAA 11–12
  demobilization 35–7, 51–2, 56–60, 63, 155, 183
  disbandment 66–8
  FALA hidden army 52–3
  incorporation into police 73–4, 75
  M'banza Congo incident 61–2
  Quilenges incident 49
  troop assembly 18–19, 25–6, 47–8, 50
FDA 99, 131
Fermor, Patrick Leigh: *Three Letters from the Andes* 171
Fernándes, Tony da Costa 23, 133
  defection 35, 89, 132
Ferreira Gómez, Péricles 14
Feyez, Shaidaft 406
Field Operations Division 43
field teams *see* UNAVEM camps
finance: UN 539–40
Financial Times 225
FLEC (Frente de Libertação del Enclave de Carinda) 7–8, 60, 145–6
  Savimbi contacts 317
Flynn, John 27, 93, 140, 248, 265, 271
  Benguela 294
  election aftermath 200
  Luanda fighting 269–91

Flynn, John *continued*
   ceasefire negotiations with Savimbi 275–81
   registration of voters 117
   summit meetings 345
FNLA (Frente Nacional de Libertação de Angola) 97, 99, 182, 235
   civil war and peace process 8
   composition 7
   election results 236
   Ethiopia peace talks 381
   origins 129–30
Food and Agriculture Organization (FAO) 24, 170
Foro Democratico Angolano (FDA) 99, 131
França, General Antonio dos Santos *see* N'dalu
France 12
   French ambassador 301–2
Franco, Antonio 454
Frank, Rank 146
'Friends of the Secretary-General' 426–7, 414
Fritz, Major 268, 285
   Abidjan meeting 454
Fubu 142, 545
   Malange incidents 80
   Futungo de, Belas 50, 97, 430

gallantry award 541
Garuba, Major General 521
'Gato', General (Ciel da Concepão — Government) 82, 140, 229, 260, 288
   Abidjan meeting 453
'Gato', General (Armindo Lucas Paulo — Unita) 140, 231, 260, 288, 293, 382
Geingob, Prime Minister Hage 519
'George' (Savimbi's secretary) 293, 314, 409, 427
   Ethiopia peace talks 368, 370, 371, 376
Germany 115
Gharekhan, Mr 478–9, 496–7, 498
global positioning systems (GPS) 191
Gonzalez, Prime Minister Felipe 100–1

Gorbachev, President Mikhail 9
Goulding, Marrack (Mig) 232
   air traffic controllers 191
   Angolan criticisms of UNAVEM 143
   on Angola mission 3–4, 5, 6
   Angolan visit 294–5, 301
   correspondence with Savimbi 315–16
   custody of weapons 49
   election aftermath 208
   election support 102, 115
   Ethiopia peace talks 368, 371–2
   FAA 64
   N'dalu's absence 320
   police 73
   transfer to Department of Political Affairs 399, 428
   UN peace-keeping 42–3
   UNAVEM funding 37–8, 39–40
Government
   Abidjan meeting 427–32, 453–65, 466–70, 479–89
   Angola Appeal 506
   attacks on MJA 528, 531–2
   ceasefire 283–4
   criticisms of UNAVEM 141–5
   deteriorating relationship with UNITA 139–40
   election aftermath 203, 213
   election support 99–100, 101
   Ethiopia peace talks 372–3, 380–5, 387–413
   formation of new administration 333–4, 335–6
   humanitarian aid 507
   illicit arms supplies 373
   incidents 78–84
   Lubango attack 357–9
   Menongue Meeting 366
   military situation 400–2, 509–10
   MJA's successor 512–13
   Namibe meetings 323–7, 351–2
   offensive 332–3
   police 70–7
   politics 127–8
   pre-election clashes 150–2
   pressure for international condemnation of UNITA 337–8

propaganda 133, 381–2
release of prisoners 134
reluctance to meet MJA 344, 347–8, 351, 348
return to negotiation 508–9
second election proposals 254–6
South African air support 107
Uige and Negage problem 331–2, 334–5, 336, 341–2, 345
UNAVEM extended role 339–40
UNITA participation in 322, 444–5, 457–8, 459–60, 461
see also Dos Santos, José
Graça, Miguel da 24, 90
Griffiths, Bob 270, 272, 290
  ceasefire 285
  Luanda attack 274, 282, 288–9
Gröbler, Ambassador Gert J. 53, 95–6, 109, 234
Grossi, Maria 105, 117, 121, 214, 218
Hannay, Sir David 520, 523
Hassan II, King of Morocco 415–16, 428
Hejny, Elisabeth *see* Sissy
Henderson, Andie 272
Higino Carneiro, General 277, 278, 285, 289–90, 348
  Abidjan meeting 430–1, 453, 456, 458, 460, 468, 470
  ceasefire 281, 358
  Ethiopia peace talks 372, 376, 381, 408, 410, 411
  FAA hostages 360
  Luanda fighting 283
  truce 415
  Uige and Negage problem 331, 335, 351
Honest, Stephen 453
Hornsby, Peter 16, 25, 28
Hossi, Victor 233–4
  appointed Minister of Culture 338
  hostages
    Capanda 295, 297, 298, 299, 300–1
    FAA 358, 359–60, 361
    Miramar 270–1, 272–3, 283
  Hotel Turismo: evacuation 274, 280, 281
Houphoüet-Boigny, Felix 415–16, 428, 429–30

Abidjan meeting 452, 459–61, 469, 489
death 475
description 450–1
relations with Savimbi 431, 443, 444, 451, 463–4, 483, 490
leaves for France 474–5
Huambo 176, 401
  elections 124
  fall of 417–19
  fighting 366, 367, 393, 395, 396, 400
  Goulding visit 305–11
  government officers held 266–7, 299
  humanitarian aid 432, 437–9, 442–3, 445–6, 507, 508
  MJA's visits 215–17, 252, 255, 256, 305–11, 349
  plight of 505
  refugees from 439–42
  UN Security Council Commission visits 220–1
  UNAVEM evacuation from 369–70
  as UNITA centre 252–3
human rights 88–9, 529
  seminar 122
Humanitarian Affairs, Department of 436, 465
humanitarian aid *see* aid, humanitarian
'humanitarian corridors' 504, 507
Hurd, Douglas 273

ICRC (International Committee of the Red Cross)
  Catumbo incident 78–9
  Chivukuvuku's wound 405
  humanitarian truce 400
  release of prisoners 134
Ilha 167
Independent 225
INMARSAT sets 188
intelligence services: lack of in UN 537–8
international community
  Angola 535–6
  condemnation of UNITA 337–8
  dos Santos on 243
  election support 39–42, 92–4, 99–103, 535

international community *continued*
  Savimbi on 241
  soldier retraining schemes 54–5
International Women's Day 418, 531
Italy: election support 101

Jamba, Jaka 378–9, 392, 396, 398, 399
Jamba
  description 179
  issue of 136–7
  MJA visits 179–80, 181
James, Henry: *The Golden Bowl* 474
Jamwal, Col 15, 324
  Lubango attack 357–8
Japan
  election aid 95
  electoral observers 187–8
Jesus, Ambassador José Luis 211, 240, 498, 523
  humanitarian aid 499, 501
  visit to Luanda 220, 222, 223, 224, 226
João (gardener) 171
João, Paulino Pinto 99, 132
Jobarteh, Ebrima 44, 117, 242, 281, 284, 291, 292 324
  Abidjan meeting 453
  election aftermath 214
  election fairness 236–7
  Ethiopia peace talks 380
  visit to Chivukuvuku 305
John Paul II, Pope: visit 138–9
Jonah, James 428, 477, 496–7
Jorge, Paulo 513
  description 175
Jornal de Angola 133, 241, 314, 382
  attacks on MJA 181, 348–9, 433, 475, 528

Kabango, Mr 99
Kakumba, John Marques 449, 481, 482
  Abidjan meeting 454
Kambandu, Mr 99
Kapralov, Yuri 21, 271
  Abidjan meeting 454, 459
  Capanda hostages 301
  description 20

Kapuscinski, Ryszard: *Another Day of Life* 15, 130, 161–2
Karasin, Ambassador 59, 137
  description 138
  see also Troika
Kassebaum, Nancy 112
Kassoma, Antonio Paulo 96–7, 99, 135
  description 97
  election support 101
  registration of voters 117, 118, 119
Kassuwma, João Batista 96
Katu, Lt. Colonel 79
Kikongo 7
Kilandamoko, Andre 132
Kimbundo 7
Kinshasa: UNITA delegation in 396
'Kito', Alexandre Rodríguez 333
Kossikov, Sergei 454
Kruger, Mr 109–10
Kuito/Bié 176, 430
  evacuation of UNAVEM staff 364
  humanitarian aid 439, 507–8
  incidents 124–5, 150
  plight of 505

leadership: political parties 129, 131–2
Lehman, Christopher 114
Leitão-Greene, Deolinda 453, 471–2
Libération 419
Lima, Victor 57, 241, 330
  Abidjan meeting 443
  complaints about UNITA 58, 143
  description 50
  election aftermath 213
  Ethiopia peace talks 394
  summit meetings 339, 345
Lisbon: MJA contacted by UNITA 378–9
Lobito
  ceasefire 292
  fighting 275, 283, 284–5, 289
  incidents 175–6
  UNITA attack on UNAVEM team 257
'Loy' 52, 109–10, 143, 151
  demobilization 57–8
  election aftermath 213, 214, 232
  supply of tents 65

Index

Uige and Negage problem 331, 332, 333
Lozinskiy, Valentin V. 211
Luanda 191, 192, 195, 200
  Boutros-Ghali's visit 141
  election incident 198
  farewell to 513–17
  fighting 130, 258–9, 265–91, 322
  International Women's Day 418
  life in 161–72
  MJA arrival in 15–25, 34–44
  and UNAVEM 386–7, 392
  and UNITA 387
Lubango 176, 400
  fighting 275, 352–3, 357–9
Luena 176, 181, 191, 192
  demobilization 35–7
  humanitarian aid 508
  registration of voters 121, 125
Lumbala N'Guimbo 121
Lunda Norte 266–7
Lusaka Protocol 543

Machado, Pedro Santis Fontes 454
'Mackenzie', General 207, 255, 284, 285
Maier, Karl 225
Mairov, Mikhail 454
Malange 155, 176, 191, 192, 200
  antiriot police 73–4
  fighting 294, 327
  humanitarian aid 507–8
  incidents 48, 80–4
  plight of 505
Mango, Aliceres 206, 288, 289
  disappearance 293
Manuvakola, General Eugenio 307, 313–14, 321, 429, 543
  Abidjan meeting 453, 468, 469, 480, 481
  Ethiopia peace talks 381–4, 388, 391, 398, 402–8, 411–12
Marcelino, Fernando 253
Marker, Ambassador 523
Marshall, Alan 272
Maseka, Mr 121
Matos, João de 334, 338, 400–1, 418
  arms 509–10

proposed meeting with Chilingutila 350, 358, 359, 360, 362–3
Mavinga 179, 180–1, 191, 192
Mbalu, Major 156–7
M'banza Congo 182
  incident 61–2
  UNITA occupation 332
M'binda, Ambassador 249, 259
  Ethiopia peace talks 371–2, 376
  summit meetings 344
McCormick, Shawn 111–12, 524–5
McCurdy, Dave 113–14
Médecins Sans Frontières
  death of doctor 311
  staff rescued 365
media 528
  Abidjan meeting 455–6
  criticisms of MJA 475–6
  Ethiopia peace talks 370
  see also specific names, e.g. Vorgan radio
Menongue 176, 191, 192, 363, 366, 430
  humanitarian aid 439, 507–8
Metelis, Mr 397, 403
Miguel, José Manuel 99, 131
Miguel, Sebastian 99
Millington, Jeffrey 21, 56–7, 109, 115
  departure 245–6
  description 20
  election aftermath 232
  election support 100, 111
  elections 87, 205, 212
  Jamba issue 136
  police 74
  registration of voters 117
  see also Troika
Mills, Christina (MJA's aunt) xiii, 341, 433, 449, 503
Miramar 246
  hostages 270–1, 272–3, 283
  incident 198, 200
  UNITA leaders dash from 288, 305
Miranda, João de 426–7
Moco, Marcolino 151, 206, 338, 509
  Abidjan meeting 427
  appointed Prime Minister 333–4
  proposed truce 416

Monteiro, Antonio   21, 27, 156, 246, 268
   Abidjan meeting   454
   ceasefire   267, 288
   ceasefire consolidation attempts   298
   description   20
   election aftermath   201, 227, 230, 232, 254–5
   elections   87, 94
   FAA   66
   Luanda fighting   271, 274, 275, 280, 281, 282, 293–4
   in Luena   36–7
   Miramar incident   198
   'Protocol of Abidjan'   477
   see also Troika
Monteiro, President Antonio Mascarenhas   347
Moose, George   524
   UN troops   510–11
Morgado, Carlos   294, 338
Morris, Hank   102–3, 191
Mortlock, General Roger   78, 179, 215, 220, 315, 321
   Goulding's visit   306, 307, 308
   Huambo evacuation   369–70
   Namibe meeting   325
   and Savimbi   150
Moussoulu   167
MOVCON (Movement Control)   163
Mozambique   341, 534–5
MPLA   99
   Chipenda in   131
   civil war and peace process   8–12
   composition   7
   criticisms of UNAVEM   141–5
   election aftermath   201–2, 206
   election campaign   122–3, 192–3
   elections   87, 90
   forms government   8
   Holden, Roberto on   131
   Malange incident   81
   opposition to South African election support   108–10
   politics   127
   support for   8–11, 127
Muekalia, Jardo   112, 113, 524
   Abidjan meeting   454, 481

Mugabe, President Robert   333, 347, 385
Muteka, Fernando Faustino   380–1, 383, 384, 453, 460
   Abidjan meeting   462–3, 468, 470, 479, 481, 485
   Ethiopia peace talks   388, 391, 404, 407, 408, 410, 411

N'dalatando   348, 358–9
   evacuation of UNAVEM staff   364
   fighting   275, 296, 347
   UNITA occupation   332, 337
   visit to   182–3
N'dalu, General   37, 139–40, 156, 265, 283
   appointed Joint Chief of General Staff   67
   Capanda   295
   ceasefire   281, 284, 286, 287, 288, 289, 290
   ceasefire consolidation attempts   292–3, 298–9, 314, 316–17
   central administration   135–6
   demobilisation   35, 52, 54
   description   21
   election aftermath   203, 207, 209, 212, 213, 230, 232
   elections 87, 93, 94, 95
   FAA 64
   Goulding's visit   301
   leaves Angola   319–20
   Luanda fighting   275
   Lubango fighting   352
   Malange incident   81–2
   military situation   256–7
   no government post for 334
   police   73, 74–6
   South African election support   109
   second election proposals   260
   street shooting   218–19
   summit meeting   242, 245–6
N'Zau Puna, Miguel   35, 132, 133
Namibe   176, 400
Namibe meeting   323–7
Namibe II meeting   351–2, 360
Namibe   419, 534
   elections   25, 38

independence 9–10
MJA's visit to 517–20
'Nando' 57, 75, 76, 268, 338
appointed Vice Minister of the Interior 334
election aftermath 203
in place of N'dalu 266, 267, 319
Namibe meeting 324–5
summit meeting 242
Nascimento, Cardinal Alexandre do 138, 150–1, 513
attack on 419
Nascimento, Lopo de 23–4, 50, 96, 131, 146
elections 88
meets Boutros-Ghali 320
no government post for 334
National Assembly of Angola 422
National Electoral Council 55, 87, 89, 99, 223–4
appointment of Director-General 96–8
election aftermath 201, 202, 206–7
election fraud investigations 209–10, 217–18, 233–4
election results 199, 200, 213
Electoral Code of Conduct 121–2
registration of voters 106, 111, 117–19
Ndaki, Grégoire 476
Ndondo, Nevile 271, 272–3
Negage 25–6, 348
problem 327–36, 341–5, 347, 349–50, 351, 360, 362
Netherlands: election support 100
Neto, Agostinho 7, 8, 131, 450
Neto, Alberto 131, 155, 236
Neto, General Alberto 251
Neto, Pedro 66
Neto, Pitra 453
Newton, Tony 115
NGOs 365
human rights 529
humanitarian aid 434–5
Nicaud, M. 274, 280
Noakes, Stephen 272
Norway: election aid 94, 115
Nujoma, President Sam 519–20, 534

Numa, General 298
disappearance 304
Uige and Negage problem 330
Nyambuya, Michael (Colonal, then Brigadier) 53, 62, 266, 268, 346, 359
Abidjan meeting 453
appointed Acting CMO 337
Ethiopia peace talks 380, 408
FAA 65
humanitarian aid 439
Lubango attack 358
Namibe meeting 324, 327
security 387, 392
Uige and Negage problem 343–4, 349, 351
UN troops 487, 511
Nzele, Gen 358

ODP (People's Vigilance Brigades) 390
Ondjiva 176–7
Ongavi 518–19
Organização da União Nacional de Cabinda 146
Organization of African Unity (OAU) 8, 13, 384–5, 509
Abidjan meeting 454
delegation visit 347
summit 510, 512
Ovimbundu people 7
Ozanne, Julian 225

PAJOCA 99
Pantaleón, Elizabeth 213, 325, 348–9, 376
Abidjan meeting 453, 471–2
Paris, Ambassador Rocha 100
Parreira, Adriano 132
Partido Angolano Independiente (PAI) 132
Partido Democrático Angolano (PDA) 131, 235, 236
Partido Democrático para o Progresso da Alianzç Nacional Angolana (PDP-ANA) 132, 235
Partido Liberal Democrático 381
Partido Nacional Democratico Angolano (PNDA) 131

Partido Renovador Democrático (PRD) 99, 131
Partido Social Democrático (PSD) 131
Partido Social Democrático Angolano (PSDA) 132, 235
parties, political 87, 99, 108
  election fraud 206
  electoral campaign 124
  Jamba issue 137
  leadership 131–2
  meeting with UNITA 235
  MJA's general meeting with 128–9
  multiparty meeting 317, 318–19
  presence at elections 92
Patricio, Ambassador José 112, 113, 114
Pavillard, Leo 121
Payhama, Kundi 207
PDA 131, 235, 236
PDP-ANA 132, 235
Peace Accords *see* Bicesse
peace-keeping
  MJA's views 341, 533
  women in 5, 530–2
Péréz de Cuéllar, Javier 5, 47
Perkins, Joseph E. 211, 223
'Petroff', General 133, 145, 163, 270, 290
  appointed Minister of the Interior 334
  ceasefire consolidation attempts 298
  election aftermath 200
Petukov, Vladimir 20, 21
  illness 299
  see also Troika
Pinheiro, Paulo João Lopes 454
Pitra, Santana Andre *see* 'Petroff'
PLD 381
Poland: election aid 94, 111
police
  antiriot 58–9, 72–7, 154–5
  Ethiopia peace talks 388, 390–1, 396, 403–4
  Bicess Peace Accords provisions 12
  issue of 69–72
Political Commission: CCPM 12, 19
Portugal 419
  Abidjan meeting 454
  Angolan elections 227
  Angolan independence 7–8

Bicesse Peace Accords 10
  election aid 93–4, 100, 101, 191
  supply of uniforms 66
Portugese citizens: incidents 79–80
Prat-Vincent, Christian 380
PRD 99, 131
Prime Minister: appointment 333–4
prisoners, release of 134
private sector: election support 100, 101, 102, 112
'Protocol of Abidjan' 463, 464, 466, 535
  versions of 477
PRS 381
PSDA 132, 235
public relations: UN 538
Puna, Miguel N'Zau General 89, 132, 133

'Quick Count' system: election results 192, 205, 313
Quilengues incident 49, 79
Quipedro 25, 26–7

radio
  BBC World Service 170–1
  propaganda 124, 133–4
  see also Vorgan radio
Rasoilo, General 453
recreation hall 168–9
Red Cross *see* ICRC
refugees
  Caimbambo 439–42, 445
  in Luanda 162
  registration of voters 118
  see also UNHCR
religion 138–9, 150–1
retraining schemes: soldiers 54–5, 534
Ribeiro, Major 134
Rindel, Fred 53, 95
Roberto, Holden 7, 97
  election results 236
  leadership 129, 130
  MJA meets 130–1
Rocha Pinto 16
Roque, Fatima 23, 271, 282, 286, 530
  after ceasefire 294
  election fraud 255

Ross, Cameron 381, 400, 402, 465
  Ethiopia peace talks 403, 407, 408
  safety of staff 364
Roth, Richard: Abidjan meeting 454
Rothwell, Ambassador Margaret 449, 451, 471–2
Rufino, Gaspar 66

Sabo, Martin Olav 113–14
Sachiambo, Paulo
  Abidjan meeting 454
  Ethiopian peace talks 382
Salim Salim, Ambassador 347, 384, 385
Salupeto Pena, Engineer Elias 23, 75–6, 100, 148, 156–7, 265
  attacks on MJA 250
  Catumbo incident 78–9
  ceasefire 283
  complaints 139, 266–8
  death 288, 289, 290, 293, 305
  demobilization 35, 52
  description 21–2
  election aftermath 200, 202–4, 207, 210, 212, 214–15, 231
  elections 88, 93, 95
  FAA 57
  hostages 272–3
  Jamba issue 136
  Luanda fighting 275, 276, 280, 281, 282, 285
  Malange incident 81–2
  outbursts 242, 254, 256–7, 260, 266, 276
  police 70, 71–2, 73
  registration of voters 117
  Savimbi on 295–6, 308–9
  second elections 251–2
  soldier retraining schemes 54
  treatment by Botha 234–5
  UNAVEM funding 37
  UNITA plan of attack 302–3
Samakuva, Brigadier 411
  Abidjan meeting 454, 460
  Ethiopia peace talks 381, 404, 408–9, 410
Sambo 178
Samondo, Marcos 73, 276, 286, 363, 396

Ethiopia peace talks 371, 381, 403–5, 408–9, 410, 411
sanctions: againt UNITA 522
Santa Clara 177–8
Santo, Armindo Espiritu 198
Saurimo 176, 181
  humanitarian aid 508
Savimbi, Jonas 7, 9, 132–3
  Abidjan meeting 464, 469–70, 481–3, 484
  alleged plot to kill 140
  Angola Appeal 504
  antiriot police 60
  armoured vehicles 150
  Cabinda 146
  ceasefire consolidation attempts 295–7, 298, 299, 321–3
  control of UNITA 330–1
  demobilisation 54, 55, 57, 63
  and democracy 127
  description 23
  disappearance 209
  election aftermath 201–2
  elections 89, 198, 240–1
  electoral campaign 123–4
  Ethiopia peace talks 368–9, 370, 371, 375–6, 392
  FAA formation 66, 67
  FAA hostages 361
  in FNLA 130
  on foreigners 80
  Holden, Roberto on 130–1
  Huambo fighting 367, 418–20
  ignorance of public opinion 431
  Jamba 136
  Luanda fighting 275–81
  Menongue meeting 366
  MJA's proposed successor 477, 520–1
  peace process 10
  police 72, 75, 76–7
  Pope's visit 139
  as presidential candidate 132
  registration of voters 110–11, 119–20
  relations with Botha 239–40, 242, 243–4
  relations with Boutros-Ghali

Savimbi, Jonas *continued*
   letters 208–9, 210, 211–12,
     213–14
   phone calls 156–7, 230–1, 232,
     249–50, 313
   talks 427–8
   relations with Dos Santos 146–8; *see also* summit meetings
   relations with Goulding 301–2, 303, 315–16
   relations with Houphoüet-Boigny 431, 443, 444, 451, 463–4, 483, 490
   relations with MJA
     attacks on 419, 421, 443
     break in communications 530
     farewell letter 514
     meetings 22–3, 51, 57, 153–6, 204, 205–6
     return to negotiations 511
   role in government 334, 395, 444, 458, 460, 461
   smuggled out of Luanda 212–13
   Uige and Negage problem 330, 332, 333, 349–50
   visit to South Africa 151
Schuster, Bud 113–14
Scott-Bowden, Peter 83, 465, 517
Scowcroft, Brent 113, 114
Sebastião, Francisco 146
Senegal: on election 205
Sigi (security guard) 228, 290
Sills, Joe 421, 443, 479
Simeão, Analia Maria Caldeira de Vitoria P.: as presidential candidate 132
Sinjela, A. Mpazi 106, 236–7
Sissy (Austrian housekeeper) 27, 162, 163–4, 228, 291, 301, 347, 517, 518
Smith, Judy 114
Snoussi, Ambassador Ahmed 211
Soares, Mario 141, 473
social life: official 169
Soderberg, Nancy 524
soldiers: vocational training programmes 54–5, 534
Soto, Alvaro de 58, 143, 498
South Africa
   Angolan elections 227
   evacuation of nationals from Luanda 300
   election support 95–6, 103, 107, 108–10
   FALA hidden army 53
   Savimbi's visit to 151
   support for UNITA 8, 9, 10, 127
     withdrawn 259
Soviet Union
   Abidjan meeting 454
   Angola 533
   Russians in UNAVEM 168
   support for MPLA 8, 9, 10, 11, 127
   see also Troika
Spain
   election support 100–1
   police equipment from 71–2
Stott, Patricia 43
Strilchuk, Dennis 103, 163, 300, 327
Sukissa, General 417
Sumbe 176, 196, 362–3
summit meeting commissions 240, 245–7, 251–2
summit meetings between dos Santos and Savimbi: before elections 10, 59, 120, 148–50, 152–7 after elections 227–8, 229–35, 239–40, 243 proposed by Boutros-Ghali 339, 340, 344–5, 350, 352, 360–1
Sweden: election support 100, 101
Switzerland 115

Tadeu, General 274, 286
Tanzania 522
television
   electoral campaign 124
   propaganda 133–4
Tempelsman, Maurice 112
tents: FAA 65
Terra Angolana 134, 250
Tiago, N'Zita 146
Tiburcio, José 146
Times 374–5
Titov, Dmitry 16, 399
   Angolan visit 295, 301
training programmes: for soldiers 54–5, 534

Index

'triple zero option'   10–11, 373, 415, 520, 522
  declared null and void   397
Troika   12, 20, 28, 59, 137–8, 149, 415, 416, 509
  Abidjan meeting   431, 458–9, 493
  aid to government   520
  in CCPM 1 2, 28
  ceasefire consolidation attempts   295
  composition   20, 137–8
  condemnation of attacks on MJA   443
  confidence in UNAVEM   144
  demobilization   51
  election aftermath   215
  elections   96–7
  Ethiopia peace talks   397, 399–400, 405
  Goulding's visit   301
  meeting with Savimbi   244
  second election proposals   254–6
  summit meetings   239, 240, 242–3
  UN approach   377
  UN troops   510–11
Trollope, Anthony: *The Small House at Allington*   171
troop assembly   10, 18–19, 47–8, 50, 60, 178–9
troop movements: UNITA   203–4, 256
truce proposals
  Ethiopian peace talks   409–11, 413
  humanitarian   393, 395, 396–7, 398, 399, 400
Truman, John   33, 43, 98

Uige   25
  air crashes   188–90
  FAA hostages   353, 358, 359–60, 361
  MJA's visits to   153–6, 182
  problem   327–36, 341–5, 347, 349–51, 360, 362
UK 12
  barracks   65
  election aid   93, 100, 101
  supply of tents   66
Ukuma, Jerónimo: Ethiopian peace talks   382

UN
  backing from   476–9
  condemnation of attacks on MJA   424
  condemnation of UNITA   385–6
  internal operations   537–41
  MJA leaves   525–6
  observers   104–5
  role in peace-keeping   42–3, 533
  women in   5, 104, 530–2
UN agencies
  humanitarian aid   434–9
  meetings   24, 170
  see also specific names, e.g. UNDP
UN Economic Commission for Africa   453
UN Security Council   340, 520–3
  Abidjan meeting   466, 467, 468–9
  condemnation of attacks on MJA   443
  condemnation of UNITA   377–8
  resolutions on Angola   9, 14, 35, 259, 331, 378, 385–6, 422–5, 499–501, 521–3
  role in truce   415
  spread of fighting   363–4
  staff   539, 540–1
  triple zero provision   373
UN Security Council Commission   210–11, 212, 219–27
  meeting with Botha   224–7
  reports   223, 240, 243
UN troops   58, 129, 316, 343–4
  Abidjan meeting   469, 486–8
  constraints on deploying   538
  support of humanitarian aid   494–8, 500–1, 510–11, 524–5
  use of   339, 360, 422, 444
UNAVEM   36
  attacks on   257–8, 267–8, 375, 386–7, 521
  Botha on   225
  campaign against   181
  Capanda hostages   300–1
  Catumbo incident   78–9
  CCPM meetings   19
  certification of elections   236–8
  communication channels   435
  conditions   27–8
  confidence in   19–20

UNAVEM *continued*
  criticisms of   141–5, 382
  death of military observer   327, 328–9
  dwindling presence   336–7
  election support   102
  establishment   9–10, 13–14
  FALA hidden army   53–4
  farewell party   515–16
  funding   24–5, 32–3, 34–5, 37–43, 223–4
  humanitarian aid   434–42
  information gathering   537–8
  living conditons   164–9
  Lubango attack   357–9
  M'banza Congo incident   61–2
  mandate
    Abidjan meeting   458, 461–2
    Bicesse Peace Accords   11, 342–3
    elections   13–14, 31–5, 58, 92, 129
    extensions   250–1, 259, 310–11, 374, 377, 385, 386, 422–3
    government wishes   303
    MJA's draft   345–6
    Namibe   326
    UNITA wishes   316
  military observer kidnapped   406, 424
  Namibe meeting   323–7
  peace-keeping medal ceremonies   169–70
  relations with Luanda   392
  relief planes shot at   456, 465–6
  role in elections   24–5, 90, 195, 197
  role in police   69–70
  safety of staff   363, 364–6
  staff evacuation plans   292
  staffing and conditions   16–18, 25, 33–4, 43–4, 104–5, 527–8
  troop monitoring   48
  Uige and Negage problem   327, 328–9, 334–5, 341–4
UNAVEM camps   83
  conditions   173–83
  Huambo   367, 369–70
  MJA's visits   104–5, 513
UNDP   24, 39, 90, 121
  election support   102, 103
  emergency supplies   400

funding for project   100, 101
humanitarian aid   438
meetings with   170
UNDTCD (UN Department of Technical Cooperation for Development)   90
UNFPA (UN Fund for Population Activities)   170
UNHCR (UN High Commission for Refugees)   24, 27, 170
  emergency supplies   400
  humanitarian aid   436, 438
UNICEF (UN Children's Fund)   24, 170
  Caimbambo refugees   439–40, 442
  emergency supplies   400
  humanitarian aid   438
uniforms: FAA   66
Unimna, Edward Ushie   15, 21, 22, 28, 294, 324
  appointment of   14
  CCPM meetings   19
  ceasefire consolidation attempts   292
  demobilization   35–6, 66
  FAA   62
  FALA hidden army   53
  field trips   173
  Goulding's visit   306
  lack of communication with   285
  Malange incident   81, 82, 83
  peace-keeping medal ceremonies   170
  police   72
  relinquishes post   337, 338
  Uige and Negage problem   333
UNITA
  Abidjan meeting   427–32, 4535, 466–70, 474, 479–89, 494
  absence from multiparty meeting   318–19
  acceptance of first election results   312–16
  admonished by US   463
  Angola Appeal   506
  antiriot police   388
  attacks on MJA   241–2, 247–50, 251, 252, 257–8, 259, 280–1
    apologies for   295, 296, 449, 456–7
  attacks on UN agencies   257–8, 267–8, 436, 456, 465–6, 521

Index

Cabinda 145
Catumbo incident 78–9
civil war and peace process 8–12
  composition 7
  condemnation of 377–8, 385–6, 521
  control of 330–1, 361
  criticism by UN 499, 500
  defections 35, 89, 132
  deteriorating relationship with
    government 139–40
  election aftermath 200–38
  election fraud 201–38
  elections 87, 88, 89
  electoral campaign 122–4, 133
  Ethiopia peace talks 366–9, 370–3,
    375–7, 378–9, 380–5, 387–400,
    402–13
  FAA hostages 353, 358, 359–60, 361
  formation 130
  Holden, Roberto on 130–1
  humanitarian aid 445–6, 507–8
  illicit arms supplies 373
  incidents 78–84
  Jamba issue 36–7
  military situation 372, 381, 401, 509
  Namibe meeting 323–7
  politics 127
  pre-election clashes 150–2
  propaganda 133–4
  MJA's public statements against 530
  release of prisoners 134
  return to negotiation 508–9
  role in government 334, 338, 457–8,
    459–60, 461
  role of UN 13
  sanctions against 522
  second election proposals 254, 259–60
  security for 316, 317, 318, 320,
    322–3, 328, 340, 425–6
  support for 8–11, 127
  UNAVEM evacuation from Huambo
    369–70
  US deadline 397–8, 399
  see also FALA; Savimbi; Vorgan radio
UNMO (UN Military Observer)
  humanitarian aid 436
  staffing and conditions 17–18, 26
UNPO (UN Police Observer) 17, 18

Updike, John: *The Coup* 171
Urquhart, Sir Brian 43
US
  Abidjan meeting 427, 428–31, 454
  admonishes UNITA 463
  election fairness 239
  election fraud 205
  election support 100, 101, 111–17,
    191
  no military aid to Angola 315
  recognition of Angola 395, 399, 486,
    510
  and Savimbi 132–3
  strategy for Angola 511–12, 533
  supply of aircraft 52, 56–7, 61–2,
    403
  supply of tents 65–6
  support for Holden Roberto 130
  support for UNITA 8, 9, 10, 11, 127
  UNAVEM expansion 522
  UNITA deadline 397–8, 399
  MJA's visits to 523–5
  see also Troika
US compound: Luanda 271, 273, 275,
  282, 286, 287

Vahekeni, João 454, 506
Valentim, Jorge 153, 433, 460, 485–6
  Abidjan meeting 429, 453, 455–8,
    462–4, 467–9, 474, 479–84,
    488–9
  election aftermath 216
  Ethiopia peace talks 398
  Goulding's visit 307, 308, 309
  humanitarian aid 438, 445–6
  relief planes shot down 466
  Uige and Negage problem 331, 333
Van Dunem, Prime Minister Fernando
  J. de França Dias 143
Van Dunem Foreign Minister Pedro de
  Castro, *see* 'Loy'
Viana 194
  ceasefire 292
Victor, Mfulupinga N'Landa 132
Vienna 3, 378, 380
Vila Espa 29
  Christmas 346–7
  description 16

Vila Espa *continued*
  explosions   228–9
  living conditions   164–9
  vulnerability of   387
Voice of America   314–15
Vorgan radio   133–4, 180
  attacks on MJA   247, 248–9, 259, 432, 442–3
  ceasefire   286–7
Vorontsov, Ambassador   498
voter education   122

Waldecir, Dr   166, 190, 305
Walker, Ambassador   399
Wambo, General   207, 287, 294, 405
Ward, Ambassador Jennifer   524
weapons: custody   48–9, 55–6, 61, 62, 63
Wenda, Brigadier   306, 307, 321
WFP   *see* World Food Programme
White, Thomas   15, 18, 27, 220, 517
  Ethiopian peace talks   403
  evacuation plan   258
  Luanda fighting   270, 281
WHO   24, 170
Windhoek   518, 519, 520
Wiyo, General   66, 321
  Goulding's visit   307, 308

women
  Angolan   163–4
  in UN   5, 104, 530–2
Woods, Jim   524
World Food Programme   24, 95, 115, 170
  Caimbambo refugees   439–40, 442
  emergency supplies   400
  humanitarian aid   435, 438, 465
World Health Organization   24, 170

Xangongo   177

Yaker, Layashi   380, 385, 414
Yamoussoukro   431–2
  MJA's visit to   472–3

Zacarias, General   207, 284, 285
  summit meeting commission   246
Zaire
  Savimbi's visit   314, 317
  support for Roberto   130
  support for UNITA   8
Zimbabwe   333
  on election   205
  UN troops   511